The New Public Contracting

The New Public Contracting

Regulation, Responsiveness, Relationality

Peter Vincent-Jones

OXFORD
UNIVERSITY PRESS

This book has been printed digitally and produced in a standard specification in order to ensure its continuing availability

OXFORD
UNIVERSITY PRESS

Great Clarendon Street, Oxford OX2 6DP

Oxford University Press is a department of the University of Oxford.
It furthers the University's objective of excellence in research, scholarship, and education by publishing worldwide in

Oxford New York

Auckland Cape Town Dar es Salaam Hong Kong Karachi
Kuala Lumpur Madrid Melbourne Mexico City Nairobi
New Delhi Shanghai Taipei Toronto

With offices in

Argentina Austria Brazil Chile Czech Republic France Greece
Guatemala Hungary Italy Japan South Korea Poland Portugal
Singapore Switzerland Thailand Turkey Ukraine Vietnam

Published in the United States
by Oxford University Press Inc., New York

Reprinted 2008

ISBN 978-0-19-929127-4

For Glynn

Preface

This book examines the deployment of contract as a regulatory mechanism in government policies across a broad spectrum of economic and social relationships in contemporary Britain. These range from the financing and provision of public services to the control of behaviour among school pupils and young offenders. My argument is that at the heart of the phenomenon of contractualization lies a distinctive mode of governance – the New Public Contracting – in which powers and responsibilities are devolved to public agencies in various contracting arrangements preserving central government controls and powers of intervention. The book demonstrates the practical problems and deficiencies in legal accountability and control associated with such policies, and suggests some ways of ensuring increased responsiveness in the performance of these public service functions. It draws on empirical and theoretical research I have carried out with colleagues over a fifteen-year period,[1] and more generally, on research on contracting, contracts and competition undertaken by academics from a variety of disciplines.[2] The analysis is distinguished from recent contributions on this topic by other writers in the traditions of private law, administrative law, and constitutional law by its scope, theoretical position, and socio-legal inter-disciplinary perspective.

Part I introduces the New Public Contracting and establishes its contemporary significance. Chapter 1 begins by distinguishing the core behavioural, legal, and rhetorical dimensions of the concept of contract. Following Macneil, the argument is that contractual relations are defined by the presence of ten essential or common contract norms in varying combinations. The traditional classification of government contracts, based on the distinction between 'external' contracts enforceable at private law and non-enforceable 'internal' contracts, is rejected in favour of a socio-legal typology that reflects the different administrative, economic, and social control functions of contemporary public contracting. Accordingly three main types of the New Public Contracting are distinguished: administrative contracts, economic contracts, and social control contracts. Each entails the deliberate attempt by the state to structure social behaviour – within government, in the economic organisation of public services, and in state–citizen relationships – through

[1] P Vincent-Jones, D Campbell, A Harries, and W Seal, *Conflict and Cooperation in Contracting for Professional Services: A Comparative Study*, (ESRC Final Report, 1998).

[2] D Campbell, and P Vincent-Jones, (eds), *Contract and Economic Organisation: Socio-Legal Initiatives* (Aldershot: Dartmouth, 1996); S Deakin, and J Michie, (eds), *Contracts, Cooperation and Competition: Studies in Economics, Management and Law* (Oxford: Oxford University Press, 1997); K Walsh, *Public Services and Market Mechanisms: Competition, Contracting and the New Public Management* (Houndmills: Macmillan, 1995).

regulatory arrangements that harness the contract norms for the attainment of determinate public policy purposes. An outline is provided of the distinctive regulatory anatomies of these types of the New Public Contracting. While administrative contracts are a form of *hierarchical regulation*, both economic contracts and social control contracts involve *regulation by contract within hierarchical regulatory frameworks.* The basic theme of the book is that while in business and other private relations contract serves as a mechanism of joint utility maximisation through which the parties may govern and adjust their on-going relationships to mutual benefit,[3] such welfare-enhancing conditions are much more problematic and difficult to attain through programmes of policy-driven regulation involving public contracting. A major concern is therefore with how inappropriate central regulation may damage the norms that support trust and cooperation in these contractual relations, and thereby impede the overall attainment of the government's public service policy objectives.

Chapter 2 locates contemporary public contracting developments in their broader policy context, tracing the genealogy of the New Public Contracting from the early 1980s through to the present day. The relationship between the New Public Contracting and the New Public Management is explored in depth. Here I suggest that the UK has been particularly influenced by a market/competition model of public management reform, in comparison with a more restricted 'managerialist contractualist' conception that has been dominant in other countries. The chapter shows how the separate administrative and economic functions of the New Public Contracting have nevertheless been brought within a coherent overall policy framework governing public services, through guidance in the form of *Better Quality Services* (BQS) in central government and the statutory regime of best value in local government. While such regimes may appear to leave senior managers free to choose how to deliver best value or better quality services at optimal cost, in practice discretion is exercised according to central standards and guidelines which favour certain competitive processes, thus limiting options and circumscribing choice. The extension and development of the New Public Contracting under New Labour is set in the context of 'centralized decentralization' and the increasing power of the 'new centre' of government (the Treasury in association with the Cabinet Office) in driving forward policies directed at raising productivity and increasing Britain's international competitiveness.

Part II develops the key theoretical concepts of regulation, responsiveness, and relationality. In Chapter 3 I suggest a synthesis between recent theories of regulation and theories of governmentality. The focus is on the necessarily limited capacities of the state in achieving regulatory goals, and on the vocabularies, technologies, and techniques through which power is exercised in contemporary societies. The New Public Contracting is shown generally to operate by rendering

[3] D Campbell, and D Harris, 'Flexibility in Long-Term Contractual Relationships: The Role of Cooperation' (1993) 20 JLS 166.

responsible (or 'responsibilizing') social agents through contractual commitments and obligations undertaken across a whole range of administrative, economic and social relationships. Chapter 4 unpacks the meaning of 'responsiveness' by distinguishing a number of dimensions of this concept in the regulation literature: regulator sensitivity; restorative justice; collaborative regulation; organizational learning; institutional adaptation; public accountability; and responsiveness to consumer/citizen needs. This discussion leads to the formula that will be used in the subsequent evaluation of the New Public Contracting: 'responsiveness = effectiveness + legitimacy'. While effectiveness denotes the efficient deployment of means to the attainment of given ends, legitimacy refers to the need both for public deliberation in the determination of fundamental policy goals, and for the nurturing of qualities of institutional morality and values of good administration within organizations engaged in public service networks. For various reasons, legitimacy is shown to be the more important of these criteria.

Chapter 5 draws together the theoretical threads of the previous two chapters and establishes more precisely the regulatory perspective informing the remainder of the book. Administrative contracts, economic contracts, and social control contracts are shown to be part of wider 'contracting regimes', deployed by the state in efforts to attain determinate policy purposes. A range of problems of unresponsiveness is predicted in the operation of such regimes. In addition to significant legitimacy deficits in the policy process, I suggest that excessive central government interference is likely to have a negative impact on the ability of public agencies to perform the regulatory functions they have been assigned in an efficient and responsive manner. There is a tendency in many cases for the New Public Contracting to undermine norms that are essential to effective contractual relations, as indicated in Chapter 1.

Part III examines in depth the institutional structures and environments of particular instances of each of the three main forms of the New Public Contracting. The focus is on governance problems that have arisen in practice both in the management of contracts and in the wider operation of contracting regimes. Chapter 6 considers two main types of administrative contract used in the restructuring of relations within government: (1) framework documents linking executive agencies and government departments; and (2) Public Service Agreements (PSAs) linking spending departments and the Treasury/new centre of government. The performance indicators and targets embodied in these administrative contracts pervade all levels of the organization and delivery of public services, and are reflected more concretely in the responsibilities devolved to public agencies in other forms of the New Public Contracting. The system of government by contractual targets is subjected to critical scrutiny. The main concern in these administrative contracts is with the operation of contract norms in structuring, confining, or checking the exercise of public power in these relationships.

Chapter 7 explores recent government policies directed at encouraging both competition for public services through outsourcing and market testing, and the quasi-market organization of entire welfare sectors on the basis of the purchaser-provider split. Rather than examine particular sectors in detail, economic contracting regimes are analysed here in terms of three sets of relationships – purchaser–provider; state–purchaser; and state–provider – illustrated with reference to a range of practical contract governance problems. My principal concern in this chapter is with the effectiveness component of responsiveness. Particular attention is paid to the manner in which the contractual purchaser–provider relationship is conditioned by the hierarchical regulatory relationship between central government and the public purchasing or commissioning agency. Complementing this analysis, Chapter 8 focuses on the role of citizens and consumers in economic contracting regimes. It considers how the development of supply-side competition in quasi-markets is being supplemented by a range of choice, voice, and exit mechanisms involving direct links between consumers and providers in service arrangements that are increasingly difficult to classify as private or public. Here I argue that we are witnessing the transition from quasi-market to regulated market organization in major public service sectors such as health and education, and suggest that in this regard the New Public Contracting may represent a temporary stage in the drift towards increasingly privatized forms of service provision.

Chapter 9 considers how relationships between the state and individual citizens are being structured increasingly through social control contracts in the fields of unemployment and employment services, criminal justice, and education. The responsiveness of these regulatory arrangements is evaluated with reference to the common contract norms of reciprocity, consent, choice, and power. Here there are particular concerns about the fairness of terms of contracts and the adequacy of safeguards against unwarranted interference by the public agency with individual autonomy. A contrast is drawn between social control strategies based on centrally determined regulatory frameworks and the more organic development of contractual techniques by professionals in the spheres of probation and social work. The agendas and rationales are shown to be entirely different, with greater governance problems being anticipated in the case of state-imposed measures.

Part IV examines in depth the role of law in the governance of the New Public Contracting. Chapter 10 reviews the deficiencies in legal accountability that have generally been identified in current debates as accompanying the developments described in the foregoing chapters. Various proposals for legal reform in administrative law, private law, and constitutional law are subjected to critical scrutiny. Rather than attempt to extend or develop private or public law in any particular direction, I suggest that a hybrid reform strategy is most likely to be successful in protecting both the public interest and the particular interests of parties with stakes in public contracting processes.

This leads naturally to the discussion of the role of law in contractual governance in Chapter 11. The first part of this chapter considers how legal procedural reforms might help increase legitimacy and effectiveness by controlling the pace and extent of contractualization across the whole range of New Public Contracting phenomena. I suggest that a major role for responsive law should be to structure the exercise of discretion by ministers and officials in respect of both the development of general policy and its implementation by public agencies in particular instances. The availability of information at all levels of decision making on public contracting is shown to be an essential component of such 'proceduralization'. One of the purposes of disclosure of information is to maximize responsiveness by improving the quality of public deliberation. Lack of democratic involvement and public deliberation is likely to increase the risk both of inappropriate selection of form of public service organization and of unresponsive regulation. The remainder of the chapter explores how legal frameworks might be reformed in order to help increase effectiveness and fairness through the strengthening of institutions governing administrative contracts, economic contracts, and social control contracts. Given the differences in the functions of these contracts, it cannot be expected that conclusions reached in one sector or setting will be applicable in another. The assumption is that public contracting, in whatever form, requires *appropriate* institutional support for any potential for increased responsiveness inherent in such arrangements to be realized.

Chapter 12 summarizes the main arguments and conclusions concerning the failures of responsiveness in the New Public Contracting, and makes a number of policy recommendations for the reform of particular contracting regimes and legal procedures aimed at improving the quality of decision making on a wide range of public service issues in contemporary Britain. Eight conditions of responsive regulation are expounded as basic elements of a theory of public contractual governance. Four such conditions are concerned mainly with the appropriate support in governance relationships of the contract norms, and four with further institutional and organizational dimensions of responsiveness in the design and implementation of contracting regimes. Finally, in lamenting the general lack of transparency and accountability in New Labour's privatization and contractualization agendas, I conclude with a plea for a new 'social contract' that might serve, at an abstract level, to orient continuing debates on how public service functions should be performed.

A brief note on the organization of material and the structure of the book may be of help to the reader. My deliberate purpose has been to address the general questions of why successive governments in modern Britain have resorted to contractual regulation across such a wide range of social relations, with what degree of success in the attainment of policy goals, and with what implications for legal governance. The analysis of particular administrative, economic, and social control contracts is subordinated to this investigation, and to the development of a general thesis about the limits of public contractual governance. This thematic approach has meant that each of the three main forms of the New Public Contracting is considered at various points throughout the book rather than in self-contained chapters. I hope nevertheless that the chapter headings, sub-headings and index enable the reader with more specialist interests in one or other of these fields to navigate the text without too much difficulty. Similarly, readers in the disciplines of public administration, public management and policy studies, as well as law and socio-legal studies, should find the relevant material accessible. Due to the range and complexity of the subject matter, the treatment of economic contracts in Chapters 7 and 8 is necessarily more synoptic than the coverage of administrative contracts and social control contracts elsewhere in Part III. These chapters need to be considered in the context of the foundational material contained in Part I. I should stress that my principal concern is with contractualization in England, leaving to one side the significant issue of policy divergence on public service reform accompanying devolution within the UK. Finally, for a legal audience, I emphasize that – consistent with the socio-legal approach and the fundamental distinction between contract behaviour and norms on the one hand, and the law governing such behaviour on the other hand – I have reserved questions of specifically legal analysis and reform for consideration in Part IV.

Acknowledgements

This book extends and completes a project for the socio-legal analysis of public contracting developed in a series of journal articles and other publications over the past fifteen years. During this period I have incurred numerous academic and other debts. I would like to thank Andrew Harries for his research role in two empirical projects based at Sheffield Hallam University in the 1990s, and for his contribution to our jointly published work on local government contracting which has been a reference point for many of the ideas developed in this book. I would like also to thank my colleagues David Campbell, Kevin Dowd, Willie Seal, and Mary Seneviratne, who contributed in various ways to the development of the research at this time. The book is the final product of these influences, and of work undertaken during a research fellowship between 2001 and 2004 for which the support of the ESRC is gratefully acknowledged: 'Regulation and Responsibilisation: The New Public Contracting in Socio-Legal Perspective' (award no R000271186). I am grateful to Richard Taylor and other colleagues in the Law School at the University of Central Lancashire for the support I received in preparing for and carrying out this research. In 2003 I was fortunate to have the opportunity to study as a Visiting Fellow in the Law Program at the Research School of Social Science, Australian National University. I am particularly grateful to Peter Cane for his critical engagement with the theme of the New Public Contracting, and to John Braithwaite, Terry Daintith, Nicola Lacey, Nick Seddon, and Colin Scott for their encouragement and comments on related papers. I thank my present colleagues at the University of Leeds, Ann Blair and Adam Crawford, for commenting on Chapter 8, and Clive Walker who read and commented on the whole draft. I received very helpful and much appreciated comments from three referees at Oxford University Press. I am particularly indebted to David Campbell for his contribution over more than a decade to my thinking on public contracts and regulation, with which I know he will profoundly disagree. Finally, I would like to thank my wife Karen for her detailed comments and efforts to persuade me to write in a more accessible and jargon-free style. While I fear she may not have succeeded in this, I can say with confidence that the sentences are shorter than they would have been without her prompting.

Some parts of the book repeat or develop arguments on public contracting that I have published in journal articles in the course of the last five years. The presentation of Macneil's contract norms in Chapter 1 is a version of the analysis in 'Contractual Governance: Institutional and Organisational Analysis' (2000) 20 *Oxford Journal of Legal Studies* 317. The discussion of the relationship between theories of regulation and governmentality in Chapter 3 is a re-statement of the position outlined in 'Values and Purpose in Government: Central-local Relations in Regulatory Perspective, (2002) 29 *Journal of Law and Society* 27. Most recently, Figs 6 and 7, and parts of Chapter 7 (on contracting regimes), Chapter 8 (on the state role in public services), Chapter 10 (on legal debates and reform strategies), and Chapter 11 (on law and contractual governance) have appeared in 'Citizen Redress in Public Contracting for Human Services' (2005) 68 *Modern Law Review* 887.

Contents

Abbreviations

ASBO	Anti-Social Behaviour Order
BPS	Better Public Services
BQS	Better Quality Services
CCT	Compulsory Competitive Tendering
CPA	Comprehensive Performance Assessment
CSR	Comprehensive Spending Review
CTC	City Technology College
DBFO	Design Build Finance and Operate
DBO	Design Build and Operate
DfES	Department for Education and Skills
DSO	Direct Service Organization
DVLA	Driver and Vehicle Licensing Authority
DWP	Department of Work and Pensions
EBPM	Evidence-Based Policy Making
FoI	Freedom of Information
FMI	Financial Management Initiative
GATS	General Agreement on Trade in Services
GATT	General Agreement on Tariffs and Trade
LEA	Local Education Authority
LGIU	Local Government Information Unit
LIFT	Local Improvement Finance Trust
LMS	Local Management of Schools
LPP	Local Performance Plan
LPSA	Local Public Service Agreement
LSVT	Large Scale Voluntary Transfer
MbO	Management by Objectives
MbR	Management by Results

NAO	National Audit Office
NDPB	Non-Departmental Public Body
NHSFT	NHS Foundation Trust
NICE	National Institute for Clinical Excellence
NPM	New Public Management
OECD	Organization for Economic Cooperation and Development
OPSR	Office of Public Service Reform
PCT	Primary Care Trust
PFI	Private Finance Initiative
PI	Performance Indicator
PMDU	Prime Minister's Delivery Unit
POS	Purchase-of-Service contracting
PPP	Public Private Partnership
PPPP	Public Private Partnerships Programme
PSA	Public Service Agreement
SDA	Service Delivery Agreement
SGI	Services of General Interest
SSAT	Social Security Appeal Tribunal
TEC	Training and Enterprise Council
TUPE	Transfer of Undertakings (Protection of Employment) Regulations 1981
YOT	Youth Offending Team
WHO	World Health Organization
WTO	World Trade Organization

Table of Cases

Table of Statutes

List of Figures

Glossary of Terms

Automaticity: A regulatory instrument or tool of government is 'automatic' to the degree that it utilizes an existing set of institutions, such as those supporting the operation of the market, rather than having to create its own special administrative apparatus.

Collibration: A regulatory strategy denoting governmental efforts to secure a policy objective through the balancing of rival forces to achieve a condition of stability or equilibrium.

Contracting regime: A regulatory regime in which the mechanism of contract plays a principal or central role, supported by a range of other regulatory resources deployed by the state in efforts to attain determinate policy purposes. Contracting regimes enable administrative, economic, and social control functions to be performed through the instrumentality of administrative contracts, economic contracts, and social control contracts.

Contractualization: The process of transition from direct state provision of public services towards more decentralized forms of organization entailing economic contracts, administrative contracts, and social control contracts. This includes both the development of general policy at the highest levels within government, and lower level decision making by public officials charged with implementing policy in particular instances.

Discreteness and presentiation: Defining features of any contractual relationship: 'discreteness is the separating of a transaction from all else between the participants at the same time and before and after . . . presentiation, on the other hand, is the bringing of the future into the present' (Macneil).

Governance: The process of governing in the wide sense (distinct from the narrower concept of 'government'), entailing the distribution of power among state and non-state actors in relationships of interdependence in networks, and the maintenance of social control through a range of techniques such as audit, accounting, and contract.

Human services: Complex public services, for example in the health, education, and social care sectors, which typically are labour-intensive and co-produced through human interaction and which may be aimed at modifying behaviour or addressing the welfare needs of disadvantaged populations.

New Contractualism: A term encompassing a range of scholarship and research focusing on the various ways in which contract has been adapted as a general mechanism of governance of social life, and its role in shaping culture and liberal democracy.

New Public Contracting: A distinctive mode of governance traceable in Britain to the early 1980s, and characterized by the delegation of powers and responsibilities to public agencies in various contracting arrangements preserving central government controls and powers of intervention.

Quasi-market: A mode of provision of public services (free at the point of delivery and financed from general taxation) combining competition between suppliers in the state, private, and non-profit sectors with either the concentration of purchasing power in a public agency acting on behalf of consumers (the purchaser-provider split), or the devolution of purchasing power to individual consumers in the form of a 'voucher' or earmarked budget.

Reactance: The psychological process whereby regulatees respond to overt governmental attempts to restrict their freedom by acting in a manner directly contrary to the intention of regulators, as a means of re-asserting their autonomy.

Regulatory regime: 'A historically specific configuration of policies and institutions which structures the relationship between social interests, the state, and economic actors in multiple sectors of the economy' (Eisner).

Relationality: The presence in contractual relationships of relational norms (reciprocity, solidarity, flexibility, power, role integrity, and proportionality) that support trust and cooperation, and which are necessary to deliver the joint welfare maximizing benefits associated with successful business and other private exchanges.

Remedial hierarchy: A form of regulation entailing the development within public service organizations of a 'ladder' of remedial measures – ranging from informal self-regulation in complaints handling and disputes resolution to legal enforcement in the courts – whose purpose in addition to redressing individual grievances is to encourage efficient administration and respect for fundamental process values of fairness and natural justice.

Responsibilization: The process through which individual subjects – including private citizens, public authorities, and independent sector organizations – are constructed as self-determining and self-willing agents through a range of governance techniques, discourses, and practices.

Social contract: A hypothetical or implicit agreement between members of a governed population and their government, which serves to legitimate and justify sovereign authority in terms of common collective benefits provided by the state in return for reciprocal obligations and commitments undertaken by individuals.

Social control: The range of formal and informal processes whereby both individual and collective behaviour is governed in contemporary societies, including both planned and programmed societal responses to deviance, and indirect practices involving socialization within institutions such as the schools and the family, and professional discourses and technologies of governance.

PART I

CONCEPTUAL FOUNDATIONS AND GENEALOGY

1

Government by Contract and the New Public Contracting

The term 'government by contract' is commonly used to describe a wide range of contractual arrangements involving public bodies, including traditional public procurement, contracting out, public/private partnerships, franchising or state concessions, agreements between the government and self-regulatory organizations, agreements between state agencies and individual citizens, and various types of agreement within government.[1] In considering such phenomena in this chapter, I suggest that the distinction often drawn between 'external' (legally enforceable) and 'internal' (legally unenforceable) contracts is of limited value in socio-legal analysis.[2] Instead, I develop an alternative typology reflecting the different administrative, economic, and social control functions of the New Public Contracting.[3]

The chapter begins by defining a meaning of 'contract' suited to the analytical tasks ahead. It then traces the historical movement from traditional public procurement to contemporary government by contract, showing how the modern state pursues a wide range of policy purposes through various forms of 'contract' and 'agreement'. The subsequent section narrows the scope of the book to a subset of government by contract – the New Public Contracting – characterized by the delegation of powers to public agencies in contractual arrangements preserving central government controls and powers of intervention. The three main forms of this novel type of regulation are identified as administrative contracts, economic contracts, and social control contracts. While administrative contracts may be conceived as instruments of hierarchical authority, economic contracts and social control contracts share a more complex dual regulatory structure involving regulation by contract within hierarchical regulatory frameworks. The chapter

[1] H Collins, *Regulating Contracts* (Oxford: Oxford University Press, 1999), ch 13; ACL Davies, *Accountability: A Public Law Analysis of Government By Contract* (Oxford: Oxford University Press, 2001); M Freedland, 'Government by Contract and Public Law' [1994] PL 86; C Harlow and R Rawlings, *Law and Administration* (London: Butterworths, 1997); J Stewart, 'The Limitations of Government by Contract' (1993) 13 *Public Money and Management* (Jul–Sep) 7–12.

[2] eg Davies, n 1 above, 42–46.

[3] P Vincent-Jones, 'Regulating Government by Contract: Towards a Public Law Framework?' (2002) 65 MLR 611.

concludes with an outline of the key issues in the relational analysis of the New Public Contracting that will be explored in the remainder of the book.

Definition of contract

We begin by clarifying an essential, or paradigmatic, meaning of contract. Three main dimensions can be distinguished: behavioural; legal; and rhetorical.

Contract behaviour and norms

Most fundamentally, contract may be conceived as a form of institutionally guided behaviour that serves to reduce complexity in social exchange.[4] Contract is distinguishable from other institutions performing similar functions (for example friendship, the family or community membership) by two main qualities. First, *discreteness* implies the deliberate and precise isolation of key aspects of the relationship in abstraction from its wider context. Secondly, *presentiation* refers to the self-conscious attempt, through planning, to bring the future into the present.[5] In other terminology, the contractualization of social life involves 'atomization' (excluding other parties or issues as irrelevant externalities) and 'narrowing' of social relations, such that the parties' conduct is valued according to specific and exclusive points of reference.[6] Contractual commitments are said to be temporary and specific, and the relationships finite and susceptible to dissolution. Business relationships are most often rendered quantifiable and measurable through the medium of money, but this is just one currency of exchange.[7] For Macneil, this contractual function is defined by the presence of relatively 'discrete' norms concerning *planning* (as a means of reducing uncertainty about the future), *consent* (involving acquiescence or choice as a basis for obligation), and *limited choice* (choices made in the present necessarily restrict those in future).

However, in all contractual relations such discrete norms exist in balance with a set of more 'relational' norms (Fig 1), namely: *flexibility* (in recognition of the need to avoid rigidity in implementation); *reciprocity* (the idea that exchange is a process of mutual benefit); *solidarity* (involving the extension of reciprocity in

[4] Collins, n 1 above, 13. According to Collins, the contractual frame of reference enables the parties to orient their conduct in relation to rights and obligations established by formal documents, explicit agreements and associated standards. For the argument that contract need not be associated exclusively with legal rights and obligations, see P Vincent-Jones, 'Contractual Governance: Institutional and Organisational Analysis' (2000) 20 OJLS 317. See also S Deakin and J Michie, 'The Theory and Practice of Contracting', in S Deakin and J Michie, (eds), *Contracts, Cooperation and Competition: Studies in Economics, Management and Law* (Oxford: Oxford University Press, 1997), 1.

[5] 'Discreteness is the separating of a transaction from all else between the participants at the same time and before and after . . . Presentiation, on the other hand, is the bringing of the future into the present. Underlying both is the ideal of 100 per cent. planning for the future' – IR Macneil, *The New Social Contract* (Yale University Press, 1980), 60.

[6] Collins (n 1 above) 16.

[7] H Collins, *The Law of Contract* (London: Butterworths/LexisNexis, 2003), 108–9.

social relations through time); *role integrity* (promoting stability through expectations about recognized social roles); *power* (to control relations of domination and subordination); *propriety of means* (placing constraints on the ways in which ends may legitimately be achieved); and *harmonization* (reflecting the need for contract norms to be consistent with wider social norms).[8] While Macneil is commonly interpreted as counter-posing 'discrete' and 'relational' contracts,[9] each associated with its own distinctive mode of legal reasoning,[10] in the present interpretation discreteness and relationality are viewed as products of the interplay of norms in the contractual environment of all exchanges. It is not that some contracts are discrete and some relational, but rather that discrete and relational norms are involved to a greater or lesser degree, and in a variety of combinations, in all human interactions.[11] A core argument of the book is that the success of contract as a governance mechanism is dependent ultimately on 'relationality' as a quality of social exchange. This shorthand term denotes the presence of relational norms in the relationship to the degree necessary to foster trust and cooperation and thereby deliver the mutual benefits intended by the parties. The importance of relationality in the analysis of the New Public Contracting is further explained below.

The contract norms have overlapping internal and external dimensions. External norms include custom, morality, conventions, and a wide range of institutional constraints in addition to those provided by the legal system.[12] Contracting

[8] Ten 'common contract norms' are considered by Macneil to run through all contracts. The original formulation was of five principles or norms – IR Macneil, 'The Many Futures of Contracts' (1974) 47 *Southern California Law Review* 691, 808–816, 809 n 32. Nine 'intermediate norms' were identified in *The New Social Contract* in 1980, (n 5 above). Ten norms were identified in a slightly different formulation in IR Macneil, 'Values in Contract: Internal and External' (1983) 78 *Northwestern University Law Review* 340. This account draws eclectically on all three sources.

[9] For a critique of the discrete–relational spectrum, see D Campbell, 'The Social Theory of Relational Contract: Macneil as the Modern Proudhon' (1990) 18 *International Journal of the Sociology of Law* 75; ibid, 'The Relational Constitution of the Discrete Contract', in D Campbell and P Vincent-Jones, (eds), *Contract and Economic Organisation: Socio-Legal Initiatives* (Aldershot: Dartmouth, 1996), 42; ibid, 'Ian Macneil and the Relational Theory of Contract' in D Campbell, (ed), *Selected Papers of Ian Macneil* (London: Sweet and Maxwell, 2001). The substance of this critique has been acknowledged by Macneil, who nevertheless regards the problem as terminological rather than fundamental. His response has been to attempt to 'resolve' the theoretical tension accompanying the dual claims that that all exchange occurs in relations so there is no such thing as a discrete contract, while at the same time discrete contracts may be found at the opposite end to relational contracts on a spectrum, by re-labelling the poles of the spectrum 'as-if-discrete' and 'relational' – IR Macneil, 'Relational Contract Theory: Challenges and Queries' (2000) 94 *Northwestern University Law Review* 877, 895.

[10] See for example K Walsh, *Public Services and Market Mechanisms: Competition, Contracting and the New Public Management* (Houndmills: Macmillan, 1995), 40–44.

[11] See P Vincent-Jones, 'The Reception of Ian Macneil's Work on Contract in the UK' (Introduction to edited collection) in D Campbell (ed), *Selected Papers of Ian Macneil* (London: Sweet and Maxwell, 2001).

[12] For a Weberian perspective, see P Vincent-Jones, 'Contract and Business Transactions: A Socio-Legal Analysis' (1989) 16 JLS 166.

<table>
<tr><th colspan="3">Common Contract Norms</th></tr>
<tr><td rowspan="3">Relatively Discrete Norms</td><td>(1) Planning</td><td>. . . involving conscious awareness of the temporal dimensions of past, present and future, and reflecting the need to cope with the uncertain future;[13]</td></tr>
<tr><td>(2) Consent</td><td>. . . 'binding people by reason of their consenting or otherwise acquiescing in being bound';[14]</td></tr>
<tr><td>(3) Choice</td><td>. . . choices made in the present necessarily restrict choices that may be made in the future;[15]</td></tr>
<tr><td rowspan="7">Relatively Relational Norms[16]</td><td>(4) Flexibility</td><td>. . . to avoid rigidity and facilitate adaptation to changing conditions,[17] in tension with norms supporting planning and consent;</td></tr>
<tr><td>(5) Reciprocity</td><td>. . . exchange is a process of mutual benefit, and that something should be received in return for something given;[18]</td></tr>
<tr><td>(6) Contractual solidarity</td><td>. . . 'belief in being able to depend on another,'[19] involving 'the projection of reciprocity through time';[20]</td></tr>
<tr><td>(7) Role integrity</td><td>. . . enabling stable and consistent behaviour to be promoted or 'effectuated' according to the different social positions occupied by the parties to exchange;[21]</td></tr>
<tr><td>(8) Power</td><td>. . . governs both the creation and restraint of the power that runs through all contract relations – the net effect 'has to be some workable balance of power';[22]</td></tr>
<tr><td>(9) Propriety of means</td><td>. . . placing constraints on the way by which ends may be legitimately achieved – 'the more complex the social relation, the more complex such principles and practices of decorum become';[23]</td></tr>
<tr><td>(10) Harmonization</td><td>. . . referring to the need to maintain consistency between contractual and more general social norms.[24]</td></tr>
</table>

Figure 1. Common Contract Norms (Macneil)

behaviour itself generates and reinforces norms internally within particular relationships; the more long-term the relationship, the more the ongoing relation becomes a source of obligation. While Atiyah is clearly correct in his assessment that contract involves 'futurity and the concept of obligation',[25] obligations may be extra-legal as well as legal, and may originate within, as well as existing independently of particular social relations. As will be seen, the *quality* of human relationships is determined by, and may be analysed according to, the precise manner in which the common contract norms are configured in different contracting environments. In this conception, any adequate description of how law governs, or prescription as to how the law ought to govern, must be founded on an understanding of the ways in which social exchange behaviour both gives rise to and is supported by the common contract norms.[26]

13 ibid 812.

14 IR Macneil, 'Political Exchange as Relational Contract' in B Marin (ed), *Generalized Political Exchange* (Frederick A. Praeger: Colorado, 1990), 166. 'Contractual exercises of choice have not only the usual effect of sacrificing other opportunities, but a very special characteristic of their own: the power in someone else to restrain one's future choices' – Macneil (n 5 above) 48.

15 Macneil (1974), (n 8 above) 810.

16 The five norms of *enhanced* importance in ongoing complex contractual relations (relational norms are always consistent with the common contract norms) are role integrity, preservation of the relation, harmonization of relational conflict, propriety of means, and the supracontract norms – Macneil (1983), (n 8 above) 361–366. *Roles* in relations include an element of utility maximisation, but involve also habits, custom, internal rules and expectations, growing in duration and range. 'If role is to serve its social function as a foundation for reliance and expectations, maintaining its integrity in the sense of keeping it together in a coherent piece is a major job of social engineering' – Macneil (n 5 above) 66. *Preservation of the relation* 'is an intensification and expansion of the norm of contractual solidarity' – ibid. Whereas discrete transactions self-destruct by reason of performance and are replaced by other such transactions, 'the ongoing character of relations is such that preservation of the relation becomes the norm'. *Harmonization of relational conflict* could be subsumed under preservation of the relation. Procedural regularity, good faith and trust are particularly important in connection with conflict resolution. The *supracontract* norms are so called because they are not particularly contractual. 'In ongoing contractual relations we find such broad norms as distributive justice, liberty, human dignity, social equality and inequality, and procedural justice' – Macneil (n 5 above) 70.

17 Macneil (1983), (n 8 above) 363.

18 ibid 347. This norm was earlier described as 'mutuality': 'The norm of mutuality calls not for equality, even were it possible to know what constitutes equality, but for some kind of evenness' – Macneil (n 5 above) 44. This norm is concretely reflected in the concepts of restitution, expectation and reliance interests;

19 Macneil (n 16 above) 153.

20 Macneil (1983), (n 8 above) 349.

21 People play roles that 'generate expectations of what their behaviour will and should be' – Macneil (n 16 above) 166.

22 ibid 167. 'Lawyers are most familiar with the creation of legal power. But power may be economic, social, and political as well; indeed at normal operating levels of contracts, it is those kinds of power, not legal power, that count the most' – Macneil (n 5 above) 56.

23 Macneil (1983) (n 8 above) 347; see fn 20 for an account of the origin of this norm, which was not included among the nine intermediate contract norms in *The New Social Contract* – Macneil (n 5 above).

24 'Norms such as those relating to privacy, liberty, social obligation, ideology, and many others, will in any given society have immense impact on contractual relations. Thus an ever-present necessity to harmonize the relations with them will exist' – Macneil (n 5 above) 58.

25 PS Atiyah, 'The Modern Role of Contract Law' in *Essays On Contract* (Oxford: Oxford University Press, 1986), 1.

26 Macneil (1974), (n 8 above) 878.

The law of contract

More familiar to lawyers is the idea of contract as a set of *legal* institutions and rules with obligational force, supported by the legal system and by judicial enforcement and dispute resolution machinery.[27] Lawyers are interested primarily in how general norms are embodied in more concrete legal obligations. From this 'law-centred' perspective, contract is defined by the creation and application of rights and duties,[28] and by the availability of legal sanctions adequate to protect reliance on promises, to prevent gain by default, and to protect expectations.[29] In critical socio-legal perspective, some contract norms (for example, reciprocity, flexibility, and contractual solidarity) have been regarded as particularly poorly served by English contract doctrine, which privileges discreteness at the expense of relationality in comparison with other jurisdictions. The need to reform contract law doctrine better to reflect and therefore to support relational norms in commercial practice is widely accepted as a central task of contemporary socio-legal scholarship.[30] In this perspective, the role of the state in the governance of market relations is to constitute contract, through private law, as a means of enabling the self-regulation of exchange according to individuals' preferences

[27] S Macaulay, 'Non-Contractual Relations in Business: A Preliminary Study' (1963) 28 *American Sociological Review* 55. This and other studies view contract as a device for conducting exchange characterised by rational legal planning for contingencies (including the possible need for legal sanctions) and the threat or use of these sanctions in practice – see also H Beale and T Dugdale, 'Contracts Between Businessmen: Planning and the Use of Contractual Remedies' (1975) 2 *British Journal of Law and Society* 45. On the relationship between contract norms and contract behaviour, see H Collins, 'Competing Norms of Contractual Behaviour', in D Campbell and P Vincent-Jones, (eds), *Contract and Economic Organisation: Socio-Legal Initiatives* (Aldershot: Dartmouth, 1996). Generally see S Macaulay, 'Elegant Models, Empirical Pictures, and the Complexities of Contract' (1977) 11 *Law and Society Review* 507; ibid, 'An Empirical View of Contract' (1985) *Wisconsin Law Review* 465; ibid, 'Relational Contracts Floating on a Sea of Custom? Thoughts About the Ideas of Ian Macneil and Lisa Bernstein' (2000) 94 *Northwestern University Law Review* 775; ibid, 'The Real and the Paper Deal: Empirical Pictures of Relationships, Complexity and the Urge for Transparent Simple Rules', in D Campbell, H Collins, and J Wightman, (eds), *Implicit Dimensions of Contract: Discrete, Relational, and Network Contracts* (Oxford: Hart Publishing, 2003).

[28] Macneil (1974) (n 8 above) 691.

[29] 'Promises are given sanctions to protect reliance on promises and to prevent unjust enrichment' – IR Macneil, 'Power of Contract and Agreed Remedies' (1962) 47 *Cornell Law Quarterly* 495, 497; 'Where legal sanctions are not adequate this power of contract is curtailed' (ibid 498); S Macaulay, 'The Reliance Interest and the World Outside the Law School's Door' (1991) *Wisconsin Law Review* 247.

[30] R Brownsword, 'From Cooperative Contracting to a Contract of Cooperation', in D Campbell and P Vincent-Jones, (eds), *Contract and Economic Organisation: Socio-Legal Initiatives* (Aldershot: Dartmouth, 1996); ibid, *Contract Law: Themes for the Twenty-first Century* (London: Butterworths, 2000), 55; D Campbell, 'Socio-Legal Analysis of Contract' in P Thomas (ed) *Socio-Legal Studies* (Aldershot: Dartmouth, 1997). Macneil, while emphasizing the need to distinguish *descriptions* of contract behaviour and law from *prescriptions* about the law that should govern, remains broadly committed to the idea that the law should generally track the relational behaviour and norms found in the relations to which it applies – Macneil (n 9 above) 877–900. 'In essential contract theory there is a somewhat general assumption that typically the law will more or less track the common contract behavior and norms. This should not, however, be overread. There may often be good reasons why the law should not track the common contract behavior and norms' (893).

and their decisions as to how to maximise their individual and joint utilities.[31] The expectations of the parties, and the relational norms of trust and cooperation embedded in business relations, are best protected through open-textured rules of private law (preventing bad faith, abuse of rights and unconscionable conduct) combined with the autonomy conferred on the parties to devise their own governance structures on the basis of negotiation and consensus. The responsive potential of private law lies in its provision of background or default rules enabling flexible and consensual self-regulation of business relationships, and experimentation with novel types of transaction that may enhance productive efficiency.[32]

Contract rhetoric and the social contract

Finally, social contract ideas perform an important legitimating function in attempting to provide an answer to the question of how, if all people are created free and equal, government rule is justified; the classical answer being that they will relinquish their natural rights to the collectivity only in return for securing certain objectives of common benefit.[33] The notion here is of an *implicit* contract (rather than of actual presentiating behaviour) involving individual members of a governed population and their government or sovereign.[34] Modern social contractarian thinking, like the classical liberal theory from which it derives, has a moral as well as a justificatory dimension.[35] It emphasizes the desirability of mutuality of obligation between individuals, and the reciprocal responsibility of citizens to the state or the communities that are charged with their support.[36]

In recent years both Conservative and Labour governments in Britain have made extensive use of social contract rhetoric in promoting a particular vision of social order and of the proper role of individuals in society. While such rhetoric neither reflects nor impacts upon contracting behaviour directly, it has provided the general ideological backdrop and justification for major changes in the welfare state and in the organisation of public services since 1979. The traditional welfare state grounded in universal social rights has been radically challenged, with the notion of entitlements being replaced by one of negotiated claims and reciprocal duties.[37] The representation of the relationship between individual citizens and

31 D Campbell and D Harris, 'Flexibility in Long-Term Contractual Relationships: The Role of Cooperation' (1993) 20 JLS 166; A Arrighetti, R Bachmann and S Deakin, 'Contract Law, Social Norms and Inter-Firm Cooperation' (1997) 21 *Cambridge Journal of Economics* 171.

32 Collins (n 1 above) 67.

33 M Loughlin, *Sword and Scales: An Examination of the Relationship Between Law and Politics* (Oxford: Hart Publishing, 2000), 162.

34 B Hindess, 'A Society Governed by Contract?', in G Davis, B Sullivan, and A Yeatman, (eds), *The New Contractualism?* (Melbourne: Macmillan, 1997).

35 A Etzioni, *The Spirit of Community* (New York: Crown Books, 1993); ibid, *The New Golden Rule* (New York: Basic Books, 1996).

36 M Dean, *Governmentality: Power and Rule in Modern Society* (London: Sage Publications, 1999) 207.

37 RH Cox, 'The Consequences of Welfare Reform: How Conceptions of Social Rights are Changing' (1998) 27 *Journal of Social Policy* 1, 12.

the state in the discourse of the 'New Contractualism'[38] is manifested more concretely in particular state programmes directed at changing individual behaviour (of welfare claimants, school children, and young offenders) through the restructuring of relationships in contractual terms. Nowhere is this shift more manifest than in New Labour's agenda for reform of welfare and of public services more generally. The 'New Deal' between the state and the individual is intended to counter perceived problems of the welfare dependency culture, spiralling expenditure, and the undermining of individual responsibility.[39] Plans for reform of the 'unaffordable' welfare system by the government's 'third way' ('promoting opportunity instead of dependence') were deliberately couched in terms of 'A New Contract for Welfare'.[40] In the 'something for something' society, the duty of the state to ensure that citizens have a stake in society's future is balanced by the acceptance of responsibility of individuals for their own improvement.[41] We examine this dimension of the New Public Contracting in greater depth in Chapter 9.

A three-way distinction may be drawn between:

1. empirically observable contracting behaviour defined in terms of the contract norms;
2. the rhetorical use of contract in the legitimation or promotion of policy programmes in political discourse; and
3. the recourse to contract terminology in efforts to conceptualize or understand social relations (involving analyses of such relations 'as if' they were contracts).[42]

38 A Yeatman, 'Interpreting Contemporary Contractualism', in M Dean and B Hindess, (eds). *Governing Australia: Studies in Contemporary Rationalities of Government* (Cambridge: Cambridge University Press, 1998) 227; A Yeatman and K Owler, 'The Role of Contract in the Democratisation of Service Delivery' (2001) 18 *Law in Context* 34.

39 E Heron and P Dwyer, 'Doing the Right Thing: Labour's Attempt to Force a New Welfare Deal Between the Individual and the State' (1999) 33 *Social Policy and Administration* 91, 100.

40 *A New Contract for Welfare*, Green Paper, (Cm 3805,1998).

41 S Prideaux, 'New Labour, Old Functionalism: The Underlying Contradictions of Welfare Reform in the US and UK' (2001) 35 *Social Policy and Administration* 85, 91.

42 Loughlin's analysis of the traditionally cooperative relationship between central and local government in terms of a 'political compact', involving collaborative relations and an informal system of governance bolstered by judicial non-interference, might be included in the 'as if' category – M Loughlin, *Legality and Locality: The Role of Law in Central-Local Government Relations* (Oxford: Clarendon Press, 1996); ibid, 'Understanding Central-Local Government Relations' (1996) 11 *Public Policy and Administration* 48. The 'incomplete contracts' tradition of economic analysis, and the contractarian perspective on corporate governance, might also be so regarded – see R Goddard, 'Enforcing the Hypothetical Bargain: Sections 459–461 of the Companies Act 1985' (1999) 20 *Company Lawyer* 66. See similarly the literature on 'psychological contracts' in employment relations – S Lo and S Aryee, 'Psychological Contract Breach in a Chinese Context: An Integrative Approach' (2003) 40 *Journal of Management Studies* 1005; D Guest, 'Is the Psychological Contract Worth Taking Seriously?' (1998) 19 *Journal of Psychological Behaviour* 649; E Morrison and S Robinson, 'When Employees Feel Betrayed: A Model of How Psychological Contract Violation Develops' (1997) 22 *Academy of Management Review* 226.

However, this distinction may be difficult to maintain in practice, especially in the case of arrangements that are proclaimed as contracts by government for political purposes. In the 1997 general election campaign Tony Blair offered a '10-point contract' to the British people, implying that he would not deserve a second term if he did not meet its promises.[43] This 'compact' might, in a weak sense, be argued to have governed (or to have been capable of governing) the behaviour of the parties to it. Nevertheless, despite the existence of elements of discreteness and presentiation, this self-proclaimed contract was lacking in reciprocity, specificity of commitments, certainty as to the identities of the parties, and any realistic sanctioning mechanism for non-performance. For similar reasons, voluntary agreements between the government and organised labour, such as the 'social compact' of 1974 in which the cooperation of the trade unions on wages was secured in return for legislation on job security and repeal of the Industrial Relations Act 1971,[44] are unlikely to satisfy the present behavioural definition of contract, although such relations have undoubted political significance and might still fruitfully be analysed with reference to the contract norms.[45]

The phenomena of public contracting

When confronted with legally unenforceable instances of public contracting (as in the use of contracts in the restructuring of relations within government, or the attempt to structure relationships between the government and citizens in contractual form) the response of lawyers tends to be to question whether the relationships are 'contractual' in any meaningful sense at all. Rejecting the use of contract terminology in these instances, Collins describes the arrangements variously as 'quasi-contracts', 'fictional contracts' and 'mere contractual metaphors'. Their limited role is 'to provide a framework of reference for the

43 A 40-page document was offered as the basis of a relationship of trust that would be developed between government and the people: 'Judge us on this agenda. Track our progress. Measure it to see if we live up to the promises that we make.' At the end of the decade, Labour returned to the contract theme in retrospective justification of its conduct after two years of office. In his introduction to Labour's 'Annual Report 1998/99', on sale in Tesco for £2.99, Tony Blair said that Labour had delivered on 90 of 177 specific election promises, a further 85 were on course, and only two had still to be timetabled.

44 C Turpin, *British Government and the Constitution – Text, Cases and Materials* (5th edn, London: Butterworths, 2002) 438.

45 Macneil has applied relational contract theory in exactly this political context, arguing that by the time of the 1978–9 winter of discontent the 'social contract' was increasingly perceived as seriously defective in respect of a large number of norms (most notably reciprocity and solidarity) necessary for the contractual relation to continue successfully – Macneil (1990) (n 16 above) 154: 'The prevailing view in 1979 Britain was that the balance of power between unions on the one hand, and companies, government, and electorate on the other, had become too one-sided. This was a significant factor in the decision of the prevailing electorate to elect a party pledged to do something about the way (general political exchange) was played' (167). However, I prefer to view this as an example of an interesting analysis of social relations 'as if' they were behavioural contracts expressing the operation of the contract norms in real social organisation.

orientation of the parties' conduct within a system of bureaucratic control,'[46] yet the existence of such control necessarily compromises the effectiveness of these arrangements. In similar fashion, Harlow and Rawlings contrast arrangements 'true to contract in the legal sense' with various forms of 'pseudo-contract' that have been deployed as tools of intra-governmental coordination, or in the remodelling of relations between the government and individuals.[47] Implicit in these accounts is the notion that the legal conception of contract is the original and true meaning, against which various contemporary manifestations are judged to be false or inauthentic. The important issue then becomes the 'lack of fit' between these emergent 'administrative' adaptations and the traditional legal framework. The simultaneous existence of the attempt to recast relations in terms of contract while denying these relationships legal recognition leads lawyers to advocate more formal legal governance, creating 'fertile territory for advocates of a special public law of contract'.[48]

My argument, by contrast, is that the 'reality' of government contracts is not dependent on the quality of legal enforceability at private law or on legal recognition more generally.[49] Legal enforceability is neither a crucial element in the definition of public contracts, nor a particularly useful point of departure for their classification.[50] The main objection to the lawyer's definition is that it underplays the behavioural dimension of contract, pre-supposing the existence of extra-legal (and 'pre-legal') norms and institutions that support social exchange.[51] A more obvious and practical problem with this starting point is that many modern public 'contracts' are not legally enforceable at private law, either because the parties lack separate legal personalities (as in the case of framework agreements linking departments and executive agencies, or contracts between public purchasers and in-house agencies following market-testing) or because legislation or regulations deliberately preclude this result (as in the case of commissioning of health care in the

[46] Collins (n 1 above) 318–9.

[47] C Harlow and R Rawlings, *Law and Administration* (London: Butterworths, 1997) 210–211.

[48] ibid 210; I Harden, *The Contracting State* (Buckingham: Open University Press, 1992).

[49] For a similar rejection of the notion that internal contracts are purely symbolic, see Davies (n 1 above) 57.

[50] What is important is enforceability in the sense of the constraining effect of contract norms together with the sanctioning of their violation. In this vein Seddon states that the essential feature of contract is 'enforceability by some means, even if not by law'. 'If it is not enforceable (in some sense) then it is futile to call it "contract" because the whole point of contractualism . . . is that the principal has a means of achieving a particular objective or outcome' – N Seddon, *Government Contracts: Federal, State and Local* (2nd edn, Sydney: Federation Press, 1999), 30. However, Seddon's rejection of the application of the 'contract' label for Activity Agreements in the context of Australian unemployment law appears to be based precisely on the lack of legal enforceability – see N Seddon, 'Activity Agreements – Are They Contracts?', in R Creyke and M Sassarella, (eds), *Targeting Accountability and Review* (Canberra: AIAL, 1998). We argue in ch 9 that such contracts are indeed enforceable, albeit indirectly, at least by the 'principal'.

[51] AW Gouldner, 'The Norm of Reciprocity' (1960) 25 *American Sociological Review* 161–178; M Weber, *The Theory of Social and Economic Organization*, translated by AM Henderson and T Parsons, (London: Collier-Macmillan, 1947).

NHS, or home-school agreements between parents and headteachers).[52] The task in such cases is to analyse the role played by contract norms in the wider context of the regulatory frameworks and associated administrative and legal governance mechanisms that constitute these public contracting arrangements.

In many instances, however, public contracting is indeed subject to the private law of contract, which reinforces the contract norms and thereby opens the way to judicial enforcement and dispute-settlement machinery. Leaving aside the question of the adequacy of contract doctrine in regulating business relations generally, the focus here is on how private law governs inter-sectoral transactions (for example involving public procurement, the Private Finance Initiative (PFI) or other forms of public-private partnership) and on how this law relates to, and impacts upon, the common contract norms. These forms of public contracting are again, to varying degrees, produced or influenced by specific government policies, so that the role of private law needs to be considered in the context of the broader regulatory frameworks and institutions that make up the governance structure.

In sum, the social process of contracting may be said to occur wherever human action is rationally oriented in accordance with what the parties engaged in exchange regard as their contract. This 'contract' – whether existing as a formal document or an informal understanding, and whether or not recognized at private law – provides a reference point for the parties' subsequent action. In this analysis, while the contract norms indeed serve to structure social relations for the participants, 'the contract' as a frame of reference should neither be reduced to, nor necessarily associated with, contractual rights and duties in the sense recognized by law.[53] Despite clear differences between the three contemporary conceptions of contract (behavioural, legal, and rhetorical), all draw on a common normative language involving core notions of reciprocity, mutuality of obligations, and rights balanced by responsibilities. All three dimensions will be shown to be relevant in the investigation of contemporary public contracting phenomena.

From public procurement to government by contract

Government contracting has traditionally been equated with public procurement, contract being 'the instrument by which the goods and services required by government departments are procured from the private sector'.[54] Traditional, or basic, public procurement remains a vitally important part of current public

52 eg School Standards and Framework Act 1998, s 111(6): 'A home-school agreement shall not be capable of creating any obligation in respect of whose breach any liability arises in contract or tort.' See also National Health Service and Community Care Act 1990, s 4(3).

53 Collins (n 1 above) 21.

54 C Turpin, *Government Procurement and Contracts* (Harlow: Longman, 1989), ix.

contracting.[55] Regulation here takes the form of relatively general rules supporting the broad policy objective of acquiring goods or services from the private sector on the best terms and on schedule. Current procurement rules are embodied in guidance and model contract conditions produced by government bodies such as the Buying Agency, the Central Computer and Telecommunications Agency (CCTA), and the joint Treasury and DTI Procurement Policy team.[56] The general guiding principle is value-for-money, defined as the optimum combination of whole-life cost and quality to meet the user's requirements, to be achieved through competitive tendering. The pursuit of value-for-money in public purchasing and the encouragement of competitiveness (and hence efficiency) of UK suppliers have been key policy objectives since the 1980s. There exists a tension between the aim of boosting national competitiveness, and the need to observe international and European treaty obligations on opening up procurement to overseas contractors. A key task of scholars in this field is understanding the inter-relationship of different (and sometimes conflicting) international, European and domestic regulatory frameworks governing public procurement.[57]

Government by contract

The general term 'government by contract' is currently used to describe a wide range of contractual arrangements involving public bodies in addition to public procurement. Such arrangements include contracting out, public/private partnerships, franchising or state concessions, contracts of employment in the public service, agreements between the government and self-regulatory organizations, agreements between state agencies and individual citizens, and various types of agreement internal to government.[58] Some aspects of government by contract will now briefly be considered, prior to narrowing the scope of the investigation in the next section to the New Public Contracting.

[55] D Kettl, *Sharing Power: Public Governance and Private Markets* (Washington DC: The Brookings Institution, 1993); D Parker and K Hartley, 'The Economics of Partnership Sourcing Versus Adversarial Competition: A Critique' (1997) 3 *European Journal of Purchasing and Supply Management* 115.

[56] P Craig, *Administrative Law* (4th edn, London: Sweet and Maxwell, 1999), 122.

[57] S Arrowsmith, 'Public Procurement as an Instrument of Policy and the Impact of Market Liberalisation' (1995), 111 *LQR* 234; C Bovis, *EC Public Procurement: Case Law and Regulation* (Oxford: Oxford University Press, 2006); R Fee, P Maxwell, and A Erridge, 'Contracting for Services: A Double Jeopardy? An Analysis of Contract Compliance in the Context of European and UK Social and Public Procurement Policy' (1998) 13 *Public Policy and Administration* 79; R Fee, 'Contract Compliance: Subnational and European Influences in Northern Ireland' (2002) 12 *Journal of European Social Policy* 107; F Sutcliffe, 'Contracting Out Public Services: UK Policy *v* EC Law' (1993) 22 *Anglo-American Law Review* 337. From the present perspective, the interesting research question is how legal structures at these different levels impinge upon the contract norms supporting public procurement behaviour.

[58] The modern tendency is to regard agreements between state agencies and individual citizens as a form of government by contract – see for example Collins (n 1 above) 317; Harlow and Rawlings (n 47 above) 211–14. For a narrower classification see Davies (n 1 above) 1–8.

Over the course of the last fifty years, contract has been used increasingly as a means of promoting policy goals that are secondary or ancillary to the government's principal procurement purposes. In the UK, economic objectives have been pursued through the positive deployment of procurement powers to assist industrial restructuring, for example in the form of 'buy national' pressures on nationalised industries and public authorities, and preference schemes aimed at regional re-development. Social policies aimed at changing and regulating behaviour have been pursued through contract compliance requirements in respect of employment practices, race and sex discrimination, and environmental protection. Conformity with such policy objectives may also be secured 'negatively' through the threat of withholding contracts or the imposition of contractual sanctions for non-compliance.[59]

On both sides of the Atlantic in the early post-war period, the term 'new contracting' was used to describe novel delegations of authority to institutions outside the direct framework of government, entailing something quite different from the 'older' pattern of contracting – the routine buying of goods and services in well-established markets. In the increasingly intricate pattern of interactions between public and private institutions, public contracting was argued to be moving from the logistic periphery of government action into the 'main arena of policy-making'.[60] In the United States, contract was increasingly viewed both as an instrument of regulation and a means of social control.[61] The emergence of regulation by contract and contracting out was seen as entailing a new concept in government and a novel development in American law. The associated breakdown of the private/public distinction was marked by a trend towards discharging governmental responsibilities at least in part by private endeavour, and by the sharing of governmental power between state officials and 'personnel who draw their pay checks from profit or non-profit private enterprise'.[62] Other writers in the United States focused on how government contracts combining 'agreement' with authority and command were being deployed in administrative actions.[63] In the UK, the increasing use by central government of its contractual powers to promote

59 Arrowsmith (n 57 above) 238; P Morris, 'Legal Regulation of Contract Compliance: An Anglo-American Comparison' (1990) 19 *Anglo-American Law Review* 87. The scope for implementation of secondary policies has been cut down by Britain's treaty commitments at European and international levels.

60 BLR Smith, 'Accountability and Independence in the Contract State', in BLR Smith and DC Hague, (eds), *The Dilemma of Accountability in Modern Government: Independence Versus Control* (London: Macmillan, 1971) 13.

61 AS Miller, 'Government Contracts and Social Control: A Preliminary Inquiry' (1955) 41 *Virginia Law Review* 27.

62 AS Miller, 'Administration by Contract: A New Concern for the Administrative Lawyer' (1961) 36 *New York University Law Review* 957, 967.

63 G Langrod, 'Administrative Contracts: A Comparative Study' (1955) 4 *American Journal of Comparative Law* 325. On the rise of contract as an administrative and regulatory insrument in the US in the context of more recent global privatization trends, see: J Freeman, 'The Contracting State' (2000) 28 *Florida State University Law Review* 155.

economic or social policy objectives without recourse to Parliament was analysed famously by Daintith in terms of the 'new prerogative' of regulation by contract, involving a shift in the mode of state control from 'imperium' to 'dominium'.[64]

Against this background, two contemporary forms of government by contract may briefly be considered to illustrate the argument that follows. First, the use of 'covenants' has become widespread throughout Europe as an instrument for achieving governmental objectives in particular sectors, for example environmental policy.[65] Covenants differ from voluntary agreements in the explicitly juridical form of the arrangement between government and industry. They tend to be regarded by both partners as a preferable alternative to formal regulation, being more flexible and more reciprocal, and according both contract partners rights and duties whereas regulation in the same field is considered to involve mainly duties.[66] Second, a different type of government by contract occurs in the form of constitutional concordats or agreements between national and state governments in federated systems such as Belgium, which has 100 such formal and legally binding agreements and protocols.[67] Elsewhere in Europe and in common law countries with federal or devolved systems of government, non-statutory and legally unenforceable agreements are used to structure relations between different levels of government. Such arrangements in the UK are found in the guise of 'concordats of the constitution' linking the UK government and devolved administrations in Scotland, Wales, and Northern Ireland.[68] Concordats of the constitution raise major concerns about the nature and quality of the emergent system of UK governance.[69]

Government by agreement

A distinction may be drawn between government by contract as just considered on the one hand, and a variety of arrangements involving government and external organizations or associations under the general rubric of 'government by agreement' on the other. Baggott includes in this category 'any agreement between the government (or one of its agencies) and a section of the community (or its representatives) whose main purpose is to establish a degree of regulation over the specific activities of the latter, and which involves a non-statutory regulatory procedure or code of practice, or both, which the latter is committed to follow

[64] T Daintith, 'Regulation by Contract: The New Prerogative' (1979) CLP 41.

[65] I Koppen, 'Ecological Covenants: Regulatory Informality in Dutch Waste Reduction Policy, in G Teubner, L Farmer, and D Murphy, (eds), *Environmental Law and Ecological Responsibility: The Concept and Practice of Ecological Self-Organization* (Chichester: John Wiley & Sons, 1994).

[66] AB Ringeling, 'European Experience with Tools of Government', in LM Salamon, (ed), *The Tools of Government: A Guide to the New Governance* (Oxford: Oxford University Press, 2002) 591.

[67] J Poirier, 'The Functions of Intergovernmental Agreements: Post-Devolution Concordats in a Comparative Perspective' [2000] PL 134.

[68] ibid 136.

[69] R Rawlings, 'Concordats of the Constitution' (2000) 116 LQR 257, 261.

under the terms of the agreement'.[70] These arrangements are not legally enforceable at private law,[71] and have nothing to do with public procurement. In the UK they include schemes of self-regulation negotiated with trade, manufacturers' or professional associations, in circumstances where legislation might otherwise have been used to achieve public policy objectives. In essence the bargain consists in the provision of a financial incentive or an assurance by the government that it will forbear from taking formal regulatory action, in return for an undertaking of self-regulation on the part of the organization.[72] Voluntary agreements between government and industry or private associations have a long history elsewhere in Western Europe. Government by agreement has tended generally to be used as a substitute for regulation, such that when agreements are reached, 'government regulation will, as a rule, not take place'.[73]

A different type of government by agreement, in this instance involving other governmental rather than private or non-state bodies, is found in Local Public Service Agreements (LPSAs) which local authorities have recently been encouraged to conclude with central government. Under such arrangements, administrative freedoms are granted and extra funds made available to councils making commitments to ambitious targets for improving services. As with many other types of government by agreement, the initiative came from the 'regulated' bodies (in this case councils represented by the Local Government Association) rather than being imposed by central government. Furthermore, while councils were given an indication of the areas in which ministers wanted to see improvements through the LPSA scheme, they made their own choices and developed their own proposals. Another example of this type of government by agreement concerns the attempt to structure the relationship between government bodies and the voluntary sector through 'compacts'.[74]

Whether the government's policy agendas are pursued through contract, compact, concordat, or agreement, and regardless of the legal enforceability of the arrangements, the administrative advantages of governing in this manner have to be balanced against disadvantages of reduced transparency and public

[70] R Baggott, 'By Voluntary Agreement: The Politics of Instrument Selection' (1986) 64 *Public Administration* 51, 52.

[71] While they cannot be directly enforced, voluntary agreements in some cases have an indirect statutory basis (in the legal requirement that such agreements be drawn up), and infringements may constitute evidence in extra-contractual private law actions – ibid 55.

[72] This category is discussed by Cane in terms of 'corporatism', considered to involve 'cooperative arrangements between government and non-governmental groups or institutions under which the latter, either in return for some benefit or in order to avoid some disadvantage, agree to act in a way which will further government policy'. Self-regulation by professional groups such as doctors and lawyers, and partnerships between governmental and non-governmental groups in pursuit of shared policy objectives, are brought within this definition – P Cane, *An Introduction to Administrative Law* (3rd edn, Oxford: Clarendon Press, 1996) 21.

[73] Ringeling (n 66 above) 591.

[74] J Morison, 'The Government-Voluntary Sector Compacts: Governance, Governmentality, and Civil Society' (2000) 27 JLS 98; Local Government Association, *Local Compact Guidelines* (London: NCVO, 2000).

accountability in policy making and implementation.[75] In many cases, the question is why more formal legal procedures have not been used where sensibly they could, the criticism being that such politically convenient arrangements lack adequate constitutional accountability.

Taking stock

In all these instances, contracting arrangements may be evaluated in terms of the balance struck between discrete and relational contract norms within the relationships and in their institutional environments. Some of the contracts are likely to fail because they are too general and nebulous, lacking the degree of discreteness and presentiation necessary for effective planning. One of Labour's major initiatives on assuming power in 1997, the compact between government and the voluntary sector, appears to be a good example of the attempt to create a 'constitution' governing relationships that in reality has had very little impact on the behaviour of the parties.[76] In other cases, the problem might concern damage to the norms of reciprocity and solidarity caused by a breakdown of trust, either within the particular contractual relationship or outside it. For example, LPSAs might founder on growing suspicion on the part of local councils of central government's unwillingness to deliver on promises of increased autonomy.[77] Local authorities might abandon LPSAs should these agreements come to be seen as a subtle attempt at micro-management of local by central government. Constitutional concordats might, like LPSAs, suffer from damage to the relational norms of reciprocity and solidarity should they be perceived as instruments of regulation by national government. The effectiveness of the various forms of government by contract may be positively related to the involvement and participation of regulated bodies in setting up the new governance structures, in contrast with the top-down imposition by central government of pre-conceived and ready-made arrangements.[78]

While the foregoing types of government by contract or agreement might be included within a broad definition of 'new public contracting', and can certainly be analysed in terms of the common contract norms, they merit separate treatment in their own right and will not be further considered here.[79] What is now required is a more precise definition of the scope of the present inquiry.

75 Baggott (n 70 above) 51.

76 *Guardian* 5 November 2003.

77 *Guardian* 4 July 2001.

78 C Pateman, *The Problem of Political Obligation: A Critical Analysis of Liberal Theory* (Chichester: John Wiley and Son, 1979). Future research might test this hypothesis.

79 Some of these forms (notably LPSAs) will be shown to be a significant feature in the environment of the New Public Contracting, while not being part of it. Other forms of government by contract that will not be considered include contracts of employment, and the public control of privatized utilities or services through franchising or licensing. Privatization raises different regulatory issues that are better addressed through other theoretical perspectives. See for example C Scott, 'Privatization, Control, and Accountability', in J McCahery, S Picciotto, and C Scott, (eds), *Corporate Control and Accountability* (Oxford: Clarendon Press, 1993); ibid, C Scott, 'Analysing Regulatory Space: Fragmented Resources and Institutional Design' [2001] PL 329.

The New Public Contracting

This section explains and justifies the narrowing of the principal focus of the book to the three main forms of the New Public Contracting: administrative contracts, economic contracts, and social control contracts. The New Public Contracting is distinguished from government by contract more generally by the delegation of powers and responsibilities to public agencies in various contractual arrangements preserving central government controls and powers of intervention.[80] In addition to governance through the contract norms, features common to each form of the New Public Contracting include the separation of interests (purchaser and provider, client and contractor, public agency and individual citizen), and the nesting of contractual relations within policy-driven regulatory frameworks directed at structuring or changing behaviour (administrative, economic, or individual).

Purposiveness: policy-driven regulation vs general regulatory control

While competitive tendering and market testing policies introduced from the early 1980s were viewed by Turpin as simply a 'special case of the search for value-for-money',[81] such developments arguably marked a more fundamental policy shift from relatively simple regulatory control through contract, to more purposive, policy-driven regulation.[82] This shift, considered by Freedland to have occurred in the Private Finance Initiative (PFI), may be argued to have begun earlier and been more far-reaching than his account suggests.

Acknowledging that governments have been engaged in contracting of various kinds in pursuit of policy for many years, including transactions in which the private contractor in some way provides capital assets or capital funding, Freedland detects a change from about 1980 that led to the programmatic initiative from 1992 onwards in the specific shape of the PFI. An important feature of the background to the PFI was the informality of the regulatory framework governing this form of public contracting. The Treasury was accordingly able easily to

80 While the New Public Contracting is claimed to be a 'new' phenomenon, it remains in some senses a development of earlier forms of government by contract. Pertinent here is Miller's prescient insight on the trend towards 'federalism by contract', consisting in the delegation of administrative responsibility by public officials who simultaneously retain powers both of supervision and of revocation of the delegation – Miller (n 62 above) 967.

81 Turpin (n 54 above) 70.

82 M Freedland, 'Public Law and Private Finance – Placing the Private Finance Initiative in a Public Law Frame' [1998] PL 288. By contrast, Turpin's main concern in the revised version of his earlier work on public procurement is with how the law and more informal influences maintain the balance between the aim of securing value-for-money through competitiveness on the one hand, and the need for close cooperation in the conduct of these relationships on the other. The policy on contracting out receives relatively scant attention, although its importance (more than half way into the eighteen year period of Conservative political dominance) is clearly acknowledged – Turpin (n 54 above).

modify both substantive norms and their mode of presentation in policy documents (typically glossy brochures, discursive in character and promotional in tone and presentation), and thereby to develop a more permissive approach to private finance contracting.[83] The rationale for the PFI at the micro-economic level is the belief that public services can be provided more efficiently by the private market than by the state directly. The macro-economic rationale concerns the supposed benefit of minimizing or deferring immediate public spending or borrowing requirements.[84] While pointing to certain tensions in the Government's overall policy, Freedland nevertheless demonstrates in the case of the PFI a marked trend away from regulatory control towards positive policy-driven regulation.[85]

This analysis may be applied more broadly. Both contracting out and internal contracting between public purchasers and in-house providers following Compulsory Competitive Tendering (CCT) or market testing display features of positive policy-driven regulation. Such novel forms of public contracting were deliberately created through regulatory frameworks promoting particular policy objectives. As is well known, public sector reform in the UK received a significant boost with the election of a Conservative administration under the leadership of Margaret Thatcher in 1979. The exposure of public bureaucracies to market oriented reforms was a crucial accompaniment to the privatization of state owned industries and public utilities.[86] While market-testing of ancillary services in central government was less obviously ideologically driven than the regime of CCT for manual and professional services in local government, public contracting here was also moulded by central government policy.[87] As with the PFI, the normative structures governing these forms of public contracting consist not just in a set of identifiable and separable rules of operation, but in 'a set of ideas or guiding principles which emerge from a large body of partly presentational and explanatory material'.[88]

A major objective of policies introducing competitive procedures is to reduce costs and to improve the quality of public services. The market, it is presumed, is more likely to be able to achieve both productive and allocative efficiency than bureaucratic organization. However, just as important as the attainment of value-for-money, and distinct from it, have been the policy goals of transferring public service functions out of the state sector, reducing the size of public bureaucracies, increasing the role of private and voluntary providers, and curbing the powers of the public sector unions. The substantive thrust of central government policy since the 1980s has been about the *transition* from bureaucratic to non-state provision through exposure to competitive processes. Following the introduction of

[83] Freedland (n 82 above) 302. [84] ibid 299.

[85] ibid 299-300. For a critique of Freedland's argument, see M Elsenar, 'Law, Accountability and the Private Finance Initiative in the National Health Service' [1999] PL 35.

[86] S Domberger, *The Contracting Organization: A Strategic Guide to Outsourcing* (Oxford: Oxford University Press, 1998), 157. [87] see ch 7.

[88] Freedland (n 82 above) 289.

market testing and the contracting out of support services in central and local government, the radical Conservative reformers turned in the late 1980s and 1990s to the reform of the welfare state. The creation of quasi-markets, which involved the separation of purchaser and provider functions in the major welfare sectors of housing, education, health and social care, was still more obviously guided by particular policy objectives (increasing responsiveness to consumer needs, reducing the power of the medical and legal professions, and again, encouraging greater reliance on the non-state sectors). The new contractual forms (for example, NHS Contracts) were the product of specific legislative schemes constituting them as key mechanisms of economic coordination.

The remainder of this and the following chapter show how, in addition to the economic reform agenda just outlined, the government has pursued substantive policy goals entailing the restructuring of relationships both within government and in the social control of individual citizens through the New Public Contracting.

Functions, forms, and variants

Three main forms of the New Public Contracting may be distinguished, together with their corresponding policy purposes and social functions.[89]

Administrative contracts

'Administrative contracts' are contractual arrangements intended (or having the potential) to increase the transparency and effectiveness of the operation of the machinery of government. These arrangements are the culmination of pressures for reduction of waste within the Civil Service that may be traced back to managerialist reforms of the 1970s, and have nothing directly to do with marketization and the exposure of government activities to competitive forces. They are associated most recently with the attempt to separate the political and managerial aspects of government, and to clarify bureaucratic roles through performance-based management systems.[90] The devolution of financial control to decentralized provider units, which have operational control of their own budgets and are accountable to politicians through monitoring systems that measure performance against targets, is a major feature of the use of administrative contracts. The attempt to distance politics from management is particularly evident in the autonomy accorded executive agencies in their relationship to their political masters. While

89 These three forms of the New Public Contracting and their variants may be considered ideal types in the Weberian sense. The classification is therefore acknowledged to be provisional and imperfect.

90 A major difference between the new managerialism and previous efforts at public management reform has been the reassertion of the dominance of the political level, 'following an era in which the distinction between the activities of the bureaucrat and the politician had become blurred' – Walsh (n 10 above) 66.

oriented to values of economy and efficiency, contracts here are primarily concerned with relationships of power within government and administration, and in that sense may be said to have a constitutional dimension. The two major variants of administrative contract are framework documents between executive agencies and government departments under the Next Steps initiative commencing in 1988, and Public Service Agreements (PSAs) between the Treasury and spending departments linked with the Comprehensive Spending Review begun in 1998 and continued at two-yearly intervals. Administrative contracts are considered in depth in Chapter 6.

Economic contracts

'Economic contracts' are contractual arrangements directed at improving public services through competition and/or the devolution of management powers to public purchasing or commissioning agencies in a variety of hybrid forms beyond simple market or bureaucratic organisation.[91] The focus on competition and marketization reflects a part of the New Public Contracting reform agenda which is distinct from managerialism. In addition to efficiency, the regulatory frameworks within which such contracts operate also embody values of social justice, equity and redistribution. Policy initiatives here are about the better use and coordination of resources that lead ultimately to the production of public services. While in a limited sense the function of economic coordination may be performed within public organizations through the device of the contract of employment, a fundamental purpose of the New Public Contracting has been to displace such bureaucratic organization. The economic organizational role of the New Public Contracting is evident in the operation of quasi-markets for education, health, and social care resulting from the major structural reorganizations of these public services since the 1980s, but it features in public service provision more generally. Since economic contracts in this sense are so varied and numerous, my treatment of them in this book is necessarily more synoptic than other forms of the New Public Contracting. The examples selected for discussion in Chapters 7 and 8 are: market testing and competitive tendering, including both external contracting and internal contracting on the basis of Service Level Agreements (SLAs); franchising and corporatization in the organization of health, social and welfare services; and Public Private Partnerships, including public infrastructure financing and procurement under the PFI and the Public Private Partnerships Programme ('Four Ps') initiatives in local government.

[91] W Powell, 'Neither Market nor Hierarchy: Network Forms of Organisation', (1990) 12 *Journal of Organizational Behaviour* 295; HA Simon, 'Organizations and Markets' (1991) 5 *Journal of Economic Perspectives* 25; E Schanze, 'Symbiotic Contracts: Exploring Long-Term Agency Structures Between Contract and Corporation', in C Joerges, (ed), *Franchising and the Law: Theoretical and Comparative Approaches in Europe and the United States* (Baden-Baden: Nomos Verlagsgesellschaft, 1991); H Thorelli, 'Networks: Between Markets and Hierarchies' (1986) 7 *Strategic Management Journal* 37.

Social control contracts

'Social control contracts' are adaptations of the contract mechanism used in the regulation of relationships between individual citizens and state authority in various guises. Of particular importance here are values of individual responsibility, fairness and justice. The variants of social control contracts that will be considered in depth in Chapter 9 are jobseekers' agreements under the Jobseekers' Act 1995; home-school agreements under the School Standards and Framework Act 1998; youth offender contracts between Youth Offender Panels and young offenders under the Youth Justice and Criminal Evidence Act 1999; and parenting contracts under the Anti-social Behaviour Act 2003.

The distinction between administrative and economic functions of the New Public Contracting may be clarified further. While both PSAs and framework documents involve the separation of roles within government and the allocation of resources in return for policy delivery, contract here performs an administrative rather than an economic function. In the absence of competition and purchaser choice, the relationships are necessarily bureaucratic in character. Executive agencies do not compete directly with one-another for departmental funding, and similarly, government departments do not compete directly for central funding. The subordinate partners in the contractual relationships (government departments in relation to the Treasury, executive agencies in relation to their parent departments) have no choice whether or with whom to contract. The administrative function of contract in this context is not affected fundamentally by the existence of internal charging, or charging user fees to the public, except in those relatively unusual cases where agencies are subject to competition in the market or for the market.[92]

Administrative contracts operate within the organizational boundaries of the state, understood as comprising central and local government and other public agencies subject to bureaucratic chain-of-command controls. Civil servants continue to operate within such boundaries despite their movement out of central government departments to executive agencies, so framework documents are included in this category. However, the fact that contracting occurs literally 'within' government organizations does not by itself render the arrangements suitable for analysis in terms of administrative contracts. For example, where contracts are awarded to in-house teams in the form of legally unenforceable SLAs following market testing, the function being performed by contract is economic rather than purely bureaucratic or administrative – assuming that in-house bidders are under

92 The levying of charges or user fees for services performs no economic function other than recovering an arbitrary level of costs, since the user cannot choose whether to consume the service, and the level of charge does not vary with the degree of usage – Walsh (n 10 above) 88.

pressure to compete with the private sector, and public purchasers have the power and incentive to choose to award the contract externally.

Conversely, where local authorities or other public bodies have developed internal trading on a voluntary basis for services that are not subject to competitive tendering,[93] the contractual arrangements are fundamentally administrative rather than economic in nature. Internal trading and charging for support and professional services (finance, IT, legal work) within central and local government organizations are thus distinguished from internal contracting for such services following market testing or competitive tendering.[94] While both relationships are commonly described as SLAs, only in the latter instance does the client have a choice whether to contract with the in-house bidder, which must compete with external providers for the right to supply the service. Whereas here prices are likely to approximate to those in the external market, internal transfer prices within organizations – in the absence of purchaser choice and provider competition – are often a political matter having little relationship to costs. My argument, therefore, is that it is better to reserve *market* (including internal market) terminology for organizational arrangements in which the elements of choice and competition associated with the generation of economic efficiencies in private business exchanges are present. Both framework documents and PSAs are thus unambiguously administrative rather than economic contracts. They are the product of a managerialist reform agenda, rather than one informed by principles of marketisation or competition.

The distinction between administrative and economic functions reflects different policy purposes in the adaptation of the contract mechanism in the two New Public Contracting forms. The purpose of administrative contracts is both to provide an incentive to separated units and agencies within the public organisation to improve performance, and to ensure, through contractual coordination, that individual units contribute to the overall goals of the organization. The purpose of the New Public Contracting in its economic organizational form, irrespective of the location of the provider within or outside the organization, is to improve public services through the stimulation of provider competition and devolution of decision-making powers, including the capacity to choose, to public purchasing agencies. In this analysis, while the objective of administrative restructuring within government has certainly been to encourage the civil service to become more innovative and financially effective, it is too simplistic to maintain that this was to be achieved by exposing them to competitive market dynamics.[95] Not all

93 M Mackintosh, 'Trading Work: Discourses of Internal Exchange in the Economic Culture of Local Government' (1997) 12 *Public Policy and Administration* 17.

94 The introduction of accurate accounting methods in local government through 'activity costing' and internal trading accounts was a necessary prelude to competitive tendering for corporate services under the Local Government Act 1992 – see M Pendlebury, 'Management Accounting in Local Government' (1994) 10 *Financial Accountability and Management* 117, 121.

95 As claimed, for example, by I Kirkpatrick and M Lucio, 'Introduction: The Contract State and the Future of Public Management' (1996) 74 *Public Administration* 1. A similar over-simplification is evident in Hunt's assertion (having noted the various ways in which contract has replaced command

forms of the New Public Contracting therefore involve the attempt to replace bureaucratic ordering with a more market-based approach to the organisation of public services. For example, executive agency status was never intended, in the British context, to be about marketization or competition: 'it is . . . unfortunate that the rhetoric of markets and competition should have become entangled with what is essentially a decentralization initiative.'[96]

Because the underlying values, or the values at stake, in administrative contracts and economic contracts are so different, it makes little sense to attempt to evaluate the two types of arrangement according to common criteria.[97] In the former case, the contract norms operate through the medium of hierarchical authority rather than price and money. Although the contract norms remain the principal focus of analysis in both cases, their precise meaning is dependent on the administrative or economic functions being performed. The significance of the distinction between administrative and economic functions of the New Public Contracting will be further explored in Chapter 2.

Regulatory structures

This section outlines the regulatory anatomy of each of the three main forms of the New Public Contracting. A basic distinction is drawn between administrative contracts, which involve hierarchical regulation by contract;[98] and both economic contracts and social control contracts, which involve regulation by contract within hierarchical regulatory frameworks. Whereas the former implies the *contractual* delegation of governmental responsibilities, the latter two forms entail the delegation of *contracting powers* to responsible public agencies (either public

and control as the paradigm of regulation) that: 'in short, the state has been reconceived on the model of market ordering' – see M Hunt, 'Constitutionalism and the Contractualisation of Government', in M Taggart, (ed) *The Province of Administrative Law* (Oxford: Hart Publishing, 1997) 21. The present argument is that administrative contracts do not involve market ordering.

96 E Mellon, 'Executive Agencies in Central Government', in A Harrison (ed), *From Hierarchy to Contract* (Oxford: Transaction Books, 1993) 31.

97 Hence, the argument that the efficiency of contractual relationships between Next Steps agencies and central government is compromised by the absence of purchaser choice and provider competition ('bilateral monopoly' in economic analysis) may miss the point that this is essentially an administrative rather than an economic arrangement, which needs to be judged in such terms – W Bartlett and J Le Grand 'The Theory of Quasi-Markets', in J Le Grand and W Bartlett, (eds), *Quasi-Markets and Social Policy* (Houndmills: Macmillan, 1993) 21.

98 There is an important sense in which all contracts, even those between private parties with equal bargaining power in markets, may be described as 'hierarchical' in character – see A Stinchcombe, 'Contracts as Hierarchical Documents', in A Stinchcombe and CA Heimer, (eds), *Organization Theory and Project Management: Administering Uncertainty in Norwegian Offshore Oil* (Oslo: Nowegian University Press, 1985). On the role of discretionary power in contractual governance, see Collins (n 1 above) 24. On the 'bindingness of planning' (drawing on Macneil), see Vincent-Jones (n 4 above) 325–8. In the analysis of the New Public Contracting, however, 'hierarchical regulation by contract' has specifically bureaucratic organizational connotations. It is this bureaucratic, intra-governmental dimension that has led many commentators to doubt the 'contractual' nature of the relationships, and to see the use of contract terminology as purely symbolic or metaphorical.

purchasers or agencies of individual social control) operating within or beyond the boundaries of formal government in accordance with central regulatory regimes.

Administrative contracts

In the case of administrative contracts the regulatory structure appears relatively simple (Fig 2(a)). Bureaucratic regulation is cast in an explicitly contractual form – contract being the mechanism linking superior and subordinate levels within the government hierarchy (hence the term 'hierarchical regulation by contract'). Accordingly, spending departments are subject to Treasury control through contractual undertakings expressed in PSAs as part of the biennial Spending Review. In addition, executive agencies are regulated by their parent departments in accordance with the conditions set out in framework documents.

The 'public service' element in the PSA label is somewhat misleading,[99] since in this type of contract services are rendered by one tier within central government to another rather than to members of the public; the services are 'public' only in the sense that they are supplied in the public domain and to a public body.[100] Admittedly, there is a direct public service element in the functions performed by some executive agencies, for example vehicle licensing and certification services provided by the Driver and Vehicle Licensing Authority (DVLA). However, in contrast with public services that are provided through quasi-markets, these functions continue to be bureaucratically organised. In many cases the inherently regulatory nature of the activities would make them difficult to operate through competition,[101] although both government departments and executive agencies are under increasing pressure to consider whether a function needs to be performed at all, and if so whether it might better be privatized or contracted out. The values typically associated with this form of the New Public Contracting include transparency, political accountability, good government, the control of discretion and the prevention of abuse of public power, and (more controversially) the 'separation of powers'.[102]

99 The confusion is still greater in the case of LPSAs. It has already been suggested that LPSAs between local councils and central government departments – despite the Public Service Agreement label – are better considered an example of government by agreement than an instance of New Public Contracting.

100 Harden (n 48 above) distinguishes 'direct' public services, ie those delivered to identifiable members of the public, and 'indirect' or general public services that benefit all citizens. Ascher draws a different distinction between products or services required to maintain internal government operations (eg window cleaning and buildings maintenance) from those enabling the authority to meet external output obligations (eg the purchase of linen or the use of agency nurses in the NHS) – K Ascher, *The Politics of Privatisation: Contracting Out Public Services* (Houndmills: Macmillan, 1987) 8.

101 In the public franchising model, some regulatory functions might be contracted out and performed quite adequately on the basis of competition for the market, rather than in the market – see Domberger (n 86 above) 159–60.

102 Harden (n 48 above); ND Lewis, *Law and Governance: The Old Meets the New* (London: Cavendish Publishing, 2001) 140–141.

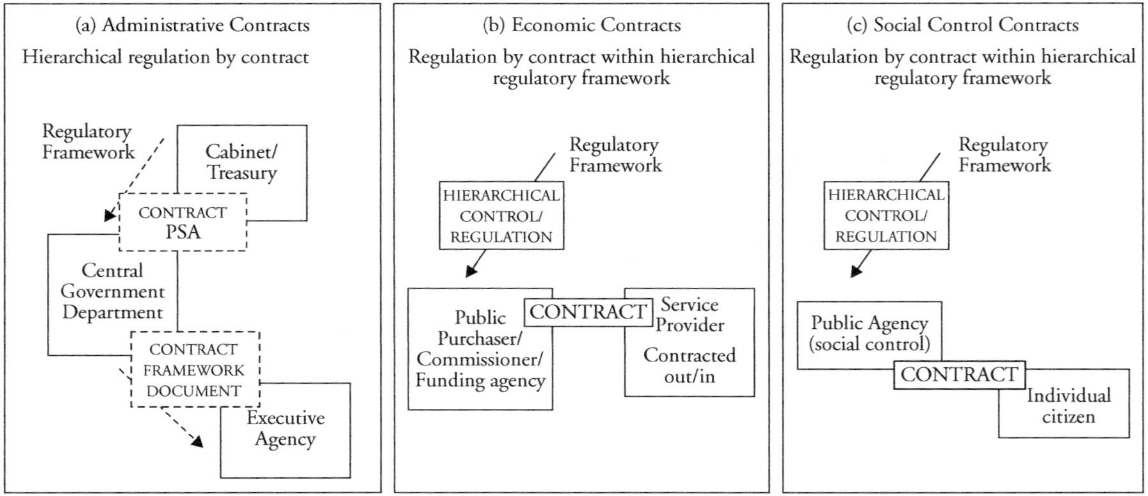

Figure 2. Anatomy of the New Public Contracting

Economic contracts

Economic contracts have a more complex 'double' regulatory structure, entailing regulation by contract within hierarchical regulatory frameworks (Fig 2(b)). The purchasing agency's use of contract as an instrument of regulation is dependent on the conditions that have been specified (extra-contractually) in the regulatory regime. The 'horizontal' contractual relationship between purchaser and provider therefore has to be considered in the context of the 'vertical' or hierarchical relationship between central authority and public purchaser.[103] Economic contracts play a central part in quasi-market organization in which there exists, on the supply side, competition between suppliers in the private, state, or non-profit sectors, combined on the demand side with the concentration of purchasing power in a public agency acting on behalf of ultimate consumers.[104] Economic coordination occurs through the devolution/granting of contractual capacities to public commissioning agencies under competitive conditions in which real choices have to be made, for example concerning the form of provision, the identity of the supplier, and the trade-off between price and quality.

The purchaser-provider relationship involves payment of money by the purchaser/client for services supplied by the contractor/provider. Whether the contract is external (enforceable at private law) or internal (not so enforceable) is immaterial to the quasi-market definition. A key difference in theory between the provision of public services through bureaucratic and quasi-market organisation is the presence of competition and choice, or at least contestability and other pressures and incentives to compete. These conditions should ideally allow comparisons to be made between internal and external suppliers, and enable the purchasing of services by public agencies in accordance with rational cost and value-for-money criteria. The advantage of quasi-markets compared with the market as a mechanism for delivering public services concerns the greater level of public control exercised through the hierarchical element in the regulatory structure. The values at stake in the operation of economic contracts therefore include distributive justice and the public interest, in addition to more familiar economic values of economy and efficiency.

Social control contracts

The third form of the New Public Contracting (Fig 2(c)) refers to adaptations of the contract mechanism in the social control of individual citizens in various relationships with state authority, for example involving the regulation of standards

[103] V Goldberg, 'Regulation and Administered Contracts' (1976) 7 *The Bell Journal of Economics* 426. On the concept of 'administered contracts' in the NHS, see D Hughes, J McHale, and L Griffiths, 'Contracts in the NHS: Searching for a Model?', in D Campbell and P Vincent-Jones, (eds), *Contract and Economic Organisation: Socio-Legal Initiatives* (Aldershot: Dartmouth, 1996).

[104] Le Grand and Bartlett (n 97 above) 10.

of behaviour among school pupils and young offenders. These arrangements are funded from general taxation as part of the public service provided by government to citizens generally. As with economic contracts, the hierarchical and contractual elements in the regulatory structure are linked – the public agency's use of contract as a mechanism of behavioural regulation being governed by the powers and duties established by the wider regulatory framework. In this type of New Public Contracting again, therefore, the contractual relationship between public agency and individual citizen has to be seen in the context of the hierarchical relationship between the public agency and central government authority. As we shall see, the values at play here include justice, effectiveness, fairness, protection of the public and the public interest, individual responsibility, and rehabilitation.

Key issues in the relational analysis of the New Public Contracting

In contemporary socio-legal scholarship,[105] the success of the law of contract as a governance framework in business and other private relations[106] is considered to lie in its capacity to permit the parties to express expectations in their own language, and so to self-regulate their relationship while avoiding distortions that might result from rigid and formal private law rules or an externally imposed regulatory framework.[107] In other words, the law of contract enables the parties to produce, for themselves, a constitution which they may use in the governance and adjustment of their on-going relationships,[108] and which may provide a basis for maximisation of their joint welfare.[109] While the interests of the parties diverge, it is of the essence of reciprocity that exchange is capable of benefiting both.[110] This perspective, as developed by Campbell and Harris, explicitly rejects the association in the dominant law and economics tradition of rational economic behaviour with narrow *individual* utility maximization. The attempt instead is 'to model the fundamental reciprocity of concerns between the parties, where each identifies its own best interest so closely with the interest of the other that it is inaccurate to view them as individual maximizers. They are joint-maximizers.'[111]

My central argument in this book is that such welfare-enhancing or joint-maximizing conditions are much more problematic and difficult to attain through programmes of policy-driven regulation involving public contracting. Leaving to one side the issue of legal enforceability and therefore of the role of the *law* of

105 See n 30 above.

106 J Wightman, 'Intimate Relationships, Relational Contract Theory, and the Reach of Contract' (2000) 8 *Feminist Legal Studies* 93.

107 Collins (n 1 above) 67.

108 Pateman (n 78 above).

109 Campbell and Harris (n 31 above).

110 Lon L Fuller, 'The Forms and Limits of Adjudication' (1978) 92 *Harvard Law Review* 353, 358; IR Macneil, 'Exchange Revisited: Individual Utility and Social Solidarity' 96 *Ethics* 567.

111 Campbell and Harris (n 31 above) 186.

contract in these relationships, the contractualization of the public sphere through the New Public Contracting involves the deliberate attempt by the state to structure social behaviour – within government, in the economic organization of public services, and in state-citizen relationships – through regulatory arrangements that harness the contract norms for the attainment of particular policy purposes. The basic issue in the analysis of administrative contracts, economic contracts, and social control contracts concerns the impact of purposive regulatory frameworks on the contract norms, and the implications for effectiveness in achieving the government's policy goals. A major focus is on the negative effects of policy-driven regulation on the relational elements of trust and cooperation that are essential to realizing the capacity of contract to benefit both the parties and society more generally. The cooperative state continues only 'so long as each party's analysis concludes that continuance is more advantageous than termination *and this essentially requires that each side can continue to trust with confidence in the other's co-operation*'.[112]

The behavioural conception of contract suggests a methodology for assessing the state of contractual relations with reference to the condition of contract norms in all three main forms and individual instances of the New Public Contracting. Where contractual relations are operating effectively, the discrete and relational norms are likely to be in balance and in 'robust' condition. Where however relations are 'in trouble', the contract norms are likely to be revealed 'in varying degrees of disarray'.[113] The separation of the transaction from its general context (discreteness), and the focusing of attention on the present to the exclusion of past and anticipated future dealings (presentiation) may go too far.[114] The associated 'magnification' of the planning and consent norms is problematic to the extent that the relational norms (such as reciprocity, solidarity, and flexibility) are under-represented or thereby weakened: 'A sufficiently serious defect in any one of the contract norms will bring a contractual relation down over time.'[115]

Legally enforceable contracts

In some inter-sectoral transactions involving legally enforceable contracts between government as purchaser and private business suppliers, the issues for socio-legal analysis appear relatively straightforward. For example, in the contracting out of basic or ancillary services in central and local government, the focus is on how relationships are affected by regulatory frameworks defining the contracting powers and areas of discretion of public agencies. The interest is in how relational contracting may be impeded by difficulties associated with competitive

[112] ibid 184. See A Fox, *Beyond Contract: Work, Power and Trust Relations* (London: Faber and Faber, 1974).

[113] Macneil (1983), (n 8 above) 351–2.

[114] Macneil (n 5 above) 60.

[115] Macneil (n 16 above) 168 fn 38: 'It is theoretically possible that all but one of the norms could be working well; however, like a spiderweb, if one pulls on one bit, the whole web will be changed.'

tendering requirements, the novelty of the type of contracting, the client's lack of contract management experience, the lack of competitiveness or contestability of the market, and insufficient expertise and capacity within it. In the case of relatively simple services, empirical research has shown how the parties' separate utilities can be jointly-maximized (at a cost) through the development of cooperative partnership relationships, even under the unfavourable conditions of CCT.[116]

In other types of public-private sector transaction, however, the increased complexity of the goods or services being procured poses greater problems. PFI contracts for hospitals and schools are not just concerned with design and building, but with the long-term management of the infrastructure and with the delivery of the service to citizens and consumers. Similarly in 'purchase-of-service' contracting in quasi-markets for human services such as health and social care, the state acts as purchaser on behalf of the ultimate service recipients, whose interests have to be taken into account in addition to those of purchasers and providers. Such consumers may for various reasons (for example due to minority, sickness, disability, or old age) not be able to articulate their needs. The existence of multiple interests complicates the assessment of the welfare-maximizing benefits of exchange that ideally characterize private business relations. The tension between public and private interests may be more difficult to resolve. For example, commercial confidentiality may suit the interests of purchaser and contractor, but may not be in the consumer interest or the public interest more generally. A major question here, where the law of contract is already involved in purchaser-provider relations, is whether contract law norms should also govern the relationship between consumer and provider.[117] A further question, given enforceability at private law, concerns the adequacy of this form of legal governance, and whether the relationships should be subject to greater public/administrative law controls.

A complicating factor in quasi-market contracting for public services is the need to reconcile internal and external welfare effects. In other words, arrangements need to be not just welfare-enhancing for parties to exchange and the third-party beneficiaries of that exchange, but also consistent with broader public policy and social welfare goals. Regulatory tasks are more complex than is the case, for example, with the control and redress of inequalities of bargaining power in markets. In that setting, socio-legal scholars have in recent years been quick to reject the traditional twentieth century 'command and control' approach of welfare or public regulation in favour of a revitalised and responsive private law. The problem of unfairness in contracts is considered best dealt with through open-textured standards

[116] See P Vincent-Jones and A Harries, 'Partnership and Cooperation in Contracting Out Local Authority Refuse Collection Services: A Case Study', in L Montanheiro, et al. (eds), *Public and Private Sector Partnerships in the Global Context*, (Sheffield: Pavic Publications, 1995), drawing on Campbell and Harris (n 33 above).

[117] J Wightman, *Contract: A Critical Commentary* (London: Pluto Press, 1996) 161–169.

such as the test of unconscionability rather than by 'clear or bright-line rules'.[118] In other situations where power imbalances cannot be justified by the contribution they make to efficiency and trust, contractual arrangements may be qualified by reference to duties to follow a fair procedure or to refrain from opportunism.[119] With regard to quality, the setting of standards by business self-regulation according to particular industrial sectors, and then the monitoring and enforcement of such standards by private law rather than by regulatory agencies, are hallmarks of efficient and responsive regulation.[120] However, while the tasks of regulation are relatively easily conceived and performed by the law of contract within markets, much greater difficulties arise in public contracting in quasi-markets. In Macneil's terminology, the problem of 'harmonization within the social matrix' is how to maintain consistency between contract and more general social norms, such as those relating to distributive justice, equity and social inclusion.

Legally unenforceable contracts

Where public contracting relationships are not governed by private law, further issues arise. In administrative and economic contracts of this sort, a key question is whether the contract norms might better be supported (and the government's policy goals thereby better served) by more explicit legal governance. For example, in the cases of internal contracting between purchasers and providers in the NHS or between government clients and in-house agencies following market testing, contractual commitments might be made more credible and binding either by making relations privately enforceable (as through corporatization involving the creation of independent legal personalities), or through the development and application of a special public law of contract. Davies argues that the advantages of internal government contracts generally could be enhanced by a greater emphasis on regulation and enforcement through an appropriate public law normative framework. My position, by contrast, following the argument that 'internal contracts' should be distinguished according to their economic and administrative functions rather than considered as a single category, is that there is no general or simple answer to the question whether the law should be more involved in these arrangements, and if so in what form. In Chapter 11 I argue that solutions to problems identified with the operation of contract norms lie as much in responsive institutional and organisational design as in the reform of legal structures.

Other legally unenforceable instances of the New Public Contracting concern agreements between state agencies and citizens directed at changing individual behaviour in the fields of education, welfare and criminal justice. In the case of social control contracts the issue again is not only whether the law should be more involved in the governance of relationships, but also whether the arrangements are capable of advancing the government's intended policy objectives – in other

[118] Collins (n 1 above) 266. [119] ibid 255. [120] ibid 296.

words whether, given the constraints of the regulatory frameworks, the contract norms can operate in a manner that jointly maximizes the utilities of the parties to the contract and delivers welfare benefits to society as a whole. The answer to this question depends on the operation of these contractual schemes in practice, and in particular on whether they enable relationships to be governed by a mutually agreed constitution from which both parties benefit.

In the behavioural/normative meaning outlined at the beginning of this chapter, contract ideally provides a mechanism by which the parties may control their relations and achieve their desires by consent. In this definition, contracting is associated with ideas of individual autonomy and self-determination. Self-assumed obligation may involve simple consent to an already-existing obligational relationship whose content has been predetermined by the stronger party; or it may involve the free creation of a new and flexible relationship of obligation, whose scope is consensually and jointly determined.[121] The latter type of arrangement is more likely to display respect for relational contract norms, and to deliver the benefits associated with the contractual governance of relationships recognized at private law. By contrast, the top-down imposition by government of social control regimes, in which the citizen has little choice over the ground-rules governing the contractual relationship or over the particular commitments undertaken, is unlikely to work effectively to the benefit of the individual, the state, or society more generally. The attempt centrally to prescribe behavioural patterns may be expected to damage the contract norms or otherwise to inhibit the development of the conditions of genuine relational contracting. Choice may be constrained or limited. Consent may be problematic.[122] Reciprocity may be asymmetrical.[123] Power may be unbalanced.[124] Such possible negative outcomes of the operation of regulatory schemes are explored in depth in Chapter 9. While the contract norms may be under strain to some degree in all private business relations, they are likely to be especially difficult to sustain in the New Public Contracting, particularly in the form of social control contracts.

Conclusion

The relationship of the New Public Contracting to other contemporary public contract phenomena is summarized in Fig 3. The degree of purposiveness in

121 Pateman (n 78 above) 20.

122 J Braucher, 'Contract Versus Contractarianism: The Regulatory Role of Contract Law' (1990) 47 *Washington and Lee Law Review* 697, 699.

123 Drewry makes this point in connection with PSAs between the Treasury and spending ministries concluded as part of the Comprehensive Spending Assessment – G Drewry, 'The Citizen and the New Contractual Public Management: The Quest for New Forms of Accountability and A New Public Law', in Y Fortin and H Van Hassel, (eds), *Contracting in the New Public Management – From Economics to Law and Citizenship* (Amsterdam: IOS Press, 2000) 255.

124 Collins (n 1 above) 24.

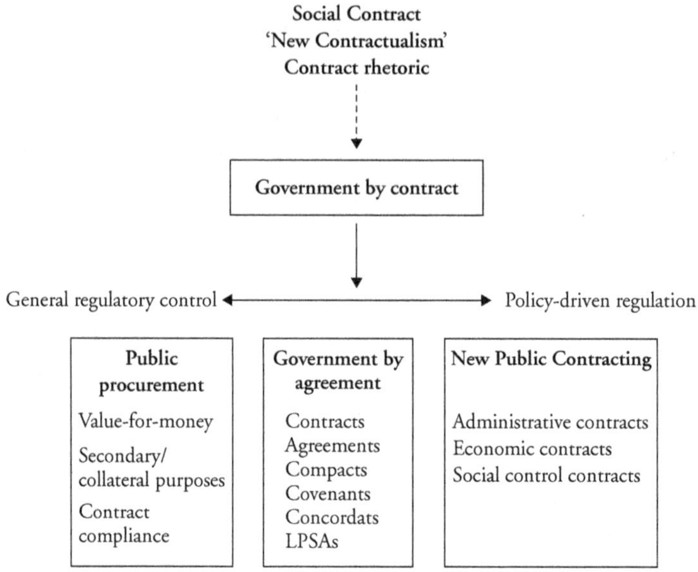

Figure 3. Government by contract and the New Public Contracting

the different types of government contract may be represented as points on a continuum, ranging from general regulatory control through procurement at one pole, to policy-driven regulation in the New Public Contracting at the other.

The distinguishing feature of the New Public Contracting is the deployment of administrative contracts, economic contracts, and social control contracts for the attainment of particular policy purposes.[125] The present concern is solely with purposive contractual mechanisms through which relations are ordered within government, or in economic organization, or between the state and individual citizens. Most instances of government by contract are beyond the scope of the present inquiry either because they are not due to any systematic initiative on the part of central government, or because they do not involve a fundamentally hierarchical relationship of authority in which powers and responsibilities are delegated to public agencies in purposive regulatory frameworks that preserve central government controls and powers of intervention. At the level of the social contract and in political rhetoric, the 'New Contractualism' provides the means by which the pursuit by recent governments of specific policy goals in respect of public administration, economic organization, and social control has been brought within an overarching political discourse.

[125] For the sake of clarity, and bearing in mind the argument that legal enforceability should not be a determinative criterion, all concordats, compacts, covenants, and associated 'contracts' are brought within the single category 'government by agreement', located at a middle point on this continuum.

In final conclusion, the paradigm meaning of contract should not be exclusively associated with, or limited to, the role of private law in supporting capitalist market exchange. Rather this is just one (albeit a highly developed and in some respects the most perfect) manifestation of a deeper and more universal meaning. The New Public Contracting is a sub-set of government by contract, which is a sub-set of the social practice or behaviour of contracting more generally. The question whether social relations are in legal terms contractual, as opposed to merely metaphorical or pseudo-contractual, appears misdirected. The proper question, posed on the basis of the distinction between behaviour and norms on the one hand and law governing those relations on the other, is how adequately the norms that are definitive of all contractual relations are represented in these regulatory arrangements.

2

Policy Context

This chapter begins with a brief account of the key public sector reforms introduced by the Conservatives from the early 1980s, showing how the period since New Labour's victory in the 1997 general election has been marked by continuity with the previous government's policies. The relationship between the New Public Contracting and the New Public Management is then explored. Here I suggest that the UK has been particularly influenced by a market/competition model of public management reform compared with a more restricted 'managerialist contractualist' conception that has been dominant in other countries. The next section shows how the separate administrative and economic functions performed by the New Public Contracting have nevertheless been brought within a coherent overall policy framework governing public services, through Cabinet Office guidance applying to central government and the statutory regime of best value in local government. The development of policy on public services is then placed in the context of the continuing centralization of power and the increasing influence of the 'new centre' (the Treasury and Cabinet Office) within government. The chapter concludes with a brief discussion of the external constraints on UK policy imposed under international treaty obligations, showing how they relate to fundamental economic rationales for the public contracting policies currently being pursued by New Labour.

Genealogy of the New Public Contracting

Policy continuity has been a feature of contractualization in the public sphere in Britain over the past twenty five years. While not suggesting that the reforms were ever conceived as a blueprint,[1] a coherent pattern is nevertheless discernible. Many of the elements of New Public Management, later to be expressed in the New Public Contracting, had cross-party support before the first Thatcher government in

[1] On a similar theme see D Oliver and G Drewry, *Public Service Reforms: Issues of Accountability and Public Law* (London: Pinter, 1996) 26. There was no 'master plan' in 1979 for the reform of local government, let alone any explicit articulation of the central role of CCT in that process – T Williams, 'Local Government Role-Reversal in the New Contract Culture', in RJ Bennett, (ed) *Local Government in the New Europe* (London: Belhaven Press, 1993) 95.

1979.[2] Since Labour's victory in the 1997 general election, the public service reforms begun by the Conservatives have been extended and deepened across a broad range of administrative, economic and social relations.[3] Despite such continuity, the ending of eighteen years of Conservative political domination remains an important watershed, justifying the rough periodization pre- and post-1997.

Pre-1997 – New Right

The origins of the economic form of the New Public Contracting may be traced (Fig 4) to the introduction of Compulsory Competitive Tendering (CCT) in local government under the Local Government (Planning and Land) Act 1980. CCT was extended by primary legislation and statutory instrument to include a wide variety manual and professional services in the 1980s and 1990s. Similar pressures encouraging contracting out at the expense of direct provision were applied through market testing, first in the NHS from 1983 and later in central government from 1991. Market testing of prisoner escort arrangements was introduced under the Criminal Justice Act 1991, followed by the contracting out of the design and management of prisons under the Criminal Justice and Public Order Act 1994.[4] The use of private finance to fund public infrastructure projects through the PFI began in 1993. Contemporaneous with these New Public Contracting developments was the related policy initiative of consumer empowerment through the Citizen's Charter, introduced in 1991 and subsequently applied in other charters in particular public service sectors. These reforms were accompanied by the creation and continuous modification of quasi-markets – in housing and education from the beginning of 1980s, and in health and social care under the National Health Service and Community Care Act 1990.

As regards administrative contracts, the restructuring of relations within government on contractual lines began in the late 1980s. From this time government departments were required to review all their functions with a view to abolition, privatization, contracting out, or creating a Next Steps agency. In the latter case the relationship between the executive agency and its parent department was governed by a framework document or agreement.

[2] For example, the recommendations of the Fulton Report on the Civil Service in 1968, precursor to the Financial Management Initiative (FMI) introduced in 1983 and the Next Steps initiative launched in 1988, had been broadly accepted by prime minister Harold Wilson. Had a Labour government been elected under James Callaghan in 1979, Next Steps might have been introduced in much the same way. One of the reasons so many public sector reforms occurred under the Conservatives was that they (and particularly Mrs Thatcher) were in office for a very long period. 'The language and the rhetoric of public service reform may change, but many ideas from the past keep resurfacing in new guises' – Oliver and Drewry (n 1 above) 15.

[3] What has changed significantly under New Labour, as Part 2 will show, is not so much the fundamental policy ends, as the regulatory means being deployed in their attainment.

[4] CCT and market testing, as much as the PFI, have been argued to be examples *par excellence* of policy-driven regulation (see ch 1).

Finally, while contract had been used as a mechanism of behavioural modification in the field of social work since the early 1980s, this social control function was extended to the sphere of unemployment through primary legislation in the form of the Jobseekers' Act 1995, which made the payment of state benefits conditional upon specific contractual undertakings entered into by welfare recipients.

Post-1997 – New Labour

New Labour's programme for 'Modernising Government', trailed in various consultation documents in the wake of the 1997 general election, led to streamlined guidance in the form of *Better Quality Services*. This guidance applied to a wide range of public contracting functions of central government, including market testing, outsourcing and public/private partnerships. In a parallel initiative, the Local Government Act 1999 (abolishing CCT from 2000) imposed on public authorities the 'best value' duty to secure continuous improvements in their performance with regard to economy, efficiency and effectiveness. The PFI was enthusiastically adopted and developed by Labour in the late 1990s, becoming the principal vehicle for the funding of new schools, hospitals, prisons, and other public infrastructure projects. The quasi-market for legal services was significantly reformed under the Access to Justice Act 1999. As will be seen, in all these instances reform has involved competition and marketization.

Relationships between the Treasury and spending departments were cast as Public Service Agreements (PSAs) as part of the first Comprehensive Spending Review in 1998, repeated in 2000, 2002, and 2004. This development has been driven by a managerialist reform agenda concerned, like Next Steps, with restructuring administration and increasing efficiency in the operation of government. The use of contract as a mechanism of social control and behavioural modification was extended beyond the field of social security under the School Standards and Framework Act 1998 and the Youth Justice and Criminal Evidence Act 1999, which introduced home-school agreements and youth offender contracts respectively. Drawing on 'new contractualist' discourse, reform here has been directed at improving standards of behaviour among deviant or 'problem' social groups, including youth offenders and school children.

After the 2001 general election, Labour's key priority became the delivery of 'better, modern public services'. The programme for achieving this was underpinned by 'four principles' of public sector reform:

- a national framework of standards and accountability;
- greater devolution of power to deliver those high standards;
- more flexible working and better rewards and incentives to keep pace with constant change; and

	Year	Normative source	Reform
NEW RIGHT	1980	Housing Act 1980	Quasi-market reform in housing
		Education Act 1980	Quasi-market reform in education
		Local Government (Planning and Land) Act 1980 Pt III	CCT (local government) building and construction services
	1983	Circular Guidance [HC (83) 18]	Market testing (NHS)
	1988	Local Government Act 1988 Pt III	CCT extended to most 'blue collar' services
		Education Reform Act 1988	LMS, corporatization (CTCs)
		Employment Act 1988	Corporatization (TECs)
	1989	Efficiency Unit, *Improving Management in Government: The Next Steps*	Next Steps Five 'key options' (Kemp)
	1990	NHS and Community Care Act 1990	NHS internal market
			Quasi-market in social care
	1991	Treasury, *Competing for Quality*	Market testing (central government)
		Criminal Justice Act 1991, ss 80, 84.	Market testing prisoner escort arrangements
		Citizen's Charter	Citizen's Charter
	1993	Treasury, *The Private Finance Initiative: Breaking New Ground*	PFI
	1994	Criminal Justice and Public Order Act 1994, ss 93, 96	Contracting out (DCMF) prisons
	1995	SI 1995/1336.	CCT ('white collar' professional support services)
		Treasury, *Private Opportunity, Public Benefit – Progressing the PFI*	PFI
		Jobseekers' Act 1995	Jobseekers' Allowance

NEW LABOUR	1997	Treasury Taskforce, *Partnerships for Prosperity – the PFI*	PFI (Treasury Taskforce)
	1998	*Better Quality Services: Creating Public/Private Partnerships through Market Testing and Contracting Out*	'Appraising options' test (abolition; internal restructuring; strategic contracting out; market testing; privatization)
		Treasury	Comprehensive Spending Review (CSR) (rd 1) – Public Service Agreements (PSAs)
		School Standards and Framework Act 1998	Home-school agreements
	1999	Local Government Act 1999	'Best Value'
		Youth Justice and Criminal Evidence Act 1999	Youth Offender Contracts
		Access to Justice Act 1999	Quasi-market for legal services
	2000	Local Government Act 2000	Powers to promote well-being, restrictions.
		Treasury	CSR (rd 2) – PSAs
	2001	Health and Social Care Act 2001	PPP powers for SHAs – LIFT. Intervention orders. Care Trusts.
	2002	NHS Reform and Health Care Professions Act 2002	PCTs and SHAs. Strengthening CHI. Patients' Forums.
		Education Act 2002, ss 1, 11, 54, 60, 65	Powers to form companies. Powers of intervention. Academies (CTCs, CAs).
		Treasury	CSR – (rd 3) PSAs
	2003	Anti-social Behaviour Act 2003	Parenting contracts
		Local Government Act 2003	Regulation capital finance.
		Health and Social Care (CHS) Act 2003	NHS Foundation Trusts. Independent regulators for health and social care.
	2004	Higher Education Act 2004	Quasi-market in HE – variable fees.
		Treasury	CSR – (rd 4) PSAs

Figure 4. The New Public Contracting – Genealogy

- more choice for customers including access to alternative provision where services are poor.[5]

The health and education sectors have been subjected to further quasi-market reforms under the Health and Social Care Act 2001 (granting Strategic Health Authorities new powers in respect of Public Private Partnerships); the Health and Social Care (Community Health and Standards) Act 2003 (creating NHS Foundation Trusts with the legal capacity to enter enforceable contracts with NHS Primary Care Trusts); the Education Act 2002 (governing the creation of Academies as corporate entities); and the Higher Education Act 2004 (introducing variable tuition fees aimed at increasing competition and student choice in tertiary education). Under the 2002 and 2003 Acts, health and education authorities that are considered to be failing in their public service duties are liable to various central enforcement measures and powers of intervention.[6] In the area of social control, the use of contract as an instrument of behaviour modification received a further boost during this period through the introduction of parenting contracts under the Anti-social Behaviour Act 2003.

The prominent role of the New Public Contracting in public service reform in England continues in Labour's third term following the 2005 general election.[7] The fundamental economic policy goal remains to increase supply-side competition and consumer choice – whether exercised directly by service recipients or indirectly on their behalf by representative public agencies – through centrally prescribed regulatory frameworks. For example, where public providers remain under government control, as in health and education, they are being encouraged to become more entrepreneurial through increased management freedoms granted in 'foundation' or other forms of corporate status. At the same time, public purchasing agencies such as Primary Care Trusts are being given greater autonomy and wider powers to commission treatment from the cheapest sources in the public, private and non-profit sectors. As will be shown in Chapters 7 and 8, even the principle that public services should be funded from general taxation, traditionally regarded by Labour as sacrosanct, appears to be being eroded. At the heart of government, PSAs and framework documents continue to embody the performance indicators and targets that are used in contractual governance across all forms of the New Public Contracting.

[5] Cabinet Office, 'The Second Phase of Public Sector Reform: the Move to Delivery', 22 March 2002.

[6] See eg s 23 of the Health and Social Care (Community Health and Standards) Act 2003 ('Failing NHS Foundation Trusts'); Pt 4 Education Act 2002 ('Powers of Intervention' in the case of 'schools causing concern').

[7] Devolution in the UK has resulted in significant policy divergence on a range of public service issues. While in England competition and market reforms are being embraced with enthusiasm, reform in Scotland and Wales is occurring within more traditional bureaucratic organization – see M Sullivan and M Drakeford, 'Devolution, Divergence and Social Policy' (2005) 3 *Wales Journal of Law and Policy* 7.

The New Public Contracting and the New Public Management

This section relates the New Public Contracting in Britain to the New Public Management (NPM) reforms that have occurred in industrialized societies throughout the western world. The purpose of the comparison is to explore common influences, but also to highlight the peculiarity of the British experience. The NPM typically is characterized by a set of managerial practices including:[8]

- the use of indirect mechanisms of control in place of direct command;
- devolution of management responsibilities to lower levels within organizational hierarchies;
- replacement of detailed central planning by decentralized management systems;
- recourse to output and outcome measures in place of input controls;
- separating of responsibilities for policy making and delivery;
- separating of purchaser and provider functions;
- splitting of bureaucracies into more autonomous units;
- creation of executive agencies within government;
- managing and monitoring of relationships through contracts; and
- the increasing role of the non-state sectors in the provision of public services.

NPM reforms are usually justified by reference to public choice and agency theories,[9] which have emphasized the untrustworthiness of state employees and the need for tighter management and discipline within public organizations.[10] Such developments are seen by some observers as challenging the foundations of the welfare state.[11] However, while often accompanied by privatization, the NPM remains fundamentally concerned with the problem of management by the state of public services for which it continues to have responsibility, and which are funded partly

[8] J Boston, (ed), *The State Under Contract* (Wellington: Bridget Williams Books, 1995), 2; T Reddel, 'Beyond Participation, Hierarchies, Management and Markets: "New" Governance and Place Policies' (2002) 61 *Australian Journal of Public Administration* 50, 55. See also C Hood, 'A Public Management for All Seasons' (1991) 69 *Public Administration* 3; ibid, 'The "New Public Management" in the 1980s: Variations on a Theme' (1995) 20 *Accounting, Organizations and Society* 93; P Dunleavy and C Hood, 'From Old Public Administration to New Public Management' (1994) 14 *Public Money and Management* (Jul–Sep) 9–16; D Shand, 'NPM: An International Perspective', *Public Finance Foundation Review* (1995) No 7 (August).

[9] P Greer, *Transforming Central Government: The Next Steps Initiative* (Buckingham: Open University Press, 1994), 14–20; MJ Ormsby, 'The Purchaser/Provider Split: A Report From New Zealand' (1998) 11 *Governance* 357.

[10] M Casson, *The Economics of Business Culture: Game Theory, Transaction Costs, and Economic Performance* (Oxford: Oxford University Press, 1991) 246. Casson points to the irony of the borrowing by Western governments of 'low-trust' public sector management from the United States, at the same time as Western private enterprises were borrowing softer, more informal business management ideas from Japan (243).

[11] For example: K Walsh, *Public Services and Market Mechanisms: Competition, Contracting and the New Public Management* (Houndmills: Macmillan, 1995) xix.

or wholly out of general taxation and are either subsidised, or free, at the point of delivery.

While commentators have in the past tended to stress the common elements in the NPM,[12] a recent strand in the public policy literature has focused on the diversity of approaches to reform across the OECD.[13] In particular, there are important differences in the way in which managerialism has (or has not) been combined with public contracting mechanisms – there being no necessary relationship between the former and the latter. For example, despite broad similarities in the reforms of financial management within government in Britain and Australia, the implementation in practice has been very different.[14] While in both countries administrative restructuring has occurred through the setting of performance objectives and targets, subject to regular monitoring and evaluation to determine how far objectives have been met, in Australia the relationships are not cast in the explicitly contractual form found in Britain.[15] In the United States, political theorists have noted the 'strange absence' of contracts as tools of public management compared with their more common use throughout Europe.[16]

Where reforms have involved the mechanism of contract, a distinction may be drawn between 'managerialist contractualism' and 'marketization' as dimensions

[12] Hood (1995), (n 8 above) 99; L Torres and V Pina, 'Changes in Public Service Delivery in the EU Countries' (2002) *Public Money and Management* (Oct-Dec), 41.

[13] Hood considers that three comparative aspects of contemporary public administration have tended to be run together: (1) why similar reforms, terminology, and recipes appeared at roughly the same time in a number of states; (2) why some states invested heavily in NPM reforms while others did not; and (3) why the NPM took different forms in different states – C Hood, 'Individualized Contracts for Top Public Servants: Copying Business, Path-Dependent Political Re-Engineering – Or Trobriand Cricket?' (1998) 11 *Governance* 443. For a discussion of why similar NPM reforms are institutionalized in different ways between countries, see O James, 'Business Models and the Transfer of Businesslike Central Government Agencies' (2001) 14 *Governance* 233.

[14] S Zifcak, 'Contractualism, Democracy and Ethics' (2001) 60 *Australian Journal of Public Administration* 86, 110; ibid, *New Managerialism: Administrative Reform in Whitehall and Canberra* (Buckingham: Open University Press, 1994).

[15] ibid (2001), 113. Here the devolution of managerial authority and its control have occurred through other mechanisms. Budgetary reforms involved the displacement of line item budgeting (which was focused on financial inputs and concerned with stewardship and financial probity) by programme management and budgeting (PMB), concerned more with the achievement of results. 'On this basis, an assessment of the efficiency and effectiveness of each programme could be made' (126).

[16] Among the Anglophone democracies the US is remarkable for the general absence of 'policy-driven' public contracting either within government or in economic organization. On the one hand, the presence of strong managerialist structures and *ex ante* controls informed by business values and an ingrained lack of trust of public managers appear to have made the development of forms of contractual governance beyond the employment relationship unnecessary – BG Peters, 'Contracts as a Tool for Public Management: Their Strange Absence in North America', in Y Fortin and H Van Hassel, (eds), *Contracting in the New Public Management – From Economics to Law and Citizenship* (Amsterdam: IOS Press, 2000) 41. On the other hand, with regard to economic organization, the limited role of the state in welfare provision and the existence of well established private markets for services have led to a more conventional public contracting agenda (smart procurement, partnership between sectors) than that associated with the development of quasi-markets and the more purposive use of public contracting as a policy instrument.

of the NPM.[17] This categorization reflects the typology of administrative contracts and economic contracts used in the analysis of the New Public Contracting in Britain, as set out in Chapter 1. The distinction is a refinement of the rather general view that the NPM represents a shift towards a single and undifferentiated 'contractual mode of government'.[18]

Managerialist contractualism

Many countries embracing the NPM have engaged in managerialist reforms directed at improving 'the public service' through the contractual restructuring of administrative relations between parts of government.[19] The contractual coordination of separated policy making and delivery functions within government is a common feature of performance-based management strategies.[20] In Britain under Next Steps, contract budgeting systems reconfigured public financing through the introduction of purchase contracts between provider agencies and central government.[21] The use of administrative contracts has arguably been more extensive and far-reaching elsewhere. Denmark established a system of contract agencies in central government in 1998.[22] In New Zealand, the State Sector Act 1998 split the civil service into departments, Crown entities, and State-Owned Enterprises (SOEs). Relationships between departmental chief executives and government ministers are governed through formal performance agreements – written contracts specifying the responsibilities of heads for the delivery of output targets,

[17] These dimensions are frequently conflated – see for example E Ferlie, L Ashburner, L Fitzgerald, and A Pettigrew, *The New Public Management in Action* (Oxford: Oxford University Press, 1996). The authors regard Next Steps as a form of quasi-market within the public sector 'whereby previously line-managed organizations disaggregate into purchasing and providing wings, with relations between them being governed by contract rather than hierarchy' (67). This account appears wrongly to attribute to the arrangement an economic function, while underemphasizing the continued hierarchical dimensions of the 'contractual' relationship.

[18] M Freedland, 'Government by Contract and Public Law' [1994] PL 86, 88. For a similarly undifferentiated view of 'government by contract' see J Stewart, 'The Limitations of Government by Contract' (1993) 13 *Public Money and Management* (Jul–Sep) 7–12.

[19] G Boyne, 'Public and Private Management: What's the Difference?' (2002) 39 *Management Studies* 97; N Carter, and P Greer, 'Evaluating Agencies: Next Steps and Performance Indicators' (1993) 71 *Public Administration* 407; T Cutler and B Waine, 'Managerialism Reformed? New Labour and Public Sector Management' (2000) 34 *Social Policy and Administration* 318. The distinction between 'managerialist contractualism' and 'marketization' is not the same as that drawn by some writers on the NPM between 'managerialism' and 'contractualism' as strands in public sector reform – see J Martin, 'Contractualism in New Zealand', in Y Fortin and H Van Hassel (n 16 above) 67.

[20] Walsh (n 11 above) 65.

[21] For a review of contractual and other output-based budgeting schemes, see M Robinson, 'Contract Budgeting' (2000) 78 *Public Administration* 75. The author concludes that the contract mechanism is not well suited to budgeting in a complex public sector.

[22] C Greve, 'Exploring Contracts As Reinvented Institutions in the Danish Public Sector' (2000) 78 *Public Administration* 153. On the position in Germany, see C Reichard, '"Kontraktmanagement" Experiences With Internal Management Contracts in German Local Government', in Y Fortin and H Van Hassel (n 16 above) 127.

and of ministers for broader strategic outcomes.[23] In addition to such contracts, 'purchase agreements' specify in detail the outputs to be delivered by departments to ministers, and the outcomes in terms of the consequences for the public resulting from the outputs and activities of government.[24]

Another form of administrative contract in New Zealand links responsible ministers to Crown entities – a type of quango owned by the government but legally separate from it, and subject to statutory regulation. Crown entities are managed by appointed boards composed of representatives of business and industry, charged under legislation with promoting the public interest. In some respects like executive agencies and Non-Departmental Public Bodies (NDPBs) in Britain, Crown entities may provide services or carry out a range of regulatory functions. For example, the Civil Aviation Authority enters into annual performance agreements with the Minister of Transport specifying objectives for the year, with outputs, performance targets and measures being set out in a schedule to the agreement.[25] New Zealand is unusual in the manner in which performance agreements of various kinds and legal status have been adapted as instruments of control and accountability at all levels of the public service.[26]

Marketization

A second variant of the NPM which is particularly evident in Britain involves marketization[27] – the attempt by the state to harness economic incentives in the organization of public services through new forms of purchaser choice and provider competition.[28] The intellectual basis of this dimension of the NPM has been the 'new institutional economics', and more particularly transaction cost theory.[29] The economic goal of opening up the public sector to market forces

[23] J Boston, 'The New Contractualism in New Zealand: Chief Executive Performance Agreements', in G Davis, B Sullivan, and A Yeatman, (eds), *The New Contractualism?* (Melbourne: Macmillan, 1997) 180.

[24] Martin (n 19 above) 71–2. Under the Public Finance Act 1989, the emphasis has been on funding of departments according to delivery of specific outputs rather than parliamentary appropriation to fund inputs. Since 1993 there has developed a sophisticated public management framework integrating the government's strategic objectives expressed as 'strategic results areas' (SRAs), with 'key results areas' (KRAs) at the departmental level allowing progress towards SRAs to be precisely measured and evaluated.

[25] ibid, 72–73; J Martin, 'Contracting and Accountability', in J Boston, (ed), *The State Under Contract* (Wellington: Bridget Williams Books, 1995).

[26] Boston (n 8 above) xi.

[27] By implication, the present analysis of the NPM distinguishes: (1) managerialism without any form of public contracting; (2) managerialism coupled with administrative contracts (managerialist contractualism); and (3) marketization involving the use economic contracts. It is suggested that this categorization is preferable to the over-simple distinction made by Reddel (n 8 above) between managerialism and marketization.

[28] S Richards and J Rodrigues, 'Strategies for Management in the Civil Service: Change of Direction' (1993) 13 *Public Money and Management* (Apr–Jun) 33.

[29] OE Williamson, *Markets and Hierarchies: Analysis and Antitrust Implications* (New York: Free Press, 1975); ibid, 'Transaction-Cost Economics: The Governance of Contractual Relations' (1979)

is far more ambitious than the relatively limited managerialist aim of gaining political control over the public service.

The extent of marketization and competition in public service reform, and the corresponding recourse to 'economic contracts' as instruments of regulation, have varied considerably across the OECD and other advanced economies.[30] In both Britain and New Zealand, administrative restructuring has been accompanied by economic regime changes entailing the displacement of the traditional welfare state by quasi-market and market-like structures. By contrast, in the Nordic countries efforts at reform have been directed at the consolidation of the welfare state, while in Germany and the Netherlands administrative and economic reforms have proceeded incrementally and not as part of connected programmes.[31] Again, while Britain and New Zealand have been enthusiastic proponents of marketization, other countries have adopted such reforms on a more pragmatic basis and with less political rhetoric.[32]

A quasi-market in health care was introduced in Italy in the early 1990s.[33] In Sweden, quasi-markets were introduced across a range of services at around the same time.[34] Many developed countries are addressing problems of how to contain the increasing cost of institutional care for older people through quasi-market reforms accompanied by manipulation of supply-side and demand-side levers.[35] Quasi-markets in education, involving varying degrees of parental choice and school autonomy, are common throughout the western world. The Belgian and Dutch education systems operate on 'voucher' principles.[36] New Zealand and

22 *Journal of Law and Economics* 233; ibid, *The Mechanisms of Governance* (Oxford: Oxford University Press, 1996).

30 On the relative absence of market reforms and lack of private sector involvement in the NPM in Denmark, see PM Christiansen, 'A Prescription Rejected: Market Solutions to Problems of Public Sector Governance' (1998) 11 *Governance* 273. Market-type reforms have been accepted more widely in Sweden – see C Green-Pedersen, 'New Public Management Reforms of the Danish and Swedish Welfare States: The Role of Different Social Democratic Responses' (2002) 15 *Governance* 271.

31 Jan-Erik Lane, (ed), *Public Sector Reform: Rationale, Trends and Problems* (London: Sage Publications, 1997) 301.

32 Green-Pedersen (n 29 above); J Boston, P Dalziel, and S St John, (eds), *Redesigning the Welfare State in New Zealand* (Auckland: Oxford University Press, 1999); J Halligan, 'New Public Sector Models: Reform in Australia and New Zealand', in Jan-Erik Lane, (ed), *Public Sector Reform: Rationale, Trends and Problems* (London: Sage Publications, 1997) 17; J Kelsey, *Rolling Back the State: Privatisation of Power in Aotearoa/New Zealand* (Wellington: Bridget Williams Books, 1993).

33 G France, 'Healthcare Quasi-Markets in a Decentralised System', in W Bartlett, JA Roberts, and J Le Grand, (eds), *A Revolution in Social Policy: Quasi-Market Reforms in the 1990s* (Bristol: The Policy Press, 1998).

34 K Walsh, N Deakin, P Spurgeon, P Smith, and N Thomas, *Contracting for Change: Contracts in Health, Social Care, and Other Local Government Services* (Oxford: Oxford University Press, 1997) 189. There is considerable local variation, with different forms of competition between public bodies and between such bodies and the private and voluntary sectors. A purchaser/provider split exists in over half of county councils, and in some communes in relation to community care.

35 J Healy, 'The Care of Older People: Australia and the United Kingdom' (2002) 36 *Social Policy and Administration* 1.

36 V Vandenberghe, 'Educational Quasi-Markets: The Belgian Experience', in W Bartlett, JA Roberts, and J Le Grand, (eds) (1998), 79.

Australia have abandoned many of the elements associated with traditional state provision such as 'zoning' (the principle that access to publicly funded education is dependent on neighbourhood with no choice for children to attend schools elsewhere).

The marketization of public services is associated not only with public contracting, but also with a range of other mechanisms supporting quasi-market organization such as corporatization.[37] For example, the health service in New Zealand was radically reformed in 1993 on the basis of a purchaser-provider split and competitive contracting combined with corporatization.[38] This type of arrangement differed from the internal market established in the UK health sector at the same time in that purchaser and provider enjoyed greater powers and greater autonomy from governmental control than their British counterparts, derived from their independent legal status. Nevertheless, the corporate entities still operated within a statutory regulatory framework.[39] Despite some retrenchment in 1996 involving the concentration of the purchasing function in a single public agency, the system retains many original features and remains more far-reaching than analogous reforms in Britain.[40] The arrangement might still be considered 'quasi-market' in the sense that a regulatory framework (for example defining the control and accountability relationship of purchasing and providing agencies to Ministers) determines the conditions under which health services are purchased on behalf of patients. In Britain, as has already been suggested, since 2002 corporatization has given a further twist to public contracting in the health and education sectors. The significance of corporatization, both for the operation of quasi-markets and for the government's competition and choice agendas, will be explored in depth in Chapters 7 and 8.

Social control

NPM reforms have been associated with the restructuring of social relations as well as with administrative and economic reorganization. Significant changes have occurred in all liberal democracies in the social regimes governing the relationship between individual citizens and the state. Echoing developments in the United States,[41] entitlements to unemployment benefits have been replaced across Europe

37 The regulation of liberalized markets provides a further example. See Peters (n 16 above) 28; Walsh (n 11 above) 185; S Domberger and C Hall, 'Contracting for Public Services: A Review of the Antipodean Experience' (1996) 74 *Public Administration* 129, 141.

38 P Barnett and K Jacobs, 'Policy-making in a Restructured State: The Case of the 1991 Health Reform Policy in New Zealand' (2000) 59 *Australian Journal of Public Administration* 73.

39 T Ashton, J Cumming, J McLean, M McKinely, and E Fae, *Contracting For Health Services In New Zealand: A Report For The World Health Organization* (WHO 2002), 22.

40 R Gauld, 'Beyond New Zealand's Dual Health Reforms' (1999) 33 *Social Policy and Administration* 567, 575.

41 On the change in welfare policy under the Personal Responsibility and Work Opportunity Act 1996, which marked the end to the Aid to Families with Dependent Children programme, see A Waddan, 'Redesigning the Welfare Contract in Theory and Practice: Just What Is Going On in the USA?' (2003) 32 *Journal of Social Policy* 19.

with 'active labour market' and 'workfare' schemes making welfare payments dependent on citizens assuming increased responsibilities to seek work and participate in training programmes.[42] Despite major differences, governments in Denmark, Netherlands, Norway, France, Germany, Australia, as well as Britain, have institutionalized the assumption that people of working age who receive benefits should take jobs if they are able to do so.[43] However, as in other aspects of public service reform, there is considerable variation in the use of the contract mechanism in such social control arrangements. While Britain and Australia have adopted a disciplinary approach based on individual responsibility and contractual obligation,[44] Denmark has arguably succeeded in achieving 'workfare in a welfare society' with a less punitive emphasis and relatively little recourse to contract and the rhetoric of rights balanced by responsibilities.[45] Overall, as we shall see in Chapter 9, the British experience is notable for the manner in which the contractual rhetoric of rights balanced by responsibilities has been embodied in programmes of behavioural modification introduced in primary legislation.

Conclusion

From this brief review it is evident that managerialist contractualism and marketization are far from peculiar to Britain. Moreover, other countries (in particular New Zealand) have in some respects been more radical in their NPM reforms. However, the New Public Contracting remains unusual in the breadth of its application across a wide range of administrative, economic, and social control contexts. The experience of the NPM in Britain may be distinguished from that in other countries also by the highly centralized and purposive nature of policy-driven regulation, as already indicated in Chapter 1. This aspect of the New Public Contracting is further explored in the remaining two sections of this chapter.

Better Quality Services and Best Value

While administrative contracts and economic contracts have been shown to perform different functions and to have separate policy origins, they began to be subject to a common rationale with the requirement, from 1989, that government activities be reviewed periodically in accordance with five options: abolition,

42 Lane (n 31 above) 301.

43 C Finn, (ed), *Sunrise or Sunset? Administrative Law in the New Millennium* (Canberra: Australian Institute of Administrative Law, 2000); JF Handler, 'Social Citizenship and Workfare in the US and Western Europe: From Status to Contract' (2003) 13 *Journal of European Social Policy* 229.

44 P Saunders, 'Mutual Obligation, Participation and Popularity: Social Security Reform in Australia' (2002) 31 *Journal of Social Policy* 21. Following a review conducted by the Reform Reference Group in 1999, recommendations have been made to further increase mutual obligation requirements on the unemployed, sole parents, and disability support pensioners – ibid 23.

45 J Torfing, 'Workfare With Welfare: Recent Reforms of the Danish Welfare State' (1999) 9 *Journal of European Social Policy* 5.

privatization, contracting out, creating an agency, or maintaining the status quo. Under the 'prior options' reviews originally introduced as part of the Next Steps initiative, the same process that led a public body to question whether a function might better be performed by an executive agency would raise questions also as to whether services might better be contracted out, or contracted in, after market testing. This section considers, first, the modern successor to the prior options reviews, and second, analogous processes of critical self-review introduced in local government under the statutory regime of best value.

BQS 'appraising options' reviews

The rationalization of the New Public Contracting as a coherent set of policies applying to both administrative restructuring and the economic reorganization of public services began with the election of New Labour in 1997. The general guidance that applied from this time until its replacement by other institutional frameworks in 2004 was contained in two documents, 'guidance for senior managers',[46] and a 'handbook on creating public/private partnerships through market testing and contracting out',[47] together known as *Better Quality Services* (BQS).[48] The guidance required permanent secretaries, chief executives, and other senior managers within departments, executive agencies, and NDPBs to ensure that their organizations were systematically seeking out ways to achieve 'better quality services at optimal cost'. While it was for the department or agency itself to decide how to achieve this goal, the factors it should take into account were subject to detailed prescription. Performance standards covering cost and quality had to be set, reflecting the views and needs of customers and users and the results of research into what could potentially be achieved for the service.[49]

Under the revised and re-named 'appraising options' reviews introduced in 1998, departments were required to consider five alternatives: abolition; internal

46 *Guidance for Senior Managers* (London: The Stationery Office, 1996) ISBN 0-11-430152-2.

47 *Better Quality Services Handbook* (London: The Stationery Office, 1998). ISBN 0-11-630964-4. The Handbook describes the policy and key processes for project managers and bidders, but is also relevant to senior managers. References to 'Departments' include their Agencies and NDPBs. Twelve 'guiding principles' in using market testing and contracting out were issued by the Chancellor of the Duchy of Lancaster in 1997 (Hansard, 4 November 1997, Col 94).

48 By 2004 the Government considered that its Modernizing Government and Service First initiatives had accomplished their reform objectives. At the time of writing in August 2005, public service reform continues to be steered by the Office of Public Services Reform and the Prime Minister's Delivery Unit, both established within the Cabinet Office in 2001, as described in ch 1. In place of detailed central guidance through BQS, responsibilities for continuous improvement have been devolved to departments and agencies in PSAs and framework documents. Other regulatory mechanisms include benchmarking. The role of the Public Sector Benchmarking Service, a partnership between the Cabinet Office and HM Revenue and Customs, is: to promote knowledge transfer and effective benchmarking, to supply practical advice and information on improvement tools, to broker learning through sharing knowledge and good practice, and to support public service improvement projects – see Public Sector Benchmarking Service, www.benchmarking.gov.uk/default1.asp accessed 11th August 2005.

49 n 46 above, para 8.

restructuring, strategic contracting out, market testing, and privatization.[50] In significant contrast to earlier guidance, maintaining the status quo was no longer an option. The reviews were subject to detailed rules for the assessment of costs and likely quality outcomes, laid down in HM Treasury's 'Green Book'.[51] This separate guidance, which continues in an updated form to play a major role in structuring decision making within central government, required comparison of: existing costs; projected costs after the efficiency exercise (for new services, there should be a comparator derived from benchmarking to help ensure that value-for-money will be achieved); and the process costs of carrying out each option. If the service was no longer needed, it should be abolished.[52] Whether the activity was required at all was to be determined according to a clear assessment of what it was intended to produce (outputs), and what the relevant policy informing the activity was intended to achieve (outcomes). Where the assessment was that the service was necessary, a choice had to be made among the service delivery options. Rather than continuing to be directly responsible for the activity, the government might better achieve its objectives by privatization with regulation. The advantage of privatization is that it allocates responsibility for funding to the private sector and generates tax revenue from the new private sector provider, therefore reducing central government's costs and demand for resources.[53] Where the assessment was that the government needed to retain responsibility for a necessary activity, the service might be restructured internally either within the department, agency or NDPB, or by merger with another department or public organization. While the approach underlying the guidance claimed to be 'pragmatic not dogmatic',[54] in practice managers attempting to demonstrate that service improvements could be attained without competition faced a heavy burden. The assumption was that, in the long term, innovation and continuous improvement were more likely to be delivered by the private sector or with private sector involvement than through internal restructuring or administrative reform.[55]

The preferred options were therefore: (1) strategic contracting out, which involves buying services from the private sector after a competition between external bidders only; and (2) market testing, in which the in-house team competes against external bidders for the right to provide the service. In the case of market testing, the service might then be contracted out to an external provider, or 'contracted in' to the winning in-house team on the basis of a (legally

[50] A further option is 'insourcing', where an activity previously provided by the private sector is integrated within the government department. The specified criteria appear particularly difficult to satisfy and in practice this option is likely to be rarely used – ibid, para 16.

[51] The 'Green Book: Appraisal and Evaluation in Central Government' presents the techniques and issues that Treasury requires to be used by all departments and agencies in assessing the benefits and costs of new policies, programmes, and projects – see http://greenbook.treasury.gov.uk/ accessed 10th August 2005.

[52] n 46 above, para 1.6.

[53] ibid para 1.6 (c).

[54] ibid '12 Guiding Principles', Principle 1.

[55] cf Richards and Rodrigues (n 28 above) 37. The authors argue that market testing policies were developed in reaction to dissatisfaction with the agency model of reorganization.

unenforceable) Service Level Agreement (SLA). While the Handbook referred to SLAs somewhat confusingly as 'quasi-contracts', the intention that they should be treated in the same manner as enforceable contracts emerges clearly:

> A contract is an agreement enforceable at law for services (or goods) in return for a consideration . . . For the purposes of this guidance, contracts are made between Departments and outside bodies following a competition. As the Crown cannot contract with itself, an in-house team winning a market test, or a successful bidder from another Government Department, is awarded a Service Level Agreement (SLA) – in effect, a quasi contract. In this guidance: "Contractor" refers to the service provider and includes in-house teams working to SLAs; "Client" refers to the Department awarding the contract or SLA; "Contract" means the agreement made with an external provider; "SLA" means the agreement with an in-house provider or a provider from another Government Department . . . The aim of awarding a contract or SLA, and of its subsequent management, is to ensure that the services required are delivered by the contractor in accordance with the quality, performance and value for money standards agreed with the Department, and to deal with any problems.[56]

Provisions for contract management, monitoring and dealing with performance problems were therefore the same despite the legally unenforceable nature of SLAs. Clauses designed to counter the effects of disruption in services were to be included in all contracts and SLAs. Hence in both cases, in the event of failure to perform:

> Service providers should be informed in writing and given a specific period in which to recover the failure and improve. Termination is the ultimate sanction, but should not be used without full consideration of the consequences. In the case of unacceptable performance of in-house organisations under SLAs, Departments should examine the causes and consider early termination of the SLA.[57]

The Handbook placed particular emphasis on the benefits of strategic contracting out, a new option which did not figure in earlier guidance issued in 1989. A problem with market testing in the past had been the perpetuation of uncertainty for directly employed staff, who could be made redundant if the in-house bid was not successful (although staff and expertise transferred to the new employer where Transfer of Undertakings (Protection of Employment) Regulations 1981 (TUPE) applied). During this period, there is some evidence of central pressure having been applied to achieve a clear-cut choice between internal restructuring and strategic outsourcing, in order to avoid this uncertainty and costs associated with postponing the decision on the future of the internal workforce.[58]

BQS therefore brought together, in a single set of policy documents, authoritative guidance encouraging both the contractual restructuring of internal

[56] n 46 above, paras 8.1-8.2. [57] ibid.

[58] ND Lewis, *Law and Governance: The Old Meets the New* (London: Cavendish Publishing, 2001) 121.

government relationships through administrative contracts, and the replacement of direct provision by internal and external forms of economic contract. Central pressures favouring increasingly privatized modes of service provision were just as much a reflection of policy-driven regulation as the more explicit programmes of market testing and CCT that operated in 1980s and 1990s. Indeed, the review process was arguably designed to facilitate the movement of central government functions progressively 'outwards' from direct bureaucratic control to executive agencies, then to external contractors, and finally to the private market – at which point the activity ceases to be governed through the New Public Contracting and becomes subject to more general forms of regulation.[59]

In spite of the withdrawal of BQS and other formal guidance, market testing and other competitive procedures remain a fundamental part of the programme for public service reform at the central government level.[60] The current trend is towards the replacement of detailed and overt central prescription with looser frameworks of guidance which, despite an apparently increased level of managerial autonomy, nevertheless strongly encourage certain forms of competitive activity or market involvement. While decision making on public service issues in central government cannot be described as 'policy-driven' in quite the same manner as in the six-year period following the introduction of BQS, the contractual relationships here may still be considered within the analytical framework of the New Public Contracting.

Best Value

One year after the launch of BQS in central government, the Local Government Act 1999 abolished CCT and imposed on public authorities the requirement to review and appraise their activities in accordance with the new regime of best value.[61] The regime applies to a wide range of local public bodies in England

59 For some self-funding non-monopoly agencies the promise of increased autonomy and reduced departmental interference should in theory provide an impetus to privatization. For a discussion of why relatively few executive agencies have taken the further step towards privatization, see F Gains, 'Implementing Privatization Policies in "Next Steps" Agencies' (1999) 77 *Public Administration* 713.

60 For example, on the Government's continuing commitment to the contracting out of prison management services, see the Criminal Justice White Paper, *Justice for All*, (Cm 5563, 2002).

61 P Vincent-Jones, 'Competition and Contracting in the Transition from CCT to Best Value: Towards a More Reflexive Regulation?' (1999) 77 *Public Administration* 273; ibid, 'Central-Local Relations Under the Local Government Act 1999: A New Consensus?' (2000) 63 MLR 84. See: G Boyne, 'Processes, Performance and Best Value in Local Government' (1999) 25 *Local Government Studies* 1; T Bovaird and A Halachmi, 'Learning from International Approaches to Best Value' (2001) 29 *Policy and Politics* 451; M Geddes and S Martin, 'The Policy and Politics of Best Value: Currents, Crosscurrents and Undercurrents in the New Regime' (2000) 28 *Policy and Politics* 379; M Lewis and J Hartley, 'Evolving Forms of Quality Management in Local Government: Lessons From the Best Value Pilot Programme' (2001) 29 *Policy and Politics* 477; S Maile and P Hoggett, 'Best Value and the Politics of Pragmatism' (2001) 29 *Policy and Politics* 509; S Martin, 'Re-evaluating Public Service Improvement: The Early Impacts of the Best Value Regime' (2001) 29 *Policy and Politics*

and Wales that have tax-raising or precepting powers,[62] including local councils, police, fire, civil defence, waste disposal, and passenger transport authorities.[63] Such authorities are subject to the statutory duty to make arrangements to secure 'continuous improvement' in their public service functions, having regard to a combination of economy, efficiency and effectiveness.[64] The duty to local people is 'to provide quality services at an acceptable cost'.[65] As with the emphasis in BQS on 'better quality services', the purpose has been to move away from the exclusive concern with cost that is widely regarded as having been detrimental to service quality under CCT.

However, although it is for local authorities themselves to devise how best value is to be achieved, this is to be done in the context of a central regulatory framework. The regime prescribes, in detail, processes that must be undertaken in order to discharge the statutory duty. Authorities must consult with representatives[66] of council tax payers, local businesses, service users and other persons who have an interest in any area of the authority's functions.[67] The authority must conduct best value reviews aimed at improving the way its functions are exercised, having regard to economy, efficiency and effectiveness.[68] It must also prepare a performance plan for each financial year,[69] which must be published by a certain deadline and in the manner and form specified by the Secretary of State.[70] Authorities are expected, through Local Performance Plans (LPPs): to report to local people on the authority's performance in achieving the previous year's targets and on these results relative to other best value authorities; to inform local people of performance targets for the forthcoming year and remedial action where previous targets have not been met; and to summarise the outcome of best value reviews, normally expressed in the form of revised targets and the future programme for achieving them.[71]

Furthermore, while best value is defined in very general terms, the Secretary of State may by order specify the performance indicators by which an authority's performance can be measured,[72] and the performance standards that must be met[73] in relation to those indicators.[74] The Secretary of State may make different orders for different authorities, applying at different times.[75] Authorities must have regard to any guidance issued by the Secretary of State concerning the consultation

447; B Walker and H Davis, 'Perspectives on Contractual Relationships and the Move to Best Value in Local Authorities' (1999) 25 *Local Government Studies* 16.

62 Local Government Act 1999, s 1(1).

63 The *de minimis* threshold of £500,000 expenditure per year means that the duty applies to only around 50 parish or town councils out of a total of 8000 councils at that level: (*Hansard*, HL vol 599, col 608 (12 April 1999) (Lord Whitty)).

64 LGA 1999, s 3(1).

65 Select Committee on Environment, Transport and Regional Affairs, Eleventh Report, *Implementation of the best value Framework* (HC 705-I, 1997/98) para 11.

66 LGA 1999, s 3(3).

67 s 3(2).

68 s 5(3)(a).

69 s 6(1).

70 ss 6(3) and (4).

71 Cm 4014, para 7. 31.

72 s 4(1)(a).

73 s 4(5).

74 s 4(1)(b).

75 s 4(2).

process,[76] the conduct of best value reviews,[77] and the making of performance plans.[78] Such guidance may relate to the timetable, procedure, form and content of the review,[79] and any performance indicators and targets that have been specified under section 4. The Secretary of State may require an authority to consider or assess its objectives, performance and progress in relation to any particular function, or whether it should be exercising the function at all.[80] The power of the Secretary of State to specify, by order, the period within which authorities must review their functions may be applied differently between authorities and functions.[81]

More detailed direction on the processes to be undertaken and factors to be considered in the discharge of best value duties is contained in guidance issued under the legislation. For example, reviews should be conducted in accordance with the 'Four Cs' – indicating the requirement on the part of authorities to *challenge* whether a service is necessary, *consult* with local people to establish standards, *compare* service performance with other providers, and (where appropriate) use *competition* to achieve value for money.[82] The 'challenge' component here is similar to the BQS option encouraging abolition of central government services or functions where they can no longer be justified. Since the ending of CCT local authorities are no longer compelled to subject activities to competition as a precondition to performing them directly. Nevertheless, 'voluntary' competitive tendering is encouraged either in order to provide incentives to in-house teams to improve their performance, or as part of the process of strategic contracting out. Strategic contracting out in local government, as in central government, may be regarded as a product of the New Public Contracting in spite of its voluntaristic appearance.[83] While no particular competitive procedure is prescribed, this is one of the ways in which public authorities are likely to be able to satisfy auditors and the government that they are complying with their duty to secure continuous improvement in their public service functions.[84]

Policy-guided choice in review processes

Much was made in BQS of the Government's approach being 'pragmatic' not 'dogmatic' – 'there should be no hierarchy or implied preference in considering these options . . . the question is which will best deliver value for money in the

76 s 3(4). 77 s 5(3)(b). 78 s 6(2)(a)–(l). 79 s 5(5). 80 s 5(4)(a)–(h).
81 s 5(2). 82 *Hansard*, HL vol 599, cols 572-573 12 April 1999 (Lord Whitty).

83 Under CCT, local authorities had an incentive 'voluntarily' to contract out services (for which credits towards competition quotas were allowed) as a means of avoiding the compulsory regime. Outsourcing or 'externalization' in such circumstances was thus an indirect result of policy-driven regulation.

84 For a sceptical view of the capacity of benchmarking to serve as an effective proxy for competition in securing improved performance, see M Bowerman and A Ball, 'Great Expectations: Benchmarking for best value' (2000) *Public Money and Management* (Apr–Jun) 21, 25.

particular circumstances?'[85] Nevertheless, just such a hierarchy appears to have existed, albeit implicitly. This reflected the presumption that too many public service functions are presently performed by government, and that policy should therefore aim to shift the provider role, or preferably the entire responsibility for the service, out of the public and into the private sector. In the eyes of government, both abolition and privatization serve to reduce public expenditure, while privatization has the added benefits of stimulating the market and raising tax revenues. Only where these options were deemed inappropriate should the service be subjected to competition through strategic contracting out or, where this was not possible, through market testing. And only if these options were in turn unsuitable should internal restructuring be considered, involving the use of benchmarking and other 'diagnostic tools' as proxies for competitive market pressures.

While the White Paper preceding the 1999 Act had considered a variety of ways in which best value might be achieved, for example through contracting out, competitive tendering, and privatization, these were not specified in the legislation in the way that options were spelled out under BQS.[86] On the face of it a public authority has the 'freedom to deliver its services using traditional or innovative methods or any other combination it chooses.'[87] However, the whole philosophy of best value and similar policies is to encourage public bodies voluntarily to adopt innovative solutions with competition at their heart. Public authorities are unlikely in practice to be able to demonstrate best value to the satisfaction of auditors and the Secretary of State by following just the 'traditional' route.[88] In one respect this is the position in which government departments and executive agencies find themselves following the withdrawal of BQS. However, as has been seen, in central government there continues to exist a strong presumption that efficiencies associated with innovation and pressures for improvement are less likely to be assured through bureaucratic organization than in the private sector or through competition.

In addition to formal and informal policy guidance, choice in review processes is further constrained by the threat of sanctions. Central powers of intervention are a defining feature of the New Public Contracting. If government agencies or public authorities are perceived to be failing properly to conduct reviews or to bring about required improvements, sanctions may be applied. As we shall see in Part II, standard-setting, monitoring, and enforcement are hallmarks of any regulatory regime. The 1999 Act provides for a range of widely drafted default

[85] n 46 above, para 9.

[86] *Hansard*, HC vol 323, col 138 (12 January 1999) (Mr Jenkin). Sceptics have speculated about the reasons for the lack of specific guidelines on the discipline of competiton: 'If the market place is so important, and it is referred to in all the options, why are the Government trying to give the impression that the need to go to the market place is being removed? Who are they trying to convince? Whose fears are they trying to allay?' HL Deb vol 599 col 591 12 April 1999 (Lord Bowness).

[87] *Hansard*, HL vol 599, col 574 (12 April 1999) (Lord Whitty).

[88] Tony Blair, 'Next on the List: Clean Up the Councils', *Guardian* 3 November 1997: 'There can be no monopoly of service delivery by councils; the 1970s will not be revisited.'

powers to be exercised by the Secretary of State where public authorities (including local councils) are considered to be failing in their best value duties. An authority may be directed to amend a performance plan, to follow specified procedures in relation to such a plan, to carry out a review of specified functions,[89] or to take any action considered necessary or expedient to secure compliance with the best value provisions of the Act.[90] The Secretary of State may direct that a specified function be exercised centrally or by a nominee,[91] and make provision for its exercise by regulation.[92] An authority must be given the opportunity to make representations about any proposed direction or report that has resulted in a proposed direction,[93] except where the direction is considered 'sufficiently urgent'[94] in which case the authority must be informed and given reasons.[95] The Secretary of State also has general powers to make regulations in relation to the keeping of accounts by best value authorities.[96]

By contrast, there was no explicit provision for enforcement under the non-statutory BQS guidance. Formal sanctions were, and continue to be, unnecessary in central government since policy may be enforced by means of hierarchical authority and chain-of-command controls. Where departments or agencies are considered to be under-performing, various sanctions may be applied including disciplining of Chief Executives responsible for delivering targets. The contractual commitments undertaken by departments and executive agencies in the form of PSAs and framework documents are, at least in theory, subject to sanctions. In the case of public authorities beyond direct central government control that are not covered by the best value regime, a wide range of other powers exist for emergency intervention to deal with perceived public service failures.[97]

In both central and local government, therefore, while senior managers are in theory free to decide how to deliver best value or better quality services at optimal cost, the choices they may make are circumscribed in a manner that is policy-guided.

Centralized decentralization

The present argument, to reiterate, is that the New Public Contracting should be understood as a set of policies entailing the delegation of powers and

89 LGA 1999, s 15(2). 90 s 15(5). 91 s 15(6). 92 s 15(7).

93 s 15(9). The Secretary of State must have regard to any statement which the authority sends regarding any report: s 15(10). 94 s 15(11).

95 s 15(12). 96 s 23.

97 Best value does not apply to central government, the Welsh Assembly, the NHS or to schools, despite various criticisms of this omission made by the Parliamentary Select Committee and during the passage of the Bill. Existing powers of intervention where authorities fail in a particular statutory duty are not affected. A full list of then existing powers in the areas of education, housing, child care, social services, planning and public health was set out in a written answer, (*Hansard*, HC vol 58, cols 249-255W, (11 April 1984).

responsibilities to public agencies in regulatory frameworks that preserve central government powers of various kinds. The apparent paradox of devolution combined with increased bureaucratic control over strategy and policy is part of a wider shift in modes of control in the public service:[98] 'The approach is one of centralization and decentralization at the same time; centralization of policy and setting the parameters within which the system works, and decentralization of operational management.'[99] The phenomenon of 'centralized decentralization'[100] is particularly evident in the economic form of the New Public Contracting, in which contract and market forces combine with, rather than substitute for, hierarchy and bureaucracy.[101] While the devolution of powers creates the possibility of increased choice and discretion on the part of public service managers, the promise of autonomy is undercut by the conditions imposed by regulatory frameworks and their sanctioning capacities.[102] Hence New Public Contracting policies reflect the continuing trend, in England at least,[103] towards centralization of power and increasing government control over the activities of sub-units of central government, local councils, and public and professional bodies in the fields of law, education, health and social services. While centralization is a familiar theme in the analysis of the relationship between central and local government,[104] it is manifested also in the restructuring of relations within government and in other public service settings such as the NHS.[105] Indeed, the commitment to national frameworks of standards and accountability in all public service fields was an explicit part of the second phase of New Labour's Modernizing Government agenda.[106]

This section considers some aspects of centralization in current policy on public services, setting the scene for the more detailed investigation in subsequent

98 P Hoggett, 'New Modes of Control in the Public Service' (1996) 74 *Public Administration* 9.

99 N Deakin and K Walsh, 'The Enabling State: The Role of Markets and Contracts' (1996) 74 *Public Administration* 33, 36–37.

100 L Kirkpatrick and M Lucio, 'Introduction: The Contract State and the Future of Public Management' (1996) 74 *Public Administration* 1, 5.

101 Walsh (n 11 above); K Shaw, J Fenwick, and A Foreman, 'Compulsory Competition for Local Government Services in the UK: A Case of Market Rhetoric and Camouflaged Centralism' (1995) 10 *Public Policy and Administration* 63.

102 J Benington, 'The Modernization and Improvement of Government and Public Services' (2000) *Public Money and Management* (Apr–Jun) 3, 6. S Cope and J Goodship, 'The Audit Commission and Public Services: Delivering for Whom?' (2002) *Public Money and Management* (Oct–Dec) 33, 35.

103 n 7 above.

104 M Loughlin, 'The Restructuring of Central-Local Government Relations', in J Jowell and D Oliver (eds), *The Changing Constitution* (3rd edn, Oxford: Clarendon Press, 1994) 261; ibid, *Legality and Locality: The Role of Law in Central-Local Government Relations* (Oxford: Clarendon Press, 1996); ibid, 'Understanding Central-Local Government Relations' (1996) 11 *Public Policy and Administration* 48; I Leigh, *Law, Politics and Local Democracy* (Oxford: Oxford University Press, 2000).

105 'Labour initiatives overwhelm NHS', article discussing King's Fund research report, *Guardian* 12 April 2002.

106 Cabinet Office, Effective Performance Division, www.cabinetoffice.gov.uk/eeg/?url=eeg/secondphase.htm, accessed 10th August 2005.

chapters of how the tension between centralization and devolution is expressed in various instances of the New Public Contracting.

Performance indicators, information, and management

The development of performance indicators (PIs) was encouraged throughout the public sector from the beginning of the 1980s as part of the Financial Management Initiative (FMI). Their significance increased further with the emphasis in Next Steps on decentralization and the 'hands-off' approach to central control. A reliable system of PIs became essential once structural reform of government had devolved financial and management responsibility for service delivery away from central departments.[107] PIs and performance measurement are core components of administrative contracts, providing a basis for evaluating the success or failure of departments and executive agencies in meeting the targets agreed in PSAs and framework documents.[108] Performance management systems have spread throughout the public sector, applying to senior civil servants and government ministers as well as to front-line staff who deliver services to the public. The use of PIs, and the publication of achievement in relation to them in an increasing array of league tables, performance rankings and star ratings, is an important technique of central monitoring and control accompanying deregulation and devolution.[109]

Local authorities have been required to collect and publish PIs annually as laid down by the Audit Commission since 1992. Under best value, a new set of indicators has been specified by central government. Best value serves as a means for controlling the behaviour of local and other public authorities through a combination of linked regulatory mechanisms and institutions involving performance targets, audit and inspection.[110] In addition to best value, local authorities since 2002 have been subject to a separate performance evaluation and inspection regime in the form of the Comprehensive Performance Assessment (CPA), carried out by the Audit Commission which rates councils as excellent, good, fair, weak, or poor. As we have seen, the best value regime reserves specific powers of intervention for central government to deal with a range of defaults by local authorities, including failure to perform to the required standard. Enforcement mechanisms, triggered by perceived performance failures measured in accordance with star ratings and league table positions, exist also in respect of health and education. Throughout the public service, under-performing local authorities, schools, and hospital trusts are variously threatened with closure, replacement of chief

[107] Carter and Greer (n 19 above). [108] Cutler and Waine (n 19 above) 325.

[109] N Harris, *Law and Education: Regulation, Consumerism and the Education System* (London: Sweet and Maxwell, 1993).

[110] G Boyne, 'External Regulation and best value in Local Government' (2000) *Public Money and Management* (Jul–Sep), 7. There are 18 'corporate health' and 104 'service delivery' indicators. These refer more to inputs and processes than outcomes (8).

executives, amalgamation or demotion in status, take-over by private contractors or management consortia, or other forms of compulsory intervention.

As is evident from the review of the NPM provided above, performance management systems are not dependent on, and indeed may exist entirely separately from, any form of contractual organization within government or of public services more generally. However, the contract mechanism is a congenial host for such techniques. All forms of the New Public Contracting operate increasingly according to a common process of specification of targets, performance indicators, regular reviews, and monitoring and reporting on performance in relation to targets. Not surprisingly, the targets set in PSAs between spending departments and the Treasury, and in framework documents between executive agencies and central government departments, are reflected directly in the contractual commitments entered into by private sector providers or in-house teams with public purchasing agencies. Contracts with external providers, and SLAs between public purchasers and in-house contractors, are required to be similarly expressed in terms of outputs and outcomes.[111] From the perspective of individual consumers these output specifications are the same as or consistent with the obligations contained in the Citizen's Charter or other charters.[112] Contract thus provides a uniform governance mechanism for coordinating public services from the macro levels of government to the more micro levels of production, exchange, and consumption.

The 'new centre' within government

The term 'new centre' has been coined to describe both the increasing concentration of policy-making authority within the Treasury and Cabinet Office in Britain, and the central prescription of national standards and detailed performance criteria governing delivery by local agencies and public bodies charged with policy implementation.[113] Following the election of New Labour in 1997, the development of policy on public services became the responsibility of specialist units within the Cabinet Office, notably the Modernizing Public Services Group and the Effective Performance Division located within it. Public sector reform is now supported at the strategic centre of government by the Prime Minister's Delivery Unit (PMDU) and the Office of Public Services Reform (OPSR), both set up in June 2001.[114] The breadth of the OPSR's public services remit is striking, including programmes for improvements in respect of departmental performance,

111 n 46 above, para. 12. 112 Oliver and Drewry (n 1 above) 28.

113 S Lee and R Woodward, 'Implementing the Third Way: The Delivery of Public Services Under the Blair Government' (2002) *Public Money and Management* (Oct-Dec) 49, 50.

114 See OPSR, www.cabinetoffice.gov.uk/opsr/; PMDU, www.cabinetoffice.gov.uk/pmdu/: 'The Delivery Unit works in partnership with the Treasury, No. 10, other parts of the Cabinet Office and stakeholder departments, to assess delivery and provide performance management for key delivery areas, and has a shared responsibility with the Treasury for the joint Public Service Agreement (PSA) target: "Improve public services by working with departments to help them meet their PSA targets, consistently with the fiscal rules." '

customer focus, project management and delivery, local government, and local public services including Primary Care Trusts and schools. The policy papers and explanatory documents produced by such specialist units are an important normative source of the New Public Contracting, either substituting for or supporting primary and secondary legislation, circular guidance and departmental directives.[115] Generally, the increasing control exercised by the new centre over departments has been effected through incremental extension of executive powers rather than by legislation.[116]

The Treasury has a particularly influential policy-making role within the new centre. Even sources within the Treasury admit to a change in the nature of the relationship between the Treasury and other departments. Whereas in the past the Treasury would scrutinise ideas put forward by spending departments, 'now we don't wait for that to happen. We try to develop ideas. We work jointly to produce a piece of work, perhaps on public services or tax credits. It means we need new people who can work in that mode, because the skills needed for a finance directorate are different from those needed for policy development.'[117] This statement illustrates how the Treasury now perceives its role in terms of policy development, including policy on how the relationships with spending departments should be managed in terms of PSAs. The policy focus on the supply side of the economy, especially productivity, has affected all departments. The traditional Treasury concern with raising money and setting interest rates has been replaced by a focus on justifying how money is spent. Treasury officials now wish not only to control expenditure but also to change the structure of incentives in society.[118] Many government initiatives originate in the Treasury. The Treasury now concerns itself with all matters affecting Britain's long-run productivity, from immigration to health policy, regional policy, planning law, and higher education funding. The Treasury operates in some ways outside the rest of government, recruiting separately from the normal civil service, and able to call on 'crack squads' of experts to deal with problems in spending departments. While there have been benefits of centralization of power, for example the increased coherence and economies of scale brought to government procurement by the Treasury's Office of Government Commerce, there remain major

[115] Together, these features of concentration and centralization of policy making, coupled with the relative informality of many policy documents and materials as normative sources, raise constitutional concerns about transparency and legitimacy. This aspect has been particularly highlighted by Freedland in his critique of the PFI, but is of more general significance. Nevertheless, many variants of the New Public Contracting are remarkable precisely for the explicitly legislative form of their implementation.

[116] Public service reforms have required only three enactments removing obstacles to specific policies: the Government Trading Funds Act 1990, the Civil Service (Management Functions) Act 1992, and the Deregulation and Contracting Out Act 1994 – T Daintith and A Page, *The Executive in the Constitution: Structure, Autonomy and Internal Control* (Oxford: Oxford University Press, 1999).

[117] Sir Andrew Turnbull, permanent Secretary to the Treasury, reported in the *Guardian* 16 April 2002.

[118] R Parry and N Deakin, 'Treasury', ESRC: Whitehall Programme project briefing 1.

concerns about the lack of constitutional control and public accountability in such developments.

The Comprehensive Spending Review (CSR) introduced in 1998, and the associated contractual mechanism for allocating funding to departments through PSAs, are at the heart of the Treasury's increasing power and influence within government. The 2000 Review was remarkable for its breadth of vision. The Government's overall aim of 'delivering stability through strong public services' involved four main objectives for the three-year period: increasing opportunity for all; building responsible and secure communities; raising productivity and sustainable growth; and securing a modern international role for Britain.[119] The argument put forward consistently since this time has been that the expansion of public services is possible only on the basis of the continued pursuit of economic stability through a tight framework of monetary and fiscal policy. Macro-economic stability is an essential pre-condition for high and stable levels of growth and employment and strong and sustainable public services.[120]

The new centre has thus played a significant part in Britain in driving forward policies aimed at restructuring the 'public service', broadly construed, through various contractual instruments. As will be seen in the remainder of the book, the existence in Britain of specific policies such as market testing and competitive tendering, and more recently of increasingly subtle forms of central regulation and direction which encourage strategic contracting out and privatization, is in contrast with the generally less prescriptive and more transparent approach to public service reform that has arguably been adopted in most other Anglophone countries.[121] The democratic deficit in the New Public Contracting in this regard will be further explored in Chapter 11.

Economic policy and international trade rules

A fundamental objective of the UK Government in the new millennium is to raise productivity and increase international competitiveness, and thereby to close the productivity gap with the US, Germany, France and Japan. National economic weaknesses are said to include insufficient domestic competition, lack of incentives and opportunities for enterprise and innovation, an under-skilled workforce, and a history of under-investment in public services.[122] The private sector is considered to have a crucial role to play in improving performance and productivity in this regard. Public Private Partnerships and the PFI form a cornerstone of the Government's strategy for investment, intended 'to deliver significantly improved

[119] 'Prudent for a Purpose: Building Opportunity and Security for All', 2000 Spending Review: New Public Spending Plans 2001–2004, July 2000 (Cm 4807, para. 1.2).

[120] ibid para 2.2.

[121] In other countries 'contracting has been used less for putting pressure on public services to become more efficient, and more as a means by which small public organizations can ensure that work which they could never do themselves is effectively performed' – Walsh (n 11 above) 111.

[122] n 119 above, para 5.1.

public services by increasing the quality of investment and by releasing the full potential of public sector assets'.[123] The fulfilment of the Government's objectives is dependent on maintaining efficiency and effectiveness in the operation of public services, hence the setting of exacting targets for improvement over the three-year cycle of the Spending Review, and the commitment to 'rooting out under-performance wherever it exists in the public service'.[124]

As the second largest exporter of services in the world,[125] the UK has a particular interest in furthering global competition. The service sector accounts for a far larger proportion of economic output than goods, contributing some 70 per cent of GDP and employing more than twenty three million people.[126] Under the system of formal requests for market liberalization that came into operation under the General Agreement on Trade in Services (GATS) in March 2003, markets for financial services abroad, for example, could be opened up for the City's business and financial services firms, in return for the grant of foreign access to domestic markets for other services. Britain has particular strengths also in education, as a net exporter of services with earnings worth £40 per capita of the population.[127] External pressures for the liberalization of trade in services come from both the EU in the form of the extension of public procurement rules, and the United States, which is keen for international markets in sectors such as health and education to be opened to competition from its major corporations.

The importance of supply-side competition in New Labour's policy for the development of quasi-markets in public services has already been demonstrated. While services are funded from general taxation and remain free or heavily subsidized for citizens at the point of delivery, a fundamental purpose of the regulatory regimes governing economic contracts is to encourage public purchasing agencies to commission services from an increasing diversity of providers in the public, private and voluntary sectors, both at home and abroad. In the health sector, Britain is promoting trans-border competition through a range of specific initiatives involving consumer choice as to when and where to have hospital operations. Many of the new specialist diagnostic and treatment centres from which PCTs are being encouraged to procure services for NHS patients are owned or managed by international corporations. British patients already have access to European health care in a landmark deal agreed by ministers in Brussels, which will have a major impact on the ability of patients to shop around the EU for the best or fastest treatment.[128] The agreement enshrines a formal right for members of the EU to

[123] ibid para 5.8.

[124] ibid para 5.23. Investment in physical and human capital is considered a key means of delivering increased competitiveness across the OECD countries. The UK suffers particularly from under-investment in physical infrastructure in comparison with the European Union average – D Heald and N Geaughan, 'The Private Financing of Public Infrastructure', in G Stoker, (ed), *The New Management of British Local Governance* (London: Macmillan, 1999), 223.

[125] The total value of service exports was £65 billion in 1999 – *Observer*, 29 April 2001.

[126] *Guardian*, 13 October 2002.

[127] *Guardian*, 3 June 2002.

[128] *Independent*, 8 October 2002.

go elsewhere in Europe for publicly funded services in the same way as for other services, if treatment is not available in their own countries within a time limit that is medically justifiable. The new opportunities created by increased competition are of interest to domestic firms as well as those based abroad. The CBI is looking for different ways of working and of improving productivity in all the 'big four' public service areas of education, transport, health, and law and order.[129] Throughout the public service, competition is being actively promoted by the UK government in the pursuit of a combination of macro- and micro-economic policy goals.

International trade rules provide a further impetus to competition. The purpose GATS, to which Britain is a signatory both directly and indirectly through membership of the EU, is to extend World Trade Organization (WTO) controls already applying to goods through the General Agreement on Tariffs and Trade (GATT) into the service sectors. While in theory GATS respects members' sovereign rights to regulate economic and non-economic activities in their territories in pursuit of public policy objectives, the effect of the application of free trade rules in areas such as banking, technical services, professional services, and tourism is likely to be restrictive of the rights of governments to protect domestic industries, limit foreign investment, impose specific regulations, and control levels of imports. The EC as signatory to GATS has already decided to undertake binding commitments in respect of Services of General Interest (SGI) that are currently open to competition within the internal market.[130] Again, while the treaty explicitly recognizes the rights of members to maintain services as public monopolies (and there is no compulsion to privatize particular undertakings or subject them to any form of competition) there are advantages for a net exporter of services such as Britain in encouraging national and international competition in service provision. The expanding role of private and non-profit providers in the health and education sectors increases the likelihood that parts of the NHS, for example, may fall under GATS rules. The Government's policy of encouraging commercialization of health provision – through corporatization of NHS Trusts, the use of overseas clinical teams and privately run diagnostic and treatment centres, agreements between the public and independent sectors for integrated care, and the routine contracting out of support and other services – raises questions about the ability of government (or indeed its intention) in the long term to keep health provision out of GATS. There is a growing concern that GATS will lead to full-scale privatization of public monopolies throughout the world.

Similarly, while the EU respects in principle the right of national, regional, and local authorities to choose the way in which public services are delivered, in

[129] 'The system has to change, money alone is not the answer'. Digby Jones, of the CBI, reported in *Observer*, 14 July 2002.

[130] Commission of the European Communities, *Green Paper on Services of General Interest*, COM(2003) 270, 21 May 2003; ibid, *White Paper on Services of General Interest*, COM(2004)374, 12 May 2004.

practice, once quasi-markets have been introduced, the *economic* activity of 'offering goods and services on a given market' will render many arrangements subject to public procurement and other rules regardless of the absence of a market for services to ultimate consumers.[131] Whatever the response to the questions raised in the present consultation regarding the extension of Community governance to SGIs, there has already occurred among member states a *de facto* fundamental transformation in the way in which a wide range of health, education, social and other welfare services is provided to citizens and consumers. Services that have traditionally been delivered directly by public bureaucracies are increasingly being organized through complex networks of public and private actors in market and quasi-market relationships. The more that services are organized on a competitive basis (for example through quasi-markets combining increased consumer choice and provider competition), the more likely they are ultimately to fall within developing market liberalization rules. Once public monopolies have been dismantled and rendered subject to EU and GATS trade regimes, it will be difficult, if not impossible, to return to conditions of public monopoly.

Conclusion

This chapter has placed the New Public Contracting in the context of economic policy rationales that are driving public service reform in contemporary Britain. The overall effect of the New Public Contracting has been to encourage and prepare the ground for the shifting of public service functions from the domain of government to that of the market. Hence the development of internal charging, budgetary devolution and other forms of administrative restructuring may be seen as the precursor to more far-reaching quasi-market reforms in which price and quality are determined by purchaser choice and external competition involving economic contracts.[132] The purchasing of services by public agencies from in-house teams may give way to purchasing from the private sector. Contracting out may in some instances be a stage on the way to more extreme forms of privatization of public services.

The quest for increased domestic productivity and international competitiveness, while clearly in Britain's economic self-interest, is being reinforced by European and international treaty obligations and commitments to market liberalization and the removal of non-tariff barriers to world trade in services generally. Administrative contracts and economic contracts provide the regulatory means by which New Labour is pursuing its policy goals of increasing efficiency and effectiveness. The contract mechanism generally is serving as a vehicle for implementing performance management reforms throughout the public service.

131 ibid (2003), para 44. 132 cf Walsh (n 11 above) 108.

The various governance problems that have arisen in the attempt to use public contracts as an instrument of regulation will be considered in Part III. Before embarking on this task it is necessary to establish an explicit theoretical framework that may serve in the process of evaluation. To this end, Part II of the book explores key concepts of regulation, governance and responsiveness.

PART II

REGULATION, RESPONSIVENESS, RELATIONALITY

3

Regulation and Governance

The regulatory structures comprising each of the three main forms of the New Public Contracting were outlined in Chapter 1. This chapter lays the foundations of the socio-legal regulation perspective which will be developed in the next two chapters, and which ultimately will inform the substantive investigation of administrative contracts, economic contracts, and social control contracts in Part III. The state is viewed as a purposeful actor engaged in the pursuit of policy goals through the deployment of regulatory instruments of force, wealth, information and persuasion, in multiple relationships of control and accountability. A synthesis is suggested between this approach and theories of governance, which focus on the vocabularies, technologies, and techniques through which power is exercised in contemporary societies. Links are made also with the theory of institutions and organizations. The chapter demonstrates how the New Public Contracting operates by rendering responsible (or 'responsibilizing') social agents through contractual commitments and obligations undertaken more or less voluntarily across a wide range of administrative, economic and social relationships.

Regulation

In its most general sense, regulation may be said to include 'all acts of controlling, directing or governing according to a rule, principle or system'.[1] Regulation typically comprises three key elements: the specification of rules or standards, the monitoring of compliance, and the existence of some form of enforcement mechanism.[2] Regulation may be distinguished from other forms of control by its

[1] T Daintith, 'Regulation', *International Encyclopedia of Comparative Law* (1997) Ch 10, 3. See also T Prosser, *Law and the Regulators* (Oxford: Clarendon Press, 1997); LM Friedman, 'On Regulation and Legal Process', in RG Noll, (ed), *Regulatory Policy and the Social Sciences* (Berkeley: University of California Press, 1985), 111. No attempt is made here to review the vast and rapidly developing literature on regulation generally. For a recent overview of different perspectives on legal regulation, see B Lange, 'Regulatory Spaces and Interactions: An Introduction' (2003) 12 *Social and Legal Studies* 411.

[2] C Hood, O James, C Scott, G Jones, and T Travers, *Regulation Inside Government: Waste-watchers, Quality Police and Sleaze-busters* (Oxford: Oxford University Press, 1999); H Collins, *Regulating Contracts* (Oxford: Oxford University Press, 1999), 62; P Vincent-Jones, 'Contractual Governance: Institutional and Organisational Analysis' (2000) 20 *Oxford Journal of Legal Studies* 317, 332; ibid,

'sustained and focused' character.[3] A further essential element in this definition is the collective intention to produce a desired outcome. While the state need not be involved,[4] a public agency usually plays a central role in the regulation of socially valued activities.[5] The state is a purposeful actor, which pursues economic and social objectives through regulatory strategies linking state law with power resources, or instruments, of force, wealth, information, and persuasion.[6] A range of other actors also participates in regulatory processes beyond the formal boundaries of the state.[7]

Regulation and self-regulation

This definition of regulation includes general rules and specific commands. Also included are more subtle forms of state intervention such as subsidies and taxation, and policy instruments such as licensing, franchising, and management by performance targets. Regulation extends to social as well as economic behaviour,[8] and

'The Regulation of Contractualisation in Quasi-Markets for Public Services' [1999] PL 303, 315. In cybernetic theory, control systems comprise 'directors', 'detectors', and 'effectors', referring respectively to methods of setting standards, gathering information, and modifying behaviour – A Dunsire, 'A Cybernetic View of Guidance, Control and Evaluation in the Public Sector', in Franz-Xavier Kaufman (ed), *The Public Sector: Challenge for Coordination and Learning* (New York: Walter de Gruyter, 1991).

3 P Selznick, 'Focussing Organizational Research on Regulation', in Noll (ed), (n 1 above) 363. Control is sustained when applied on a regular or continuous rather than a once-and-for-all basis, and focused when it 'systematically attends to selected activities, values, or industries' (364). See L Nader and C Nader, 'A Wide Angle on Regulation: An Anthropological Perspective', in ibid: 'Government regulation is an accumulation of social values that translate into legal mandates to redress power imbalances and the abuse of power' (146–147).

4 Black thus decouples the activity of intentionally attempting to control from government as an actor. What remains important in this definition is purposiveness: 'Regulation is a process involving the sustained and focused attempt to alter the behaviour of others according to defined standards or purposes with the intention of producing a broadly defined outcome or outcomes' – J Black, 'Decentring Regulation: The Role of Regulation and Self-Regulation in a "Post-Regulatory" World' (2001) CLP 103, 142.

5 In his definition of regulation Selznick emphasizes that the control exercised by a public agency is over 'activities that are valued by a community' – (n 3 above) 363.

6 Daintith (n 1 above) 24; see also ibid, 'State Power', in P Newman, (ed), *The New Palgrave Dictionary of Economics and the Law* Vol 3 (P-Z), 524 (London: Macmillan, 1998). This classification of regulatory resources is a refinement of Daintith's earlier analysis based on the distinction between imperium (characterised by commands backed by force, and by duties or rules whose breach is accompanied by negative sanctions) and dominium (referring to the employment of wealth, usually in the form of government grants or contracts, as incentives to comply with central policy); this analysis allows that compliance with rules may be rewarded through their relaxation, and that withdrawal of wealth benefits may serve a sanctioning purpose – ibid, 'The Techniques of Government', in J Jowell and D Oliver, (ed), *The Changing Constitution* (Clarendon Press: Oxford, 1994) 212.

7 J Black, 'Enrolling Actors in Regulatory Systems: Examples from UK Financial Services Regulation' [2003] PL 63; C Scott, 'Private Regulation of the Public Sector: A Neglected Facet of Contemporary Governance' (2001) 29 JLS 56.

8 R Baldwin, C Scott, and C Hood, 'Introduction' in R Baldwin, C Scott, and C Hood, (eds), *Regulation* (Oxford: Oxford University Press, 1998); R Baldwin and M Cave, *Understanding Regulation: Theory, Strategy, and Practice* (Oxford: Oxford University Press, 1999).

incorporates unconscious and non-deliberate as well as intentional action.[9] And it includes 'bureaucratic regulation' – referring to the control of public bureaucracies by other public agencies other than through direct command and authority, and beyond orthodox constitutional checking mechanisms such as the legislature and the courts.[10] Bureaucratic regulation takes place against a backdrop of various types of control over government, with traditional oversight by 'arm's-length' inspectorates, audit bodies, and ombudsmen increasingly being supplemented by other mechanisms including competition (control through rivalry and choice), 'mutuality' (control through professional and collegial influences), and 'contrived randomness' (control through unpredictable processes).[11] While bureaucratic regulation is mainly concerned with the control of public organizations by other public bodies, private actors (accountants, auditors, private sector inspectors) also figure in the regulatory process. This form of regulation is becoming increasingly important as traditional hierarchical controls are replaced by private management techniques, and as the public sector becomes more fragmented through the creation of semi-independent government agencies, client-contractor splits, and the separation of responsibilities for policy making and service provision.

In this light, the New Public Contracting may be viewed as a complex control system combining contractual and extra-contractual regulatory mechanisms of standard-setting, performance monitoring, and enforcement. All forms of the New Public Contracting involve an element of bureaucratic regulation, coupled in some way with contractual governance. In administrative contracts, bureaucratic regulation occurs through the medium of contract. In economic contracts and social control contracts, by contrast, the bureaucratic and contractual regulatory dimensions are separate. The contractual regulatory function of standard-setting, monitoring, and enforcement is performed by public agencies in relation to the other contracting party, in accordance with the powers and responsibilities delegated bureaucratically in the regulatory regime.[12]

Self-regulation may be variously understood as an option for policy makers confronted with intractable control problems; as delegation of public powers to private bodies, often accompanied by the threat of statutory regulation;[13] as collective self-regulation of whole sectors of business activity; as intra-firm regulation within a

9 Baldwin and Cave (n 8 above) 2. The attempted exercise of systematic control for the attainment of public policy objectives is likely to impact upon a variety of state and non-state actors and institutions in unforeseeable ways. All such repercussions need to be taken into account in the analysis and evaluation of the success or failure of regulation in any particular regulatory context.

10 Hood et al (n 2 above); C Hood, O James, and C Scott, 'Regulation of Government: Has It Increased, Is It Increasing, Should It Be Diminished?' (2000) 78 *Public Administration* 283. On the different position in Scotland, see A Midwinter and N McGarvey, 'In Search of the Regulatory State: Evidence From Scotland' (2001) 79 *Public Administration* 825.

11 Hood et al (n 2 above) 13–17.

12 see ch 1, above, and Fig 2.

13 C Graham, 'Self-Regulation', in G Richardson and H Genn, (ed), *Administrative Law and Government Action: The Courts and Alternative Mechanisms of Review* (Oxford: Clarendon Press, 1994) 203.

single organization; or as self-control by individual subjects.[14] Self-regulation is at the heart of theories of autopoiesis and reflexivity, which focus on the self-organization of social systems as a possible solution to the problem of regulatory failure.[15] As discussed in Chapter 1, the notion of contract as self-regulation applies both to agreements between private individuals and to 'government by agreement' involving compacts between the state and private or public bodies. The existence of self-regulation in so many forms implies the need for governments (if they are to be successful) to pursue policy objectives through 'indirect steering', involving 'adjusting, balancing, structuring, facilitating, enabling, negotiating, but never directly telling and never directly trying to control'.[16] Most useful for present purposes is the broad definition of self-regulation as an internal regulatory process induced by government or public authority.[17] Despite an apparent relaxation of control, 'the standards to be achieved, the limits to be observed are still set from above, or outside'.[18]

Self-regulation is of fundamental importance to the present analysis for two reasons. Firstly, with regard to economic contracts and social control contracts, relational theory predicts that where contracts are successfully established and operating effectively, they are likely to be strongly self-regulatory. Where the contract norms are optimally configured,[19] the arrangements should be inherently reflexive in allowing the parties to make adjustments according to the constitution they have established for themselves and from which they may jointly benefit. Conversely, deficiencies in some of the contract norms or in their overall balance may be reflected in limited self-regulatory capacity, and in the corresponding absence of joint-maximising benefits associated with relational contracting.

Secondly, again in the case of economic contracts and social control contracts, self-regulation is relevant to the analysis of the hierarchical relationship between central government and the public agency charged with implementing the New Public Contracting scheme. Self-regulation in this context is associated with low levels of central interference in the agency's operations and hence with a high degree of autonomy and discretion in the conduct of its contracting activities. Here again, self-regulation is likely to be indicative of regulatory effectiveness, compared with the converse situation in which the public agency is subject to high levels of external intervention and prescription limiting its discretionary contracting powers.

[14] See J Black, 'Constitutionalising Self-Regulation' (1996) 59 MLR 24; ibid, n 4 above; A Ogus, 'Rethinking Self-Regulation' (1995) 15 OJLS 97.

[15] M Aalders and T Wilthagen, 'Moving Beyond Command-and-Control: Reflexivity in the Regulation of Occupational Health and Safety' (1997) 19 *Law and Policy* 416, 428. The significance of these theories for the analysis of the New Public Contracting is considered in ch 4.

[16] Black (n 4 above) 126.

[17] cf Aalders and Wilthagen (n 15 above) 427.

[18] A Dunsire, 'Holistic Governance' (1990) 5 *Public Policy and Administration* 4, 6.

[19] Ch 1, above.

Tools of government and collibration

Consistent with this broad regulation perspective, a body of recent literature in the United States has focused on the variety of instruments or 'tools of government' deployed by the state as alternatives to direct command and control in efforts to achieve policy objectives. A 'tool of government' is defined as 'an identifiable method through which collective action is structured to address a public problem.'[20] Such instruments include grants, contracts, insurance, loan guarantees, tortious liability, vouchers, and information, as well as economic and social regulation narrowly conceived. Tools of government are said typically to operate indirectly in organizational networks characterized by complex exchanges and inter-dependencies, rather than directly within hierarchies.[21] The focus is on the network of actors engaged in the implementation of public programmes, rather than on the internal workings of public organizations. Responsibility for the operation of programmes is shared by a range of 'third parties' in the public, private and non-profit sectors, including local governments, hospitals, universities, private companies, commercial banks, and community organizations.

Tools of government may be analysed according to four main variables. Firstly, the degree of *coercion* refers to 'the extent to which a tool restricts individual or group behavior as opposed to merely encouraging or discouraging it'.[22] Secondly, *directness* is concerned with 'the extent to which the entity authorizing, financing, or inaugurating a public activity is involved in carrying it out'.[23] Thirdly, policy tools may be differentiated according to the level of *automaticity* they embody, where 'automaticity measures the extent to which a tool utilizes an existing administrative structure to produce its effect rather than having to create its own special administrative apparatus'.[24] And finally, *visibility* measures 'the extent to which the resources devoted to a tool show up in the normal government budgeting and policy review processes'.[25]

20 LM Salamon, 'The New Governance and the Tools of Public Action: An Introduction' in LM Salamon, (ed), *The Tools of Government: A Guide to the New Governance* (Oxford: Oxford University Press, 2002), 19. The operation of such instruments is necessarily indirect and contingent, reflecting the mixture of public and private resources and different styles of management at play in modern 'third-party' government, and the emphasis on networks and collaboration in place of hierarchy and control.

21 ibid. The new governance paradigm displays a number of contrasts with traditional public administration, including the shift from hierarchy to network, from 'public vs. private to public + private', and from command and control to negotiation and persuasion.

22 ibid 25.

23 'A direct tool is one in which authorization, funding, and execution are all carried out by essentially the same entity' – ibid 29. In the ranking of governance tools, there is considerable overlap between the degree of coerciveness and the degree of directness. Hence tort liability, vouchers, loan guarantees and grants are all low or medium on both scales. The correspondence is far from complete, however. Public information is said to operate highly directly, but to be one of the least coercive tools.

24 The greater the reliance on market forces, the more automatic are governance tools in their implementation – ibid 32. Again there is considerable, but not total, overlap with other dimensions. Not all indirect tools are automatic in operation, and not all automatic tools are indirect (33).

25 ibid 35.

Contract tends to be rather narrowly defined in this literature, and to be sharply distinguished from economic and social regulation. Hence public contracting is viewed as a business arrangement between a government agency and a private or non-profit entity in which that entity promises, in exchange for money, to deliver certain products or services.[26] As a sub-category of this general tool, 'purchase of service' (POS) contracting entails delivery by the private or non-profit entity directly to service consumers or citizens, on the basis of a contract with the government agency. As has been seen, however, the New Public Contracting involves regulatory arrangements that are more complicated than this analysis would suggest. In economic organization and social control, contract is both a tool deployed by central government in the policy decision to regulate through the New Public Contracting framework, and a tool governing the relationship between public agencies and service providers/citizens in accordance with the powers and responsibilities defined in the regulatory regime. The regulatory structures constituting economic contracts and social control contracts consist of complex combinations of tools of government. In addition to the contract mechanism, they include a range of instruments involving elements of hierarchy, incentives, financial inducements, grants, and the control of information. The suggestion that contract as a regulatory instrument occupies a 'medium' position on the analytical dimensions of coercion, directness, automaticity, and visibility will be subjected to critical evaluation in the detailed discussion of economic contracts in Chapter 7. The interesting feature of the New Public Contracting is that it is at once coercive and non-coercive; direct and indirect; and automatic and non-automatic in its operation. Parts 3 and 4 of this book will explore in depth the tensions and contradictions resulting from this mode of regulation.

The notion of 'collibration', which denotes governmental efforts to maintain stability or equilibrium through the balancing of rival forces,[27] is also useful in understanding regulation. The capacity to maintain such equilibrium has been described as the central logic of the 'steering state'.[28] Rather than implying an absence of government, collibration suggests government by means other

[26] J Steven Kelman, 'Contracting' in LM Salamon, (ed) *The Tools of Government: A Guide to the New Governance* (Oxford: Oxford University Press, 2002), 282.

[27] A Dunsire, 'Modes of Governance' in J Kooiman, (ed), *Modern Governance: New Government-Society Interactions* (London: Sage Publications, 1993), 30; ibid, 'Tipping the Balance: Autopoiesis and Governance' (1996) 28 *Administration and Society* 299.

[28] This logic concerns 'the capacity to steer an equilibrium by intervening in a pent-up balance of opposed forces. Collibration in this sense requires that institutionalised forces be configured into units pulling in contradictory directions in such way that a relatively puny force can alter the settings of the equilibrium between them' – C Hood, 'Which Contract State? Four Perspectives on Over-Outsourcing for Public Services' (1997) 56 *Australian Journal of Public Administration* 120, 124. This concept is consistent with the notion that in modern governance networks there are many centres of power that both steer and row – J Braithwaite, 'Accountability and Governance under the New Regulatory State' (1999) 58 *Australian Journal of Public Administration* 90.

than command and control.[29] While this concept has been developed mainly in connection with theories of governance, it may be deployed just as usefully in the context of regulation.[30] Contractual regulation through the New Public Contracting occurs in 'regulatory spaces'[31] in which power resources (force, wealth, information, and persuasion) are not just linked with law, but combined and balanced in various ways. The notion of collibration as the 'balancing' of regulatory forces is central to the analysis of the New Public Contracting. For example, the market testing and contracting out of public services may be viewed as a deliberate strategy directed at adjusting the balance between state and private sector provision. The recent trend in England towards corporatization of service provider functions that have previously been organized bureaucratically may also be considered in such terms. These and other regulatory strategies focusing on consumer voice, choice, and the control of information will be examined in detail in Chapters 7 and 8.

Control and accountability

Accountability may be described as a process whereby individuals are required to explain or justify their decisions or acts to another person or body in accordance with certain criteria, and then to make amends for any fault or error.[32] Accountability processes help to guard against the abuse of delegated power and also serve the more constructive purpose of promoting efficient and effective performance through the exchange of ideas and provision of information. Within government, internal accountability refers to the mechanisms for holding lower administrative tiers accountable to higher levels and ultimately to ministers, whereas external accountability involves the holding to account of those who govern by the courts, parliament and members of the public. In this perspective, government contracts may be analysed in terms of their performance of four 'key accountability tasks': setting standards against which to judge accounts, obtaining accounts, judging accounts, and deciding what consequences should follow from judging of the accounts.[33]

While accountability is of undoubted importance in the analysis of the New Public Contracting, it is best considered in the wider context of regulation.

[29] Dunsire (n 27 above) 34.

[30] C Scott, 'Accountability in the Regulatory State' (2000) 27 JLS 38.

[31] L Hancher, and M Moran, (eds), *Capitalism, Culture and Economic Regulation* (Oxford: Clarendon Press, 1989); T Daintith, 'A Regulatory Space Agency?' (1989) 9 OJLS 534.

[32] ACL Davies, *Accountability: A Public Law Analysis of Government By Contract* (Oxford: Oxford University Press, 2001) 79. Oliver and Drewry distinguish the concepts of *accountability* ('having the exclusive right to explain, having a duty to explain, and making amends without accepting blame') and *responsibility* ('having a job to do, including making sure that new systems are properly established, and taking the blame when things go wrong') – D Oliver and G Drewry, *Public Service Reforms: Issues of Accountability and Public Law* (London: Pinter, 1996) 13.

[33] Davies (n 32 above) 81.

Indeed, it may be argued that regulatory control and accountability are complementary concepts, the analysis of one requiring consideration of the other; or even that accountability is a form of control over those to whom power is delegated.[34] This control may be seen as comprising two elements or stages: the prior specification of obligations or standards, and the subsequent monitoring of the activity or decisions reached by the regulated body or other contracting party.[35] In circumstances where a high degree of independence of the regulated body is regarded as desirable, *ex ante* control/direction may be minimal, with a greater emphasis on *ex post* control through monitoring (there is no implication that accountability in such a case should also be minimal[36]). Where regulation takes the form of contract, it is particularly difficult to distinguish accountability and control dimensions. Information about performance does not serve just to call the other contracting party to account, rather it is part of (and feeds back into) the controlling function through contract monitoring. As has been seen, the various forms of the New Public Contracting facilitate control by designated public authorities within policy-driven regulatory frameworks in which the controlling capacities of public agencies are themselves subject to regulation by central government.

The analysis of the New Public Contracting requires simultaneous consideration of the control and accountability dimensions of regulation. A narrow accountability perspective fails adequately to recognize the fragmentation of responsibilities for oversight and provision accompanying many contemporary public sector reforms.[37] By comparison with traditional public administration, the separation of purchaser and provider roles introduces a further party, the contractor, to the existing system of elected politicians, administrators, and citizens. Contractors are involved as agents in the implementation of government policy, as this is mediated through the contracting activities of the public purchasing or commissioning body. The complex relationships resulting from growing reliance on contractors pose new challenges for public managers. One problem may be the fracturing of the agency relationship where contractors create independent political ties with policy makers and thus 'outflank' their administrative overseers.[38] In other cases, the problem may be that contractors have become

[34] LR Bruce Smith 'Accountability and Independence in the Contract State' in LR Bruce Smith and DC Hague, (eds), *The Dilemma of Accountability in Modern Government: Independence Versus Control* (London: Macmillan, 1971) 17–18. Scott presents these concepts as linked on a continuum: '*managerial* control refers to the right to *ex ante* involvement in decision making, while *accountability-based* control refers to *ex post* oversight' – Scott (n 30 above) 39.

[35] P Craig, *Administrative Law* (4th edn, London: Sweet and Maxwell, 1999). While this point is made by Craig in relation to the degree of precision of legislation, and the monitoring of decisions taken by an executive agency, it is valid for internal contracts more generally.

[36] ibid.

[37] Scott (n 30 above).

[38] 'In such cases contractors are less agents than partners, helping to shape the very design of the program, free of any significant oversight, and beneficiary of state and local governments' dependence on their performance' – D Kettl, *Sharing Power: Public Governance and Private Markets* (Washington DC: The Brookings Institution, 1993) 176.

too close to administrators, escaping the control of and accountability to elected politicians.

Public contracting is best analysed by focusing on how traditional institutions of accountability operate in conjunction with more indirect mechanisms and processes as part of a complex system of checks and balances that serves to inhibit or encourage particular forms of behaviour.

Governance

The term 'government' has traditionally been associated with the concept of the state, the sovereign body exerting power within a nation and having the monopoly of legal force. Correspondingly, constitutional theorists have been concerned principally with the sources of power residing within the state and with their legitimacy.[39] Contemporary commentators, by contrast, have shifted attention away from govern*ment* onto a broad range of political govern*ance* mechanisms beyond the sovereign state.[40]

Governance and responsibilization

The OECD defines governance as 'the act of governing seen in a wide sense ... The term includes public administration and the institutions, methods and instruments of governing ... it further incorporates relationships between government and citizen (including business and other citizen groupings) and the role of the State'.[41] For Rhodes, 'governance refers to self-organizing, inter-organizational networks'.[42] The term 'intergovernmental relations' is used to describe the network of organizations (public, private, and voluntary) existing in relations of power-dependence in a differentiated polity within which the central state exerts only limited control. Governance in this 'network theory' sense implies a number of key features: inter-dependence between organizations, including non-state actors; the blurring of the boundaries between public, private and voluntary sectors; the ongoing process of negotiation among network members over their shared

39 M Dean, *Governmentality: Power and Rule in Modern Society* (London: Sage Publications, 1999) 9.

40 B Jessop, 'The Regulation Approach, Governance and Post-Fordism: Alternative Perspectives on Economic and Political Change?' (1995) 24 *Economy and Society* 307, 311; H Aquina and H Bekke, 'Governance in Interaction: Public Tasks and Private Organisations', in J Kooiman, (ed), *Modern Governance: New Government-Society Interactions* (London: Sage Publications, 1993), 159.

41 OECD, *Responsive Government: Service Quality Initiatives* (Paris: Organisation for Economic Cooperation and Development, 1996) 158.

42 RAW Rhodes, *Understanding Governance: Policy Networks, Governance, Reflexivity and Accountability* (Buckingham: Open University Press, 1997) 53; ibid, 'Interorganizational Networks and Control: A Critical Conclusion', in Franz-Xavier Kaufman, (ed), *The Public Sector: Challenge for Coordination and Learning* (New York: Walter de Gruyter, 1991) 525.

purpose and the exchange of resources; and a significant degree of autonomy of self-organizing networks from the state.[43]

Other critics of the traditional notion of government, drawing on Foucault, maintain that while the language of political philosophy (state and civil society, freedom and constraint, sovereignty and democracy, public and private) plays a key role in the organization of modern political power, it contributes little to our understanding of modern 'problematics of government'.[44] Instead, government is defined as 'any attempt to shape with some degree of deliberation aspects of our behaviour according to particular sets of norms and for a variety of ends'.[45] In this perspective, governmentality refers to the relationship between government, power, and thought.[46] The method of inquiry here involves examination of the intermeshing of 'regimes of practices', defined as 'more or less organized ways . . . we think about, reform and practice such things as caring, administering, counselling, curing, punishing, educating and so on'.[47] The notion of governmentality focuses attention on the techniques, forms of knowledge, and calculative vocabularies that constitute relationships of unequal power in modern societies.[48]

In governance theory, the term 'responsibilization' refers to the range of techniques and practices through which individual subjects are constructed as

43 ibid (1997). See also C Knill and D Lehmkuhl, 'Private Actors and the State: Internationalizaton and Changing Patterns of Governance' (2002) 15 *Governance* 41. In the new institutional economics tradition, see W Powell, 'Neither Market Nor Hierarchy: Network Forms of Organization' (1990) 12 *Research in Organizational Behaviour* 295; ibid, 'Hybrid Organizational Arrangements: New Form or Transitional Development?' (1987) *California Management Review* 67.

44 N Rose and P Miller, 'Political Power Beyond the State: Problematics of Government' (1992) 43 *British Journal of Sociology* 173, 201.

45 Dean (n 39 above) 10. Again, 'government refers to all endeavours to shape, guide, direct the conduct of others, whether these be the crew of a ship, the members of a household, the employees of a boss, the children of a family or the inhabitants of a territory', involving 'more or less rationalized schemes, programmes, techniques and devices which seek ... to achieve certain ends' – N Rose, *Powers of Freedom: Reframing Political Thought* (Cambridge: Cambridge University Press, 1999), 3. Compare Kooiman 'By governing we mean all those activities of social, political and administrative actors that can be seen as purposeful efforts to guide, steer, control or manage (sectors or facets of) societies . . . Social-political forms of governing are forms in which public and private actors do not act separately but in conjunction, together, in combination, that is to say in "co arrangements"' – J Kooiman, 'Social-Political Governance: Introduction' in J Kooiman, (ed), *Modern Governance: New Government-Society Interactions* (London: Sage Publications, 1993) 2.

46 'Govern*mentality* is a way of problematizing life and seeking to act upon it. It both extends the concerns of rule to the ordering of the multitudinous affairs of a territory and its population in order to ensure its well being, and simultaneously establishes divisions between the proper spheres of action of different types of authority' – N Rose, 'Government, Authority and Expertise in Advanced Liberalism' (1993) 22 *Economy and Society* 283, 288.

47 Dean (n 39 above) 22; ibid, 'Governing the Unemployed Self in An Active Society' (1995) 24 *Economy and Society* 559; ibid, 'Liberal Government and Authoritarianism' (2002) 31 *Economy and Society* 37.

48 Dean (n 39 above) 16. Governmentality is linked with the historical emergence of new forms of governing in certain societies – at the time when the exercise of power on the basis of sovereignty, rules and constitutions came to be supplemented by the exercise of disciplinary power over individuals in schools, hospitals, workhouses, armies and other modern institutions (19). See K Jones, and K Williamson, 'The Birth of the Schoolroom' (1979) 6 *Ideology and Consciousness* 59.

self-determining and self-willing agents.[49] The associated notion of mutuality makes citizenship entitlements contingent upon the performance of reciprocal obligations to the state, the community, and other citizens.[50] For Rose, this development is a logical accompaniment to autonomization – the process whereby social actors are 'set free' to find their own destiny, but simultaneously 'made responsible for that destiny, and for the destiny of society as a whole, in new ways'.[51] Responsibilization in this sense is linked historically in Britain with the Conservative election victory in 1979 and the mobilization of 'individual responsibility' against what was regarded as the dominant culture of collectivism and welfare dependency.[52]

The concept of responsibilization is not confined to the structuring of relations between citizens and the state. Strategies for business regulation may involve attempts to foster industrial morality and to 'institutionalize responsibility' on the part of organizations that are resistant to other more direct government interventions.[53] Again, regulatory initiatives in the field of criminal justice have been built around the delegation of responsibilities to a wide range of agencies and organizations with roles to play in crime prevention, including residents, retailers, manufacturers, and town planners.[54] Responsibilization in this sense should not be confused with simply 'hiving off' or privatizing crime control; rather it involves a new mode of governing crime, with its own knowledge, techniques and apparatuses. The state does not diminish or become merely a nightwatchman, rather it takes on a new set of coordinating and activating roles. 'Where it works ... the responsibilization strategy leaves the centralized state machine more powerful than before, with an extended capacity for action and influence'.[55] The strategy in this instance involves establishing cooperative, inter-agency networks comprising public and private organizations dedicated to the pursuit of a common purpose. The message is that the state is not, and cannot be, alone responsible for preventing and controlling crime.[56]

Responsibilization is unlikely to be achieved through authoritative direction or coercion. Various techniques and methods have been deployed more

49 A Yeatman, 'Interpreting Contemporary Contractualism' in M Dean and B Hindess, (eds), *Governing Australia: Studies in Contemporary Rationalities of Government* (Cambridge: Cambridge University Press, 1998) 232–234.

50 Dean (n 39 above) 207.

51 Rose (n 45 above) 174.

52 ibid 139. Responsibilization becomes associated from this time also with entrepreneurialization, reflecting the function of the state in improving economic performance by motivating individuals to be more active in the labour market.

53 N Gunningham and J Rees, 'Industry Self-Regulation: An Institutional Perspective' (1997) 19 *Law and Policy* 363, 380; F Haines, *Corporate Regulation: Beyond 'Punish or Persuade'* (Oxford: Clarendon Press, 1997).

54 D Garland, 'The Limits of the Sovereign State: Strategies of Crime Control in Contemporary Society' (1996) 36 *British Journal of Criminology* 445, 453. For an account of the responsibilization of local authorities, see P Vincent-Jones, 'Values and Purpose in Government: Central-local Relations in Regulatory Perspective, (2002) 29 JLS 27.

55 Garland (n 54 above) 454.

56 ibid 453.

or less successfully in practice, including government exhortation and persuasion through publicity campaigns and schemes directed at encouraging participation of particular 'targets' or designated groups.[57] Obligations and commitments, whether involving individual citizens, communities or society generally, are most likely to be honoured where they have been negotiated and agreed. The contract mechanism and supporting norms therefore have an important part to play in responsibilization strategies, whether embodied in specific behavioural or other contracts, or as represented more generally in the social contract.

With reference to the New Public Contracting, theories of governance and responsibilization are of most obvious relevance in the analysis of the use of contract as a mechanism of social control. Social control contracts are directly concerned with relationships between the state and citizens constituted as deviant or problem subjects, and with governmental efforts to change individual behaviour. Through these arrangements individuals are made contractually responsible for their predicaments (as offenders, unemployed job seekers, or parents whose children are disruptive at school) in ways that differ significantly from the governance of social relations by hierarchical authority. Contractual strategies here serve to shift responsibility for their own condition to citizens and users of welfare services themselves, 'binding them to professional powers and expert norms in new ways'.[58]

However, the governance perspective is of broader significance for regulatory analysis. Modern public services are increasingly delivered through complex networks and partnerships involving multiple actors, posing new problems of economic coordination. A range of parties including purchasers, specialist suppliers, local councils, professional bodies, and workers in the public and voluntary sectors may all have parts to play in typical service provision. In the absence of simple hierarchical direction or control through the market, such networks are coordinated through responsibilization strategies entailing various forms of exhortation and facilitation. The special attraction of contract as a mechanism of responsibilization lies in its distinctive qualities of voluntariness, consent, and choice. How far the potential of contract in this regard is realized in practice is the main subject of this book.

Institutions and organizations

The distinction between institutions and organizations is also useful in analysing the contractual governance of human behaviour. Insights drawn from the theory

[57] ibid. [58] Rose (n 45 above) 165.

of institutions are particularly helpful in further elaborating the present regulatory perspective.[59] In North's classic definition:

> Institutions are the rules of the game in a society or, more formally, are the humanly devised constraints that shape human interaction. In consequence they structure incentives in human exchange, whether political, social, or economic. Institutional change shapes the way societies evolve through time and hence is the key to understanding historical change.[60]

While institutions establish the ground rules that apply to all exchange, organizations are 'purposive entities designed by their creators to maximize wealth, income, or other objectives defined by the opportunities afforded by the institutional structure of society.'[61] Whereas institutions are relatively stable and rigid over time, organizations are more flexible.[62] Organizations thus defined include political bodies such as parties and councils, economic bodies such as firms and trade unions, social bodies such as churches and clubs, and educational bodies such as schools and universities. While institutions provide the *rules*, the objective of the team of *players* in organizations 'is to win the game – by a combination of skills, strategy, and coordination; by fair means and sometimes by foul means'.[63]

While institutions may be valued by society as a whole,[64] they cannot be 'neutral' in their social effects since they necessarily 'embody, preserve, and impart

[59] According to Goodin, the 'new institutionalism' spans a number of disciplines (history, sociology, economics, political science and social theory). The common element in all these disciplines is the focus on 'the various contextual settings within which social action is set' – RE Goodin, 'Institutions and Their Design', in RE Goodin, (ed), *The Theory of Institutional Design* (Cambridge: Cambridge University Press, 1996) 19.

[60] DC North, *Institutions, Institutional Change and Economic Performance* (Cambridge: Cambridge University Press, 1990) 3. This account focuses particularly on the relationship between institutional change/persistence, and comparative performance of national economies.

[61] ibid 73.

[62] S Deakin and F Wilkinson, 'Contracts, Cooperation and Trust: The Role of the Institutional Framework' in D Campbell and P Vincent-Jones, (eds), *Contract and Economic Organisation: Socio-Legal Initiatives* (Aldershot: Dartmouth, 1996) 112. Compare: PA Hall and D Soskice, (eds), *Varieties of Capitalism: The Institutional Foundations of Comparative Advantage* (Oxford: Oxford University Press, 2001) 9 (institutions are rules that actors generally follow; organizations are durable entities with formally recognized members); Goodin (n 59 above) 19 (institutions comprise 'organized patterns of socially constructed norms and roles, and socially prescribed behaviours expected of occupants of those roles'); C Offe, 'Designing Institutions in East European Transitions', in Goodin (ed) (n 59 above) 199 (the relationship between social actors and institutions is reciprocal, such that 'social actors generate, support and enact institutions, (while) these institutions, in turn, generate social agents capable of observing social norms'). The term institution may be used to refer to groups as well as social practices. The process of institutionalization describes: 'the emergence of orderly, stable, *socially integrating* patterns out of unstable, loosely organized, or narrowly technical activities' – P Selznick, *The Moral Commonwealth: Social Theory and the Promise of Community* (Berkeley: University of California Press, 1992) 232.

[63] North (n 60 above) 4–5.

[64] Goodin (n 59 above) 19. In its simplest form, an institution may be defined as a stable, *valued* and recurring pattern of social behaviour (21, emphasis supplied). This echoes Selznick's definition of regulation as control exercised by public agencies over activities that are valued by a community – n 3

differential power resources with respect to different individuals and groups.'[65] The function of promoting a common good or benefit serves usefully to distinguish institutions in this sense from a narrow conception of regulation concerned with the prevention or avoidance of harm.[66] The adoption of a broad conception of regulation in this chapter brings institutions and institutional design to the forefront of socio-legal analysis. The institutions of law are of obvious relevance to the analysis of the New Public Contracting.[67] The institutions found in the spheres of politics and economics, which concern respectively the control of the use of force within a society and the regulation of the production, distribution and consumption of goods and services, are also of central importance.

Of further interest for present purposes is the notion of 'institutional intervention', which has been used to describe the way in which institutional development consists in attempts to alter or adapt existing institutions, rather than to create entirely new arrangements.[68] In this sense institutions (like regulation) may be described as 'purposeful'. Government interventions occur through the use of a range of instruments for 'altering the opportunities and incentives of individual agents and, thereby, their aggregate behaviour'.[69] Pettit's analysis in this vein distinguishes two basic instruments, sanctions and filters. First, in contrast to the narrow conception of sanctions as penalties for breach of formal legal or other rules, sanctions may be viewed as incentives (positive as well as negative) that affect the choice among available options for social action. 'Sanctions operate on the set of options before an agent, making some options more attractive or less attractive than they would have been had the sanctions not been in place; they affect the relevant incentives.'[70] Sanctions may take the form of financial or other rewards and deterrents. Sanctions may be directly taken into account by the parties or agents they affect, or may be so deeply embedded in institutional structures that they do not feature in conscious deliberations. A second type of instrument available to the institutional designer is the filter or screen. Whereas sanctions apply to a given set of agents or options, screens operate by affecting the opportunities available to defined classes of agents. In the case of negative screens, certain agents and options are thereby excluded from an activity. Positive screens, on the other hand, serve 'to empower individuals who were previously not

above. Institutions similarly are value-laden, or 'infused with value' beyond the technical requirements of any particular task in hand.

65 Goodin (n 59 above) 20.

66 P Pettit, 'Institutional Design and Rational Choice', in RE Goodin, (ed), *The Theory of Institutional Design* (New York: Cambridge University Press, 1996) 59.

67 Goodin does not mention law in his list including family and kinship, education, cultural institutions, and stratification. The institutions of 'contract', as will be seen, span all three spheres and are not confined to the legal domain.

68 Pettit prefers this term to the more usual 'institutional design' – (n 66 above) 55.

69 ibid 57. The state and supporting institutions are necessary on the assumption that, in the absence of some form of 'intervention', individuals or groups are not motivated (according to rational choice theory) to comply with relevant behavioural norms (70).

70 ibid 57.

involved, giving them an opportunity to act that they didn't have before, or they may empower the individuals already involved in the relevant situation, putting a new option on the list of alternatives before them.'[71]

Applying this approach to the New Public Contracting, regulation may operate not just through the penalties or rewards attaching to given types of behaviour, but by altering the capacities of the agencies involved in the production of services. Arrangements for public service provision in quasi-markets are characterized by complex and multiple screens that indirectly affect the opportunities open to individuals and agencies. Changing the legal capacity of bodies in sectors such as health or education may, through the mechanism of screening, affect organizational behaviour by exposing purchasers or providers to new pressures and incentives. In pointing to the importance of this regulatory strategy, institutional theory confirms an insight already suggested in the notion of collibration.

In sum, the New Public Contracting may be viewed as a set of institutions and organizations structuring social behaviour. On the one hand, specific regulatory frameworks – together with other institutional influences (the legal system, economic controls, industrial policy, informal associations) – constitute the basic contractual and other 'rules of the game' by which public agencies and other players must abide. On the other hand, organizations (including public bodies such as local authorities, hospital trusts, and executive agencies, as well as particular markets, quasi-markets, and firms) also operate as forms of governance, structuring the behaviour of actors within the parameters set by the institutional frameworks. All forms of the New Public Contracting have entailed simultaneous institutional and organizational reform to a greater or lesser degree. Where novel public contracting arrangements are imposed by central government without adequate consultation or involvement of the public bodies and other parties involved in them, problems of institutional conflict and lack of 'fit' with existing institutions may be expected. In such circumstances the contract norms both within and surrounding the contractual relationship may become strained or damaged. The quality of institutions that support contractual relationships is of fundamental importance in the analysis of the New Public Contracting.

Conclusion

At first sight, notions of governance and responsibilization may appear at odds with the emphasis at the beginning of this chapter on the state as a purposeful actor and a key player in regulatory processes. The idea in governance theory of the 'centreless society',[72] for example, appears to be in tension with the view

[71] ibid 58.

[72] Rhodes (n 42 above) 8. Network analysis implies scepticism not only of the traditional view of Britain as a unitary state but also of the centralization thesis, which maintains that central government power is increasing at the expense of that of other bodies such as local councils.

of the centralization of state power underpinning the New Public Contracting regulation thesis. Again, while the regulation approach emphasizes policy making and evaluation, in governance theories the policy process is either of less central importance or completely irrelevant.[73] And certainly, the focus on techniques, forms of knowledge, and calculative vocabularies in the governmentality perspective differs markedly from conventional regulatory analyses based on institutions, organizations and structures.[74]

Similarly, there are important differences between the notions of self-regulation and self-governance. Analyses of self-regulation tend to be applied to whole business sectors or organizational groupings, whereas self-governance focuses on individual subjects, albeit corporate bodies as well as human individuals. Self-regulation tends to be advocated by regulationists in situations where it works and because it works, even though more direct and overt forms of control are regarded as possible. Governmentalists, on the other hand, regard self-governance as the essence of governance, to which there is no theoretical or practical alternative. The governance approach is intimately and directly concerned with practices and processes through which subjects come to govern themselves.[75] The basic ideas of self-direction, self-guidance and self-conduct have important implications for the way in which the freedom of the subjects of governance is conceived.[76] Modern political power 'does not take the form of the domination of subjectivity . . . rather, (it) has come to depend upon a web of technologies for fabricating and maintaining self-government'.[77] In this conception, power is exercised through the active rather than the passive or submissive subject. Subjectivity is constructed and harnessed rather than coerced. The effect of new technologies and rationalities of power is to stimulate agency while reconfiguring (rather than removing) constraints on the freedom of choice of agents, resulting in 'governing through freedom' and 'responsibilized autonomy'.[78]

Despite their different theoretical underpinnings, however, there is ultimately no contradiction between the regulation and governmentality perspectives. Both recognize the limited effectiveness of state interventions based on crude command and control, and acknowledge various theoretical and practical obstacles to the attainment of policy objectives through direct regulation. Both may incorporate the notion of collibration or balancing of regulatory forces. Both stress the problems associated with attempts to shape, influence or 'steer' social and economic processes, and the complexity of the networks of actors involved in such

[73] The refusal of governance theorists to engage in policy evaluation is quite explicit. 'Policy studies tend to be concerned with evaluating policies, uncovering the factors that led to their success in achieving their objectives or, more usually . . . their failure. We, on the other hand, are not concerned with evaluations of this type, with making judgements as to whether and why this or that policy succeeded or failed' – P Miller and N Rose, 'Governing Economic Life' (1990) 19 *Economy and Society* 1, 4.

[74] Dean (n 39 above) 16.

[75] ibid 10–11.

[76] Rose (n 45 above) 3.

[77] Miller and Rose (n 73 above) 28.

[78] J Morison, 'Democracy, Governance and Governmentality: Civic Public Space and Constitutional Renewal in Northern Ireland' (2001) 21 OJLS 287.

activities.[79] Both accept nevertheless that social organization entails deliberate or purposive control.[80] And while the regulation approach is indeed concerned with institutions and structures, the emphasis on 'controlling or governing' according to 'principles or systems' implies that governance techniques, forms of knowledge and expertise may be accommodated within the regulatory analysis. There is sufficient common ground between the regulation and governance approaches to suggest that a synthesis is possible and may be useful in the theoretical analysis of contemporary public contracting.[81] The concepts of regulation, tools of government, self-regulation, collibration, responsibilization, governmentality and governance, may be treated for present purposes as complementary. The value of this theoretical synthesis will be demonstrated in the more detailed regulatory perspective developed in Chapter 5.

[79] For Dunsire, the term 'governance' is used in preference to 'government' to convey the twin notions of 'social turbulence kept within bounds, and change steered in desired directions . . . so "governance" preserves order and continuity, but is not necessarily the maintenance of the status quo' – Dunsire (n 18 above) 18.

[80] 'Control (or governance) is always for some purpose, even if it is only survival (in living systems)' – ibid 16.

[81] For an exploration of the relationship between regulation and governmentality specifically in the field of housing, see D Cowan and A Marsh, 'Making Connections', in D Cowan and A Marsh, (eds), *Two Steps Forward: Housing Policy into the New Millennium* (Bristol: The Policy Press, 2001) 363.

4

Responsiveness

This chapter explores key dimensions of the term 'responsiveness' in the context of related concepts of reflexivity, juridification, purposiveness, and meta-regulation. It proceeds to unpack the meaning of the formula: 'responsiveness = effectiveness + legitimacy' that will be used in the evaluation of the various forms of the New Public Contracting in Part III. I argue that the more important of these criteria is legitimacy, defined by the presence of qualities of public deliberation and institutional morality in government decision making on public service issues and in the policy process.

Dimensions

A number of dimensions of responsiveness may be distinguished in the current research and scholarship on regulation (Fig 5): regulator sensitivity; collaborative regulation; restorative justice; organizational learning; institutional adaptation; consumer/citizen needs; and public accountability. I will consider these analytical dimensions in turn, indicating briefly their significance for the analysis of the New Public Contracting.

Regulator sensitivity

The core meaning of responsiveness in the business regulation literature implies sensitivity on the part of regulators to the conditions in which regulation occurs. The emphasis is on appropriate 'responses' to the behaviour of regulatees, in contrast with regulatory formalism – the attempt to define regulatory problems and responses in advance and to write rules to mandate those responses.[1] Responsive regulation is distinguished from more direct strategies of governance by both what triggers a regulatory response and what the regulatory response will be.[2] In Braithwaite's recent formulation:

The basic idea of responsive regulation is that governments should be responsive to the conduct of those they seek to regulate in deciding whether a more or less interventionist

[1] J Braithwaite, *Restorative Justice and Responsive Regulation* (Oxford: Oxford University Press, 2002) 29.

[2] I Ayres and J Braithwaite, *Responsive Regulation: Transcending the Deregulation Debate* (Oxford: Oxford University Press, 1992) 4.

response is needed . . . In particular, law enforcers should be responsive to how effectively citizens or corporations are regulating themselves before deciding whether to escalate intervention.[3]

This notion of responsiveness is associated with Ayres and Braithwaite's metaphor of the regulatory pyramid.[4] Persuasion is located at the base of the pyramid and more punitive sanctions such as licence revocation at its apex, with various warnings and penalties of increasing severity in between. Regulatory objectives are ideally achieved not through direct 'command and control', but through the incentive and deterrent effects associated with the threat of escalation of sanctions. Under 'enforced self-regulation', rules may be written, monitored and enforced by companies themselves in conjunction with the government and state agencies. Most effort is concentrated on persuasion, with the severest sanctions being reserved for the relatively small number of worst regulatory failures.

Dimension	Referring to:
(1) Regulator sensitivity	. . . the sensitivity of regulators to the conditions in which regulation occurs, with particular attention to the capacity for adjustment of regulatory strategies to the behaviour of regulatees;
(2) Collaborative regulation	. . . the quality of the regulator-regulatee relationship in terms of the degree of collaboration and cooperation in, and surrounding, that relationship;
(3) Restorative justice	. . . the capacity of the regulatory system to facilitate restoration by regulatees to those harmed by their behaviour, as opposed to just punishing rule violation;
(4) Organizational learning	. . . the relationship of organizations to their environments, focusing on their capacity for innovation, learning and adaptation;
(5) Institutional adaptation	. . . the relationship of institutions to their environments, in terms of the combination of institutional qualities of robustness with revisability and openness to change;
(6) Consumer/citizen needs	. . . the responsiveness of government and/or public service providers, and of the policy process generally, to the needs and preferences of users and citizens;
(7) Public accountability	. . . the accountability of bureaucratic and other actors performing public service functions to legitimate sources of authority or influence.

Figure 5. Dimensions of responsiveness

3 Braithwaite (n 1 above) 29.
4 'The most distinctive part of responsive regulation is the regulatory pyramid' – ibid. 20.

The regulatory pyramid has been variously criticized for its distorted representation of regulatory processes that in reality do not take the form of a 'ranking' or orderly sequence of enforcement measures,[5] and for underestimating the diversity of sources and forms of regulation.[6] Nevertheless, the metaphor will be useful at various points in the following analysis in exploring the tension in the New Public Contracting between devolution and voluntarism on the one hand, and centralization and compulsion on the other.[7] Since 1997, regulatory regimes such as best value might be regarded as displaying greater regulator sensitivity than the overtly compulsive and prescriptive legal frameworks that governed public contracting under the Conservatives. Central intervention and the ultimate sanction of incapacitation (eg involving placing failing schools under 'special measures', or sending management teams into under-performing local councils and hospital trusts) are used only where persuasion through a range of more subtle incentives and deterrents has failed. However, as we shall see, the crucial issue in the ultimate evaluation of responsiveness concerns not so much the degree of coercion or its explicitness, as the overall legitimacy of regulatory regimes.[8]

Collaborative regulation

For a number of writers, responsiveness implies the existence of collaboration and cooperation in regulator-regulatee relationships.[9] Responsive regulators 'participate with business and other institutions in a cooperative effort to make the law effective.'[10] The extent of collaboration between the various parties in regulatory frameworks is a major focus of the subsequent analysis of the New Public Contracting. As was explained in Chapter 1, economic contracts and social control contracts have in common a complex dual regulatory structure, entailing regulation by contract within hierarchical regulatory frameworks. I will argue that trust and cooperation are essential to the effectiveness of such regulation, as regards both

5 F Haines, *Corporate Regulation: Beyond 'Punish or Persuade'* (Oxford: Clarendon Press, 1997) 221.

6 N Gunningham, P Grabosky, with D Sinclair, *Smart Regulation: Designing Environmental Policy* (Oxford: Clarendon Press, 1998) 93. The authors criticize the notion of the regulatory process as 'a dance between two participants – government and business, with the former acting in the role of regulator and the latter as regulatee'. In reality a variety of instruments is used by a multiplicity of regulatory participants, with informal social orderings playing as significant a role as formal ones. The notion of regulation as involving two participants is particularly inappropriate in the context of complex public service organization.

7 See for example the discussion of 'remedial hierarchies' in Chapters 10 and 11.

8 P Vincent-Jones, 'Responsive Law and Governance in Public Services Provision: A Future for the Local Contracting State' (1998) 61 MLR 362; ibid, 'Competition and Contracting in the Transition from CCT to Best Value: Towards a More Reflexive Regulation?' (1999) 77 *Public Administration* 273.

9 H Collins, *Regulating Contracts* (Oxford: Oxford University Press, 1999), 65; J Freeman, 'Collaborative Governance in the Administrative State' (1997) 45 *UCLA Law Review* 1.

10 P Selznick, 'Self-Regulation and the Theory of Institutions', in G Teubner, L Farmer, and D Murphy, (eds), *Environmental Law and Ecological Responsibility: The Concept and Practice of Ecological Self-Organization* (Chichester: John Wiley & Sons, 1994) 401.

the 'horizontal' relationship between public agencies and the other contracting party, and the bureaucratic or 'vertical' relationship between central government and public agencies to whom contractual regulatory powers have been devolved.

Restorative justice

In his recent work, Braithwaite has sought to link responsiveness in the senses just considered with restorative justice. Restorative justice at the base of enforcement pyramids is considered appropriate in dealing with 'virtuous' actors; deterrence occupies a middle position and is associated with rational actors; and incapacitation at the pyramid's apex is reserved for incompetent or irrational actors.[11] Rather than simply punishing the rule-breaker for breach of a duty owed to the state, the principle of restoration brings into the equation stakeholders such as victims and communities,[12] giving them a role in determining the consequences of the regulatory infraction.[13] In this way offenders, victims and communities affected by crime can resolve collectively how to deal with the aftermath of an offence and its future implications. What is to be restored is determined by the process of deliberation, but the subject-matter of restoration may include property loss, personal injury, and harms to individual dignity and to the community. Values such as retribution, just deserts and fair punishment, it is argued, have no place within the restorative justice framework.[14] The basic idea is that the parties adversely affected by regulatee behaviour are those to whom restoration should be made.

While restorative justice has traditionally been associated with a relatively narrow range of criminal behaviour, Braithwaite considers that the perspective may be applied much more broadly, for example, to war crimes and the 'commanding heights' of business power and political power. The restorative justice framework is thus argued to be relevant in such varied contexts as trade practices enforcement, community policing, and nursing home regulation: 'In most cases justice works best by empowering affected communities to deal with the consequences of injustice and transform private troubles into public issues, as by advocacy of

[11] J Braithwaite, 'Meta Regulation for Access to Justice', Presentation to *General Aspects of Law* (GALA) Seminar Series, (University of California, 13 November 2003) 7.

[12] Braithwaite (n 1 above) 42.

[13] Restorative justice is defined as a deliberative process involving 'bringing together all stakeholders in an undominated dialogue about the consequences of an injustice and what is to be done to put them right' – ibid 12. Restorative justice can be seen as a 'third way' alternative to the retributive/punitive and welfare/rehabilitation models (10).

[14] ibid 16. The relationship between values and process is complex. In some instances the former will 'trump' the latter, as where limits are imposed on the type of punishment that can be imposed through stakeholder deliberation. In other instances, restorative process should be permitted to trump restorative values. The stakeholder conference should be permitted to decide the outcome, however apparently unreasonable, provided it is consistent with fundamental human rights and otherwise within the law (12). 'Republican normative theory' is used to decide in what circumstances values or process should predominate – J Braithwaite and P Pettit, *Not Just Deserts: A Republican Theory of Criminal Justice* (Oxford: Oxford University Press, 1990).

preventive measures'.[15] It is acknowledged that not all problems can be dealt with by the restorative justice approach. Hence one of the key issues is how theory may be used to predict when restorative justice may be inappropriate, and what the alternatives are when restorative justice fails.

Subsequent chapters will explore how far the link between responsiveness and restoration suggested in this account is useful and applicable in the analysis of the New Public Contracting. The principle of restoration may simply be applied to the bilateral relationship (whether or not contractual) between regulator and regulatee.[16] Usually, however, restoration refers to other parties beyond that relationship who may have been affected by regulatee actions. The interesting point to note here is the focus on the existence of interests and stakes in the regulatory process beyond the principal contractual relationship. The link between responsiveness and restoration is of obvious importance in social control contracts involving criminal justice. In youth offender contracts, for example, offenders typically undertake to make reparation to their victims. The restorative justice model may also be relevant to the analysis of quasi-market organization of human services such as nursing home care. The regulatory frameworks governing economic contracts might embody a principle, to be included within all purchase-of-service contracts agreed with service providers, that effective restoration should be made directly to consumers on whose behalf the public agency has purchased the service. Restoration to the putative beneficiaries of nursing home regulation (ie residents) could be equated with restoration to the victim in criminal justice contexts.[17] The implications of this insight are considered in greater depth in Chapters 10 and 11.

Organizational learning

Another strand in the regulation literature links responsiveness with the capacity of organizations to adapt to and learn from their environments, taking account of new information and adjusting their activities to their own core values and purposes.[18] This notion of responsiveness is associated with 'system reflexivity', the modern equivalent of collective learning theories that explain

15 Braithwaite (n 1 above) 26.

16 In terms of the contract norms, reciprocity is reflected at a concrete level in the concept of restitution. The management of contractual relationships in cooperative and non-adversarial ways is likely to place heavy reliance on 'restorative' processes such as client-contractor meetings and fora for user-involvement, akin to the stakeholder 'conferences' advocated by restorative justice theorists. (The opposite strategy is the adversarial one of going straight to penalties and sanctions). Braithwaite's more recent emphasis on punishment and sanctions as a background support for more cooperative strategies involving persuasion at the base of the regulatory pyramid echo the empirical findings of non-contractual relations in business.

17 The shift towards a consumer-centred discourse in this sense parallels the victim-centred discourse in criminal justice – Braithwaite (n 1 above) 17.

18 M Considine, 'The End of the Line? Accountable Governance in the Age of Networks, Partnerships, and Joined-Up Services' (2002) 15 *Governance* 21, 29.

organizational performance in terms of positive and negative feedback. Regulatory strategies built on this approach are concerned not only to ensure that resources are properly accounted for, but also to foster creativity and innovation on the part of regulated entities. For Sabel, 'learning by monitoring' as a form of economic cooperation works by creating a common framework of understanding that allows actors constantly to assess the shortcomings of their joint activities, and to adjust their strategies accordingly.[19] Beyond their particular relationship, actors are obliged 'to take notice of the unintended burdens created by their transactions and to arrive at a common view of how to reshape their activities so as to avoid them.'[20] The reflexive conditions for the successful operation of collective learning in these senses cannot be taken for granted. Rather the task for institutional designers is both to identify these conditions and determine the role of the state in their affirmative creation.[21] What mechanisms might function as incentives for social actors to reflect on the extent to which their present understandings are necessarily limited, and open to revision in the light of experience?[22]

This dimension of responsiveness also focuses on processes of decision-making and control, and on procedures and structures that provide overall direction within regulated organizations.[23] In local government, organizational learning is implicit in the Widdicombe Committee's definition of responsiveness in terms of 'sensitivity, initiation and coordination.'[24] In the analysis of the New Public Contracting, such qualities are most obviously relevant in the performance of public agencies to whom contractual responsibilities have been delegated, who are required to learn how effectively to manage contractual processes and relationships. I will argue that the ability of local councils and other public agencies to learn from their environments may be undermined by excessive central prescription and top-down interventions that stifle innovation and creativity on the part of professionals and other workers who have the task of implementing contractual schemes.[25]

19 CF Sabel, 'Learning by Monitoring; The Institutions of Economic Development', in NJ Smelser and R Swedberg, (eds), *The Handbook of Economic Sociology* (New York: Russell Sage Foundation, 1994), 155.

20 ibid 158.

21 O De Schutter and S Deakin, 'Reflexive Governance and the Dilemmas of Social Regulation', in ibid (eds), *Social Rights and Market Forces: Is the Open Coordination of Employment and Social Policies the Future of Social Europe?* (Bruxelles: Bruylant, 2005).

22 J Lenoble, 'Open Method of Coordination and Theory of Reflexive Governance', in O De Schutter, and S Deakin, (eds), (n 21 above); J Lenoble and M Maesschalck, *Toward a Theory of Governance: The Action of Norms* (London: Kluwer Law International, 2003).

23 R Hodges, M Wright, and K Keasey, 'Corporate Governance in the Public Services: Concepts and Issues' (1996) 16 *Public Money and Management* (Apr–Jun) 7.

24 M Radford, 'Competition Rules: The Local Government Act 1988' (1988) 51 MLR 747, 763; *Report of the Committee of Inquiry into the Conduct of Local Authority Business* (Cm 9797, 1985/86).

25 I Sanderson, 'Performance Management, Evaluation and Learning in "Modern" Local Government' (2001) 79 *Public Administration* 297.

Institutional adaptation

In a related sense, responsiveness concerns the relationship between institutions and their environment. The importance of institutional theory for the understanding of governance was indicated in Chapter 3. For example, Goodin argues that what is required for good governance is a set of principles of institutional (and we might add regulatory) design, comprising revisability, robustness, variability, and sensitivity to motivational complexity.[26] Given the fallibility of human beings and the inevitably changing nature of societies, institutions should be designed to be *revisable* to allow for development and evolution. A closely related quality is *variability* in institutional arrangements, reflecting the need to encourage 'learning by doing' and experimentation with different structures in different places. The principle of robustness implies the need for institutions (in spite of their flexibility) to be adaptable to new situations only to the degree that is appropriate or relevant. The principle of robustness balances those of revisability and variability. Effective institutions are responsive only to relevant changes in their environments, ignoring others which are not.[27] We return to the issue of the precise role of legal institutions in the governance of the New Public Contracting in detail in Chapters 10 and 11.

Citizen/consumer needs

Responsiveness is used in contemporary debates on public services, and in New Labour's 'Modernizing Government' political rhetoric, to describe forms of organization and provision that meet the needs of businesses and consumers:[28]

> We must deliver services and programmes that are not only efficient and effective but also joined up and responsive . . . In short, we want public services that respond to users' needs and are not arranged for the provider's convenience.[29]

The implication here is that public services should be arranged in a manner that both maximizes consumer influence and increases sensitivity on the part of bodies

26 RE Goodin, 'Institutions and Their Design', in RE Goodin, (ed), *The Theory of Institutional Design* (Cambridge: Cambridge University Press, 1996).

27 ibid 39. Goodin acknowledges that what is 'desirable' or 'relevant' is highly contested and politically controversial. This serves to reinforce the importance of the design aim of creating and supporting the conditions under which such controversial issues may adequately be debated.

28 The requirement here is that public officials be 'responsive to the needs of their clients in a way analogous to private sector firms being sensitive to consumer demands' – R Mulgan, ' "Accountability": An Ever-Expanding Concept?' (2000) 78 *Public Administration* 555, 566.

29 Cabinet Office, *Modernising Government*, White Paper (Cm 4310, March 1999) (ch 3 – Responsive public services, para 3.1). This concern with the balance of consumer and producer interests, and the emphasis on redistributing power in favour of the former at the expense of the latter, is associated with public choice theory. This approach arguably underplays the critical question of what sort of services should be provided – J Potter, 'Consumerism and the Public Sector: How Well Does the Coat Fit?' (1988) 66 *Public Administration* 149, 155.

engaged in the provision of public services to such signals. What is important is the quality of interaction between public administrators and clients and consumers, including the comprehensibility and accessibility of administration, the degree of public involvement, and the availability of redress.[30] In a variation on this theme, the 'responsive state' is one that is responsive not only to the users of public services but also to the needs, problems, and preferences of citizens,[31] implying public participation in policy development and political decision making.[32] The state does not have a monopoly on defining and pursuing the public interest, rather regulated entities are involved with regulators in forming the public interest.[33] This dimension raises fundamental questions about the design of mechanisms for increasing civil dialogue and public involvement in policy making, implementation, and evaluation.[34]

It goes without saying that responsiveness to the needs of consumers is fundamental to the success of quasi-market contracting. The relationship between responsiveness to consumers and to citizens raises complex governance issues that will be considered in depth in Chapter 8.

Public accountability

A final dimension of responsiveness refers to the expectation that public officials will be accountable to other actors within the political system, particularly to elected politicians.[35] In this sense, bureaucratic actors are expected to be 'responsive to' legitimate sources of authority or influence.[36] The current literature distinguishes between 'upwards' accountability to parliament and the courts, 'horizontal' accountability to broadly parallel institutions and grievance handlers,

30 OECD, *Governance in Transition* (Paris: OECD, 1995) 159; R Sheaff, S Pickard, and K Smith, 'Public Service Responsiveness to Users' Demands and Needs: Theory, Practice and Primary Healthcare in England' (2002) 80 *Public Administration* 435.

31 W Wirth, 'Responding to Citizens' Needs: From Bureaucratic Accountability to Individual Coproduction in the Public Sector', in Franz-Xavier Kaufman, (ed), *The Public Sector: Challenge for Coordination and Learning* (New York: Walter de Gruyter, 1991) 73; W Thomson, 'Realising Rights Through Local Service Contracts', in A Coote, (ed), *The Welfare of Citizens – Developing New Social Rights* (London: IPPR, 1992) 129.

32 TB Jorgensen, 'Modes of Governance and Administrative Change', in J Kooiman, (ed), *Modern Governance: New Government-Society Interactions* (London: Sage Publications, 1993) 223. The White Paper *Modernising Government* considered mechanisms for increasing responsiveness in this sense through the setting up of a 5000 strong nationally representative Peoples Panel – ch 3, 'Responsive public services', Cabinet Office, *Modernising Government*, White Paper (Cm 4310, March 1999).

33 E Bregman and A Jacobson, 'Environmental Performance Review: Self-Regulation in Environmental Law', in G Teubner, L Farmer, and D Murphy, (eds), *Environmental Law and Ecological Responsibility: The Concept and Practice of Ecological Self-Organization* (Chichester: John Wiley & Sons, 1994).

34 On the link between citizen participation and organizational learning, see R Rowe and M Shepherd, 'Public Participation and the New NHS: No Closer to Citizen Control?' (2002) 36 *Social Policy and Administration* 275.

35 Mulgan (n 28 above) 566; ibid, *Holding Power to Account* (London: Palgrave, 2003).

36 'The question of how to achieve such responsiveness results in the quest for political control of or participation in administrative performance' – Wirth (n 31 above) 69. On accountability of public servants to those they serve, see also Considine (n 18 above) 37.

and 'downwards' accountability to lower level institutions such as consumers and the market. However, such conceptual sophistication has arguably failed to keep pace with the transformations wrought by the fragmentation of responsibilities for oversight and provision accompanying public sector reforms.[37] For this and other reasons explained in Chapter 3, the principal focus in the analysis of the New Public Contracting is on regulation rather than accountability.

Two general points may be made as a prelude to further conceptual analysis. Firstly, responsiveness invariably describes a relationship with separate 'of' and 'to' components (of regulators to regulatees, of regulators to the conditions of regulation, of organizations or institutions to their environments, of those organizing or providing public services to consumers or legitimate sources of authority). Responsiveness is therefore defined differently according to whether it refers to the regulatory system, to administrative arrangements within regulatory or regulated bodies, or to the performance of a service for a third-party constituency such as citizens or consumers. It will also be necessary shortly to distinguish more specifically between responsiveness as a quality of law, regulation, and governance.

Secondly, the dimensions of responsiveness are not necessarily complementary, indeed they may exist in mutual tension or conflict. The different responsiveness benefits and losses accompanying particular forms of organization may have to be traded off against one another.[38] Hence increased responsiveness in the sense of upwards accountability to those in hierarchical or political authority for the design and operation of public services may impede responsiveness to consumers, for example by making public employees excessively risk-averse.[39] The implication for reform debates is that a holistic approach is necessary in order properly to identify and address responsiveness deficits in public service organization. This preliminary analysis serves as a warning against regulatory reform strategies that attempt to address governance deficits on a single dimension,[40] with inadequate regard to the impact on other aspects. The concept of collibration as previously defined suggests a positive outcome of the mixing of regulatory mechanisms in

37 C Scott, 'Accountability in the Regulatory State' (2000) 27 JLS 38.

38 Mulgan argues that it is mistaken to conflate issues of responsiveness and accountability, which are better treated separately – R Mulgan, 'Comparing Accountability in the Public and Private Sectors' (2000) 59 *Australian Journal of Public Administration* 87, 115. William Waldegrave argued famously that responsiveness to consumers is more important than political accountability – W Waldegrave, *The Reality of Reform and Accountability in Today's Public Service* (London: Public Finance Foundation, 1993); see N Deakin and K Walsh, 'The Enabling State: The Role of Markets and Contracts' (1996) 74 *Public Administration* 33, 41–42.

39 R Mulgan, 'Contracting Out and Accountability' (1997) 56 *Australian Journal of Public Administration* 106, 110: 'One of the reasons for the comparative inefficiency of service provision by public servants compared with contractors is that public servants are subject to additional pressures of accountability which help to make them more risk-averse than their private sector counterparts.'

40 For example, improving 'upwards' accountability by extending the scope of judicial review. On the relationship between accountability, efficiency, and effectiveness, and in particular on how accountability may impede effectiveness, see D Oliver, *Government in the United Kingdom: The Search for Accountability, Effectiveness and Citizenship* (Milton Keynes: Open University Press, 1991).

efforts to increase responsiveness in the pursuit of public service goals. However, a negative outcome would be one where the mechanisms cancelled one another out, or operated to the detriment of other values or desired goals.[41] The outcome would also be negative where the mechanisms did not conflict, but where there was duplication of effort, or inefficiencies resulting from poor communication between agencies performing complementary tasks.

Concepts

Reflexivity and juridification

Reflexivity refers to an organization's 'relationship with itself' or, more simply, to self-regulation.[42] This concept implies limits to external or direct control, and hence to the regulatory capacities of the state. The success of law and regulation in achieving policy goals is, therefore, necessarily dependent on the facilitation and reinforcement of 'internal' or reflexive processes within organizations, involving the 'regulation of self-regulation'.[43] The notions of reflexivity and responsiveness are closely related, with some commentators using the terms interchangeably. Hence Collins contrasts command and control techniques with 'responsive or reflexive regulation.'[44] The argument is that regulation works best, ie reflexively/responsively, through the 'collaboration and participation' of those subject to regulation; and that the private law of contract meets this condition by allowing individuals in markets to negotiate their own standards against the background of known monitoring arrangements and enforcement mechanisms.[45] In the context of environmental and health and safety regulation, Aalders and Wilthagen consider the importance of regulatee collaboration and participation in similar terms, arguing that a 'reflexive administrative law' can serve to promote such qualities in business self-regulation.[46] Reflexivity in this sense is closely linked with the collaborative regulation and organizational learning dimensions of responsiveness discussed in the previous section.

In Teubner's interpretation, however, reflexivity and responsiveness are more sharply distinguished. Disenchanted in the early 1980s with the goals and structures of the regulatory state in the advanced democracies, Teubner argued that

[41] For example, there may be a tension between the free availability of information necessary for consumers to make choices about public services and for providers to be held to account, and the need for commercial confidentiality to prevent the substance of contracts and negotiations leading up to their award becoming public and so undermining competition.

[42] M Aalders and T Wilthagen, 'Moving Beyond Command-and-Control: Reflexivity in the Regulation of Occupational Health and Safety' (1997) 19 *Law and Policy* 415.

[43] ibid 428.

[44] Collins (n 9 above) 65: 'I prefer the terminology of reflexivity, because it recognises that the fundamental problem for regulation consists in the interaction between the operationally closed systems of legal regulation and contractual agreements . . . . However, little turns on the distinction in terminology for my argument' (fn 14).

[45] ibid.

[46] Aalders and Wilthagen (n 42 above).

Nonet and Selznick's notion of responsive law, while containing elements of reflexivity,[47] was contaminated with 'substantive rationality' – the ultimate cause of the state's regulatory failures. The resolution of the resulting contradiction was considered to require the substitution of the typology of legal *orders* (from repressive, to autonomous, to responsive) with an evolutionary typology of modern legal *rationalities* (from formal, to substantive, to reflexive). Far from being synonymous with responsiveness, reflexivity here is based on the fundamental distinction between the substantive rationality of results on the one hand, and 'the "reflexive" rationality of the process-oriented structuring of institutions and the organizing of participation' on the other'.[48] For present purposes, it appears sensible to maintain a distinction between the two meanings, and to consider reflexivity in its non-dogmatic sense as referring to an organization's relationship with itself and its environment, as just one dimension of the broader concept of responsiveness.[49]

Whereas reflexivity is positively associated with responsiveness, juridification implies unresponsiveness. As has been seen, a potential difficulty with all forms of regulation concerns the limited capacity of the legal system directly to control the operation of other social systems or spheres. The concept of juridification provides a useful way of thinking about the potentially damaging effects of legal regulation in 'steering' complex social and economic processes that are resistant to top-down policy initiatives.[50] Juridification refers to the process whereby relations hitherto governed by extra-legal norms and expectations come to be subjected to specifically legal values and rules that are inappropriate to the particular conditions.[51] The juridification of central-local government relations in the 1980s, for example, was both a response to and a product of the 'normative gulf' that opened up following the breakdown of the institutions that had hitherto served this governance purpose.[52] Where law had traditionally provided a facilitative framework for negotiation, its role was transformed into that of establishing a regulatory

47 G Teubner, 'Substantive and Reflexive Elements in Modern Law' (1983) 17 *Law and Society Review* 239, 256.

48 ibid 251. In contrast to substantive legal rationality, which attempts to regulate social structures by legal norms even though these structures do not easily bend to legal regulation, reflexive law operates by fostering mechanisms that 'systematically further the development of reflexion structures within other social systems' (275).

49 For a relational critique see IR Macneil, 'Contracting Worlds and Essential Contract Theory', (2000) 9 *Social and Legal Studies* 431.

50 B Jessop, 'The Regulation Approach, Governance and Post-Fordism: Alternative Perspectives on Economic and Political Change?' (1995) 24 *Economy and Society* 307, 314; R Laughlin and J Broadbent, 'Accounting and Law: Partners in the Juridification of the Public Sector in the UK?' (1993) 4 *Critical Perspectives on Accounting* 337.

51 C Scott, 'The Juridification of Regulatory Relations in the UK Utilities Sector', in J Black, P Muchlinski, and P Walker, (eds), *Commercial Regulation and Judicial Review* (Oxford: Hart Publishing, 1998) 19.

52 M Loughlin, 'The Restructuring of Central-Local Government Relations', in J Jowell and D Oliver, (eds), *The Changing Constitution* (4th edn, Oxford: Clarendon Press, 2000), 137; ibid, 'Innovative Financing in Local Government: The Limits of Legal Instrumentalism – Part I', [1991] PL 372, ibid (Part II) [1991] PL 568.

regime.[53] Juridification was therefore intimately connected with Conservative efforts to centralize power at the expense of local government, and with the ensuing resistance on the part of local authorities to this process through constant challenges in the courts. Juridification had various negative consequences, expressed in the increased prominence of lawyers in the policy making process, the increasing submission of disputes to formal dispute-resolution, and the generally heightened legal consciousness of actors. For Loughlin, regulatory problems are:

> . . . common to all complex systems in which attempts are made to improve the effectiveness of the system through the imposition of some central will. Such action often fails simply because of the systemic limits imposed, whether through a limited knowledge of particular facts or a limited understanding of how the system works, or the centre's ability to reconstruct such systems afresh.[54]

The ultimate failure of CCT was arguably attributable to juridification and the associated problem of legal formalism – the highly specific nature of rules and regulations inviting their manipulation and subversion through 'creative compliance',[55] leading eventually to the defeat of legal policy.[56]

Like the concept of reflexivity, juridification also has a more technical meaning, in this instance associated with the theory of autopoiesis. According to this theory, external regulation that fails to take account of the autopoietic and self-reproducing nature of social systems, and of the need for law and politics to exhibit 'structural coupling' with them, is likely to be ineffective or to have destructive effects. In the 'regulatory trilemma', which arises wherever the limits of structural coupling are overstepped, the regulatory intervention 'is either irrelevant, or produces disintegrating effects on the social area of life, or else disintegrating effects on law itself'.[57] More specifically:

> This means: either law, politics and/or the social area of life will be mutually indifferent, or juridification will have disintegrating effects on politics and/or social sectors concerned, or, finally, law itself will be exposed to the disintegrating pressures to conform of politics and/or social sectors.[58]

[53] M Loughlin, *Legality and Locality: The Role of Law in Central-Local Government Relations* (Oxford: Clarendon Press, 1996) 367.

[54] ibid 382.

[55] Creative compliance may be described as 'the process whereby those regulated avoid having to break the rules by using legal techniques to achieve non-compliance with the intention of the law without technically violating its content' – R Baldwin, 'Governing With Rules: The Developing Agenda', in G Richardson and H Genn, (eds), *Administrative Law and Government Action: The Courts and Alternative Mechanisms of Review* (Oxford: Clarendon Press, 1994) 172; see J Braithwaite and V Braithwaite, 'The Politics of Legalism: Rules Versus Standards in Nursing-Home Regulation' (1995) 4 *Social and Legal Studies* 307.

[56] D McBarnet and C Whelan, 'The Elusive Spirit of the Law: Formalism and the Struggle for Legal Control' (1991) 54 MLR 848; P Vincent-Jones, 'The Regulation of Contractualisation in Quasi-Markets for Public Services' [1999] PL 303.

[57] G Teubner, 'Introduction to Autopoietic Law', in G Teubner, (ed), *Autopoietic Law: A New Approach to Law and Society* (1987) 21.

[58] ibid 27.

Successful structural coupling, which is associated with genuinely reflexive law, may therefore come about only where the limits of self-reproduction of political decision-making, legal norm-making and social guidance are observed.[59]

While in my view a useful metaphor, the 'regulatory trilemma' ultimately adds little to the explanation of juridification. Again, therefore, this concept will be used in its less technical sense in the subsequent analysis of the New Public Contracting. The question I address in depth in Part III is how far this mode of regulation avoids the problems of juridification, and ultimately of policy failure, associated with earlier attempts to achieve central policy purposes through more overt direction and compulsion.

Purposiveness

Purposiveness is central to Nonet and Selznick's original notion of responsiveness. Whereas autonomous law encouraged a restrictive view of official obligation and was concerned mainly with the restraint of authority, responsive law is purposive and concerned with substantive outcomes, paying due regard to the values implicit in rules and policies which may be flexibly interpreted and applied to new institutional settings.[60] Responsive law proceeds through the assignment of responsibilities to various state agencies, allowing them 'initiative in selecting ways and means and emphasising their active organisational role and responsibility to enlist participation of the public'.[61] In this manner law becomes a 'facilitator of response to social needs and aspirations'.[62] Responsive law is a problem-solving enterprise, bringing to bear a variety of powers and mobilizing an array of intellectual and organizational resources in dealing with change, and implying the 'capacity for responsible, and hence discriminate and selective, adaptation'.[63] The distinctive contribution of responsive law is 'to facilitate public purpose and build a spirit of self-correction into the governmental process'.[64]

Teubner's rejection of this notion of responsiveness and his preference for the concept of reflexivity, as just discussed, are intimately connected with his critique of substantive rationality. The argument is that the contemporary crisis of the state, expressed in regulatory ineffectiveness combined with challenges to the legitimacy of its actions, is due to excessively particularistic and substantive forms of legal intervention entailing: purposive programmes implemented through regulations,

59 ibid 21. In another context, see J Broadbent and R Laughlin, 'Contracts, Competition, and Accounting in Health and Education: An Example of Juridification at Work?', in S Deakin and J Michie, (eds), *Contracts, Cooperation and Competition: Studies in Economics, Management and Law* (Oxford: Oxford University Press, 1997).

60 P Nonet and P Selznick, *Law and Society in Transition: Toward Responsive Law* (Harper Torch Books, 1978), 79.

61 ibid 101.

62 ibid 14. This notion, which involves a commitment to the achievement of substantive as well as procedural justice, is rooted in the legal realist tradition of Jerome Frank and the sociological jurisprudence of Roscoe Pound (73).

63 ibid 110.

64 ibid 113.

standards and principles;[65] the authoritative prescription of 'ways and means of social integration';[66] and the attempt generally 'to regulate social structures by legal norms, even though these structures do not always or easily bend to legal regulation'.[67] In contrast, reflexive law (founded on reflexive rationality) is not purposive in this sense. It 'retreats from taking full responsibility for substantive outcomes',[68] instead seeking 'to design self-regulating social systems through norms of organization and procedure',[69] and restricting itself to 'the installation, correction and redefinition of democratic self-regulatory mechanisms'.[70]

Against this argument, I contend that the 'sovereignty of purpose' in Nonet and Selznick's conception of responsive law does not necessarily imply a commitment to substantive state interventions involving either particularistic regulatory goals, or detailed prescriptions as to the means by which such goals should be achieved.[71] The solution to problems associated with the failures of state interventionism and welfarist regulation might be found in a more subtle conception of purposiveness than Teubner allows, either in the original concept of responsive law, or in analogous theoretical perspectives.[72] My argument in Part 3 is that the regulatory failures accompanying the New Public Contracting are not attributable to purposiveness *per se*, but rather to problems associated with the lack of legitimacy and transparency of policy objectives being pursued by recent governments in their restructuring of administrative, economic, and social relations.

Aside from this theoretical debate, the centrality of policy and purpose has been lost in subsequent adaptations of 'responsiveness' in the regulation literature. In their seminal work on responsive regulation, Ayres and Braithwaite comment only in passing on the similarity of their usage of this term with that of Nonet and Selznick, voicing scepticism of the evolutionary model of legal development and concerns about the risks of jettisoning the safeguards against repression provided by autonomous law.[73] A tradition of responsive regulation studies has grown up in which the fundamental purposes of regulation and the values underpinning policy-making processes have not been central issues. This may be due partly to the fact that in many fields, the fundamental regulatory objectives and underlying values are relatively self-evident or uncontentious, as in the control of recognised 'harms' involving accidents and ill-health at work, cataclysmic damage to

[65] Teubner (n 47 above) 254. [66] ibid 255. [67] ibid 274. [68] ibid 254. [69] ibid 255. [70] ibid 239.

[71] Teubner's analysis does appear to allow for purposeful state activity in an analogous sense. Reflexive rationality 'shares with substantive law the notion that focused intervention in social processes is within the domain of law' – ibid, 254. This begs the question of the nature of the 'focus', and how it is produced. See also J Black, 'Proceduralizing Regulation: Part I' (2000) 20 OJLS 597, 604–5.

[72] As has been seen, governance theories emphasize purposiveness: 'Practices of government are *deliberate* attempts to *shape conduct* in certain ways in relation to *certain objectives*' – N Rose, *Powers of Freedom: Reframing Political Thought* (Cambridge: Cambridge University Press, 1999), 4 (emphasis supplied).

[73] Ayres and Braithwaite (n 2 above, 53).

the environment, or high prices caused by producers' inefficiencies and excessive profits and wages.[74] As will be demonstrated, research in this tradition has tended to reduce the assessment of regulation to the technical evaluation of efficiency and effectiveness in the attainment of given ends.

The emphasis on purposiveness, by contrast, places questions of legitimacy at the forefront of analysis. Such questions are particularly important in the overall evaluation of the New Public Contracting due to the policy-driven and politically contentious nature of this mode of regulation.

Law and governance

Nonet and Selznick's principal concern is with the evolution of forms of legal order – from repressive, to autonomous, to responsive. The emphasis is on *law* as a 'facilitator of response' and a 'problem-solving enterprise'. The notion of responsive *regulation* emerges against this background. Responsive regulation is just one facet of a more general quest for the development of responsive law and a responsive legal order:

> If there is a paradigmatic function of responsive law, it is regulation, not adjudication. Broadly understood, regulation is the process of elaborating and correcting the policies required for the realization of a legal purpose. Regulation thus conceived is a mechanism for clarifying the public interest. It involves testing alternative strategies for the implementation of mandates and reconstructing those mandates in the light of what is learned.[75]

Other commentators have focused similarly on the relationship between law and regulation. As we have seen, Collins argues that the self-regulatory potential of contractual arrangements derives from the responsive or reflexive properties of the private law of contract. For Teubner, reflexivity is illustrated by the way in which labour law shapes collective bargaining by providing a general framework for negotiation, consumer law fosters organisations for the representation of consumers and the articulation of their 'voice' and interests, and the law of private organizations 'constitutionalizes' participatory governance structures for corporations.[76]

74 In other cases regulatory goals are not so obvious, or the harms are not so clear-cut, or there are choices to be made between conflicting public goods. Generally, 'optimality' is harder to assess when objectives of equity and political acceptability have to be considered alongside those of efficiency and effectiveness – Gunningham and Grabosky (n 8 above) 26. In the UK privatized utilities sector, economic policy objectives are overlain with social and distributive goals, based on the desire to counter the effects of unequal distribution of wealth and opportunity – T Prosser, *Law and the Regulators* (Oxford: Clarendon Press, 1997) 10; hidden economic objectives, garnered from the behaviour of regulators rather than policy statements, include the development of competitive markets (13–14). The more complex or politically sensitive the regulatory arena, the more problematic becomes the task of evaluation.

75 Nonet and Selznick (n 60 above) 108–9.

76 Teubner (n 47 above) 276–278. It is specifically reflexive *law* that performs the role of the 'installation, correction and redefinition of democratic self-regulatory mechanisms' (239).

Again, administrative law may be regarded as inherently responsive or reflexive as a mode of regulation.[77]

However, responsiveness may be considered a quality not just of law and regulation but of social organization more generally. This implies both a plurality of sources of law and law-making within the framework of modern government, and public participation in the making and interpretation of legal policy.[78] The hallmark of the responsive legal order is *competence* in the exercise of public powers and functions by the legislature, executive, and administration. This achievement is dependent on responsive political and administrative processes. These should be characterized by decentralization and the broad delegation of authority; the creative use of planning, evaluation and development; and participatory decision making as a source of knowledge, a vehicle of communication, and the foundation of consent:

> The special problem of post-bureaucratic organisation is to enlist participation, to encourage initiative and responsibility, to create cooperative systems tapping the contributions of multiple constituents ... authority must be open and participatory: consultation is encouraged; reasons for decisions are explained; criticism is welcome; consent is taken as a test of rationality.'[79]

The suggestion here is that responsiveness, in the senses in which this term has been earlier defined, cannot be reduced to law or regulation. Responsiveness is ultimately a product of specific governance arrangements both within regulated agencies, and between these bodies and external parties with interests or stakes in the performance of the tasks in question. Responsive or reflexive law may help secure the preconditions and determine the parameters of the operation of responsive governance. Responsive governance is founded at least to some degree on responsive law. However, responsive governance is dependent on organisational, economic, administrative and political arrangements that have their own existence and influence outside the ambit of law and legal norms. As was made clear in the previous chapter, the contemporary social order is the product of a complex combination of regulatory mechanisms and governance techniques, among which law is not necessarily the only or the most important component.

Meta-regulation

The term 'meta-regulation' has been used recently in the regulation literature to describe the process whereby corporations are required 'to evaluate and report on their own self-regulation strategies so that regulatory agencies can determine

77 Aalders and Wilthagen (n 42 above). According to Nonet and Selznick, however, administrative law 'is better understood as an heir of autonomous law than as a harbinger of responsive law ... responsive law aims rather at "enablement and facilitation" ' – n 60 above, 111. 78 ibid 95.
79 ibid 99.

whether the ultimate substantive objectives of regulation are being met'.[80] Clearly there are overlaps between this concept and those of self-regulation and reflexivity already considered in this and the previous chapter. Braithwaite has used meta-regulation in this sense to restate the relationship between restorative justice and responsive regulation in terms of a meta-regulatory strategy for access to justice.[81] This notion may be regarded as complementary to the core conception of the enforcement pyramid, with its emphasis on self-regulation at the base and recourse to formal sanctions at the apex only as a last resort.

In a second interpretation drawing on systems theory, meta-regulation is more sharply distinguished from conventional responsive regulation accounts by the absence of hierarchical authority relations and of 'the credible threat of the big stick'.[82] Instead, for example in the case of auditing practices, 'the application of sanctions is substantially limited to naming and shaming through the publication of reports and, in respect of regularity or certification audits, qualification of accounts'.[83] The capacity to impose sanctions for performance failures lies not with the auditor but with other parties outside the particular regulatory process, for example ministers, who exercise enforcement powers 'according to the normative structures of the political rather than the audit system.'[84] This implies a new and radically different way of thinking about governance, which is in tension with the traditional paradigm of responsive regulation. However, while individual governance techniques such as audit and accounting may indeed lack the capacity for sanctions, and cannot therefore be considered regulatory mechanisms in the full sense in their own right,[85] the important point for the present analysis concerns the way in which such governance techniques are incorporated within wider regulatory regimes. As we saw in Chapter 3, the New Public Contracting entails the combination and coordination of a range of instruments and tools of government, which together constitute the regulatory regime.

In a further sense sense, meta-regulation refers more simply to a 'set of institutions and processes that embed regulatory review mechanisms on a systematic basis into the every-day routines of governmental policy-making, such that a particular form of economic rationality becomes part of the taken-for-granted ways of policy-making.'[86] There is arguably a strong meta-regulatory dimension to the

80 C Parker, *The Open Corporation: Effective Self-Regulation and Democracy* (New York: Cambridge University Press, 2002) 245; Gunningham et al (n 6 above). 'The notion of meta-regulation is simple at heart: it captures a desire to think reflexively about regulation, such that rather than regulating social and individual action directly, the process of regulation itself becomes regulated' – B Morgan, 'The Economization of Politics: Meta-Regulation as a Form of Nonjudicial Legality' (2003) 12 *Social and Legal Studies* 489, 490.

81 Braithwaite (n 11 above). Following Parker, this strategy might entail making large organizations themselves responsible for preparing access to justice plans that would benefit the various constituencies affected by their actions.

82 C Scott, 'Speaking Softly Without Big Sticks: Meta-Regulation and Public Sector Audit' (2003) 25 *Social and Legal Studies* 203, 205.

83 ibid.

84 ibid 214.

85 ie combining elements of standard-setting, monitoring and enforcement.

86 Morgan (n 80 above), 490.

processes of self-review required of government departments and local authorities respectively by guidance such as *Better Quality Services* (BQS) and the statutory regime of best value. The focus in the analysis of the New Public Contracting is on the tension between the devolution of responsibilities and powers – including those of self-review – to public agencies on the one hand, combined with continued central control and oversight through conditions established in regulatory frameworks on the other hand. The question is whether, in economic contracts and social control contracts that decouple the regulatory function performed by public contracting agencies from direct bureaucratic authority, this tension is managed in a way that enables or inhibits the attainment of the state's policy goals.

Criteria

This section establishes the criteria by which regulatory regimes might be judged more or less responsive. I argue that the formula: 'responsiveness = effectiveness + legitimacy' may be used to evaluate not only the operation of particular instances of the New Public Contracting, but also the policy process whereby public contracting initiatives are developed and implemented.

Efficiency and effectiveness

Effectiveness measures the extent to which a regulatory activity achieves its intended objectives.[87] The issue of efficiency is usually regarded as part of this assessment, so the question becomes whether regulatory goals are being achieved at the minimum reasonable level of inputs or costs.[88] This criterion implies that regulation cannot be responsive if policy goals either are not achieved, or are incapable of achievement. Neither can regulation be responsive if the costs associated with the mechanisms implementing the policy are excessive. However, a number of questions is raised by the attempt to use this criterion in practice. How and when can success or failure be judged, especially in the case of general or nebulous goals? Can any policy ever be said to be finally and completely successful? How do we measure the efficiency of new relative to previous regulatory arrangements? At what level do costs become regarded as excessive and therefore

[87] LM Salamon, 'The New Governance and the Tools of Public Action: An Introduction', in LM Salamon, (ed), *The Tools of Government: A Guide to the New Governance* (Oxford: Oxford University Press, 2002), 23.

[88] See R Baldwin and M Cave, *Understanding Regulation: Theory, Strategy, and Practice* (Oxford: Oxford University Press, 1999) 81–82. But Salamon argues that effectiveness judgements may be made independently of costs. 'The most effective tool is the one that most reliably allows action on a public problem to achieve its intended purposes' – Salamon (n 87 above) 23. In this case, efficiency is a separate criterion of evaluation, balancing results against costs. This suggests a tension between efficiency and effectiveness: 'The most efficient tool may not be the most effective one. Rather, it is the one that achieves the optimum balance between benefits and costs' (23).

indicative of regulatory ineffectiveness? How do we identify and assess the costs associated with unintended consequences or negative externalities?[89] And what kinds of costs (economic, social) should be taken into account in the evaluation process?[90] Trebilcock has criticised the view that a neat distinction may be drawn between means and ends such that efficiency becomes a purely technical issue of how to produce any given policy result:

> Choices among policy instruments for the realization of given policy objectives are not a substitute for choices among policy objectives (or political interests or values). Rethinking *how* governments might do their work better is not to be confused with *what* governments should be working at.[91]

The relationship between the economic goal of efficiency and distributional and political considerations is particularly problematic.[92] The question is how and to what extent the burden of paying for public goods might be shared between disadvantaged and advantaged groups in the community.[93] The regulatory frameworks governing complex public services are likely to be especially difficult to evaluate in these terms.[94] Policies on public services may not be amenable to simple regulatory impact assessments.

A further problem with this criterion is that it assumes that policy objectives are plain or easily identifiable. In many cases, however, goals may be implicit

[89] Hood stresses that the effects of policy are always likely to be different than expected or anticipated by originating reformers. Counter-productive effects can be expected whenever 'what are claimed to be business practices are carried over into public service employment contracts' – C Hood, 'Individualized Contracts for Top Public Servants: Copying Business, Path-Dependent Political Re-Engineering – Or Trobriand Cricket?' (1998) 11 *Governance* 443, 460. On 'unintended consequences' of CCT (including worsening working conditions, damaging structural disturbances, declining service quality, deterioration in the position of vulnerable groups, and increased economic and social costs to the state generally) see K Escott and D Whitfield, *The Gender Impact of CCT in Local Government*, EOC Research Discussion Series No. 12 (Manchester: Equal Opportunities Commission, 1995).

[90] Even in narrow economic terms, the evidence suggests a relative lack of awareness of the cost of regulation in local government, and a tradition of 'overlapping and cost-unconscious' regulation in the growth of inspectorates, overseers, ombudsmen and auditors – see C Hood, O James, C Scott, G Jones, and T Travers, *Regulation Inside Government: Waste-watchers, Quality Police and Sleaze-busters* (Oxford: Oxford University Press, 1999), 98–101. Salamon makes similar points: programme purposes are often ambiguous, there may be disagreements over what are the principal purposes of public programmes. The assessment of efficiency should included the costs of nongovernmental institutions in complying with regulation, which do not normally appear in government balance sheets – Salamon (n 87 above) 23.

[91] MJ Trebilcock, 'Can Government Be Reinvented?', in J Boston, (ed), *The State Under Contract* (Wellington: Bridget Williams Books, 1995) 30.

[92] J Prager, 'Contracting Out Government Services: Lessons from the Private Sector' (1994) 54 *Public Administration Review* 176, 183. Even if an economic cost-benefit analysis can satisfactorily be conducted of government policy on contracting out, such an evaluation does not take account of the success or failure of arguably more important political imperatives driving such public management reforms.

[93] Trebilcock (n 91 above) 25.

[94] Prosser argues that maximising economic efficiency is not and should not be an overriding regulatory goal given commitments to universal service and other social obligations in the regulatory regimes governing utilities – Prosser (n 74 above).

or reflect hidden agendas.[95] Economic objectives may be inextricably bound up with political ones.[96] I will argue in Chapter 5 that, by comparison with other countries, the policy goals informing public management reforms in Britain have been particularly opaque.[97] The whole notion of measuring effectiveness by reference to goal attainment, and of accountability in the sense of ensuring that the investment of resources has achieved its intended result, may be based on the questionable assumption that the political process is capable of generating clear-cut and precise objectives.[98] Such difficulties point to a need to 'bring values back in',[99] and to a prominent role for legitimacy in the evaluation of responsiveness.

Legitimacy

Legitimacy may be regarded as just one element to be taken into account in evaluating responsiveness. According to Salamon, the basic criterion for gauging the success of public action is effectiveness, followed by efficiency, equity, implementability, and only finally legitimacy.[100] Others, however, see legitimacy as of more central importance. Hence Baldwin and Cave argue that all regulatory regimes and actions should be basically assessed according to the merits of their claims to legitimacy in the sense of whether they are 'worthy of public support'. Five criteria for measuring such worthiness are identified: (1) the existence of legislative authority or mandate; (2) the existence and appropriateness of schemes of accountability; (3) the fairness, accessibility and openness of procedures (due process); (4) the degree of expertise of regulators; and (5) the efficiency of the action or regime.[101] These criteria cannot be applied mechanistically:

> What matters is the collective justificatory power of the arguments that can be made under the five headings. Strong claims across the board point to regulation that deserves support, generally weak claims indicate low capacity to justify.[102]

This suggests that legitimacy is the master criterion, rather than just one factor to be traded off against others. In emphasizing the contested nature of regulation and the difficulty of reaching definite conclusions in regulatory assessments, this approach points to the fundamental importance of public debate and deliberation in the policy process. We return to such features of responsiveness in advocating an increased procedural role for law in contractual governance in Part 4.

95 Perri 6, 'Giving Consumers of British Public Services More Choice: What Can Be Learned From Recent History?' (2003) 32 *Journal of Social Policy* 239: 'Assessing goals is not always easy, for overtly avowed goals may not, of course, be the true goals' (239).

96 Prager (n 92 above).

97 J Rehfuss, 'The Competitive Agency: Thoughts From Contracting Out in Great Britain and the United States' (1991) 57 *International Review of Administrative Sciences* 465.

98 P Day and R Klein, *Accountabilities: Five Public Services* (London: Tavistock, 1987) 28.

99 A Waddan, 'Redesigning the Welfare Contract in Theory and Practice: Just What Is Going On in the USA?' (2003) 32 *Journal of Social Policy* 19, 31 (in connection with problems of evaluating the 'success' of the US welfare-to-work experiment).

100 Salamon (n 87 above) 23.

101 Baldwin and Cave (n 88 above) 76–95.

102 ibid 82.

It has already been suggested that the regulation approach generally has failed to engage sufficiently with the values and purposes informing the state's regulatory endeavours. While the technical and moral or normative aspects of a regulatory strategy cannot in reality be considered in mutual isolation, the new orthodoxy in regulation studies appears to have divorced means and ends, and to have accorded primacy to the former.[103] Against this position, the ideal of responsive regulation implies not just effectiveness, but the harnessing of all regulatory forces and 'governmental' resources to achieve legitimate regulatory purposes. This issue is particularly relevant to the analysis of the New Public Contracting. Urgent questions of legitimacy have arisen here due to the inevitably contentious nature of attempts by central government to restructure and reform public services and the organizations involved in their delivery, for example local government and the NHS. Here more than anywhere the state's regulatory efforts need to be subjected to critical scrutiny, with particular attention to their underlying values, legitimacy and accountability.

I will argue that the legitimacy of government policies on public contracting is dependent, firstly, on the quality of public deliberation and participation in the determination of regulatory objectives; and secondly, on the ethical environment of decision-making and the associated quality of 'institutional morality' within governmental organizations.[104] These aspects may be considered in turn.

Public deliberation

A number of writers have sought recently to develop the implications of Habermas' theory of communicative action and of deliberative democracy. In one view, the ideal of deliberation involves the principle that everything done by government or by public agencies, or claimed to be in the public interest, should be 'contestable' by the people. What is paramount is reason rather than consensus, the goal being 'to create a testing environment for the selection of laws, rather than to have laws that are consensually designed'.[105] This implies that citizens should have maximum opportunity for challenging government actions and their underlying rationales. Responsiveness here equates with the openness of decision-making processes to challenge and contestation, in contrast with notions of democracy based on the aggregation of individual wills or interest-group pluralism:

> The notion of a deliberate democracy is rooted in the intuitive ideal of a democratic association in which the justification of the terms and conditions of association proceeds through public argument and reasoning among equal citizens. Citizens in such an order

103 J Black, 'Proceduralizing Regulation: Part II' (2001) 21 OJLS 33, 57.

104 There is, however, a significant difference of emphasis and methodology in these positions. Whereas Black develops an analysis of proceduralization based on a critique of Habermas, my concern here is more with Nonet and Selznick's original notion of responsiveness and its later refinement in Selznick's work on institutional morality.

105 P Pettit, *Republicanism: A Theory of Freedom and Government* (Oxford: Blackwell, 1997) 278.

share a commitment to the resolution of problems of collective choice through public reasoning, and regard their basic institutions as legitimate insofar as they establish the framework for free public deliberation.[106]

On another view, which rejects the purely procedural approach to legitimacy, the democratic deficits in current social-democratic government must be addressed through 'thick proceduralization'. This implies a need for positive action on the part of the state to overcome barriers to public participation associated with class, ethnic, and gender differences in modern societies. Tackling these obstacles requires the *mediation* of deliberative democracy. Such mediation might provide the conditions of effective communication and public reason in various ways, by mapping differences and conflicts between deliberants, 'translating' otherwise incommensurate languages, making deliberants aware of the inclusionary and exclusionary effects of problem definition and modes of discourse, and facilitating strategies of dispute resolution.[107] This raises questions as to the precise role of the state in policy-formation, in particular regarding the locus of decision-making and whether regulators can act as mediators:

> A proceduralist model of regulation in which the deliberants themselves decide is indeed a qualitative shift in the nature of regulation. For no longer is the question how best to ensure that the ends that the state has determined are achieved within society, but how to arrange matters such that participants themselves can make the decisions *as to what those ends should be*.[108]

This implies that the proper role of the state might be to structure deliberations among decision-making fora beyond its formal boundaries, rather than just to guarantee the conditions of communication necessary for effective debate and public reason within the legislature.[109] This analysis raises further questions, concerning the precise stages in the regulatory process deliberation might be expected to occur effectively, and the likelihood that thick proceduralization might need ultimately to abandon the search for full normative consensus and integration in favour of developing policies of tolerance to deal with irreconcilable difference. The relationship between deliberation, representation, and participation raises particular difficulties. Responsiveness requires that service recipients, local citizens and communities are given the opportunity not just to express views or contribute to debates, but to assume responsibility for decisions themselves.[110]

[106] AR Oquendo, 'Deliberative Democracy in Habermas and Nino' (2002) 22 OJLS 189, 192. The ideal of deliberation is equated with an ideal constituent convention, or 'an extraordinary university faculty meeting' (220).

[107] Black (n 103 above) 57.

[108] ibid 54 (emphasis supplied).

[109] Habermas's conception of procedural law is ultimately limited 'in not providing for sufficient pluralism in norm formation or in the loci of regulation' – Black (n 103 above) 57.

[110] J Potter, 'Consumerism and the Public Sector: How Well Does the Coat Fit?' (1988) 66 *Public Administration* 149, 154–5.

The notion of proceduralization in this broadly Habermasian sense will be further developed in the analysis of legal governance of the New Public Contracting in Chapter 11.[111]

Institutional morality

A different approach to 'thickening' the notion of legitimacy focuses on institutional morality and the ethical frameworks governing organizational behaviour. The issue of legitimacy is addressed only indirectly in Nonet and Selznick's original analysis of responsive law. The general argument is in favour of broadening legal and political participation and increasing the involvement of groups and organizations in the making of public policy through legal action and social advocacy.[112] On its own, this plea offers not a solution but a new set of questions.[113] However, Selznick's later work on the morality of institutions and organizations suggests how 'self-regarding or reflexive responsibility' might contribute to increased legitimacy and responsiveness:

> Responsibility runs to an institutional self or identity; to those upon whom the institution depends; and the community whose well-being it affects. Thus responsiveness entails reconstruction of the self as well as outreach to others. Established structures, rules, methods, and policies are all open to revision, but revision takes place in a principled way, that is, while holding fast to values and purposes.[114]

The notion of reflexive responsibility adds a moral and normative dimension to the definition of responsiveness as organizational learning or system reflexivity considered earlier in this chapter. The organization's relationship with itself and its environment is conditioned by the embodiment within it of values. Again this implies the need for a radically different form of state direction to that entailed in command and control approaches to regulation:

> Rule-centred law tends to expend authority on securing conformity to rules, not on solving problems. Responsive regulation is less interested in rule-compliance for its own sake than in mobilizing energies for the achievement of public purposes. Therefore the enterprise must be perceived as, and must become, a resource for public policy. Although this requires respect for and deference to its special needs and purposes, it also requires a reconstruction of the enterprise to enhance its capacity of responsible conduct.[115]

111 J Habermas, *Between Facts and Norms: Contributions to a Discourse Theory of Law and Democracy* (Oxford: Polity Press, 1996). For a comparison and evaluation of the relative merits of Habermas's procedural paradigm based on the theory of communicative action, and Teubner's reflexive law associated with the theory of autopoiesis, see J Paterson, 'Trans-science, Trans-law and Proceduralization' (2003) 12 *Social and Legal Studies* 525.

112 Nonet and Selznick (n 60 above) 96.

113 Black (n 103 above) 37.

114 P Selznick, *The Moral Commonwealth: Social Theory and the Promise of Community* (Berkeley: University of California Press, 1992) 338: 'This we might call self-regarding or reflexive responsibility.'

115 Selznick (n 10 above) 401.

'Thick institutionalization' is considered by Selznick to be part of the process of transformation of organizations into institutions. This entails the sanctifying or hardening of rules and procedures, administrative rituals, symbols, and ideologies. It is strongly associated with the intensification of purposiveness and the commitment to unifying objectives, and the embedding of organizations in their social environment.[116] Institutionalization in this sense is associated also with the building of moral competence into the structure of the enterprise, and with the development of capacities for self-regulation.[117] Responsive institutions avoid insularity but without embracing opportunism.[118] Institutional integrity is linked with internal morality: 'An internal morality is the set of standards that must be honoured if the distinctive mission of an institution or practice is to be achieved.'[119] Where an organization has a well-developed internal morality, the significance for regulation is that this becomes a resource for public policy and 'the community's strategy may well shift from *external* to *internal* control'.[120]

Thick institutionalization combines responsive formal structures of official design with organic or informal structures consisting of attitudes, relationships and practices that evolve through social interactions. This development is associated with the realization of core values on which moral experience is based, such as responsibility, autonomy, integrity, reason, fairness, equality, and democracy. These values go beyond the rational instrumental perspective that is concerned with technical excellence, effectiveness and efficiency in the attainment of policy ends. Ethical decision-making in public organizations should be informed by 'process values' (eliminating bias, providing opportunities for reasoned argument, assuring accurate and reliable determination of facts, upholding legal stability, and so forth) underlying formal administrative and legal procedures:

> The idea of process is richer than that of procedure. It contains the whole matrix of values, purposes, and sensibilities that should inform a course of conduct. The integrity of process, thus understood, cannot be protected unless we appreciate those values, purposes and sensibilities. Therefore process requires the integration of means and ends.[121]

This analysis mirrors the emphasis placed on internal morality and organizational virtue in such fields as environmental regulation and corporate governance. The normative culture of organizations shapes the ways in which individuals reflect and act within them. The task of Occupational Health and Safety (OHS) regulators, for example, is to 'operationalize' organizational virtue by recognizing, encouraging and nurturing firms with cultures that accept good health and safety practice as integral to their business.[122]

This focus on the institutional morality and responsibility of organizations might be further developed to provide a theoretical framework for the ethical evaluation of decision making in public institutions, so grounding a new ethics

116 ibid 397. 117 ibid 398.

118 'which arises where an institution is too weak or inept to defend its integrity, associated with uncontrolled adaptation and capitulation to pressure' – ibid 399. 119 ibid 400.

120 ibid 400. 121 Selznick (n 114 above) 331. 122 Haines (n 5 above).

for public administration.[123] Within public sector organizations, ethical problems (most obviously concerning financial waste and misallocation of funds, conflicts of interest, improper influence, and outright fraud and corruption) have arguably been exacerbated by deregulation, contractualization, and new public management reforms.[124] On the broadest definition, public sector ethics may be argued to be about 'good governance', and to include the whole range of attempts to mould the practice and policy of government in the service of the common good.[125] The proper focus of administrative ethics is not just the decisions and conduct of managers, but the institutions and associated values and principles that define the duties and obligations attaching to individual roles.[126] Prescriptions for ethical reform need to be directed at institutional frameworks, and to challenge organisational cultures.[127] The reiteration of core public service values (such as honesty and integrity, impartiality, respect for law and persons, diligence, selflessness, accountability, objectivity and openness) does little to address the problem of the difficult choices that increasingly confront public servants where there is no obviously 'right' or 'wrong' answer.[128] The dilemmas posed by value-conflicts in ethically ambiguous situations can only be resolved ultimately at a deep institutional level through responsive regulatory strategies that build respect for core values into decision-making processes both within public organisations and in their relationships with consumers and citizens.

This perspective should not be confined, however, to public bodies such as local councils that traditionally have been regarded as ethically deficient or vulnerable to fraud and corruption. I will argue in Part 4 that it should be applied at the heart of government, encompassing the institutional and organizational environments of central decison-making and the processes whereby New Public Contracting policies are developed and implemented.

Policy process and institutional design

The 'policy process' refers to the entire process whereby state purposes are conceived and translated into programmes through the medium of legislation, policy

[123] B Dorbeck-Jung, 'Towards Reflexive Responsibility. New Ethics for Public Administration', in A Hondeghem, (ed), *Ethics and Accountability in a Context of Governance and New Public Management* (Amsterdam: IOS Press, 1998) 45; R Gregory and C Hicks, 'Promoting Public Service Integrity: A Case for Responsible Accountability' (1999) 58 *Australian Journal of Public Administration* 3.

[124] P Bishop and N Preston, (eds), *Local Government: Public Enterprise and Ethics* (Sydney: The Federation Press, 2000).

[125] N Preston, 'Public Sector Ethics: What Are We Talking About', in ibid.

[126] T Cooper, 'Ethical Issues in Citizen Participation and Representation in Local Government', in ibid.

[127] 'Whilst the conduct of individual public officials is important, a sound approach to public sector ethics is a multi-dimensional institutionalised, long-term project integrated into strategic planning and corporate governance' – Preston (n 125 above) 20.

[128] M Maguire, 'Ethics in the Public Service', in A Hondegem, (ed), *Ethics and Accountability in a Context of Governance and New Public Management* (Amsterdam: IOS Press, 1998).

documents, or other authoritative sources.[129] Increased transparency and deliberation in the policy process, coupled with an emphasis on institutional morality and reflexive responsibility, should both enhance legitimacy and lead to more effective policy-making and better regulatory outcomes.[130] Ultimately the New Public Contracting will be judged in terms of the responsiveness of the policy process.

The critique of effectiveness as a criterion of responsiveness, above, has already indicated the limits of the rational choice model of the policy process. In practice alternative options are investigated to the point where a satisfactory solution is found, rather than to the point of discovery of the ideal solution assumed to exist by rational decision theory.[131] Politics and ideology have played an important role in the choice of instruments for programme implementation, in addition to criteria such as effectiveness, efficiency and reliability.[132] Political objectives may override or take precedence over economic goals.[133] In Britain, as has been seen, contracting out has been orchestrated through particularly strong central government pressures promoting a reduction in the direct providing role of the state, relative to many other countries where decision-making on this issue has tended to be more pragmatic. Even if it were a technical exercise, devoid of political content and influence, policy making would not be a simple matter.[134] Policy instruments do not have inherent characteristics that cause them always to operate in the same way. The rationalist assumption that technical knowledge and expertise can be used to calculate the most economical means to the attainment of a given end is strongly associated, in one interpretation, with juridification and unresponsive regulation.[135]

129 As an expression of 'attempts at governing', the policy process may be formally rationalized in programmatic statements, policy documents, pamphlets and speeches. Less formal 'attempts at governing', embodied in the practical rationalities of professional work in areas such as police work and social work, are not part of the policy process in this sense – see Rose (n 72 above) 4.

130 J Steele, 'Participation and Deliberation in Environmental Law' (2001) 21 OJLS 415.

131 On 'satisficing' as a characteristic of administrative decision-making, implying an orderly process involving the following of a procedure or routine, rather than rational calclulation on individual cases, see HA Simon, 'Rational Decision-Making in Business Organizations (1979) 69 *American Economic Review* 493.

132 BG Peters, 'The Politics of Tool Choice', in LM Salamon, (ed) *The Tools of Government: A Guide to the New Governance* (Oxford: Oxford University Press, 2002) 563; Arthur B Ringeling, 'European Experience with Tools of Government', in LM Salamon, (ed), *The Tools of Government: A Guide to the New Governance* (Oxford: Oxford University Press, 2002) 594.

133 Escott and Whitfield (n 89 above).

134 For a critique see C Lindblom, *The Intelligence of Democracy: Decision-making Through Mutual Adjustment* (New York: Free Press, 1965). In many cases old instruments are applied in new contexts through a process of imitation rather than rational selection – C Hood, *The Tools of Government* (London: Macmillan, 1983) 129.

135 Loughlin (n 53 above) 374. Against this instrumental conception, an emphasis on practical reason and on traditions of administration better acknowledges the complexity of government and the difficulties caused by the mechanistic separation of means and ends. If the means to ends cannot be scientifically and rationally known, then policy goals themselves certainly cannot. Again the key issue is one of legitimacy of the policy process, and the procedures whereby policies are deliberated, determined, implemented, revised, and abandoned.

While it is generally accepted that the selection of regulatory instruments should be based on some understanding of 'how to match instruments to circumstances',[136] the theoretical and practical obstacles to this goal need squarely to be recognized. Responsiveness in the policy process needs to be informed by regulatory design principles that are sensitive to the complexity of different regulatory environments, and to the difficulty if not impossibility of determining an 'optimal mix' of regulatory instruments.[137] Policy making is a continuous process, always incremental and provisional rather than comprehensive and once-and-for-all.[138] Due to historical and cultural differences, an instrument may work well in one country but not in others, despite apparently similar or identical conditions.[139] Policy decisions in reality are constrained and influenced by many factors, including policy transfer, social learning, and path-dependency.[140] Policy learning through the dissemination of good practice, for example among the advanced industrial economies by the OECD, is as much about the circumstances in which particular innovations succeed or fail as about the innovations themselves.[141]

The question of what constitutes responsiveness in institutional design raises similar issues to those already considered in relation to regulation and the policy process. The difference is that the focus on institutions is at a higher level of abstraction. Corresponding with the unrealizable ideal of the rational policy maker is the 'myth of the institutional designer'.[142] Institutions cannot be created from scratch. Their continuity and relative stability limits the creative capacity of policy makers, helping to explain the accidental and evolutionary character of much institutional development. Nevertheless, Goodin's discussion of criteria of institutional design is useful in this preliminary analysis of the New Public Contracting. A first, 'internal' criterion refers to the quality of fit between the designed institution

136 Hood (n 134 above) 137.

137 Such principles, relating to efficiency and effectiveness, might emphasize the complementarity of regulatory instruments; parsimony; the empowerment of third parties as surrogate regulators; and the maximizing of opportunities for 'win-win' outcomes – G Gunningham and D Sinclair, 'Designing Environmental Policy', in N Gunningham, P Grabosky, with D Sinclair, *Smart Regulation: Designing Environmental Policy* (Oxford: Clarendon Press, 1998) 377 (in the context of environmental regulation).

138 M Aronson, 'A Public Lawyer's Responses to Privatisation and Outsourcing', in M Taggart, (ed), *The Province of Administrative Law* (Oxford: Hart Publishing, 1997) 58.

139 Ringeling (n 132 above) 594.

140 I Greener, 'Understanding NHS Reform: The Policy-Transfer, Social Learning, and Path Dependency Perspectives' (2002) 15 *Governance* 161; R Mannion and P Smith, 'How Providers are Chosen in the Mixed Economy of Community Care', in W Bartlett, JA Roberts, and J Le Grand, (eds) *A Revolution in Social Policy: Quasi-Market Reforms in the 1990s* (Bristol: The Policy Press, 1998) 111; D Hughes, L Griffiths, and J McHale, 'Do Quasi-markets Evolve? Institutional Analysis and the NHS' (1997) 21 *Cambridge Journal of Economics* 259. Generally see M Granovetter, 'Economic Action and Social Structure: The Problem of Embeddedness' (1985) 91 *American Journal of Sociology* 481; M Roe, 'Chaos and Evolution in Law and Economics' (1996) 109 *Harvard Law Review* 641.

141 R Klein, 'Learning From Others; Shall the Last be the First?' (1997) 22 *Journal of Health Politics, Policy and Law* 1267. Policies cannot be copied in a straightforward manner between countries. Their 'effective transplant' depends on the institutional compatibility of donor and recipient.

142 Goodin (n 26 above) 28.

and its environment, such that it is 'in harmony with the social order in which it is set.'[143] The second, 'external' criterion concerns the institution's 'moral worth' or consistency with some larger moral code.[144] These criteria correspond very broadly with the criteria already suggested for the evaluation of responsive regulation, namely effectiveness/efficiency and legitimacy respectively. The complex and inevitably controversial nature of institutional reform reinforces the importance of the design aims of facilitating the development of 'internal morality', and of creating and supporting the conditions under which contested issues may adequately be debated. The Kantian 'publicity principle' might be particularly helpful in regard to public involvement and deliberation in decision making. The principle theoretically requires that all institutional actions be publicly defensible. It does not require that every political action literally be publicized, but rather that such action has the capacity to withstand publicity.[145]

Not surprisingly, the four principles of institutional and regulatory design considered earlier (revisability, robustness, variability, and sensitivity to motivational complexity) are consistent with certain dimensions of responsiveness outlined at the beginning of this chapter. Organizations, including public agencies, should have some discretion in framing the rules (or designing the institutions) according to which they act. If the degree to which social outcomes can be the subject of intentional change or design is limited, attention should be devoted 'one level up' to altering or affecting the selection mechanisms that guide institutional development.[146] Hence:

> Even within the realm of our intentional interventions, what we should be aiming at is not the design of institutions directly. Rather, we should be aiming at designing schemes for designing institutions – schemes which will pay due regard to the multiplicity of designers and to the inevitably cross-cutting nature of their intentional interventions in the design process.[147]

Conclusion

The New Public Contracting is characterized fundamentally by the delegation of powers to public agencies in various contractual arrangements for the attainment of particular policy purposes. The formula: 'responsiveness = effectiveness + legitimacy' provides a useful starting point for the analysis and evaluation of this highly purposive mode of regulation. The designation 'responsive' implies efficiency and effectiveness in the use of regulatory means to the attainment of given ends.[148] The mechanisms and processes constituting 'smart' or 'optimal'

[143] ibid 37. [144] ibid 39. [145] ibid.

[146] 'Outcomes may be the product of accident, but accident rates might be intentionally altered. Outcomes may be the product of evolutionary forces, but the selection mechanisms that guide that evolution might be intentionally altered' – ibid 29. [147] ibid 28.

[148] On the theoretical difficulties of maintaining a distinction between means and ends, see Selznick (n 114 above) 328–330.

regulation are an essential part of any adequate analysis of regulation, or indeed of governance. However, the more important criterion of responsiveness is legitimacy. This may be considered with reference either to the quality of deliberative processes leading to policy formulation ('thick proceduralization'), or to the inner morality and 'process values' at work in public institutions ('thick institutionalization'), or to their combination. Just as purposes are central to the debate on regulation, so too are values. Given the various reasons for distrusting both technical experts and politicians, democratic values of probity, transparency and public deliberation need to be applied at all stages and at all levels of decision-making in the performance of public service functions.[149] Political legitimacy consists in the provision of maximum opportunity for deliberation over the merits of various forms of government action on a wide range of public service issues.[150] Responsiveness is not just a quality of particular policies that are judged 'effective' or 'legitimate', but is dependent ultimately on the responsiveness of the policy process itself.

149 For example, the pre-contracting stage, prior to the decision to contract out a service – S Zifcak, 'Contractualism, Democracy and Ethics' (2001) 60 *Australian Journal of Public Administration* 86.

150 P Vincent-Jones, 'Values and Purpose in Government: Central-local Relations in Regulatory Perspective, (2002) 29 *Journal of Law and Society* 27; J Chalmers, and G Davis, 'Rediscovering Implementation: Public Sector Contracting and Human Services' (2001) *Australian Journal of Public Administration* 74.

5

The New Public Contracting in Regulatory Perspective

This chapter draws together the threads of the foregoing theoretical discussion, and situates the New Public Contracting fully in a regulatory perspective. We begin by considering a range of problems of unresponsiveness associated with legitimacy deficits in the policy process. We then explore regulatory relationships through the notion of 'contracting regimes'. I suggest that the success of such regimes depends on an appropriate balance being struck between central direction on the one hand, and autonomy on the part of the bodies charged with performing public service functions on the other. I further argue that the effectiveness of the New Public Contracting is dependent on the quality of the contract norms governing relationships between public purchasing agencies and providers in economic contracts, between public authorities and individual citizens in social control contacts, and between government bodies in administrative contracts.

New Public Contracting policy

The previous chapter emphasized the essentially purposive character of regulation, and the centrality of this element to the understanding of the New Public Contracting. An immediate problem here, however, is that regulatory purposes or rationales cannot simply be deduced or read-off from political statements or policy documents, and may have to be found in other sources, or induced from the practical operation of regulatory schemes.[1] As has been seen in Chapter 2, the British experience of the NPM has been particularly marked by a lack of clarity and explicitness in the goals of public service reform. For example, the case for privatization has never been fully justified, and appears to have shifted over time.[2]

[1] T Prosser, *Law and the Regulators* (Oxford: Clarendon Press, 1997) 10.

[2] 'No grand theological debate has taken place; nor is there an obvious theatre for such an event' – ND Lewis, *Choice and the Legal Order: Rising Above Politics* (London: Butterworths, 1996) 123. There is uncertainty as to whether the policy aim is less government or increased efficiency, which could be achieved without privatization through administrative reforms and better 'value for money' by public employees – J Rehfuss, 'The Competitive Agency: Thoughts From Contracting Out in Great Britain and the United States' (1991) 57 *International Review of Administrative Sciences* 465, 478.

Similarly, the Next Steps programme gathered momentum through the market-testing programme, but without any statement of overall purpose or direction.[3] This is in sharp contrast with other common law countries such as New Zealand, where the public management and public service reforms have been accompanied by greater transparency.[4]

Motives and foreseeable consequences

Even when policy goals are explicitly proclaimed, there is the question of how far they can be taken at face value: 'overtly avowed goals may not, of course, be the true goals'.[5] There is a gulf between official statements of policy objectives accompanying the New Public Contracting, and what academics and political commentators have seen as the underlying purposes of regulatory programmes. The social and public policy literature is replete with accusations of duplicity, deception, and 'hidden agendas' in public management reforms. For example, the rhetoric of increasing participation and responsiveness accompanying the Tenants' Choice provisions of the late 1980s arguably masked a specific central government agenda aimed at reducing the size of the council sector and encouraging confrontation between tenants and council landlords.[6] Similarly, the 1998 school choice reforms were presented by ministers as promoting greater diversity in school provision, yet the real agenda was arguably one of centralization. Here the introduction of the national curriculum and league tables as the principal or even sole basis of competition, coupled with tighter systems of financial management and greater regulation of local authorities generally, could be said to have undermined diversity.[7] Again, with regard to best value, despite the avowed commitment to pragmatism and to allowing local authorities to choose how to fulfil the 'compare' and 'compete' requirements of the regime, the government appears to have decided that benchmarking is incapable of providing a test of competitiveness or even a basis for comparison among alternative service providers.[8]

[3] P Greer, *Transforming Central Government: The Next Steps Initiative* (Buckingham: Open University Press, 1994) 132.

[4] The requirement that goals of departments, agencies and individual public servants be clearly stated is built into the administrative process – J Boston, (ed), *The State Under Contract* (Wellington: Bridget Williams Books, 1995); ibid, 'The Use of Contracting in the Public Sector – Recent New Zealand Experience' (1996) 55 *Australian Journal of Public Administration* 105. On principles governing asset sales, see Lewis (n 2 above) 122–123.

[5] 'Sometimes the avowed goals and the foreseeable consequences of the measures (foreseeable, that is, within what the ideological blinkers of the government of the day would allow) seem to coincide . . . other cases are harder to understand' – Perri 6, 'Giving Consumers of British Public Services More Choice: What Can Be Learned From Recent History?' (2003) 32 *Journal of Social Policy* 239.

[6] H Carr, D Sefton-Green, and D Tissier, 'Two Steps Forward for Tenants?, in D Cowan, and A Marsh, (eds), *Two Steps Forward: Housing Policy into the New Millennium* (Bristol: Policy Press, 2001) 161.

[7] Perri 6 (n 5 above) 244.

[8] M Bowerman and A Ball, 'Great Expectations: Benchmarking for Best Value' (2000) *Public Money and Management* (Apr–Jun), 21, 25.

The legitimacy of the exercise of regulatory power is dependent on the reasons for desired behaviour being made explicit both to regulatees and to wider society. The absence of such explanation denotes unresponsiveness and may be evidence of manipulation.[9] The notion of the 'hidden agenda' implies the concealment of 'true' or ulterior motives behind 'false' or deliberately misleading ones. The development of policy on the PFI has been characterized arguably by bad arguments and bad motives, thus inhibiting necessary policy deliberation and evaluation.[10] This is an example to which we shall return on a number of occasions in the argument that follows. Government claims that private companies in the health sector are preferable to NHS providers due to their superior efficiency may disguise a more subterranean purpose of encouraging the development of markets as a prelude to further privatization.[11] Beneath the rhetoric of responsiveness to consumer needs, the real targets of many public service reforms implemented by the New Right in the 1980s were the powerful professional interest groups perceived as being 'embedded in the welfare system'.[12] Again, the objective of policies directed at reforming the education and housing sectors through the introduction of various exit mechanisms was to weaken the influence of local councils and local education authorities.[13]

However, the argument as to the existence of responsiveness deficits in the New Public Contracting is not dependent on proof of bad motives on the part of politicians and policy makers. Policies may have different layers or levels of meaning, expressing multiple purposes rather than any single or principal policy agenda. Best value, for example, might be about improving local authority performance as well as expanding the private sector role in public service provision. In addition to the absence of bad faith, legitimacy in the political and administrative process requires that all foreseeable and unintended consequences be properly explored, and that all dimensions of policies be analysed, with particular attention to ambiguities, contradictions or incoherence in government reasoning. The coherence and transparency of the discourse on the PFI, for example, may be contested by scrutinizing the claim that a private contractor is 'better placed to manage a risk' than a government department or public authority.[14] Again, efficiency claims made in connection with privatization may be challenged on their own terms. The empirical evidence on market testing is that increased efficiency may

9 'It is clear that manipulation cannot be legitimate power, since in the case of manipulation there is no recognition by the subordinated individual that an act of power has been effected' – H Goldhamer and E Shils, 'Types of Power and Status' (1939) 45 *American Journal of Sociology* 171, 171.

10 D Heald and N Geaughan, 'The Private Financing of Public Infrastructure', in G Stoker, (ed), *The New Management of British Local Governance* (London: Macmillan, 1999) 222.

11 A Talbot-Smith, S Gnani, A Pollock, and D Gray, 'Questioning the Claims from Kaiser' (2004) 54 *British Journal of General Practice* 415.

12 P Hoggett, *Modernisation, Political Strategy and the Welfare State* (Bristol: SAUS, 1990), 32.

13 I Leigh, *Law, Politics and Local Democracy* (Oxford: Oxford University Press, 2000) 179.

14 M Freedland, 'Public Law and Private Finance – Placing the Private Finance Initiative in a Public Law Frame' [1998] PL 288, 307.

be achieved through pressures associated with competition or contestability, and is not dependent therefore on change of ownership per se.[15] The need for constitutional mechanisms and procedures for subjecting official decision making on public services to detailed scrutiny is a recurring theme of the argument in Parts 3 and 4 of the book.

Policy purposes

The policy agenda underpinning the New Public Contracting may be explored in accordance with the methodology suggested by Perri 6. This entails deducing governmental purposes with reference to the 'foreseeable consequences' of the design of regulatory schemes, with due regard to policy statements and available published materials.[16] The aims of CCT and related public service reforms beginning after 1979 thus included:[17]

- reducing the size of the public sector and therefore public expenditure;
- limiting the adverse impact of local government spending on macro-economic policy;
- increasing the efficiency of public bodies by subjecting them to competitive pressures;
- expanding opportunities for private enterprise and encouraging the development of private markets;
- weakening the power of the public service trade unions and undermining national pay bargaining;
- protecting industrial ratepayers from higher local taxation; and
- encouraging local authorities to adopt market solutions to service delivery problems.

After the 1983 general election CCT and market testing crystallized as coherent policies with both economic and political objectives.[18] Policy developments at this time were part of a wider governmental effort addressing a range of economic, ideological, and political dimensions of the crisis of the modern welfare state. Local authorities were an obvious target of the Conservative reformers, perceived as bastions of socialism ideologically committed to policies incompatible with

[15] Lewis (n 2 above) 122.

[16] Perri 6 (n 5 above) 245. The methodology suggested by Perri 6 involves following explicitly claimed intentions wherever possible, then reconstructing goals from foreseeable consequences of the design of schemes only where that method fails. However, purported intentions should arguably be treated with greater circumspection.

[17] See B Abbott, R Blackburn, and J Curran, 'Local Authority Privatisation and Markets for Small Business' (1996) 22 *Local Government Studies* 72; C Harlow and R Rawlings, *Law and Administration* (London: Butterworths, 1997) 252; D Oliver, *Government in the United Kingdom: The Search for Accountability, Effectiveness and Citizenship* (Milton Keynes: Open University Press, 1991) ch 5; M Radford, 'Competition Rules: The Local Government Act 1988' (1988) 51 MLR 747.

[18] Radford (n 17 above) 749.

those of central government, involving high public spending, stimulating local employment, and promoting industrial democracy.[19]

The overarching theme of New Labour policy on public services has been restated on a number of occasions since the 2001 election.[20] Coupled with the continuing commitment to the principle of free access to public services according to need, the reform agenda requires the development of a competitive mixed economy of provision. Public service quasi-markets are to be made responsive through mechanisms of consumer choice, enabling pressures to be exerted by the ultimate service recipients on public managers performing public purchasing functions on their behalf. Purchasing agencies are being encouraged to award contracts to providers who offer the best value regardless of their location in the public, private or non-profit sectors. Public purchasers and providers are subject to pressures from central government through national frameworks of standards accompanied by performance indicators and targets, with failure resulting in sanctions and ultimately central intervention, while success is rewarded with increased freedoms from central control in accordance with the principle of 'earned autonomy'. These developments are examined in detail in Chapter 8.

At a deeper level, state power in capitalist societies is conceived in Marxist analysis as being exercised for the purpose of maintaining and restoring the conditions of capital accumulation. The reason why public service organization through the market is preferred to direct state provision is that it is more consistent with this goal, avoiding the negative effects associated with withdrawing money from the 'immediate circuit of capital'.[21] A similar logic underlies policies directed at improving domestic productivity and thereby increasing international competitiveness. Here New Labour faces a dilemma. On the one hand it remains committed to the principle of public services paid for out of general taxation and free at the point of delivery. In order to counter decades of under-investment and to improve public services to a standard comparable with the rest of Europe, an increasing proportion of GDP will be devoted to public services over the next five years. On the other hand, given very low economic growth, there is the problem of how such increased funding will be sustained while meeting tight public borrowing and fiscal targets.

This dilemma is being addressed in various ways through the New Public Contracting. This mode of regulation may be regarded as a mechanism for promoting changes in administrative and economic organization entailing: the reduction of the Public Sector Borrowing Requirement (PSBR) and state expenditure on certain forms of public service; the shifting of responsibilities for funding into

[19] Oliver (n 17 above) 71; J Painter and M Goodwin, 'Local Governance and Concrete Research: Investigating the Uneven Development of Regulation' (1995) 24 *Economy and Society* 334, 352.

[20] T Blair, *The Courage of Our Convictions: Why Reform of the Public Services is the Route to Social Justice* (London: Fabian Society, 2002).

[21] B Jessop, *State Theory: Putting the Capitalist State in its Place* (Cambridge: Polity Press, 1990) 354.

the private and voluntary sectors; and the avoidance of short-term costs of financing public infrastructure in key areas such as health and education through the PFI. Savings may be made through abolition of publicly funded activities that can no longer be justified, or through privatization. The transfer of responsibility for funding to the private sector has the twin merit of reducing central government's demand for resources, and generating tax revenues from the new private sector provider. Regardless of the ultimate coherence of these policies, the 'savings' thereby generated have enabled the Government (at least until very recently) to target increased public spending elsewhere without violating its own or EU limits on the budget deficit. Savings may be made also through increased efficiencies resulting from greater productivity in the coordination of resources involved in the production of public services.

Overall, there has been continuity with the policies on privatization and contractualization begun in the 1980s. If anything, New Labour has re-invigorated and extended such policies into new areas of the public service. The major difference between Labour and Conservative approaches to reform, following widespread acknowledgement of the failures of crude 'command and control', lies not in policy ends but in the regulatory means being deployed for their attainment.[22]

Policy development

The New Public Contracting has been marked by a general lack of transparency in policy development and implementation. The period of Conservative government from 1979 saw a decline in public consultation and debate in the legislative process, with a trend away from Royal Commissions, official inquiries and Green Papers, and fewer White Papers.[23] Changes in parliamentary procedure further restricted the opportunity for debate through 'guillotine' motions, and there was a marked increase in provisions enabling primary legislation to be amended by ministers in secondary legislation without full parliamentary scrutiny. Major structural reforms were implemented, for example in local government, with little consultation or debate in contrast to earlier reforms that had been preceded by years of deliberation.[24] Given the general lack of debate and consultation over the principles and purposes of legislation both in Parliament and in the public arena more generally, it is unsurprising that law-making in this period is widely considered to have lacked legitimacy.

[22] P Vincent-Jones, 'Values and Purpose in Government: Central-local Relations in Regulatory Perspective, (2002) 29 JLS 27.

[23] The general experience was of 'fewer consultative documents being issued, containing less information and analysis, and often being produced on a timetable which seems to defeat the ostensible objective of the exercise' – M Loughlin, *Legality and Locality: The Role of Law in Central-Local Government Relations* (Oxford: Clarendon Press, 1996) 387. Consultation documents assumed an increasingly promotional rather than exploratory form.

[24] Leigh (n 13 above) 16–22.

Since Labour came to power following the 1997 general election there has arguably been greater consultation over the agenda for modernizing government, and legislative programmes appear to have had a more popular mandate. The replacement of CCT by the less prescriptive regime of best value under the Local Government Act 1999 was proclaimed as marking a new spirit of consensus and cooperation following a period in which public services had been marred by conflict and the 'the trench-warfare of centralism'.[25] There was a two-year period of consultation, following widespread publicity given the twelve core 'principles' of best value. The legislative process followed the traditional pattern involving Green and White Papers. Policy was refined in light of the experience of pilot schemes conducted in England and Wales. The Government took account of academic research on the on-going experiences of best value pilot authorities. There was similar cooperation between affected interests in efforts to resolve problems with existing regulations that might interfere with best value arrangements, in the areas of contract compliance and TUPE.[26] Generally, affected bodies and interests were consulted and involved in key aspects of the policy process,[27] for example in relation to the development of best value performance indicators and inspections.

Despite the appearance of increased public participation and democratic involvement, however, Labour's version of the New Public Contracting falls far short of responsiveness in the sense of collaborative regulation discussed in Chapter 4. The policy process continues to be highly centralized and top-down in character. In Labour's second and third terms, this persisting trend has been accompanied by the attempt to de-politicize the trajectory of policy development through 'evidence based policy-making' (EBPM). 'What matters is what works' has become a favourite mantra of New Labour, constantly reiterated in government pronouncements and official documents. The rise of EBPM is explained by a range of factors, including the erosion of public trust in professionals and in privileged expertise, the wider availability of data in electronic forms, increasing capabilities in the research community, the demands of government for new measures of productivity driven by international competitiveness, and technological progress in the IT industry.[28]

However, claims that ideological and political considerations in policy development are being forsaken in favour of pragmatism are open to criticism on

[25] *Hansard*, HC (series 6) vol 323, col 171 (12 January 1999) (Dr Whitehead).

[26] There is now general agreement, for example, on the areas where it would be legitimate to ask questions about a contractor's employment record: *Hansard*, HC (series 6) vol 323, col 180 (12 January 1999) (Mrs King).

[27] The Improvement and Development Agency for local government, successor to the Local Government Management Board, was launched on 1 April 1999. Its mission is to assist local authorities improve their performance, encourage training and peer review, develop skills of council members, managers and staff, and to commission, evaluate and disseminate best practice.

[28] H Davies, S Nutley, and P Smith, 'Introducing Evidence-based Policy and Practice in Public Services', in HT Davies, SM Nutley, and PC Smith, (eds), *What Works? Evidence-based Policy and Practice in Public Services* (Bristol: The Policy Press, 2000) 2.

a number of grounds. This philosophy tends to presuppose that policy goals are non-problematic or uncontentious, focusing attention narrowly on the strategies or interventions necessary to implement them. The assumptions of rationality in the policy process in some versions of EBPM are difficult to sustain, displaying a naïve modernist faith in progress informed by reason.[29] Evidence of what works does not feed automatically into the policy process in a linear fashion; rather responsive policy-making and evaluation requires that deliberations should be 'evidence-influenced' or 'evidence aware'.[30]

Again, piloting may be regarded as a potentially responsive form of policy-making. It suggests a provisional, experimental approach, as seen for example in schemes for beacon councils, education action zones, best value, and health action zones.[31] It is suggestive of a more consultative and collaborative style of regulation than was typically the case under the Conservatives. The attempt to ground policy making in more reliable knowledge of what works may be defended as an element of governance of complex social systems through 'reflexive social learning'.[32] Piloting may in theory be associated with a bottom-up policy process in which implementation by practitioners is dialectically related to the development and refinement of policy, a form of organizational learning or learning by doing as these terms have been defined in Chapter 4. However, the suggestion that policy making is more responsive in this sense under Labour compared with the Conservatives is again open to challenge. On a more cynical view, piloting may be used as a means of undermining resistance to the introduction of unpopular or contentious policies. The policy and the form of its implementation may already have been decided. A related criticism of piloting is that the benefits of openness and participation in the early stages may be lost when the policy is adopted and 'finalized', preventing further refinement. The responsive potential of piloting depends on how the exercise is conducted. Any limited democratization of the policy process as might have occurred over the past ten years does not begin to address the fundamental problems of legitimacy surrounding the New Public Contracting.

Contracting regimes

A regulatory regime may be defined as 'a historically specific configuration of policies and institutions which structures the relationship between social interests,

[29] I Sanderson, 'Evaluation, Policy Learning and Evidence-Based Policy Making' (2002) 80 *Public Administration* 1; J Newman, '"What Counts Is What Works"? Constructing Evaluations of Market Mechanisms' (2001) 79 *Public Administration* 89.

[30] Davies et al (n 28 above) 10; I Sanderson, 'Performance Management, Evaluation and Learning in "Modern" Local Government' (2001) 79 *Public Administration* 297.

[31] J Benington, 'The Modernization and Improvement of Government and Public Services' (2000) *Public Money and Management* (Apr–Jun) 3, 6.

[32] Sanderson (n 29 above).

the state, and economic actors in multiple sectors of the economy'.[33] Accordingly, a 'contracting regime' is a regulatory regime in which the mechanism of contract plays a principal or central role, supported by a range of other regulatory resources deployed by the state in efforts to attain determinate policy purposes.[34] The regulatory structures constituting administrative contracts, economic contracts, and social control contracts, as outlined in Chapter 1, may thus be conceived as contracting regimes. In practice these regimes are super-imposed, overlapping and reinforcing one-another in particular sectors. Hence the performance targets agreed in administrative contracts between parts of government in PSAs and framework documents are reflected more concretely in the commitments undertaken by public agencies in social control contracts and economic contracts.

Cascades of contracts

Another way of conceptualizing the relationship between different regulatory structures comprising the New Public Contracting is through the metaphor of a cascading series of contracts. This notion originates in Boston's account of the reformed health care sector in New Zealand.[35] Here there are 'contracts' of various kinds between the Minister of Health and the Ministry of Health, between the ministry (the main funder) and the regional health authorities (the purchasers), between those authorities and the major providers (including Crown health enterprises, private commercial suppliers and the voluntary sector), and between the major providers and sub-contractors. A similar set of relationships between different levels of administration of public services can be seen in the United States.[36] In Britain also, the metaphor of a cascade captures the manner in which particular contracting roles performed by public agencies are the result of contractual policy objectives expressed at higher levels within government, reflecting the system of overall management of public services through target outputs and outcomes oriented to frameworks of national

[33] MA Eisner, *Regulatory Politics in Transition* (Baltimore: John Hopkins University Press, 2000). The term is understood here to refer to the structuring of relations more broadly, within government and in the maintenance of social control as well as in economic organization. A key question is how to make regulatory regimes accountable – J Freeman, 'Private Parties, Public Functions and the New Administrative Law' (2000) 52 *Administrative Law Review* 814, 857–8.

[34] For a different usage of 'contract regime' see M Considine, 'Contract Regimes and Reflexive Governance: Comparing Employment Service Reforms in the United Kingdom, the Netherlands, New Zealand and Australia' (2000) 78 *Public Administration* 613.

[35] Boston (1996) (n 4 above).

[36] Freeman notes that 'the delivery of social welfare and services is accomplished through a series of contracts: those struck between governments and those subsequently negotiated between a government agency and a private provider. Government-provider contracts are meant to specify the terms under which private providers will implement the agency's policy decisions (which themselves are ostensibly designed to implement legislative will)' – J Freeman, 'The Private Role in Public Governance' (2000) 75 *New York University Law Review* 543, 597.

standards. The different New Public Contracting forms thus embody a common contractual governance technique for organizing public services, from the highest echelons of public administration and management to the lower levels at which discretion is exercised by public purchasers in economic decision making, or by other public agencies performing social control functions.[37] The cascade of contracts in Britain may be distinguished from that in other countries by the particularly high degree of central coordination and the role of central government in setting standards, monitoring performance, and ultimately enforcing compliance.[38]

In this light contracting regimes may be considered a form of government 'at a distance',[39] a complex mechanism of coordination combining central steering with the devolution and delegation of powers to responsibilized public agencies. In economic contracts, for example, the purchaser-provider relationship and the contracting process are relatively independent of direct government control. In place of bureaucratic organization is a network model in which 'multiple organizations of different types, sizes and missions often collide and conflict as much as they cooperate to serve human needs'.[40] Contracting regimes link members of heterogeneous networks in particular ways.[41] Public purchasing agencies (such as local councils, health and education authorities) exercise a range of discretionary contracting powers, monitoring and evaluating the performance of service providers in accordance with contract terms, specifications and standards. In many cases their discretion extends to the prior decision whether a service should be outsourced (rather than remain in-house) or provided under some other arrangement such as a public/private partnership.

Despite such autonomy, however, these agencies are themselves subject to varying degrees of regulation and control by central government, in accordance with the arrangements established in their governing contracting regimes. The operation of contract as a system of regulation which is itself subject to regulation is

37 For example, the targets agreed by the Department of Health with the Treasury, which are part of the 'New NHS Plan', are reflected in the contractual planning of PCTs as public purchasing agencies. These output specifications are oriented to the standards that are published in documents such as the Citizen's Charter and other charters to help inform service users of the nature and quality of services they can reasonably expect.

38 This idea is implicit in Freedland and King's notion of 'hierarchy', or pyramid of contracts comprising micro- and macro- levels of operation of governmental contractualism – M Freedland, and D King, 'Contractual Governance and Illiberal Contracts: Some Problems of Contractualism as an Instrument of Behaviour Management by Agencies of Government' (2003) 27 *Cambridge Journal of Economics* 465, 470.

39 Miller and Rose stress the importance of indirect mechanisms of government that link the conduct of individuals and organizations to political objectives through 'action at a distance' – P Miller and N Rose, 'Governing Economic Life' (1990) 19 *Economy and Society* 1.

40 DeHoog, Ruth Hoogland, and LM Salamon, 'Purchase-of-Service Contracting', in LM Salamon, (ed), *The Tools of Government: A Guide to the New Governance* (Oxford: Oxford University Press, 2002) 331.

41 On private sector network relations see H Collins, 'Ascription of Legal Responsibility to Groups in Complex Patterns of Economic Integration' (1990) 53 MLR 731.

suggestive of meta-regulation, as defined in Chapter 4.[42] The powers devolved to public agencies are set within national frameworks of public service standards. Local and public authorities are under continuing pressure through market testing and similar policies to deliver high standards through contracting out and other competitive arrangements rather than direct provision. This highly purposive form of regulation preserves central government controls and powers of intervention for the enforcement of government policy. The freedom of public purchasing agencies under economic contracting regimes is strictly limited and contingent. The question to be explored in Chapters 7 and 8 is whether this mode of governance succeeds, or is capable of succeeding, where markets and hierarchies are regarded for various reasons as having failed.

Regulatory mechanisms

As we saw in Chapter 4, the state may be viewed as a purposeful actor pursuing determinate policy objectives through the deployment of regulatory instruments of force, wealth, information, and competition. I will illustrate the use of such instruments, and the important link with the regulatory strategy of collibration in the regulatory environment of contracting regimes, before considering the role of complementary governmental techniques in the subsequent section.

Firstly, as regards force, the prominent role of compulsion in early forms of the New Public Contracting is well illustrated in the regulation of local authority public services through CCT.[43] Under New Labour, there has been a distinct shift towards greater reliance on other regulatory mechanisms, with increasingly varied 'dominium' incentives and competitive pressures being combined with more subtle forms of 'imperium'.[44] Nevertheless, legislative commands backed by monitoring and sanctioning machinery remain a fundamental feature of the New Public Contracting. The change in regulatory style under New Labour implies neither decentralization nor the disappearance of force. Although public agencies involved in the organization of housing, education, and health services enjoy a degree of autonomy in the exercise of purchasing and other coordinating functions, their freedom is circumscribed by various forms of central oversight and control. Widely drafted default powers in best value and other legislation leave considerable scope for central 'emergency intervention' in the affairs of both service providers and public purchasing agencies.[45]

[42] C Parker, C Scott, N Lacey, and J Braithwaite, (eds), *Regulating Law* (Oxford: Oxford University Press, 2004).

[43] P Vincent-Jones, 'Hybrid Organization, Contractual Governance, and Compulsory Competitive Tendering in the Provision of Local Authority Services', in S Deakin and J Michie, (eds) *Contracts, Cooperation and Competition: Studies in Economics, Management and Law* (Oxford: Oxford University Press, 1997), 143.

[44] Vincent-Jones (n 22 above).

[45] See Ch 2, above.

A feature of economic contracting regimes is the ease with which rules and commands may be fine-tuned to the particular circumstances of agencies performing public functions.[46] Less obviously, regulatory fine-tuning occurs through the selective *relaxation* of prohibitive rules, for example those governing the finances of local authorities and NHS Trusts. 'Beacon' authorities and hospitals that meet central government's criteria of excellent performance may be exempted from financial controls and restrictions that would otherwise apply, reflecting the philosophy that central interference should vary inversely with the demonstrable ability of authorities to manage their own affairs.[47] The relaxation of financial prohibitions has also been used, in conjunction with the granting of new powers for specific purposes, as a means of inducing public authorities to explore new forms of service provision in partnership with the private sector.[48] Contractors (whether in the private, voluntary or public sectors) are subject to various forms of direct and indirect regulation by government.[49] The relationship with government is underpinned by the principle of 'earned autonomy'. Increased freedoms for the best-performing authorities are balanced by sanctions for persistent under-achievers. Rewards take various forms,[50]

46 For example, public authorities must have regard to any guidance issued by the Secretary of State concerning the conduct of best value reviews and the making of performance plans. Additional duties may be imposed individually on different authorities, applying at different times. Authorities may be required to consider or assess their objectives, performance and progress in relation to any particular function, or whether they should be exercising the function at all.

47 P Vincent-Jones, 'Central-Local Relations under the Local Government Act 1999: A New Consensus?' (2000) 63 MLR 84.

48 P Vincent-Jones, 'From Housing Management to the Management of Housing: The Challenge of Best Value', in D Cowan and A Marsh, (eds), *Two Steps Forward: Housing Policy Into the New Millennium* (2001) (Bristol: Policy Press, 2001). Where councils have decided to retain housing stock, they are being encouraged to separate this ownership function from that of housing management through the PFI. Such schemes allow access to private finance unencumbered by public expenditure controls, without having to transfer ownership. In this type of PFI arrangement, the winning bidder is responsible for raising the funds to do the work (eg refurbishment works, continuing management, repairs and maintenance services) with payment by the authority on a performance basis and in the form of annual service fees under a long-term contract rather than initial capital expenditure. In a separate initiative, new regulations will permit the setting up of arm's-length companies, *controlled* or *influenced* by the local authority, to perform the specific function of housing management, so bypassing the normal rule that capital expenditure restrictions apply to local authority companies unless ownership is completely transferred to the voluntary sector.

49 For an account of the informal 'Compact' governing the relationship between government and the voluntary sector in the UK after 1997, see J Kendall, 'The Mainstreaming of the Third Sector into Public Policy in England in the Late 1990s: Whys and Wherefores' (2000) 28 *Policy and Politics* 541.

50 Enhancing market rewards for desired behaviour may under certain conditions be an effective regulatory strategy – J Braithwaite, 'Rewards and Regulation', (2002) 29 JLS 12. Braithwaite argues against the use of rewards as a form of persuasion, unless they are produced by the market as opposed to government: 'My conclusion that rewards in markets are effective in shaping behaviour implies that *indirect regulatory strategies which have the effect of enhancing market rewards for desired behaviour* can be effective' (24) (emphasis supplied). Non-market rewards are argued to be inappropriate in the business sector due to problems of psychological reactance.

from direct financial inducements to the differential application of prohibitive rules.[51]

Secondly, the role of competition as a means of modifying the behaviour of local authorities and other public agencies has increased in recent years,[52] despite the demise of CCT and other explicit guidance. Government policy since 1997 has deliberately prioritized competition and other market arrangements involving public-private partnerships as methods for securing best value and better quality services. The key difference between Labour and previous Conservative policies is that competition is now being encouraged in a more subtle and less coercive manner. Rather than being prescribed for any particular function, the spirit of competition pervades entire regulatory frameworks. Local authorities, government departments, and executive agencies are under continuing pressure to outsource ancillary services to the private or voluntary sectors rather than provide them directly. They are likely to want to embrace competition and its corresponding contractual forms as a means of staving off more radical service-providing options that might involve the complete transfer of functions to the private sector or to independent companies beyond their control.[53]

In another sense, local authorities and public bodies are competing among themselves – for the achievement of performance targets and for position in league tables, for the rewards attaching to Beacon or foundation status, for the financial benefits associated with qualification for PFI and 'arm's-length' company schemes, and for the right to transfer housing stock to the private sector. Public sector providers are increasingly being required to compete for the right to supply core public services such as housing and education with providers in the private and voluntary sectors. Local authorities are required similarly to compete for recognition as primary vehicles for the promotion of innovation and partnership in the performance of public functions.[54] In a further sense, the rationale for encouraging public-private sector partnerships and joint ventures is to improve performance of public functions through the involvement of private management skills honed in organizations that have been operating under competitive market conditions.

Thirdly, the availability and circulation of information is playing an increasingly important part in regulatory processes. The relative performance of providers in the same and different sectors is being made increasingly transparent through information published in performance tables, which may inform future choices made by public purchasers or enable pressure to be brought to bear by consumers. Chapters 7 and 8 will consider in detail how the best value regime and initiatives

[51] Compliance with rules may be rewarded through their relaxation, while withdrawal of wealth benefits may serve a sanctioning purpose – T Daintith, 'The Techniques of Government', in J Jowell and D Oliver, (eds), *The Changing Constitution* (Clarendon Press: Oxford, 1994).

[52] C Hood, O James, C Scott, G Jones, and T Travers, *Regulation Inside Government: Waste-watchers, Quality Police and Sleaze-busters* (Oxford: Oxford University Press, 1999) 94.

[53] Vincent-Jones (n 43 above). [54] Loughlin (n 23 above) 108.

such as Service First (successor to the Citizen's Charter) have contributed to this process. The publication of performance information serves as a method for calling officials to account, requiring them to justify their priorities in comparison with other public agencies. Such information may also reveal disparities between providers that are not the product of conscious choice, may provide politicians with clear evidence of how officers are performing, and may enable any improvement or deterioration of performance within given authorities to be plotted over time.[55]

Finally, government routinely influences the behaviour of public agencies through the selective allocation of financial resources. Some public authorities performing New Public Contracting functions (for example the Legal Services Commission) are entirely dependent on central government funding. Others, such as local councils, have become dependent on government largesse through the successive imposition of public borrowing regulations and expenditure controls that have increasingly eroded their financial autonomy.[56]

The notion of balancing of forces in the regulatory environment of the New Public Contracting is central to the analysis sketched above and will be developed in greater detail in Part III. Overall, the operation of contracting regimes may fruitfully be analysed in terms of the balance struck between elements of coercion and directness on the one hand, and 'automaticity' on the other.[57] Competitive incentives associated with market testing and contracting out may be viewed as a deliberate strategy directed at adjusting the balance between state and private sector provision: 'If public bureaucracies are indolent or unreliable, contracting out key functions may increase rulership.'[58] State intervention in the contracting environment may also take the form of manipulating markets in order to increase competitive incentives in areas where they are weak or have not hitherto operated, as in the opening up of educational or health services to competition.[59] Facilitating competition between potential providers in the same sector, and between providers in different sectors, may be part of an overall regulatory strategy involving 'balancing operations' between different types of actor.[60] Maintaining the conditions of effective competition (combating monopolies,

[55] Leigh (n 13 above) 146. [56] Vincent-Jones (n 48 above). [57] See ch 3, above.

[58] C Hood, 'Which Contract State? Four Perspectives on Over-Outsourcing for Public Services' (1997) 56 *Australian Journal of Public Administration* 120, 124. This suggests a need for an ongoing process of competition between public and private sectors through market testing exercises, and the maintenance of direct state capacity to engage in such competition. 'Over-outsourcing', involving loss of that capacity and excessive reliance on external single suppliers where there is insufficient market competition, would be damaging to the functioning of the steering contract state thus conceived (125).

[59] For an account of the way in which quasi-markets in human services such as long term care may be structured according to various policy levers, such as cost capping, reduction in supply, means testing, and capital subsidies, see D Gibson and R Means, 'Policy Convergence: Restructuring Long-Term Care in Australia and the UK' (2000) 29 *Policy and Politics* 43.

[60] For example, performance improvements among local authorities are being sought by encouraging competition within the sector, and competition with the private and voluntary sectors.

ensuring transparency and fairness in tendering processes) is a major task of regulation.[61]

The balance of forces in the contracting environment is subject to adjustment through other policy instruments. The recent trend in England towards corporatization of service provider functions that have previously been organized bureaucratically may also be analysed in terms of collibration. The granting of legal capacities to hospital trusts (Foundation Hospitals) and education and training bodies (Academies, Training and Enterprise Councils), which formerly lacked legal personalities separate from public authorities, may be regarded as an attempt to create incentives for improved performance by altering the balance of power among key players in these sectors.[62] The increased autonomy of these public service providers is justified on the basis that it has been 'earned' through compliance with the government's strategy for public service reform. Corporatization in this sense may be implemented in a manner that preserves the susceptibility of the service provider to administrative law controls, in spite of the contractual basis of the relationship with the sponsoring public agency.[63]

Other regulatory strategies have focused on increasing opportunities for consumer 'voice' and 'choice' rather than on the creation of substantive rights exercisable against the service provider.[64] Present government policy on quasi-markets is placing ever-greater emphasis on such strategies for empowering users of welfare services.[65] Where competition exists or can be stimulated, the devolution of purchasing power to consumers to choose among alternative providers through earmarked budgets (vouchering) is being used increasingly as a mechanism for encouraging service improvements.[66] In sectors where competition is weak or there is monopoly of supply, 'voice' mechanisms may be

[61] Domestic and EU competition policy and public procurement rules set particular requirements for public services regarding the forms of competition and competitive tendering – Local Government Act 1988, s 17 (non-commercial considerations); Services Directive 92/50/EEC [1992] OJ L209; Public Services Contracts Regulations 1993, SI 1993/3228.

[62] Training and Enterprise Councils (TECs) were established through general powers exercised by the Secretary of State under s 25(1) of the Employment Act 1988 (amending s 2 of the Employment and Training Act 1973), to make arrangements for training for employment. City Technology Colleges (CTCs) were established under the Education Reform Act 1988, s 105(1), giving the Secretary of State powers to enter into agreement with any person for establishing and maintaining a CTC.

[63] *R v Governors of Haberdashers' Aske's Hatcham College Trust, ex p Tyrell* [1995] COD 399; The Times, 19 Oct. 1994.

[64] R Means, L Hoyes, R Lart, and M Taylor, 'Quasi-Markets and Community Care: Towards User Empowerment?', in Bartlett et al (eds) (1994), 174.

[65] Leigh (n 13 above) 147–158.

[66] Vouchering is much closer to the market than quasi-market purchasing by representative public agencies, and the most radical form of privatization short of outright service shedding – ES Savas, *Privatizing the Public Sector: How To Shrink Government* (Chatham House, 1982) 68–69. There is an ambiguity about vouchering: it may be considered a distinctive means of social welfare provision with a more client-centred emphasis than traditional mechanisms, or be part of a strategy of gradual progression towards real market organisation – AG Watts, 'Applying Market Principles to the Delivery of Careers Guidance Services: A Critical Review', in W Bartlett, JA Roberts, and J Le Grand, (eds) (1998), 249.

expected to play a more important role.[67] These aspects are examined in depth in Chapter 8.

Techniques of responsibilization

As we have seen in the discussion in Chapter 3, from the perspective of governmentality many of the regulatory processes just considered are expressed in (and synonymous with) the responsibilization of public agencies charged with the performance of public functions.[68] The focus here is on how actors operating at various levels within contracting regimes are made responsible, and more specifically on how power relations are constituted through forms of knowledge, calculation and evaluation that supplement regulatory institutions and mechanisms. The techniques and practices of accounting and audit are given particular attention. This perspective helps explain the apparent paradox of continuing centralization involving erosion of the traditional powers and autonomy of public authorities on the one hand, combined with less prescriptive regulation and even increased powers in certain fields on the other. The fundamental shift in the roles of a wide range of public authorities in fields such as education, health, and housing is being achieved, not by command and control, but through 'responsibilized autonomy'. The selective granting by central government of *increased* powers (to certain authorities for certain purposes and subject to certain conditions) is illustrative of responsibilization. The New Public Contracting implies a strong governance relationship between the state and public agencies, through the regulatory conditions attaching to powers granted and the subjection of these bodies to on-going monitoring and supervision by central government.

The theme of responsibilization in current political thinking is not necessarily linked with contract, having originated in and been associated with various other neo-liberal and communitarian agendas concerned with the balancing of rights and responsibilities.[69] The theme emerges clearly in government policy documents in such apparently diverse fields as the Treasury's Spending Reviews, and the Prison Service's efforts at rehabilitation.[70] Responsible behaviour (by

67 A Hirschman, *Exit, Voice and Loyalty: Responses to Decline in Firms, Organizations and States* (Cambridge, Mass: Harvard University Press, 1970). The encouragement of 'exit' from government services may be part of a load-shedding strategy in which competition is envisaged as occurring in the private and voluntary sectors, rather than between private/voluntary and public sector organizations.

68 The concept of responsibilization has not generally been developed in the business regulation literature. The 'nurturing of virtue' within organizations might be described as dependent on responsibilization, the process whereby the logic and rationality of regulatory aims becomes owned by and part of the modus operandi of the regulated entity – see F Haines, *Corporate Regulation: Beyond 'Punish or Persuade'* (Oxford: Clarendon Press, 1997) 235.

69 See chs 2 and 3, above.

70 In relation to prisoners, see S Pryor, 'The Responsible Prisoner: An Exploration of the Extent to which Imprisonment Removes Responsibility Un-necessarily and an Invitation to Change', Autumn 2001, www.homeoffice.gov.uk/docs/the_responsible_prisoner.pdf, accessed 23 August 2005. In education, the aim is to enable 'well led schools to take full responsibility for their mission' (para

government departments, education authorities, hospital trusts, local councils, youth offenders) is rewarded by freedoms from central controls that would otherwise continue to apply. Nevertheless, contract has a special contribution to make to responsibilization. The power of contract here stems partly from the voluntaristic ethos that ideally surrounds the making of contractual commitments. As has been seen, the New Public Contracting is not just an institutional response to the need for links between more fragmented agencies (public, private and voluntary) performing local public functions, rather it entails a distinctive way of thinking about public organization, with its own rationality and logic. The penetration of contracting as a technique of governance is evident in the increasingly varied use of contractual terminology and discourse in social contexts far removed from the lawyer's traditional concerns.[71] Contract provides a powerful basis, through its voluntaristic connotations of agreement, commitment and responsibility, for the *disciplining* of a wide range of social 'bodies'.

The processes of responsibilization that operate through the New Public Contracting are reinforced by governmental techniques of accounting and audit.[72] As regards accounting, the gradual imposition of new modes of financial calculation has been crucial to the transformation of the public sector. Financial management regimes have played a major part in reforming public bureaucracies and in displacing governance by traditional hierarchical norms. Developments in accounting technology have resulted in the incursion of financial rationality, with its vocabulary of costs, incomes, savings and profits, into all aspects of the operation of public authorities. Like other public sector organizations, local authorities have become increasingly accountable in these financial, rather than bureaucratic or professional terms. Under CCT, direct service organisations (DSOs) became cost centres with trading accounts, subject to 'accounting logic'.[73] Where NPM reforms have devolved decision making power to individuals or business units within organizations, the activities have been rendered governable in new ways, through the neutrality and objectivity of accounting.

Within the complex of financial techniques for the government of bureaucratic and professional expertise, audit is playing a key role.[74] Audit is part of a more general process that renders modern government possible and judgeable

1.5); the reform of secondary education is to be achieved, among other means, by 'giving successful schools the freedom they need to excel and innovate' (para 1.6); the problem of disruption in schools and promoting good behaviour is to be tackled by 'legislating to require parents to take greater responsibility for their children's behaviour' (para 3.33) – DfES, *Schools Achieving Success*, (Cm 5230, 2001).

71 P Vincent-Jones, 'Contractual Governance: Institutional and Organisational Analysis' (2000) 20 OJLS 317.

72 M Power, *The Audit Society: Rituals of Verification* (Oxford: Oxford University Press, 1997); ibid, 'Evaluating the Audit Explosion' (2003) 25 *Law and Policy* 185.

73 R Laughlin, 'Accounting Control and Controlling Accounting: The Battle for the Public Sector?, Sheffield University Management School Discussion Paper No 92.29 (1992).

74 N Rose, *Powers of Freedom: Reframing Political Thought* (Cambridge: Cambridge University Press, 1999) 153.

through quantitative information in the form of rates, tables, graphs, trends and numerical comparisons that enable the scrutiny of authority in contemporary society.[75] Through enumeration and quantification, governance is organized through objective principles and neutral 'facticity'. The formal autonomy of public authorities or of departments or business units within them may increase, at the same time as they become more governable through the use of techniques that render activities and decisions more visible and amenable to external scrutiny.

In essence audit involves the use of routines that 'purport to enable judgements to be made about the activities of professionals, managers, business people, politicians and many others'.[76] Government by audit 'transforms that which is to be governed' in a similar manner to accounting, in this instance through the emphasis on defined and measurable goals and targets, the setting of objectives, the standardization of forms of assessment, and new systems of record-keeping and accountability. In local government, the function of audit has shifted from ensuring that public money is spent lawfully and without fraud, to checking the reasonableness of discretionary expenditure and value for money in the delivery of services. Since 1982 the Audit Commission has been an enthusiastic promoter of NPM reforms, assuming an increasingly pro-active role in disseminating private management practice, undertaking studies into specific areas of public services, and overseeing and coordinating audit processes.[77] What is significant in the present context is not the statutory duties of the Commission or its oversight functions, but the methods and techniques on which its judgements are based. Under both best value and the Service First initiatives, audit takes the form of comparative evaluation of the relative performance of public authorities with reference to centrally determined performance indicators and standards, involving a combination of flat-rate and flexible (self-imposed) targets. The impact of audit (rendering transparent the decisions of councillors and officials over their priorities, revealing disparities that are not the product of conscious choice, providing politicians and consumers with evidence on how authorities are performing, and enabling comparison of performance over time within particular authorities[78]) is magnified through the increasingly detailed and sophisticated presentation of comparative information.

Relationality in regulatory relationships

The quality of relationality in the regulatory linkages and relationships comprising contracting regimes is a vital factor contributing to the responsiveness of the New Public Contracting. We saw in Chapter 1 how this quality denotes the presence

[75] ibid 198. [76] ibid 154.

[77] Leigh (n 13 above) 128. The Commission's role is expanding through increased powers under recent legislation to undertake comparative reviews of local authority functions as well as services – LGA 1999, s 19. [78] ibid 146.

of relational norms in those relationships to the degree necessary to foster trust and cooperation and thereby deliver both the mutual benefits intended by the parties, and the wider policy goals intended by government. Where regulatory linkages involve contract (ie in the restructuring of relations within government, and in the 'horizontal' purchaser–provider and state–citizen relationships in economic contracts and social control contracts respectively) responsiveness may be assessed with regard to the balance between discrete and relational norms within the contractual relationship and in its institutional environment. The 'extra-contractual' regulatory relationships between central government and regulated public agencies to whom contracting powers have been devolved in the economic organization and social control contexts may also be analysed in terms of relationality.[79]

As we shall see in the analysis of economic contracting regimes in Chapters 7 and 8, the complexity of quasi-market organization poses particular problems for regulatory design. The existence of multiple regulatory tiers is in contrast to the relative simplicity of self-regulation against the background of broad and open-textured standards that has been argued to characterize responsive market regulation.[80] The radical nature of quasi-market reforms and the rapidity of changes to traditional bureaucratic organization brought about by the process of contractualization might be expected to be the source of relational problems at all levels of the regulatory system. Where quasi-market organisation is promoted dogmatically in circumstances where hierarchical or other planned arrangements might have been more suitable, then 'trouble' for the contract norms can be expected. The highly substantive policy-driven welfare state reforms of the 1980s and 1990s may be considered in relational terms as having had various negative effects on the norms of solidarity, role integrity, power and the implementation of planning. Many of the reforms were imposed in the face of fierce opposition and with little public consultation, evaluation or debate.[81] In the hierarchical relationship between central government and public agencies performing public purchasing functions, the cooperation and mutual respect that characterized relationships between central government and public sector organizations in the immediate post-war period were replaced in many cases by antagonism and mistrust. Norms of reciprocity were undermined and eroded, and planning and consent norms enhancing discreteness and presentiation became intensified,[82]

79 In the 'as if' contractual sense, as explained in ch 1.

80 H Collins, *Regulating Contracts* (Oxford: Oxford University Press, 1999).

81 D Hughes, 'The Reorganization of the NHS – The Rhetoric and the Reality of the Internal Market' (1991) 54 MLR 88.

82 Problems associated with such intensification include ineffectiveness, game-playing and 'creative compliance'. Creative compliance may be described as 'the process whereby those regulated avoid having to break the rules by using legal techniques to achieve non-compliance with the intention of the law without technically violating its content' – see R Baldwin, 'Governing With Rules: The Developing Agenda', in G Richardson, and H Genn, (eds), *Administrative Law and Government Action: The Courts and Alternative Mechanisms of Review* (Oxford: Clarendon Press, 1994) 172;

particularly in local government where the costs of rule-making, monitoring and enforcement were excessive under CCT.

At the level of purchaser–provider relationships, the contract norms were particularly damaged by government policies enhancing discreteness at the expense of relationality. Many of the dysfunctional consequences of the introduction of contracting regimes in the health, education and local government sectors have arguably been attributable to the implementation of artificially discrete models of contracting. Trust and cooperation are hallmarks of responsiveness. While we established in Chapter 1 that responsiveness is not exhaustively defined by trust and cooperation,[83] it is unlikely that efficient and effective outcomes will be achieved where the contract norms are damaged or 'in trouble'. This responsive regulation/relational contract approach stresses the need to take into account all the constituencies involved in contractual processes, beyond the interests of 'the parties' whether as individuals or as contracting pairs.

The question for empirical analysis is whether the New Public Contracting, in its most recent incarnation under New Labour, avoids the costs of the failure of previous policy-driven contracting regimes in their undermining of conditions of relationality. The aim of my substantive analysis of the New Public Contracting in Part 3 is fully to locate administrative, economic, and social control contracts in their wider regulatory context. The focus therefore is on: (1) the balance of the contract norms (discrete and relational) within the contractual relationships and in their immediate institutional environment; and (2) the effects of any other regulatory processes, systems, or instruments on the operation and governance of the contractual relationships. The latter dimension is in recognition of the fact that contract as a tool of government is necessarily surrounded by, and operates in the context of, other regulatory mechanisms.[84]

Conclusion

The analysis in Part III will focus on how the conditions of responsiveness in all the senses considered in this chapter are affected by the regulatory constraints inherent in contracting regimes. For example, the performance of bodies such as local councils, education authorities, or health service purchasers in their public contracting roles is dependent on the policy climate set by central government, and in particular on the degree to which this fosters or constrains innovation at the local level. The prescription of policy in minute detail by civil servants is not

D McBarnet and C Whelan, 'The Elusive Spirit of the Law: Formalism and the Struggle for Legal Control' (1991) 54 MLR 848, 873.

[83] W Seal and P Vincent-Jones, 'Accounting and Trust in the Enabling of Long-Term Relations' (1997) 10 *Accounting, Auditing and Accountability Journal* 406, 410.

[84] J Kooiman, 'Social-Political Governance: Introduction', in J Kooiman, (ed), *Modern Governance: New Government-Society Interactions* (London: Sage Publications, 1993) 2.

conducive to the development of a culture of creative adaptation and problem-solving that is necessary for responsive public services.[85] A common theme across all forms of the New Public Contracting is the stifling of innovation by the proliferation of centrally driven targets and performance indicators. The nature of the performance management regime in Britain, in particular, has been argued to hamper rather than promote organizational learning and improvement.[86] In local government, the tight coupling of central government policy and local authority implementation under best value has been argued to inhibit the capacity of local authorities to respond to local issues and agendas.[87] Yet local government is widely recognized as having greater potential than central government in responding to local needs.[88]

There is an obvious tension in New Labour's public service vision between the benefits that are claimed to have accompanied the devolution of powers to public service managers and front line staff on the one hand, and continuing central government control and restrictions imposed on local policy development and adaptation on the other.[89] The Government claims that its current philosophy is distinguished from that of the post-1945 welfare state by the movement away from the 'top-down, one-size-fits-all, command and control' approach to one that empowers consumers by giving them choice,[90] yet many economic contracts, as will be seen in Chapters 7 and 8, are characterized by excessive central control and the weakness or complete absence of genuine consumer choice or citizen empowerment. In administrative contracts also, regulatory problems are associated with the failure to develop bottom-up approaches to policy making and implementation that might lead to more genuinely responsive public services.

The main question for substantive analysis in the remainder of the book is whether the New Public Contracting, in its attempt to combine central control and local autonomy, is capable of overcoming this tension and of increasing responsiveness in the performance of public service functions.

85 J Newman, J Raine, and C Skelcher, 'Transforming Local Government: Innovation and Modernization' (2001) *Public Money and Management* (Apr–Jun), 61.

86 Sanderson (n 29 above).

87 Newman *et al.* (n 85 above).

88 As is recognized in the principle of subsidiarity in EU law – see D Oliver, *Government in the United Kingdom: The Search for Accountability, Effectiveness and Citizenship* (Milton Keynes: Open University Press, 1991) 72.

89 K Ascher, *The Politics of Privatisation: Contracting Out Public Services* (Houndmills: Macmillan, 1987) 269. In the late 1980s Ascher's early study of privatization and contracting out noted the highly politicized nature of the policy, and warned that effectiveness and responsiveness might be compromised by the highly centralized nature of the policy initiatives, by comparison with earlier voluntary pragmatic developments in local government.

90 *Guardian* 29 April 2003.

PART III

THE NEW PUBLIC CONTRACTING

6

Administrative Contracts

This chapter charts the shift away from traditional bureaucratic organization towards the use of contract as a mechanism for structuring relations within government. Two main variants of administrative contracts are considered: framework documents linking executive agencies and government departments, and Public Service Agreements governing relationships between the Treasury and spending departments. With reference to the concept of contracting regimes introduced in Chapter 5, I examine the operation of contract norms in structuring, confining, or checking the exercise of public power in these relationships. The particular focus is on how the regulatory arrangements impact on the autonomy of subordinate parties (spending departments, executive agencies), as regards both the fairness of terms of contracts and safeguards against unwarranted interference by the dominant party (the Treasury, parent departments). The final section subjects to critical scrutiny the system of performance management running through all levels of the contractual organization of public services.

From public administration to administrative contracts

The traditional model of the civil service built on the Northcote-Trevelyan reforms of the nineteenth century entailed organization of governmental functions in and through departments.[1] The first half of the twentieth century saw a gradual process of centralization, with many public functions that had previously been performed by local government or boards being transferred to new departments or sections of existing departments in central government. Problems of size and inefficiency with the central departmental structure were first identified in the 1960s in the Fulton Committee Report,[2] which recommended clearer allocation of responsibilities and authority, and the movement of some activities outside the departmental framework. While this led to the creation of a number of agencies with specific regulatory roles,[3] the real spur to the development of agencies within government

[1] The constitutional basis of this model was ministerial responsibility with the corollary of civil service neutrality and anonymity – P Craig, *Administrative Law* (4th ed, London: Sweet and Maxwell, 1999), 89.

[2] *Report of the Committee on the Civil Service 1966–68* (Cmnd. 3638, 1968).

[3] For example, the Health and Safety Commission, the Manpower Services Commission, and the Civil Aviation Authority.

came in 1979 with the establishment of the Efficiency Unit, under first Lord Rayner and then Sir Robin Ibbs. The Ibbs ('Next Steps') Report in 1988 was the culmination of various scrutinies aimed at reducing waste and improving efficiency in the civil service. Government departments were already being encouraged to clarify financial responsibilities and management objectives under the Financial Management Initiative (FMI). Next Steps took this a stage further, recommending the splitting of policy-making and service-providing roles, and increasing the devolution of management powers to a larger number of executive agencies with greater financial autonomy and responsibility for service delivery. Together these developments represented a radical shift in governance, reflecting a 'neo-liberal strategy of anti-bureaucracy':

> No longer would bureaucracy authorize itself through its ethical claims: it would focus on the delivery of services, and be judged according to its capacity to produce results. It would be governed indirectly, through contracts, targets, performance measures, monitoring and audit.[4]

In contrast to other types of agency based on statute or the prerogative,[5] the powers and responsibilities of a Next Steps agency are contractually defined in the framework document agreed with its parent department. Agencies are responsible for the attainment of performance targets set out in annual business plans drawn up in accordance with their framework documents.

The introduction of Public Service Agreements (PSAs) in 1998 as part of the first Comprehensive Spending Review may be considered an extension of the contractual approach already established in relationships between central departments and executive agencies. The aim was to help deliver better value-for-money in public services by replacing the annual Public Expenditure Survey with firm plans set for three years. The claimed advantage for departments is greater certainty in planning expenditure. For its part the Treasury is freed from the process of annual bidding rounds, and able to take a more strategic view of the effectiveness of public spending. A further benefit in theory is that the 'new centre' is able to exert increased control by making the allocation of funding contingent upon specific service commitments which are expressed as outcomes to be achieved by spending departments.

Administrative contracting regimes

Chapter 1 outlined the relatively simple regulatory structure of administrative contracts as a form of the New Public Contracting. Here bureaucratic/hierarchical regulation is cast in an explicitly contractual form – contract being the mechanism

[4] N Rose, *Powers of Freedom: Reframing Political Thought* (Cambridge: Cambridge University Press, 1999) 151.

[5] Craig (n 1 above) 95.

linking superior and subordinate levels within the government hierarchy (hence the term 'hierarchical regulation by contract').[6] This section shows how relations within government are structured through overlapping administrative contracting regimes.

Separation of interests

While both PSAs and framework documents entail contractual governance, they differ considerably in their nature and operation. Firstly, the creation of executive agencies implies the separation of political from certain administrative aspects of the work of government. A new type of relationship is thereby established between ministers responsible for policy making, and agency chief executives responsible for policy delivery. In the case of PSAs, by contrast, while again there is a distinction between strategic and service delivery roles, the division is drawn at the political level between Treasury/Cabinet Office ministers and secretaries of state of spending departments. Secondly, the separation of interests takes different forms in the Treasury–spending department and the department–agency relationships. In the former case the PSA regime serves to reinforce an already-existing organizational distinction by differentiating more clearly the respective roles of government departments. The use of framework documents, on the other hand, presupposes the specific creation of an agency in preference to continued departmental performance of the function. Framework documents are used to govern the separate interests thus created.

The arrangements differ in another important respect. Framework documents exhibit some of the characteristics of secondary or 'power-conferring' contracts,[7] serving as 'constitutions' or sets of rules governing processes of target-setting and performance management. Next Steps involves the deliberate attempt 'to restrict ministers to a strategic role in which they do not interfere in management decisions'.[8] A basic rationale for structuring relationships through framework documents is to guarantee the managerial autonomy of agency chief executives, subject to performance targets set out in business plans. PSAs, on the other hand, are far simpler in their nature and operation. In this respect they are more like primary contracts – substantive statements of the projected financial requirements and intentions of spending departments in their biennial bids for resources and negotiations with the Treasury, without a 'constitutional' dimension.

Nevertheless, framework documents and PSAs both operate as contractual mechanisms linking separate or separated interests within government. Policy making is undertaken at senior levels within government by the Treasury/new centre in relation to spending departments, and by all central departments in

[6] Donald F Kettl, 'Managing Indirect Government' in LM Salamon, (ed) *The Tools of Government: A Guide to the New Governance* (Oxford: Oxford University Press, 2002) 502.

[7] I Harden, *The Contracting State* (Buckingham: Open University Press, 1992) 31–32.

[8] ibid 35.

relation to executive agencies. Responsibility for policy delivery and service provision rests with both departments and executive agencies, in accordance with the strategic objectives set out in PSAs and framework documents respectively.

It was established in Part 1 that administrative contracts do not involve markets and competition. Only where there exists an explicit market orientation in the adoption of managerialist culture is it appropriate to describe the contracts as economic in nature.[9] While the use of administrative contracts changes the incentive structures under which civil servants operate in the attempt to make them more efficient and managerial in outlook, there is limited scope for entrepreneurial incentives or for encouraging bureaucrats to be more risk-taking.[10] In the absence of supply-side competition and purchaser choice, the relationships are necessarily hierarchical rather than quasi-market in character.[11] The Next Steps and PSA initiatives are informed by a managerialist agenda rather than by the logic of competition that applies, for example, to market testing and contracting out.[12] Market forces are associated with factors such as the emphasis on property rights as a source of power and control, an understanding of outputs as alienable commodities to which a price may be attributed, and some degree of freedom of choice in trading.[13] Whereas in the case of economic contracts the relationship between the parties is accurately expressed in the terminology of the 'purchaser-provider split', in the present instance the separation of interests is less complete. While PSAs and framework documents both literally involve the separation of roles and the payment of money (in the sense of the allocation of funding or resources) in return for implementing policy and delivering services,[14] contract here is about public administration rather than the economic coordination of public service production.

Governance issues

The separation of interests as just described need not be based on contract. Public management systems involving target setting and performance monitoring and evaluation can be hierarchically implemented within bureaucratic structures,

9 For a similar distinction between two forms of managerialism – one involving 'client' and the other 'market place' cultures – which corresponds broadly with the present distinction between administrative contracts and economic contracts, see E Wilson and A Doig, 'The Shape of Ideology: Structure, Culture and Policy Delivery in the New Public Sector' (1996) *Public Money and Management* (Apr–Jun) 53.

10 K Dowding, 'Managing the Civil Service', in R Maidment and G Thompson, (eds), *Managing the United Kingdom* (London: Sage, 1993) 241.

11 See ch 1, above.

12 G Jordan, 'From Next Steps to Market Testing: Administrative Reform as Improvisation' (1994) 9 *Public Policy and Administration* 21.

13 'Real trading implies the users of the services would have complete freedom to buy from where they wanted, and the provider of services would have complete freedom whether or not they wanted to deal with the user' – M Mackintosh, 'Trading Work: Discourses of Internal Exchange in the Economic Culture of Local Government' (1997) 12 *Public Policy and Administration* 17, 23.

14 M Robinson, 'Contract Budgeting' (2000) 78 *Public Administration* 75.

as is commonly the case in North America and Canada, without the need for specifically *contractual* governance. The use of contracts in such contexts may be problematic for various reasons. The 'separation within' public bodies may confuse lines of responsibility and accountability, and restrict organizational learning and the sharing of information between separated purchaser and provider units.[15] The potential efficiency and accountability benefits of contracting have to be balanced against the drawbacks of any contracting system, including increased transaction costs, monitoring problems, loss of micro-management capacity, and difficulties associated with contractual incompleteness and rigidity.[16] Accordingly the analysis of policy-guided choice in Chapter 2 has established that the scope of investigation of the responsiveness of administrative contracts includes consideration of the decision-making processes resulting in their adoption. We return to this issue in the discussion of procedural legal reform in Chapter 11.

As we have seen, contract ideally provides a mechanism by which the parties may achieve their desires through relationships of mutual benefit that jointly maximise their individual utilities. By definition, all contracting behaviour displays elements of discreteness and presentiation – reducing uncertainty about the future, excluding irrelevant externalities, and narrowing social relations. The relatively discrete norms of planning, consent, and choice exist in balance with more relational norms, namely flexibility, reciprocity, solidarity, role integrity, power, propriety of means, and harmonization.[17] The task in the analysis of both types of administrative contract is therefore to illuminate and explain contracting behaviour with reference to the common contract norms. The main governance issues concern:

- the 'bindingness' of the arrangements in terms of both the credibility of commitments and the ability of the parties to enforce contractual obligations, supported by appropriate sanctioning machinery;
- the strength of representation of the norms of choice, consent, and reciprocity in the making of contracts;
- the quality of fairness in the performance of contracts, as regards both the application of sanctions by the dominant partner and the ability of the subordinate partner to enforce reciprocal commitments;
- the balance of power in terms of the autonomy of subordinate partners in the relationship (spending departments in relation to the Treasury, executive

15 J Stewart, 'The Limitations of Government by Contract' (1993) 13 *Public Money and Management* (Apr–Jun) 7–12.

16 BG Peters, 'Contracts as a Tool for Public Management: Their Strange Absence in North America', in Y Fortin, and H Van Hassel, (eds), *Contracting in the New Public Management – From Economics to Law and Citizenship* (Amsterdam: IOS Press, 2000).

17 IR Macneil, 'Relational Contract Theory: Challenges and Queries', (2000) 94 *Northwestern University Law Review* 877, 879–80.

agencies in relation to central departments), and freedom from unwarranted interference by the dominant partner; and

- the overall quality of contractual relationships, assessed in terms of the balance of relatively discrete and relational norms both within the relationship and in the institutional environment ('relationality').

Treasury–spending department relationship

As expressions of policy at the highest levels of government, PSA commitments have a significant influence on how public services are provided through contractual networks within and outside government.[18] The operation of these arrangements in practice may be compared with the management rhetoric of contractual targets, performance standards and increased public accountability surrounding them. The Spending Review process is considered across the four cycles that have taken place to date, in 1998, 2000, 2002, and 2004.

Public Service Agreements and Service Delivery Agreements

PSAs are 'statements of the aims and objectives of the various parts of government, together with a statement of the resources available and targets for the performance expected of them'.[19] They are negotiated and agreed in accordance with detailed guidance issued by the Treasury.[20] PSAs were published for the first time in December 1998, marking a 'fundamental change in the accountability of government to Parliament and the public.' The first PSAs were criticised for their variable and amorphous targets. Half the four hundred targets set in the 1998 review had been axed by 2000. In addition to the reduction in number, the targets were claimed to be better focused.[21] The 2000 Spending Review built on the earlier experience:

> The new PSA targets focus on key strategic objectives. These new PSAs set out for every major government department an aim, objectives and the targets against which success will be measured – including tough targets on improving value for money and efficiency across the public sector. They ... provide a clear commitment to the public on the improvements in services they can expect to receive for their money. Each agreement makes clear which Minister is accountable for delivering on the targets that underlie that

[18] S Lee and R Woodward, 'Implementing the Third Way: The Delivery of Public Services Under the Blair Government' (2002) *Public Money and Management* (Oct–Dec) 49, 51.

[19] *Treasury Select Committee, 7th Special Report of Session*, HC Paper (1998–99 no 849).

[20] HM Treasury paper PES (98) 29, 'Guidance on Public Service Agreements', 14 September 1998.

[21] per N Macpherson, head of Treasury's public services directorate, reported in *Guardian* 16 April 2002.

commitment. Progress in delivering the targets will be monitored closely and will be reported in departments' annual Departmental Reports.[22]

The 2000 review set new three-year spending plans up to 2003–04, using 2001–02 (the last year of the plans set in the 1998 CSR) as the first year of the new plans. The review concluded in July 2002 covered the period 2003–2006. There is some confusion caused by the rolling three-year review every two years. Many of the targets set in 2002 for 2005, for example, were modified or abandoned in the 2004 review, which covers the period 2005–2008.

Taking just one example from the 2000 round, the stated aim of the PSA for the Department for Education and Employment was 'to give everyone the chance, through education, training and work, to realise their full potential, and thus build an inclusive and fair society and a competitive economy'. The Department expressed three objectives, each with associated performance targets. The objectives were, first, to ensure that all young people reach sixteen with the skills, attitudes and personal qualities that will give them a secure foundation for lifelong learning, work and citizenship in a rapidly changing world; second, to develop in everyone a commitment to lifelong learning, so as to enhance their lives, improve their employability in a changing labour market, and create the skills that the economy and employers need; and finally, to help people without a job into work. The PSA specified responsibility and accountability in the following terms:

> The Secretary of State for Education and Employment is responsible for the delivery of this PSA. The Welfare to Work targets ... are the joint responsibility of the Secretary of State for Education and Employment, the Secretary of State for Social Security, and the Chancellor of the Exchequer. The Secretary of State for Education and Employment is also responsible at Cabinet level for the work of the Sure Start unit. The Minister for Public Health has day-to-day responsibility for the unit.[23]

The accompanying Technical Notes described in detail how progress with the PSA would be measured and monitored.

Since 2002, PSAs have been accompanied by Service Delivery Agreements (SDAs). These focus on the processes adopted by departments to ensure that their PSA targets are met, and include additional targets and commitments undertaken as part of the Government's wider programme for public service reform. For example, the 2002 PSA for the Department for International Development (DfID) specified four main objectives and six targets, covering poverty, international coordination, education and health, and value for money and effectiveness. A separate SDA elaborated in greater depth how the department would deliver

[22] *Prudent for a Purpose: Building Opportunity and Security for All, 2000 Spending Review: New Public Spending Plans 2001–2004* (Cm 4807, 2000) para 2.24. The review reiterates and brings together in a single document the commitments of all the spending departments, integrated into an overall plan for the forthcoming three-year period.

[23] *Department for Education and Employment, 2000 Spending Review: Public Service Agreements 2001–04* (Cm 4808, 2000).

the main objectives. The PSA and SDA were accompanied by Technical Notes containing statistical references and describing how progress would be measured.

Contract norms

The problems of attempting to implement performance management through PSAs may be analysed with reference to the common contract norms. The following assessment of the overall effectiveness and integrity of PSAs as a management technique focuses on the 2002 round, paying particular attention to the relationship between financial allocations then made and performance targets set in 2000.

The norm of consent is strongly associated with the existence of choice, or at least 'acquiescence' in being bound.[24] In practice, however, spending departments have 'little choice but to accept the deal proposed by the Treasury and backed by prime minister and cabinet',[25] even where they enjoy trading fund status and are self-supporting. The conditions under which consent or acquiescence in PSAs are obtained may impede the effectiveness of contract as a governance mechanism. While 'negotiations' over PSAs have often been protracted and in some cases may have involved mutual concessions,[26] there is little doubt where the ultimate authority lies. In 2002, PSA targets were set jointly by the Treasury and the No 10 Delivery Unit, headed by Michael Barber, confirming the power of the 'new centre' within government as discussed in Chapter 1. While the norm of choice further implies the ability of both parties to exit the relationship, spending departments cannot obtain funding other than through the Treasury, which in turn cannot transfer business to a different provider. The only sanction available to the 'purchaser' lies in de-prioritizing poor performers in failing areas at the expense of better performing departments. However, most governmental functions are of such significance that they could not be de-prioritized in this way. Furthermore, poor performance begs the question of the reasons for failure,[27] which may have as much to do with social problems and inadequacy of resources in addressing them, as with inefficiency on the part of the service providing department.

As regards the balance of power in the performance of PSAs, the Treasury Select Committee Report in 1998–99 specifically welcomed the potential for enhanced

[24] Macneil's analysis allows that acquiescence may be a basis of obligation. However, in such cases the norm of consent may only be weakly represented in the relationship – see ch 1.

[25] G Drewry, 'The Citizen and the New Contractual Public Management: The Quest for New Forms of Accountability and A New Public Law', in Y Fortin and H Van Hassel, (eds), *Contracting in the New Public Management – From Economics to Law and Citizenship* (Amsterdam: IOS Press, 2000) 259.

[26] The PSAs finalised in 1988 were the product of 'lengthy discussions' between Treasury and government departments – Treasury Select Committee Report (n 19 above) para 11.

[27] Targets might not be met for many reasons. For example, the dropping of the target by the Department of Transport for increasing rail use measured by passenger kilometres by 50% between 2000 and 2010 was obviously affected by the Hatfield train disaster.

autonomy of departments over the three-year period of the review, compared with the traditional annual cycle. But there is little evidence of such autonomy in practice. While an imbalance of power is arguably inherent in PSAs, in the sense that all administrative contracts necessarily involve 'hierarchical regulation by contract', there appears to be no constraint on the power of the Treasury, which is free to act in violation of the terms of the agreement. It is surely inconceivable that financial allocations are in any way guaranteed under the PSA, or that the centre lacks the power to alter or reduce projected spending commitments for a host of reasons unconnected with poor performance or 'breach' on the part of the ministry concerned.

In the rhetoric surrounding PSAs, much is made of the reciprocal nature of the arrangements. It is through qualities such as reciprocity that PSAs are supposed to supply motivation to deliver the Government's policy priorities, from enhancing literacy and improving numeracy to restructuring the armed forces.[28] A principal claim is that money is 'allocated in return for agreements to achieve quantified improvements in public services.'[29] The Chancellor has stated explicitly that investment in public services that are provided by government departments is 'in return for' reform in the way in which the services are managed. The implication is that departmental budgets will be linked increasingly to performance judged in relation to PSAs, and that increases in funding are therefore dependent on demonstrable achievement of departments in meeting targets. In practice, however, the allocation of resources appears to have little bearing on past or projected performance, having more to do with factors beyond the control of spending departments such as the rate of growth of GDP and Treasury-imposed borrowing constraints. A further problem with reciprocity concerns the ambiguous position of members of the public who are not signatories to the PSA, but for whose benefit the service functions are ultimately performed. In some government pronouncements PSAs are described as agreements with the public,[30] while in others the implication is that services are delivered to the public as third parties to the contract between the Treasury and spending departments.[31]

This discussion leads to issue of the 'bindingness' of PSAs, as regards both the credibility of commitments undertaken by the parties and the availability or use of sanctions for breach of the agreements. What happens if departments fail to achieve targets, or to adhere to agreed commitments? There are obviously no legal sanctions since there is no contract recognized at private law. As for extra-legal sanctions usually associated with contractual behaviour, we have already noted

[28] *Spending Review 2000* (n 22 above) para 2.23. [29] ibid para 2.22.

[30] *HM Treasury Comprehensive Spending Review Public Service Agreements 1999–2002* (Cm 4181, 2000). In Alan Milburn's Foreword to the accompanying White Paper, PSAs are similarly described as 'a contract with the people' – HM Treasury, White Paper, *Public Services for the Future: Modernisation, Reform, Accountability* (Cm 4315, 2000).

[31] Hence the PSAs published as part of the 2000 Spending Review were described 'outcomes that every part of government will deliver *to the public* in return for resources,' *2000 Spending Review* (n 22 above).

the lack of an option on the part of the Treasury to withdraw from relationships regarded as unsatisfactory. While the Chancellor made clear in planning for the Summer 2002 Spending Review that departments that did not meet targets set in the previous round would not receive extra cash,[32] in regard to this as other aspects of PSAs, the rhetoric has not been matched by the reality. The PSA regime appears not to provide incentives for performance through sanctions attaching to 'breach' of contract in any sense. In the 2002 review a minority of departments was judged to have met few targets while the majority failed to meet some, yet all major public service sectors benefited from massive increases in resources. Certain departments may have done better than others in this spending round due to the skill with which the ministers concerned presented their performance record or negotiated their cases for increased investment. The general view of outcomes measured against performance targets set in 2000, however, was that 'Ministries Fail to Measure Up.'[33] The reasons for the across-the-board increases in spending had more to do with the Chancellor's long term plans for investment following earlier prudence, and the need to be seen to be closing the gap between Britain and other social-democratic countries in expenditure on public services as a proportion of GDP, than with rewarding good performance. The proportion of national wealth devoted to education, for example, was set to increase to 5.6 per cent by 2005–6, rivaling the average in the EU and in other industrialized countries. The £14.7bn allocated to the DfES over three years amounted to an increase of 8.1 per cent, despite failure to meet key targets set in 2000. The Government was under intense political pressure to increase resources in this sector, spending on education having been lower in the first two years of the Blair government than at any time since the early 1960s.

Similarly, the Department of Health will see large increases in the proportion of GDP allocated to health spending, rising from 7.7 per cent in 2002 to 9.4 per cent in 2007–8 (the only area in which funding was committed beyond the period of the 2002 review). The extra £40bn over this period is despite failure to meet targets, or even to demonstrate progress in their attainment.[34] There are many other examples of increases in funding allocations despite poor performance on targets set in earlier PSAs. The Home Office was allocated a 5.6 per cent increase over three years despite evidence of exceptionally poor performance in managing the previous budget. The budget for asylum was increased to around £750m, in spite of the Department's failure to meet its target for ensuring that 60 per cent of substantive asylum applications were decided within two months, and for removal of asylum seekers with failed applications. The Department was not on course to meet its target of 30 per cent reduction in vehicle crime by 2004, or to have cut robbery and violent crime as measured by the British Crime Survey, or to have

[32] *Guardian* 16 April 2002. [33] *Guardian* 15 July 2002.

[34] For example: to reduce to three months the maximum wait for an outpatient appointment, and to six months the maximum wait for an inpatient by 2005; and to guarantee access to a primary care professional within 24 hours, and to a GP within 48 hours.

reduced by a quarter the proportion of people under twenty five using class A drugs by 2005. In the 2002 round, some of these targets were 'revised', 'renegotiated', or dropped completely, with little explanation for the change. Targets in relation to asylum seekers and drug use were abandoned as 'unrealistic', and replaced with more 'aspirational' targets such as 'removing a greater proportion of failed asylum seekers'.

There appears to be little evidence, therefore, that any sanctions have been applied in disciplining spending departments that have performed poorly in relation to PSA targets.[35]

Accountability and transparency

Whatever the failures of PSAs measured in contractual terms, it can be argued that their introduction has led to improved accountability and transparency in the allocation of funding for major public services compared with the previous system of annual spending rounds. Ministers are clearly accountable to Parliament for the performance of their departments against PSA targets.[36] The Government generally is accountable to the electorate for its collective performance, through the publication of PSAs and annual departmental reporting on progress on targets. PSAs provide a basis also for holding civil servants to account to ministers for their performance.[37]

One of the public accountability benefits claimed for PSAs is increased clarity in the presentation of the Government's policy objectives on public services. Defenders of PSAs might argue that they operate in a more subtle manner than suggested by the emphasis in the contractual analysis on incentives and sanctions. Rather than holding individual ministers or civil servants literally and directly responsible for performance, the potential of the PSA system may lie in the encouragement of public debate over the setting of policy goals and associated targets; in the subsequent public deliberation over success or failure in achieving them; in the opportunity for consideration of reasons for poor performance; and finally in informing further policy making and target setting. The success or failure of PSAs in these terms will be subject to detailed scrutiny in Part 4. Here it may be noted that the lack of public involvement and participation in target setting, monitoring of performance, and policy making generally raise major questions about the ability of PSAs in their current form to realize any such potential.

[35] The absence of any apparent sanctioning of poor performance by spending departments on PSAs does not mean that poor performance by the agencies delivering services will not escape financial sanctions. The windfall for education, for example, was accompanied by clear warnings that money would be withheld from school heads and LEAs who failed to improve standards, and that 'failing institutions' would be dealt with firmly.

[36] 'The constitutional provision that it is ministers who are accountable to Parliament should be preserved . . . Ministers should take responsibility for their departments' performance against PSA targets' – Treasury Select Committee (n 19 above) para 25.

[37] ibid para 24.

Transparency in the PSA system implies the existence and publication of reliable information on performance against targets. However, in many cases performance has proved difficult or impossible to measure in such terms. Information on outcomes may not be available, either because evaluations have not been undertaken or the research has not been published. The political stakes in performance information are particularly high due to the priority accorded improvements in public services by New Labour in its second and third terms of office. At the time of the announcement of PSAs for 2002, ministers were accused by the opposition of fudging performance information and of watering down, refining or abandoning many public service targets. The shadow Chancellor, Michael Howard, alleged that the Government had missed almost 40 per cent of the targets it set in 1998, and had failed or was on course to fail to meet 75 per cent of the goals it set in 2000. 'The latest figures show that PSAs are being failed, but the money is still going in. This is at the heart of Labour's failure to deliver improvements to public services. Increased spending has not been tied to reform as Labour promised.'[38] Accurate and independently validated performance data is necessary both to prevent the Government making political capital from extravagant claims of success on public service targets, and to counter unfair allegations of performance failure.

The Treasury's dual role in conducting the Spending Review and in administering PSAs raises particular accountability concerns. One of the reasons for the creation of policy units after the 2001 general election reporting directly to the PM, such as the Prime Minister's Delivery Unit (PMDU) and the Office of Public Services Reform (OPSR), was to provide a counterpoint to the increasing power of the Treasury.[39] The perception of the growing influence of one part of the 'new centre' within government served therefore as the justification for further increasing the power of another part of that centre. However, there is some evidence of increased transparency of the PSA process as a result of provisions in 2002 for quarterly independently audited reports on targets, such that the public may now have access to information previously known only to Treasury officials and those in the No 10 Delivery Unit. There is also an increased role for both the National Audit Office (NAO) and the Audit Commission.

Conclusion

PSAs do appear to exhibit characteristics of discreteness and presentiation in the explicitly contractual ordering of relationships between the Treasury and spending departments. On closer examination, however, the norms of planning, consent and choice are so weakly represented as to render any benefits associated with genuinely contractual processes extremely unlikely. There is a significant gap between

[38] Quoted in *The Independent* 5 December 2002.

[39] *Guardian* 16 April 2002.

the rhetoric and the reality of PSAs, especially as regards the claim that the funding of spending departments is conditional and dependent upon the attainment of performance targets. The use of the term 'hierarchical contract' reflects the fundamentally administrative/managerial character of this variant of the New Public Contracting. Given the weakness of the relatively discrete norms, it cannot be maintained that the experience of renegotiation, revision, and refinement of PSA targets is an expression of relational contract norms such as flexibility and solidarity. To the degree that PSA relationships express relational features of trust and cooperation, these qualities cannot be ascribed to any specifically contractual mode of social ordering.

Despite such contractual shortcomings, PSAs appear to offer some prospect of increased accountability in the organization of public services: by requiring government policy to be specifically expressed in the form of targets; by separating policy making and service delivery roles; and by increasing the potential for public discussion and debate on public service targets and performance. PSAs may therefore be viewed as providing a more transparent framework for decision making on public services and subsequent policy evaluation than the previous system of annual allocations. The question for legal governance, to be considered in later chapters, is how the potential for increased accountability in the Spending Review process might better be realized.

Department–executive agency relationship

Relationships resulting from the separation of policy making and policy delivery functions within government have typically (but not always) been organized on a contractual basis.[40] One of the advantages claimed for contracts in this context is the capacity for quicker and more effective decision making. Authorization of action is unnecessary within the terms of the contractual grant of powers, the need for permission being replaced by the requirement on the part of agencies periodically to provide information on decisions and outcomes.[41] We saw in the discussion of 'managerialist contractualism' in Chapter 2 how a radical separation of interests within government was effected in New Zealand through the introduction of a new form of contractual relationship between ministers, who remain responsible for broad strategic outcomes, and heads of departments and agencies responsible for delivering specified output targets. The rationale was increased transparency, greater clarity in the policy-making role, and improved

40 Governance structures have varied considerably. The restructuring of relations within government in Germany and Japan has not drawn on the Anglo-American model of corporate governance in the manner of UK executive agencies – see O James, 'Business Models and the Transfer of Businesslike Central Government Agencies' (2001) 14 *Governance* 233.

41 A Vermeulen, 'Contract Management in the Netherlands' (1988) 54 *International Review of Administrative Sciences* 201, 205.

accountability of officials committed to specific targets. The autonomy of public bodies charged with policy delivery was clearly established through the granting of independent legal status and the corresponding legal enforceability of contracts. Similarly in Sweden, the relationship between agencies and departments is clearly defined in law, and arguably not subject to confusion surrounding 'outmoded doctrines of ministerial responsibility'.[42] By contrast in Britain:

> The government has chosen not to give its agencies independent status, so that they are still subject to the direct exercise of ministerial authority. Compared to other countries the freedom of agencies, and the clarity of the system in which they operate, can be seen as limited, as indeed it is in comparison to some other areas of British government organisation.[43]

The implications of this important difference for debates on the reform of legal governance will be specifically considered in Chapter 10.

Framework documents and business plans

The introduction of framework documents preceded by a decade the implementation of the PSA framework. In addition to formalising the split between policy-making and service delivery and serving as a mechanism for devolving powers and responsibilities, framework documents may be regarded as providing a 'constitution' governing the relationship between executive agencies and their parent departments.[44] The source of the power of agencies is contractual rather than statutory. One implication of the increased autonomy accorded to agency chief executives compared with ordinary civil service employees is the attenuation of ministerial responsibility. Framework documents, which typically run for a period of between three and five years, define the scope of legitimate departmental interest and involvement in agency activities and provide the governance framework for various procedural matters, including processes of negotiation and representation in setting PIs and targets.[45] Framework documents vary widely in their contents, particularly as regards the powers and responsibilities of chief executives, who are personally responsible for the attainment of targets and for performance in delivering the service generally. Supplementing framework documents, agencies are

[42] D Oliver and G Drewry, *Public Service Reforms: Issues of Accountability and Public Law* (London: Pinter, 1996) 125.

[43] K Walsh, *Public Services and Market Mechanisms: Competition, Contracting and the New Public Management* (Houndmills: Macmillan, 1995) 189.

[44] But this constitution is not legally binding, in the sense of legally enforceable power-conferring contracts at private law – indeed for Harden (n 7 above) this is a significant governance deficit. See P Greer, 'The Next Steps Initiatives: An Examination of Agency Framework Documents' (1992) 70 *Public Administration* 89.

[45] N Carter and P Greer, 'Evaluating Agencies: Next Steps and Performance Indicators' (1993) 71 *Public Administration*, 411. For example, Jobcentre Plus is an executive agency of the DWP, created in June 2001. Its business plan for 2004/05 can be found at: www.jobcentreplus.gov.uk/pdfs/BP_English.pdf, accessed 24th August 2005.

required to produce a corporate plan covering the same period. In addition, PIs and specific targets must be set out in an annual business plan for the forthcoming year, which serves as the substantive 'contract' by which agencies undertake to deliver specified performance within a given level of resources.[46]

The commitments contained in these documents are the result of negotiations involving the Treasury, the Minister for the Civil Service, and the department and agency, conducted in accordance with central guidelines. The drafting process and procedures have been criticized for being excessively centrally driven. Similarly with annual business plans setting out PIs and targets for the forthcoming year, the criticism is that these have been too top-down and centrally prescribed.[47] In one sense this is hardly surprising, since framework documents – like PSAs – have been shown to be a form of hierarchical regulation by contract. The issue for further investigation, however, concerns the nature of the equilibrium between hierarchy and contract in these regulatory arrangements.

Autonomy

The fundamental problem in the relationship between departments and executive agencies is how to maintain an appropriate balance between central control, and agency autonomy and flexibility.[48] As far back as 1992, the Fraser Report had recommended that departments reduce their involvement in agency affairs.[49] As many commentators have noted, the limited independence of agencies raises similar issues to the problems encountered by the old nationalized industries in preserving managerial freedoms to make commercial judgements against the constant threat of ministerial interference.[50] The absence of formal independent legal status, and the fact that legal actions can be brought only against the minister/department rather than the agency, are arguably a source of tensions that run through the whole Next Steps regime.[51] While the clear intention behind framework documents as originally conceived was that they should be binding (albeit revisable) statements of the respective rights and responsibilities of the department and agency, the constitutional obstacle of the inability of the Crown to contract with itself was not properly addressed in the original Treasury and Civil Service Committee Report in 1988.[52] Critics point to a number of governance deficits associated with the unenforceability of internal contracts and the corresponding absence of effective sanctions. These range from the difficulty of ensuring compliance with controversial or challenging targets on the one hand, to

[46] Carter and Greer (n 45 above) 409.

[47] P Greer, *Transforming Central Government: The Next Steps Initiative* (Buckingham: Open University Press, 1994) 75.

[48] Carter and Greer (n 45 above) 411.

[49] Greer (n 47 above) 65.

[50] The difference is that the relationship between departments and chief executives of agencies is contractual rather than statutory – Harden (n 7 above) 35.

[51] Craig (n 1 above) 108–9.

[52] Harden (n 7 above) 27, 44; Oliver and Drewry (n 42 above) 68–70.

the constant threat of unwarranted departmental interference in agency affairs – including varying the terms of the contract without appropriate contractual justification or consent – on the other.[53]

Problems of central government interference have been particularly acute in respect of politically controversial issues. 'Ministers have been unwilling to allow chief executives in agencies providing politically sensitive services to act autonomously.'[54] Where chief executives have been appointed from the ranks of the civil service, there may have been insufficient challenge to traditional approaches and impetus to independence from within the agencies themselves. Even given the absence of overt ministerial involvement or interference in most agencies, recent research has found general disappointment with the structural lack of autonomy in executive agency status.[55] The assumption has been that 'the agency and its chief executive must justify changes, rather than having freedom to adopt the approaches they think necessary'.[56] One reason why departments have been reluctant to relinquish control over their agencies is that they themselves are subject to increasing Treasury control through PSAs. Agencies with trading fund status tend to enjoy greater autonomy than those dependent on the civil service budget. The extent of autonomy depends on such factors as whether the agency can generate income rather than having to operate within a cash limit allocated at the beginning of the year, and whether it is free from the requirement to match income and expenditure each year ('annuality').[57]

Accountability

There is a substantial critical literature focusing on the negative implications of Next Steps for political accountability, particularly that of ministers to Parliament. The main argument is that the separation of policy and operational interests has contributed to the erosion of ministerial responsibility. However, such claims may exaggerate the effectiveness of this accountability mechanism prior to the creation of executive agencies.[58] Rather than giving rise to new accountability problems, Next Steps may have revealed long-standing deficiencies with the UK constitution in this regard.[59] Furthermore, the existence of 'layers of accountability' in the relationship between agencies and departments may compensate for any reduction in the direct responsibility of ministers.[60]

[53] ACL Davies, *Accountability: A Public Law Analysis of Government By Contract* (Oxford: Oxford University Press, 2001) 71. [54] Walsh (n 43 above) 187.

[55] B Hogwood, D Judge, and M McVicar, 'The Audit of Accountability – Agencies and their Multiple Constituencies', ESRC Whitehall project briefing 12, http://ncl.ac.uk/geps/about/politics/whitehall/riefings/briefing12.html, accessed 20th August 2003.

[56] Walsh (n 43 above) 188. [57] ibid. [58] Dowding (n 10 above) 256.

[59] C Polidano, 'The Bureaucrat Who Fell Under a Bus: Ministerial Responsibility, Executive Agencies and the Derek Lewis Affair in Britain' (1999) 12 *Governance* 201.

[60] For example, scrutiny by Commons committees, and meetings between ministers and chief executives – Hogwood et al (n 55 above).

More fundamentally, the issue of accountability is not confined to the governance of relationships once executive agencies have been created, but refers to the decision to organize services on this basis in preference to departmental organization. While not doubting the potential benefits of the separation of policy making and service delivery roles, some commentators have expressed concerns over the pace of the reforms and the absence of collective dialogue over their implementation. We noted in Chapter 2 various criticisms of the excessive secrecy and lack of transparency surrounding 'appraising options' reviews.[61] Britain compares unfavourably in such respects with other jurisdictions, such as Sweden and New Zealand, in which choices concerning the organization and operation of public services are made more openly and within a statutory framework.[62] In New Zealand, the programme for the restructuring of relations between parts of government has been marked by a general commitment to procedural openness and transparency, with the goals of departments, agencies and individual public servants being required to be clearly stated in the reform process.[63]

A further accountability issue in the department–executive agency relationship in Britain concerns the lack of independent external validation of agency performance against publicly announced targets. As with PSAs, maintaining proper accountability is dependent upon accurate and reliable information. The NAO has called for more extensive and systematic reporting of performance information to Parliament in annual reports.[64]

Contract norms

We have seen how public service reformers originally intended framework documents to operate on an explicitly contractual basis. The purpose of Next Steps was to create a relationship based on a 'bargain' between the ministers and chief executive.[65] Agencies would enjoy increased freedoms including latitude in deciding how to implement government policy *in return for* the commitment to deliver certain outputs or standards with available resources.[66] While the norm of reciprocity, expressing the fundamental notion of exchange for mutual benefit, is arguably more strongly present in framework documents than in PSAs, the balance of power in the department–agency relationship is undoubtedly weighted

61 N Lewis, 'Reviewing Change in Government: New Public Management and Next Steps' [1994] PL 105, 108 see also C Harlow, 'Accountability, New Public Management, and the Problems of the Child Support Agency' (1999) 26 JLS 150.

62 Oliver and Drewry (n 42 above) 143.

63 J Boston, J Martin, J Pallot, and P Walsh, *Public Management – The New Zealand Model* (Oxford: Oxford University Press, 1996) 4.

64 National Audit Office *Good Practice in Performance Reporting in Executive Agencies and Non-Departmental Public Bodies* (HC 272 Session 1999–2000, 9 March 2000). www.nao.gov.uk/publications/nao_reports/9900272.pdf, accessed 26 August 2005.

65 D Goldsworthy, *Setting Up Next Steps – A Short Account of the Origins, Launch and Implementation of the Next Steps Project in the British Civil Service* (London: HMSO, 1991) 30.

66 Greer (n 47 above) 60.

in favour of central departments. Again, the conditions under which 'consent' is obtained may be expected to have implications for the effectiveness of contract as a governance mechanism. Negotiations over framework documents may be more genuinely consensual than PSAs, reflecting a less directly hierarchical relationship. Chief executives in theory have considerable leeway in the specific commitments they undertake in formulating annual business plans, although these are subject to departmental oversight and approval. However, executive agencies have no choice other than to agree framework documents with their parent department on a three to five year basis. For departments there is more room for manoeuvre, since they are not locked into relationships with agencies. They may choose to change the basis on which a function is performed, for example by contracting out or privatization. Poor performance by an agency may therefore be sanctioned extra-contractually. This possibility provides an incentive for the agency to meet performance targets set out in its business plan.[67] The quality of bindingness in these administrative contracts may therefore be described as asymmetrical, with the parent department being able to sanction poor performance by the agency through various exit options,[68] while the agency has no extra-contractual sanctions or alternative to continuing to deal with the department.

As in all contractual relations, the discrete norms of planning and consent are in tension with the relational norm of flexibility, which emphasizes the need to avoid rigidity and to adapt to changing conditions. An institutional environment that is supportive of trusting and cooperative relations should permit such flexible adaptation, and enable problems and disagreements to be resolved before they become disputes. For example, in relation to the targets and PIs contained in agency business plans, there is a need for flexibility and for adjustment in the light of changing circumstances. However, the contractual machinery does not always appear to allow this.[69] Furthermore, there is a danger that framework documents may impede flexibility, and compromise the ability of agencies to adapt to a changing policy environment.[70] As in other instances of the New Public Contracting, there is a potential here for the development of adversarial or 'hard' contractual relations, which are destructive of trust and cooperation and unsuited to the tasks of public administration.[71]

Conclusion

Experience in other countries has shown that an appropriately implemented contract management model can deliver benefits in restructuring relations within

[67] Similarly, where one agency carries out work for another and supplies services on the basis of an SLA, there may be no formal sanctioning such as penalty clauses, but an informal sanction exists in the threat on the part of the agency to subject the function to market testing – ibid 79.

[68] While again there appears to be little empirical evidence of the use of contractual and extra-contractual sanctions in disciplining executive agencies, framework documents exhibit stronger potential for bindingness in this regard than PSAs.

[69] Greer (n 47 above) 74.

[70] ibid 79.

[71] On the experience of Danish 'contract agencies' in this regard, see C Greve, 'Exploring Contracts As Reinvented Institutions in the Danish Public Sector' (2000) 78 *Public Administration* 153.

government. Where administrative contractual relationships are embedded in a supportive institutional environment, benefits have been shown to include more expeditious decision making, more economic use of resources, greater job satisfaction, and increased capacity for organizational learning through experimentation.[72] Where problems with contract performance arise, they are likely to be resolved through consensus. Conflicts and disputes are likely to be relatively rare. Under such supportive conditions, the contract mechanism offers particular advantages over earlier public management reforms such as Management by Objectives (MbO) and Management by Results (MbR). While both these initiatives tended in varying degrees to involve top-down management,[73] a properly designed scheme of contractual governance has the potential to facilitate more bottom-up solutions to organizational problems based on voluntarism and the joint ownership of commitments by the contracting parties. On this argument, the major problem with framework documents in Britain remains the lack of security or guarantees offered in the 'constitution' of the contractual relationship against unwarranted (ie unjustified according to the terms of the framework document) interference by departments with agency affairs, including revision of the framework document itself, for short-term gain or other political reasons.

However, we have seen that the issue of governance extends beyond the regulation of the department–executive agency relationship to the initial decision to organize governmental functions on an agency basis. Empirical research has shown the difficulty in practice of separating responsibility for policy making and the operational management of services on the Next Steps model.[74] In the case of some existing agencies, the solution to governance problems may lie not in the more rigid separation of policy making and operational management, but in the greater integration of these functions. In their recent research, Day and Klein conclude that the freestanding agency model may not be appropriate in complex public services with high political salience such as health and social security, where service delivery is inescapably bound up with political issues.[75] This analysis has major implications for the way in which the role of legal governance of the New Public Contracting is conceived in Chapter 11, pointing to a need for greater deliberation, democratization and increased public involvement in decision making over how public services and associated governmental functions should be organized.

[72] N Hyndman and R Eden,'Rational Management, Performance Targets and Executive Agencies: Views From Agency Chief Executives in Northern Ireland' (2001) 79 *Public Administration* 579; A Vermeulen, 'Contract Management in the Netherlands' (1988) 54 *International Review of Administrative Sciences* 201, 211.

[73] A Wegener, 'Management Contracts in International Comparative Perspective: Experience From Leading-Edge Local Governments', in Y Fortin and H Van Hassel, (eds), *Contracting in the New Public Management – From Economics to Law and Citizenship* (Amsterdam: IOS Press, 2000) 107. This study was in local government, but is relevant for contract management in central government. Contract management may incorporate the best features of MbR, with its emphasis on 'steering' by broad specification of outcomes to be achieved, and emphasis on strategic management processes and feedback systems for monitoring of performance.

[74] P Day and R Klein, 'Steering but not Rowing?' ESRC Whitehall Programme project briefing 4. www.ncl.ac.uk/geps/about/politics/whitehall/briefings/briefing4.html, accessed 20th July 2003.

[75] ibid.

Government by (contractual) targets

Advocates of performance management systems argue that the clear specification of roles and service objectives, and the measurement and evaluation of progress in relation to targets, together create the potential both to improve organizational performance and to increase transparency and accountability in public services.[76] While performance indicators (PIs) had been used throughout the public sector from the beginning of the 1980s, they took on increased significance with decentralization and the 'hands-off' approach to central control accompanying Next Steps.[77] A reliable system of PIs became essential once financial and management responsibility for service delivery had been devolved away from central departments.[78] PIs were used to measure progress on PSAs in 'output and performance analyses' (OPAs) published for the first time in 1999.[79] In 2002 the Treasury began setting out in a single document the annual progress of departments against PSA targets across Whitehall. The publication of information on progress in achieving targets serves as a fundamental governance technique at all organizational levels in the management and delivery of public services.[80]

According to the Treasury, PSA targets have played a key role in raising standards in public service sectors such as health and education. They are argued to be most successful where:

- they focus on outcomes rather than process, thus empowering providers to develop their own approach to service delivery;
- they are stretching but achievable;
- service providers are selective in their use – the trend in successive spending reviews has been towards fewer rather than more targets;
- they are part of a coherent package of mechanisms to drive performance – targets complement but cannot substitute for management; and
- front-line service providers are fully involved in target setting, maximizing ownership and minimizing perverse incentives.[81]

76 Public Administration Select Committee (Fifth Report) *On Target? Government by Measurement* (HC 62-1 2002–03).

77 T Cutler and B Waine, 'Managerialism Reformed? New Labour and Public Sector Management' (2000) 34 *Social Policy and Administration* 318, 325.

78 Carter and Greer (n 45 above).

79 HM Treasury, *The Government's Measures of Success: Output and Performance Analyses*, 31 March 1999.

80 N Harris, *Law and Education: Regulation, Consumerism and the Education System* (London: Sweet and Maxwell, 1993).

81 HM Treasury, *Public Services: Meeting the Productivity Challenge* (London: The Stationery Office, 2003) para 4.9.

In practice, however, there is a range of obstacles to the realization of this ideal. The assumption that performance management systems drive up standards by raising aspirations and increasing motivation is open to question.

There are fundamental problems in attempting to measure and evaluate performance in relation to targets. Even given the experience of one full round of review by the second round of PSAs, more than one-third of the headline targets set in 2000 still lacked any method of measuring performance. There is considerable variation between departments in the specificity and measurability of their targets. Where targets have been achieved, there is the question of how far such success correlates with real improvements in the service. There is a general overemphasis on quantitative targets that are relatively easy to measure at the expense of 'effectiveness' targets that are more likely to lead to service improvements.[82] Service quality is particularly difficult to measure. On this issue the Treasury Select Committee concluded:

> We welcome the increased emphasis on outcome targets and the determination to ensure that the right targets are chosen, even if they are more difficult to measure. However, we believe that insufficient attention has been paid to building quality of service into the targets, and that this must be remedied to avoid quantity being achieved at the expense of quality.[83]

It remains doubtful whether the tension between quality and other aspects of performance has been properly addressed within the PSA framework, although later policy documents do emphasise the quality aspect as a core component of value for money.[84]

A related problem concerns the reliability and integrity of performance information. In the worst cases there is evidence of outright fraud or manipulation in the presentation of data, associated either with management pressures within the provider organization to meet its contractual commitments,[85] or political pressures within departments protecting their own or the Government's wider political interests. For example, a report commissioned by the Ambulance Services Association in 2002 found that the achievement of the government's target that 75 per cent of ambulance responses to emergency calls should be within eight minutes may in some areas have been due to delaying the start time of the clock measuring performance by up to three minutes.[86] The fiddling of response times only became apparent when these were compared with the survival rates of patients. Since the improved performance claimed by some trusts had not been accompanied by

[82] Carter and Greer (n 45 above) 413.

[83] Treasury Select Committee (n 19 above) para 20.

[84] HM Treasury (n 81 above).

[85] An added problem in these cases has been damage to relationships of trust and cooperation necessary for the public service to run efficiently and effectively. For example, relations between ambulance workers and senior management within the service have been damaged by the culture of fear accompanying the oppressive and dictatorial management style adopted to meet government targets – *Guardian* 15 October 2002.

[86] *Guardian* 8 August 2002. 'Ambulance services accused of fiddling 999 response times'.

improved survival rates, either there had been a deterioration in clinical performance by ambulance and hospital staff, or the response times were worse than had been reported.[87] Where data are properly recorded and accurately presented, just as worrying from the viewpoint of regulatory effectiveness are the incentives to rule-bending and creative compliance that may become part of performance target culture.[88]

Since PSAs and associated targets apply not just to the whole of central government but to services carried out by local government and non-government organisations, there is an issue of coordination among these bodies in both target-setting and the organization of services to meet targets.[89] Where commitments are undertaken by several departments in cross-departmental PSAs, there may be confusion or at least lack of clarity over where precisely responsibility lies, particularly where the commitments are jointly expressed. Lines of accountability need to be clear if initiatives promoting 'joined up' government either by cross-departmental PSAs or less formal arrangements are to be successful.[90]

In the higher education sector, performance evaluation and the publication of results in league-tables may measure everything except what really matters, such as quality in teaching and innovation, risk-taking, and challenging orthodoxy in research.[91] In the NHS, constantly changing targets may hinder strategic planning in the medium and long term. The significance attributed to performance measured by star ratings has arguably been at the expense of real improvements in hospital practice. The system of rewarding success and punishing failure in league-table culture may deny resources necessary to address deep-rooted causes of under-performance. Negative ratings may lead to low morale among nursing and other staff in hospitals whose poor record might be due to factors beyond local managerial control.[92] An undue emphasis on meeting targets may distort clinical priorities, for example forcing doctors to prioritize those waiting longest over the sickest patients.[93] In 2003 there was well-documented evidence that patients with diabetes and glaucoma had actually lost their sight as a result of delayed follow-up caused by diversion of resources.[94] Again, pressures to attain targets for the diagnosis of cancer sufferers within two weeks may have drained resources from the treatment of confirmed cancer patients. Generally there is evidence of inappropriate hospital admission and discharge of patients in order to meet central targets.

In the field of criminal justice, one criticism has been that the police are encouraged to chase easier cases that will improve performance on targets while ignoring

[87] ibid. [88] ibid. [89] Treasury Select Committee (n 19 above) para 28.

[90] ibid para 32.

[91] P Scott, 'High wire – performance culture may measure everything except what really matters' – *Guardian* 13 May 2003.

[92] In prison league tables, naming and shaming is unhelpful to staff and damaging to morale where problems such as overcrowding are due to inadequate resources rather than poor management – *Guardian* 15 November 2003. [93] *Guardian* 10 May 2002.

[94] *Guardian* 22 July 2003.

more serious crimes, for example concentrating resources on motoring fines rather than tackling joyriding.[95] Unresponsiveness in this and other public services is associated with the 'top-down' manner in which targets have been set by central government.[96] For example, during Labour's first two terms of office schools were expected to achieve objectives determined at the highest levels of government through PSAs.[97] By 2004 there was increasing recognition of the ineffectiveness of many Whitehall-driven targets.[98] There are considerable administrative and opportunity costs in conforming with externally imposed performance management regimes, which may impair the efficiency of the service provider. Resources and expertise may be diverted to satisfy bureaucratic requirements at the expense of the front-line service. A simulacrum of efficiency may thereby by created for audit purposes, but this is achieved only by burdening the best people or indeed all the people in the organization.[99]

We saw in Chapter 2 that performance management systems are not dependent on, and indeed may exist entirely separately from, any form of contractual organisation within government or of public services more generally.[100] Targets do not have to be expressed as *contractual* commitments on the part of those to whom they apply. In the UK, however, all forms of the New Public Contracting operate increasingly according to the contractual specification of targets, regular progress reviews, and monitoring and reporting on performance in relation to targets. Some of the governance deficiencies noted in this chapter may be attributable to the way in which performance management systems have been embodied in administrative contracts. For example, there may be a lack of fit between centrally determined targets, and the public service priorities of departments and agencies. The targets in many administrative contracts are unlikely to have been genuinely agreed, negotiated or bargained, but rather imposed on the 'contracting' partner by hierarchical authority. If targets are not the product of consensus and voluntary commitment, the welfare-maximising benefits associated with relational contracting are unlikely to be realized. Contractual targets are only likely to be of value as drivers of improvement if they are consensually determined and reflect the needs of the ultimate consumers of services. If these conditions are not met, management by targets cannot be expected to contribute to increased effectiveness.

Beyond the relationships between parent departments and executive agencies and between spending departments and the 'new centre' within government,

[95] *Guardian* 7 May 2003.

[96] I Sanderson, 'Performance Management, Evaluation and Learning in "Modern" Local Government' (2001) 79 *Public Administration* 297.

[97] Cutler and Waine (n 77 above).

[98] The system has now been reformed to allow schools to set their own targets for attainment by the final year of primary school at age 11 – *Guardian* 21 May 2003.

[99] *Guardian* 26 May 2002.

[100] In the United States, the performance management regime applying to federal agencies under the Government Performance and Results Act 1993 (requiring federal bodies to develop strategic plans, performance measurement, and reporting) is not explicitly contractual – see D Kettl, 'Measuring Performance When There Is No Bottom Line', in J Boston, (ed), *The State Under Contract* (Wellington: Bridget Williams Books, 1995); Peters (n 16 above).

targets form part of a wider social contract with the people. PSAs are contracts for the benefit of third parties, whether they be 'citizens' generally, or particular public service recipients. The government is accountable to the public for success or failure of departments, agencies, and state bodies generally in their public service performance assessed in these terms. Reflecting this social contract dimension, criticism of public services has tended to be directed at the government generally, rather than focusing on the performance of particular departments or agencies comprising it. In 2002, only thirty three of two hundred and fourteen hospitals in England met the national targets stipulating the time within which heart attack patients should receive life-saving care, for example treatment with clot-busting drugs within thirty minutes of arrival in hospital.[101] The Joseph Rowntree Foundation's verdict on Labour's performance in its first and second terms of office was that the majority of fifty targets on poverty and social exclusion would not be met, although on most indicators there was evidence of improvement and on only six was there significant deterioration.[102] Education ministers have historically been particularly sensitive to empirical embarrassment of missed targets. The Secretary of State, Estelle Morris, resigned in light of failure to meet the government's target that 85 per cent of primary school children would achieve level four in English and maths by 2004.[103] Ministerial resignation may be regarded as the ultimate political price for breach of social contract commitments made by government with the electorate.

Because of the high political salience of performance against targets as a measure of public services in the social contract, governments have an obvious incentive to present data in the most favourable manner. Complex performance information may easily be 'spun' or manipulated, as in the widely criticized general claim made by the Treasury in 2003 that 90 per cent of all targets had been met.[104] In the same year the chief executive of the British Medical Association alleged that NHS doctors and managers had been pressurized by the Department of Health to collude in cheating on certain performance indicators to serve the Government's political purposes.[105] A properly thought-out governance structure for management by targets in public services would need to protect against any such political interference or bias in the presentation of performance data.

Conclusion

Both PSAs and framework documents are hybrid forms of governance combining hierarchical and contractual elements. The attempt to evaluate the effectiveness of these administrative contracts is complicated by the hierarchical performance

101 *Guardian* 20 November 2002, reporting results of audit by Royal College of Physicians.
102 *Guardian* 12 December 2002. 103 *Guardian* 21 May 2003.
104 *Guardian* 14 July 2003. 105 *Observer* 29 June 2003.

management dimension. Operational problems may be due either to the nature and style of performance management systems, with their emphasis on centrally prescribed PIs, targets and monitoring processes, or to the specifically contractual mode of their implementation.

One problem with performance management regimes, as presently conceived, may be the lack of integration between the culture of *performance* which is about building an organization's capacity, and the culture of *measurement* which is more concerned with the tracking of quantitative achievement in public services. The goal of increasing efficiency and effectiveness in public administration may be impeded by processes of measurement and evaluation intended not primarily to improve performance but to increase accountability for the use of public funds.[106] What is required on this view is the better integration of these cultures, for example by encouraging the construction of fewer and more meaningful targets that focus on key outcomes; widening the target consultation process to involve professionals, service users, Select Committees and parliament generally; and reforming target-setting processes to encourage greater local involvement. The institutional reforms required to support such integration might include independent assessment of progress in meeting targets, an increased role for the NAO in this assessment and in validating annual reporting on performance by government to parliament, and a framework for the development of action plans to enhance performance management skills at both local and central levels.

As to the contractual mode of implementation, while it would be missing the point to expect administrative contracts to resemble the economic contracts found in competitive markets and quasi-markets, certain conditions still need to be satisfied if the relationships are to deliver the benefits associated with relational contracting. The relatively discrete norms of planning and consent must be present in order to structure relationships and to establish a reference point for future conduct. Contractual commitments must be credible and regarded as binding, with the potential for sanctioning of non-compliance. Without these conditions, the casting of relationships in 'contractual' form is unlikely to result in any administrative efficiency gains over and above what could have been achieved through pure bureaucratic organization. PSAs are significantly weaker on all dimensions of the contract norms than framework documents, which appear to exhibit some genuinely contractual characteristics.

Despite their common function in ordering relations within government, framework documents and PSAs have been shown to be markedly different in their structure and operation. I will argue in Part IV that clarity in the legal reform debates surrounding these contracts can be achieved only through recognition of the fundamental differences between them. The point to emphasize at this stage is the rejection of the categorization of these forms of the New Public Contracting as

[106] *Public Administration Select Committee On Target? Government by Measurement* 5th Report (HC 62–1 2002–03).

'internal contracts'. In the department–executive agency relationship, framework documents arguably serve an explicit regulatory purpose involving constitutional values associated with the separation of powers.[107] There is a need to safeguard managerial autonomy against interference by politicians in the running of services once the parameters for their operation have been set. By contrast, PSAs appear to lack any coherent regulatory rationale. Given the fundamental deficiencies in the contractual foundations of these administrative contracts, it is unlikely that the arrangements could ever be made to work more effectively through organizational or institutional reinforcement of whatever kind. Disregarding such specifically contractual deficiencies, I have suggested that the real value of PSAs may lie in the placing of information in the public domain about what citizens may reasonably expect from government, and about the performance of government in meeting those expectations. The question to be explored in Chapter 11 is how these governance objectives may best be achieved.

107 Where important constitutional issues are at stake, as in the relationship between ministers and executive agencies in government, some loss of efficiency may have to be accepted as a reasonable trade-off for the safeguarding of constitutional values – MJ Ormsby, 'The Purchaser/Provider Split: A Report From New Zealand' (1998) 11 *Governance* 357, 358.

7

Economic Contracts

This chapter examines economic contracting regimes governing competition for public services generally, and the quasi-market organization of particular public service sectors such as health and social care on the basis of the purchaser-provider split. The focus is on three main relationships in these contracting regimes: purchaser–provider; state–purchaser; and state–provider (the relationships between citizen/consumers and public purchasers, and between consumers and service providers, are dealt with in Chapter 8). The principal concern is with the effectiveness component of responsiveness, and in particular with efficiency. Particular attention is paid the manner in which the *contractual* purchaser–provider relationship is conditioned by the *hierarchical* regulatory relationship between central government and the public purchasing or commissioning agency. These contracting regimes exemplify the regulatory mode described in Chapter 1 as 'regulation by contract within hierarchical regulatory frameworks'.

The state role in public services

We saw in Part II how quasi-market contracting and other competitive arrangements including franchising and corporatization may be considered particular forms of regulatory intervention in the economy. The changing state role in public services will briefly be considered before the more detailed examination of economic contracts in the remainder of the chapter.

Public and private services

A public service exists 'not because of choices in the market but because of a public decision that it should exist'.[1] The designation 'public' therefore implies a role for the state or public authority beyond the provision of formal institutional supports (a legal framework and enforcement machinery guaranteeing exchange) for the private operation of markets. This raises the question of whether a given service

[1] I Harden, *The Contracting State* (Buckingham: Open University Press, 1992) 76.

should be public at all. The advantage of private services in theory is that demand decisions are made according to 'automatic links' established in the market, and on the basis of consumer sovereignty.[2]

However, markets tend to suffer from fundamental structural problems such as information asymmetries and various economic and social inequalities. Private provision may not be a viable option where market deficiencies cannot be addressed by regulation, or where the costs of regulation are prohibitive compared with alternative bureaucratic or quasi-market arrangements. Many services have a public dimension precisely because of 'market failure', reflecting the inability of private initiative to perform the task adequately.[3] The market model may be particularly inappropriate in the provision of core welfare services, or where equity goals are paramount.[4] Welfare-consuming differs from market-consuming in a number of respects. Many of the goods are 'experience goods', which are co-produced through interaction between provider and recipient of the service, and conditioned by a need to consume rather than by pleasure in their consumption.[5] The distribution of such services is often mediated by a professional agency or other body with the role of assessing the needs of the user, deciding how they might best be met, and arranging for delivery by care providers. In other cases, assuming that equality barriers (knowledge, information, wealth) have been or are capable of being addressed, the public interest in the service may lie in the promotion of a public good such as social solidarity and social cohesion.[6]

The main question for present purposes, therefore, is what the nature of the state's involvement in these public services should be.[7] In the definition of a public service as 'an activity with respect to which the public administration fulfils a fundamental role', there is nothing to imply that the state should perform

[2] ibid. While characterized by 'automaticity' in this sense (see ch 3) markets are highly constituted through regulation – see C Shearing, 'A Constitutive Concept of Regulation', in P Grabosky and J Braithwaite (eds), *Business Regulation And Australia's Future* (Canberra: Australian Institute of Criminology, 1993).

[3] EM Garcia, 'Public Service, Public Services, Public Functions, and Guarantees of the Rights of Citizens: Unchanging Needs in a Changed Context', in M Freedland and S Sciarra, (eds), *Public Services and Citizenship in European Law – Public and Labour Law Perspectives* (Oxford: Oxford University Press, 1998) 80. 'The origin of every public service lies in an essential or collective need which is recognized in the community at large as being impossible for private initiative to fulfil adequately', 81.

[4] HM Treasury *Public Services: Meeting the Productivity Challenge April 2003* (London: The Stationery Office, 2003).

[5] K Walsh, N Deakin, P Spurgeon, P Smith, and N Thomas, *Contracting for Change: Contracts in Health, Social Care, and Other Local Government Services* (Oxford: Oxford University Press, 1997) 30.

[6] M Feintuck, *'The Public Interest' in Regulation* (Oxford: Oxford University Press, 2004).

[7] Salamon is concerned to overcome the traditional ideological divide between opponents and supporters of state action, arguing that 'third-party government' necessarily involves a mixture of the two – LM Salamon, 'The New Governance and the Tools of Public Action: An Introduction', in LM Salamon, (ed), *The Tools of Government: A Guide to the New Governance* (Oxford: Oxford University Press, 2002).

the activity directly.[8] That role may take various forms, ranging from full public ownership and direct provision on the one hand, to the statutory regulation of markets involving independent regulatory agencies on the other. In this and the following chapter, I will argue that economic contracting regimes occupy a middle position on this spectrum, reflecting a process of transition towards increasingly privatized modes of public service provision.

De-bureaucratization and privatization

In Britain there has existed an unusually strong tradition of bureaucratic organization of public services, involving direct provision by state employees coupled with commitment to the principle that services should be free at the point of delivery and funded from general taxation.[9] Local authorities in particular have been large-scale employers of direct labour, with wider responsibilities than is typical elsewhere in Europe. The development of the economic form of the New Public Contracting may be understood as a response to the perceived obstacles to modernization posed by this bureaucratic tradition. Whereas the private sector role in public services arguably became established in the US, Europe and Japan in a pragmatic and relatively haphazard fashion, in Britain central control and compulsion have been at the heart of the government's agenda for public service reform.[10]

From the end of the 1970s, the trend towards privatization and contracting out expressed in New Right policies was buttressed by various academic critiques of public bureaucracies and 'big' government. Osborne and Gaebler argued famously for a reduced government presence and a greater role for market mechanisms in terms of the need for the state 'to steer rather than row', and 'to empower rather than serve'.[11] The prescription was that government had to learn how better to delegate public service functions, to share power, and to work in partnership with the private sector.[12] Public choice theorists also challenged public bureaucracy

[8] Garcia (n 3 above) 62–63. 'A public service is therefore an activity of general interest which is performed or, depending on the circumstances, merely supervised by a public authority on the basis of its special powers' – E Picard, 'Citizenship, Fundamental Rights, and Public Services', in M Freedland and S Sciarra, (eds), *Public Services and Citizenship in European Law – Public and Labour Law Perspectives* (Oxford: Oxford University Press, 1998) 89.

[9] Government bureaucracies differ from other bureaucracies such as charitable bodies, whose income is similarly not dependent on market sale, in being funded by taxation rather than by voluntary subscription – D Beetham, *Bureaucracy* (2nd edn, Buckingham: Open University Press, 1996).

[10] K Ascher, *The Politics of Privatisation: Contracting Out Public Services* (Houndmills: Macmillan, 1987) 20–1.

[11] D Osborne and T Gaebler, *Reinventing Government: How the Entrepreneurial Spirit is Transforming the Public Sector* (Reading, Mass: Addison-Wesley, 1992); J Donahue, *The Privatization Decision: Public Ends, Private Means* (New York: Basic Books, 1989); ES Savas, *Privatizing the Public Sector: How To Shrink Government* (Chatham House, 1982).

[12] D Kettl, *Sharing Power: Public Governance and Private Markets* (Washington DC: The Brookings Institution, 1993).

and the tradition of direct provision.[13] In this view, bureaucracies as monopoly suppliers tend inevitably to look after the producer interests of professionals and trade unions, and over-produce to levels not required by consumers. Waste and 'X-inefficiency' (the non-optimal use of resources) are associated with lack of adequate cost control and monitoring of performance by managers. Bureaucrats are rewarded for increasing the size of their budgets and empire building, not for efficiency; for expanding their power, not for responsiveness to citizen and consumer needs.[14]

However, rather than implying the shrinking or rolling back of the state, debureaucratization has entailed increasing central government power and an intensification of governmental activities – for example directed at building markets, responsibilizing a range of public and private agencies engaged in public service networks, and establishing other regulatory conditions for the more effective or efficient provision of public services.[15] Economic contracting regimes may be considered part of a deliberate strategy aimed at adjusting the balance between state and private sector provision of public services in favour of the latter.[16] Such regimes determine how public services are provided either to third-party consumers and citizens ('direct public services') or in support of the administrative operations of the public bodies ('indirect public services').[17]

As suggested in Chapter 2, two main forms of policy-driven regulation of competition may be distinguished. Firstly, with regard mainly to ancillary or support services, public bodies generally have been required increasingly either to contract out, or to organize internal provision on a comparable contractual basis following external competition.[18] Contracting out implies a less radical type of restructuring than full privatization. While the means of provision of the service are located in the private sector, the state retains overall responsibility for the function.[19] Again, whereas privatization is defined by the sale of physical assets,[20]

[13] P Dunleavy, *Democracy, Bureaucracy and Public Choice – Economic Explanations in Political Science* (Hemel Hempstead: Harvester Wheatsheaf, 1991); P Self, *Government by the Market? The Politics of Public Choice* (Houndmills: Macmillan, 1993).

[14] Kettl (n 12 above) 1; W Niskanen, *Bureaucracy and Representative Government* (Chicago, Il: Aldine-Atherton, 1971).

[15] A Sbragia, 'Governance, the State, and the Market: What is Going On?' (2000) 13 *Governance: An International Journal of Policy and Administration* 243, 246.

[16] C Hood, 'Which Contract State? Four Perspectives on Over-Outsourcing for Public Services' (1997) 56 *Australian Journal of Public Administration* 120. 'If public bureaucracies are indolent or unreliable, contracting out key functions may increase rulership,' 124.

[17] Harden (n 1 above).

[18] S Domberger, *The Contracting Organization: A Strategic Guide to Outsourcing* (Oxford: Oxford University Press, 1998). Contracting in this sense is defined by 'the application of competition to a set of economic activities which were previously immune to it,' 160.

[19] M Freedland, 'Government by Contract and Public Law' [1994] PL 86, 87. In the case of privatization, by contrast, responsibilities for both the function and the organization of provision are transferred.

[20] M Aronson, 'A Public Lawyer's Responses to Privatisation and Outsourcing', in M Taggart, (ed), *The Province of Administrative Law* (Oxford: Hart Publishing, 1997) 41.

indeed the raising of revenues from sale may in some cases be the principal object of the exercise, outsourcing does not necessarily imply such a transfer.[21] Secondly and more fundamentally, economic contracts serve in the quasi-market organization of whole welfare sectors on the basis of the purchaser-provider split, with public agencies being assigned specific contractual powers and responsibilities appropriate to the discharge of a wide range of newly designated purchaser functions. These dimensions of competition regulation are considered in detail in subsequent sections.

Regulatory coordination

Both forms of contractualization combine elements of public control with private enterprise. The increasing dependence of the state on private action for the attainment of public purposes immediately raises questions of regulatory coordination. A variety of policy instruments may be used in the organization of public services beyond direct state provision or command and control regulation. We have seen how the 'tools of government' literature in the United States focuses on networks of actors, and on the sharing of responsibilities among a range of third parties engaged in the implementation of public programmes.[22] In this perspective, regulatory instruments may in theory be analysed along four dimensions: coercion; directness; automaticity; and visibility.[23] The different types of economic contract (involving competitive tendering, franchising, corporatization, and particular quasi-markets) operate through complex combinations of governance instruments with varying characteristics. We have noted now economic contracting regimes are at once coercive and non-coercive; direct and indirect; and automatic and non-automatic in their operation. In this sense public contracting in Britain involves particularly complicated regulatory relationships by comparison with the experience of contracting as a tool of government in America.[24] Many of the problems with economic contracts concern 'implementability', referring to the ease or difficulty of operating policy programmes. Institutional weaknesses and governance difficulties associated with the operation of these contracts may be a reflection of fundamental problems with quasi-market organization:

The more complex and convoluted the tool, the more separate actors are involved, the more difficult it is likely to be to manage. Some tools are more cumbersome to operate

[21] Domberger (n 18 above) 160. [22] See ch 3. [23] Salamon (n 7 above).

[24] Contracting is regarded by Salamon as a 'medium' tool on the four dimensions. In the British case this judgement is complicated by the way in which contracting co-exists with other policy instruments (vouchering, franchizing, corporatization). Because economic contracting regimes comprise 'suites' of governance instruments, they are difficult to assess in accordance with the dimensions of coerciveness, directness, automaticity, and visibility that are supposed to characterize individual tools.

than others. While they may promise great efficiency and effectiveness in theory, they are unlikely to deliver it in practice because of the managerial difficulties they pose.[25]

These epithets ('cumbersome', 'complex', 'convoluted') aptly describe the problems of regulatory coordination posed by economic contracting regimes which involve the delegation of contracting powers to public purchasing agencies within detailed and prescriptive central policy frameworks.

Over the course of their development since the 1980s, economic contracting regimes have varied in the manner in which the elements of coerciveness, directness, and automaticity have been combined. Under New Labour, there has been a discernible shift towards indirectness, non-coerciveness, and automaticity.[26] However, contracting is an automatic tool only to the extent that competitive markets exist for the goods and services needed to address public problems.[27] Furthermore, while economic contracting regimes seek to embrace the virtues of the market in terms of automaticity, this is on the basis of complex administrative arrangements that are far from automatic.

Competition in public services

The notion that government should not carry out any commercial activity where goods or services could be procured more cheaply or effectively from private enterprise was current in the United States in the 1950s. In Britain, contracting out became generally accepted as a principle of public sector management only much later. The transition from bureaucratic to contractual organization was effected initially through policies of Compulsory Competitive Tendering (CCT) in local government, and market testing which applied to central government and other monopoly public services. These arrangements are considered briefly before turning to contracting regimes involving Public Private Partnerships (PPPs), franchizing, and corporatization.

Market testing and (compulsory) competitive tendering

From its inception in 1980 to its abolition in 1998, the statutory regime of CCT dictated that 'defined activities' could be provided by local authority direct labour only where they had been subjected to external competition in accordance with

[25] Salamon (n 7 above) 24.

[26] Salamon hypothesizes that the more coercive the tool, the more effective it is likely to be. The problem with coercive instruments is said to be that they are inefficient, both for government and for society at large – ibid 26. By contrast, I have suggested that early forms of the New Public Contracting in Britain that relied on coercion (for example CCT) were both inefficient and ineffective.

[27] The same problem affects the use of vouchers in quasi-market organisation. 'The effectiveness of vouchers depends critically on the responsiveness of markets to the kind of demand that voucher recipients will make and on the ability of voucher recipients to make wise decisions' – ibid 34.

detailed regulations.[28] In central government and other public bureaucracies, policies of market testing similarly required the costs of internal and external provision of goods or support services to be compared through competitive tendering. The assumption of policy makers was that the private sector was inherently more efficient than state bureaucracy, and hence would win a significant proportion of tendered work. However, in-house teams in both central and local government proved remarkably successful in competing with the private sector.[29] The resulting internal 'contractual' relationships were governed through Service Level Agreements (SLAs). These arrangements resembled contracts with external service providers in many respects, with the important difference that they were unenforceable at private law. Most manual services subject to CCT under the Local Government Act 1988 were internally provided by Direct Service Organizations (DSOs),[30] while central and other services were retained in-house after market testing in approximately 60 per cent of cases.[31]

While market testing and competitive tendering have been adopted in various forms in other countries, their use has not been as politically confrontational or controversial as in Britain. In the United States, for example, competitive in-house agencies have developed mainly to suit local conditions and for pragmatic reasons, unconnected with resistance on the part of public employees to the threat of redundancy and/or deteriorating working conditions posed by compulsory competition. A further distinctive feature of the British experience is the relative formality of internal contractual relationships. Contractual formalities introduced under CCT continued under Better Quality Services (BQS).[32] The purpose of applying the same stringent contract award, monitoring and accounting requirements to internal and external providers is to ensure fair competition and discourage anti-competitive practices. Regardless of whether the winning bidder is the DSO or an external contractor, the relationship is contractual.[33] In the

[28] 'Defined activities' under the Local Government (Planning and Land) Act 1980 were new building, building repair, and construction and highways maintenance, followed by refuse collection, catering, street and buildings cleaning, and vehicle and ground maintenance under the Local Government Act 1988. Sports and leisure services management were added by secondary legislation in 1989 (SI 1989/2488), on-street parking and vehicle fleet management in 1994 (SI 1994/2884). Following the Government's statement of intention in the Citizen's Charter in July 1991 (Cm 1559), CCT was further extended by statutory instrument to include legal, construction, property, IT, finance, personnel and housing management services in 1994 and 1995 (SI 1994/1671, 1994/2884, 1994/2888 and 1995/1915).

[29] In the UK as in the US, estimated savings from market testing or competitive tendering are similar to those claimed for contracting out: 'Where public sector agencies are required to compete with the private sector . . . productivity differences often largely disappear' – MJ Trebilcock, 'Can Government Be Reinvented?', in J Boston, (ed), *The State Under Contract* (Wellington: Bridget Williams Books, 1995) 20.

[30] Local Government Management Board, *CCT Information Service Survey Report* (London: LGMB, 1994).

[31] Audit Commission *Realising the Benefits of Competition: The Client Role for Contracted Services* (London: Audit Commission, 1993).

[32] See ch 2, above.

[33] K Walsh and H Davis, *Competition and Service: The Impact of the Local Government Act 1988* (London: HMSO, 1993).

United States, where about half the cost comparisons between public and private provision conducted in the federal A-76 programme have been won by in-house providers,[34] there is little evidence of such formality in internal contractual relationships.[35] This is explained by the more pragmatic approach to outsourcing and the relative absence of bureaucratic regulation.

A distinction may be drawn between contracting out in consequence of (and in accordance with) economic contracting regimes, and outsourcing resulting from the *strategic* management decision that public services hitherto provided directly would better be performed privately.[36] The latter situation may be likened to the 'make or buy' decision by firms to outsource functions to the market rather than perform them in-house. In theory the strategic decision is influenced by a variety of pragmatic financial and commercial considerations, including the nature of the market and the assessment of transaction costs. In contrast with the uncertainty surrounding New Public Contracting policies encouraging contracting out, the outcome (if not the identity of the private contracting party) is entirely predictable. Local and other public services have been strategically outsourced in such a manner in the United States,[37] the Netherlands,[38] and other European countries.[39] In Britain, by contrast, although local councils such as Westminster and Wandsworth began outsourcing services such as refuse collection and buildings cleaning on a voluntary basis in the 1970s, the tradition of direct provision of most services continued until the 1980s.[40] A key governance issue in the evaluation of economic contracting regimes concerns the compulsive regulatory environment in which the decision to cease direct provision is taken. We saw in Chapter 2 that, despite the more voluntaristic appearance of best value and BQS relative to market testing and CCT, these policies may be regarded as the modern successors to compulsory regimes originally introduced under the Conservatives.

Nevertheless, the distinction between voluntariness and compulsion in the outsourcing decision may be harder to sustain in practice than this analysis would suggest. For example, the term 'externalization' has been used in the local government sector in Britain to describe situations where a particular service is voluntarily transferred, either to an existing company in some form of partnership arrangement, or to a specially established company following an employee or management

34 Kettl (n 12 above) 47.

35 see eg J Rehfuss, 'The Competitive Agency: Thoughts From Contracting Out in Great Britain and the United States' (1991) 57 *International Review of Administrative Sciences* 465.

36 T Stott, 'Market Testing and Beyond: Privatisation and Contracting Out in British Central Government' (1994) XI V *Teaching Public Administration* 36.

37 RK Common, 'Privatisation Through Contracting: The View From Local Government in the United States' (1994) 20 *Local Government Studies* 379.

38 S Snape, 'Contracting Out Local Government Services in Western Europe: Lessons from the Netherlands' (1995) 21 *Local Government Studies* 642.

39 Council of Europe, *The Role of Competitive Tendering in the Efficient Provision of Local Services* (Strasbourg: Council of Europe Press, 1993).

40 Ascher (n 10 above).

buy-out.[41] In these cases the former workforce is employed in the same capacity by the new business, which enters a legally enforceable contract with the local authority for provision of the service.[42] In the 1980s and 1990s, many local authority functions were externalized in such a manner deliberately as a means of avoiding competitive tendering provisions that would otherwise have applied under CCT regulations. The 'voluntary' externalizations were the indirect result of the compulsory regime of CCT.

Public Private Partnerships and the Private Finance Initiative

The idea of 'partnering' between public and private sectors is at the heart of economic contracting regimes. All forms of contracting out and market testing may be considered to involve partnering to some degree. The term Public Private Partnerships (PPP), however, is reserved for a particular type of partnering relationship between public and private (or voluntary) bodies characterized by risk-sharing agreements directed at the attainment of specific policy objectives. While PPPs may include a range of cooperative arrangements beyond simple 'arm's length' contracting, including benchmarking, the presumption is that there should be a strong competitive element. Where the partnership involves private sector financing of public infrastructure such as schools, roads and hospitals, the PPP is subject to special Treasury regulation in the form of PFI rules and guidance. The private financing of public infrastructure under New Labour has been a logical development of earlier Conservative policies. The PFI and PPP regulatory frameworks permit a high degree of central control to be exercised by the Treasury, while avoiding the burden on the Public Sector Borrowing Requirement (PSBR) that would otherwise accompany public financing and procurement.

Government departments are under pressure to explore PPP options in regard to their use and exploitation of assets.[43] In addition to commitments undertaken in PSAs, each department is required to have a Departmental Investment Strategy (DIS), setting out its long-term strategic plans for investment, the condition and suitability of its existing asset base, and the systems that will ensure value-for-money in delivery. 'A central aim is to improve the use of the Government's existing assets. This means working existing assets harder, looking at Public Private

[41] The difference between externalization and outright privatization lies in the continuing local authority interest in the company, as defined and regulated by Part V of the Local Government and Housing Act 1989, ss 68–71. On the limited extent of buy-outs in the 1990s, see K Robbie and M Wright, 'Local Authorities, Compulsory Competitive Tendering and Buy-Outs' (1996) 22 *Local Government Studies* 127.

[42] P Vincent-Jones, 'Hybrid Organization, Contractual Governance, and Compulsory Competitive Tendering in the Provision of Local Authority Services', in S Deakin and J Michie, (eds), *Contracts, Cooperation and Competition: Studies in Economics, Management and Law* (Oxford: Oxford University Press, 1997).

[43] HM Treasury, *Public Services: Meeting the Productivity Challenge* (London: The Stationery Office, 2003).

Partnership and commercial opportunities and disposing of those assets which are no longer required.'[44] Under the new method of resource accounting and budgeting introduced in 2000, departments are required to produce financial statements similar to those in commercial accounts, in particular a balance sheet and the equivalent of a profit and loss statement, and to use this information as the basis for planning and controlling expenditure. These requirements all serve to increase the motivation of departments to explore novel forms of service delivery involving partnership with the private sector.

Public infrastructure PPPs may take one of two forms. In Design Build and Operate (DBO) contracts, finance is publicly provided. In Design Build Finance Operate (DBFO) projects, by contrast, the private sector provides part or all of the finance in accordance with strict PFI guidelines. The only type of relationship for which the PFI is considered unsuitable is standard procurement, for which 'arm's-length' contracting out is the most appropriate route. In other circumstances either contracting out or the PFI might be adopted to achieve the same result in relationships characterized (in progressive degrees of 'partnership') by *shared understanding* of both parties' strategic agendas; *shared commitment* to both parties' strategic agendas; and *joint development* for separate but complementary benefits.[45]

In the local government sector, the Local Authorities (Capital Finance) (Amendment No 3) Regulations 1996, SI 1996/2539, created a statutory financial framework aimed at facilitating local authority PFI schemes.[46] The Public Private Partnerships Programme Ltd ('Four Ps') was set up by local authority associations in England and Wales with all party support in April 1996, with the purpose of delivering increased investment through local partnerships. In light of its remit to assist local authorities in progressing PFI and other partnership schemes, its objectives are to lobby government for changes to regulations that hinder development of PFI and other forms of partnership, to assist the Audit Commission in providing guidance on PFI and partnerships to district auditors, and to maintain a database of projects and private sector companies working in public-private sector partnerships.[47]

Franchising and corporatization

As a mode of state control of economic activity, franchising entails granting to a private business the exclusive or protected right to provide a given service for

[44] *HM Treasury Prudent for a Purpose: Building Opportunity and Security for All 2000 Spending Review: New Public Spending Plans 2001–2004* (Cm 4807 2000) para 2.26.

[45] HM Treasury (n 4 above) 59.

[46] Details of the new framework were published on 19 November 1997 (DETR, *A New Framework for Local Authority PFI Projects*).

[47] Committee of Public Accounts, *Managing the Relationship to Secure a Successful Partnership in PFI Projects*, 42nd Report of Session 2001-02, (The Stationery Office, London. HC 460, 11 July 2002).

a limited period.[48] Whereas in commercial franchising the franchisor is seeking to make a profit, the purpose of public franchising is to secure the delivery, to individual consumers or the public generally, of an efficiently produced and competitively priced service.[49] Control is exercised by the franchisor (the state) through contractual conditions of the grant, by the monitoring and enforcement of performance in accordance with it, and by incentives for the franchisee including the prospect of franchise renewal. From the government's viewpoint, the advantage of this arrangement compared with contracting out is that the revenue risk may be allocated to the service provider. Furthermore, where the service is provided to identifiable public consumers, payment may be made by them to the franchisee directly at the point of consumption.[50] On the other hand, the franchising mechanism may feature in the provision of services that remain publicly funded. The PFI building programme in the health sector may be considered in this light as a type of public service franchising, with hospital services remaining free to patients at the point of delivery. The supply-side conditions of quasi-market organization are met by the existence in theory of competition *for* the market, whereas traditional public procurement generally entails competition *within* already established markets. The organization of legal services under the Access to Justice Act 1999 serves as another example. Only firms that have bid successfully and been awarded contracts with the Legal Services Commission can provide specified legal services on a publicly funded basis.

For present purposes, corporatization may be understood as the process whereby bodies performing public service functions are constituted as distinct legal entities, separate from the public organizations of which they have hitherto been part.[51] Like other types of economic relationship in the New Public Contracting, corporatization implies a movement away from bureaucratic monopoly provision towards increasing independent sector involvement, and the increasing exposure of public services to competitive market incentives.[52] As we have seen in the discussion of governance techniques in Chapter 3, corporatization shifts the balance of power among key players in sectors such as health and education and training by altering the legal status and capacities of certain agents. Corporatization is associated with

[48] S Domberger, 'Economic Regulation Through Franchise Contracts', in J Kay, C Mayer, and D Thomson, (eds), *Privatisation and Regulation: The UK Experience* (Oxford: Clarendon Press, 1986) 269. In the UK franchising is used as a mode of regulation of broadcasting and transport services, including bus and rail. See H Collins, *Regulating Contracts* (Oxford: Oxford University Press, 1999) 304; R Baldwin and M Cave, *Understanding Regulation: Theory, Strategy, and Practice* (Oxford: Oxford University Press, 1999) 297.

[49] Baldwin and Cave, ibid 258.

[50] ibid 42.

[51] Corporatization in this sense is distinguishable from corporatism as a method of governance involving 'cooperative arrangements between government and non-governmental groups or institutions under which the latter . . . agree to act in a way which will further the governmental policy' – P Cane, *An Introduction to Administrative Law* (3rd edn, Oxford: Clarendon Press, 1996), 21–22.

[52] J Farrar, and B McCabe, 'Corporatisation, Corporate Governance and the Deregulation of the Public Sector Economy' (1995) 6 *Public Law Review* 24.

the granting of increased autonomy to provider units such as hospitals, schools, and education and training bodies, for example through their creation as not-for-profit Public Interest Companies (PICs). Such arrangements have been described as a halfway house between full state ownership and the PFI.[53] PICs combine both private and public sector characteristics, while remaining independent of direct public management. They may be required to operate according to market principles (borrowing, competing, generating revenue to pay debts, and investing) but in the public interest, and without having to pay dividends to shareholders. Any operating surplus may be required to be reinvested in the service. Assets may continue to be publicly owned, and be specifically protected from private sector take-overs.

Under legislation introduced in the late 1980s, Training and Enterprise Councils (TECs)[54] and City Technology Colleges (CTCs)[55] were constituted either as charitable bodies or private companies limited by guarantee, with dual legal accountability to shareholders and the Secretary of State. This model has been adopted by New Labour as a mechanism for the creation of other corporate bodies separate from but regulated by central government, such as Academies.[56] Corporatization here serves to increase the involvement and influence of local business communities, and to inject an element of competitive discipline into the design and implementation of educational and training programs. Contract functions here as a regulatory mechanism in a similar manner to PPPs and the PFI. While the government is a 'purchaser' of services only in a loose sense, and there is no supply-side competition involving competitive tendering, the services are provided in partnership with

[53] *Observer* 6 October 2002.

[54] Training and Enterprise Councils (TECs) were established through powers exercised by the Secretary of State under s 25(1) of the Employment Act 1988 (amending s 2 of the Employment and Training Act 1973) to make arrangements for training for employment – see D Vere, 'Training and Enterprise Councils: Putting Business in the Lead', in A Harrison, (ed), *From Hierarchy to Contract* (Oxford: Transaction Books, 1993).

[55] City Technology Colleges (CTCs) were established under the Education Reform Act 1988, s 105(1), which gave the Secretary of State powers to enter into agreement with any person for establishing and maintaining a CTC. While CTCs are not subject to the same controls as schools in the maintained sector, they must be run in accordance with their funding agreements and schemes of governance. Regulation takes the form of monitoring of performance by the DfES, and inspection by the Office for Standards in Education (OfSTED) in the same way as for maintained schools.

[56] City Academies were first introduced in 2000 under s 482 Education Act 1996 as replacements for failing or under-achieving inner-city schools. They became simply Academies under s 65 Education Act 2002. Academies are all-ability schools established by sponsors from business, faith or voluntary groups working in partnership with central government and local education authorities. Sponsors contribute to capital costs, most of which are borne by the Department for Education and Skills (DfES). Running costs are met in full by the DfES. In any agreement made in the exercise of powers under s 482, payments made by the Secretary of State are dependent on the fulfillment of specified conditions (s 4). The intention is that Academies will generally replace an existing poorly performing school, or be part of a proposal to tackle a group of under-performing schools. Where the demand for new places justifies it, an Academy may be established without the closure of an existing school.

the private sector and in a management environment subject to competitive discipline.[57]

In the health sector, corporatization describes the process of conferment of legal autonomy and associated increased powers on NHS Foundation Trusts (NHSFTs)[58] and Primary Care Trusts (PCTs).[59] While the internal market has been formally abandoned as an organizational model for health care, a more genuine quasi-market is emerging in England through the redefined roles of PCTs and NHSFTs, coupled with increasing competition among a diversity of providers in the public, private, and non-profit sectors. Freedoms enjoyed by NHSFTs may include local pay determination, and the right to earn income from fee-paying patients. Where PICs such as NHSFTs have access to capital markets, services may be funded in a similar manner to the PFI, but with the benefit for ministers of reduced complexity and greater freedom from Treasury control. Corporatization in the health sector is also taking the form of local improvement finance trusts (LIFTs). Like the PFI, LIFT schemes are a means of obtaining finance for public services infrastructure and management. They are likely to be managed by a relatively small number of multi-national specialist private companies. PCTs may have no practical option other than to enter into LIFT schemes to effect improvements in their areas.

Such economic organizational arrangements in the major public service sectors exemplify a mode of regulation which may be described as 'corporatization + contract'.[60] Whether the powers of the newly corporatized entity are given in statute or under contract, its freedom is circumscribed by the conditions of the grant. Central government typically reserves the right in 'operating agreements'

57 It is these bodies, for example TECs, that act as the public agencies entering contracts (or more properly sub-contracts) for the work they have contracted with government to deliver. This is therefore a good example of a double contractual relationship, involving the corporatized body both as provider (to the government) and purchaser (from the private and voluntary sectors).

58 Part 1 of the Health and Social Care (Community Health and Standards) Act 2003 establishes NHSFTs as a new form of NHS organization. s 1 defines FTs as public benefit corporations authorized under the Act to provide goods and services for the purposes of the health service in England. The process of creation of NHSFTs involves 'authorization' following application by NHS Trusts or other bodies to the Independent Regulator established under s 2, provided in both cases that the application is supported by the Secretary of State. The authorization may specify conditions, such as the provision of certain goods and services by the Trust for the purposes of the health service (s 14(4)), and restrictions on private work undertaken (s 15(1)). Failure to comply with a term of authorization may result in the application of various sanctions by the Regulator, including the removal of existing directors or board of governors and the appointment of others to perform these functions (s 23), and ultimately dissolution of the Trust itself (s 25).

59 The National Health Service Reform and Health Care Professions Act 2002 provided for many of the functions performed by health authorities to be transferred to PCTs, and for resources to be allocated directly by the Secretary of State to support their enlarged planning and commissioning role. In contrast with 'NHS contracts' governing relations between PCTs and ordinary Trusts, contracts with NHSFTs are legally binding.

60 Employment training could have been provided within government through the creation of an executive agency of the then Department of Education, but instead was placed more squarely in the market place through the creation of TECs.

to revoke the privileged status where the conditions are breached, or where performance is judged to be inadequate. As in other variants of the economic form of the New Public Contracting, increased autonomy of agencies and bodies performing public service functions is balanced by central powers of intervention. This type of arrangement is distinguishable from more radical forms of corporatization involving the creation of private corporations with greater autonomy and market freedoms.[61]

Quasi-markets for welfare services

The main alternative to direct state provision of major public services such as health and education is quasi-market organization. These sectors were untouched by the first two Thatcher administrations, but began to be restructured on a quasi-market basis from the end of the 1980s.[62] Just as there was no blueprint for the New Public Contracting, so there appears to have been no coherent programme for the development of quasi-markets. The reforms occurred at different points in time and resulted from varied central government initiatives.[63] The NHS and Community Care Act 1990, for example, involved the 'big bang' introduction of a completely novel set of institutional and organizational arrangements for the delivery of health care and social and community care. As we have seen, the British experience of the NPM has been unusual in both the strength of the political commitment to weakening established bureaucracies, and the manner in which radical and controversial reforms have been imposed by government from above. This is in contrast with the more pragmatic nature of developments and the more dispassionate tenor of debates on public services elsewhere in Europe and in the United States.

Quasi-markets combine elements of central direction with managed and regulated competition. Their appeal across the political spectrum lies in their potential for avoiding some of the deficiencies of both bureaucracies and markets.[64] Quasi-markets are 'markets' in the sense that competition among independent suppliers displaces monopoly provision by state bureaucracies. They differ from conventional markets on the supply-side, however, in that competition is between

[61] For example, take-overs are permitted among mutualized non-profit companies or voluntary associations operating in the social housing sector.

[62] J Le Grand and W Bartlett, (eds), *Quasi-Markets and Social Policy* (Houndmills: Macmillan, 1993) 2. Social housing reforms form a more complicated jigsaw, with earlier roots – G Bramley, 'Quasi-Markets and Social Housing', in ibid 155.

[63] K Walsh, N Deakin, P Spurgeon, P Smith, and N Thomas, *Contracting for Change: Contracts in Health, Social Care, and Other Local Government Services* (Oxford: Oxford University Press, 1997) 20.

[64] Walsh has pointed out that the recognition of market failures does not imply that 'government need necessarily employ any staff or own any productive resources at all' – K Walsh, *Public Services and Market Mechanisms: Competition, Contracting and the New Public Management* (Houndmills: Macmillan, 1995) 12.

a range of types of organization, not all of which are privately owned or necessarily out to make a profit.[65] This is particularly true of the social and community care sector, which historically has comprised a large proportion of charitable and voluntary bodies. On the demand side, the distinctive feature in comparison with conventional markets is the absence of a direct relationship or cash nexus linking service recipients and providers. Instead, purchasing power is either centralized in a state commissioning agency acting on behalf of ultimate consumers (the 'purchaser-provider split'), or takes the form of an earmarked budget or 'voucher' allocated to users for the consumption of specific services.[66] These quasi-market forms will briefly be considered in turn.

The purchaser-provider split

In this type of quasi-market purchasing power is concentrated in state agencies representing the consumers to whom services are ultimately delivered. Quasi-market contracting in this sense closely resembles the contracting out of local authority services such as refuse collection that are also delivered directly to consumers. The common feature is the agency process of securing another party (organizationally separate from the purchaser or commissioner) to provide goods or services on a competitive basis to a third party.[67] Nevertheless, in the social policy literature the term 'quasi-market' has a narrower and more specific meaning, referring to the radical reorganization of the major public welfare sectors such as health and education from the beginning of the 1990s.

In the health care sector, the separation of purchaser and provider roles under the NHS and Community Care Act 1990 Act was intended to subject NHS Trusts to competitive pressures that would result in better cost control and increased efficiency.[68] The resulting internal market satisfied quasi-market criteria in only a limited sense, since competition was restricted to providers within the NHS.

65 'They are "markets" because they replace monolithic state providers with competitive independent ones. They are "quasi" because they differ from conventional markets in a number of key ways. The differences are on both the supply and demand sides' – Le Grand and Bartlett (n 62 above) 10.

66 W Bartlett, JA Roberts, and J Le Grand, (eds), *A Revolution in Social Policy: Quasi-Market Reforms in the 1990s* (Bristol: The Policy Press, 1998) 1.

67 'Under the new quasi-market arrangements the functions of service provision and purchase have been split. Designated purchasers now enter into contracts with providers for services to meet the needs of the population for which they are responsible. The services provided, the level of output and the quality of that output are determined by contracts between the purchaser-provider pair' – C Propper, 'Quasi-Markets and Regulation', in J Le Grand and W Bartlett, (eds) (n 62 above) 183.

68 W Bartlett, and L Harrison, 'Quasi-Markets and the National Health Service Reforms', in ibid; C Bennett and E Ferlie, 'Contracting in Theory and In Practice: Some Evidence From the NHS' (1996) 74 *Public Administration* 49; R Flynn and G Williams, (eds), *Contracting for Health: Quasi-Markets and the National Health Service* (Oxford: Oxford University Press, 1997); R Flynn, G Williams, and S Pickard, *Markets and Networks: Contracting in Community Health Services* (Buckingham: Open University Press, 1996).

While under New Labour the internal market experiment has been formally abandoned, a more genuine quasi-market is being developed in England through the corporatization of provider functions coupled with the encouragement of competition among an increasing diversity of providers in the public, private, and non-profit sectors, with the commissioning role being streamlined in PCTs. The 1990 Act also implemented a purchaser-provider split in social and community care. The more radical objective here was to shift the centre of gravity of provision from the public to the non-state sectors.[69] The role of local authorities became that of enabling and developing markets through community care planning.[70] The transition from a predominantly internal market to an external one was immediately facilitated through guidelines which specified that a relatively high proportion of local authority budgets had to be spent on non-statutory organizations in the private and voluntary sectors.[71] We saw in Chapter 2 how the pace of quasi-market reforms in the health and education sectors has accelerated under New Labour, for example through the granting of new powers to health authorities in respect of Public Private Partnerships, the creation of NHS Foundation Trusts with the legal capacity to enter enforceable contracts with PCTs, the creation of Academies as corporate entities with contractual capacities, and the introduction of variable tuition fees aimed at increasing competition and student choice in tertiary education. Under the Education Act 2002 and the Health and Social Care (Community Health and Standards) Act 2003, education and health bodies that are considered to be failing in their public service duties are liable to various central enforcement measures and powers of intervention.

The splitting of purchaser and provider functions is considered by advocates of quasi-markets to have various advantages compared with direct government provision. These include: weakening the influence of vested interests which tend to result in services reflecting the needs of providers rather than users; strengthening commissioning functions (needs analysis, specification of outcomes, costing, and evaluation and review) by separating these from day-to-day management; increasing responsiveness to users by allowing purchasers to focus on local needs and preferences; and improving service outcomes through competition among a larger number and wider range of provider organizations.[72]

Vouchering

While traditionally associated with the New Right, in recent years there has been increasing interest in vouchering from the political left. One advantage claimed

[69] L Challis, P Day, R Klein, and E Scrivens, 'Managing Quasi-Markets: Institutions of Regulation', in ibid 20.

[70] Walsh et al (n 63 above) 81.

[71] M Knapp, G Wistow, J Forder, and B Hardy, 'Markets for Social Care: Opportunities, Barriers and Implications', in W Bartlett, C Propper, D Wilson, and J Le Grand, (eds), *Quasi-Markets in the Welfare State: The Emerging Findings* (Bristol: SAUS, 1994) 130.

[72] ibid 133.

for this form of quasi-market organization is improved transparency and accountability. In theory vouchering should lead to superior allocative efficiency in public services through the operation of the price mechanism. Putting purchasing power in the hands of the consumer should result in a more optimal pattern of distribution of services than may be achieved by concentrating that power in a representative public agency.[73] Allowing prices a clearer role in reflecting demand and determining resource allocation may also avoid various problems traditionally associated with public provision. These problems (such as waste associated with administrative costs, and over-production due to opportunity costs not being taken into account by users) may be said to occur whether public services are provided directly or through the purchaser-provider split. The allocative benefits of vouchering, however, can only fully be realized where charges are related to the level of output, usually where the consumer is free to choose whether or not to use the service, and this choice has an effect on the amount of service produced.[74]

A further advantage of vouchering lies in the relative empowerment of service recipients. Choice is exercised directly by consumers rather than on their behalf by state agencies, thereby resolving the problem of how to ensure the responsiveness of purchasing decisions. Users not only choose their service provider, but may also in theory 'exit' from unsatisfactory relationships so long as there is sufficient competition. In comparison with market organization (which theoretically also permits choice and exit) vouchering enables equity and redistributive goals to be achieved through subsidies to disadvantaged individuals and groups. Vouchering may therefore be regarded as compatible with the commitment that public services should remain free at the point of delivery and funded from general taxation. This form of subsidy may be argued to be preferable to the unintended subsidization that occurs where there is no effective pricing of any kind, as is currently the case with most public services.

Hence many of the quasi-market reforms in education and housing operate, not through the separation of purchaser and provider roles in the sense so far considered, but primarily through the creation of consumer choice and exit mechanisms. The delegation of choice to individuals, coupled with continued state funding and stimuli to increased competition, has the effect of giving 'vouchers' to consumers of these services.[75] In the quasi-markets for primary and secondary (and now tertiary) education, parents and students have become directly engaged in the selection function.[76] Some degree of parental choice over schools was

73 Walsh et al (n 63 above) 91; EC Steuerle and EC Twombly, 'Vouchers', in LM Salamon, (ed), *The Tools of Government: A Guide to the New Governance* (Oxford: Oxford University Press, 2002).

74 These conditions do not normally apply in cases of charging for bureaucratic services (passport applications, vehicle tax registration), whereas the whole point of quasi-market organization is to generate efficiencies through supply-side competition.

75 Le Grand and Bartlett (n 62 above) 10.

76 Challis et al (n 69 above) 16; G Johnes and M Cave, 'The Development of Competition Among Higher Education Institutions', in Bartlett et al (eds) (1994).

introduced under the Education Act 1980. This was extended in the Education Reform Act 1988 through 'open enrolment', and through the establishment of grant-maintained schools which could obtain funding directly from central government. The bureaucratic allocation of pupils and resources was thereby replaced by a quasi-market system in which school budgets depended primarily on success in attracting pupils.[77] Similar quasi-market reforms in housing created exit mechanisms through rights granted tenants to opt out of the council housing sector and local authority control. The 'right to buy' provisions of the Housing Act 1980 had resulted in the sale of 20 per cent of council housing stock by the mid-1980s. The Housing Act 1988 gave tenants the choice of opting for non-public sector landlords through the change of landlord and Housing Action Trust schemes. The Housing Act 1985 enabled councils to dispose of their entire housing stock to the private sector through Large Scale Voluntary Transfer (LSVT) with the consent of the secretary of state. In theory tenants of social housing are able to choose between competing providers, with the cost being borne at least to some degree by the state through housing benefit funded from general taxation.

The devolution of decision-making powers to consumers rather than to public purchasing agencies removes exactly that element of delegation subject to central control and supervision that has been argued to characterise economic contracting regimes. The significance of New Labour's current interest in this form of quasi-market, and the associated regulatory mechanisms of choice and exit, will be further considered in Chapter 8.

Organizational problems

Where public agencies are charged with commissioning services on behalf of third parties, ie consumers, the problem arises of how to ensure that purchasing decisions are responsive to the needs and preferences of service recipients and citizens. The present section outlines some of the main obstacles to increasing the efficiency of public services through quasi-market organization.

First, the effective operation of purchaser-provider quasi-markets ideally requires multiple purchasers and providers. On the supply side, efficiency benefits associated with the ability of prices to move freely in response to changes in supply and demand may still accrue in the absence of actual competition provided that the market is contestable, ie one that new competitors may enter at relatively low cost. On the demand-side, while there are circumstances where a monopoly may be justified, a number of purchasers is usually considered necessary to represent the range of individual and group interests, to ensure that resources are drawn into

[77] R Levacic, 'Evaluating the Performance of Quasi-Markets in Education', in Bartlett et al (eds) (1994), 35; W Bartlett, 'Quasi-Markets in Educational Reforms', in Le Grand and Bartlett (n 62 above) 125. Generally see M Feintuck, *Accountability and Choice in Schooling* (Buckingham: Open University Press, 1994); S Gewirtz, SJ Ball, and R Bowe, *Markets, Choice and Equity in Education* (Buckingham: Open University Press, 1995).

their highest valued uses, and to attract new market entrants and to discourage exit by efficient suppliers.[78] Secondly, accurate and reliable information is necessary for various reasons: for central government to allocate budgets; for public purchasers to manage contracts and monitor quality; for providers to price their activities appropriately; and for consumers indirectly to influence purchasing and demand decisions. Where such basic conditions are established in a particular sector, the additional transaction costs of obtaining information, preventing opportunism, dealing with uncertainties, and of writing and monitoring contracts need to be taken into account in assessing the efficiency benefits of quasi-markets compared with markets and hierarchies.[79]

In practice, a growing body of empirical evidence has revealed structural problems with quasi-markets similar to those that occur in real markets.[80] In many cases there is considerable doubt as to the existence of effective competition between providers.[81] The markets may not be contestable, either because of the relative novelty of competition and the lack of competitors, or because features of the particular type of service (for example quality in health and social care) are not readily quantifiable or otherwise easily subject to competitive discipline.[82] Such arrangements may fail to deliver value-for-money due to a combination of ineffective competition, monopoly market conditions, and problems following the award of contracts on the basis of impossibly low bids.[83] The attainment of efficiency and equity goals may be impeded by various information asymmetries, barriers to entry, and monopolistic relationships across the whole range of welfare quasi-markets. Other problems include opportunities for 'cream skimming',[84] the priority given cost reduction over service improvement, and the lack

78 W Bartlett and J Le Grand, 'The Theory of Quasi-Markets', in J Le Grand and W Bartlett, (eds) (n 62 above) 21.

79 P Vincent-Jones and A Harries, 'Conflict and Cooperation in Local Authority Quasi-Markets: The Hybrid Organisation of Internal Contracting Under CCT, (1996) 22 *Local Government Studies* 187.

80 While the ideal market structure should be sufficiently diverse that neither purchasers nor providers can exert a significant influence on it, empirical studies of public contracting have shown that public authorities are often monopsonistic purchasers of services which themselves tend to monopoly in provision – Walsh et al (n 63 above) 31. Various factors serve to restrict competition. For example, public services must be delivered in particular localities, and there may be barriers to market entry for smaller firms where there are considerable economies of scale, or high levels of asset specificity in equipment or expertise.

81 W Bartlett, JA Roberts, and J Le Grand, (eds), *A Revolution in Social Policy: Quasi-Market Reforms in the 1990s* (Bristol: The Policy Press, 1998). For an analysis of such problems under the Access to Justice Act 1999, see H Sommerlad, '"I've lost the Plot": An Everyday Story of Legal Aid Lawyers' (2001) 28 JLS 335.

82 C Propper and W Bartlett, 'The Impact of Competition on the Behaviour of National Health Service Trusts', in R Flynn and G Williams, (eds), *Contracting for Health: Quasi-Markets and the National Health Service* (Oxford: Oxford University Press, 1997); L Hoyes and R Means, 'Markets, Contracts and Social Care Services: Prospects and Problems', J Bornat, C Pereira, D Pilgrim, and F Williams, (eds), *Community Care* (London: Open University Press, 1993).

83 *Guardian* 12 November 1998.

84 In quasi-markets for welfare and health and social services, cream-skimming is associated with perverse incentives for purchasers (or providers) to discriminate between users in favour of those who

of management skills on the part of the public agencies which perform purchasing functions on behalf of consumers. Debates in the social policy literature now centre on whether such deficiencies can be corrected through regulation, beyond that already implied in the constitution of quasi-markets and the state's involvement in setting budgets, limiting entry to markets, setting quality standards, and determining the form of contracts between purchaser and provider. The question is whether the benefits of further regulation outweigh the drawbacks of increased complexity and distortion.[85]

While vouchering systems may avoid some of the above difficulties, the drawback with this form of quasi-market organization is that it may benefit privileged and well-educated individuals and fail to protect the disadvantaged and the vulnerable. In making service provision dependent on individual choice, vouchering also removes an element of public control that is a feature of the purchaser-provider split. It may furthermore create structural inefficiencies (for example, several care agencies working in the same building with different clients) and reduce provider accountability where there is no-one other than the client to hold the provider to account.[86] And the potential for vouchering is arguably limited in the case of complex human services, which rely on professional assessment and require services to be brokered or commissioned by an agency on behalf of the consumer.

Economic contracting regimes

We now consider in greater depth the relationships comprising economic contracting regimes. These may be modelled along five separate axes (Fig 6):[87] (a) purchaser–provider; (b) state–purchaser; (c) state–provider; (d) citizen/user–purchaser; and (e) user–provider. Here we focus on the institutions of purposive regulation comprising the top half of the diamond, paying particular attention to the manner in which the contractual purchaser–provider relationship is conditioned by the hierarchical relationship between central government and the public purchasing or commissioning agency.[88]

are least expensive, so threatening the equity and social justice goals of quasi-market organisation – Bartlett and Le Grand (n 78 above) 31–3.

85 C Propper, 'Quasi-Markets and Regulation', in Le Grand and Bartlett (eds) (n 62 above) 184.

86 Walsh et al (n 63 above) 198.

87 cf H Schoombee, 'Privatisation and Contracting Out – Where Are We Going?', in J McMillan, (ed), *Administrative Law Under the Coalition Government* (Canberra: AIAL, 1997): 'Contracting out gives rise to a triangular relationship between, firstly, the government body which does the out-sourcing and acts as a "purchaser" of the services; secondly, the party contracting with the government . . .; and thirdly, the members of the public to whom the service is delivered' (136). The position taken in the present paper differs in the broader emphasis on citizenship, and in the situation of this 'triangle' within a more complex web of relationships constituting the regulatory framework of contracting for human services (see below).

88 The bottom half of the figure, which refers to issues of citizen and consumer representation in public service organization, is considered in Chapter 8. A further dimension, already touched on at

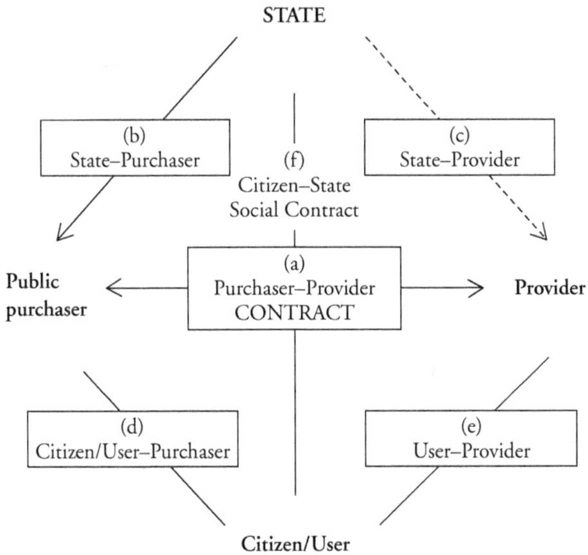

Figure 6. Economic contracting regime

State–public purchaser relationship

In the *hierarchical* relationship between central government and public purchasers (Fig 6(b)), major governance issues concern:

- the nature and form of responsibilities of the purchasing agency, in terms of duties, standards, and performance targets;
- the definition and ambit of contractual powers of the purchasing agency, regarding when, with whom, and on what terms to contract;
- the scope of discretion and freedom from central interference of the purchasing agency in the exercise of contracting powers; and
- the overall quality of the regulatory relationship (relationality) – the more relational the regulatory linkage, the more likely the attainment of regulatory purposes.

A first major dimension of the analysis of the state–public purchaser relationship concerns the adequacy of legal powers and the resulting capacity of public agencies to discharge the responsibilities that have been assigned to them. Public purchasing and procurement are subject to detailed EU regulations, which cover

various points and to which we shall return, is the 'social contract' relationship between citizen and state (Fig 6(f)).

a wide range of matters including planning and contract initiation, solicitation of bids, contract award, contract management and monitoring, and contract renewal or termination.[89] In addition to such general regulation, domestic contracting regimes define and circumscribe the legal powers of public agencies in various ways. The regulatory framework governing the role of local authorities may be argued to be particularly restrictive.[90] The power under the Local Government Act 2000 to do anything which local authorities consider likely to promote or improve the economic, social, or environmental well-being of their areas is heavily qualified by a plethora of earlier legislation,[91] for example preventing them from taking account of non-commercial considerations when awarding contracts. If the idea of community leadership is to be taken seriously, it implies more discretion than councils currently enjoy, and powers which distinguish them from other agencies and actors operating on the local stage.[92]

We have seen in the discussion of policy-guided choice in review processes in Chapter 2 how contracting regimes impose various constraints (direct and indirect, formal and informal) on the role performed by senior managers in central and local government. While they are in theory free to decide how to deliver best value or better quality services at optimal cost, in practice discretion is exercised according to central standards and guidelines favouring certain competitive processes, limiting options, and circumscribing choice. Economic contracting regimes embody policies and regulatory instruments directed specifically at reducing public monopoly provision of public services. The possibility that administrative efficiencies may be obtained merely by applying private management techniques in the management of directly employed staff is deliberately discounted.[93] This structural bias is likely to interfere with the transaction cost considerations that should determine whether the function is performed directly,[94] under contract with an in-house or external provider, or in some form of

[89] S Arrowsmith, J Linarelli, and D Wallace, *Regulating Public Procurement: National and International Perspectives* (London: Kluwer International, 2000); S Arrowsmith, 'The EC Procurement Directives, National Procurement Policies and Better Governance: The Case for a New Approach' (2002) 27 *European Law Review* 3.

[90] I Leigh, *Law, Politics and Local Democracy* (Oxford: Oxford University Press, 2000).

[91] ibid 61. [92] ibid 346.

[93] Ascher (n 10 above) 16; D Adams and M Hess, 'Alternatives to Competitive Tendering and Privatisation: A Case Study from the Australian Health Industry' (2000) 59 *Australian Journal of Public Administration* 49.

[94] A Harries and P Vincent-Jones, 'Housing Management in Three Metropolitan Local Authorities: The Impact of CCT and Implications for Best Value' (2001) 27 *Local Government Studies* 69; P Vincent-Jones, 'Hybrid Organization, Contractual Governance, and Compulsory Competitive Tendering in the Provision of Local Authority Services', in S Deakin and J Michie, (eds), *Contracts, Cooperation and Competition: Studies in Economics, Management and Law* (Oxford: Oxford University Press, 1997); P Vincent-Jones and A Harries, 'Conflict and Cooperation in Local Authority Quasi-Markets: The Hybrid Organisation of Internal Contracting Under CCT, (1996) 22 *Local Government Studies* 187; P Vincent-Jones, D Campbell, A Harries, and W Seal, *Conflict and Cooperation in Contracting for Professional Services: A Comparative Study*, (ESRC Final Report, 1998).

partnership arrangement,[95] for example analogous to supply chains in the private sector.[96] In the quasi-market organization of major public service sectors such as health and social care, the role of the public agency is even more tightly defined. Here there is no discretion at all whether, but only how, to perform the designated purchasing or commissioning function. Again, this may impede the attainment of economic benefits that are assumed to accompany the devolution of managerial responsibilities to lower levels within the state bureaucracy or to public agencies implementing welfare programmes.

The concern here is that economic contracting regimes frequently deny the degree of autonomy and flexibility in the choice of mode of public service organization that is required for responsive public services.[97] The selection of the PFI over other procurement options, for example, is supposed to depend on detailed cost-benefit analysis, in particular as regards risk transfer to private investors and the consideration of practical alternatives. Yet the available evidence suggests that this option is being routinely adopted in circumstances where it is more expensive for government in the long term, both as a consequence of the higher cost of private sector borrowing and the profits paid to shareholders, while at the same time failing to transfer risk to the private sector.[98] Continued attempts to justify the PFI on value-for-money grounds appear to involve creative compliance by the government's accountants with the government's own policy.[99] The suspicion remains that the PFI is a political project which cannot be justified in terms of economic efficiency.[100]

In addition to such constraints, the autonomy of public agencies may be further restricted by direct central government interference in the commissioning

[95] On the general tendency of outsourcing pressures associated with the NPM to undermine the conditions of effective decision-making by public service managers, see J Stewart, 'Purchaser-Provider – Are the Purchasers Ready for It?' (1999) *Australian Journal of Public Administration* 105. On the outsourcing of professional and white-collar services, see: J Boston, 'Purchasing Policy Advice: The Limits to Contracting Out' (1994) 7 *Governance* 1; ibid 'Inherently Governmental Functions and the Limits to Contracting Out', in J Boston, (ed), *The State Under Contract* (Wellington: Bridget Williams Books, 1995); P Vincent-Jones, D Campbell, A Harries, and W Seal, (n 94 above).

[96] M Sako, *Prices, Quality and Trust: Inter-Firm Relations in Britain and Japan* (Cambridge: Cambridge University Press, 1992); RJ Admiraal and G Jan van Helden, 'Benchmarking in the Dutch Waste-Water Treatment Sector' (2003) *Public Money and Management* (April), 113.

[97] On the mixed evidence concerning best value, see S Martin, 'Implementing Best Value: Local Public Services in Transition' (2000) 78 *Public Administration* 209; ibid 'Re-evaluating Public Service Improvement: The Early Impacts of the Best Value Regime' (2001) 29 *Policy and Politics* 447; S Martin and H Davis, 'What Works and For Whom? The Competing Rationalities of Best Value' (2001) 29 *Policy and Politics* 465; S Martin and A Boaz, 'Public Participation and Citizen-Centred Local Government: Lessons From the Best Value and Better Government for Older People Pilot Programmes' (2000) *Public Money and Management* (Apr–Jun), 47.

[98] D Asenova and M Beck, 'The UK Financial Sector and Risk Management in PFI Projects: A Survey' (2003) *Public Money and Management* (July), 195; R Ball, M Heafey, and D King, 'Private Finance Initiative: A Good Deal for the Public Purse or a Drain on Future Generations?' (2000) 29 *Policy and Politics* 95.

[99] J Michie, *Public Services Yes. Euro No* (London: New Europe Research Trust, 2002).

[100] *Guardian* 27 July 2004.

function.[101] In the NHS, for example, there is no institutional mechanism structuring the discretion of ministers and safeguarding the autonomy of PCTs against hierarchical intervention by the Department of Health.[102] Where such interventions are perceived as lacking in legitimacy, or where competitive contracting solutions are imposed dogmatically in circumstances where other planned arrangements might have been more suitable, then tensions in the regulatory regime are inevitable. The various constraints on the role of public agencies do not mean that managerial autonomy is completely denied, or that discretion may not be exercised to some degree.[103] The problem, however, concerns regulatory ineffectiveness, and the high costs associated with the implementation of these economic contracting regimes.

Central government interventions in the 1980s and 1990s may generally be considered, in relational terms (in the 'as if' contractual sense[104]), to have had various negative effects on the norms of solidarity, role integrity, power, and planning in the relationship between public purchasing agencies and central government. Many of the reforms were imposed in the face of fierce opposition and with little public consultation, evaluation or debate.[105] The cooperation and mutual respect that characterised relationships between central government and public sector organisations in the immediate post-war period were replaced by antagonism and mistrust. The costs of rule-making, monitoring and enforcement were excessive. During this period local authorities devoted considerable time and effort to 'creative compliance' – 'the process whereby those regulated avoid having to break the rules by using legal techniques to achieve non-compliance with the intention of the law without technically violating its content'.[106] While the development of economic contracting regimes under New Labour has arguably been marked by a more permissive and collaborative regulatory style than in the Conservative era, various constraints on the role and autonomy of public agencies remain.

101 K Shaw, J Fenwick, and A Foreman, 'Compulsory Competition for Local Government Services in the UK: A Case of Market Rhetoric and Camouflaged Centralism' (1995) 10 *Public Policy and Administration* 63.

102 *Guardian* 1 June 2004 ('NHS Trusts bullied into private contracts'). See J Le Grand, 'Competition, Cooperation, or Control? Tales from the British National Health Service' (1999) 18 *Health Affairs* 27; ibid, J Le Grand, 'Further Tales from the British National Health Service' (2002) 21 *Health Affairs* 116.

103 In quasi-market organisation, there is choice among competing providers. In the local government sector, even under the highly prescriptive CCT regime, there was considerable scope for councils in deciding precisely how to organize the separation of purchaser and provider functions, ie through what form of departmental or agency structure – see Walsh et al (n 63 above) 83–90; P Vincent-Jones and A Harries, 'CCT, Conflict and Cooperation in Local Authority Quasi-Markets', in Bartlett et al (eds) (n 66 above).

104 see ch 1, above.

105 D Hughes, 'The Reorganization of the NHS – The Rhetoric and the Reality of the Internal Market' (1991) 54 MLR 88; M Loughlin, *Legality and Locality: The Role of Law in Central-Local Government Relations* (Oxford: Clarendon Press, 1996).

106 R Baldwin, 'Governing With Rules: The Developing Agenda', in G Richardson and H Genn, (eds), *Administrative Law and Government Action: The Courts and Alternative Mechanisms of Review* (Oxford: Clarendon Press, 1994), 172; D McBarnet and C Whelan, 'The Elusive Spirit of the Law: Formalism and the Struggle for Legal Control' (1991) 54 MLR 848, 873.

The decision-making capacity of public agencies is unduly impeded by purposive regulation and the constant threat of central interference. The economic benefits of relational contracting in purchaser–provider relationships depend at least in part on the qualities of regulatory sensitivity, collaboration, and cooperation in the hierarchical relationship between central government departments and public purchasing agencies.

Purchaser–provider relationship

In the *contractual* relationships between purchasers/commissioners and providers (Fig 6(a)), governance issues concern:

- the strength of representation of the norms of planning, consent, choice, and reciprocity in the making of contracts;
- the 'bindingness' of the arrangements in terms of the credibility of commitments and the ability of the parties to enforce contractual obligations, supported by appropriate sanctioning machinery;
- the quality of fairness in the performance of contracts, particularly as regards the application of sanctions;
- the balance of power in the relationship, including the structuring of the discretionary exercise of public power by the purchaser;
- the capacity of the agency to manage the relationship in terms of the managerial skills and abilities that are necessary for effective contract letting, monitoring, and enforcement; and
- the overall quality of contractual relationships, assessed in terms of the balance of relatively discrete and relational norms both within the relationship and in the institutional environment ('relationality').

In discussing these questions, a broad distinction is drawn between normative aspects of contract, and contract design and management issues. First, as regards the former aspect, purchaser–provider relationships require appropriate support of the contract norms. In the case of legally enforceable contracts, bindingness and other basic conditions of exchange are assured by private law institutions in conjunction with the norms that have developed within particular relationships and sectors through custom, convention, and business practice.[107] In economic transactions between the public and private sectors, as in other business exchanges,

[107] P Vincent-Jones, 'Contract and Business Transactions: A Socio-Legal Analysis', (1989) 16 JLS 166; L Bernstein, 'Opting Out of the Legal System: Extralegal Contractual Relations in the Diamond Industry' (1992) XXI *Journal of Legal Studies* 115; ibid L Bernstein, 'Merchant Law in a Merchant Court: Retinking the Code's Search for Immanent Business Norms' (1996) 114 *University of Pennsylvania Law Review* 1765; D Charny, 'Nonlegal Sanctions in Commercial Relationships' (1990) 104 *Harvard Law Review* 375; RB Ferguson, 'The Adjudication of Commercial Disputes and the Legal System in Modern England' (1980) *British Journal of Law and Society* 141.

the institutional framework enables the parties to plan their relationship and to undertake mutual obligations with recourse where necessary to the threat of legal sanctions and the ultimate guarantee of judicial enforcement.[108] However, the balance of power in these relationships remains in some respects unfairly weighted in favour of the public agency. In Chapter 11 we consider how provider interests might better be protected through the strengthening of contract norms of fairness and power.

Where economic contracts are not legally enforceable in this way, bindingness may nevertheless be assured by a range of incentives which encourage compliance and provide informal sanctions for 'breach' of contract. For example, internal contracts between in-house providers and central government or local authority clients following market testing or competitive tendering occur in a highly competitive or contestable environment. The ultimate sanction for contractor failure or poor performance is termination of the contract, and the prospect that the function will be outsourced in any subsequent tendering exercise. Despite the presence of such incentives, a major question here is whether contractual commitments might be rendered more credible either by making relations privately enforceable (as through corporatization involving the creation of independent legal personalities), or through the development and application of a special public law of contract. We return to this issue in Chapters 10 and 11.

In both internal and external contracts, the hierarchical dimension of the contracting regime is likely to have an important bearing on the quality of purchaser–provider relationships. Some choices of organizational arrangement are likely to be better than others, with implications for the cooperative or conflictual nature of contractual relationships.[109] High levels of trust and cooperation are indicative of optimal service provision,[110] and should enhance the capacity for organizational learning on the part of purchasers and providers in public service networks. By contrast, conflict and the absence of trust are suggestive of both dynamic inefficiency (poor information flows and lack of responsiveness to changing environmental conditions) and operational inefficiency (poor utilization of productive resources).[111] Empirical socio-legal research in Britain has

[108] S Macaulay, 'Non-Contractual Relations in Business: A Preliminary Study' (1963) 28 *American Sociological Review* 55.

[109] Vincent-Jones (1997) (n 94 above).

[110] M Casson, *The Economics of Business Culture: Game Theory, Transaction Costs, and Economic Performance* (Oxford: Oxford University Press, 1991).

[111] S Deakin and F Wilkinson, 'Contracts, Cooperation and Trust: The Role of the Institutional Framework', in D Campbell, and P Vincent-Jones, (eds), *Contract and Economic Organisation: Socio-Legal Initiatives* (Aldershot: Dartmouth, 1996); S Deakin, C Lane, and F Wilkinson, 'Contract Law, Trust Relations, and Incentives for Co-operation: A Comparative Study', in S Deakin and J Michie, (eds), *Contracts, Cooperation and Competition: Studies in Economics, Management and Law* (Oxford: Oxford University Press, 1997) 105. Whilst the high costs of managing and adjusting conflictual transactions might be outweighed by financial savings in some cases, there is likely to be a strong association between cooperation and efficiency. A high level of defaults and terminations is also likely to be culturally damaging in terms of antagonistic relations within the organization, and to detract from the quality of the service (through interruptions, poor morale etc) to the ultimate consumer.

shown repeatedly how the contract norms governing purchaser-provider relations have been damaged or strained by policies such as CCT and market testing.[112] Many of the dysfunctional consequences of the introduction of quasi-market contracting in the health, education and local government sectors have arguably been attributable to artificially discrete models of contracting, implemented in accordance with central prescriptions or guidelines. It is hardly surprising that the experience of problems with some PFI projects mirrors that of contractual arrangements for service provision made under CCT,[113] since competitive tendering operates in a similar way and the public 'partner' is under similar pressures to give high priority to price over quality considerations.

Again as with CCT, the major contractors (such as Amec, Balfour Beatty, McAlpine, and WS Atkins) have the incentive to create monopolies by making loss-leading bids as part of a long-term strategy to drive competitors out of the market. Information technology PFI projects have run into particular difficulties, resulting from the award of contracts on the basis of impossibly low bids. The public benefits of PFI projects are particularly doubtful in the longer term. The need for the private sector to obtain a return on its investment means that efficiency gains in the operation of facilities may be made at the expense of service quality, and the total cost of schemes may be higher than if public bodies had been able to raise finance directly. In cases where the private partner has got into financial difficulties, the risks supposedly transferred to the private sector appear to have been borne by the taxpayer. Critics argue that the financial problems besetting PFI contractors such as Jarvis in 2005 are the tip of an iceberg, and a disaster not only for the Treasury and taxpayers, but also for citizens who bear the brunt of uncompleted PFI projects such as schools and hospitals.[114] Legal bindingness may be futile where central pressures lead to the inappropriate tendering or letting of contracts, or if the contract is not properly managed by the purchaser, or if the contract fails for some other reason.

This discussion leads to the second set of governance issues in the purchaser–provider relationship, concerning the capacity of public agencies to manage the contracting process.[115] Even if the potential exists for the efficient and effective operation of economic contracts, whether this result is achieved in practice depends on the details of contract design, award, monitoring and enforcement.[116]

See also SB Sitkin and NL Roth, 'Explaining the Limited Effectiveness of Legalistic "Remedies" for Trust/Distrust' (1993) 4 *Organization Science* 367.

112 Vincent-Jones (1997) (n 94 above).

113 P Vincent-Jones and A Harries, 'Conflict and Cooperation in Local Authority Quasi-Markets: The Hybrid Organisation of Internal Contracting Under CCT, (1996) 22 *Local Government Studies* 187. See E Capen, R Clapp, and W Campbell, 'Competitive Bidding in High Risk Situations' (1971) 23 *Journal of Petroleum Technology* 641.

114 *Guardian* 27 July 2004.

115 Schoombee (n 87 above).

116 DeHoog, Ruth Hoogland, and LM Salamon, 'Purchase-of-Service Contracting', in LM Salamon, (ed), *The Tools of Government: A Guide to the New Governance* (Oxford: Oxford University Press, 2002) 326: 'Award decisions are a critical point in the contract process. Public officials

The challenges of contract management here differ from those in traditional procurement, for example in the competitive pressures placed on public agencies and the relative lack of previous contracting experience on which to draw. Nevertheless, some basic principles of contract design are clear. There is a growing consensus among economists and public administration experts that the fixed-price contract is rarely optimal in government contracting. While the winning bidder has the incentive to reduce costs in order to win the contract in a competitive tendering exercise, this may be at the expense of quality of service. On the other hand, cost-plus contracts, in which the provider receives all costs plus a fee, may result in high quality services but encourage cost-padding.[117] This form of contract is more attractive to bidders than the fixed-price contract since risk is shared rather than borne by the supplier.

One method of addressing concerns over quality where there is limited observability of output is to specify inputs or 'throughput' standards in contracts.[118] However, a lengthy contract-specification process increases the transaction costs of both tendering and bidding, and is likely also to reduce significantly the number of bidders. Detailed input specification is also likely to both inhibit improvements in quality and impede dynamic efficiencies that may result from innovation in the methods of service delivery. An alternative is to leave to providers the choice of the most efficient production process.[119] This regulatory strategy depends on the attainment of consensus on appropriate output standards, and on the credibility of sanctions for non-performance.[120] In economic contracts there may be a private law sanction for non-compliance, or failure may be met with financial penalties or have negative administrative repercussions. The targets specified in contracts between purchasers and providers in the primary health care sector, for example, occupy a mid-way position on a spectrum of regulation ranging

must be aware of the potential threats to the fairness of the process – primarily corruption, collusion, fraud, favoritism, and conflict of interest.' On the need for appropriate contract design in the residential care sector, see J Kendall, 'Of Knights, Knaves and Merchants: The Case of Residential Care for Older People in England in the Late 1990s' (2001) 35 *Social Policy and Administration* 360, 371–3.

117 C Propper, 'Quasi-Markets, Contracts and Quality in Health and Social Care: The US Experience' in J Le Grand and W Bartlett, (eds), (n 62 above) 62.

118 ibid 64; K Walsh, 'Quality and Public Services' (1991) 69 *Public Administration* 7.

119 De Hoog and Salamon (n 116 above) 334. Performance contracting focuses attention 'more on the results or client outcomes of contracts while giving contractors more leeway on the process. The general assumption is that free of process constraints, agencies will have the incentive to find the most effective approach.' The main problem here is that the behaviour of agencies may simply be oriented to what is being measured, especially where there are difficulties of independent evaluation of performance and scrutiny of self-reporting records for accuracy. 'The greatest responsibility for implementing performance contracting lies with government – it must have the resources to create the measures, the data collection systems, and the enforcement mechanisms' (335).

120 Propper (n 117 above) 64. The contract design issues here are analogous to those of regulatory design more generally. As normally understood, the 'standards' technique in business regulation 'allows the activity to take place without any *ex ante* control, but the supplier who fails to meet certain standards of quality commits a criminal offence' – A Ogus, *Regulation: Legal Form and Economic Theory* (Oxford: Clarendon Press, 1994) 150.

from the most precise (input standards) to the most general (output or performance standards).[121] Generally, economic contracts may be viewed as combining the regulation of process (for example, the requirement of service reviews) with a degree of regulation of output, with performance of service providers judged according to centrally determined standards.[122] A major question here concerns the extent of discretion of public purchasing agencies in determining the form of contract, and how far contract design is by contrast centrally prescribed.

The governance problems associated with the contracting process may be expected to vary according to the complexity of the service. Information asymmetries and difficulties of measuring quality of output in some public services sectors may be overcome by careful design of the contract and appropriate choice of the method by which contracts are awarded.[123] However, the structural characteristics of quasi-markets for complex human services raise more intractable contract governance issues. For example, the problems of specifying, monitoring and managing contracts in health and social care are much greater than in the municipal services sector.[124] Clearly the quality of residential care for elderly people is harder to specify and evaluate than the quality of refuse collection or buildings cleaning. In addition, there are particular difficulties of contract design associated with relatively high transaction costs, and high levels of risk and uncertainty.[125]

A further aspect of the purchaser role with a vital bearing on the attainment of the government's regulatory objectives concerns the allocation and management of risk. According to government guidelines, the nature of contractual relationships should be carefully matched to the circumstances and to the assessment of risk. 'Arm's-length' contracting is considered suited to low-risk situations where the activity is not critical to the department's strategic objectives, there are many suppliers, and the costs of changing to another provider would be low.[126] Here the degree of openness in the relationship is limited to a 'need to know' basis, and the nature of risk sharing determined solely by the client. At the other extreme is a form of 'partnering' characterized by strong incentives for joint development for separate but complementary benefits. This is considered more suited to situations in which the service is critical to the client's strategic objectives, where requirements are changing or developing and the market is continually evolving, and

[121] ibid 167.

[122] Propper (n 117 above) 66. Propper concludes in relation to quasi-markets for health and social care: 'Each aspect of contract and franchise design has associated advantages and disadvantages. The relative balance of incentives will depend on the technology of production, the verifiability of output, the extent of information asymmetry between provider and purchaser and the degree of relative risk aversion of provider and purchaser.'

[123] ibid 35.

[124] M Mackintosh, 'Flexible Contracting? Economic Cultures and Implicit Contracts in Social Care' (2000) 29 *Journal of Social Policy* 1.

[125] 'Although several countries' reform programmes incorporate an intention to shift from contracts which focus on inputs to performance-oriented contracts, in practice the measurement of performance is underdeveloped and contentious. The role for users in this is a particularly neglected area' – Walsh et al (n 63 above) 197; Kendall (n 116 above).

[126] *Treasury Taskforce, Partnerships for Prosperity – The Private Finance Initiative* (1997) 59.

where there is potential for exploiting irreducible spare capacity.[127] Here there is a greater degree of openness, with proportionately more risk being allocated to whichever party is agreed to be in the better position to manage it. The emphasis on partnering reflects the acknowledgement by government of the importance of trust and cooperation in economic exchanges, and of the need to avoid damaging these aspects of relational contracting through an exaggerated and distorted ideal of competition.[128]

The risks involved in contracting for simple public services, for example buildings cleaning and refuse collection in local government, are relatively clear and straightforward to manage.[129] Contract conditions and specifications tend to allocate risk to the contractor, who can make accurate risk assessments and adjust prices accordingly. In social care, there has been generally a less commercial attitude and greater emphasis on risk sharing, especially in purchaser dealings with voluntary organisations.[130] In this and other human service sectors, contracting relationships are complicated by the existence of multiple parties performing different roles. In the NHS risk has tended to be shared between purchasers and providers. The internal market in health, at least until now, has been marked by the reluctance of central government to allow unhindered operation of contracts, with political considerations and values often in tension with the efficiency goals of the contracting regime.

State–provider relationship

In economic contracting regimes, central government takes a direct regulatory interest in the performance of service providers as well as public purchasers (Fig 6(c)). The central determination of performance indicators, the specification

[127] 'Partnering' in this sense does not imply partnership with a private company, which involves the sharing of responsibilities or each other's debts. Public bodies cannot enter such arrangements other than through a special purpose company created for a joint venture – *Better Quality Services Handbook* (London: The Stationery Office, 1998) para 4.15.

[128] De Hoog and Salamon argue that management challenges can be addressed partly through improving contracting procedures. The standard *competitive approach* is suitable only for those circumstances in which there are several potential service suppliers, uncertainty is low, and there are sufficient resources available for the full competition process. The *cooperative* or *partnership* model is suitable under conditions of uncertainty and scarcity of resources, where there is insufficient knowledge of the service or clients (perhaps the service has not previously been performed in house), and where there are relatively few eligible suppliers. This model may be adopted for contract renewals, but also for new relationships – 'in this relationship, the government and the contractor are relatively equal partners' – De Hoog and Salamon (n 116 above) 334. The benefits of this model include flexible adaptation to changing conditions, without 'artificial' deadlines and complex procedures; it encourages cooperation, learning and ongoing problem solving. *The negotiation model* is particularly appropriate for contract renewals, and may also be used for new contracts – but only where there are relatively few providers interested in bidding for the contract.

[129] P Vincent-Jones and A Harries, 'Limits of Contract in Internal CCT Transactions: A Comparative Study of Buildings Cleaning and Refuse Collection in "Northern Metropolitan"' in D Campbell, and P Vincent-Jones, (eds), *Contract and Economic Organisation: Socio-Legal Initiatives* (Aldershot: Dartmouth, 1996).

[130] Walsh et al, (n 63 above) 177.

of targets in relation to these, the evaluation of performance against targets, and the publication of results in league tables, together with various other forms of direct and indirect regulation, serve as governance techniques and as mechanisms for the control of service outputs by schools, hospitals, and local authorities.

For example, performance league tables have been operating on a 'star rating' system in the health sector for several years. The tables published in July 2002 revealed that of the one hundred and fifty eight acute hospital trusts in England,[131] forty seven improved their rating, thirty six did worse and seventy five stayed the same. The number of top-ranking three star hospitals rose from thirty five to forty six.[132] The publication of the 2002 tables was accompanied by government warnings to the poorest performers that they would be taken over by private contractors, external management teams, voluntary bodies, universities or other hospitals if they did not rapidly improve. A register of interested parties was established in Autumn 2002. The winners in the selection process were awarded franchises to manage failing hospitals on a contractual basis. At the other extreme, three star trusts were rewarded with between £250,000 and £1m extra to spend on investment projects. In line with the philosophy of earned autonomy, these trusts also became eligible to apply for the coveted foundation status, giving them greater freedom from Whitehall control over pay rates and investment strategy.

NHS Foundation Trusts (NHSFTs) are placed in a direct regulatory relationship with central government through the process of bidding for and being awarded foundation status. This regulatory linkage is in addition to regulation by PCTs through the purchaser–provider contract. The new arrangement, described by one commentator as being at 'the heart of the next wave of public service reform',[133] is of considerable significance for the issue of governance. NHSFTs and other Public Interest Companies (PICs) could, in theory, be granted a degree of constitutional autonomy protecting them against the types of political interference and excessive central control that have been features of the NHS internal market. The granting of such status, involving the provision of safeguards through a range of already-existing private and public governance regimes, might be considered an alternative reform strategy to devising new forms of governance of 'internal' market relationships. As presently constituted, NHSFTs do not enjoy such autonomy from central government. Nevertheless, the underlying issue in the privatization

[131] Also rated were ambulance services and specialist trusts such as childrens hospitals, mental health trusts, and more than 300 Primary Care Trusts (which were given responsibility for commissioning health NHS services early in 2002).

[132] Eight trusts received no stars at all (*Guardian* 25 July 2002). The ratings were based on 37 measurements, the most important of which were: no patients waiting more than 18 months for inpatient treatment; fewer patients waiting more than 15 months for inpatient treatment; no patients waiting more than 26 weeks for outpatient treatment; fewer patients waiting on trolleys for more than 12 hours; less than 1% of operations cancelled on the day; no patients with suspected cancer waiting more than two weeks to be seen in hospital; improvement to the working lives of staff; a high standard of hospital cleanliness; a satisfactory financial position.

[133] W Hutton, 'War looms between Blair and Brown', *Observer* 6 October 2002.

debate is whether PICs are a stepping-stone on the way to private corporate status, in which a greater degree of independence would be assured and in which market risks would be underwritten ultimately by private shareholders rather than the Treasury.

Conclusion

The form of public service organization imposed by the Conservatives and encouraged by New Labour typically involves the constitution of public agencies as purchasers engaged in the award and management of contracts. Despite the enthusiasm of proponents,[134] the real efficiency benefits of contracting out and quasi-markets compared with alternative or pre-existing arrangements remain notoriously difficult to assess. A balanced view of the research on contracting out reveals some cost savings in some sectors.[135] But the interpretation of the evidence is hotly contested even in simple cases,[136] and has little bearing on more complex contracting for human services in quasi-markets.[137]

While the establishment of quasi-markets was supposed to have been part of a general move towards deregulation, the powers devolved to public purchasing agencies have in practice been exercised within a system of regulation in which central government continues, in many respects, to determine the nature and allocation of services. Some of the governance problems associated with these regulatory arrangements are being tackled through organizational reforms directed at increasing 'automaticity', as this has been defined in Chapter 3. The role of market forces is being expanded in various ways, for example by stimulating supply-side competition and devolving choice to consumers. Such developments are considered in depth in the next chapter. Again, the creeping corporatization of service providers such as hospital trusts and education and training bodies illustrates the increasing exposure of public services to competition. This transition resolves certain governance problems (eg by permitting contracts enforceable at private law between purchaser and provider bodies that were previously part of the same organization) while raising others. For example, the drift to privatization may be accompanied by the loss of an element of control by

[134] S Domberger, SA Meadowcroft, and D Thompson, 'Competitive Tendering and Efficiency: The Case of Refuse Collection' (1986) 7 *Fiscal Studies* 69; S Domberger and S Rimmer, 'Competitive Tendering and Contracting in the Public Sector: A Survey' (1994) 1 *International Journal of the Economics of Business* 440.

[135] K Hartley and M Huby, 'Contracting-out Policy: Theory and Evidence' in J Kay, C Mayer, and D Thomson, (eds), *Privatisation and Regulation: The UK Experience* (Oxford: Clarendon Press, 1986) 284; Audit Commission, *Realising the Benefits of Competition: The Client Role for Contracted Services* (London: Audit Commission, 1993); ibid *Making Markets: A Review of the Audits of the Client Role for Contracted Services* (London: Audit Commission, 1995).

[136] GA Boyne, 'Bureaucratic Theory Meets Reality: Public Choice and Service Contracting in U.S. Local Government' (1998) 58 *Public Administration Review* 474.

[137] A Pollock, *NHS plc: The Privatisation of our Heatlh Care* (London: Verso, 2004).

government in its pursuit of equity and distributional goals through quasi-market organization.

Where the conditions of efficient exchange have been established in a given purchaser–provider relationship, a range of other issues remains in the ultimate assessment of responsiveness. A narrow concern with efficiency may be at the expense of unfairness to particular firms bidding for public contracts, or may fail to take sufficient account of the interests of vulnerable or disadvantaged groups, or of the costs to society generally. For example, in the case of policies encouraging contracting out, the evidence suggests that women have borne the brunt of redundancies and deterioration in pay and conditions, while taxpayers and citizens have had to bear the economic and social costs of increased unemployment.[138] There is an obvious and unresolved contradiction here between the Government's economic reform agenda on the one hand, and its proclaimed commitment to gender equality and to increasing the participation of economically marginalized and otherwise disadvantaged citizens on the other hand. Again, in complex quasi-markets for human services such as health and social care, the achievement of efficiency in the purchaser–provider relationship may be in tension with responsiveness to the needs or preferences of service recipients. Most fundamentally, there remain questions concerning the lack of legitimacy of the purposes being pursued through economic contracting regimes, and the absence of deliberative conditions necessary for responsive policy-making on public services. We return to these issues in Chapters 10 and 11.

[138] K Escott and D Whitfield, *The Gender Impact of CCT in Local Government*, EOC Research Discussion Series No 12 (Manchester: Equal Opportunities Commission, 1995).

8

Citizens, Consumers, and Public Services

This chapter focuses on the relationships between citizens and consumers on the one hand, and the various public and private bodies involved in the organization and delivery of public services on other.[1] Since in administrative contracts there is no legal distinction between departments and executive agencies, the relationship of citizens/consumers is to 'government' generally. In the case of economic contracts, by contrast, the more formal separation of purchaser and provider roles gives rise to two sets of relationships – between citizens/consumers and public purchasing agencies, and between citizens/consumers and service providers. These dimensions occupy the lower half of the 'diamond' figure used in the previous chapter to depict economic contracting regimes (Fig 6(d) and (e) respectively).

We begin by exploring the position of citizens – conceived variously as users, consumers and customers – in different forms of market, bureaucratic and quasi-market organization. The next two sections examine government attempts since the 1990s to connect consumers with public services through the Citizen's Charter and Service First, and the part played by mechanisms of choice, voice, and exit in the reform of public services. Attention is then turned to citizen and consumer involvement in decision making by public agencies, and the role of contractual and performance information in regulatory frameworks governing public services. Finally, I suggest that economic contracting regimes may represent a temporary stage in the transition towards increasingly privatized forms of service provision.

Citizens and consumers

One of the most criticized aspects of the self-styled Citizen's Charter was that it tended to reduce citizenship interests to those of mere consumption of public services:[2]

> The more that citizenship is spoken of in terms of market provision of services and the expectations which citizens have of these services, the more our citizen looks like what is

[1] D Oliver and G Drewry, *Public Service Reforms: Issues of Accountability and Public Law* (London: Pinter, 1996) 28.

[2] D Prior, J Stewart, and K Walsh, *Citizenship: Rights, Community and Participation* (London: Pearson Professional, 1995) 22; M Barnes 'Users as Citizens: Collective Action and the Local Governance of Welfare' (1999) 33 *Social Policy and Administration* 73; M Barnes and D Prior, 'Spoilt for Choice? How Consumerism Can Disempower Public Service Users' (1995) 15 *Public Money and Management* (Jul–Sep) 53.

generally thought of as a consumer. By consumer we mean someone who enters transactions and through exercise of market power (including economic strength, knowledge, bargaining skill and choice) exercises some control over the quality of the service which he receives and the price which the supplier charges.[3]

It is trite to maintain that individual members of society may at the same time be both citizens and consumers. The real question is when it is appropriate to view public service relationships in terms of citizenship, and when in terms of consumption.

In the broadest sense, the 'public service' is equated with the role of government in providing public goods that are both non-excludable and non-rival, such as defence and criminal justice.[4] There are no identifiable individual consumers of such governmental functions, which are performed by the state for citizens generally. Because the services are not marketable they cannot be charged for directly, so are financed from general taxation. There is no choice whether to accept these services, other than by influencing policy through the political process or by some other means. The citizenship interest is not confined to public goods, however, but extends to the manner of organization of public services more generally. Services that are not public goods may be provided to individual citizens as identifiable consumers in a variety of ways. The distinction between consumers, users, clients, and customers is notoriously difficult to draw.[5] What is important for present purposes is the difference between market, state, and quasi-market organization, and what this implies for the structuring of relationships

[3] P Rawlings and C Willett, 'Consumer Empowerment and the Citizen's Charter', in C Willett, (ed), *Public Sector Reform and the Citizen's Charter* (London: Blackstone Press Ltd, 1996) 26. See also G Amato, 'Citizenship and Public Services – Some General Reflections', in M Freedland and S Sciarra, (eds), *Public Services and Citizenship in European Law – Public and Labour Law Perspectives* (Oxford: Oxford University Press, 1998) 145; N Deakin and A Wright, (eds), *Consuming Public Services* (London: Routledge, 1990); S Easton, 'The Meaning of Citizenship', in C Willett, (ed), above; N Ryan, 'Reconstructing Citizens as Consumers: Implications for New Modes of Governance' (2001) 60 *Australian Journal of Public Administration* 104.

[4] R Geuss, *Public Goods, Private Goods* (Princeton: Princeton University Press, 2001). A public good is 'non-rival' in the sense that once it has been produced, each person can benefit from it without diminishing another's enjoyment; it is 'non-excludable' in the sense that people generally cannot be prevented from gaining access to the good – see further n 47 below.

[5] In many local government services, users are referred to as clients. These may be individual (users of residential care services) or institutional, for example schools or departments. Purchasing or commissioning officers acting on behalf of clients are referred to as 'client agents' – K Walsh, N Deakin, P Spurgeon, P Smith, and N Thomas, *Contracting for Change: Contracts in Health, Social Care, and Other Local Government Services* (Oxford: Oxford University Press, 1997) 105. Harden suggests that the terms 'consumer', 'citizen' and 'customer' represent three overlapping 'ways of expressing categories of legitimate interest in relation to public services,' without attempting to define these categories – Harden, *The Contracting State* (Buckingham: Open University Press, 1992) 1. While in theory a distinction may be drawn between customers who pay, providers who deliver, clients who co-produce, and citizens who indirectly fund and benefit from public services, in practice there are considerable difficulties in deciding who exactly fills these roles – L McGuire, 'Service Delivery Contracts: Quality for Customers, Clients and Citizens', in G Davis, B Sullivan, and A Yeatman, (eds), *The New Contractualism?* (Melbourne: Macmillan, 1997) 113.

between service recipients and the parties involved in the production of public services.

Market organization

In private markets there exists a direct relationship between the provider of goods or services and purchasing consumers. In its simplest form, the relationship involves the exchange of money at the point though not necessarily the time of delivery. Services are funded by payments from those who receive them. The term 'customer' is usually applied to consumers who purchase goods and services on a regular basis, implying a past history of repeat dealings and/or the prospect of future dealings with the same or similar supplier.[6] Consumers who are dissatisfied with a particular supplier may choose to exit the relationship and transfer their custom elsewhere, given a competitive market.[7] Private goods and services are by definition marketable, in the sense that they may be charged for, there is demand for them, and price is a reflection of supply and demand. The price mechanism enables consumers and customers to make market comparisons and an optimum pattern of production and consumption to emerge. Overall supply is determined by the aggregation of consumer preferences expressed through multiple decisions to purchase the goods or services in question.

In efficient market organization the issue of consumer involvement is non-problematic. Allocations are made according to 'automatic links' established in the market, on the basis of sovereign decision-making predicated on private property rights.[8] Allocative efficiency is associated with the maximization of marginal utilities through the purchasing decisions of individual consumers, whose preferences can be inferred from their behaviour. Productive efficiency is reached at the point where the cost to the consumer at any given level of quantity and quality is minimized. In theory, markets may be regarded as naturally responsive in the sense of having the potential to deliver efficient satisfaction of wants by empowering individuals to act in their own self-interest.[9] Consumers as direct purchasers may choose between different products and services according to their needs and their own assessment of the trade-off between quality and price.[10]In practice, however,

6 Users of government services who receive a service regularly may also be referred to as 'customers', for example in charters and government documents, even though the service is free at the point of delivery and not paid for directly.

7 Hence it is incongruous to portray claimants of the Jobseeker's Allowance as 'customers', since there is no choice among bodies with whom to contract for the provision of employment services. In the more radical Australian system, by contrast, individual exit is possible at least in theory due to competition between service providers, enabling 'clients' to transfer 'custom' – T Carney and G Ramia, *From Rights to Management: Contract, New Public Management and Employment Services* (The Hague: Kluwer Law International, 2002).

8 Harden (n 5 above) 12.

9 H Collins, *Regulating Contracts* (Oxford: Oxford University Press, 1999) 70.

10 ibid 305. Even in the case of private provision through the market, the state has an important regulatory role in establishing and maintaining the conditions in which contracts can operate as reflexive mechanisms.

we have seen that there remain significant physical, financial, and social obstacles to individual involvement and participation, which limit the capacity of citizens to realize their human potential through choices they make in markets. The response to market failure has been the societal designation of services as 'public' in nature, implying a role for the state beyond simply providing the formal institutional framework and enforcement machinery for guaranteeing exchange.

State provision, quasi-markets, regulated markets

I suggested in Chapter 7 that three forms of state involvement in public services may ideally be distinguished: direct state provision by a government body; quasi-market organization involving 'purchase-of-service' contracting by a public body representing the consumer interest;[11] and provision by a private body under a public law duty or statutory regulation.[12] Here we explore the implications of these different modes of public service organization for the nature of the relationship between citizens/consumers and other parties in contracting regimes.

In direct provision (Fig 7(1)), there is no competition or choice of supplier, while in quasi-markets involving the purchaser-provider split (Fig 7(2)), public purchasing agencies exercise choice among competing providers on behalf of consumers. Despite this difference, in both these forms of organization the demand function is concentrated in a public body or agency. The links between such 'demand' and individual preferences are 'complex and contingent'.[13] The demand function includes responsibilities for deciding the overall level of resources devoted to a service, the price paid, and the quality of provision. We have seen that private services (Fig 4(4)), by contrast, are allocated on the basis of choice exercised directly by sovereign consumers. A key difference between private and public services is that standards are set through the market rather than by administrative fiat. Again, whereas these public services are usually funded from general taxation and are free or subsidized, private services are paid for at the point of consumption. Where a public service is marketable, it may be charged for in the form of a user fee. However the distinction with private services remains in that the supply of the service is not determined by the aggregation of consumer preferences expressed through decisions to purchase, and the fee charged is relatively arbitrary compared with market prices.

While a basic distinction may be maintained between public and private services in these terms, there is a blurring of the boundary between private markets

[11] Because Collins' analysis in *Regulating Contracts* is built on the market paradigm, he does not consider how the alternative organizational form of quasi-markets might provide solutions to the problems he poses of how to combine welfare regulation with the utility-maximising potential of markets. The result is a rather narrow treatment of public contracting in 'Government by Contract' (ch 13), which misses a range of increasingly important 'hybrid' contractual relationships and the nuances of the regulat*ing* and regulatory functions of contract in quasi-market processes.

[12] cf Harden (n 5 above) 9.

[13] ibid 6.

Type of service	Public Services			Private Services
Form of Economic Organization	(1) Bureaucratic	(2) Quasi-market	(3) Regulated market	(4) Private market
State Involvement	Traditional bureaucratic organization (including CIG)	CEO contracting regime Purchaser-provider split 'Purchase of service' contracting	Independent regulatory agency Privatized utilities, telecommunications	General institutional framework Legal enforcement machinery
Demand Function	Representative government/state	Representative purchaser agency, competition/ contestability	Limited consumer sovereignty, choice, competition	Consumer sovereignty, direct choice, competition
Funding and Payment	Publicly funded, free at point of consumption		Individually funded, payment at point of consumption	

Figure 7. Consumer role in public and private services

(Fig 7(4)), and regulated markets (Fig 7(3)). In the latter case, the consumer exercises a degree of choice, but typically in an environment in which competition between alternative providers is limited. Services are paid for at the point of consumption, but prices and other conditions are determined by a regulatory agency. In practice, the picture is considerably more complicated in all these cases, with elements of choice increasingly pervading all forms of public service organization. The more that consumers are involved in demand decisions or are brought into direct relationship with non-state providers, for example through vouchering, the more the arrangement resembles a regulated market rather than a quasi-market.

Whatever the precise mode of organization, current consumers have an obvious interest in how public services are provided. At the same time, individuals who are not consuming a given public service, such as health or education, have a legitimate citizenship interest as members of society and as taxpayers in the conditions under which the service is delivered to others, including family and dependants. Similarly, individuals have an interest in services not consumed at present but which may be required in future, for example in old age or retirement. Again, individuals may be applying for or intending to receive a service, access to which depends on satisfying eligibility conditions or rationing criteria. Whether direct public services are organized on the basis of administrative contracts or economic contracts, the same governance issues arise. How can users and citizens be connected with the public bodies that perform demand functions on their behalf in ways that ensure that their interests are adequately represented? In this regard, quasi-markets may be viewed as inherently more responsive than bureaucratic organization due to the potential created by the purchaser–provider split for increased consumer involvement in 'purchasing' matters such as service specification, standard-setting, and contract management. The next section examines governmental efforts to empower users and citizens in both economic and administrative contracting regimes through the Citizen's Charter and Service First.

Citizen's Charter and Service First

The use of charters was pioneered in the 1980s as a part of an initiative by progressive local authorities such as York City Council to improve the responsiveness of local public services. Only later was the idea taken up by central government and embodied in national policy. The Citizen's Charter presented to Parliament in 1991 was one of the Major government's most significant contributions to the Conservative reforms begun under Margaret Thatcher.[14] While 'charterism' could

14 A Barron and C Scott, 'The Citizen's Charter Programme' (1992) 55 MLR 526; BBC News Archive, 22 July 1991 – http://news.bbc.co.uk/onthisday/hi/dates/stories/july/22/newsid_2516000/2516139.stm accessed October 4 2005.

have developed quite independently of the New Public Contracting, in practice these initiatives have been intimately connected.[15] Consumer empowerment by such means was a logical accompaniment to the reform of public administration through the creation of executive agencies. Generally, the introduction of charters served 'to increase the pace of change, and to act as a banner under which to organize the new public management initiative.'[16]

Charters define standards of service that users can expect in their dealings with a wide range of public and private bodies. Despite the language of 'entitlement',[17] charters do not entail legally enforceable rights. Indeed the lack of adequate enforcement procedures and mechanisms for the redress of citizen grievances have long been regarded as a major weakness.[18] The main themes of the original Citizen's Charter included an emphasis on greater consultation with consumers and customers on public service standards and quality, and the publication of information on the performance of public service bodies in relation to targets and Performance Indicators (PIs). Also part of the charter philosophy were the development of novel mechanisms enabling recognition of the achievement of standards (as in the Charter Mark scheme), tougher regimes of independent inspection and audit, and better complaints machinery. Under Service First, the successor to the Citizen's Charter introduced in 1998 and managed under the Better Public Services division within the Cabinet Office, public service providers were enjoined to respect nine core principles of service delivery:

1. Set clear standards of service that users can expect; monitor and review performance; and publish the results, following independent validation wherever possible.
2. Be open and communicate clearly and effectively in plain language, to help people using public services; and provide full information about services, their cost and how well they perform.
3. Consult and involve present and potential users of public services, as well as those who work in them; and use their views to improve the service provided.
4. Make services easily available to everyone who needs them, including using technology to the full, and offering choice wherever possible.

[15] 'In many ways Next Steps is the vehicle for the delivery of the Citizen's Charter in central government through the agencies which serve the public' – Oliver and Drewry (n 1 above) 27. 'The charter has been seen by the government as an evolution of, and therefore intimately linked with, the executive agency approach and the other reforms in the NHS, privatized industries and local government which were introduced in the 1980s' (28).

[16] Prior et al (n 2 above) 28.

[17] ibid 24.

[18] Where charter commitments reflect targets set out in framework documents and PSAs, the failure by a government department or agency to meet published standards might in theory be sanctioned in accordance with the terms of those administrative contracts (see ch 6 for problems of enforcement in practice). Where organizations other than executive agencies or government departments are subject to charter standards (eg the BBC), there is no such method of contractual enforcement even in theory.

5. Treat all people fairly; respect their privacy and dignity; be helpful and courteous; and pay particular attention to those with special needs.
6. Put things right quickly and effectively; learn from complaints; and have a clear, well publicised, and easy-to-use complaints procedure, with independent review wherever possible.
7. Use resources effectively to provide best value for taxpayers and users.
8. Always look for ways to improve the services and facilities offered.
9. Work with other providers to ensure that services are simple to use, effective and coordinated, and deliver a better service to the user.[19]

Most executive agencies responsible for direct public services were required to develop individual charters, and some departments also had their own charters.[20] By the end of the decade, charters had been produced covering a vast range of public services including social security allowances and benefits, education, employment, health, housing, law and legal services, travel and immigration, and transport. In this period charters became an integral part of the regulatory framework underpinning increasingly complex organizational arrangements for the delivery of public services. While in some respects charters entailed a reduction in direct central prescription through the devolution of standard-setting to departments and agencies,[21] in overall context the arrangements were no less centralized than the bureaucratic system of state direction that the New Public Management sought to replace.

Under Service First, detailed guidance and databases of information were published in respect of quality networks, complaints procedures, benchmarking, performance tables and indicators, the Charter Mark scheme, and best practice.[22] Service First was gradually absorbed into New Labour's wider Modernizing Government reform agenda. For example, the Patient's Charter was abolished in the year 2000 as part of changes introduced under the ten-year 'NHS Plan'.[23] Modernizing Government has itself evolved into the current public services initiative,

[19] Cabinet Office archive, http://archive.cabinetoffice.gov.uk/ accessed 4 October 2005.

[20] For example, the Benefits Agency had several charters including 'Caring for the Carer', 'Charter Standard Statement for People with Disabilities', and a general 'Benefits Agency Charter Standard Statement'. In the Department for Trade and Industry there were charters for Companies House, the Employment Appeal Tribunal, the Insolvency Service, the Patent Office, and the Employment Tribunals Service. The Department of Health had separate charters for Maternity Services, the Medicines Control Agency, the Medical Devices Agency, the Mental Health Service, and the National Blood Service, in addition to 'The Patients Charter and You – A Charter for England'. The Department of Education had separate charters for further and higher education, and for parents with children with special needs.

[21] 'It is clear that the Charter approach is one *which gives less of a role to the State* in the setting of standards and the delivery of services' (emphasis supplied) – Rawlings and Willett (n 3 above) 34.

[22] Cabinet Office archive (n 19 above).

[23] 'The Patient's Charter and You – A Charter for England' can be found at http://www.pfc.org.uk/medical/pchrt-e1.htm accessed 31 August 2005.

known simply (at the time of writing in October 2005) as 'Better Public Services', under overall coordination by the Office of the Deputy Prime Minister (ODPM).[24] The Prime Minister's Delivery Unit (PMDU) continues to have responsibility for assessing delivery and providing performance management for key delivery areas, and has a shared responsibility with the Treasury for the joint PSA target: 'Improve public services by working with departments to help them meet their PSA targets, consistently with the fiscal rules'.[25]

The only remaining vestige of the charterism as a centrally coordinated policy appears to be the Charter Mark scheme.[26] The official government website describes this as a registered certification mark, owned by the OPSR in the Cabinet Office, whose purpose is to serve as 'a positive force for change and customer service improvement'.[27] A review of the Charter Mark Standard was announced by the Minister responsible in 2005.[28] This scheme operates in conjunction with other more facilitative resources, such as the Public Sector Benchmarking Service.[29] Some of the elements of charterism have been incorporated within the system of targets and performance measures pervading PSAs and the Spending Review.[30] For example, the six general service standards that applied across the whole of government from 1997,[31] which entailed the setting of targets and the collation and publication of information on performance by departments and agencies on an annual basis, have become part of the PSA regime. Public service standards, the setting of targets in relation to these standards, and reporting on performance in relation to targets are core features of overlapping administrative and economic contracting regimes. While the rhetoric of charters appears to be in decline, the spirit of charterism lives on as part of the wider public service reform agenda.

[24] www.odpm.gov.uk/stellent/groups/odpm_control/documents/contentservertemplate/odpm_index.hcst?n=1949&l=1 accessed 4 October 2005. The Cabinet Office's archive site (n 19 above) states: 'The Service First and Modernising Government programmes have now been completed. The information held on this site is no longer being maintained but is retained for archive purposes'.

[25] www.cabinetoffice.gov.uk/pmdu/ accessed 4 October 2005.

[26] www.cabinetoffice.gov.uk/chartermark/ accessed 4 October 2005. According to the Cabinet Office website, 'The benefits to the Charter Mark holder are not just the satisfaction of offering an improved service but also the feedback and recognition that guides development and boosts staff morale.'

[27] ibid.

[28] John Hutton, 'Public Service Reform: The Key to Social Justice', speech to Social Market Foundation, 25 August 2005 – see www.cabinetoffice.gov.uk/chartermark/downloads/doc/jh_smf_speech_24aug05.doc accessed 4 October 2005.

[29] The Public Sector Benchmarking Service, which was launched in February 2001, claims to provide a comprehensive service on benchmarking and good practice to those seeking to deliver better public services – see www.benchmarking.gov.uk/default1.asp accessed 4 February 2005.

[30] G Drewry, 'Whatever Happened to the Citizen's Charter?' [2002] PL 9, 12.

[31] All departments were required to set targets and publish performance information recording success or failure in meeting the standards in relation to core activities such as responding to letters from members of the public; seeing callers without appointment; answering telephone enquiries, publicizing complaints procedures; providing service information; and making services available to those with special needs.

Choice, voice, and loyalty in public services

A range of choice, voice and exit mechanisms has served in structuring the roles of citizens, consumers, and public purchasing agencies in economic contracting regimes. The operation of such mechanisms is likely to have a strong bearing on responsiveness of public services in particular sectors. In Hirschman's seminal analysis, exit and choice were regarded as alternative means by which customers or members of an organization could express dissatisfaction with deteriorating management performance, whether of the firm producing saleable outputs for its customers or of other groups such as political parties or voluntary associations.[32] On the premise that either the exit option (where customers stop buying the firm's products or members leave the organization) or the voice option (where customers or the organization's members express dissatisfaction directly to management or engage in some other form of public protest) might trigger a search by management for the causes and possible cures of customers' and members' dissatisfaction, the focus was on the comparative efficiency of the two 'mechanisms of recuperation'. In the New Public Contracting, however, while government policy might be interpreted as attempting to create the conditions in which exit and voice signals serve as spurs to management innovation and reform of public services, the fostering of exit is being vigorously pursued as a policy end in its own right.[33] The common thrust of both Conservative and Labour governments since 1979 has been to privilege exit over voice, reinforcing the structural bias in government policy in favour of increasingly privatized forms of provision.

Exit and choice

Exit implies the exercise of choice in ending an unsatisfactory relationship. It may also involve the transfer of custom or support to another supplier or organization offering the prospect of better performance. In the New Public Contracting, exit/choice options may be exercised to a limited degree by public managers in administrative contracting regimes, and to a greater extent by public purchasers and individual service recipients in economic contracting regimes. Choice is playing a prominent role in New Labour's programme for modernizing public services. The Government's fourth principle of public sector reform following the 2001

[32] A Hirschman, *Exit, Voice and Loyalty: Responses to Decline in Firms, Organizations and States* (Cambridge, Mass: Harvard University Press, 1970) 3.

[33] In any case, Hirschman questioned the mainstream assumption of the efficacy of exit as a means of guiding a firm or organization back to efficiency. In many situations exit drives out voice and assumes a disproportionate share of the burden in the attempted attainment of this end – ibid 120.

general election was 'more choice for customers and the ability, if provision is poor, to have an alternative provider'.[34]

In economic theory the power of exit as a recuperation mechanism is considered to lie in the ability to inflict revenue losses on delinquent management.[35] The assumption is that competition and associated pressures are the key drivers of peak performance. Given the British tradition of state monopoly provision of public services and the absence of alternatives, however, exit has been a very weak or a non-existent option for dissatisfied consumers.[36] To the limited degree that exit is possible, it does not inflict revenue losses on the public provider in the majority of cases where services are free at the point of delivery and funded through general taxation. Therefore there is no connection between customer desertion and the perception of the need to repair management failings. On this analysis, the public sector has derived no benefit from the defection of middle class consumers of education, housing and health services to the private sector.

In one sense there is nothing new about the decision of consumers to withdraw from the public sector and to receive services instead from a private or independent supplier.[37] Consumer exit from public services may be analysed on a number of dimensions. Consumers may opt out of a whole range of major public services such as health, education and housing, or only one or two. Exit may be permanent or confined to singular events, such as a private hospital operation. Exit may be complete, as where individuals fund private services themselves, or be more partial, as where a patient receives private health treatment, but the purchasing function remains in the NHS and paid for out of general taxation.[38] However, since 1979 de-bureaucratization has taken the form of specific policies of state assistance and encouragement for those wishing to exit from public to private provision, supplementing the transition from bureaucratic to quasi-market organization. Radical changes in particular service sectors have been effected through a variety of exit and choice mechanisms. In housing, the dramatic increase in home ownership and the shifting of the boundaries of state and private provision were accomplished by a combination of strong economic incentives and legal rights under the 'right

[34] Cabinet Office *The Second Phase of Public Sector Reform: the Move to Delivery* 22 March 2002 – see www.cabinetoffice.gov.uk/pmdu/ accessed 4 October 2005.

[35] Hirschman (n 32 above) 21. However, even in competitive markets there are various problems with the exit strategy – ibid 22–29.

[36] Exit is theoretically possible through the political exercise of choice between parties offering traditional policies on public policies against radical programmes such as privatization. 'Exit' in this sense may be illustrated by the defection from Labour and the election of a radical Conservative governments in 1979.

[37] G Annas, 'Patients' Rights to Managed Care – Exit, Voice and Loyalty' (1997) 337 *New England Journal of Medicine* 219; P Gillette, 'Opting Out of Public Provision' (1996) 73 *Denver University Law Review* 1185; I Leigh, *Law, Politics and Local Democracy* (Oxford: Oxford University Press, 2000) 148. On the UK healthcare sector, see C Propper, 'The Demand for Private Health Care in the UK' (2000) 19 *Journal of Health Economics* 855.

[38] By contrast, the encouragement of owner-occupation and private health care through tax reliefs and other financial incentives entails complete transfer out of the public sector.

to buy' provisions of the Housing Act 1980.[39] This policy was extended through 'collective' exit rights allowing council tenants to transfer out of the public to the private or non-profit sectors in the 'change of landlord' scheme introduced under the Housing Act 1988. Other policies encouraging individual exit have included explicit vouchering and assisted places schemes in education, and various other incentives involving tax relief or transferable state set-off against the full market cost of services. Also in education, parents have been able to express a preference of school for their children to attend, so exercising limited choice against the traditional system of Local Education Authority (LEA) allocation. In a further sense, the exit mechanism is built into public service quasi-markets involving the purchaser-provider split through the exercise of choice by public agencies acting on behalf of the consumer. The question here is how the choice is made among competing providers, and with what input or involvement of the final service recipient.

Voice

Exit is the dominant mode of consumer reaction in normally competitive business markets. In the case of public services, by contrast, given the historical lack of exit options in traditional bureaucratic organization, the task of keeping public service managers on their toes has fallen to voice:[40]

> Voice is here defined as any attempt to change, rather than to escape from, an objectionable state of affairs, whether through individual or collective petition to management directly in charge, through appeal to a higher authority with the intention of forcing a change in management, or though various types of actions and protests, including those that are meant to mobilize public opinion.[41]

In the case of many complex public services, however, consumers and citizens have been unable or reluctant to articulate dissatisfaction or to apply effective pressures for improvement. Hirschman pointed out in 1970 that the effectiveness of voice was dependent on the invention of institutions that can communicate complaints cheaply and effectively.[42] Recent public service reforms directed at increasing participation may be viewed as merely the latest in a long history of attempts to empower consumers and citizens through more and better voice mechanisms. But while voice has undoubtedly been on the Government's agenda for modernizing public services, it has tended to be narrowly conceived and restricted in scope. Citizen debate around the more controversial and fundamental

39 Leigh (n 37 above) 149.

40 For a critique of the Government's vision of consumer empowerment based on market participation rather than voice, see G Howells, 'The Potential and Limits of Consumer Empowerment by Information' (2005) 32 JLS 349. 'The voice option is the only way in which dissatisfied customers or members can react whenever the exit option is unavailable' – Hirschman (n 32 above) 33.

41 ibid 30.

42 ibid 43.

issues of public service organization and delivery, such as the contracting out of services or the private financing of public infrastructure, has not been encouraged. The governance issue here concerns the level within the political system at which voice mechanisms operate. The 'voice' or form of participation that government is keen for citizens to enjoy may not be the kind they either need or want.[43] One of the characteristics of the exit option, when exercised by public purchasers in the form of strategic outsourcing or contracting out following market testing, is the difficulty of reversing the decision and bringing the service back in-house. Where contestable or competitive markets conditions have been established, the public purchaser may of course choose a different private or voluntary provider, but the option of direct provision is limited if not gone forever.

Once the decision has been taken to outsource public service functions, the contracting process (specification, tendering, bidding, selection) opens up a space for consumer participation that does not exist in bureaucratic organization. Empowerment here depends on increasing the influence of citizens and consumers on the commissioning functions performed on their behalf, for example in selecting the provider, determining the trade-off between price and quality, monitoring delivery, and sanctioning poor performance. However, the realization of this potential is again dependent on connecting citizens/consumers with public purchasing agencies through appropriate voice mechanisms.

Loyalty and problems with exit

Recent policy initiatives encouraging consumer exit from public services are problematic for a number of reasons. Exit may undermine the potential of voice to recuperate defects in the existing mode of provision by draining the underperforming organization of its most alert and potentially effective customers or members. In the education sector, for example, mass exit by articulate middle class parents to private schools for their children has arguably paralyzed voice by removing its principal agents.[44] In addition to depriving under-performing services of champions for improvement, exit may lead to the creation of second-class services for those too poor or unable, for other reasons, to go elsewhere. There may, in other words, be externalities – hidden costs and unintended negative consequences both for exiting individuals and for society more generally. Hence the increase in owner-occupation achieved through the sale of council houses has arguably led to a marginalization of the council housing sector, and contributed to social exclusion. Rather than serving to discipline failure, exit may compound the structural

43 P Vincent-Jones, 'Contracting for Public Services: Trust, Accountability and Consumer Participation in UK Local Authority Quasi-Markets', in Y Fortin and H Van Hassel, (eds) (2000), 143.

44 Hirschman (n 32 above) 47.

social problems that have given rise to poor performance in the first place.[45] In these situations 'full exit is impossible; in some sense, one remains . . . a member of the organization in spite of formal exit'.[46] The reason has to do with the 'public' rather than 'private' nature of the goods in question, irrespective of whether they are publicly or privately provided.[47] The relationship between the individual and society cannot be terminated: 'In spite of exit one remains a consumer of the output or at least of its external effects from which there is no escape.'[48]

Even where exit is possible in the narrow sense, and there clearly exists a better private sector alternative on present performance, it may be rational for citizens/consumers to remain loyal to the public sector and to attempt to achieve change 'from within'.[49] 'The loyal customer-member of an under-performing organization may be prepared to trade off the certainty of exit against the uncertainties of an improvement in the deteriorated product.'[50] Assuming that the Government's regulatory purpose is, as claimed, to achieve the best possible service performance regardless of the public or private character of the provider, a better result in the long term may be achieved by 'locking in' the most active and vocal consumers of public services, thereby increasing the effectiveness of voice as a mechanism of recuperation. Defenders of the public sector often concede that current performance is poor compared with what could be obtained privately, but maintain that similar or better results could be achieved through public management reforms. The beneficial effect of enforced loyalty through locking in may be that members are encouraged to use the voice option with greater determination and resourcefulness than might otherwise be the case, thus saving the organization and society from the damage caused by excessive and premature exit.[51] In this way, the norm of loyalty can serve a socially useful purpose in 'preventing deterioration from becoming cumulative, as it so often is when there is no barrier to exit'.[52] The functional value of loyalty is to encourage members of an organization, by raising the costs of exit, to discover new ways of exerting influence and pressure towards recovery. The 'normal rule' in Hirschman's analysis is that 'loyalty holds exit at bay and activates voice'.[53]

Of course, loyalty may be argued to have become dysfunctional in the case of monopoly state provision. The lack of responsiveness of bureaucratic organization could be attributed to an imbalance in the relationship between loyalty and exit.[54]

45 This point applies particularly strongly to competition within the state sector. For example, the privileged status accorded Academies and NHS FTs may lead to service improvements based on expansion and increased resources, but at the expense of poor-performing schools and hospitals.

46 Hirschman (n 32 above) 100.

47 Hirschman defines public goods as 'goods which are consumed by all those who are members of a given community, country, or geographical area in such a manner that consumption or use by one member does not detract from consumption or use by another . . . The distinguishing characteristic of these goods is not only that they *can* be consumed by everyone, but that there is *no escape* from consuming them unless one were to leave the community by which they are provided' – ibid 101.

48 ibid 104. 49 ibid 38. 50 ibid 77. 51 ibid 82. 52 ibid 79.

53 ibid 78. 54 ibid 93.

Traditional public service arrangements were unsatisfactory precisely because 'irrational' loyalty was not countered by effective exit mechanisms, justifying the creation of new forms of exit. Conservative governments after 1979 were particularly concerned to undermine the loyalties of local electorates, left-controlled councils and trade unions within local government, which were increasingly regarded by right-wing radical reformers as irrational obstacles to change. This pattern has continued under New Labour, which has further contributed to lowering the barriers to exit and thereby further weakened the functional value of loyalty. In this view, the New Public Contracting and associated policies may be interpreted as an attempt deliberately to break the loyalties of citizens, consumers and public managers to traditional forms of service provision.

However, if responsiveness in public services is dependent on the maintenance of a balance between exit, voice and loyalty as mechanisms of recuperation, policies that are structurally biased in favour of exit from the state to the independent sectors may be expected to result in service arrangements that are just as flawed as under direct monopoly provision, albeit for different reasons.

Demand decisions

The challenge of regulatory design in the public services field is finding adequate substitutes for the qualities of consumer sovereignty and direct choice that make markets *theoretically* a superior form of organization. Since the commitments agreed in administrative contracts determine the parameters of the operation of economic contracts, the interests of citizens and consumers need to be properly represented at that level of decision making in regard to such matters as the determination of PIs, the setting of targets, and policy evaluation. In economic contracting regimes, as we have just seen, the question is how to link initial demand and subsequent contract management decisions of purchasing agencies to inputs from consumers and citizens through appropriate voice mechanisms and fora of public participation.

The most fundamental governmental decision, given the societal judgment that the service is public in nature,[55] concerns how the public service function will be organized, ie whether on the basis of directly employed labour, privatization with regulation, strategic outsourcing, internal contracting following market testing, or some other competitive arrangement involving partnership between public and private sectors. In economic contracting regimes, the responsibility for the decision is devolved to the relevant department, agency, or other government body. The assumption that this decision can be reduced to a rational

[55] Harden (n 5 above) 76; EM Garcia, 'Public Service, Public Services, Public Functions, and Guarantees of the Rights of Citizens: Unchanging Needs in a Changed Context', in M Freedland and S Sciarra, (eds), *Public Services and Citizenship in European Law – Public and Labour Law Perspectives* (Oxford: Oxford University Press, 1998) 80.

choice among alternative institutional arrangements, analysed in accordance with transaction cost economics and principal-agent theory,[56] has already been contested. The political dimension of public services means that tool selection can never be just a technical exercise.[57] Nevertheless, I argued in Chapter 4 that the 'make or buy' decision is excessively influenced by the structural bias towards market competition and privatized modes of public service organization. Increased citizen/consumer involvement might provide a counter-weight to such central pressures which have arguably led in many cases to 'over-outsourcing'.[58] Democratic values of probity, transparency and public accountability need to be applied at this stage in the decision-making process.[59] Political legitimacy requires the provision of maximum opportunity for deliberation over the merits of various forms of government action on public service issues.[60] Lack of democratic involvement and of adequate public deliberation is bound to have an impact on the quality of decision making, and to increase economic and other costs associated with inappropriate tool choice or instrument selection.[61]

Standards and target setting

Citizens and consumers have various interests in the demand function performed by public agencies on their behalf.[62] The quality of public services is regulated through standards and performance targets, procedures for inspection and monitoring, and restrictions on market entry through registration.[63] Standards vary widely in their degree of precision and explicitness, and in the extent to which

56 OE Williamson, *The Mechanisms of Governance* (Oxford: Oxford University Press, 1996); C Althaus, 'The Application of Agency Theory to Public Sector Management', in G Davis, B Sullivan, and A Yeatman, (eds), *The New Contractualism?* (Melbourne: Macmillan, 1997).

57 For a critique of rationalist assumptions, see C Lindblom, *The Intelligence of Democracy: Decision-making Through Mutual Adjustment* (New York: Free Press, 1965). In many cases old instruments are applied in new contexts through a process of imitation rather than rational selection – C Hood, *The Tools of Government* (London: Macmillan, 1983) 129.

58 C Hood, 'Which Contract State? Four Perspectives on Over-Outsourcing for Public Services' (1997) 56 *Australian Journal of Public Administration* 120.

59 S Zifcak, 'Contractualism, Democracy and Ethics' (2001) 60 *Australian Journal of Public Administration* 86.

60 P Vincent-Jones, 'Values and Purpose in Government: Central-Local Relations in Regulatory Perspective' (2000) 29 JLS 27; J Chalmers and G Davis, 'Rediscovering Implementation: Public Sector Contracting and Human Services' (2001) *Australian Journal of Public Administration* 74.

61 Public participation is necessary throughout the 'policy cycle', in evaluation as well as initial design – A Yeatman, 'Contracting Out and Public Values: A Symposium' (2001) 60 *Australian Journal of Public Administration* 71, 72. Programme accountability is directed at determining the aims of the programme, who is responsible for the work, and whether the programme has achieved its goals – David Z Robinson, 'Government Contracting for Academic Research', in Bruce LR Smith and DC Hague, (eds), *The Dilemma of Accountability in Modern Government: Independence Versus Control* (London: Macmillan, 1971) 108–113.

62 For an attempt to distinguish public service users' 'demands' and 'needs', see R Sheaff, S Pickard, and K Smith, 'Public Service Responsiveness to Users' Demands and Needs: Theory, Practice and Primary Healthcare in England' (2002) 80 *Public Administration* 435.

63 L Challis, P Day, R Klein, and E Scrivens, 'Managing Quasi-Markets: Institutions of Regulation', in W Bartlett, C Propper, D Wilson, and J Le Grand, (eds), *Quasi-Markets in the Welfare State: The Emerging Findings* (Bristol: SAUS, 1994) 11.

they involve measurable targets. Standards of performance for the provision of public services may be specified in contractual terms, or through the law of tort, administrative law or constitutional law.[64] Whereas in bureaucratic organization the assumption was that hierarchical management systems would play a significant part in quality assurance, standards of various kinds are assuming an increasingly important role in administrative and economic contracting regimes.

The role of citizens and consumers in standard and target setting has been downplayed in government discourse on the reform of public services.[65] Whether implemented through contracts, charters, or some other regulatory mechanism, the tendency in Britain has been for standards to be centrally prescribed in national frameworks, in pursuit of the government's declared objective of reducing local variations in quality and 'post-code lotteries', for example in the provision of education and health services. In relation to schools, the high water mark of Labour's central target setting was reached in February 2001 with the publication of the Green Paper, *Schools Building on Success*, with the commitment to a target that 85 per cent of primary school children would achieve level four in English and Maths by 2004.[66] But regulation cannot be responsive where standards and related contractual targets do not reflect the needs of service recipients, for example residents in nursing homes, or fail to take account of regional differences and preferences.

A minimum condition of responsiveness in target setting at the highest levels of government through PSAs and framework documents is dialogue between central government and the local public agencies responsible for delivering the services.[67] Empirical research on the contracting out of a range of services in English local government has shown the benefits of increased responsiveness associated with the involvement of local citizens in the contracting process.[68] In the council housing sector, for example, competitive tendering for housing management services has been conducted in some authorities on the basis of elaborate procedures for involving council tenants at every stage, from the drawing up of contract specifications and allocation of responsibilities through to tender evaluation, contractor selection, and the monitoring and enforcement of contracts.[69] However, increased consumer and purchaser involvement in standard-setting processes is in

64 Rawlings and Willett (n 3 above) 28.

65 In Australia, such dimensions were excluded from the terms of reference of the ARC investigation into contracting out – Administrative Review Council, *The Contracting Out of Government Services*, Report No 42 (Canberra: Commonwealth of Australia, 1998) para 1.9.

66 *Guardian* 21 May 2003.

67 In education, this means cooperation between DfES and LEAs and schools. At a lower level, schools and LEAs need to ensure that the views and preferences of local citizens and parents are taken into account in standard setting.

68 P Vincent-Jones, and A Harries, 'Limits of Contract in Internal CCT Transactions: A Comparative Study of Buildings Cleaning and Refuse Collection in "Northern Metropolitan"', in D Campbell and P Vincent-Jones, (eds), *Contract and Economic Organisation: Socio-Legal Initiatives* (Aldershot: Dartmouth, 1996).

69 P Vincent-Jones and A Harries, 'Tenant Participation in Contracting for Housing Management Services: A Case Study', in D Cowan, (ed), *Housing: Participation and Exclusion*, (Aldershot: Dartmouth, 1998).

tension with the centralising spirit of contracting regimes as presently constituted. The responsiveness of economic contracting regimes generally will be shown in Chapter 11 to depend on the part played by active citizens in setting, monitoring and enforcing service standards.

Resource allocation and rationing

A further dimension of the citizen/consumer interest in demand decisions concerns resource allocation and rationing. Where public services were provided directly by the state, such decisions were based on the professional assessment of individual need. Rationing was largely implicit rather than conducted according to explicit criteria.[70] In modern welfare systems, publicly funded services are not available simply on demand. Given demographic factors and the squeeze on public resources throughout the OECD, there is a perceived need for strategies to moderate and control access to such services. In human service quasi-markets the allocation issue is more complex than for other collectively consumed resources such as telecommunications and the utilities. In such cases involving privatization with regulation, resources are allocated through the market in accordance with statutory conditions. But in quasi-markets for health, community and welfare services the demand function is concentrated in the public agency acting on behalf of consumers and citizens, who have no direct contractual or market relationship with service providers. To the extent that quasi-markets are successful in responding efficiently to the needs and preferences of citizens and consumers for a wider range of more flexible services, increasing cost pressures are bound to result.[71] Potentially insatiable demand creates a problem of rationing access to particular services, and allocating resources between competing claims.

The issue of how to prioritize competing claims to scarce resources is no more reducible to rational calculation than the question of whether the service should be outsourced or provided directly.[72] Rationing as a purely technical exercise is impossible due to difficulties of comparison and the complexity of information required in order to make a judgement. It may also be inequitable if it privileges professional expertise at the expense of broader public participation in decision making.[73] In bureaucratic organization, the role of the state in demand decisions

70 Rationing here refers to the allocation of resources under conditions of scarcity. Palmer uses the term in a different sense 'to connote both the refusal and the withdrawal of services from individuals previously assessed as eligible to receive them' – E Palmer, 'Should Public Health Be a Private Concern? Developing a Public Service Paradigm in English Law' (2002) 22 OJLS 663, 664 n 6. For present purposes, however, decisions by contractors to reduce or terminate service provision on economic grounds have nothing to do with rationing.

71 P Travers, 'Quasi-Markets for the Social Services' (1995) 54 *Australian Journal of Public Administration* 346, 352; L Griffiths and D Hughes, 'Purchasing in the British NHS: Does Contracting Mean Explicit Rationing?' (1998) 2 *Health* 349.

72 T Tenbensel, 'Health Prioritisation as Rationalist Policy-Making: Problems, Prognoses and Prospects' (2000) 28 *Policy and Politics* 425.

73 ibid 427.

was relatively opaque. Popular consciousness of the rationing issue has increased in recent years partly due to the heightened visibility of quasi-market purchasing.[74] The methods deployed in health service prioritization have been particularly controversial. Greater transparency in the criteria whereby health services are rationed has resulted in those criteria being subjected to scrutiny, and in many cases found wanting.[75]

If the 'abhorrent choices' involved in the allocation of scarce resources cannot be avoided,[76] then the creation of representative institutions appears an attractive option for promoting fairness in rationing decisions.[77] In the UK health sector, some steps in this direction have arguably been taken through the role assigned the National Institute for Clinical Excellence (NICE) under the NHS Plan.[78] However, while a form of unaccountable discretion was thereby removed from local clinicians and health authorities, this reform was not accompanied by the creation of democratic structures that might be regarded as necessary to improve the legitimacy of rationing decisions.[79] In other human service sectors also, there may be a need for more explicit legal regulation of purchaser decisions, for example regarding assessments made by local social service departments as to whether a particular client should be cared for in an institution or at home. We return to these issues in the discussion of law and contractual governance in Chapter 11.

74 In the UK quasi-market for long-term care for the elderly, 'it is up to local authorities to decide what proportion of (that) funding will be allocated to providing what kind of care to which people in either a home-based or an institutional context. In direct terms, the centrally determined funding cap limits the amount of services which may be purchased, but not the nature of those services' – D Gibson, and R Means, 'Policy Convergence: Restructuring Long-Term Care in Australia and the UK' (2000) 29 *Policy and Politics* 43, 49.

75 *R v Cambridge Health Authority Ex p B* [1995] 1 FLR 1055; [1995] 2 All ER 129 (concerning the fairness of a health authority's decision to refuse medical services). On the negative impact of recent reforms on the citizenship status of disabled and older people, see K Rummery, and C Glendinning, 'Access to Services as a Civil and Social Rights Issue: The Role of Welfare Professionals in Regulating Access to and Commissioning Services for Disabled Older People Under New Labour' (2000) 34 *Social Policy and Administration* 529.

76 E Palmer and M Sunkin, 'Needs: Resources and Abhorrent Choices' (1998) 61 MLR 401 (discussing *R v Gloucester CC Ex p Barry* [1997] 2 All ER 1). In Australia, see *Yamirr v Australian Telecommunications Corp* (1990) 96 ALR 739.

77 What remains problematic is the nature and form of public input. In the health sector in the US, the 'Oregon experiment' showed that there are inherent difficulties in involving the public in assigning different values to medical illnesses and conditions. Here, public forums and survey methodology produced results that frequently were incompatible with the principle of rational economic allocation. Cost-utility analysis in the New Zealand health sector has been particularly criticised for its utilitarian assumption that costs and benefits of treatment for different illnesses can be directly compared and reduced to a single measure – Tenbensel (2000), (n 72 above) 428.

78 *Delivering the NHS Plan* (Cm 5503 2002).

79 J Montgomery, *Health Care Law* (2nd edn, Oxford: Oxford University Press, 2003) 61. Since creation of the new body, NICE has been involved in various controversial decisions over the adoption or non-adoption of certain drugs, notably Beta-interferon for MS-sufferers. 'The legal mechanisms needed to enforce and challenge these new rationing processes are as yet largely untested' (62).

Information

Information is vital to the responsiveness of public services in various senses. The availability of information may be regarded as a necessary precondition for the effective operation of the voice mechanism, and a key element connecting citizens and consumers with both providers and public purchasers in economic contracting regimes. It should further enable public agencies and individual citizens to make informed choices, and contribute to increased transparency and accountability in decision making on public service issues. However, as we saw in Chapter 6, performance information also forms a fundamental part of the system of public management based on targets and performance indicators that pervades all contracting regimes.

Contractual information

From the consumer's viewpoint, contractual information regarding service standards, provisions for defective performance, and complaints handling and dispute resolution procedures is of similar importance regardless of whether public services are provided under contract by an external body or under an SLA with an in-house team:

> Service components of contracts or SLAs should be published in order to keep customers/users informed of the service and standards they should expect. Customers/users should be actively involved in contract management arrangements. Formal arrangements should be made for them to offer feedback on contractors' performance or changes in their requirements. If relevant, there should be arrangements for complaints and redress in individual cases when services do not meet contract/SLA standards.[80]

Over and above the interests of particular consumers or citizens, there is a *public* interest in the availability of information concerning the contract letting process, specification, price, and terms of provision. In order for market testing effectively to succeed in comparing the costs and quality of internal and external provision, similar information concerning price and performance should be available to all parties with stakes in the contracting process.

Secrecy and commercial confidentiality tend to inhibit proper accountability on the part of public managers and agencies performing contracting functions, as well as limiting the potential benefits of competition. Lack of transparency in contracting processes may in some circumstances suit the interests of both purchaser and provider, but may not be in the interests of consumers or the public more generally. Freedom of information is thus essential to the responsiveness of

[80] *Better Quality Services Handbook* (London: The Stationery Office, 1998) para 8.17.

contracting regimes in this regard.[81] Under the PFI, the secrecy surrounding the award of contracts and the confidentiality of contractual information generally have made it difficult to evaluate government claims that this method of financing of public infrastructure represents overall good value-for-money. Many of the details of PFI contracts are not disclosed at the time of signing. In early 2004 a furore developed over the revelation of additional payments being made by several NHS Trusts to private consortia running hospitals financed under the PFI, triggered by unexpectedly high bed occupancy and numbers of patients treated. While the Department of Health denied there was any problem with contractual mechanisms that varied rental payments to reflect increased maintenance and service costs, the real issue was the lack of information about such 'penalty clauses' at the time the contracts were awarded. The extent of the additional payments only came to light indirectly as a consequence of investigations into financial difficulties of the trusts concerned, which had been exacerbated by increased payments to PFI landlords. The general lack of transparency surrounding PFI deals raises worrying issues about probity, value-for-money, the effect of perverse incentives, and the competence of public management that should be in the public domain.[82]

Performance information

The Government's strategy for improving public services under best value and in its latest *Better Public Services* (BPS) programme is heavily reliant on the dissemination of performance information.[83] We have seen in earlier chapters how such information may be used in calling officials to account, requiring them to justify their priorities in comparison with those of other bodies performing similar quasi-market functions. It may also reveal disparities between providers, and enable performance trends to be plotted over time.[84] In all service sectors, the relative performance of state and non-state providers is being rendered more transparent through the publication of information which may inform choices made by public purchasers and consumers. The explicit purpose of the library of resources and internet links posted on the Cabinet Office's BPS website is to enable the public to understand processes of target-setting, measurement, and evaluation, and to make it possible to compare service quality across different areas

81 Schoombee notes that effective citizen redress is dependent not only on specificity in the obligations of the contractor, but also on *public disclosure* of those obligations – H Schoombee, 'Privatisation and Contracting Out – Where Are We Going?', in J McMillan, (ed), *Administrative Law Under the Coalition Government* (Canberra: AIAL, 1997).

82 *Observer* 28 March 2004. The perverse incentive lies in the apparent penalization of Trusts that are successful, for example in exceeding government targets for rates of bed occupancy.

83 G Boyne, J Gould-Williams, J Law, and R Walker, 'Plans, Performance Information and Accountability: The Case of Best Value' (2002) 80 *Public Administration* 691.

84 Leigh (n 37 above) 146.

and sectors.[85] The importance of information as a purposive regulatory instrument lies in establishing the conditions that will allow a mixture of public, private and voluntary provision to be determined by competitive forces. This information is also being used to trigger and justify external intervention in a wide range of 'failing' public services. A number of examples may briefly be considered in the health, education, and criminal justice fields.

Performance league tables have been operating on a 'star rating' system in the health sector for several years. For example, the information published in 2002 covered acute hospitals, ambulance services, specialist trusts such as children's hospitals and mental health trusts, and more than three hundred Primary Care Trusts (PCTs), which were given responsibility for commissioning NHS services early that year.[86] Performance was measured in accordance with the targets set in the Department of Health's PSA in the 2000 Spending Review. Not all targets were required to be fully achieved in order for three stars to be awarded, although no three-star trusts 'underachieved' on more than one target. Most trusts that achieved one star or no stars 'significantly underachieved' on at least one target and 'underachieved' on a number of others. The ratings were based on thirty seven measurements,[87] combined with the rating by the Commission for Health Improvement (together with the Health Inspectorate) which graded hospitals as having significant strengths, many strengths, some strengths, and significant area of weakness. The publication of the 2002 tables was accompanied by government warnings to the worst performing trusts that they could be taken over by private contractors or other hospitals if they did not rapidly improve.[88] Similarly, secondary schools regarded as 'failing' in light of the league tables published in 2003 were placed under 'special measures' by the DfES, and required to produce emergency action plans for improvement.[89] The explicit threat was that failure to produce satisfactory plans or to implement acceptable ones would result in closure

[85] www.odpm.gov.uk/stellent/groups/odpm_control/documents/contentservertemplate/odpm_index.hcst?n=1949&l=1 accessed 4 October 2005.

[86] The tables revealed that of the 158 acute hospital trusts in England, 47 improved their rating, 36 did worse and 75 stayed the same. The number of top-ranking three-star hospitals rose from 35 to 46. Eight trusts received no stars at all – *Guardian* 25 July 2002.

[87] The most important of which were: no patients waiting more than 18 months for inpatient treatment; fewer patients waiting more than 15 months for inpatient treatment; no patients waiting more than 26 weeks for outpatient treatment; fewer patients waiting on trolleys for more than 12 hours; less than 1% of operations cancelled on the day; no patients with suspected cancer waiting more than two weeks to be seen in hospital; improvement to the working lives of staff; hospital cleanliness; a satisfactory financial position.

[88] The threat was carried out in several cases – see BBC News Archive, 'Managers take over failing hospitals' – http://news.bbc.co.uk/1/hi/health/1974659.stm

[89] The School Inspections Act 1996 defines a school requiring special measures as 'failing or likely to fail to give its pupils an acceptable standard of education'. 'A school is removed from special measures (other than through closure) when Her Majesty's Inspectors judge the school to be providing for its pupils an acceptable standard of education and no longer in need of special measures to help remedy its weaknesses' – Department for Education and Skills Standards Site, www.standards.dfes.gov.uk/otherresources/special/removed accessed 4 October 2005.

of the school, compulsion to join a 'federation' of schools, or change of status to a City Academy.[90] In both the health and education sectors, the publication of performance information has been used consistently by central government as a means of legitimating the use and threat of emergency powers of intervention.

In local government, councils are rated excellent, good, fair, weak, or poor on a system introduced under the Comprehensive Performance Assessment (CPA). The scheme applied initially to one hundred and fifty metropolitan, unitary and county councils, but was extended to second tier district authorities in 2003. In the first results published by the Audit Commission in 2002, thirty two councils were top-rated, while thirty five of one hundred and fifty largest councils in England graded weak or poor. Again, the information served to justify the threat by government of a tougher approach to deal with councils, such as Hull, that in the view of the Audit Commission 'did not have the capacity to improve'.[91]

A new system of league tables for prisons was introduced in July 2003, grading one hundred and thirty seven prisons in England and Wales on one of four performance levels based on a range of criteria including costs, performance against targets, and compliance with standards, combined with findings from independent inspectors and monitoring boards, and taking account also of views of area managers and more subjective factors.[92] A similar system of performance tables for privately managed prisons is under development. In this instance the purpose of publication of information is obviously not to inform individual choice. However, performance information may be expected to be of increasing relevance in public decision making on whether and with whom to contract out following market testing, which continues to play a major role in this part of the criminal justice system. Comparison between public and private sectors is likely to increase as prison management is opened up to competition from private firms.

General problems with top-down performance management systems and management by contractual targets have been considered in Chapter 6. That discussion will not be repeated here. If PIs, service standards, and targets fail adequately to reflect citizen and consumer needs, then it cannot be expected that the publication of performance information will achieve the beneficial effects intended. This focuses attention on the nature of quantitative data, and the processes whereby targets are set and outcomes are measured. Even simple services such as hospital cleaning may be hard to specify and to evaluate. As has been seen, in the case of complex human services such as health and social care the problems are still greater.[93] Service quality here is inherently difficult to measure and may require more qualitative evaluation. What are significant outcomes and outputs

90 *Guardian* 23 January 2003.

91 *Guardian* 12 December 2002.

92 *Guardian* 15 November 2003.

93 T Cutler, and B Waine, 'Advancing Public Accountability? The Social Services "Star" Ratings' (2003) *Public Money and Management* (April) 125.

can only be defined through dialogue with patients and consumers.[94] For example, the 2002 league tables for hospital trusts were criticized for lacking a target or measure of the standard of nursing care. In secondary education, a 'value-added' performance measure was included for the first time in league tables published in 2003. This aimed to take into account the level of attainment of pupils on entry, so that the school would receive credit for subsequent improvements. However, education experts argued that this merely served to add sophistication to a flawed system.[95] Further distortions may be introduced by the manner in which performance is evaluated and information presented to the public. The Local Government Information Unit (LGIU) criticized the CPA performance tables as misleading, and the evaluation exercise an expensive control device that failed to reflect local priorities and did little to improve services.[96] Similarly in education, secondary school league tables have been branded 'crude and confusing' for parents.

The plea for information means not just any information, but reliable information presented in a form that can both contribute to the efficiency of allocation and demand decisions, and facilitate collective debate and public deliberation. Such debate should extend to the nature and determination of standards and PIs by which attainment is measured, and how that information is presented.[97] For example, school league tables should include a meaningful value-added element. The role of evaluating performance and publishing information also needs to be conducted independently of government. The Audit Commission has been given increased responsibilities in this regard, for example in the conduct of performance assessment of local councils under the CPA, and having won the contract for monitoring productivity in the fire service following the Bain Report.[98] The degree to which the Audit Commission may be regarded as really independent, however, is open to question.[99] In Part IV we consider how the institutional framework might be strengthened in order to increase the transparency of performance management processes and improve the quality of appropriate information informing public service decision making.

94 In the regulation of the nursing home sector, see J Braithwaite, T Makkai, V Braithwaite, and D Gibson, *Raising the Standard: Resident Centred Nursing Home Regulation in Australia* (Canberra: Australian Government Publishing Service, 1993) 14; J Braithwaite, 'The Nursing Home Industry', in A Reiss and M Tonry, (eds), *Organizational Crime: Crime and Justice – A Review of Research*, Vol. V. (Chicago, Il: University of Chicago Press, 1993).

95 *Guardian* 23 January 2003. See T Cutler and B Waine, 'Performance Management – The Key to Higher Standards in Schools?' (2001) *Public Money and Management* (Apr–Jun), 69.

96 *Guardian* 12 December 2002.

97 L Gaster, *Quality in Public Services: Managers' Choices* (Buckingham: Open University Press, 1995).

98 *Guardian* 19 February 2003. The Audit Commission lost its inspection function in respect of the NHS to the new inspectorate created in 2003, but has retained the audit role. It also gained a widened housing remit, taking over scrutiny of housing associations from the Housing Corporation.

99 S Cope and J Goodship, 'The Audit Commission and Public Services: Delivering for Whom?' (2002) *Public Money and Management* (Oct–Dec) 33.

From public service quasi-markets to regulated markets?

The increases in public spending announced in the 2002 Spending Review appear to involve a recommitment on the part of New Labour to the principle of free health and welfare services at the point of delivery. Some form of quasi-market organization seems therefore to continue to be the preferred 'third way' alternative to both traditional bureaucratic and market governance. In another sense, however, policies encouraging consumer choice, coupled with the trend towards co-payments and user fees as a means of topping-up state subsidies, suggest that economic contracting regimes may be a transitional stage in the development of a model of public service organization involving increasing privatization and a diminishing role for the state. For example, while domiciliary or long term care for the elderly is publicly funded at least in part, and depends on an initial assessment of need and subsequent referral by a public agency or professional body, this is combined with an element of consumer choice as to where and how the budget earmarked for the purpose designated is spent. Where the consumer is required to pay a top-up fee directly to the provider, there is a private market aspect to the service. Similarly, since 1999 the public funding of legal services has been organized on a quasi-market basis combining limited consumer choice with the control of cost and quality through franchising of service providers.[100] Only firms that have bid successfully and been awarded contracts with the Legal Services Commission can provide specified legal services on a publicly funded basis. Consumers are required to pay privately for a proportion of the cost of the service, which is means-tested. Again, dental and optical services, NHS prescriptions, and tertiary education all involve state funding combined with user charges or co-payments for which consumers are directly liable.

In the terms suggested at the beginning of this chapter, quasi-markets may be giving way to regulated markets (Fig 7(3)). 'Privatization' no longer refers just to the increasing role of non-state bodies supplying public services under contract with public purchasing agencies in purchaser-provider quasi-markets, together with the development of supply-side competition. It further implies the devolution of demand functions and of responsibilities for public service decision making to private individuals, on the basis of direct links with providers in competitive markets through a range of choice and exit mechanisms.

Looking further into the future, the longer-term trend may be away from regulated *public* contracting towards regulated *private* contracting in the organization and provision of public services.[101] With this development, as I have already

[100] G Bevan, 'Legal Aid: A Case Study in Quasi-Market Failure', in W Bartlett, JA Roberts, and J Le Grand, (eds), *A Revolution in Social Policy: Quasi-Market Reforms in the 1990s* (Bristol: The Policy Press, 1998).

[101] The degree to which this shift entails the displacement of public law governance by a new 'postmodern' legal order is open to question – see B Edgeworth, *Law, Modernity, Postmodernity: Legal*

suggested, the boundary between regulated markets for public services (Fig 7(3)) and wholly private services (Fig 7(4)) becomes increasingly blurred. The trend is already evident in the privatized utilities and telecommunications sectors, in which public services are provided by private corporations to consumers who pay for the services at the point of consumption. The public interest in these services is maintained through controls exercised by independent regulatory agencies over the operation of markets. As such substantive regulation diminishes with the progressive liberalization of markets and the development of competition, so the distinction between 'public' and 'private' services becomes increasingly hard to sustain. With the increase in vouchering and co-payments, there is little to prevent certain other public services developing in a similar direction. This analysis supports the suggestion already made in Chapter 2 that policy-guided review processes may be interpreted as facilitating the movement of central and local government functions 'outwards' from direct bureaucratic control to the market, at which point the activity ceases to be governed through the New Public Contracting and becomes subject to more general forms of regulation.

Conclusion

There exists a tension between the Government's purported aim of harnessing competitive incentives to improve public services by whatever form of public or private provision is deemed appropriate, and the more fundamental policy goal of reducing the financial burden on the public purse, and hence the level of public sector borrowing, by transferring responsibilities for funding and provision to the private and non-profit sectors.[102] The latter can be achieved in one of two ways – either through consumer exit from the public sector to fully-privatized provision entailing a market relationship between the provider and service recipient, or by public purchasing from private providers in a quasi-market. According to the analysis of policy purposes in terms of 'foreseeable consequences',[103] the suggestion here is not that there exists necessarily a deliberately hidden or secret agenda, but rather that there are various policy aims that have not been properly explained or understood, and whose inter-relationship has not been articulated. The result is that fundamental tensions in government policy on public services remain unresolved.

Change in the Contracting State (Aldershot: Ashgate, 2003); C Scott, Review of Edgeworth (2004) 31 JLS 284.

102 The two aims need not be mutually exclusive. However, a critical analysis should seek to tease out the tensions implicit in the simultaneous pursuit of both goals. For example, even taking the Government's claims of policy neutrality at face value, cuts in public funding and restrictions on the autonomy of direct providers and public purchasing agencies may increase the attractiveness of exit by dissatisfied individuals into private markets in sectors such as housing, health, and education.

103 ch 5 above.

The shift to regulated markets avoids some of the problems associated with the complexity of quasi-markets based on the purchaser-provider split. Most importantly, choice may be exercised directly by consumers rather than on their behalf by public purchasing agencies. Increased automaticity need not imply the complete loss of public control, which may continue to be exercised through regulation, for example by independent regulatory agencies. However, the drift towards privatization of public services remains problematic and controversial. This has tended to be accompanied by a downgrading of the 'voice' interest of citizens relative to the 'choice' interest of consumers. There may also be losses with respect to the capacity of the state to achieve its equity and redistributive goals. Where service recipients are vulnerable and for this reason incapable of exercising choice or voice, then the public interest might better be protected through bureaucratic or quasi-market organization. As in the previous chapter, this serves to focus attention on the issue of legitimacy in the decision-making process as a crucial element in the ultimate evaluation of responsiveness. In the current mixed economy of public service provision, there is also the more immediate problem of deficiencies in the redress of citizen grievances. We return to these issues in Part IV, following the analysis of social control contracts in Chapter 9.

9

Social Control Contracts

This chapter considers how relationships between the state and individual citizens have been structured through social control contracts. In the field of unemployment and employment services, the focus is on jobseeker's agreements and the New Deal. With regard to education and the control of deviance, separate consideration is given youth offender contracts, acceptable behaviour contracts, rehabilitation contracts for convicted prisoners, education maintenance allowance contracts, home-school agreements, and parenting contracts in respect of anti-social behaviour and exclusion from school and truancy.

While all these behavioural contracts perform social control functions, they vary considerably in their nature and policy objectives. Youth offender contracts and rehabilitation contracts are triggered by breach of the criminal law or conviction involving a custodial sentence. Acceptable behaviour contracts and parenting contracts may be used in the attempt to control young persons suspected of involvement in criminal or anti-social behaviour. Jobseeker's agreements and home-school agreements are not predicated on breach of the law or suspicion of legal wrongdoing but apply rather to whole classes of citizens (respectively parents of school children and welfare claimants). In some instances the contracts are compulsory, while in others apparently voluntary arrangements are entered into against the background threat of more coercive measures if the individual fails to agree or to sign the contract. Incentives to individuals to enter contracts with public agencies may be financial, or consist in the avoidance of burdens or penalties than might otherwise be incurred. There is considerable variation also in how the subjects of social control are constructed in official discourses. The jobseeker is regarded as the 'customer' of Jobcentre Plus, an executive agency of the Department for Work and Pensions (DWP). Parents of school children are also described as 'customers' of the services provided by the Department for Education and Skills (DfES) and its executive agencies. Citizens caught up in the criminal justice system are generally referred to as 'clients'; only in a tenuous sense are they customers, since they are not willing recipients of correctional services in the same way that parents desire education for their children, or the unemployed desire help with jobs or at least unemployment benefits on which to subsist.

The responsiveness of these social control arrangements is evaluated with reference to the contract norms introduced in Chapter 1, with particular attention to voluntariness, reciprocity, consent, choice, and power. Where these norms are damaged or are otherwise not functioning properly, it cannot be expected that the obligations will be fulfilled or that the contracts will operate relationally. Attempts at behavioural modification through top-down, policy-driven regulatory frameworks and associated contracting techniques are contrasted with the bottom-up development of contracts by professionals in the spheres of probation and social work. These have quite different agendas and rationales.[1] I suggest that governance problems are likely to be significantly greater in state-imposed programmes.

'New Contractualism'

For the purposes of this chapter, social control refers to the whole range of formal and informal processes whereby both individual and collective behaviour is governed in contemporary societies. It encompasses planned and programmed societal responses to deviance,[2] including the official use by the state of force and sanctions, and the use by public agencies of incentives and rewards to encourage desirable behaviour. It further includes indirect practices involving professional discourses and technologies,[3] and socialization processes that occur within institutions such as schools and the family. The recent deployment of social control contracts in policy-driven regulation may be argued to form part of an 'inclusionary' strategy of governance. In contrast to more formal 'exclusionary' modes of control based on segregation, expulsion, and stigmatization,[4] this strategy entails the attempt by the state to deal with offenders and other deviants within the communities in which the problem behaviour is deemed to have arisen.

The deployment of contract as a mechanism of social control may usefully be considered in light of the burgeoning literature on the 'New Contractualism'.[5] This scholarship has sought to explain why contract has been adapted as a general mechanism of governance of social life, and its role in shaping culture and structuring liberal democracy.[6]

[1] M Freedland and D King, 'Contractual Governance and Illiberal Contracts: Some Problems of Contractualism as an Instrument of Behaviour Management by Agencies of Government' (2003) 27 *Cambridge Journal of Economics* 465, 467–8.

[2] S Cohen, *Visions of Social Control: Crime, Punishment, and Classification* (Cambridge: Polity Press, 1985) 17.

[3] See ch 3.

[4] Cohen (n 2 above) 19–20.

[5] P Vincent-Jones, 'New Labour and the New Contract: Law and Social Relations in the Age of Privatisation', Professorial Lecture, University of Central Lancashire, 17 November 1999.

[6] A Yeatman, 'The New Contractualism: Management Reform or a New Approach to Governance', in P Weller and G Davis, (eds), *New Ideas, Better Government* (Sydney: Allen and Unwin, 1996).

Models of welfare

The Marshallian model of welfare in the post-war period was based on citizenship entitlements and the principle that protection and security should be provided according to need.[7] The new welfare settlement, by contrast, involves rights balanced by responsibilities, with more limited entitlements contingent upon something being given in return for something received.[8] All western societies have been affected by this transition to some degree, driven by common economic pressures for reform.[9] The result is that current debates on welfare are conducted in a language alien to traditional social policy analysis. Issues are presented increasingly in terms of problems of dependency rather than poverty or inequality, with a focus on changing people's behaviour rather than altering the distribution of resources in society.[10] As we saw in Chapter 1, contract lies at the heart of the new discourse, being concretely embodied in new forms of relationship between individual citizens and the state.[11] Social life generally is increasingly governed through the contractual specification of roles and responsibilities of all social agents, whether government departments, public agencies, private bodies, or individual citizens.[12]

7 RH Cox, 'The Consequences of Welfare Reform: How Conceptions of Social Rights are Changing' (1998) 27 *Journal of Social Policy* 1, 3.

8 A Giddens, *The Third Way: The Renewal of Social Responsibility* (Cambridge: Polity Press, 1998) 65; P Dwyer, 'Conditional Citizens? Welfare Rights and Responsibilities in the Late 1990s' (1998) 18 *Critical Social Policy* 493; M Muetzelfeldt, 'The Facilitative State and the Symbolic Potency of Mutual Obligation' (2001) 60 *Australian Journal of Public Administration* 99.

9 Hence despite major differences, governments in the UK, the US, and the Netherlands are 'institutionalizing the assumption that *all* people of working age who receive benefits should take jobs if they are able to do so' – C Finn, (ed), *Sunrise or Sunset? Administrative Law in the New Millennium* (Canberra: Australian Institute of Administrative Law, 2000) 53. The anticipated increase in labour market participation is seen as an essential tool for both tackling dependency and social exclusion, and reducing costs and caseloads.

10 A Deacon and K Mann, 'Agency, Modernity and Social Policy' (1999) 28 *Journal of Social Policy* 413, 423. On Australian welfare reform emphasising the role of the market and the family as preferred institutions of social support, against the dependency and moral hazard associated with 'passive welfare', see S Shaver, 'Australian Welfare Reform: From Citizenship to Supervision' (2002) 36 *Social Policy and Administration* 331, 343; C MacIntyre, 'From Entitlement to Obligation in the Australian Welfare State' (1999) 34 *Australian Journal of Social Issues* 103; M Considine, 'Markets, Networks and the New Welfare State: Employment Assistance Reforms in Australia' (1999) 28 *Journal of Social Policy* 183.

11 G Davis, 'Implications, Consequences and Futures', in G Davis, B Sullivan, and A Yeatman, (eds), *The New Contractualism?* (Melbourne: Macmillan, 1997) 227. Carney and Ramia describe the New Contractualism as rooted not only in the notion of the social contract between ruler and subjects, and between subjects and other subjects, but also in neo-liberal, governmental efforts to regulate a whole spectrum of public and private relationships in new ways – T Carney and G Ramia, *From Rights to Management: Contract, New Public Management and Employment Services* (The Hague: Kluwer Law International, 2002), 26; see ibid 'Contractualism and Citizenship: Rivals or Bedfellows?' (2001) 18 *Law in Context* 8.

12 Contractual instruments, accompanied by mechanisms for monitoring and sanctions, serve to specify reciprocal expectations of social agents in all sectors and walks of life, not just in those areas of government traditionally associated with the NPM – cf J Martin, 'Contractualism in New Zealand',

The main components of the New Contractualism have been described by Yeatman as informed consent, negotiation by mutual consent, and accountability.[13] Other interpretations of the contractualist ethos have emphasized reciprocity and the mutuality of obligation.[14] The guiding principle here is that 'those who willingly share in the social product have a corresponding obligation to make a reasonable (relevantly proportional) productive contribution to the community in return'.[15] Far from indicating a retreat on the part of the state from the organization of welfare, this implies an increased role for public agencies in coordinating and integrating welfare systems based on contractual principles.[16]

These developments have been argued to be reconcilable with the Marshallian philosophy of social rights and citizenship, interpreted as rights of *reasonable* rather than unconditional access to a given resource.[17] A similarly benign view of mutuality, which attempts to allow for the dependence of citizens on welfare at some time in their lives, suggests that reciprocal obligations need not be performed 'synchronously', ie in the present, but may be deferred to some time in the future.[18] Against this, critics argue that welfare contractualism is inherently conducive to a moralistic, populist and censorious political discourse which can quite readily overwhelm any potential advantages that may rationally be argued to accompany it.[19] Problems include the unequal power relationship between the state and individual citizens, the lack of negotiation and consensus in the determination of

in Y Fortin and H Van Hassel, (eds), *Contracting in the New Public Management – From Economics to Law and Citizenship* (Amsterdam: IOS Press, 2000), 74; Davis (n 11 above) 224.

13 A Yeatman, 'Interpreting Contemporary Contractualism', in M Dean and B Hindess, (eds). *Governing Australia: Studies in Contemporary Rationalities of Government* (Cambridge: Cambridge University Press, 1998) 231.

14 L Mead, 'Citizenship and Social Policy: T. H. Marshall and Poverty', in E Paul, F Miller, and J Paul, (eds), *The Welfare State* (Cambridge: Cambridge University Press, 1997) 209–210; Carney and Ramia (n 11 above).

15 S White, 'Social Rights and the Social Contract: Political Theory and the New Welfare Politics' (2000) 30 *British Journal of Political Science* 507, 513.

16 On new forms of state involvement and institutionalization of welfare and social services across Europe, see T Bahle, 'The Changing Institutionalization of Social Services in England and Wales, France and Germany: Is the Welfare State On the Retreat?' (2003) 13 *Journal of European Social Policy* 5. 'The State does not diminish or become merely a Nightwatchman, rather it takes on a new set of coordinating and activating roles' – D Garland, 'The Limits of the Sovereign State: Strategies of Crime Control in Contemporary Society' (1996) 36 *British Journal of Criminology* 445, 454.

17 White (n 15 above) 510; see also A Deacon, 'An Ethic of Mutual Responsibility?: Towards a Fuller Justification for Conditionality in Welfare', in C Beem and L Mead, (eds), *Welfare Reform and Political Theory* (New York: Russell Sage Foundation, 2005); ibid 'Justifying Conditionality: The Case of Anti-Social Tenants' (2004) 19 *Housing Studies* 911.

18 The problem with the 'synchronous' interpretation is that it 'demands payment from the weak, when they are weak', reinforcing relations of social disadvantage and subordination – RE Goodin, 'Structures of Mutual Obligation' (2002) 31 *Journal of Social Policy* 579, 592; AW Gouldner, 'The Norm of Reciprocity' (1960) 25 *American Sociological Review* 161.

19 Freedland and King (n 1 above) 471, in a critique of White (n 15 above). For a general critique of the illiberal basis of welfare-to-work programmes in Britain and the US, see D King, *In the Name of Liberalism: Illiberal Social Policy in the United States and Britain* (Oxford: Oxford University Press, 1999).

many of the 'contracts', and the general absence of substantive individual rights and procedural safeguards in respect of contractual processes. The effect in many cases is to discipline and sanction those who are already vulnerable and socially excluded for non-compliance. Behind the rhetoric of mutuality, contractual systems erode the social protection and security associated with traditional welfare policy, and mark a 'shift towards personalisation of risk rather than its collective assumption by the state'.[20] Current expressions of mutuality in welfare policy generally may place unreasonable burdens on affected citizens, while being unduly lax on the obligations of government in such matters as subsidies, training, and child care.[21] We return to this debate in discussing the potential for a responsive welfare contractualism in the concluding section of this chapter.

Responsibilization

We established in Chapter 3 that responsibilization refers to the range of techniques and practices whereby individual citizens are constructed as self-determining and self-willing agents in control of their own destinies. This discourse focuses on agency rather than structure, implying that all actions, activities, decisions and behaviours represent some measure of meaningful choice.[22] However constrained the circumstances in which choice is exercised, the implication is that there are always alternatives or at least one other option.[23] The use of contractual mechanisms in social control both draws upon and reinforces these notions of agency and choice. While responsibilization might be achieved through authoritative and coercive measures quite independently of contract, the contract norms (voluntariness, consent, choice) may be especially effective in this process. Social control contracts render individuals responsible for their predicaments (as offenders, unemployed job seekers, parents whose children are disruptive at school) in ways that differ significantly from the governance of relations by hierarchical authority.

Like the New Contractualism in general, responsibilization has been strongly associated with a moralistic right wing agenda directed at reducing welfare and increasing the personal responsibility of citizens to be self-supporting.[24] New

[20] Carney and Ramia (n 11 above) 165. [21] ibid 150.

[22] Deacon and Mann (n 10 above) 423.

[23] ibid 413; cf Macneil's insistence that choice exists even highly pressured circumstances – (n 106 below).

[24] Mead (n 14 above). On Australian welfare reform, see Shaver (n 10 above). For analysis of the ideological underpinnings of the introduction in the US by President Clinton of the Personal Responsibility and Work Opportunity Act 1996, see A Waddan, 'Redesigning the Welfare Contract in Theory and Practice: Just What Is Going On in the USA?' (2003) 32 *Journal of Social Policy* 19. Deacon and Mann conclude that 'moralists' such as Etzioni, Field and Mead 'share a belief in the need to restructure welfare in ways that encourage and reward responsible behaviour' (n 10 above) 413, driven by a 'rejection of non-judgementalism and a belief in the need for moral leadership' (ibid 430).

Public Contracting policies pursued by Labour governments since 1997 appear to have been concerned with promoting just such a moral order, in which individuals are urged to 'do the right thing' – to take control of their own welfare and ultimately provide for their own needs wherever possible.[25] The 1998 Green Paper, *A New Contract for Welfare: New Ambitions for Our Country*,[26] set the tone for subsequent Labour policy on welfare and employment services. Whereas the first 'age of welfare' was concerned with the prevention of destitution, and the second with the alleviation of poverty through cash benefit systems, the current third age is argued to be characterized by 'opportunity instead of dependence', with governments being responsible for providing positive help and claimants being responsible for taking it up.[27] A similar theme was pursued in the field of criminal justice in White Paper proposals for youth offender contracts, eventually introduced under the Youth Justice and Criminal Evidence Act 1999.[28] In Labour's second term of office, rehabilitation policies involving contracts were developed on the basis that 'prisoners serving custodial sentences (should) accept responsibility for their actions, and understand the consequences of offending on both their victims and themselves'.[29] A central theme of the White Paper on anti-social behaviour in 2003 was 'people taking responsibility for their own actions and behaving in a way that does not harass or intimidate others'.[30] In this vision responsibility for anti-social behaviour attaches not just to individual wrongdoers, but to their families, neighbours, and entire local communities.[31]

Parents have become specific targets of responsibilization strategies. The Government's view is that offending is strongly associated with inadequate parental supervision. Where the individual offender is unable or unwilling to accept the burden, responsibility is transferred to the parents. Complementing the system

[25] 'Labour aims to forge a new deal between the state and the individual. It is a deal based firmly on a new reciprocal relationship that it hopes will counter the perceived problems of a welfare dependency culture, rising public expenditure and a system of welfare that is sees to be generally failing to meet the financial and moral needs of vulnerable citizens' – E Heron and P Dwyer, 'Doing the Right Thing: Labour's Attempt to Force a New Welfare Deal Between the Individual and the State' (1999) 33 *Social Policy and Administration* 91, 100.

[26] *A New Contract for Welfare: New Ambitions for Our Country*, Green Paper, (Cm 3805, 1998). This was followed by: *A New Contract for Welfare: Principles into Practice*, White Paper, (Cm 4101, 1998); *A New Contract for Welfare: The Gateway to Work*, White Paper, (Cm 4102, 1998); *A New Contract for Welfare: Support for Disabled People*, White Paper, (Cm 4103, 1998).

[27] Green Paper (n 26 above) para. 11. The fourth and final age of welfare, tellingly expressed in the form of the social contract, remains a future aspiration: 'By 2020 there should be in place a new welfare contract between the citizens of the country and the Government. This will deliver greater trust, transparency, responsibility and responsiveness and people will be empowered to seize the opportunities to lead independent lives' (para. 30).

[28] *No More Excuses – A New Approach to Tackling Youth Crime in England and Wales*, Home Office White Paper, (Cm 3809, 1997).

[29] *Justice for All*, White Paper (Cm 5563, 2002) para 6.12.

[30] *Respect and Responsibility – Taking a Stand Against Anti-Social Behaviour*, White Paper, (Cm 5778, 2003).

[31] 'Our aim is a 'something for something' society where we treat one another with respect and where we *all share responsibility* for taking a stand against what is unacceptable' (emphasis added) – ibid, Foreword by David Blunkett.

of parenting orders under the Crime and Disorder Act 1998, Part 3 of the Anti-social Behaviour Act 2003 ('Parental Responsibilities') introduced two new forms of 'parenting contract', in respect of exclusion from school or truancy, and criminal conduct and anti-social behaviour. With regard to school attendance and truancy, guidance states: 'Parenting contracts, parenting orders and penalty notices . . . are intended to help ensure that parents take seriously their responsibilities to ensure their children regularly attend school and behave well when they get there.'[32] Other parties allocated specific responsibilities for implementing policies combating anti-social behaviour include youth offending teams, youth offender panels, local education authorities, governing bodies of schools, employment advisers, and managers of Jobcentres. A key governmental purpose in casting these various social control relationships in a contractual regulatory form is to deflect responsibilities away from central government and onto public service professionals and their clients.[33]

The particular variants of social control contracts in the education, welfare, and criminal justice sectors function as supports for the contractual organization of public services in society more generally. Criminal, disruptive or anti-social behaviour obviously has a direct and damaging effect on the quality of public services such as housing, education, and health care.[34] The role of the social contract in promoting socially desirable behaviour in public life more generally is less obvious.[35] Models of the empowered and prudent individual in the new liberal politics stress 'care of the self' in all aspects of modern living.[36] Official guidelines were issued in 2003 requiring doctors to advise patients identified as being at particular risk to change their lifestyle. The National Institute for Clinical Excellence (NICE) has suggested expressly that patients have a responsibility to make lifestyle changes to help professionals manage progressive diseases.[37] The Labour party has consulted its members on whether the Government should

[32] Guidance on Education-Related Parenting Contracts, Parenting Orders and Penalty Notices, DfES/0234/2004, paras 1–2.

[33] Freedland and King (n 1 above) 467.

[34] In education, for example, information about home-school agreements appears on the DfES website under the banner of the Service First New Charter Programme (in spite of the declaration on other Government websites that the Service First programme has been completed – see ch 8). This confirms the shift already noted in the previous chapter from the notion of charterism as rights of consumers in respect of public services, to charterism as a 'contractual' relationship involving rights balanced by responsibilities of individual citizens in relation to the state – www.dfes.gov.uk/hsa/contents.shtml 5 October 2005. Social control in education is closely connected with school standards, as indicated by the inclusion of home-school agreements within the School Standards and Framework Act 1998.

[35] cf. F Lumley, *Means of Social Control* (New York: Century, 1925): 'All social problems are ultimately problems of social control – capital and labour, prostitution, taxes, crimes, international relations', 14.

[36] P O'Malley, 'Uncertain Subjects: Risks, Liberalism and Contract' (2000) 29 *Employment and Society* 460; ibid *Risk, Uncertainty and Government* (London: Glasshouse Press, 2004).

[37] In advice issued on 23 July 2003, people with chronic heart failure were told to play their part in managing the disease by giving up smoking, exercising regularly, and abstaining or cutting down on alcohol.

bring in formal contracts between doctors and patients, which would not be legally binding but express 'mutual good intent' in making such changes.[38]

Governance issues

As we saw in Chapter 1, the regulatory frameworks governing social control contracts have in common with economic contracting regimes a relatively complex double regulatory structure. Not surprisingly, therefore, the governance issues in this form of the New Public Contracting are in certain respects similar to those discussed in Chapter 7. First, in the hierarchical relationship between central government and the public agency to which contracting powers are delegated, they concern:

- the nature and form of responsibilities of the public agency/case worker, in terms of duties and performance targets;
- the definition and ambit of contractual powers of the public agency/case worker regarding when, with whom, and on what terms to contract;
- the scope of discretion and freedom from central interference accorded the public agency/case worker in the exercise of contracting powers;
- the adequacy of resources assigned by central government to the public agency, and the degree to which the policy objectives are capable of being realized within the designated regulatory structures; and
- the overall quality of the regulatory relationship in relational terms.

Whereas economic contracting regimes have been shown to be concerned as much with limiting the powers of public purchasing or commissioning agencies as with facilitating their contracting activities, in the social control context the less complicated purpose is the attainment of substantive policy goals in the regulation of standards of behaviour and the control of deviance.

Secondly, the responsiveness of contracting regimes is dependent on the configuration of contract norms within particular contracts and in the institutional environments in which they are made and operate. The focus here is on:

- the 'bindingness' of the arrangements, and the ability of the parties to enforce contractual obligations supported by appropriate sanctioning machinery;
- the balance between discrete and relational norms governing the relationship;
- the balance of power in the relationship, and the existence of fairness in both the making and performance of contracts;

[38] *Guardian* 24 July 2003. But patients who refused to sign the contract would still be treated.

- the autonomy of citizens/clients as regards both the conditions under which contractual commitments are made, and unwarranted interference or amendment by the public agency in the performance of the contract; and
- the overall quality of the contractual relationship (relationality) – the more relational, the greater the likelihood of attainment of the regulatory goals of the contracting regime.

We shall see that in practice there are significant problems with the operation of social control contracts on all these dimensions. The fact that these contracts are not recognized at private law does not mean that they lack obligational content or are incapable of enforcement. Nevertheless, I will argue that some form of sanctioning mechanism is necessary to support planning and to ensure the credibility of contractual commitments. Where the basic elements of contractual relations are established, these need to be balanced by relational norms such as reciprocity, solidarity, and role integrity if the regulatory objectives of the contracting regimes are to be achieved. Reciprocity is particularly problematic in these relationships due to the structural imbalance of power between the client and the public agency. As regards protection of the interests of the weaker party against unwarranted or unfair variation of the contract, a fundamental question is whether the contracts serve as 'constitutions' governing the parties' future relationships, as opposed to being static statements of obligations involving consent to a relationship of obligation.[39] As already considered in relation to administrative contracts, the distinction is between primary contracts as substantive statements of obligations, and 'power-conferring' contracts that specify processes and procedures for the future management and adjustment of relationships.[40]

Unemployment and employment services

The Department for Work and Pensions (DWP) is responsible for a major part of the Government's welfare reform agenda. Its stated purpose is 'to promote opportunity and independence for all' by delivering support and advice through a network of services to people of working age, employers, pensioners, families and children, and disabled people. Employment services are provided to 'customers' by Jobcentre Plus, an executive agency of the DWP, in accordance with charter obligations including published procedures for complaints and disputes resolution.[41] Case workers in Jobcentres operate in accordance with the terms of

39 C Pateman, *The Problem of Political Obligation: A Critical Analysis of Liberal Theory* (Chichester: John Wiley and Son, 1979) 20.

40 I Harden, *The Contracting State* (Buckingham: Open University Press, 1992) 31–32.

41 Jobcentre Plus was created as a part of the DWP in April 2002, replacing the Employment Service, which ran Jobcentres, and those parts of the Benefits Agency which provided services to people of working age through social security offices.

framework documents agreed between the agency and the DWP, and the PSA which governs the relationship between the DWP and the Treasury.

Jobseeker's Agreement

The concept of contract provided an attractive basis for the Conservative government's reform of social security through the Jobseekers Act 1995, which made entitlement to the new Jobseeker's Allowance dependent on claimants entering a Jobseeker's Agreement with an employment officer.[42] One of the main purposes of the reform was to bring the relatively generous system of unemployment benefits based on the contributory insurance principle into line with the stricter means-tested regime of social security and income support.[43] The change in terminology from 'unemployment benefit' to 'jobseeker's allowance' clearly indicated the shift from a system of entitlement based on a record of contributions, to one of conditional payments dependent on claimants being 'available for employment' and 'actively seeking employment'.[44] The 1995 Act and accompanying regulations brought to a climax a process of progressive tightening up of the unemployment benefits regime since the inception of unemployment insurance in 1911. This has involved increasingly lengthy disqualification periods for voluntarily leaving work, compulsory training, and various provisions denying benefit to claimants refusing to apply for jobs or take up training opportunities 'without good cause'.

The responsibility for specifying the content of the Jobseeker's Agreement and how it is implemented is delegated to the Secretary of State through wide enabling powers in the Act.[45] Despite this, a positive by-product of the legislative scheme has been increased transparency in comparison with previous guidance.[46] The agreement is required to be in writing and signed by both parties,[47] and a copy must be provided to the claimant.[48] Regulations specify the matters to be contained in the agreement, including the claimant's name, the type of work sought, the steps to be taken in looking for work and improving chances of finding work, and the help to be provided by Jobcentre Plus. The process for variation of the terms of the agreement closely follows that for its creation.[49] The purpose of the

[42] Jobseekers Act 1995, s 1(2)(b), s 9.

[43] The New Contractualism requires a present and immediate commitment on the part of individuals claiming welfare, distinguished from previous programs based on past record of contribution or on current need as the foundation of entitlement – Carney and Ramia (n 8 above) 146.

[44] s 1(2)(a) and (c). The change in terminology reflected changes that had already significantly restricted entitlement to unemployment benefit, involving disqualifications for voluntary unemployment and job-seeking requirements in various formulations since the 1920s.

[45] s 9(1), (8), (10), and (11).

[46] J Fulbrook, 'The Job Seekers' Act 1995: Consolidation with a Sting of Contractual Compliance' (1995) 24 *Industrial Law Journal* 395, 399.

[47] s 9(3).

[48] s 9(4).

[49] The agreement can be varied only in the prescribed manner by agreement between the claimant and an employment officer, s 10(1). The variation must be in writing and signed by both parties (s 10(2)), with a copy of the varied agreement being given to the claimant (s 10(3)).

variation provisions is to ensure that the agreement can be adapted flexibly to changes in the labour market or the claimant's circumstances.

The Jobseeker's Allowance is payable to men and women between eighteen and retirement age who are not working more than sixteen hours per week, who are capable of working, available for work, and actively seeking work.[50] Claimants who have paid National Insurance contributions may be entitled to a contribution-based allowance, while those who have not may be eligible for an income-based allowance. The former is paid at a fixed rate depending on age for up to twenty six weeks, while the latter is subject to means testing. Rules provide that new claimants must register for work and training at a local Connexions Service or Careers Service office,[51] which is responsible for helping find a job or training place and for arranging an interview at the local Jobcentre. Following the interview the claimant and employment adviser agree and sign the Jobseeker's Agreement. Monitoring of the agreement is conducted periodically in detailed interviews, supplementing the requirement to attend the Jobcentre to confirm continued entitlement to the allowance every two weeks.

On request by the claimant, the employment officer is required to refer a proposed agreement to an adjudication officer who will determine whether the availability and activity conditions specified under s 1 are satisfied,[52] and whether it is reasonable to expect the claimant to comply with the proposed agreement.[53] Any determination by the adjudication officer in accordance with this section, including any directions made as to the terms of the agreement,[54] is binding.[55] The employment officer may similarly refer a proposed variation to an adjudication officer for binding determination.[56] The adjudication officer, in addition to powers to make directions in respect of the variation,[57] may bring the agreement to an end where the claimant fails, within a prescribed period, to comply with a direction made under the section.[58] A claimant who is dissatisfied with the decision of an adjudication officer is required first to seek review by a different officer,[59] before then appealing to a social security appeal tribunal (SSAT).[60] The SSAT has powers to issue directions in a manner similar to the adjudication officer under the previous two sections,[61] with the adjudication officer retaining the power following the appeal to bring the agreement to an end for failure to comply with SSAT directions.[62] Any 'appropriate person',[63] in addition to the adjudication officer and the claimant, may appeal to the Commissioner

[50] www.jobcentreplus.gov.uk. accessed 5 October 2005. An income-based Jobseeker's Allowance may be available to unemployed 16 or 17 year olds in special circumstances.

[51] Connexions is the government's support service for all young people aged 13 to 19 in England. The service aims to provide integrated advice, guidance and access to personal development opportunities for this group and to help them make a smooth transition to adulthood and working life – see www.connexions.gov.uk accessed 5 October 2005.

[52] s 9(6)(a)(i) and (ii).

[53] s 9(6)(b).

[54] s 9(7)(b).

[55] s 9(9).

[56] s 10(5)

[57] s 10(5)(a), (b).

[58] s 10(6)(c).

[59] s 11(1).

[60] s 11(3).

[61] s 11(4).

[62] s 11(5).

[63] As defined in s 11, including a trade union or other association representing the interests of its members in prescribed circumstances – s 11(7)(c), (d).

against the decision of the SSAT on the ground that it was erroneous on a point of law.[64]

New Deal

'New Deal' is the name given to a package of government programmes ostensibly directed at giving unemployed people help and support in acquiring work skills and finding jobs. This initiative is an extension of the case management approach accompanying the Jobseeker's Agreement, in which the 'personal advisers' who implement the schemes are responsible for preparing suitable work plans tailored to the experiences, interests and goals of clients. The New Deal for Young People, for example, applies to those aged between eighteen and twenty four who have been unemployed and claiming the Jobseeker's Allowance for six months or more. In a number of meetings taking place over a period of four months, the personal adviser is responsible for drawing up an action plan, helping overcome any difficulties that might be interfering with jobseeking (such as transport or literacy problems), and identifying any extra support needed. If a job has not been secured by the end of this period, the personal adviser is responsible for arranging a package of full-time help to meet the customer's specific needs. This may involve work experience with an employer or voluntary organization, training for a specific job, enrolling on courses to develop the skills that employers want, practical help with applying for jobs, and interview practice. Similar 'workfare' schemes have been adopted throughout the developed world.[65]

The launch of the original New Deal for Young People in 1998 was followed by New Deal programmes directed at people over twenty five, those over fifty, disabled people, lone parents, partners, the self-employed, and musicians. In 2002 a further StepUp scheme was introduced in six regions requiring the long-term unemployed, defined as those not in work within six weeks of passing through a New Deal programme, to accept jobs with local employers at the minimum wage, subsidized by government. Work preparation for this form of employment was made compulsory, with failure to attend or to accept the opportunity offered being regarded as a breach of the Jobseeker's Agreement and leading to withdrawal of benefits.

Discussion

As has been seen, the New Contractualism entails the progressive displacement of citizenship rights by entitlements contingent upon reciprocal responsibilities.

[64] s 11(6)

[65] Echoing the New Deal in Britain, Australia's 'Mutual Obligation Initiative' (MOI) of 2002 may be regarded as the latest in a long line of attempts to link work to welfare going back to the Poor Law of 1834 – Goodin (n 18 above) 580. MOI applies to long-term recipients of unemployment benefit for more than 6 months (12 months if over 25), requiring them to spend a 'compliance period' in specified forms of paid, unpaid, or caring labour, or working at various educational, military, or conservationist tasks (582).

The Jobseeker's Agreement between the claimant and employment adviser is concluded in the context of a wider 'compact' between the individual and the state, as expressed in various documents such as the Jobcentre Plus Customers' Charter, first published in April 2002.[66] The DWP is engaged in a dual role, in one sense providing a public service to customers just like any other government department, while at the same time participating in governmental efforts directed at modifying the behaviour of unemployed 'clients'. Contract here also performs a macro-economic function,[67] serving as a mechanism of social control of the conditions of unemployment. The policy behind the introduction of the Jobseeker's Agreement was explicitly framed in terms of the needs of the job market. The objectives were to combat various structural disincentives to work in the employment benefits system, to motivate the unemployed to seek work, and to encourage them to develop the skills necessary to make them employable.[68]

In one sense the new scheme appears little different to the system it superseded based on the 'back to work plan'. This was a proforma document on which claimants were asked, at the time of a case review by an employment officer, to agree appropriate job search steps. Non-compliance with the plan might provide grounds for the withdrawal of benefit where this was interpreted as failure actively to seek work. Despite the promise in the White Paper of a radical shake-up of unemployment benefits law, the 1995 Act was for the most part a consolidating statute, a logical development of existing policies presented in a new language of contracts and jobseeking.[69] However, the Jobseeker's Agreement differs from the 'back to work plan' in certain important respects. It is expressly stated in the legislation to be a mandatory requirement and an essential condition of eligibility for the Jobseeker's Allowance. Furthermore, the ideological significance of the shift to a more explicitly contractual basis for income support should not be underestimated. As will be shown in the analysis of other types of social control contract, the Jobseeker's Agreement was the first of a number of measures embodying the philosophy and ethos of New Contractualism in concrete contractual arrangements.

An immediate problem in attempting to evaluate the effectiveness of the policy at the macro-level is that declining unemployment since 1995 may be attributable to a range of factors unconnected with contract, such as incentives associated with the New Deal or simply a relatively strong economy with low unemployment. Each month between ten and twenty thousand people enter the New Deal for Young People, with similar numbers leaving. Since the programme's inception, the proportion of long-term unemployed (defined here as those out of work

66 Jobcentre Plus Customers' Charter, Ref No. JCPCCA5 July 2003, www.jobcentreplus.gov.uk/cms.asp?Page=/Home/Customers/OurCharter, accessed 5 October 2005.

67 J Torfing, 'Workfare With Welfare: Recent Reforms of the Danish Welfare State' (1999) 9 *Journal of European Social Policy* 5.

68 *Guardian* 26 March 2003. Other policy aims arguably included the attempt to change attitudes to work, and to redistribute job opportunities to those who usually miss out, equalising job chances.

69 Fulbrook (n 46 above).

for two years or more) fell from 4.6 per cent to 1.6 per cent.[70] However, a study by the National Audit Office concluded that such reductions are due to economic buoyancy and improved employment prospects generally, rather than to any particular government employment programme.[71] The effectiveness of the contractual mechanism can only be established through careful qualitative research into how the agreements operate in practice, including any effects on the motivation of welfare claimants, their skills development, their success in finding work, and their acceptance of responsibility for their unemployed status.[72]

Such a narrow calculus would in any case fail to take account of a range of other issues concerning fairness, social exclusion, social marginalization, and negative consequences for society as a whole. The progressive tightening of disqualification rules in conjunction with workfare schemes may be expected to have a disproportionate impact on disadvantaged groups, particularly ethnic minorities. Government statistics reveal particularly high rates of use of New Deal sanctions in areas of chronic job shortage such as the North-East, indicating that those suffering most from the vagaries of the market economy are also those who are the most penalized.[73] Despite claims of improvements in the system of matching jobseekers with job opportunities made by supporters of workfare programmes, there is disturbing evidence that the most vulnerable are being excluded. A common problem is cream-skimming, whereby the 'best' clients (those already closest to the labour market) are selected for the 'best' opportunities, leaving the less socially desirable options for those most in need.[74]

At the micro-level, the element of mutuality in New Contractualist policies might be regarded as potentially advantageous to claimants. Guidelines require officials to be specific about what jobseekers must do in order to demonstrate 'actively seeking employment', with the prospect of negotiation over the details of how that obligation might be performed.[75] The Jobcentre's side of the bargain might include responsibilities for skills development, the provision of training opportunities, and other help in overcoming obstacles to employability. As a dimension of mutuality, 'individualization' in theory implies the tailoring of services to the particular needs of clients by a designated single-point case coordinator or service broker.[76] In practice, however, the New Deal has failed to deliver on the promise of individualization. Empirical research has revealed a tension between

70 *Guardian* 26 March 2004.

71 National Audit Office, *The New Deal for Young People* (London: The Stationery Office, 2002) paras 2.1-2.18.

72 Waddan (n 24 above).

73 *Guardian* 26 April 2002.

74 JF Handler, 'Social Citizenship and Workfare in the US and Western Europe: From Status to Contract' (2003) 13 *Journal of European Social Policy* 229, 235.

75 'There arises a suspicion, of course, that the opportunities for negotiation will be slight, and that the requirements will be offered like an adhesion contract on a take it or leave it basis' – H Collins, *Regulating Contracts* (Oxford: Oxford University Press, 1999) 317.

76 Carney and Ramia consider mutuality in terms of three elements: individualization, choice, and partnership – (n 11 above) 88–91.

the brokerage concept and the imperatives of the market. The contract with the jobseeker tends not to reflect client preferences, and is seldom aimed at improving substantive skills or addressing major barriers to employability.[77]

Despite the appearance of reciprocal commitments, the Jobseeker's Agreement approximates more to a model of conditional welfare than contract.[78] A number of criticisms may be made of the operation of these contracting regimes. Genuine options are not always offered, and the quality of training is often poor or non-existent. The most popular option of full-time education and training is not available in many areas, and claimants may be compelled, or feel impelled, to accept unpopular options such as placements in the voluntary sector or with the environmental task force. Choice is both limited and restricted.[79] Claimants enrolled on New Deal programmes are often scornful of their individual action plans.[80] Jobseekers' Agreements tend to be mechanically drawn up, forcing the unemployed into meaningless activities involving 'make-work' or broom-pushing.[81] Employment service workers are similarly frustrated in many cases by the absence of suitable job opportunities, the significant personal barriers to employability faced by claimants, and by lack of time and resources to perform their tasks properly. Welfare departments are typically under-staffed and under-resourced, making it difficult for staff to take any genuine interest in clients' own long-term goals and perceptions.[82]

The rhetoric of agreement is difficult to reconcile with the legislative phraseology of 'directions', the imposition by an adjudication officer of conditions considered 'appropriate', and the 'prescription' of matters concerning Jobseekers' Agreements by the Secretary of State in secondary legislation.[83] The agreements qualify for consideration as 'contracts', on the present definition, by virtue of their explicit planning function and the practical involvement of norms that support discreteness and presentiation. The problem concerns the coercive nature of the process whereby agreement is secured, and the implications for the quality of the relationship in terms of the norms of consent, choice, solidarity and reciprocity. There appears to be little leeway in practice for the 'meeting of minds', the contractual arrangement better being described as one of 'take it or leave it'. Beneath the rhetoric of contract the 'agreement' potentially involves the obtaining of the claimant's signature under duress coupled with the 'blackmail threat that benefit

77 ibid discussing research reported in M Considine, *Enterprising States: The Public Management of Welfare to Work* (Cambridge: Cambridge University Press, 2001) 178.

78 Carney and Ramia (n 11 above) 7 and 134–5.

79 The promise of genuine choice and of open and flexible negotiation over workfare options is rarely realized in practice in other workfare regimes. In the Australian system of 'activity agreements', applicants may choose one of among up to 15 or so 'additional activities' in which they have to be involved as a condition of obtaining benefit, but in reality there is little scope for negotiation and choice is restricted, ibid.

80 Handler (n 74 above) 236.

81 *Guardian* 26 March 2004. This criticism has been made particularly in relation to placements with the environmental task force.

82 Carney and Ramia (n 11 above) 91. While this point is made in the Australian context it is likely to be applicable to Britain.

83 Fulbrook (n 46 above) 400.

will be denied if the unilateral document is not signed'.[84] Other commentators have regarded these agreements as a particularly coercive example of the use of behaviour management contracts as instruments of illiberal policy marked by illiberal process.[85] There is a strong contrast between 'liberal virtues of consent, freedom of choice and the willing assumption of mutual responsibility' and illiberal processes which are 'arbitrary, oppressive or one-sided in character'.[86]

Even if it is acknowledged that these social control contracts are capable of benefiting clients, there is the issue of lack of adequate safeguards preventing abuse in particular cases, for example through the illegitimate or inappropriate use of sanctions. Non-compliance with terms and conditions of workfare regimes has the appearance of an 'offence' for which individuals may ultimately be held quasi-criminally responsible and punished.[87] The excessive use of sanctions may serve to reinforce social exclusion. The evidence from the United States is that contractual enforcement procedures do not change behaviour, and that they are frequently abused. Employment workers there have tended to resort to sanctions routinely as a means of avoiding tackling the fundamental problems which underlie the most difficult cases.[88] In Britain, there appears to be little concrete evidence of such overt abuse or of conflict in the implementation of these social control contracts. Yet conflicts might be expected to have occurred and to be reflected to some degree in disputes over the contents of the agreements, their variation, or disqualifications based on failure of claimants in performing their contractual commitments. It might be inferred from the lack of evidence of such relational difficulties that contracts are operating smoothly and effectively. However, clients might have grievances that are not addressed by the current system of review and appeals. For example, the mandatory internal review procedure (involving review by a different adjudication officer before appealing to an SSAT) may discourage claimants from pursuing appeals. Another interpretation of the absence of evidence of adversarial relations or disputes might be that the contractual scheme is completely ineffective, and that the relationships are lacking in elements necessary to make them really contractual. Further research is needed to establish which, if any, of these explanations is the most plausible.

Regardless of how the Jobseeker's Agreement itself is agreed, and with what degree of respect for the contract norms, the institutional environment is one of compulsion and the principal policy objective that of labour market discipline. This feature of current policy should be squarely acknowledged, rather than disguised in the language and rhetoric of agreement, customer services, and individual empowerment. There needs to be more public debate on this aspect, and on the question of how far other desirable objectives such as redistributing job

84 ibid.

85 Freedland and King (n 1 above) 466. The contracts are only 'ostensible contractual or contract-like arrangements between public authorities and members of society whose behaviour it is judged necessary to manage and control', 465.

86 ibid.

87 ibid 476.

88 Handler (n 74 above) 239.

opportunities and equalizing job chances are being achieved or impeded under present workfare programmes. We return below to the question of whether the principle of welfare contractualism can be reconciled with responsive regulation.[89]

Education and the control of deviance

Governmental processes of individual responsibilization are well established in the fields of education, criminal justice, and the control of deviance.[90] What appears new is the systematic use of contract as a mechanism of social control and behavioural modification, and the detailed specification of contractual regulatory schemes in primary legislation and accompanying guidance.

Youth Offender Contracts

Part I of the Youth Justice and Criminal Evidence Act 1999 gives magistrates the power to sentence young offenders by way of referral to a Youth Offender Panel.[91] Referral orders became available as a sentencing option for young offenders in England and Wales from 1 April 2002. The purpose of the sentence is 'to provide an opportunity for the young offender to consider, with his or her parents and the Panel, how best to address the offending behaviour and prevent its re-occurrence'.[92] At a first meeting, the Panel is under a duty to reach agreement with the offender on a 'programme of behaviour', the principal aim of which is the prevention of re-offending.[93] The terms of the programme, which become the terms of the Youth Offender Contract,[94] might require the offender to make financial or other reparation to the victim of the offence, to attend mediation sessions, to be at home at specified times, to attend school or other educational establishment or place of work, to stay away from specified places or persons, or to carry out unpaid work or services to the community.[95] The contract must be properly explained, set out in writing and signed by both the offender and a representative member of the Panel, with a copy being given to the offender.[96] The contract runs from the date of agreement for a period between three and twelve months as determined in the referral order. Guidance specifies that contracts

89 The Danish experience of 'welfare-workfare' suggests that there may potentially be benefits for all stakeholders in organizing welfare relationships between the state and individual citizens on a more genuinely contractual basis – Torfing (n 73 above).

90 Garland (n 16 above).

91 s 1. The local Youth Offending Team (YOT) named in the order is responsible for establishing the Panel. Most young offenders pleading guilty and appearing before a Youth Court for the first time are given a referral order. For an analysis of the Act focusing on restorative justice dimensions, see A Crawford, and T Newburn, *Youth Offending and Restorative Justice: Implementing Reform in Youth Justice* (Cullompton: Willan, 2003).

92 *No More Excuses*, White Paper (Cm 3809 1997).

93 s 8(1). Home Office guidance provides that victims may attend Panels or, if they prefer, have their views represented.

94 s 8(6).

95 s 8(2).

96 s 8(5), (6)

should contain an element of reparation to those affected by the offence if they consent (where there is no identifiable victim, reparation may be made 'to the community at large').

Where there is no agreement at this meeting and no prospect of agreement following a second meeting,[97] or where agreement is reached but the offender refuses unreasonably to sign the contract,[98] the Panel may refer the offender back to the appropriate court for re-sentencing. Section 11 provides for meetings during the course of the contract to monitor progress. A meeting must take place if the offender notifies the Panel of a desire to vary the terms of the contract,[99] and may take place where it appears to the Panel expedient to review the offender's progress in implementing the programme of behaviour.[100] Where the Panel decides that there has been a breach of the contract without good reason, it may refer the offender back to the appropriate court for a 'normal' sentence.[101] Where the Panel decides that the terms of the contract may be varied (as in the case of genuine difficulties preventing compliance), the same general rules govern the variation as are applied in the making of the original contract.[102] The contract may be brought to an end by the decision of the Panel following a final meeting that compliance with the terms of the contract has been satisfactory, so discharging the referral order.[103]

These behavioural modification contracts pose a number of relational problems. The norm of consent implies voluntariness or at least acquiescence in being bound by contract planning, but for youth offenders choice and therefore consent may be limited. If young people 'simply feel that they are doing what they are being forced to do, that they have no alternative, they will participate with much less enthusiasm, and that will make it more difficult for the scheme to have the desired therapeutic effect'.[104] Although the Government has been adamant that there is real choice, and that the effect of the measures is to give young offenders 'ownership of their own redemption,'[105] there is a danger that the choice and consent norms will be only weakly supported in these regulatory arrangements. The issue here is how far the pressured circumstances in which consent is given may damage the prospects of successful completion of the contract.[106] If the contractual process established under the Act is inherently coercive, the referral order is itself likely

[97] s 10(1), (2) [98] s 10(3). [99] s 11(3) [100] s 11(2) [101] s 11(5)
[102] s 11(6)–(8).
[103] s 12(1), (2). s 12(5) provides that the referral order may be discharged where appropriate in the absence of the offender.
[104] *Hansard*, HL (series no 5) vol 595, col 1281 (15 December 1998), Lord Northbourne.
[105] *Hansard*, HL (series no 5) vol 595, col 1304 (15 December 1998), Lord Williams of Mostyn.
[106] Macneil includes 'strongly pressured circumstances', even quite extreme forms of coercion, within the realm of contract – IR Macneil, 'The Many Futures of Contracts', (1974) 47 *Southern California Law Review* 691, 703–706. This 'should not, of course, be taken to suggest that highly coerced pattern is either the ideal prototype or current stereotype', 705. In this interpretation the problem is not so much the absence of choice, as the nature of the circumstances in which the weaker party is required to exercise choice.

in practice to prove as coercive as any other criminal disposal. All the negotiating power appears to be in the hands of the Panel, which may in effect dictate terms to the offender, who has little with which to bargain. The threat of referral back to the appropriate court if either there is no prospect of agreement or the offender refuses to sign the contract hangs over the first and second meetings to agree a programme of behaviour, and over any subsequent progress meetings to monitor compliance or vary the terms of the contract.

The norm of reciprocity implies mutual benefit and the notion that something should be received in return for something given. The problem with these contracts in practice is that the proceedings may lack this crucial element. The young offender may receive little benefit other than the avoidance of a harsher alternative sentence, although on successful completion of the contract the conviction is considered spent for the purposes of the Rehabilitation of Offenders Act 1974. The norm of proportionality and associated values of fairness are under constant threat since, in the event of failure to reach agreement, referral back to court for re-sentencing could lead to a harsher sentence (taking into account the offender's failure to agree or sign the contract) than if the referral order had not been made in the first place.[107] At the same time there is no sanction on the Panel for failure to reach agreement.[108] 'In normal contract theory, this is called a contract which is voidable for duress. In criminal law it is called a sentence.'[109] Linked with the weakness of the norms of consent and reciprocity, the power norm, which governs both the creation of contractual relationships and the restraint of power in their operation, is clearly inadequately served in these agreements. The limited degree of flexibility that is built into the statutory scheme in the provisions for variation of the terms of the contract is undermined by the lack of procedural safeguards.

There are concerns more generally regarding the absence of procedural safeguards or resources normally available to offenders in other forms of criminal disposal. For example, no lawyer will usually be present to advise on the terms being offered, and there is no legal aid for this purpose in any event.[110] This may be

[107] While the original draft Guidance to Magistrates Courts specifically prohibited harsher sentences being imposed where a young person is referred back to court for re-sentencing, this provision is absent from the Guidance published in 2002. This states that 'In reaching a decision on re-sentencing, the court will consider the youth offender panel's report, and take into account how far the offender may already have complied with the contract.'

[108] C Wonnacott, 'The Counterfeit Contract – Reform, Pretence and Muddled Principles in the New Referral Order' (1999) 11 *Child and Family Law Quarterly* 271, 281. Failure to reach agreement might be due to unreasonableness on the part of the Panel as much as the recalcitrance of the offender. The court cannot then consider any such evidence, and has no power to refer the matter to a differently constituted panel.

[109] ibid.

[110] There is uncertainty whether the 'adult supporter' permitted at meetings can be a paid lawyer. Wonnacott argues that if the purpose of meetings is to negotiate a genuine contract, then lawyers should be present to advise offenders and to close the deal. 'The presence of lawyers is destructive to the objects of the Act because the Act is not really about making a contract at all. It is about imposing terms' – ibid 285.

in breach of Art 6(3)(c) of the European Convention, which provides for entitlement to legal representation in criminal proceedings. There is no requirement that the young offender or his/her parent (if under sixteen) participate in the meeting or be informed of their rights, in contrast with the children's panel in Scotland, where the panel is legally obliged to obtain the views of the child, and parents both have a right to attend hearings and are encouraged to participate.[111] The provision that one of the members of the Panel may be police officer, even though not directly involved in the case, raises questions about the adequacy of separation of roles of judge and prosecutor.[112] The principles of restorative justice underlying the referral order may be undermined by ancillary, more punitive criminal orders which the court has powers to make at the same time. Most importantly, there is a lack of adequate provision for challenging bad decisions of the Panel.[113]

There is no obligation on the Panel to keep a record of proceedings other than in respect of the terms of the programme of behaviour and compliance with the contract. There is no right of appeal by either offender or the Panel against the court's finding of fact in regard to a Panel report, nor is there provision in the Act for complaint by the young offender concerning treatment by the Panel. Wonnacott's analysis implies both that the language of contract is a sham and should be abandoned, and that referral orders (assuming they are to be retained) should be subject to the same safeguards as other criminal proceedings.[114] The findings of research evaluating national pilots for referral orders reveals a number of concerns stemming from the constitution and operation of Panels, most notably the nature of lay representation and tensions between communitarian appeals to local justice and managerialist pressures.[115]

While this analysis points to significant problems with Youth Offender Contracts concerning the sincerity of contractual undertakings, the pressured circumstances in which choice is exercised, the existence in reality of consent, and the overall fairness of the bargain, it is important not to dismiss out of hand the potential benefits of these regulatory arrangements for all stakeholders. As with other social control contracts, whether this potential is realized is likely to depend on how the schemes are implemented in practice. While the Home Office contract proforma does not require the obligations of the Panel to the young person to be expressly stated, the 2002 Guidance makes clear that the contracts

[111] ibid 282. [112] ibid 283.

[113] The conclusions of this commentator are emphatic: 'A contract agreed under compulsion is not a contract at all, and it is dishonest to suggest otherwise. An offender will see no difference between being told what he must do by a panel and being told what he must do by a court' – ibid 286. The essential problem disguised in contract terminology concerns the basic function of the Panel, which 'is actually to sentence the offender for his crime'. [114] ibid.

[115] A Crawford and T Newburn, 'Recent Developments in Restorative Justice for Young People in England and Wales: Community Participation and Representation' (2002) 42 *British Journal of Criminology* 476.

are intended to be two-way agreements with responsibilities on both parties.[116] Empirical research in some areas has shown how members of the Youth Offending Team (YOT) often go out of their way to assist the young person, for example with travelling to and from locations, and with gaining access to training and employment opportunities.[117] In many cases the contracts are couched in terms of shared and agreed targets rather than obligations just on the young offender. The joint responsibility of the parties is reinforced by incentives on the part of YOTs for the contracts to succeed, due to the management culture in which performance is monitored, evaluated and compared. Despite the formal appearance of lack of reciprocity and power imbalance in the relationship, the importance of successful outcomes for the public service professionals charged with drawing up and managing these contracts also gives the young person something with which to bargain. Available empirical evidence shows that contracts are often light or minimal in the obligations placed on the young person, and that YOTs tend to be flexible and lenient in their interpretation of 'breach' or non-compliance. With regard to fairness, the implementation research reveals that young people and parents in practice experience the referral order process as fairer than other forms of criminal disposal. Overall, therefore, the contract norms may be better served in practice than the formalistic legal analysis might suggest.[118]

Evidence of policy success and therefore of effectiveness might be sought in empirical data on reconviction rates under referral orders compared with ordinary criminal disposals. The Home Office claims that pilot projects demonstrate a reduction in such rates,[119] and independent research of the national cohort in 2003 has reached similar conclusions.[120] As was the case with Jobseekers' Agreements, however, the problem is determining whether any success in these terms (assuming the accuracy and reliability of the findings) is due to the system of referral orders

116 Home Office/Lord Chancellor's Department/Youth Justice Board, 'Referral Orders and Youth Offender Panels: Guidance to Courts, Youth Offending Teams and Youth Offender Panels', February 2002. www.youth-justice-board.gov.uk/NR/rdonlyres/7A25AD98-8515-427F-8976-A6625789B54C/0/referral_orders_and_YOPs.pdf accessed 5 October 2005.

117 A Crawford and T Burden, *Integrating Victims in Restorative Youth Justice* (Bristol: Policy Press, 2005).

118 The lawyer's riposte, while accepting the empirical evidence, might be to point to the lack of safeguards against abuse of the contractual procedure in other geographical areas, or under different government guidelines, or given the reduction of resources made available to YOTs in implementing the scheme.

119 According to the Home Office, the pilot projects show that three quarters of young offenders successfully completed the order. Over two thirds said they had a clearer idea of how people had been affected by their offence; 78% said the contract helped keep them out of trouble. On the whole, all participants, including parents and victims, were positive about their experience of the referral order process. In 23% of cases following the initial Panel meeting, the young person was convicted of a further offence before the end of the order. In three quarters of those cases the order was revoked and the offender resentenced – www.homeoffice.gov.uk/documents/faqs.pdf accessed 14 September 2005.

120 Crawford and Burden (n 117 above).

and the supervisory role of the Panel generally, or to the specifically contractual nature of the governance arrangements and the commitments undertaken by the offender. Such claims might also need to be weighed against negative effects or unintended consequences of the policy. The suggestion that these are inherently coercive quasi-criminal proceedings serves to focus attention on the absence of safeguards or resources normally available to offenders in other forms of criminal disposal.

'Acceptable Behaviour' and 'Going Straight' contracts

According to the 2002 White Paper, *Justice for All*, the purpose of the 'acceptable behaviour contract' is to provide an alternative and less severe option in dealing with problem behaviour on the part of young people than resort to a statutory anti-social behaviour order (ASBO).[121] Following the White Paper proposals, acceptable behaviour contracts have been adopted as national policy modelled on the scheme originally pioneered in Islington, north London.[122] These contracts result from an informal meeting between the young person and their parents and a representative of the local authority housing department together with a police officer, at which the parties agree a contract specifying how the individual should behave, for example requiring them not be abusive towards others. Guidance states:

> An Acceptable Behaviour Contract (ABC) is a written agreement between a person who has been involved in antisocial behaviour and one or more local agencies whose role it is to prevent such behaviour. ABCs are most commonly used for young people but may also be used for adults. The contract is agreed and signed at a meeting with the individual and the lead agencies. Where the person whose behaviour is at issue is a child or young person, parents or guardians should be encouraged to attend. The contract specifies a list of anti-social acts in which the person has been involved and which they agree not to continue. Where possible the individual should be involved in drawing up the contract. This may encourage them to recognise the impact of their behaviour and take responsibility for their actions. Support to address the underlying causes of the behaviour should be offered in parallel to the contract. This may include diversionary activities (such as attendance at a youth project), counselling or support for the family.[123]

Whereas ASBOs are civil court orders prohibiting the offender from engaging in specific anti-social acts, breach of which constitutes a criminal offence, acceptable behaviour contracts are stated to be 'voluntary written agreements'. While there is no formal sanction for breach of the contract, this may result in formal application

121 ASBOs were created under the Crime and Disorder Act 1998.

122 On ABCs specifically in the context of housing, and policing through social housing tenancies, see A Crawford, 'Contractual Governance of Deviant Behaviour' (2003) 30 JLS 479, 491–493.

123 Home Office Guidance, 'A Guide to Anti-Social Behaviour Orders and Acceptable Behaviour Contracts', November 2002, 52.

being made by a public agency for an ASBO or possession order (if the young person is in social housing).[124] By April 2002, there were over one hundred and seventy such schemes across the country and over eighteen hundred individual contracts in place.[125] The latest figures show that over five thousand contracts were made in the twelve months between October 2003 and September 2004 alone.[126]

The White Paper also proposed to extend use of the contractual mechanism further into the area of prisoner rehabilitation.[127] In the programme being piloted for eighteen to twenty-year old prisoners from 2002, the 'Going Straight Contract' is a new measure intended to address the factors associated with the prisoner's offending or reoffending, with inputs from all the organisations responsible for delivery of the criminal justice service.[128] The contract, which is signed by the offender at the time of conviction, covers the whole period of the sentence in and out of custody (including any period to be served in the community). 'The aim is that this will include rewards for participation and sanctions for non-participation. To fulfil their side of the contract, prisoners would be required to follow their agreed programme. They would also make payments from their prison pay, both to make reparation to the victims and to help finance the support the case manager would provide on release.'[129] The contract is between the offender and the case manager, a member of the Probation Service with primary responsibility for drawing up the programme of behaviour and for implementing the scheme. This contractual scheme is part of a deliberate attempt to improve the success rate for rehabilitation by making prisoners accept responsibility for their actions. The programme currently under development through the pilot projects lacks a statutory basis of the sort underpinning Youth Offender Contracts. 'Going Straight' contracts are unlikely, in practice, to differ significantly from earlier arrangements involving the

[124] This possibility may be included as a provision of the ABC, though it appears that there is nothing to prevent application for an ASBO in the absence of such an express provision. 'The threat of legal action provides an incentive to ensure that the contract is adhered to' – ibid.

[125] www.crimereduction.gov.uk/asbos9.htm?fp accessed 5 October 2005.

[126] Home Office Guidance, 'A Guide to Anti-Social Behaviour Orders and Acceptable Behaviour Contracts', November 2002.

[127] White Paper, *Justice for All*, (Cm 5563 2002). Ch 6, 'Punishment and Rehabilitation'.

[128] *Justice for All*, para 6.28. See the report of the Social Exclusion Unit, Cabinet Office, *Reducing Re-offending by Ex-prisoners*, para 18, which originally recommended the piloting of the Going Straight Contract. 'To fulfil their side of the Going Straight contract, prisoners should be required to participate in a range of programmes and activities. They should be rewarded for participation and sanctioned for non-participation. Prisoners should contribute towards a reparation fund, which should be used to redress the damage caused by their offences – either for individual victims or for wider community safety' (para 18.11). 'The programmes necessary to the delivery of the Going Straight contract should be achieved through a combination of better coverage and bringing the best existing programmes into a joined-up regime focused on learning and employment' (para 18.12). 'The active participation of mainstream agencies, such as Jobcentre Plus, and local authority housing departments, would also be essential to enable the Going Straight contract to be delivered. In addition to other public bodies, voluntary and private sector organisations should play an important role' (para 18.13).

[129] ibid para 6.29.

signing of 'compacts' between prisoners and the prison service on admission to prison.[130]

There is insufficient evidence on which to base an assessment of whether the relational problems identified with Youth Offender Contracts exist in either of these contexts. There must be significant doubts about the operation of these schemes, however, concerning the balance of power and the nature of the circumstances in which the agreements are negotiated and consent obtained. An immediate question is whether the new contracts can be tailored sufficiently to the needs of individual offenders and young people. On the assumption that meaningful commitments are undertaken by public agencies, for example in respect of education and training, participation in drug and alcohol programmes, and addressing housing, income and family issues, a key question is whether adequate resources are provided to enable delivery of the state's side of the bargain.[131] As elsewhere, much will depend on how the schemes are interpreted and implemented by public agencies, and on how seriously the contractual procedures are taken by all parties.

The lack of a statutory basis and the relatively minimal official guidance in the case of both types of contract is in sharp contrast with the detailed statutory provisions and formal guidance that regulate Youth Offender Contracts. While the latter arrangements are clearly made in accordance with contracting regimes in the full sense, the former are governed by little more than policy statements.

Home-School Agreements

The policy informing the introduction of Home-School Agreements under the School Standards and Framework Act 1998 aims to combat truancy, bullying and other forms of unacceptable behaviour at school, and more generally to 'help pupils achieve.'[132] Governing bodies of maintained schools and City Technology Colleges are under an obligation to adopt such an agreement,[133] defined by the Act as a statement specifying the school's aims and values, the relative responsibilities of the school and parents, and the school's expectations as to the

130 On the judicial decision that such a compact did not give rise to a legitimate expectation on the part of the prisoner that home leave would be permitted after one third of the sentence, despite clear representations to that effect in the compact, see P Birkinshaw, 'By Command of Her Britannic Majesty's Government: Let There Be Government By Contract', conference paper for *The Constitutional Implications of Participation*, Sheffield (1997) 6.

131 Cabinet Office, *Reducing Reoffending by Ex-prisoners*, para 18.10. Even where credible commitments are made by the case manager, there are likely to be problems in implementation, given the large number of public government departments, agencies and statutory and non-statutory bodies involved in rehabilitation. The 'contract' is with the case manager, not directly with these bodies.

132 Consultation documents have been explicit in their recognition of links between educational achievement, the support and involvement of parents in educational processes, and the creation of strong local communities: *Excellence in Schools* (Cm 3681 1997), para 6.1; J Bastiani, *Home-School Contracts – Opportunities or Threats* (London: Royal Society of Arts, 1996).

133 School Standards and Framework Act 1998, s 110(1).

conduct of its registered pupils.[134] The governing bodies are required also to adopt a 'parental declaration',[135] defined as 'a document to be used by qualifying parents for recording that they take note of the school's aims and values and its responsibilities and that they acknowledge and accept the parental responsibilities and the school's expectations of its pupils'.[136] The governing body must take 'reasonable steps' to ensure that the declaration is signed by all parents.[137] The declaration may be signed also by pupils at the discretionary invitation of the governing body 'as an indication that he acknowledges and accepts the school's expectation of its pupils'.[138]

The Labour party had been committed to introducing 'contracts' of some kind between all maintained schools and parents since 1995. The Conservative Education Act 1997, which was never implemented due to the change of government that year, would have made the admission of a child to a school conditional upon the parent signing a 'home-school partnership document'.[139] The 1998 Act expressly prohibits governing bodies from imposing such a condition,[140] and provides that 'a home-school agreement shall not be capable of creating any obligation in respect of whose breach any liability arises in contract or tort'.[141] The resulting contractual arrangements are therefore neither directly nor indirectly enforceable.

The effectiveness of the contract mechanism depends on the contract norms being configured in a manner appropriate to the assigned regulatory task. Compared with the other social control contracts so far considered, Home-School Agreements appear to allow greater scope for the norms of choice and consent. Neither pupils nor parents are required to sign the declaration, although in practice most parents will feel obliged to do so.[142] On the other hand, the role of specifying the school and parental responsibilities falls entirely to the school, subject to the requirement that the governing body shall consult all qualifying parents and other prescribed persons prior to adopting or revising either the agreement or the parental declaration.[143] There is an obvious disjunction here between the drawing up of the agreement and the signing of the parental declaration. While the Home-School Agreement is referred to as a 'statement',[144] it is the parental declaration which (as a record that notice has been taken by the parent of the

134 s 110(2) 'The detail will differ from school to school, but all agreements are likely to include expectations about the standard of education, the ethos of the school, regular and punctual attendance, discipline, homework, and the information schools and parents will give one-another' (n 128 above, para 6.8). Governing bodies are required to have regard to guidance issued by the Secretary of State (s 111(1)).

135 s 110(1)

136 s 110(2).

137 s 110(3).

138 s 110(5).

139 s 13 Education Act 1997.

140 SSFA s 111(4). The governing body must not: invite any person to sign the parental declaration at a time when the child has not been admitted to the school; make it a condition of a child being admitted to the school that the parental declaration be signed in respect of the child; or make any decision as to whether or not to admit a child to the school by reference to whether such a declaration is or is not likely to be signed in respect of the child.

141 s 111(6).

142 In this sense the regulatory arrangements have a stronger element of compulsion compared with previous local initiatives in some schools.

143 s 110(9).

144 s 1(2).

statement) might more properly be regarded as constituting the 'agreement' at the moment of signing.[145] By this time, however, the respective responsibilities have already been determined, and the role of parents is merely to 'take note' and to 'acknowledge and accept' them. There appears to be little room here for negotiation or bargaining, any 'contract' being one of adhesion.[146]

In contrast with the formal lack of mutuality in Youth Offender Contracts, Home-School Agreements might be regarded as more genuinely reciprocal in that the school is expressly required to undertake certain commitments to parents.[147] The main issues here, however, concern the lack of specificity of these commitments and whether anything of tangible benefit is given or received by either side. Again, the problem may be not that sanctions are available to one party and not the other, but rather that enforcement is not a realistic option for either party.[148] Clarity in the allocation of responsibilities in these arrangements is impeded by the three-way division of responsibilities between the school, parents, and children in the form of 'the school's expectations of its pupils'.[149] The tripartite nature of the relationship is confirmed in the provision that both the qualifying parent and the registered pupil may be signatories to the parental declaration. There is also confusion in the definition of roles, with parents being presented as consumers of education, partners with the school in the education of their child, and a 'problem' for the school at one and the same time.[150] For various reasons, it might be unfair that there should be adverse consequences for the child in the event that parents fail to comply with their contractual obligations.[151]

The impression of confusion in the policy surrounding these regulatory arrangements is reinforced by the lack of substance in supporting information or guidance, whether in the form of official circulars or material available via

[145] The discretion on the part of the school to invite the pupil to sign the parental declaration, which was not a feature of the unimplemented Education Act 1997 s 13, adds further confusion. Elsewhere the Act is unclear as to whether provisions in regard to signing the parental document apply to the child as well as the parent (s 111(5) – 'No person shall be excluded from such a school or suffer any other adverse consequences on account of any failure to comply with any invitation to sign the parental declaration').

[146] Fulbrook, n 46 above.

[147] For case studies reporting experiences with home-school agreements, see the 'parental involvement' section of DfES Standards Site, www.standards.dfes.gov.uk/parentalinvolvement/hsa/hsa_case/ accessed 4 October 2005.

[148] However, making the commitments enforceable would merely create a fresh set of problems. Blair argues that by the time of the Education Act 1997, the original notion of modifying the child's behaviour based on the granting and withholding of rewards had 'metamorphosed' into contracts as statements of obligations of parents and schools, involving a 'second tier of indirectly enforceable legal norms in addition to the statutory obligations of parents'. Had the contracts been implemented in this form, mechanisms designed to regulate the abuse of power would have been circumvented posing significant new problems for legal governance – A Blair, 'Home-School Agreements: A Legislative Framework for Soft Control of Parents' (2001) *Education Law Journal* 79, 80.

[149] s 110(2)(d).

[150] A Blair, and M Waddington, 'The Home-School "Contract": Regulating the Role of Parents' (1997) 9 *Education and the Law* 291.

[151] ibid.

the DfES website. The general impression of policy ineffectiveness is confirmed by an apparent change of tack in government policy in the recent introduction of parenting contracts, which may have been intended to address some of the 'weaknesses' identified with Home-School Agreements.[152]

Education Maintenance Allowance

The national scheme for Education Maintenance Allowances was announced on 19 April 2004, under powers conferred on the Secretary of State by the Education Act 2002.[153] The operation of the scheme is set out by the DfES in the form of a 'Guidance Overview'.[154] The main policy objective is to broaden participation by improving retention and attainment of young people in post-compulsory education. This is to be achieved by offering financial assistance to those aged between sixteen and nineteen currently living in households with incomes below £30,000, around 50 per cent of all households, who will be eligible for an allowance to cover the costs of continuing education.[155] The payment of the allowance is conditional upon specific contractual undertakings on the part of the pupil, balanced in theory by reciprocal commitments on the part of the school or college. A 'learning agreement' or contract sets out the terms and conditions that have to be satisfied by the pupil in order to receive the allowance and bonuses.[156] Weekly payments of up to £30 made direct to the young person are supplemented by bonuses of £100, payable in January and July in the first year of study, and in September, January and July in subsequent years, dependent on continued attendance on the course and the demonstration of learning progress.[157] The Learning and Skills Council will usually play the leading role in coordinating the other partners involved in implementing the scheme, including LEAs, the Connexions service, jobcentres, youth services, and various voluntary and other support organizations. LEAs will be specifically responsible for promotion, support and monitoring activities, as agreed within their 'partnership group'.[158]

The Education Maintenance Allowance contract is in two parts. The first part, signed at enrolment, is a generic document provided by the Assessment and

[152] There is some doubt as to the validity of the conclusion that 'the likelihood is that home-school agreements will become a more important means of regulating behaviour in schools' – Crawford (n 122 above) 491.

[153] s14 gives the Secretary of State (England) powers to make arrangements for the giving of financial assistance in connection with certain educational purposes specified in s 14(2) – see SI 2002/2439 art 3 1 October 2002. In relation to Wales see SI 2002/3185 art 5 sch, pt II, 31 March 2003.

[154] DfES, Guidance Overview 2004/05, Version: 1.0, Issued: 27/02/04.

[155] ibid para. 1.2.

[156] The guide to applicants states: 'Once you enroll, you must sign an EMA Contract with your school or college and attend all your course sessions. This contract will set out what is expected of you in terms of: attendance; coursework; progress' – *A Student's Guide to Education Maintenance Allowance*, www.dfes.gov.uk/financialhelp/ema/uploads/docs/ema_8ppa5_0304.pdf accessed 5 October 2005.

[157] DfES (n 154 above) para 1.7.

[158] ibid para 2.16.

Payment Body (APB), setting out attendance requirements which must be met for the student to receive their weekly allowance. The second part covers learning progress, specifying how the achievement of goals will be rewarded with periodic bonus payments. The APB provides a template for this contract which schools and colleges are able to adopt. This part of the contract may be signed immediately at enrolment, or later in the student's first term.[159] The guidance continues: 'Schools and colleges need to ensure that they operate effective systems to monitor attendance and whether students have conformed to the terms of the . . . contract. As school and college decisions in effect determine whether or not a student will receive an allocation of public money, there will be a need for their . . . systems and processes to be auditable.'[160]

Much is made in the guidance of the importance of 'evidence-based policy making' and the experience of pilot projects conducted in fifteen different LEA areas in England since 1999, and extended to approximately one third of the country between 2000 and 2004. The aim was to see if a 'something for something' cash incentive would improve participation, retention and achievement among young people from lower income families. Some young people drawn into education by the scheme were not in any form of employment, education or training; others came from work with no training; and a smaller group (less than 10 per cent of the 'EMA effect') were from training programmes. Evidence from the pilots indicates that pupils who are receiving allowances are achieving to the same level as their peers despite a lower average attainment at age sixteen. The Government claims also that the findings demonstrate that the contracts have a marked positive effect on attendance and behaviour.[161] An evaluation by independent researchers concluded: 'There is no doubt that the evidence demonstrates that the financial element of the EMA initiative can, and does, have clear effects on the way in which some young people consider and undertake their participation in post-compulsory education.'[162]

The available evidence thus suggests that Education Maintenance Allowances are an effective strategy in delivering the Government's stated policy objectives.[163] What remains unclear, however, is how far the scheme's presumed success is due to its specifically contractual operation.[164] The same or similar improvements in participation, retention and educational attainment might have been achieved by a simpler system of means-tested conditional grants. The key factor behind

159 ibid para 2.4. 160 ibid para 2.5.

161 ibid para 1.6. More detailed research findings are available on the DfES website www.dfes.gov.uk/research accessed 5 October 2005.

162 R Legard, K Woodfield, and C White, *Staying Away or Staying On? A Qualitative Evaluation of the Education Maintenance Allowance* (DfES Research Report RR256, 2001), para 1.9.

163 Braithwaite argues that the naked attempt to control associated with the offering of rewards conveys negative information about the identity of regulated bodies or subjects against which they may be expected to react unfavourably – J Braithwaite, 'Rewards and Regulation', (2002) 29 JLS 12, 17. This point is made about regulation generally. Market rewards (where appropriate) are not associated with such negative information.

164 The brief for the pilot project evaluations does not appear to have focused on this aspect.

improved rates of retention may be the staggering of conditional payments and bonuses, rather than the contractual nature of commitments. Indeed, the DfES guidance contains very little detail on the contractual process, focusing more on financial management, means assessment, and the division of responsibilities among public agencies. The contractual provisions appear to offer some potential for adding value to what remains basically a system of means-tested grants. Whether benefits associated with contract norms of planning, reciprocity, choice and consensus are realized in practice is likely to depend on how seriously the two-stage contract process is taken by both parties. The risk of governance problems associated with claims of breach of contract appears minimal. This is the least bureaucratic, prescriptive, and coercive form of social control contract so far considered – a classic instance of regulation based on incentives (dominium) rather than compulsion (imperium).

Parenting contracts

Parenting contracts cut across the spheres of education and the control of deviance so far discussed. These social control measures merit separate consideration due to the responsibilities placed directly on parents of children whose behaviour is deemed criminal or anti-social, both within and outside the school environment.[165]

Criminal conduct and anti-social behaviour

The Anti-social Behaviour Act 2003 makes provision for a member of a YOT to enter into a parenting contract with a parent of the child or young person where there is reason to believe that the young person has engaged, or is likely to engage, in criminal conduct or anti-social behaviour.[166] A 'parenting contract' is defined as a document which contains both a statement by the parent of agreement to comply

165 All social control contracts involving young people seek to responsiblize parents in some way. For example, implementation research shows that in areas such as Leeds the proforma for Youth Offender Contracts refers specifically to ways in which the parent/carer will the support the young person in completing the contract – see Crawford and Burden (n 117 above). However, parenting contracts are addressed to parents directly. While parents are also directly involved in HSAs, these arrangements are not of the same order. They neither meet threshold critera of contractual relations, nor carry such serious implications for the parents involved.

166 Anti-social Behaviour Act 2003, s 25(2). Sections 25–29 came into effect on 27 February 2004 – The Anti-social Behaviour Act 2003 (Commencement No. 1 and Transitional Provisions) Order 2003 (SI 2003/3300). The intention was to supplement provisions for the making of parenting orders under the Crime and Disorder Act 1998 (White Paper, *Respect and Responsibility – Taking a Stand Against Anti-Social Behaviour* (Cm 5778, 2003), 24–6). Local Youth Offending Teams (YOTs) had been running counselling classes both for parents subject to compulsory parenting orders and for other parents on a voluntary basis for some years. The proposal was that such support be made more widely available to parents, 'on a voluntary basis in the first instance.' (*Respect and Responsibility*, para 2.16).

with specified requirements, and a statement by the YOT that it agrees to provide support to the parent for the purpose of complying with those requirements.[167] The contract, which is expressly stated not to create any obligations in contract or tort,[168] must be signed both by the parent and on behalf of the YOT.[169] As usual with this type of legislation, duties under the sections are to be exercised with regard to any guidance issued by the Secretary of State.[170] While the White Paper had emphasised that parenting contracts should be 'voluntary', failure to enter into such a contract by the parent or to abide by its terms[171] must be taken into account by a court in considering whether to make a compulsory parenting order[172] on application by the YOT.[173]

Guidance was issued by the Home Office in collaboration with the Department for Constitutional Affairs and the Youth Justice Board in February 2004.[174] Throughout the guidance the term 'parenting programmes' is used to refer to the variety of different approaches that may be used by YOTs to help parents address their child's misbehaviour as part of an overall parenting intervention.[175] Parenting contracts include a 'parenting programme' designed to cover this aspect, together with a second element requiring parents to exercise control over their child's behaviour in specific ways, for example by ensuring attendance at school.[176] The contracts 'can provide a formal framework for work YOTs carry out with parents on a voluntary basis'.[177]The Guidance summarizes three ways of working with parents: voluntarily without a contract or order; voluntarily with a parenting contract;[178] or through application for or recommendation of a parenting order. 'As contracts are voluntary there is no penalty for refusing to enter into or failing

167 s 25(3). 168 s 25(7) 169 s 25(6). 170 s 25(8).

171 s 27(1)(a) and (b) respectively.

172 Crime and Disorder Act 1998, as amended by s 18 Anti-social Behaviour Act 2003. This Act and the Criminal Justice Act 2003 increase the flexibility and widen the availability of parenting orders. Such orders may require parents to comply with specified conditions including attendance at a counselling or guidance programme.

173 s 26. An appeal lies to the Crown Court against the making of a parenting order under s 26.

174 Home Office/Department of Constitutional Affairs/Youth Justice Board, 'Parenting Contracts and Orders Guidance', February 2004. The 'technical guidance' issued with the Circular (considered below) is highly detailed and prescriptive. The elaboration of policy frameworks in secondary legislation and such guidance is a characteristic feature of the New Public Contracting. For example: 'The parents and where appropriate their child should be asked to outline their views on the misbehaviour, how they believe it should be tackled and what they think of the idea of a parenting contract. The YOT worker should outline what a parenting contract is and why one may be appropriate. The parents and YOT worker will also be able to discuss support the parents would like and what the YOT is able to provide. The aim should be to work in partnership to improve the behaviour of the child or young person' (para 3.10).

175 These include cognitive behaviour therapy, mentoring, parenting advice, individual family based therapy, functional family therapy, solution focused therapy, family group conferencing, and group based programmes. Guidance, para 2.3.

176 Guidance (n 174 above) para 2.9. The two elements are also found in parenting orders.

177 ibid para 2.12.

178 This option may be suggested by the YOT 'if a more formal approach is useful or the parents are unwilling to cooperate'. The fact that refusing to enter a contract 'can be used as evidence to support an application for an order . . . may persuade a reluctant parent to engage' – ibid para 2.14.

to comply with one. However, failure to co-operate with support offered through a contract is a relevant consideration for a court when deciding whether to make a parenting order.'[179] The Guidance revealingly continues: 'Therefore contracts provide YOTs with additional authority when attempting to secure voluntary co-operation from parents.'[180]

Allusions to the voluntary nature of parenting contracts both in the White Paper and in the Guidance (but not in the Act), and references to 'negotiation' in the Guidance,[181] are in tension with the pressured circumstances in which these contracts are likely to be made in practice. The Guidance expressly acknowledges the combination of elements of voluntariness and the threat of compulsion, but not the contradiction that this entails. It is questionable whether the full benefits associated with voluntary and consensual contractual undertakings can be realized under such conditions, which are likely to place significant limits on the effectiveness of contract as a mechanism of behaviour modification.

As with other forms of social control contract, leaving to one side the issues of consent and choice, there is also the question of reciprocity in the existence and discharge of obligations by the YOT to the parents. In addition to detailed prescriptions as to the circumstances in which the parenting contract should be made and negotiated and the procedure to be followed where parents refuse to enter or agree a contract,[182] the circular contains guidance on non-compliance by both parents[183] and the YOT with the contract. As to the latter,

> The YOT worker responsible for the contract should ensure that the parents receive all the support that the YOT agreed to provide. Where for any reason the YOT fails, or will clearly fail to meet one of the contract's requirements, the YOT worker should contact the parents and provide a full explanation. As with non-compliance by parents, this should be recorded on file. The YOT worker should also encourage the parents to voice any concerns they have about the delivery of the YOT's side of the contract and explain how they can make a complaint to the YOT manager if concerns cannot be addressed.[184]

An obvious problem here concerns the absence of procedural safeguards against unfair action on the part of the YOT, and the lack of provision for informing

179 ibid para 2.13.

180 ibid. 'When parents are unwilling to engage with parenting support on a voluntary basis and a YOT assesses that a parent could be supported to improve the child's behaviour, YOTs can apply for a free-standing parenting order' – para 2.14.

181 ibid para 3.5. 'A parenting contract is an agreement negotiated between a YOT worker and the child involved or likely to become involved in criminal conduct or anti-social behaviour' – para 2.8.

182 ibid para 3.22

183 ibid para 3.23. Because breach of contract may constitute evidence that may be used in application for a more coercive parenting order, failures to comply with the contract 'must be recorded and acted upon' – para 3.24. Where there is no satisfactory explanation of non-compliance or the parents appear to be at fault, the Guidance specifies procedure for written warnings and further meetings. 'In light of this meeting, the YOT worker should decide whether the noncompliance is undermining the contract to the extent that the YOT needs to apply for a parenting order or whether to persevere with the contract. The YOT worker must record the decision and reasons. This can be used in any future application for a parenting order' – para 3.25.

184 ibid para 3.26.

parents as to how they may enforce the obligations of the YOT. In general, there are likely to be limits on the willingness and ability of state agencies to provide the kind of support that might address the underlying social problems (poor housing, inequality of income, education) that would help parents to fulfill their side of the bargain.

Exclusion from school or truancy

Complementing the above provisions, the White Paper *Respect and Responsibility* proposed the introduction of parenting contracts to deal with truancy and problems of exclusion of children from school.[185] The Anti-social Behaviour Act 2003 accordingly provides that an LEA or the governing body of a relevant school may enter into a parenting contract with the parent of a pupil or child,[186] where either the pupil has been excluded from the school on disciplinary grounds,[187] or where a child of compulsory school age has failed to attend school regularly.[188] The parenting contract is defined in the same way as that for criminal conduct or anti-social behaviour.[189] As regards exclusion from school (but not truancy), the authority may similarly apply to a magistrates court for a formal parenting order.[190] In deciding whether to make the order, a court must take into account any refusal by the parent to enter into a parenting contract in respect of a child excluded from school on disciplinary grounds,[191] or any failure by the parent to comply with requirements stated in the parenting contract where the parent has entered into such a contract.[192] With regard to truancy, the Act makes provision for a penalty notice to be given by an authorized officer to a person who has committed the offence of failing to secure regular attendance at school of a registered pupil.[193]

The DfES has issued extensive regulations and guidance relating to parenting contracts in cases of exclusion from school or truancy, parenting orders in cases of exclusion from school, and penalty notices in cases of truancy.[194] Entry into

185 White Paper, *Respect and Responsibility – Taking a Stand Against Anti-Social Behaviour* (Cm 5778, 2003), para 2.34.

186 Anti-social Behaviour Act 2003, s 19(3). This section was brought into force in England on 27 February 2004. The Anti-social Behaviour Act 2003 (Commencement No. 1 and Transitional Provisions) Order 2003 (SI 2003/3300).

187 s 19(1)

188 s 19(2)

189 s 19(4). The parenting contract is again required to be signed by both the parent and on behalf of the education authority (s 19(7)), and does not create legal obligations in contract or tort (s 19(8)).

190 s 20(2).

191 s 21(1)(a)

192 s 21(1)(b). Appeal lies to the Crown Court against the making of a s 20 parenting order (s 22(1)).

193 s 23(1), amending s 444 Education Act 1996. The new sections introduce penalty notices as an alternative to prosecution under s 444, enabling parents to discharge potential liability for conviction for that offence by payment of a penalty.

194 DfES, Guidance on Education-Related Parenting Contracts, Parenting Orders and Penalty Notices, DfES/0234/2004. The Guidance runs to some 70 pages, compared with 40 for the analogous

parenting contracts is voluntary, with no obligation on the part of the LEA or governing body to offer such a contract.[195] There is detailed guidance on the procedure for meeting with parents and drawing up a contract with them.[196] Depending on the pupil's age and understanding, 'the pupil should also be invited to attend the meeting'.[197] Before the meeting, the LEA or governing body should write to the parent making clear that the parenting contract 'is not a punitive or compulsory measure'.[198] Once the requirements and support elements of the contract have been agreed, the governing body or LEA and the parent should write up the contract together and sign it. The contract should be written in language that the parent can easily understand.[199]

> The governing body or LEA's side of the contract is a statement that it agrees to provide the parent with support for the purpose of complying with the requirements and should specify the types of support that will be provided under the contract .... The parent and a representative of the governing body or LEA (preferably the person who will deliver the governing body or LEA's part of the contract) must sign the contract and all parties should be given a copy. It may also be appropriate to give a copy to other agencies working with the family.[200]

The guidance on 'breach of contract'[201] provides that while there can be no liability in contract or tort, failure by the parent to comply with the contract in cases of exclusion from school is a relevant consideration for the LEA in deciding whether to apply for a parenting order.[202] Similarly, in cases of truancy, failure to comply with a contract may lead the LEA or school to consider issuing a penalty notice to the parent or may lead the LEA to consider prosecuting the parent for failing to ensure their child attends school regularly in which case evidence that the parent failed to comply with the contract could be presented to the court.[203]

However, in dealing with parents who refuse to enter into a parenting contract or with whom it is impossible to agree a contract, every effort should be made constructively to meet legitimate concerns of parents. The LEA officer or member of staff responsible for liaising with the parent should also inform the parent of alternative courses of action that are available in the event of continued refusal, and the implications for application for a parenting order or criminal prosecution for irregular attendance.[204] Procedures are specified also for contacting parents

Home Office circular issued in respect of parenting orders and contracts for criminal conduct and anti-social behaviour. The accompanying Education (Parenting Orders)(England) Regulations 2004 (SI 2004/182) came into effect on 27 February 2004.

195 DfES, ibid paras 34, 133. Failure to comply with parenting contracts in neither case may lead to an action for breach of contract or for civil damages (paras 38, 137 respectively) Part 5 of the Guidance is entitled 'Common Considerations for Parenting Contracts', applying to both variants (paras 223–256).

196 ibid para 232.

197 ibid para 233.

198 ibid para 234.

199 ibid para 236.

200 ibid paras 242–243.

201 ibid paras 247–254.

202 ibid para 249

203 ibid para 250.

204 ibid paras 255–6.

to ask for explanations for non-compliance, for the writing of letters, keeping of records, the invitation of parents to further meetings, and the making of decisions as to whether the contract is being undermined to the extent that it is no longer useful and an alternative course of action is needed.[205]

In addition to the criticisms already made of analogous arrangements in the criminal justice context, other problems with these parenting contracts may briefly be noted. The burden of making, specifying and managing contracts is placed on the LEA or governing body.[206] The question here is whether such authorities have adequate resources to discharge this function. A further problem concerns the number of parties involved in implementing the contracts and the complexity of their relationships with one-another. While the regulatory structure of these contracting regimes has been portrayed theoretically in simple terms, in practice the linkages are more complicated. There are thus likely to be significant problems of coordination and liaison.[207] Particular difficulties may be expected to arise where parenting contracts in respect of both s 19 and s 25 of the 2003 Act are in place, ie where the contracts apply to criminal conduct and anti-social behaviour, coupled with exclusion from school or truancy.[208] Lack of clarity in the allocation of contractual responsibilities is likely to confuse accountability and leave considerable scope for buck-passing.

Responsiveness

Against the view that behavioural contracts are *necessarily* illiberal and repressive,[209] this section suggests that such arrangements may be compatible with increased individual freedom and autonomy,[210] and may *under certain conditions* satisfy the criteria of effectiveness and legitimacy set out in earlier chapters. If social control is essential to social organization, and the adaptation of contracts

[205] ibid paras 252–4.

[206] The party entering into the parenting contract with the parent (namely the LEA or the governing body of a school) is responsible for bearing the costs of any support provided under a parenting contract – ibid para 230. The cost of a parenting contract will be largely dependent on the type of support provided. LEAs and schools are encouraged to use parenting contracts innovatively, making use of existing resources where appropriate. This might include, for example, the facilities of the local extended school, the local Citizens Advice Bureau, on-site learning mentors, educational psychologists, an existing parenting peer group, or asking another parent to act as a mentor – para 231.

[207] 'A multi-agency approach is necessary to ensure that all work being carried out with the pupil and their parent fits well together and avoids duplication' – ibid para 226.

[208] ibid para 227. 'Governing bodies and LEAs should consider in each case whether the contract should cover both exclusion and truancy and/or criminal conduct and anti-social behaviour. If the youth offending team agrees that the order should cover these areas, they would usually, depending on the circumstances of the case and local arrangements, be the lead agency in bringing the application and supervising the order. Local protocols will need to be agreed about cooperating and supplying resources for such cases' – para 228.

[209] Freedland and King (n 1 above).

[210] N Rose, *Powers of Freedom: Reframing Political Thought* (Cambridge: Cambridge University Press, 1999).

to this end is not ruled in principle unacceptable, the question becomes how to distinguish responsive from unresponsive instances of this form of the New Public Contracting.

Contract norms and relationality

Firstly, problems of regulatory ineffectiveness may be due to the absence of the discrete norms that are the basis of any functioning contractual relationship. Some types of social control contract, it has been suggested, fail to satisfy the threshold conditions of discreteness and presentiation. This is in spite of the existence in most cases of a more or less elaborate regulatory framework which specifies procedures and formalities for the making of 'agreements' or 'contracts', including requirements that documents be signed and copies provided to the parties. However, the presence of such formalities does not necessarily equate with the social processes that have been argued to be definitive of contractual relations, ie atomization (excluding other parties or issues as irrelevant externalities) and narrowing (abstracting from the general context of the relationship and focusing on core aspects). What is important is not the form of the agreement or understanding, but its content. In the absence of discrete norms, any appearance of relationality is illusory. If nothing of value is given or received, there can be no reciprocal benefit and welfare cannot be jointly maximized by contractual means.[211] To the extent that a balance may be said to exist in such relationships, it is likely to be one of powerlessness rather than power. Generally, the absence of governance problems may indicate not a successful contractual relationship, but a relationship that is not really contractual at all.

The foregoing analysis suggests that Home-School Agreements are most ineffective in this sense. To the extent that commitments are made, these are of a vague and general rather than specific and individualized nature. These arrangements appear not to permit discreteness and presentiation to the degree necessary to structure the parties' relationship in any meaningful sense.[212] The tensions between different models of 'contract' remain unresolved.[213] The conclusion is that the 1998 Act in this regard is a muddled piece of legislation betraying its origins in the period of transition between Conservative and Labour governments.

[211] The norm of reciprocity in contexts of constrained choice requires that the individual receive some benefit over and above not being subject to a more severe criminal or quasi-criminal sanction than would be applied but for the agreement constituting the contract.

[212] In the case of Youth Offender Contracts, by contrast, such elements are present at least to some degree, even if not involving genuine reciprocity.

[213] One is directed at modifying the behaviour of the pupil, another at encouraging parental participation and involvement, while a third involves enforceable contracts – Blair and Waddington (n 150 above) 296. Blair suggests that the legislation ultimately satisfies the proponents of none of these models – ibid (n 148 above); the policy aim of encouraging partnership between parents and schools is undermined by the compulsory nature of the contractual arrangements; meanwhile this form of parental regulation as 'soft control' is criticized from the right as lacking 'teeth' – ibid 86.

Secondly, in those social control arrangements (the majority) where the threshold conditions of contract have successfully been established, regulatory ineffectiveness may be due to the inappropriate configuration of discrete and relational norms within the relationship or in the contractual environment. Where contract norms are damaged or are otherwise not functioning properly, it cannot be expected that obligations will be fulfilled or that the contracts will operate relationally. Without trust and cooperation and the support of associated relational norms, contractual relationships are likely to remain formal and lacking in substance. The more that relationships become defined exclusively by reference to documents divorced from their social contexts, the more likely it is that disputes and conflicts will result and the less likely it is that policy objectives will be achieved.[214] In some social control contracts, the failure of relational norms may be expressed also in adverse reaction or 'reactance' on the part of citizens to the state's efforts at social control. Reactance in this context refers to the psychological process whereby regulatees respond to overt governmental attempts to restrict their freedom by acting in a manner directly contrary to the intention of regulators, as a means of re-asserting their autonomy.[215] Reactance is less likely where the subject of control perceives that the relationship is reciprocal in that something is being given for something received. In the social control context, reciprocity is strongly associated with the perception on the part of regulatees of the legitimacy of the contractual process.

Contractual ineffectiveness in either sense considered here may have various policy implications, depending on the circumstances. In some contexts the use of behavioural contracts might be regarded as fundamentally inappropriate, and the policy abandoned. In other instances problems might be addressed through governance reforms directed at adjusting the balance of the contract norms, or through more radical modification of the contracting regime. We return to the question of institutional and organizational reform in this connection in Chapter 11.

Regulatory design – bottom-up vs top-down initiatives

A further dimension of responsiveness concerns the origins and mode of development of contract as a mechanism of social control. A contrast may be drawn between the 'top-down' imposition of regulatory regimes by central government, and the more organic development of contractual techniques by the professionals and case workers who have been responsible for dealing directly with a range of post-war social problems.[216] The 1960s and 1970s saw the evolution of various

[214] Contract is unlikely to succeed where other interventions have failed unless contractual obligations are supported by other norms and pressures in the contractual environment (family, peer group, professional, etc).

[215] Braithwaite (n 163 above) 17.

[216] D Nelken, 'The Use of "Contracts" as a Social Work Technique' (1987) 40 *Current Legal Problems* 207.

forms of contract in the fields of social work, specialist teaching, marriage guidance, divorce mediation, and the treatment of offenders, in countries as diverse as Scandinavia, the United States, France, and Australia, as well as in the UK. Nelken's study of the use of behaviour modification contracts in social work in Britain documented a range of devices, both oral and written, with some measure of 'agreement' as the common denominator. The increasing popularity of such techniques was due partly to the changing nature of social work, influenced by factors such as the movement of clients out of direct control within institutions and into the community, the shift to management by measurable results, and increasing pressures to clarify accountability for professional decision making.[217] A number of advantages were claimed for social work contracts by their supporters, such as improved coordination and liaison with other professions, greater clarity in planning and specifying social work interventions, and better client-social worker relationships based on greater mutual respect. Further benefits included increased motivation of public sector workers through greater visibility of progress towards goals, and improved accountability, both within the contractual relationship and in enabling outside scrutiny.[218]

By contrast, the major regulatory regimes involving social control contracts which were introduced in Britain from the mid-1990s were informed by centrally driven policy rationales, even where the initiatives were accepted by, or developed in collaboration with, professional groups.[219] Indeed, the restructuring of public and welfare services through the New Public Contracting has deliberately sought to marginalize the influence of the professions, regarded as representing entrenched interests and posing obstacles to effective NPM reforms. The point here is not that the development of social control mechanisms through professional practice is necessarily more effective than centrally coordinated regimes. Even in the relatively limited field of social work contracts, Nelken found a number of problems and differing opinions expressed by those operating contractual schemes.[220] The public service bodies implementing such arrangements may themselves be more or less responsive in their organization and operation. The use of contract as a technique of social control inevitably involves a problematic marriage of social engineering with individual freedom, the success of the strategy being dependent ultimately on moral codes being embodied rather than imposed.[221] What I am suggesting, however, is that centrally imposed regulation may give rise to a new set of problems by comparison with more locally based initiatives. These social control regimes may be informed by a number of different

217 ibid 210–213. 218 ibid 215–217. 219 Freedland and King (n 1 above) 467.

220 Nelken (n 216 above). As expressed by the 'doubtful' and the 'opponents' of social work contracts, as distinct from the 'enthusiasts'. Social work was the setting for observing a range of difficulties in securing 'agreement' in structured situations of unequal power.

221 Deacon and Mann (n 10 above) 433. In this analysis, the element of choice implies treating individuals as moral agents rather than moral defectives.

and possibly contradictory policy goals.[222] They are likely to be relatively complex and costly to administer, and may be prone to inefficiencies associated with the distance of the regulatory centre from front-line delivery of the service in question.

A similar pattern may be observed in other fields such as education. In this instance the original development by professionals of a range of agreements, aimed at individual behaviour modification and with the child as subject, has been displaced by central government policies directed at the control of parents in which the child has become the object of policies rather than the main participant in the contracting process.[223] In the control of deviance and anti-social behaviour, informal 'acceptable behaviour contracts' between young people and local public agencies (a partnership between the police and local housing department) were pioneered as a method of tackling anti-social behaviour long before the idea was taken up by Whitehall. Local initiatives by some London councils were borne out of frustration with the inability of more formal measures to deal with problems of vandalism, racist abuse, harassment and graffiti on problem housing estates. The failure of ASBOs in particular was attributed to the lack of trust between police and the local community necessary to gather evidence for formal proceedings. In one informal scheme, only four of sixty two agreements resulted in breach, and all these cases were resolved without resort to eviction proceedings.[224] Consistent with relational contract theory, the scheme was marked by increased trust and improved relationships between troublesome youngsters and individual police and housing officers, and better police-community relations generally. To the extent that such schemes are regarded as having been successful, this may be due at least in part to their local character and the active involvement and participation of public service workers in their development.

A responsive welfare contractualism?

For welfare contractualism to serve more responsively as a principle of organization of relationships between the state and citizens in the welfare arena, various conditions would have to be satisfied. The core norm of mutuality might be more precisely defined, for example in terms of 'fair reciprocity and fair play'.[225] White has suggested that the 'threshold conditions' of fair reciprocity might include:

- a decent share of the social product for those meeting minimum standards of productive participation;
- the acceptance of responsibility by the state for promoting the availability of productive participation;

[222] For example, social control rationales may conflict with those aimed at economic restructuring or public management reform.
[223] Blair (n 148 above) 84.
[224] *Guardian* 29 August 2001.
[225] Goodin (n 18 above).

- equitable treatment of different forms of participation; and
- universality of application of the reciprocity principle.[226]

Fair reciprocity in this sense implies an obligation on the part of the state actively to reduce barriers to inequality and social exclusion. While obligations should be reciprocal, they need not be synchronous.[227] The limits of the principle of mutuality in cases of individual need and dependence should be acknowledged. For example, an explicit purpose of employment service programmes should be to help rather than humble, in recognition of the circumstances giving rise to a need for public assistance.[228] Agreements should be the result of genuine negotiation and a process of bargaining. The making, monitoring and enforcement of contracts should be governed by procedures designed to ensure fairness and mutual respect. There should be a real possibility of sanctions proportionate to breaches on both sides, but also safeguards against their inappropriate or excessive use.[229] An appropriate dispute resolution machinery should be available and particularly attuned to protecting the contractual interests of the weaker party.

Such desiderata may be too much to expect from a contractualist framework in the current economic and political climate. In the employment services field, it might be argued that current workfare and 'active labour market' policies are fundamentally incompatible with genuine mutuality. The problem with attempting to use workfare as a policy of social inclusion is that it may be self-contradictory, necessarily tending to result in exclusion of those who are not able to negotiate structural barriers to participation in the labour market.[230] On the other hand, this rather negative assessment might be countered by evidence of the more successful implementation of welfare-contractualist policies in other countries. For example, Denmark has a relatively liberal welfare and employment policy, embracing contractual techniques that appear to involve greater respect for the relational contract norms. The Danish workfare model is based on 'needs-orientated' action plans agreed and signed by the employment exchange and the individual claimant. Despite similarities with the jobseeker's agreement in Britain, there are significant differences. The Danish provisions are articulated within more traditional welfare

226 White (n 15 above) 515–9. The last point implies a radical challenge to inheritance of wealth, since those enjoying the social product in this form make no personal contribution to its generation.

227 There are many established examples of the temporal decoupling of reciprocal obligations, for instance contributory social insurance and the graduate tax (now a feature of funding of higher education in Britain as well as Australia).

228 Goodin (n 18 above) 591. 'Good workfare policies would genuinely aim to *help*, to get people out of their predicament, with genuine opportunities. Bad workfare aims merely at humiliating and harassing the subordinate classes until they finally accept their inferior status and are dropped from their welfare roles', 592.

229 Handler argues that if one of the purposes of employment services is to combat social exclusion, then there should be no sanctions. This conclusion is drawn from the US experience, in which there is evidence of abuse of sanctions as a means of avoiding the most difficult cases: 'Without sanctions, agency workers have to work harder with the more difficult clients ... incentives have to be restructured ... workers have to be rewarded for progress' – Handler (n 74 above) 239.

230 ibid 230.

state values, with less emphasis on the responsibilities of the individual. Negotiated work plans appear to be the product of more genuine consensus, and are less punitive and disciplinary in their operation.

In contrast with the UK (and also the US) the Danish economic miracle of low unemployment and low inflation has not been achieved at the expense of a reduction of real wages and social benefits, and is not founded on a new underclass of working poor.[231] Despite obligations on the unemployed to engage actively in the labour market, and some reduction in unemployment benefits, the maintenance of relatively generous social assistance is associated with low levels of social marginalization and polarization.[232] The commitment to upgrading skills and qualifications is a key component of the government's strategy for enhancing the competitiveness of a small open economy, and the evidence appears to indicate a relatively high level of motivation of the unemployed through programmes of training and education.[233] However, the Danish model of 'workfare in a welfare society' is arguably based on various country-specific conditions that are only partly met elsewhere in Europe.[234] The comparison is likely ultimately therefore to be of limited significance for debates on the design of welfare contractualist policies in Britain. Nevertheless, the comparison is useful in pointing up certain tensions in the contractual organization of welfare, and in highlighting the question of how far objectives such as redistributing job opportunities and equalizing job chances are being achieved or impeded under present workfare programmes.

Conclusion

Following the pattern set during the Conservative era, Labour governments since 1997 have extended the New Public Contracting further into the personal sphere through various new forms of behavioural contract. While the ethos of New Contractualism is playing an important role in social organization in many western societies, in Britain it has been manifested in a particularly wide range of social control policies involving individual responsibilization. Some types of behavioural contract are directed at modifying deviant or anti-social behaviour while others support economic policy and serve the needs of the labour market. All the contractual arrangements perform a more or less overt disciplinary function, with non-compliance by individuals being potentially sanctioned by alternative and more direct exercise of hierarchical authority.

[231] Torfing (n 67 above) suggests that New Labour workfare strategy is a hybrid, combining elements of US-style policies (including benefit cuts, disciplinary measures, the involvement of employment agencies in surveillance and control) with Danish-style commitments to a minimum wage, education and training.

[232] ibid 19.

[233] Even this generally positive evaluation of the Danish experience acknowledges a range of problems with the operation of the scheme, including: the uneven quality of action plans and activation offers; cream-skimming; difficulties of activating weak and marginalized groups; and problems in dealing with the most difficult residual cases – ibid 21.

[234] ibid 24.

This chapter has established the importance of social control contracts to the Government's overall strategy for improving public services in the key areas of education, employment, criminal justice and the control of deviance. Socially disadvantaged or marginalized citizens are likely to be signatories to a number of behavioural contracts in some or all of these sectors, for example as unemployed jobseekers, young people subject to referral orders, tenants on poor housing estates subject to acceptable behaviour contracts, or parents of children suspected of anti-social behaviour either at school or in the community. The majority of citizens not directly involved in these social control regimes have an obvious interest in their operation, due to the negative impact of social problem behaviour of whatever kind on the overall quality of people's experience of public services.

In theory, the contractualization of social control relationships might be welcomed for a variety of reasons. The self-regulatory mechanism of contract provides an inherently reflexive mode of governance. There is a significant difference between an obligation voluntarily undertaken and one imposed by command of the state,[235] the former being more likely to result in change of behaviour.[236] There is also a difference in the way in which the consequences of norm violation can be presented, with the punishment following breach of 'promise' being easier to justify both to the party who has broken the obligation and to society as a whole, ie, 'You did not have to enter the contract, but since you did and broke its terms, you got what you bargained for.'[237] The casting of individual responsibilities in contractual terms may be used to focus attention on the state's own reciprocal obligations, and on whether it is delivering its side of the bargain. This opens up new possibilities for increased accountability. On the Government's own analysis, the current 'third age of welfare' is characterized by responsibility on the part of governments for providing help to individuals in discharging their individual and social responsibilities.[238] A further positive element is the reduction of social distance between public service providers and clients compared with previous bureaucratic arrangements.

Contract differs from other techniques of social control in mobilizing specifically contractual norms in the governance of state-citizen relationships, both generally in the ideology and rhetoric surrounding the social contract and in particular behavioural contracts. In Cohen's terms, it is indirect and 'inclusionary' in its mode of operation, rather than direct and 'exclusionary'.[239] In all the

[235] For example, consider the Government's recent proposals that parents should be liable to fines of up £2,500 for persistent truancy on the part of their children. Such schemes have been rejected or abandoned in the past simply because they have failed to produce changes in parental behaviour.

[236] In relation to Home-School Agreements, 'it must be the hope of the Secretary of State that by signing the document, parents will somehow implicate themselves in the policy, and having implicated themselves will feel a moral obligation to fulfil their part of what he would describe as a bargain', *Hansard*, HC (series 6) vol 309, col 341 (25 March 1998), Mr Letwin.

[237] P Vincent-Jones, 'Contractual Governance: Institutional and Organisational Analysis' (2000) 20 OJLS 317.

[238] Green Paper (n 26 above) para 11.

[239] Cohen (n 2 above).

social control contracts considered in this chapter, the success of the governance arrangements in achieving their integrative policy goals is connected in some way with the configuration of the discrete and relational norms. Where the minimum conditions of contractual relations are established, the contract norms must be in appropriate balance. Reciprocity is of particular importance in these relationships. Public agencies must have powers and resources appropriate to the performance of the functions delegated to them. As we have seen, employment service workers managing Jobseekers' Agreements are routinely frustrated by lack of time and resources needed to perform their tasks properly. Welfare departments are typically under-staffed and under-resourced, making it difficult for officials to take any genuine interest in clients' own long-term goals and perceptions. In education, significant burdens of making, specifying and managing parenting contracts have been placed on the LEA or governing body, arguably without sufficient resources or training provision. In the criminal justice field, as regards commitments of public agencies to young offenders in respect of education and training, participation in drug and alcohol programmes, and addressing housing, income and family issues, a key question is whether adequate resources are provided to enable delivery of the state's side of the bargain.[240] In all the statutory and centrally driven social control regimes, there is a significant danger that excessive central direction and prescription will inhibit the conditions necessary for effective contractual relations to develop. The social control contracts most likely to be effective are those that have evolved in a close and organic relationship with the public service workers and professionals who manage the contractual process.

Where governance deficiencies in the operation of social control contracts in particular settings have been identified, the key question for Chapter 11 is whether the problems can be addressed through legal reform. As we shall see, the interests of the weaker party in these relationships might be safeguarded through various substantive and procedural reforms. However, where the relationships are inherently exploitative, disciplinary, or one-sided, there are obvious limits to how far relational deficiencies can be addressed by reform of the legal framework. The fundamental problem may concern the policy, or the manner of its implementation. If fair reciprocity and mutuality cannot be maintained or guaranteed by institutional reform,[241] the obvious implication is that the contractual mode of

240 Cabinet Office, *Reducing Reoffending by Ex-prisoners*, para 18.10.

241 The failure of contractual schemes might be due to practical obstacles encountered in particular instances, or to the fundamental incoherence of the application of principles of reciprocity and mutuality in the context of structural inequalities and chronic individual need and dependence – ie the very notion of welfare contractualism may be fundamentally flawed. Freedland and King (n 1 above) represent the latter view, White (n 15 above) the former.

regulation has failed.[242] In that case the hierarchical and compulsive nature of authority relations should be squarely acknowledged, rather than disguised inappropriately in the language and rhetoric of agreement, customer services, and individual empowerment.

There needs to be greater critical scrutiny of claims made on behalf of New Contractualist policies that the policies are capable of empowerment of individuals as opposed to merely providing a more narrowly effective means of social control. A fundamental criticism of the use of contracts as a means of dealing with social problems is that the emphasis on 'future-orientation' may obscure the need for 'backward looking' work which is necessary 'to find out *why* problematic behaviour is taking place'.[243] In the long term solutions are likely to require not just individual but collective strategies to deal with the underlying causes of social problems. Contractualization may have negative effects in concealing real underlying problems and preventing proper engagement with them, while misdirecting time and effort through requirements imposed on public agencies to comply with bureaucratic processes.

242 'A strong commitment to principles of fair reciprocity does not automatically commit us to workfare of any sort' – Goodin (n 18 above) 593.

243 Nelken (n 216 above) in the context of social work contracts.

PART IV

LAW AND CONTRACTUAL GOVERNANCE

10

Legal Debates and Reform Strategies

This chapter begins by identifying some of the criticisms made by lawyers of the legal governance and accountability deficits accompanying the New Public Contracting. It goes on to consider various proposals for reform of administrative law, private law, and constitutional law. I argue, with regard to economic contracts, that a hybrid reform strategy, rather than one that attempts just to extend or develop private or public law in any particular direction, is most likely to be successful in addressing these governance deficiencies, and in protecting both the individual interests of parties with stakes in public contracting processes and the public interest more generally.

Legal governance deficits

Public accountability

Public lawyers argue that constitutional law fails adequately to control the executive decision to use contract, whether in the provision of services by a non-state body or in the restructuring of relationships within government along contractual lines.[1] Where there exists legislation on government contracts, this amounts to only a partial constitutional law check.[2] Once the policy decision has been taken to organize public services on a contractual basis, there are further constitutional weaknesses. These include the absence of procedures for calling to

[1] 'Contractualization is a matter for the government . . . no parliamentary authority is required' – ACL Davies, *Accountability: A Public Law Analysis of Government By Contract* (Oxford: Oxford University Press, 2001) 9; H Street, *Governmental Liability: A Comparative Study* (Cambridge: Cambridge University Press, 1953).

[2] The Deregulation and Contracting Out Act 1994 empowers ministers to delegate discretions to a contracting partner in the same way that delegation to civil servants operates under the *Carltona* doctrine, but without imposing any significant constraints; s 72 appears to provide that in cases of contracting out the department continues to be legally responsible, although the Act will not apply in all cases and the common law is uncertain – ibid 23–24. Domestic and European regulation in various areas has rendered the exercise of contracting powers by public bodies more than merely a matter of private law – S Fredman and GS Morris, 'The Costs of Exclusivity: Public and Private Re-examined' [1994] PL 69, 77. But only local and certain other public authorities are regulated, not central government.

account those performing public contracting functions, the inadequate representation or involvement of service recipients and citizens in decision making on public contracting issues, and the failure to articulate policy purposes with sufficient precision.

As we have seen in Part III, internal contracts are not subject to any form of law, public or private.[3] For example, executive agencies are prevented from entering legally binding contracts or bringing proceedings in judicial review by the lack of corporate personality. Since framework documents are not legally enforceable, there is nothing to prevent ministers interfering with the operation of agencies, and no adequate constraint on ministerial discretion.[4] Even in the case of NHS Trusts, which are statutory corporations with some degree of organizational independence, contracts with other NHS bodies are subject to only limited public law controls.[5] A similar problem of lack of effective separation of interests arguably exists in 'internal' contracts between local authority clients and in-house contractors in the local government sector.[6]

Where public services are provided under contract with external bodies and private law applies, neither the government agencies that exercise contractual powers nor the private bodies that perform public functions are properly accountable. The fundamental legal governance deficit stems from the dispersal of public powers beyond the state's traditional boundaries into a 'private' sphere beyond the reach of public law.[7] The general absence of public law controls is in contrast with the specific regulatory frameworks that govern other public service arrangements, for example in the privatized utilities sectors.[8] Firstly, the exercise of contractual powers by statutory authorities or governmental bodies is amenable to judicial review only in respect of decisions that are underpinned by statute, or which involve 'some other sufficient public law element'.[9] Otherwise the relationship is

[3] Davies (n 1 above) 11.

[4] This problem might be overcome if the 'self-denying ordinance' (the assurance by ministers that they will not interfere but refer questions on operational matters to agency chief executives) could acquire a binding quality, for example as a constitutional convention. In this case, there would remain uncertainty as to interpretation of the document and the resolution of disputes – I Harden, *The Contracting State* (Buckingham: Open University Press, 1992) 46.

[5] ibid 47.

[6] ibid 50.

[7] 'The great irony is that, just as the English courts are on the verge of articulating for themselves a version of constitutionalism which gives them a legitimate role in the protection of constitutional values in the administrative state, that state, as it has traditionally been conceived, is starting to disappear, as the political branches promote the private over the public' – M Hunt, 'Constitutionalism and the Contractualisation of Government', in M Taggart, (ed), *The Province of Administrative Law* (Oxford: Hart Publishing, 1997) 26.

[8] The operation of such regulatory frameworks is subject to judicial review – *Mercury Communications Ltd v Director General of Telecommunications* [1996] 1 WLR 48 (HL). 'No such regulatory regimes exist . . . where the relationship of private organizations with the State is governed solely by contract, a relationship whose operation traditionally concerns only the contracting parties' – Fredman and Morris (n 2 above) 69.

[9] *R v Lord Chancellor, ex p Hibbit & Saunders (A Firm)* [1993] COD 326 (per Rose LJ); *R v Legal Aid Board, ex p Donn & Co* [1996] 3 All ER 1.

governed solely by the ordinary private law of contract, leaving a range of individual and public interests unprotected. While tendering for government contracts is covered by domestic and European public procurement directives, procedural protections here serve a different purpose and are of a limited nature compared with natural justice. In any case they do not extend beyond the initial award of the contract to its performance.[10]

Secondly, as regards decision making by private contractors, while judicial review may be possible on the basis that the body is exercising discretions as agent of the public authority,[11] delegations of authority are rarely so complete as to imply an agency relationship.[12] Agency aside, amenability to judicial review depends on factors such as the governmental nature of the body,[13] its performance of a public function,[14] and the origin of its jurisdiction in a source other than contract.[15] The effect of these restrictions is an increasing potential for the abuse of discretionary powers by a range of 'private' or non-public bodies, unsupervised by the administrative law jurisdiction of the courts and disengaged from the formal accountability processes that apply in bureaucratic organisation.[16] Again, while the common law has been supplemented by a new basis of review through the European Convention on Human Rights rights incorporated by the Human Rights Act 1998, the application to private bodies remains uncertain.[17] Not only may activities of private contractors be beyond judicial review, they may also be

10 Davies (n 1 above) 18.

11 For example, where the function that is contracted out includes the making of decisions as to eligibility for services, as opposed to delivering a service in accordance with purchaser instruction – N Seddon, *Government Contracts: Federal, State and Local* (2nd ed, Sydney: Federation Press, 1999) 281; see P Craig, *Administrative Law* (4th edn, London: Sweet and Maxwell, 1999) 772.

12 *R v Servite and Wandsworth LBC, ex p Goldsmith and Chatting* [2001] LGR 55. Here Moses J. rejected the argument that Servite Houses (a charitable housing association) was acting as agent, on the ground that the local authority lacked the power to delegate its obligations under s 21 of the National Assistance Act 1948.

13 It is clear that private bodies performing public regulatory or governmental functions, which are integrated directly or indirectly into a system of statutory regulation or which the government would otherwise have to step in and provide, are subject to judicial review – but see *R v Chief Rabbi of the United Hebrew Congregations and the Commonwealth, ex p. Wachmann* [1993] 2 All ER 249; *R v Football Association, ex p Football League Ltd* [1993] 2 All ER 833.

14 *R v Panel on Take-overs and Mergers, ex p Datafin plc* [1987] QB 815. *Datafin* established that the body need not itself be public, nor did its powers have to originate in statute or prerogative, provided it was under some 'public duty' (per Lloyd LJ, Nicholls LJ) or there was otherwise a 'public element' in the case (per Sir John Donaldson MR).

15 The courts have been reluctant to include powers *derived from* contract or even *associated with* contract within the scope of judicial review – *R v Disciplinary Committee of the Jockey Club, ex p Aga Khan* [1993] 2 All ER 853; M Loughlin, 'Courts and Governance', in P Birks, (ed), *The Frontiers of Liability* (Oxford: Oxford University Press, 1994) 98.

16 'We have no systematic response, either in common law or statute, to the problems presented by the expansion of the private provision of public services' – C Newdick, 'The NHS in Private Hands? Regulating Private Providers of Health Services' (2000) 3 *Current Legal Issues* 1, 25.

17 Section 6(3)(b) of the HRA 1998 defines public authority as including 'any person certain of whose functions are functions of a public nature.' Sub-section (5) states that in relation to a particular act, a person is not a public authority by virtue only of s (3)(b) if the nature of the act is private.

outside the jurisdiction of other administrative mechanisms such as merits review in tribunals or the Ombudsman.[18]

Stakeholder interests

In addition to this public accountability deficit, it may be argued that the legal framework fails adequately to protect the particular interests of public purchasers, potential contractors, and service recipients in the public contracting process.

Firstly, public purchasing and commissioning agencies such as government departments, local authorities, and Primary Care Trusts have an obvious interest in the use of contract as a management tool to achieve their public service aims. Yet as we saw in the discussion of the state–public purchaser dimension of economic contracting regimes in Chapter 7, central government has placed significant constraints on the autonomy of many public bodies in their performance of public contracting functions. For example, local councils are not permitted to pursue 'ancillary' or 'secondary' purposes through contract terms requiring compliance with policies on a range of matters including local employment and equal opportunities.[19] Contract compliance is regarded as undermining competitiveness where potential burdens are placed on private sector bidders that do not normally arise in the market and which are already built into the costs of in-house provision.[20] In other respects, the government has indicated that it is keen for local authorities to use contractual powers imaginatively in exploring new forms of relationship and new ways of working in partnership with the private sector.[21] Despite some recent clarification, however, there is continuing uncertainty about the extent of contractual powers of public bodies.[22] The legal framework continues

[18] However, in the case of publicly funded health and social care services the actions and decisions of contractors are generally within the Ombudsman's jurisdiction – s 7(2)(a) Health Service Commissioners Act 1993; see M Seneviratne, *Ombudsmen: Public Services and Administrative Justice* (London: Butterworths, 2002) 70–71, 162–167. In Australia, the diminution in legal accountability following contracting out appears particularly acute given the relative strength of remedies that were, and continue to be, available against government bodies through the 'administrative law package' (judicial review, merits review, freedom of information, and the Ombudsman). For example, the jurisdiction of the Ombudsman applies to government departments and 'prescribed authorities' (Ombudsman Act 1976 (Cth) s 5(1) and (2)). It does not extend to private bodies performing functions previously carried out by government.

[19] Local Government Act 1988, ss 17, 18.

[20] P Morris, 'Legal Regulation of Contract Compliance: An Anglo-American Comparison' (1990) 19 *Anglo-American Law Review* 87.

[21] The contracual powers of local authorities generally have been clarified in the Local Government (Contracts) Act 1997. The Act is intended to allay the fears of banks and financial institutions that their investments might be lost where local authorities are held to have acted outside their legal powers – see *Credit Suisse v Allerdale BC* [1996] 4 All ER 129. The Act introduces a certification procedure for partnership contracts establishing their lawfulness (ss 2–4), limits the circumstances in which such contracts may be argued to be unenforceable in private law proceedings (s 5), and provides for compensation to be paid to private contractors where a public law challenge is successful and the contract is set aside by the court (s 6).

[22] S Arrowsmith, 'Judicial Review and the Contractual Powers of Public Authorities' (1990) 106 LQR 277.

to discriminate unfairly against local government by imposing restrictions that do not apply to central government. Generally, where purchasers lack adequate powers to implement locally mandated goals or to perform centrally imposed tasks, the responsive potential of public contracting and of quasi-market organization is unlikely to be realized. The capacity of public agencies to use contract effectively as a mechanism of regulation may be further undermined by policy-driven regulation. The PFI may be a good example of an arrangement which, beneath the rhetoric and formal justifications of value-for-money and risk transfer, deprives the public partner of adequate control through the delegation to private contractors of decision-making powers affecting the interests and the welfare of citizens.[23]

Secondly, potential contractors, whether private firms or their in-house competitors, have interests in the fairness of processes of tendering and decision making in the award of contracts. Regulation at national and EU levels has been directed at encouraging competition and tackling problems of discrimination and unfair trade practices. Despite the proliferation of competition regulation and increasing judicial control of tendering procedures, contractor interests arguably continue to lack sufficient protection, for example as regards unfairness in the tendering and letting of contracts.[24] Furthermore, the *ultra vires* doctrine currently enables the government too easily to avoid liability by pleading fettering of discretion, or to escape bad bargains on grounds of incapacity. The difference in the legal frameworks governing public contracting by central government departments and local authorities is particularly anomalous from the viewpoint of private contractors bidding for public sector work with both types of body.

Finally, as we saw in Chapter 8, existing or prospective public service recipients again have a range of interests in the public contracting process. Responsiveness to the needs of citizens and consumers depends ultimately on the appropriateness of the service arrangement and, where the decision has been taken to organize provision on a contractual basis, on the form of contract and the method and criteria of selection of the contractor. The specification of the contract also needs to be appropriate to the needs and preferences of service users. Again, there should be procedures for rectifying problems with service delivery, for the redress of grievances, and for the resolution of contractual disputes. In private law, the

23 M Freedland, 'Public Law and Private Finance – Placing the Private Finance Initiative in a Public Law Frame' [1998] PL 288, 307.

24 *Hibbit* (n 9 above) The Lord Chancellor's Department, in putting out to tender the contract for shorthand reporting of court proceedings, had acted unfairly in breaching a legitimate expectation of the applicants (the firm which had held the contract for ninety years) that none of the interested parties would be permitted to amend their offers following submission of bids based on a firm price. Despite the acknowledgement that the Department had acted unfairly by giving other bidders the opportunity to submit lower bids, the decision was held to be not subject to judicial review on the ground that contractual obligations are enforceable by ordinary action. On private law control of fairness in tendering for public contracts, see *Blackpool and Fylde Aero Club Ltd v Blackpool BC* [1990] 3 All ER 25.

fundamental legal governance problem here stems from the restrictive doctrines of privity and consideration, which prevent the creation of a direct legal relationship between the consumer and service provider. These elements are similarly lacking in the relationship between the service recipient and public purchaser. Even where public services are marketed and paid for directly by consumers, the law of contract often does not apply where the provider is carrying out a public legal duty. Where there are legal entitlements, these are a patchwork of legislation and judicial decision-making concerning the tort of breach of statutory duty.[25]

Partly as a result of this deficiency, the present legal framework governing public contracting does not protect against various types of harm to the interests of actual or potential service recipients. Examples of unregulated or under-regulated situations include:

- unfairness in decision making by private bodies in the award of educational and training opportunities;
- unfairness in the process of allocation of scarce resources (rationing) involving the denial of a service to a claimant where other needs are accorded higher priority;
- unlawful termination of contracts by private providers, with deleterious consequences for service recipients;
- lack of control by consumers over the terms of contracts between purchasers and providers;
- the withdrawal or withholding of services by a private provider, typically associated with a claim that the user no longer qualifies for the service; and
- decisions of a public body to withdraw direct services and to arrange for their provision instead by a private business.

Filling the accountability vacuum

In contemporary legal debates, constitutional and administrative law reforms are widely regarded as fundamental to securing improvements in accountability to both the general public and particular consumers. However, a degree of circumspection is needed in assessing the merits of different legal reform proposals. The basic governance question raised by the foregoing analysis of the New Public Contracting is how to facilitate increased responsiveness in the organization and delivery of public services. I have suggested that the answer in some cases requires organizational change rather than institutional reform. Where the institutions that support relational contracting do require strengthening, this result is not

[25] J Wightman, *Contract: A Critical Commentary* (London: Pluto Press, 1996) 161–169.

necessarily best achieved through the reform of specifically *legal* institutions, whether relating to substance or procedure.

Solutions to regulatory problems depend on the particular public service setting.[26] In many cases formal remedies or disputes resolution procedures may not be necessary and the interests of consumers may best be advanced through practical rectification of the defect that has given rise to the grievance.[27] Responsiveness in this sense is likely to depend on whether consumers are able to articulate and communicate service delivery problems, for example through complaints mechanisms,[28] and on the ability of providers and client agencies to respond appropriately. In other areas, victims of poor performance may have grievances that require administrative redress,[29] or redress and compensation through the application of law and resort to the courts. The legal accountability vacuum needs to be considered in such different contexts. In many instances the parties involved in purchasing and provision in quasi-markets may not be legally accountable, in the sense of having to make amends for the consequences of poor performance to wronged consumers. But the clarity with which their roles have been defined and distinguished, and their greater visibility and responsibility in consequence, may render them more easily accountable in other ways, for example through performance on individual contracts of employment.[30] The main issue is likely to concern what forms of sanction or incentive are necessary to facilitate performance. These may be economic, bureaucratic, administrative or operational, rather than narrowly legal or contractual. Where problems arise that require formal redress as opposed to rectification, recourse to the courts should generally be a last rather than a first resort. We return to the issue of the design of responsive 'remedial hierarchies' in Chapter 11.

Furthermore, while it is self-evident that contracting out has entailed a diminution in public law accountability,[31] this does not necessarily imply overall or net accountability losses.[32] A narrow public law approach tends to exaggerate the effectiveness of traditional accountability mechanisms, as well as ignoring the potential of new forms of accountability which may accompany contracting out.[33]

[26] P Vincent-Jones, 'The Regulation of Contractualisation in Quasi-Markets for Public Services' [1999] PL 303.

[27] P Vincent-Jones and A Harries, 'CCT, Conflict and Cooperation in Local Authority Quasi-Markets', in W Bartlett, JA Roberts, and J Le Grand, (eds), *A Revolution in Social Policy: Quasi-Market Reforms in the 1990s* (Bristol: The Policy Press, 1998).

[28] N Lewis and P Birkinshaw, *When Citizens Complain: Reforming Justice and Administratation* (Buckingham: Open University Press, 1993).

[29] P Birkinshaw, *Grievances, Remedies and the State* (2nd edn, London: Sweet and Maxwell, 1994) 187–245.

[30] C Scott, 'The "New Public Law"', in C Willett, (ed), *Public Sector Reform and the Citizen's Charter* (London: Blackstone Press Ltd, 1996) 53–60.

[31] R Mulgan 'Contracting Out and Accountability' (1997) 56 *Australian Journal of Public Administration* 106; N Seddon 'Is Accountability a Cost of Contracting Out?' in C Finn (ed), *Sunrise or Sunset? Administrative Law in the New Millennium* (Canberra: AIAL, 2000) 37.

[32] Scott (n 30 above). [33] ibid.

The assumption that the application of traditional mechanisms to private bodies is desirable may also be challenged.[34] Similar legal accountability benefits might be achieved by different means that are both more suited to the fields being regulated, and more sympathetic to the quasi-market policy objectives of increasing efficiency and competitiveness. A related argument is that some reduction in legal accountability for public services may have to be accepted as the price that must be paid for the attainment of wider individual and social benefits.[35] In this view, public accountability (whether under private or public law or some hybrid combination) might be subordinated to the goal of increasing responsiveness on the part of public service providers to consumers and citizens in other senses.[36]

The questioning of the importance of traditional public law notions of accountability is not unique to Britain. In the United States there have been calls for different standards of accountability and frameworks of reference to deal with the shift to 'third-party government', in which government agencies are inevitably no longer exclusively in control of the programmes they administer.[37] In light of this development the traditional focus on controlling the exercise of discretion by administrative agencies is no longer appropriate. Administrative law procedures, which are designed to force administrative discretion into the open and ensure fairness in its exercise, may be unsuited to circumstances where discretion and responsibilities for the implementation of public programmes are widely dispersed among different actors in the public and private sectors. The phenomenon of third-party government:

> . . . parcels out to the variety of third-party partners who come to share with the government administrators the authority to shape program operations. This has the result, however,

[34] In the US, even if the state action doctrine or its common law equivalent were applied to private decision making, for example in the nursing home sector, quality of care would not thereby be ensured given the fragmentation of responsibility among different levels of government and private actors – J Freeman, 'The Private Role in Public Governance' (2000) 75 *New York University Law Review* 543, 602.

[35] Wirth defines accountability broadly in terms of responsiveness to legitimate sources of authority and influence (including the public at large and the intended recipients and actual clients of services), operating in addition to bureaucratic and other formal institutional controls. The various accountabilities deriving from different sources are not necessarily cumulative, but may be at odds with one another. Satisfying accountability in one sense may involve denying it in another – W Wirth, 'Responding to Citizens' Needs: From Bureaucratic Accountability to Individual Coproduction in the Public Sector' in Franz-Xavier Kaufman, (ed), *The Public Sector: Challenge for Coordination and Learning* (New York: Walter de Gruyter, 1991) 72–73.

[36] Some of the advantages of contracting out derive precisely from the reduction in *certain forms* of accountability: 'One of the reasons for the comparative inefficiency of service provision by public servants compared with contractors is that public servants are subject to additional pressures of accountability which help to make them more risk-averse than their private sector counterparts' – Mulgan (n 31 above) 110. However, even where contracting out demonstrably can be shown to increase *responsiveness* in the sense of increasing choice and competition, it is mistaken to associate any such improvement with increased *accountability* – ibid 115. Generally see R Mulgan, *Holding Power to Account* (London: Palgrave, 2003).

[37] LM Salamon, 'The Tools Approach and the New Governance: Conclusion and Implications' in LM Salamon, (ed), *The Tools of Government: A Guide to the New Governance* (Oxford: Oxford University Press, 2002) 604.

of placing significant portions of the discretionary authority over the operation of public programs beyond the reach of classic administrative law. Indeed, to operate most effectively, third-party tools require that program managers have wide latitude to bargain with their third-party partners, in direct opposition to the prohibitions on *ex parte* contacts stipulated in administrative law.[38]

This argument implies that efforts simply to extend administrative law controls into the private sphere are misplaced. The problem for administrative law is rather how to reconcile the 'new discretion' with more traditional procedural safeguards.[39] Similarly, the New Public Contracting necessarily entails the wide dispersal of discretion and responsibilities among a variety of public and independent sector bodies. What is necessary for the effective operation of economic contracting regimes, it may be suggested, is increased discretion (in certain crucial respects) on the part of actors engaged in the performance of public service functions, rather than any further constraint on their autonomy.

Nevertheless, despite such reservations, where contractualization has been accompanied by a reduction in public law accountability there is *prima facie* a strong case for redressing that loss, whether by administrative law or other means.

Administrative law

Extending the scope of judicial review

The argument for extending the scope of judicial review has been pursued in two main directions. First, as regards the exercise of contractual powers by public bodies, Craig has suggested that the 'public law element' necessary to render the activity subject to judicial review 'might be found in cases where ... there was some *special aim* being pursued by the government through the tendering process which set it apart from *ordinary commercial tender*'.[40] This avoids the inference that the substantive and procedural principles of public law should be applied to all public contracts.[41] It also addresses the absence of logic in the current position that the contracting functions of local authorities (just because they are governed by statute) should be subject to judicial review, whereas those of central government departments are not. The issue of amenability to judicial review turns on whether 'the task being performed by the public body when it makes the contract really partakes in some manner of "governing" or "public regulation" as opposed to private contracting'.[42]

38 ibid 605.

39 ibid citing M Shapiro, 'Administrative Law Unbounded: Reflections on Government and Governance' (2001) 8 *Indiana Journal of Global Governance Studies* 369; J Freeman, 'Collaborative Governance in the Administrative State' (1997) 45 *UCLA Law Review* 1.

40 Craig (n 11 above) 773, emphasis supplied.

41 'These principles may not be appropriate when a public body makes an ordinary commercial contract for furniture, a lease or the like' – ibid 773.

42 ibid 773–4.

Such a public regulatory element may clearly be found in *Donn*, where the decision of a legal aid committee to award a contract for the conduct of litigation was held to be amenable to judicial review due to its association with the policy of state provision of legal aid. Less obviously, the situation in *Hibbit* might also be argued to come within this redefined test, on the ground that the arrangement was entered into pursuant to a specific policy encouraging the creation of a new form of competitive relationship between government and suppliers.[43] This line of argument might find support in the fundamental distinction drawn in the present work between traditional public procurement and policy-driven regulation in the New Public Contracting. The acknowledgement of a blurring of the distinction between policy and formal legislation, and the growing importance of the regulatory status of policy documents and associated materials, reinforces the argument that a 'public element' may be found in the purposive nature of economic contracting regimes.

An alternative position on the question of how to increase the scope of judicial review of the exercise of contractual powers by public bodies without exposing all government contracting to administrative law principles is taken by Arrowsmith. The conclusion reached in her survey of English law in this regard is that 'the time has come to put to rest the perception of contract as a private activity and to recognise that for the purposes of judicial review, at least, such activities are truly within the ambit of "public law"'.[44] Rather than continuing the search for some 'public law' element as a justification for applying public law doctrines, the argument here is that there should be a general presumption in favour of judicial review of contractual powers of public authorities. While the principle of reviewability of contractual powers would be accepted by the courts in principle, the review might be negated or limited by specific policy factors.

Secondly, as regards the problem of diminished legal accountability of private or non-state bodies which provide public services in contractual relationships with public purchasing agencies, an obvious legal reform argument is that judicial review could be made more generally available through a liberal interpretation of the 'public function' test. Increasing the scope of public law jurisdiction in this way may be regarded as part of the modern 'expansionist' tendency in the field of judicial review.[45] Support for the view that that the nature of the function being exercised, rather than the source of the power, should be the key factor in deciding amenability to administrative law controls comes both from the development of English law on the public/private divide and s 6 of the Human Rights Act

[43] n 9 above. However, the cases might be distinguished, and the facts of *Hibbit* still considered as falling within the unreviewable category, on the ground that the service being procured was indirect rather than direct, ie for the benefit of a public body rather any particular class of public consumer.

[44] Arrowsmith (n 22 above) 292.

[45] Elliott distinguishes between extending the scope of review on the one hand, and broadening of the range of grounds of supervision, as under the Human Rights Act, on the other hand – MC Elliott *The Constitutional Foundations of Judicial Review* (Oxford: Hart Publishing, 2001) 4–5.

1998.[46] EU law has added a further impetus to this trend, inspired by continental jurisprudence which has traditionally placed greater emphasis on the *function* than the identity of the *actor* (whether private, public or voluntary) as the crucial determinant of the legal relationship between user/citizen and service provider.[47]

On a liberal interpretation of *Datafin* – the seminal case which established that public law standards could in certain circumstances be applied to private contractors – a body would be performing a public function, and so be amenable to judicial review, 'when it seeks to achieve some collective benefit for the public or a section of the public and is accepted by the public or that section of the public as having the authority to do so'.[48] The aim here is to avoid the danger of technical procedural barriers becoming 'obstacles to the redress of legitimate complaints by those aggrieved by unlawful, unfair or unreasonable decisions'.[49] Judicial review might thus be extended to cover any body exercising authority or power over another in a manner prejudicing the rights or interests of that party, provided that there is no suitable alternative remedy.[50] A related approach, while sceptical whether institutions or functions are capable of intrinsic definition in this way, argues that the application of public and private law should be based on a close examination of the *reasons or justifications* for drawing the distinction in particular contexts, notably whether they relate to access to government information, the extent of government power, the separation of powers, or procedural protections for public authorities.[51]

[46] Advocates of the extension of public law controls into the contracted out sector have tended to argue that both forms of review, at common law and under the HRA, should be available – see P Craig, 'Contracting Out, The Human Rights Act and the Scope of Judicial Review' (2002) 118 LQR 551; E Palmer, 'Should Public Health Be a Private Concern? Developing a Public Service Paradigm in English Law' (2002) 22 OJLS 663.

[47] M Ross, 'Article 16 E.C. and Services of General Interest: From Derogation to Obligation?' (2000) 25 *European Law Review* 22, 34.

[48] SA de Smith, Lord Woolf and J Jowell, *Judicial Review of Administrative Action* (5th edn, London: Sweet and Maxwell, 1995) 167. The most radical argument for extending the scope of review is that the test of amenability should be *monopolistic* rather than *governmental* power, so that the controlling bodies of sporting and religious bodies might also be subject to review – Lord Woolf, '*Droit Public* – English Style' [1995] PL 57; MJ Beloff, 'Judicial Review – 2001: A Prophetic Odyssey' (1995) 58 MLR 143.

[49] Woolf and Jowell (n 48 above) 167.

[50] Lord Woolf, 'Judicial Review: A Possible Programme for Reform' [1992] PL 221, 235. Hunt takes a similar position, arguing that there is a basis in the common law for the courts to assert general public law principles over all exercises of power, regardless of the source of that power – Hunt (n 7 above) 38.

[51] P Cane, *An Introduction to Administrative Law* (3rd edn, Oxford: Clarendon Press, 1996) 12–18. Cane argues generally in support of a public function test of amenability to judicial review. 'A public function is a function peculiar to government, or a function not peculiar to government *the performance of which has an important impact on society at large* (17, emphasis supplied). In this interpretation, while the criterion of amenability is broader than the *governmental* nature of the function, the argument appears circular – 'public functions are functions which ought to be subject to public law controls', 18. Whether a function is a public function therefore can only be resolved through a rational process of reasoning and deliberation. Furthermore, such deliberation is considered to occur within the courtroom rather than in any broader forum; the court has to make a '*normative judgment* about the desirable scope of judicial review' (25, emphasis supplied). But there

Such extension of the scope of judicial review would bring arrangements governing provision by private and voluntary sector bodies into line with those applying to public providers, in relation to whom citizens have traditionally had recourse to judicial review for the enforcement of individual rights.[52] All these bodies would be under duties at common law to act within the terms of any empowering legislation, to take into account all relevant considerations and not to take into account irrelevant considerations, and to act according to standards of procedural fairness. To take a concrete example, residents of private nursing homes would have the same rights as enjoyed by citizens in the state sector as regards procedural fairness and the protection of legitimate expectations,[53] irrespective of the private identity of the service provider.[54] The common factor justifying judicial control would be the impact of decisions of service providers on the rights of individual citizens, and their significance for the interests of the public at large.[55]

The argument that the scope of judicial review is capable of being extended by the courts, provided they are prepared to act boldly in developing the notion of reviewability of all exercises of power,[56] has been criticized for uncertainty, and for leaving the courts 'armed with a concept in a theoretical twilight zone'.[57]

is no easy answer to the question whether services such as health care, housing and education should be considered 'essential' in the same way as transport and the utilities.

52 Palmer (n 46 above) 663 – citing *R v Cambridge Health Authority, ex p B* [1995] 2 All ER 129; *R v North Derbyshire Health Authority, ex p Fisher* [1997] 8 Med LR 327

53 *R v North Devon Health Authority, ex p Coughlan* [2000] 3 All ER 850; [2001] QB 213; MC Elliott, '*Coughlan*: Substantive Protection of Legitimate Expectations Revisited' [2000] *Judicial Review* 27.

54 Palmer (n 46 above) 664. Despite setbacks acknowledged to have occurred in *Servite* and *Heather*, Palmer argues that there is no logical reason why the result achieved in *Coughlan* (where the Court of Appeal decided that the closure of a NHS nursing home amounted to a breach of the applicant's legitimate expectation that it would remain open for the rest of her life) should not be applied in the context of private nursing home provision.

55 ibid 670. 'It is not difficult to postulate a range of factors by which courts could identify core public functions in accordance with their impact on the rights and interests of citizens', 682. In relation to the delivery of welfare services, relevant factors might include the extent to which the activities of providers impinge on the health, human dignity, and social development of citizens. The vulnerability of service users would be particularly important in such an assessment. Other factors that might lend weight to, or detract from, the inference that a body is performing a public function, and should therefore be subject to judicial review, might include whether the service is publicly funded, and 'the degree of choice in succumbing to its provision', 670. The absence of choice on the part of the user, and the absence of a contractual nexus in the form of direct payment for services at the point of delivery (ie exactly the condition under which contracted out services are typically provided in quasi-market organisation) would support the inference of public function. But payment for a service does not necessarily indicate choice, as for example in the case of residential care services, where 'the fact of payment depends on the fortuitous financial position of vulnerable clients at the time when the need for residential care arises', 682.

56 Hunt argues that all that is holding the courts back from this task is excessive adherence to the Diceyan tradition and failure to embrace its logical successor, modern constitutionalism – Hunt (n 7 above).

57 J Allison, 'Theoretical and Institutional Underpinnings of a Separate Administrative Law', in M Taggart, (ed), *The Province of Administrative Law* (Oxford: Hart Publishing, 1997) 89. The author argues that the reason why none of the attempts to extend the scope of administrative law is successful is that English lawyers and academics cannot escape, but continually fail to confront, the issue of the

An obvious criticism is that this task is beyond judicial interpretation and development, and requires legislation.[58] More fundamentally, however, many administrative lawyers are dubious about the extension of judicial review by whatever means as a response to the accountability deficits accompanying outsourcing and contractualization. Aronson has been particularly pessimistic about the 'Datafin project'.[59] The failure of the attempt to develop *Datafin* as a basis for progressive legal reform is deserved, in this view, because the project is fundamentally unviable, due to the rigid dichotomy of public and private power that it assumes. Real situations are likely to include elements of both, resisting attempts to force facts into one or the other.[60] While the importance of public law qualities such as openness, participation, fairness, impartiality, accountability, and rationality is acknowledged, the argument is that the implementation of such values within administrative practices might better be promoted through legal mechanisms other than judicial review.

The expansionist judicial review project may be criticized for other reasons. For example, a practical problem with the argument that protection of the kind afforded residents in local authority nursing homes should be extended to residents in private or independent sector homes is that a 'rights' strategy based on holding the contractor to account is in many cases likely to be futile. The underlying problem here concerns the nature of the market for residential and community nursing services. Private or non-profit providers cannot be compelled to maintain a non-profitable business, or one that cannot break even. The quasi-market in long term care in the UK has been particularly vulnerable to changing market conditions.[61] In extreme cases, contractors may have no choice other than bankruptcy where businesses cannot be run at a profit. In public service sectors where market structures are more robust and where transfer of risk to private or non-profit bodies is both appropriate and practicable, the question is

state. The province of public law cannot be successfully demarcated without such a confrontation, which is necessary to give a separate administrative law theoretical justification. Yet this project is impractical, and wholly incompatible with the Diceyan tradition of the common law which refuses to countenance a separate public law or jurisdiction through which public officials would be held accountable.

58 Palmer argues that the continuing tendency of the courts to interpret 'public function' restrictively, both in judicial review and in relation to the Human Rights Act, means that parliament must step in to clarify those public functions that should be regulated by the courts in accordance with public law standards – Palmer (n 46 above) 665. 'There is a great deal wrong with administrative law in the UK and it is highly unlikely that the judiciary can come to terms with the changes (required) . . . without legislative support' – ND Lewis, *Choice and the Legal Order: Rising Above Politics* (London: Butterworths, 1996) 174.

59 M Aronson, 'A Public Lawyer's Responses to Privatisation and Outsourcing' in M Taggart, (ed), *The Province of Administrative Law* (Oxford: Hart Publishing, 1997) 46; M Chen, 'The Reconfiguration of the State and the Appropriate Scope of Judicial Review' in J Boston, (ed), *The State Under Contract* (Wellington: Bridget Williams Books, 1995) 112.

60 See also Allison (n 57 above).

61 D Gibson, and R Means, 'Policy Convergence: Restructuring Long-Term Care in Australia and the UK' (2000) 29 *Policy and Politics* 43.

whether judicial review is the best way of holding providers to account and of promoting values of good administration and fair decision making.[62] The more traditional and limited forms of procedural review that are likely to be involved in the majority of cases might be ineffectual in controlling the behaviour of contractors, being 'subject to all the usual defects of judicial review generally, with some peculiar to that area.'[63] For a variety of reasons, therefore, judicial review may not be the answer to the legal governance and accountability problems raised by contracting out.

Human rights and public authorities

The Human Rights Act 1998 incorporating the European Convention on Human Rights into UK law may be expected to be of increasing significance in controlling the contractual activities of public authorities. By comparison with common law judicial review, the jurisdiction asserted on human rights review has been described as 'relatively intrusive'. It is concerned with substantive values rather than procedural norms, with the content and effect of decisions as well as the process of decision making, and ultimately with justifiability and proportionality rather than with reasonableness.[64] Human rights law encompasses a broad range of substantive fundamental rights, as distinct from the largely process-oriented rights conferred by the common law. The effect of s 6(1) is to create a new ground of judicial review on which an act, decision or failure to act may be held unlawful. There are likely to be many cases involving human services in which the claims of dissatisfied citizens and consumers will be cast in these terms.

However, the Act has full direct effect only in respect of public authorities such as the government, police, local authorities, courts or tribunals.[65] Its application to other bodies is limited to their performance of functions that are public in nature,[66] so that a given body may be subject to human rights review in respect

62 In cases of legitimate expectation there remain doubts about the propriety of the judicial role in reviewing the substance of administrative decisions, and concerns about interfering with the capacity of contractors to deliver benefits of increased efficiency and responsiveness through business restructuring. (The closure in *Heather* was part of a restructuring operation in which the original home was to become a high dependency unit to meet the pressing need for such facilities, with existing residents being relocated in community-based units in neighbouring towns).

63 Aronson (n 59 above) 47. 'Even if judicial review did start to move into the "private" area of government contracts, the results would not be very startling. This is because . . . there is not much that judicial review can deliver . . . in the area of contracted out services' – Seddon (n 11 above) 300.

64 Elliott (n 45 above) 203.

65 Decisions as to the scope of supervisory jurisdiction will be informed (in addition to domestic law) by the test applied by the European Court of Justice in deciding whether a respondent is a state body in respect of which a directive should have direct effect – see *Aston Cantlow PCC v Wallbank* [2001] 3 WLR 1323; [2001] 3 All ER 393; Loughlin (n 15 above) 98.

66 n 17 above. In *Poplar Housing and Regeneration Community Association Ltd v Donoghue* (2001) 33 HLR 823-846, the Court of Appeal held that a registered social landlord (Poplar Housing) was a public authority for the purposes of s 6 HRA 1998 – see M McDermont, 'The Elusive Nature of the "Public Function": Poplar Housing v Donoghue' (2003) 66 MLR 113.

of some activities but not others.[67] The meaning of 'public function' in this context is proving as problematic as the common law test of amenability to judicial review under *Datafin*. Contrary to Parliament's original intention, the courts appear to be adopting a restrictive interpretation,[68] with the result that citizens are being denied human rights protection on the relatively arbitrary criterion of the body's administrative links with state institutions.[69] The recent report of the Joint Committee on Human Rights considers that all bodies delivering public services should be subject to human rights obligations, and that all citizens should enjoy the same protection under the Convention regardless of the private or public identity of the service provider.[70] In addition to being indefensible in principle, the current gaps and inconsistencies in human rights protection are likely to mean that the UK is falling short of its international obligations to secure effective protection of Convention rights (art 1) and to provide an effective remedy for their breach (art 13).[71] Rejecting various reform options including statutory amendment, supplementing the Act with a scheme of ministerial designation of public authorities, and using purchaser-provider contracts as a means of requiring adherence to Convention rights, the Joint Committee concluded that a human rights culture across all sectors might best be developed through clear principles of interpretation: 'As a matter of broad principle, a body is a functional public authority performing a public function under s 6(3)(b) of the Human Rights Act where it exercises a function that has its origin in governmental responsibilities, in such a way as to compel individuals to rely on that body for realization of their Convention human rights.'[72]

While the argument for legal reform is more clearly established in principle in relation to human rights than common law judicial review, similar practical problems are likely to remain. A more generous interpretation of s 6(3)(b) through judicial regard to principles of interpretation is but a small part of the solution to the overall problem of the present inadequacy of citizen redress in public

[67] D Oliver, *Common Values and the Public-Private Divide* (London: Butterworths, 1999) 227; ibid, 'Functions of a Public Nature under the Human Rights Act' [2004] PL 329.

[68] See *R (on the application of Heather)* v *Leonard Cheshire Foundation* [2002] 2 All ER 936; C Donnelly, 'Leonard Cheshire again and Beyond: Private Contractors, Contract and s 6(3)(b) of the Human Rights Act' [2005] PL 785. However, some bodies previously outside the scope of judicial review may now, following incorporation of the Convention, be regarded as public authorities amenable to judicial review where their decisions are not subject to some other remedy – AW Bradley and KD Ewing, *Constitutional and Administrative Law* (Harlow: Pearson Education, 2003) 738.

[69] Joint Committee on Human Rights, 'The Meaning of Public Authority under the Human Rights Act', Seventh Report of Session 2003-04, HL Paper 39, HC 382, p 52 para 1.

[70] Even were the Act recognized as having indirect horizontal effect between private parties, victims of human rights violations would not have a cause of action against the provider of a public service that was not a public authority – ibid para 58.

[71] ibid para 73.

[72] ibid para 31. 'Under section 6 of the Human Rights Act, there should be no distinction between a body providing housing because it itself is required to do so by statute, and a body providing housing because it has contracted with a local authority which is required by statute to provide the service. The loss of a single step in proximity to the statutory duty does not change the nature of the function, nor the nature of its capacity to interfere with Convention rights' – para 26.

contracting for human services. As to the possibility of using the HRA to enforce Convention rights against private contractors,[73] there is little prospect of the courts recognizing any form of direct 'horizontal effect'. In the absence of contract, it is difficult to see how a cause of action necessary to extend the rights of the citizen can be grounded in the common law in this context.[74] Overall, the principal concern of the HRA with individual rights rather than with the regulation of decision making may be expected to limit its significance for the governance of the New Public Contracting.

Limits of administrative law

There is some disagreement among public lawyers as to how far the governance issues raised by contractualization and outsourcing amount to a crisis in administrative law.[75] Responses range from the argument that legal processes and institutions are capable of reform and of playing an increased role in securing accountability (a 'revitalization of administrative law' project), to the position that the courts and formal legal processes should be marginalized in favour of non-legal forms and methods of accountability.[76]

Certain widely acknowledged deficiencies in administrative law might be dealt with relatively easily through incremental reforms.[77] More fundamentally, Sir William Wade (and later Wade and Forsyth) have criticized the distinction between public law and private law proclaimed in *O'Reilly* in 1983, but rooted in the procedural reforms of 1977. Without 'procedural exclusivity', contractualisation and outsourcing would arguably have posed fewer problems of legal definition. Complainants could have challenged decision-making processes regardless of the 'private' or 'public' status of bodies concerned through application by writ or originating summons for a declaration or injunction in the Queens Bench or Chancery Division of the High Court. Alternatively, they could pursue an application to the Divisional Court of the Queens Bench Division for judicial review, where prerogative orders (certiorari, mandamus, prohibition) could be granted

[73] M Hunt, 'The Horizontal Effect of the Human Rights Act' [1998] PL 423; G Phillipson, 'The Human Rights Act, "Horizontal Effect" and the Common Law: A Bang or a Whimper?' 62 (1999) MLR 824; R Buxton, 'The Human Rights Act and Private Law' (2000) 116 LQR 48; HWR Wade, 'Horizons of Horizontality' (2000) 116 LQR 217.

[74] Bradley and Ewing (n 68 above) 421. 'Plaintiffs seeking to invoke Convention rights in private common law cases will not be able to rely solely on the right in question, but will have to anchor their claim in an existing common law cause of action' – Phillipson (n 73 above) 847.

[75] Cane is sceptical of the somewhat apocalyptic tenor of many 'crisis' commentators. While acknowledging the problems posed by contractualization for the traditional conception of judicial review, he considers that many of the problems are capable of being addressed by careful mapping of its various frontiers – P Cane, 'Mapping the Frontiers' in P Birks, (ed), *The Frontiers of Liability* (Oxford: Oxford University Press, 1994) 137.

[76] ibid 152; C Harlow, 'Public Service, Market Ideology, and Citizenship' in M Freedland and S Sciarra, (eds), *Public Services and Citizenship in European Law – Public and Labour Law Perspectives* (Oxford: Oxford University Press, 1998) 54.

[77] See ch 11, above.

and, from 1977, injunctions, declarations and even damages. While the prerogative orders were only available against public bodies and other bodies exercising public functions, 'the extent of their applicability was not often tested, as alternative remedies were available in the Queens Bench or Chancery Divisions'.[78] This implies that a partial administrative law solution to contemporary governance difficulties might be sought in the adoption of a unified procedure, in effect reversing *O'Reilly*. The supervision of the use of executive powers involving contract might then occur in a single forum, regardless of the public or private dimensions of the particular case.[79]

However, such a unified procedure could not resolve the fundamental problems associated with the blurring, in practice, of the boundary between public and private spheres through privatization, de-bureaucratization, and the development of new forms of hybrid economic relationship. On a more radical interpretation, the increasingly ineffectual role of the courts in the domain of administrative law may be a reflection of the failure of the legal order to respond to new challenges of social complexity. The result has been the displacing of law as an active regulatory mechanism over great areas of public life.[80] The modernizing of the machinery of judicial review, and the attempts after *O'Reilly* to differentiate public law and private law spheres, have merely exposed the lack of an adequate jurisprudence in English public law. The alternative to the doomed attempt to rationalize the common law is to accept that:

> . . . the basic function of public law is to develop criteria for guiding, controlling and evaluating governmental performance. It is by adopting this orientation that we can best make sense of the contemporary relationship between courts and governance. The foundations of judicial review are no longer to be found in the idea of jurisdiction but in a sense of governmental function.[81]

In this vein, Aman has provided a critique of the conception of the state/civil society relationship on which traditional legal analysis in the common law countries rests. The role of the new administrative law should be 'to legitimate new forms of public, private, state and federal partnerships. Unlike the transformations in administrative law in the past, however, the primary source of the new administrative law will be the executive and legislative branches. Given clear signals from those branches, the courts will follow.'[82] In this radical critique, the role of the courts becomes deeply problematic. 'The new administrative law of market

78 Oliver (n 67 above) 72. *O'Reilly* required a conceptual distinction to be drawn between matters of public law and private law, a distinction arguably alien to the Diceyan tradition – *O'Reilly v Mackman* [1983] 2 AC 237. Nevertheless, the creation of an exclusive procedure was regarded by some as a step towards a more rigorous and comprehensive system of administrative law.

79 Fredman and Morris (n 2 above) 81.

80 Loughlin (n 15 above). In this view, the 'court-centred focus' of the common law has vested too much importance in the position of the judiciary within the structure of governance.

81 ibid 111.

82 AC Aman, 'Administrative Law for a New Century' in M Taggart, (ed), *The Province of Administrative Law* (Oxford: Hart Publishing, 1997) 117.

approaches and structures is largely the creation of the legislative and executive branches of government. It is unclear just what the role of the courts will be.'[83]

This line of argument casts doubt on the likely efficacy of strategies for the better governance of the New Public Contracting which involve simply the removal of procedural obstacles, or the extension of the ambit of judicial supervision further into the sphere of the 'private'.

Constitutional law

Constitutional reform

Some public lawyers have seen in the increasing use of contracts a genuine potential for promoting constitutional values, through the institutional separation of responsibility for deciding what services there shall be from responsibility for service delivery. In this interpretation, contractualization produces a 'structural bias' in favour of two constitutionally valuable developments connected with the rule of law: the reduction of unnecessary administrative discretion, and the delegation of decision-making authority to accountable and effective units. The problem in realizing this potential, as we have seen, is that constitutional law fails adequately to control executive decision making in regard to contractualization. A radical reform option here might be to establish central government contract powers on a statutory basis. This would solve the problem of amenability to judicial review, replacing the 'third source' as a basis of the exercise of powers and problems associated with it.[84] The detailed statutory regimes governing local authority contracting make all the more obvious the lack of any such regulatory framework for central government. Given that such fundamental constitutional change must be considered unlikely, however, some other means must be found to govern the separation of purchaser and provider functions, and to ensure the proper representation of interests of consumers and citizens through individual rights in public service organization.[85]

83 ibid 95. In posing the question of what role can be played by the state as a regulator, in the light of the collapse of the distinction between public and private, Aman considers two main options: the delegation of public functions to the private sector, and the application of market organisational models involving corporatisation – ibid 92. These regulatory transformations are argued to require a radical shift in the focus of administrative law and the legal system, from one of legitimating extensions of public power and increased state intervention, to that of 'legitimating new mixes of public and private power, new uses of private power, and increased reliance on market approaches to further public interest goals', 92. The emphasis is on the new forms of *involvement* of the private sector in the realization of public purposes.

84 B Harris, 'The "Third Source" of Authority for Government Action' (1992) 109 LQR 626. In this account the 'third source' is the freedom (or prerogative in the broad sense) enjoyed by the government to do anything that is not prohibited by law.

85 'The mechanism of contract can itself play a valuable role, within a broader legal and constitutional framework. Both accountability and individual rights can be promoted by an organizational separation of decisions as to what services there should be from the delivery of those services, and by

To this end, the new legal framework advocated by constitutional reformers of the 'Sheffield school' eschews any simple dichotomy of private and public law. Individual rights in this perspective are best conceived as rights *in respect of* the purchaser–provider contract for the public service, rather than *contractual rights* as normally understood by private law.[86] The separation of roles 'offers the opportunity not only to pursue economy, efficiency and effectiveness, but also to enhance both individual rights and the accountability of government for policy decisions'.[87] The publication of contractual information regarding the primary obligations of the parties might give rise to citizens' entitlements in various ways, for example through the public law doctrine of legitimate expectations. The provider might thereby be made accountable for performance of the contract, overcoming the obstacles to consumer enforcement posed by the private law doctrine of privity.[88] The publication of service standards creates the potential for increased accountability in other ways, since failure to meet the promised standard provides a legitimate basis for criticism and complaint. Individual rights might serve thereby as a means both of securing redress for individual consumers whose reasonable expectations are not satisfied, and of structuring the exercise of discretionary power by those performing public functions.[89]

The representation of citizen and consumer interests in decision making on public services might be facilitated through the creation of legally guaranteed procedures.[90] The emphasis on proceduralization involves both accountability for performance, and establishing the regulatory conditions through which decision making can be more optimally and openly conducted. In the utilities sector, specific organs of consumer representation have been argued to be necessary due to the inability of the unregulated market to produce equitable and socially acceptable allocative outcomes.[91] Such representation is still more essential in the human

these responsibilities being negotiated in a binding agreement between the organisations concerned' – Harden (n 4 above) 77–78.

86 Harden's argument is brought together in his final chapter entitled 'Towards a constitutional framework for public services', 69.

87 ibid xi.

88 'Publication creates the possibility of legitimate expectations, but this is not yet a well developed area of law' – ibid 45. However, the scope for judicial development of the doctrine of legitimate expectations into a 'citizen's charter' for services provided through contract is considered limited. There remain also uncertainties regarding the scope of the doctrine, and whether it could give rise to substantive rather than procedural rights.

89 ibid 61.

90 On the analogous regulatory context of privatized utilities, see C Graham, *Regulating Public Utilities: A Constitutional Approach* (Oxford: Hart Publishing, 2000). 'If discretion is a necessary part of the regulatory task, then it is important that the regulator is able to "hear" the consumer voice', 89. While arrangements for consumer representation in the utilities sector may be seen as simply tokenistic, they are argued to have a broader significance 'as embryonic forms of a new proceduralism, regardless of the particular legal form taken', 105.

91 'In a perfect market consumer representation, in the sense of specific institutions, would be unnecessary. The consumer would have a choice of producers, no one producer would dominate the market, therefore consumers could respond to price and quality differences in the products and thereby send signals to the producers . . . The privatised utilities are far removed from the model of a perfect market, even though there are differences in the degree of competition existing within the various markets. Important decisions about the rules of the market, and indeed the extent of the

services context, where the decision-making role of the public purchasing agency appears particularly onerous and complex. The contractual organization of public services has the potential to increase the accountability of public agencies in decisions regarding the level of resources to be allocated to a particular service, and the standards of quality to be achieved.[92] There is a strong case for a judicially monitored public law procedural framework surrounding sites of demand decisions, including the allocation of resources and the setting of service priorities and standards.[93] We revisit the issue of procedural reform in Chapter 11.

Subsidiarity and local autonomy

The weakness of local government contracting powers compared to those enjoyed by central government has been noted at various points in the foregoing discussion. Local authorities as organizations are restricted in their activities in a much more fundamental sense than businesses.[94] Whereas the objectives and powers of the private corporation may be covered by wide objects clauses in standard memoranda and objects of incorporation, in local government the legal parameters are imposed by tightly drawn statutory powers and duties that cannot be changed by the authority itself.[95] Furthermore, under the UK constitution there is no protected core of local government safe from central interference. Given the wide range of public service functions performed by local councils and other public authorities not directly linked with central government, an obvious reform strategy might involve establishing local autonomy on firmer constitutional foundations.

In other words, there is a strong case for greater constitutional subsidiarity,[96] as envisaged in the European Charter on Local Self Government. The concept of 'local self-government' denotes 'the right and the ability of local authorities . . . to regulate and manage a substantial share of public affairs'.[97] The Charter stipulates that 'public responsibilities shall generally be exercised . . . by those authorities which are closest to the citizen',[98] and that 'administrative supervision of local authorities shall be exercised in such a way as to ensure that the intervention of

market, will be made, not by impersonal economic forces, but by the policy decisions or non-decisions of the regulators' – ibid 88.

92 ibid 63.

93 'In effect, this means creating a procedural alternative to ministerial responsibility and expertise as the basis for the legitimacy of public sector organizations making demand decisions' – Harden (n 4 above) 74.

94 While in company law 'the legal regime is concerned with procedural matters only, leaving the raison d'etre of the enterprise to those who control and own it, in local government the law governs both' – I Leigh, *Law, Politics and Local Democracy* (Oxford: Oxford University Press, 2000) 36.

95 ibid 38.

96 ND Lewis, *Law and Governance: The Old Meets the New* (London: Cavendish Publishing, 2001).

97 European Charter on Local Self-Government, art 3(1).

98 art 4(3).

the controlling authority is kept in proportion to the importance of the interests which it is intended to protect'.[99] Were the spirit of the Charter to be complied with, the position in Britain would be brought into line with the constitutional recognition of local government enjoyed in other countries. Such reform would enshrine the principle of pluralism within the state, and ensure a degree of financial and legal independence that would enable local authorities to experiment with different forms of organization and provision of public services. More generally, it would help counter the manifest distrust of representative democracy which underlies contemporary legislative and judicial developments and which the legal framework permits and encourages.

However, advocates of this position acknowledge both the political difficulties of reversing the long-term trend towards increasing centralization, and the problems that would inevitably be involved in defining precisely the boundaries of any new constitutional settlement.[100] The case for the central state having ultimate authority and control subject to proper democratic accountability is compelling. Central government has superior resources and better access to information in determining local issues, and is also in a position to coordinate reform on the basis of best local management practice among all authorities. Central controls over local taxation and expenditure are necessary in order to maintain international competitiveness and to pursue national economic and social policy goals. For these and other reasons there would be considerable difficulties in defining the minimum core of local government functions that should be constitutionally guaranteed. Such a guarantee might also carry the danger of preventing or impeding forms of centrally imposed reorganization necessary to deal with local authorities that had become unresponsive.[101]

A more modest reform strategy might be directed at increasing the legal powers of local authorities to the level necessary to enable them to discharge the ever-widening range of responsibilities with which they are being burdened by central government, including public contracting functions. As we have seen, the role of local authorities as community leaders and coordinators of partnership initiatives implies more discretion than councils currently enjoy.[102] While the debate continues regarding the creation of a power of general competence, and/or an overarching duty ('of quasi-constitutional significance') defining the mission and

99 art 8(3) stipulates that 'In strict legal terms the Government would be unlikely to have difficulty defending the new legislation against charges of breach of the Charter, given its vagueness and the margin of appreciation it permits.'

100 See Leigh (n 94 above) 38 (What are the quintessential local functions that should be guaranteed? What would there be to stop them being undermined by (for example) government sponsorship of parallel providers, rather than frontal attack? Should the powers be exclusive or concurrent with those of regional and central government?)

101 'A constitutional provision which prevented, for example, a future reorganization of a form of local government which because of social changes had become unresponsive would be a mixed blessing' – ibid 32. 'We must not be starry-eyed about local government' – M Loughlin, *Legality and Locality: The Role of Law in Central-Local Government Relations* (Oxford: Clarendon Press, 1996) 380.

102 ibid 346.

purpose of local government,[103] such reform also would pose a fundamental challenge to the present balance of power in central-local relations which is likely to be strongly resisted by Whitehall.

A 'public law contract'?

Some constitutional theorists have further argued that a 'public law contract' is needed to help secure the organizational independence of purchasers and providers across the whole range of internal and external public contracting relationships. On analogy with the doctrine of the separation of powers of legislative, executive, and judicial branches within the state, the public law contract would serve as a constitutional framework guaranteeing the separation of purchaser and provider functions, so helping to combat the 'failures and the evasions of ministerial responsibility'.[104] Establishing the purchaser/provider relationship on solid constitutional foundations would limit the potential for abuse of discretion in the exercise of powers in relation to public services. In the case of a primary contract this goal might be achieved by turning the obligations of the service provider into legally enforceable entitlements of individuals. However, 'to create a public constitutional dimension for a secondary contract between public sector bodies means confining and structuring ministerial responsibility and finding a new basis for legitimate authority in the space thus created'.[105]

The case for a special public law of contract is asserted particularly strongly in relation to internal contracts.[106] Davies argues that the effectiveness of these contracts is presently compromised by the lack of legal enforceability at private law, and by the absence of structural conditions (competition, economic incentives) that would encourage compliance and provide informal sanctions for breach of

[103] The absence of sufficient powers has been argued to be particularly serious in the light of the 'communitarian twist' that New Labour has given the original Conservative idea of the 'enabling council', involving the imposition of new responsibilities for community leadership and coordination – Leigh (n 94 above) 61.

[104] Lewis (n 96 above) 140–1 (Evidence to the Treasury and Civil Service Committee on the Role of the Civil Service, Session 1993-4, HC 27-1, HMSO, Vol 11, p.173).

[105] Harden (n 4 above) 35–36. The problem identified by Harden in internal government contracts is the lack of organizational independence between purchaser and provider. Once responsibility for deciding what services there should be has been separated from responsibilities for delivering those services, the relationship between the separate public entities should be negotiated in a binding agreement. Private law is not suited to this task primarily because the parties are prevented from making enforceable contracts due the absence of separate legal personalities. But even were they able to do so (as with contracts with external bodies) the 'default constitution' of the private law of contract could be used (either in collusion or by pressure exerted by the dominant party) to revise whatever private constitution they have agreed, contrary to the public interest. 'To have legal validity, organizational independence in the public sector must originate in public law' – ibid 75. Harden advocates a general public law contract, modelled on a revised form of 'NHS Contract'.

[106] Davies (n 1 above) 11. Internal contracts are here defined as 'agreements between two public bodies in which one undertakes to perform specified activities in return for a budget supplied by the other.'

contract. Furthermore, contrary to the government's rhetoric of citizen empowerment and increased responsiveness to consumer needs, the law has failed to protect the public interest in participation and involvement in these arrangements. Public law reform would compensate for these weaknesses and address two associated problems: the inadequate protection of the provider against unwarranted interference by the purchaser, and the inability of the purchaser to enforce the contract and to hold the provider to account for performance.[107] The core argument is that the quality of decision making, and of regulation and accountability, would be improved if internal contracts were governed by a public law framework embodying natural justice norms, applied if necessary in an internal enforcement and dispute resolution forum or 'arbitral tribunal'.[108] In short, a public law of internal contracts would make contractualization policies more successful.[109]

The main difficulty with this argument in favour of a public law contract is how to determine precisely the circumstances in which it would be applicable. Firstly, in the case of contracts with external bodies enforceable at private law, Harden argues that the special law should apply wherever a shared 'public service mission' renders this governance structure appropriate as a means of constitutionalizing the relationship, for example imposing a wider range of good faith duties than usually apply in public procurement. Such a common interest might be found in various types of contractual relationship between public purchasers and private, voluntary and non-profit organizations. Many of the partnership or partnering arrangements being created in pursuance of current government policy on PPPs might be considered as falling into this category. However, contracts with commercial firms would normally be quite satisfactorily governed by the ordinary law of contract. The public law contract would not be appropriate in such cases due to the absence of shared values and purposes. In particular, 'a public law contract ... is clearly not compatible with competitive tendering'.[110] The problem with this analysis is that competition is at the heart of economic contracting regimes, and is not considered by policy makers to be inconsistent or incompatible with the notion of partnership and a shared public service mission.

Secondly, with regard to internal contracts, the argument in favour of a public law contract fails to distinguish between different internal contracting arrangements,[111] insisting that that internal contracts may be treated as a coherent category due to common features of unenforceability, lack of organizational separateness, and absence of choice.[112] In relation to Next Steps agencies, for example, Harden

107 ibid 52–3. 108 ibid 70. 109 ibid 185. 110 Harden (n 4 above) 76.

111 For a critique of Davies' argument that internal contracts can be treated as a coherent category, regulated by an 'Internal Contracts Act' (n 1 above, 206) see P Vincent-Jones, 'Regulating Government by Contract: Towards a Public Law Framework?' (2002) 65 MLR 611.

112 The significant differences in the NHS, Next Steps, and local government settings are acknowledged – Davies (n 1 above) 42–46. Nevertheless, it is the similarities that are stressed. Internal contracts are said to have three common (and unusual) features: they are not legally enforceable; they take place between organizations which need not be formally separate; and they do not necessarily

states: 'there is a split between departments and agencies *like that between* a local authority and its DSOs, or between a DHA and NHS provider'.[113] However, while acknowledging certain similarities, I have argued that there are significant differences in the role of contract as a mechanism of economic organization and administrative restructuring, and in the functions of the variants within the main forms of the New Public Contracting. The contractual arrangements are not directly comparable. Some are best considered as administrative contracts, others as economic contracts. Furthermore, the focus on individual accountability and liability,[114] implicit in the notion that the special law might be applied to all internal contracts, may be inappropriate in addressing problems of defective performance in many public service settings. Economic contracts are fundamentally about the coordination of the resources needed to produce or co-produce efficient and effective public services. The adoption of a relatively narrow and exclusive accountability perspective may tend to distort the common purpose of improving public services and rectifying problems, for which the parties are often jointly responsible. Internal contracts might better be analysed by focusing on how traditional institutions of accountability operate in conjunction with more indirect mechanisms and processes as part of a complex system of checks and balances that serves to inhibit or encourage particular forms of behaviour. In this 'extended accountability' perspective, accountability processes are not directly 'programmable' with the legal norms (fairness, legality, rationality, and so on) recognized by public lawyers.[115]

Hybrid approaches

Limits of private law

From a private law perspective, a different strategy for securing the increased accountability of contractors for the exercise of 'public' power is through the creation of private rights on the part of consumers and other affected members

result from freely given promises in competitive markets. These common features make it appropriate to consider internal contracts together for the purposes of research and reform – ibid 46.

113 Harden (n 4 above) 28 (emphasis supplied).

114 'It is a basic principle of our legal system that judgments of liability should be made only after a full investigation of the relevant evidence, during which the 'accused' should be given an opportunity to refute allegations being made against him or her. Hence one requirement of a good accountability process is observance of principles of natural justice' – Davies (n 1 above) 86.

115 C Scott, 'Accountability in the Regulatory State' (2000) 27 JLS 38, 59. The aim is not to judge accountability outcomes in 'negative' or 'positive' terms, but to analyse how strategic interventions, through the shifting of balances, might be made in order to correct a system which is malfunctioning. One accountability resource that may be drawn upon in such strategic interventions is 'redundancy'. This describes a situation in which 'overlapping (and ostensibly superfluous) accountability mechanisms reduce the centrality of any one of them', 52. This perspective might be applied in assessing the issues of duplication and reinforcement of contractual accountability referred to by Davies.

of the community.[116] This approach suggests that the administrative law goals of increasing public accountability and participation may be achieved by means other than public law.[117] For example, in addition to providing enforceable substantive rights to certain standards of service, contract may also be the basis of procedural protection in the form of duties of fairness, considerate decision making and good faith.[118] However, we have seen that the fundamental problem with this avenue of redress is the absence of a contractual relationship between service recipient and provider.[119] The purchaser-provider contract may contain terms and conditions in respect of the nature and quality of service delivery, but the consumer is denied access to the courts for redress for poor performance or dispute resolution.[120]

The uncertainty and inconvenience associated with the doctrine of privity in commercial business relationships are well known. If the doctrine can be challenged and a coherent alternative suggested in the ordinary commercial context, for example in cases involving building contracts and carriage contracts, then such principles might certainly be expected to apply in quasi-market organization. Adams and Brownsword have argued that restrictive rules of privity should not apply to linked commercial contracts that in effect comprise a 'network', defined as 'a group of contracts which have collectively as their object the attainment of a common underlying purpose . . . in which each contract in the group contributes in some way towards the achievement of that purpose'.[121] Applying this line of argument in the quasi-market context, the consumer would be able

116 M Allars, 'Private Law But Public Power: Removing Administrative Law Review From Government Business Enterprises' (1995) 6 *Public Law Review* 44; ibid, 'Citizenship Rights, Review Rights and Contractualism' (2001) 18 *Law in Context* 79.

117 While public law and private law have different starting points rooted in the primacy of 'other-regarding' or 'self-regarding' behaviour respectively, the results of private law analysis may approximate to those derived those derived from administrative law – M Taggart, 'The Province of Administrative Law Determined?' in M Taggart, (ed), *The Province of Administrative Law* (Oxford: Hart Publishing, 1997) 5.

118 The potential flexibility of the common law in implying a term of fair dealing into all contracts is illustrated by the Australian case of *Hughes Aircraft Systems International v Airservices Australia* (1997) 146 ALR 1 (where the term was implied in a pre-award contract involving a commercial tender). In the US the courts have similarly been eager to 'proceduralize' private relationships by importing public law due process norms into contracts – see Freeman (n 34 above) 589. However, such developments are of limited significance for the user-provider relationship in quasi-market organization, since in this instance there is no contract into which a term may be implied.

119 See n 25 above.

120 Where the public purchaser can be persuaded to sue on the consumer's behalf, the problem with a damages claim would normally be proving loss to the government, in cases where the harm had in fact been done to the citizen – Seddon (n 11 above) 34.

121 J Adams and R Brownsword, 'Privity and the Concept of a Network Contract' (1990) 10 *Legal Studies* 12. The main objective of relaxing the privity rule would be to allow a third party to take the benefit of a contract to which she was not party. A legal framework could be provided for dealing with disputes between contractors in the network, with the parties being held to the obligations and the allocations of risk as contained in the various contracts comprising the network (36); see also ibid, 'Contract, Consideration and the Critical Path' (1990) 53 MLR 536.

to sue either the public purchaser or the private provider to enforce the terms of the contract between them, while either principal party might be able to rely on contract in response to the consumer's action.[122]

A related attempt to circumvent the privity rule involves the argument that all the parties with stakes or interests in a given public service should be regarded as linked by virtue of their membership of a 'complex economic organization'. Such membership would have significant implications for the purposes of both ascribing legal responsibility and determining the boundaries of contractual liability in private law.[123] Economic contracting regimes might be regarded as giving rise to such complex organizational forms, entailing the creation and maintenance of definite relationships between purchasers, providers, and consumers for the furtherance of particular policy purposes, and implying the existence of legal rights enforceable by service recipients against the principal contracting parties.[124] The question arises whether responsibilities may be ascribed to the parties engaged in the provision of public services in quasi-markets in the same manner as Collins argues in relation to liability in tort on the part of corporate bodies forming complex economic organizations in the business sector.[125] What is important for present purposes are the rights of consumers in relation to both public purchasing agencies and service providers, regardless of the absence of any direct contractual link and of the public or private identity of the service provider.

In the UK the Contracts (Rights of Third Parties) Act 1999 provides a statutory exception to the doctrine of privity.[126] The benefit of such measures may, however, be limited in practice. Remedies may not be available to a person affected by the actions of the service provider, but who is not currently a service recipient. Assuming that a contractual claim against the service provider can be established in principle, liability depends on the terms of the contract, and on the prior willingness and ability of the purchaser to include terms that protect the consumer interest. Even where service standards and the provider's obligations have been adequately specified in the contract, the consumer may face formidable obstacles in finding out that information, or in gaining access to contractual documentation. This court-based remedy suffers from disincentives to enforcement associated

122 The situation is less complex than in the commercial setting, where none of the parties is in a position akin to that of the consumer of public services, and there are more permutations in the combinations of possible plaintiffs and defendants – ibid (10 *Legal Studies* 12) 28.

123 H Collins, 'Ascription of Legal Responsibility to Groups in Complex Patterns of Economic Integration' (1990) 53 MLR 731, 744.

124 See ch 5, above.

125 Collins distinguishes three forms of bond tying together companies with distinct legal personalities: ownership, contract, and authority – (n 123 above). While authority relations may be hard to pin down in the corporate governance context of parent holding companies with multiple subsidiaries, such relations are relatively easy to establish in quasi-market organization

126 See Law Commission *Privity of Contract: Contracts for the Benefit of Third Parties* (Law Com No 242, 1996); E Palmer, 'Residential Care: Rights of the Elderly and the Contracts (Rights of Third Parties) Act 1999' (2000) 22 *Journal of Social Welfare and Family Law* 461.

with the disproportionate expense and time involved in pursuing legal action, particularly given the relatively small size of many claims. If the prospect of private law actions to enforce breaches of contract is remote, incentives to perform fairly and efficiently may be lacking. Private law might, under certain conditions, provide redress in the form of compensation for non-performance or poor quality in service delivery, but it is unlikely to serve as a substitute for administrative law in upholding 'public' values and controlling the exercise of power in decision-making processes.[127]

Whatever the merits of the argument as to the inherent responsiveness of the private law of contract as a regulatory mechanism,[128] its potential in the governance of complex public services appears limited. As has been seen, quasi-market organization involves a tripartite relationship between service recipients, contractors and public purchasers. Even assuming the construction of a legal nexus between service recipient and contractor, for example through relaxation of the privity rule, the advantages claimed for private law regulation in standard-setting, monitoring and enforcement presumably could not apply in the absence of consumer engagement in these contracting activities.[129] This leaves open the question of whether such involvement is practicable in quasi-market organization, or whether responsiveness in this sense is dependent on a more direct market relationship between consumers and service providers.[130]

In the law of tort, legislation would be required for the public agency to be vicariously liable for the actions or omissions of the service provider, since under common law the provider in the vast majority of cases is an independent contractor rather than agent of the authority.[131] Were this option to be adopted, the public body would in effect accept liability on the basis that the contractor was acting as its agent, and then seek redress from the contractor under the terms of the

127 cf Freeman (n 34 above) 590. Even assuming the standards imposed in private law actions become more demanding, 'their chances of achieving a public law resolution in private law seem slim'. The parties might also minimize or avoid new obligations by contracting out of them.

128 H Collins, *Regulating Contracts* (Oxford: Oxford University Press, 1999).

129 ibid 56–93.

130 In purely private markets for services such as social and residential care, there remain however significant problems of market structure. Consumers have limited capacity to articulate demands and assert their interests. In the empirical research study reported by Ryan, 'market mechanisms were considered to be particularly imperfect in situations where proprietors were able to persuade, influence or even intimidate their clients' – N Ryan, 'The Competitive Delivery of Social Services: Implications for Program Implementation' (1995) 54 *Australian Journal of Public Administration* 353, 355.

131 For an argument in favour of vicarious liability as a reform strategy, see N Seddon, 'Commentary: Privatisation and Contracting Out – Where are We Going?' in J McMillan, (ed), *Administrative Law Under the Coalition Government* (Canberra: AIAL, 1997): 'Why should the government not be responsible for what contractors do? This of course requires an agency relationship between the government and the contractor, the latter simply being an extension of the government for the purpose of achieving some public purpose. Yet, the common practice in government contracts is to ensure by a suitably drawn clause that the contractor is *not* an agent of the government', 150.

head contract.[132] This option would have the benefit of convenience for the individual consumer. However, there would be additional costs for the public agency in administering the contractual relationship with the service provider, whose incentive to efficient and fair administration and to developing adequate internal complaints mechanisms might thereby be weakened. The economic benefits of more direct responsibility for harms caused would not be achieved.

Transcending the public/private divide

Rather than seeking to extend the ambit of private or administrative law, a different reform strategy challenges the assumption that the problems associated with the blurring of public and private spheres can be addressed through doctrinal clarification or development within either branch of law.[133] The attempt here is to transcend artificial limits associated with the public/private distinction.[134] The traditional dichotomy is regarded as no longer helpful in constructing the key tasks of administrative law. Rather, regulatory reforms that rely on the private sector and market incentives represent 'the beginnings of a new model of administrative law in which the line between the public and private is no longer distinct'.[135] The necessary co-existence of public and private elements in modern public service organization is reflected in notions of 'hybridity', 'mixed administration', and the sharing of regulatory roles among various actors in government and the non-state sectors.[136]

One example of this type of hybrid analysis discerns in modern public service organization the evolution of a 'third sector' distinct from the public and private sectors.[137] The third sector is:

> . . . the sector of the economy in which services or activities, recognized as public in the sense that the State is seen as ultimately responsible for the provision of them, are nevertheless not provided by the State itself but by institutions which are intermediate between the market and the State. These institutions are, on the one hand, too independent of the State to be regarded as part of the State, but are, on the other hand, too closely and distinctively

[132] Seddon (n 11 above) 34. A contract term might be included stipulating that damages could be recovered on breach measured by the loss suffered by the citizen.

[133] There should be 'clear criteria for identifying the kinds of official decision that are subject to public law and a clear division in a modern state as to what constitutes the "public" and the "private" realm' – Woolf and Jowell (n 48 above) 163.

[134] Aman's analysis of the prospects for regulatory reform views contemporary developments such as contractualisation and corporatisation as novel forms of arrangement that transcend the simple public/private dichotomy – (n 82 above).

[135] ibid 116.

[136] Aronson (n 59 above) 52–53.

[137] This is considered to justify the conception of legal governance in terms of a distinctive body of public services law based on notions of citizenship – M Freedland, 'Law, Public Services, and Citizenship – New Domains, New Regimes?' in M Freedland and S Sciarra, (eds), *Public Services and Citizenship in European Law – Public and Labour Law Perspectives* (Oxford: Oxford University Press, 1998) 2.

associated with the goals, activities and responsibilities of the State to be thought of as simply part of the private sector of the political economy.[138]

Oliver has contested the contemporary significance of the public/private divide in other terms, suggesting that the common law should require powerful bodies to act fairly and with due regard to individual interests and the public interest irrespective of whether the power they exercise lies in public or private hands.[139] The emphasis here is on the underlying 'common values', notably autonomy, dignity, respect, status, and security, that operate increasingly across both private and public law. While the movement in the direction of these values may clearly be seen in employment, family and welfare law, the trend can also be observed in contract, for example in the increased protection of security and status through the development of concepts of legitimate expectations and reliance interests.[140] Rather than denying the differences between public and private bodies, this analysis challenges the significance of such differences for the issue of legal governance.[141]

Similarly, a direct legal relationship between the private service provider and citizen or consumer might be constructed on the basis of obligations in respect of essential public services. In this view, the fact that administrative law has usurped many of the functions of control of what happens in the public sphere does not mean that the common law might not be developed or adapted in this direction. Three inter-related but distinct doctrines can be traced in the common law requiring certain services to be provided to the public at reasonable prices and without discrimination: the law relating to common callings, the law regulating monopolies in the public interest, and the doctrine of 'prime necessities'. While

138 ibid 3. The continued regulatory role of the state in respect of privatized functions is explained in terms of the partial or incomplete nature of transfers to the private sector, 'leaving the activity in question perched between the public and private sectors in a genuinely distinctive situation, which should be regarded as constitutionally a third sector', 4.

139 There is a 'developing common law right of those seriously affected by decisions taken by powerful bodies to have the effects of a decision on them considered and taken into account fairly and rationally before a decision is made' – D Oliver, 'Common Values in Public and Private Law and the Public/Private Divide' [1997] PL 630, 638. See also C Harlow, '"Public" and "Private" Law: Definition Without Distinction' (1980) 43 MLR 240.

140 D Oliver, 'The Underlying Values of Public and Private Law' in M Taggart, (ed), *The Province of Administrative Law* (Oxford: Hart Publishing, 1997) 233–239. Oliver has argued that the 'supervisory jurisdiction' of the courts, by which is meant the imposition of duties of legality, fairness and rationality, or more generally 'principles of good administration', can be grounded in private law: in contract through the presumed intentions of the parties, or in the law of trusts through the duties imposed on trustees and derived from the presumed intentions of the settlor – (n 139 above) 631–632.

141 Both public law and private law are argued to be concerned with the control of power and with the protection of individuals against abuses of power, and with upholding common values of respect for the interests of individuals. Both are concerned with standards of considerate action and decision-making, and with balancing this quality against the need to uphold authority and protect the interests of good administration – Oliver (1999), (n 67 above) 11. However, the differences between private law and administrative law doctrine in other respects should be emphasized – see J McLean, 'The Crown in Contract and Administrative Law' (2004) 24 OJLS 129.

the latter two became the basis of American public utilities law in the nineteenth century, in Britain these bodies of law became progressively marginalized as the regulatory role was assumed by the legislature. Only after the privatization of the public utilities in the 1980s has public utility law begun to develop in the direction of recognizing duties in respect of essential public services.[142] This strategy avoids the public/private dichotomy, or more precisely, the issue of classifying law as public or private.[143] On the other hand, it is vulnerable to criticism on the ground that it is unhelpfully antiquarian. While of theoretical interest, there are significant practical obstacles to the rediscovery of common law powers based on essential service obligations in common law jurisdictions.[144]

All these critiques serve to highlight the partial and limited nature of public law reform strategies built simply around extending the scope of administrative law controls such as judicial review. Such strategies, in addition to posing all sorts of doctrinal and practical difficulties, may be fundamentally flawed. Indeed, the crisis that has afflicted public law doctrine as a result of contractualization and privatization may be argued to lie precisely in the failure of traditional legal analysis to recognize the true nature of the evolution of public service organization, and its significance for the public/private divide.[145] The pressing need is for legal doctrine and legal reasoning to take adequate account of what is primarily an economic and political development.[146] Public law needs to redefine itself in relation to the public service sector 'if it is to resist the highly sophisticated project of transferring that sector largely into the domain of private law'.[147] The emphasis in hybrid approaches on the breakdown and incoherence of the separation of public and private, of state and civil society, appears fully consistent with the governmentality approach indicated in Chapter 3. It is consistent also with the long-standing acknowledgement by commentators in the United States of the 'shared' nature of government power, and of the significance of contract in its exercise.[148]

[142] Taggart (n 117 above) 7; T Prosser, 'Public Service Law: Privatization's Unexpected Offspring' (2000) 63 *Law and Contemporary Problems* 63.

[143] Taggart suggests, for example, that there is no good reason (given the argued artificiality of the public/private divide) why the civil law 'abuse of rights' doctrine might not ultimately be developed in the English common law context. 'This French-inspired doctrine is widely accepted in civil law countries and the Canadian civil law Province of Quebec, and basically prevents a right-holder abusing the right by exercising it for the sole purpose of harming another or for a purpose other than that for which it was granted or in an unreasonably disproportionate fashion.' By contrast, the common law has refused to 'investigate the motives or reasons for the exercise of lawful powers by private individuals or corporations, no matter how discriminatory or harmful to the public interest' – ibid 16.

[144] Aronson disagrees particularly with the idea of a common law power to set a reasonable price, arguing that the recognized difficulties in this function (determining the value of assets, return on capital, level of investment in infrastructure) make it much better suited to performance by a regulatory agency with a specific remit – Aronson (n 59 above) 48–51.

[145] Freedland (n 137 above) 6. [146] ibid 3. [147] ibid 11.

[148] D Kettl, *Sharing Power: Public Governance and Private Markets* (Washington DC: The Brookings Institution, 1993).

Services of general interest in EU law

In contemporary European debates the notion of rights in respect of essential services is strongly associated with the increasing influence of EU law in the telecommunications and utilities sectors.[149] More generally, the term 'services of general interest' (SGI) has been adopted in recent European Commission policy statements as a vehicle for the encouragement of further political and economic integration. The Communication of September 1996 on *Services of General Interest in Europe* has been described as 'in effect the White Paper or definitive policy document for the development of a Community public service sector, or services of general interest sector'.[150] The core values of the EU are said to include access for all members of society to universal services of general benefit that contribute to social solidarity, equality of treatment, and European citizenship. Continental jurisprudence may be regarded as useful in helping to provide a 'framework within which issues of how to develop principles of public service can be debated'.[151]

While it is clear that the ambit of any SGI regime will extend to private businesses as well as public bodies, there is less certainty over the range of economic activity that might come within the definition of a service of general interest.[152] Obviously included are the telecommunications and postal service sectors, which have traditionally been regarded as involving universal service obligations. Other sectors identified in the 1996 Communication were transport, electricity, and broadcasting. However, the more complex the service and the less obviously it may be regarded as an essential component of modern daily living, the harder the task of justifying its special treatment in terms of minimum standards governing the citizen-provider relationship. In quasi-markets for human services the existence of multiple relationships poses particular difficulties. The services are not natural monopolies, although the supplier may have won the exclusive right to perform the function for a specified period (competition for the market rather than in the market) through a franchise or contracting out following competitive tendering. Assuming the existence of a legal basis to the relationship between the citizen and service provider, it is difficult to see how human services could be brought within the realm of essential services in the same manner as say the utilities and telecommunications.

149 W Sauter, 'Universal Service Obligations and the Emergence of Citizens' Rights in European Telecommunications Liberalization' in M Freedland and S Sciarra, (eds), *Public Services and Citizenship in European Law – Public and Labour Law Perspectives* (Oxford: Oxford University Press, 1998).

150 Freedland (n 137 above) 15 – referring to COM(96)443, 11 Sept. 1996. For more recent Green and White Papers on Services of General Interest, see respectively COM(2003)270, 21 May 2003; COM(2004)374, 12 May 2004.

151 T Prosser, *Law and the Regulators* (Oxford: Clarendon Press, 1997) 292.

152 Freedland (n 137 above) 16.

Then there is the question of the content of the duties/rights that attach to the function of providing public services:

> The rules widely accepted among legal scholars as being common to all public services consist in the trinity of continuity, equality, and constant adaptation (or adaptability and adjustment in step with technical progress). In other words, functions of general interest must be provided uninterruptedly, over the whole of the geographical area concerned, to all users at uniform prices and must comply with standards of quantity and quality that are regulated by the public administration. However, although it may be true that these rules apply to all public services, *it is equally true that the degree to which they apply is not uniform.*[153]

This depends on the characteristics of the public goods provided – whether they are 'essential' or 'complementary', and whether they address 'special needs' or 'general needs'.[154] The question then is in what sense such 'rules' may be said to apply in the context of quasi-market contracting for human services, and with what implications and effects on the provider-user relationship. This is the crucial point at which the circumstances of provision of services in the utilities and human service sectors need to be distinguished. The scope of application of the concept of 'services of general interest', and the precise definition of the 'public service sector' remain uncertain. Where should the line be drawn, and on what basis, between public utilities and other services that may be argued to be necessary for economic and social wellbeing?

Nevertheless, the developing law and practice on public services in the EU has provided a significant impetus to debates emphasizing various hybrid aspects of contemporary legal governance:

> It is in Continental systems, diffused through the organs of the European Union, that answers to the problems created by contemporary downsizing and downloading of the public service will have to be found. In this way, public law can renew the cycle by *recolonizing private law.*[155]

Again, the significance of the possible construction of a 'European conception of contract' is that 'it cuts across the traditional continental division between private and public law, by applying its requirements of fairness and transparency to an important class of public contracts, the supply of public services to consumers'.[156] Whittaker, like Harlow, argues that such a conception would not be just a matter of private law, 'rather it would straddle the private/public divide, recognizing the role of public participants in the modern market ... and the importance of

[153] ibid 68 (emphasis supplied). [154] ibid 81.

[155] For Harlow, it is *private law*, albeit in some hybrid form, that is regarded as offering an escape route from the inadequacies of administrative law doctrines and the 'malaise of complex administrative regulation' – C Harlow, 'Public Service, Market Ideology, and Citizenship' in M Freedland and S Sciarra, (eds), *Public Services and Citizenship in European Law – Public and Labour Law Perspectives* (Oxford: Oxford University Press, 1998) 54.

[156] S Whittaker, 'Unfair Contract Terms, Public Services and the Construction of a European Conception of Contract' (2000) 116 LQR 95, 120.

the regulation of that market in the interests of consumers'. Hence the effect of EU regulation through Directives aimed at harmonizing aspects of contract law is not confined to the realm of the private, since lying at the heart of such measures is a judicial power to review the terms on which contracts are made – 'and judicial power to review administrative decisions is central to traditional concerns of public law'.[157] This supports Harlow's implicit suggestion that a 'public law of contract' may emerge indirectly through the impact of EU Directives informed by Continental public services jurisprudence.

Conclusion

This brief review might be expected to conclude that a mix of strategies is needed to address the legal governance deficits currently posed by privatization and contractualization.[158] However, a smorgasbord approach to reform is likely to generate confusion and incoherence. While some of the foregoing proposals might be regarded as complementary, others are alternatives or appear mutually contradictory. A more discriminating, theoretically coherent, and overarching approach is called for in dealing with the problems currently confronting the common law. The public/private divide no longer empirically reflects the reality of modern governance.[159] Doctrinal difficulties are a reflection of fundamental transformations in economic and social relations and of the intermingling of the public and private sectors in new ways, expressed in the essentially hybrid character of contemporary public service organization. A hybrid reform strategy, rather than one that attempts just to extend or develop private or public law in any particular direction, is most likely to be successful in addressing accountability deficits.

While administrative law has not ignored the interests of persons affected by administrative decisions, the principal concern is with the creation of a set of

157 ibid. EU regulation may itself be regarded as a type of 'hybrid', transcending the public/private categorization.

158 In an exhaustive review of the law governing contracting out in Australia, the Administrative Review Council concluded that the preservation of government accountability and avenues of redress for aggrieved individuals could be achieved through a 'mix' of public and private law mechanisms – Administrative Review Council, *The Contracting Out of Government Services*, Report No 42 (Canberra: Commonwealth of Australia, 1998). In the UK, there has been no such comprehensive review of the problems of reduced public accountability and individual legal redress associated with contracting out. However, the recommendation of so many individual reforms, including extension of the entire 'administrative law package' to private contractors, appears unrealistic and lacking in overall coherence – A Tang, 'The Changing Role of Government in Community Services: Issues of Access and Equity in Administrative Review' (1997) 56 *Australian Journal of Public Administration* 95.

159 Freedland (n 137 above); G Airo-Farulla, 'Public and Private in Australian Administrative Law' (1992) 3 *Public Law Review* 186; ibid, 'Administrative Law and "Governance"' in C Finn, (ed), *Sunrise or Sunset? Administrative Law in the New Millennium* (Canberra: Australian Institute of Administrative Law, 2000); Freeman (n 34 above).

'principles of good administration' which administrators are required by the courts to obey.[160] On the other hand, while the protection of individual interests at private law may be regarded as including duties of natural justice and fairness that mimic those applied in judicial review, this appears clumsy and awkward as a way of controlling the exercise of administrative powers.[161] A more satisfactory approach may be to think across traditional legal boundaries and consider hybrid solutions combining elements of public and private law. As we have seen seen, regulatory developments at EU level may appropriately be conceived and analysed in hybrid terms. In the UK, the regulation of the liberalized utilities markets involves hybrid elements,[162] while one of the effects of litigation accompanying market liberalization in the telecommunications sector is arguably the emergence of a hybrid contractual form that combines characteristics of private and public law.[163] Other common law jurisdictions may be further advanced than Britain in acknowledging the potential for hybrid solutions to legal governance problems posed by privatization and contractualization. In Australia, for example, the courts have already recognized hybridity in the nature of obligations owed by public bodies to prospective tenderers in the tendering process,[164] and debates on legal reform generally have adverted specifically to the potential of hybrid combinations of contractual and administrative law devices in increasing accountability to consumers of public services.[165]

More than simply transcending the doctrinal public/private distinction, however, the concept of hybrid regulation implies the combination of formal law and legal procedures with more informal institutional processes that operate within all organizations, private as well as public, engaged in the performance of public

160 Elliott (n 45 above) 17. 161 ibid 187.

162 J Black, 'Reviewing Regulatory Rules: Responding to Hybridisation' in J Black, P Muchlinski, and P Walker, *Commercial Regulation and Judicial Review* (Oxford: Hart Publishing, 1998) 123.

163 ibid; C Scott, 'The Juridification of Regulatory Relations in the UK Utilities Sector' in J Black, P Muchlinski, and P Walker, (eds), *Commercial Regulation and Judicial Review* (Oxford: Hart Publishing, 1998).

164 Finn J's judgment in *Hughes* specifically refers to the interpenetration of private and public law – see *Hughes Aircraft Systems International v Airservices Australia* (1997) 146 ALR 1, 25. The case is generally regarded as significant in forging a new kind of relationship between administrative law and contract law – see M Allars, 'The Commercialisation of Administrative Law' in S Kneebone, (ed) *Administrative Law and the Rule of Law: Still Part of the Same Package?* (Canberra: Australian Institute of Administrative Law, 1999) 167.

165 There are hybrid elements in the ARC report's acknowledgement of the benefits of the blending of public and private law in some recommendations. For example, agencies should ensure under the terms of the contract (a private law device) that any decision taken by a merits review tribunal in respect of the contractor's function (as required by public law) should be binding on the contractor. The resulting remedy might be more flexible than a simple public law duty imposed on the contractor in all cases. The argument in favour of a simple and inexpensive system for awarding compensation to citizens aggrieved by improper administrative action, including abuse of discretion and denial of natural justice, may be regarded as blending elements of public and private law – see H Whitmore, 'Administrative Law Reform: A Personal Recollection' (2001) 8 *Australian Journal of Administrative Law* 144.

service functions. In the next chapter, I will argue that the goal of legal regulation should be to facilitate, within all such bodies, the development of public service values, processes, and principles of good administration, including mechanisms for the redress of grievances of individuals with interests or stakes in the public services in question.

11

Law and Contractual Governance

This chapter begins by considering how the reform of legal procedures might contribute to increased responsiveness by controlling the pace and extent of contractualization in contemporary Britain. I will argue that a major role for responsive law should be to structure the exercise of discretion by ministers and officials in respect of both general policy and its implementation by public agencies in particular instances. The availability of information at all levels of decision making on public contracting is an essential element of proceduralization. The disclosure of information should serve to promote transparency and facilitate public deliberation. Lack of democratic involvement and public participation is likely to have a negative impact on the quality of decision making, increasing the risk of inappropriate choice of mode of organization and of regulatory instrument.

The remainder of the chapter provides a critical analysis of the legal frameworks governing the various relationships comprising the three main forms of the New Public Contracting, once the decision has been taken to organize the public service function on a contractual basis. The purpose here is to explore how legal reform might help increase effectiveness and fairness through the strengthening of contractual institutions. The final section on the governance of economic contracts shows how a hybrid reform strategy might contribute to increased responsiveness through the development of remedial hierarchies in public, private, and voluntary sector organizations engaged in public service networks. .

Contractualization

'Contractualization' refers to the process of transition from the direct performance of public service functions by the state towards more decentralized forms of organization entailing economic contracts, administrative contracts, and social control contracts. This process includes both the development of general policy on the New Public Contracting at the highest levels within government, and lower level decision making by public officials charged with implementing such policy in particular instances. My basic argument is that the responsiveness of contracting regimes is dependent on the provision of maximum opportunity for public deliberation and debate over the merits of various forms of government action. This requires more accessible, equitable, and democratic administrative procedures; greater freedom of information; and greater inclusiveness across a wide range of decision making processes.[1]

Proceduralization: regulating regulation

For advocates of proceduralization, what is required in the policy process generally is 'a commitment to procedural formality, to openness and transparency, to the disclosure of information, and to the need for explanation for and justification of the course chosen'.[2] Proceduralization is built on an acknowledgement of the limits of public law and of court-based proceedings as a means both of calling to account,[3] and of facilitating the effective and efficient organization of public services.[4] In contrast with the protection of the substantive rights of individuals by the legal framework, proceduralism is directed at 'offloading some of the weight of social regulation from the legal system to other social actors ... Rather than detailed pronouncements of acceptable behaviour, the law adopts procedures for regulated entities to follow.'[5] The 'regulated entities' to which procedures apply include government and other public bodies engaged in developing and implementing policy on public services. Proceduralization may thus serve as a means of regulating regulatory processes themselves, through the application of norms of conduct governing rule-making and other regulatory activities at all levels of government and public administration.[6]

As we have seen in the discussion of the democratic elements of responsiveness in Chapter 3, modern constitutional theorists in the Habermasian tradition have rejected the idea that procedures should serve merely to provide opportunities for the representation of views and interests of different constituencies in the

[1] The design and implementation of purposive programmes should 'serve democracy and engage participation' – S Rathgeb Smith and H Ingram, 'Policy Tools and Democracy' in LM Salamon, (ed), *The Tools of Government: A Guide to the New Governance* (Oxford: Oxford University Press, 2002).

[2] DJ Galligan, *Due Process and Fair Procedures: A Study of Administrative Procedures* (Oxford: Clarendon Press, 1996) 482; ibid, 'Procedural Rights in Social Welfare' in A Coote, (ed), *The Welfare of Citizens – Developing New Social Rights* (London: IPPR, 1992) 55.

[3] J Black, 'Decentring Regulation: The Role of Regulation and Self-Regulation in a "Post-Regulatory" World' (2001) CLP 103.

[4] Administrative law exerts relatively little control over the reasons and motives behind policy development and decision making on public contracting. For example, the rules on improper purpose and irrelevant considerations are limited in scope and operate 'after the event', whereas proceduralization implies more positive structuring of administrative discretion.

[5] EW Orts, 'Reflexive Environmental Law' (1995) 89 *Northwestern University Law Review* 1227, 1264.

[6] H Janisch and R Levi, 'Criminal Justice From the Bottom-Up: Some Thoughts on Police Rule-making Processes, in M Taggart, (ed), *The Province of Administrative Law* (Oxford: Hart Publishing, 1997) 266.

policy-making process. The goal of 'contestatory' democracy is to create a testing environment for the selection of policies, rather than to have policies that are consensually designed by the aggregation of the wants and preferences of citizens.[7] Constitutionalism in this view should be directed at maximizing the scope for reasoned debate and deliberation, thereby reducing the scope for arbitrary decision making and the inappropriate or illegitimate exercise of discretion. Rather than presuming that objectively correct policy choices will emerge through rational debate, the assumption is that alternative options can be investigated only to the point where satisfactory solutions may provisionally be adopted.[8] We have seen that a commitment to 'thick' as opposed to 'thin' proceduralization might further require the state actively to pursue strategies of translation, mapping, and dispute resolution, directed at mediating and overcoming problems of inequality, misunderstanding, and under-representation that arguably characterize the liberal pluralist model of the democratic process.[9]

In the public contracting context, an appropriately designed legal procedural framework would require policy purposes to be explicitly stated and defended, choices between competing or incommensurate values justified,[10] and the relative costs and benefits of proposed arrangements assessed against alternatives. In this regard, constitutional reformers in Britain have drawn inspiration from the US Administrative Procedure Act 1946.[11] The Act requires that notice of proposed rule making be published in a national register. Interested persons have the opportunity to comment in writing, and in some circumstances to present oral argument. The basis and purpose of rules is ultimately required to be publicly justified on promulgation.[12] Similarly in the UK, the exercise of discretion by public purchasing agencies making demand decisions on behalf of consumers and citizens in public service quasi-markets, for example in relation to the prioritization of welfare needs, should be structured according to procedural principles. Such principles would aim to ensure that individuals are treated fairly in the

7 P Pettit, *Republicanism: A Theory of Freedom and Government* (Oxford: Blackwell, 1997) 278.

8 K Hawkins, 'The Use of Legal Discretion: Perspectives from Law and Social Science' in K Hawkins, (ed), *The Uses of Discretion* (Oxford: Clarendon Press, 1992) 20.

9 J Black, 'Proceduralizing Regulation: Part II' (2001) 21 OJLS 33, 57; Richardson contrasts 'liberal pluralism' with 'strong democracy' involving public deliberation and the institutionalization of processes affecting the substance of decisions – G Richardson, 'The Legal Regulation of Process' in G Richardson and H Genn, (eds), *Administrative Law and Government Action: The Courts and Alternative Mechanisms of Review* (Oxford: Clarendon Press, 1994) 105.

10 Alder argues that values are inherently incommensurable, with the implication that those making policy choices should identify values and justify them against alternatives as clearly and openly as possible – J Alder, 'Incommensurable Values and Judicial Review: The Case of Local Government' [2001] PL 717, 735.

11 For an argument in favour of a British Aministrative Procedure Act, see I Harden and N Lewis, *The Noble Lie: The British Constitution and the Rule of Law* (London: Hutchinson, 1986) 302–11.

12 For the case against the introduction of notice and comment procedures in Britain, see R Baldwin, 'Governing With Rules: The Developing Agenda', in G Richardson and H Genn, (eds), *Administrative Law and Government Action: The Courts and Alternative Mechanisms of Review* (Oxford: Clarendon Press, 1994) 169–70.

determination of entitlements in the implementation of policy, in addition to protecting the wider public interest in open government.

The procedures governing contractualization might be set out within legislation and overseen by a specialist administrative law body whose role would be to monitor compliance, hear complaints, and adjudicate disputes.[13] Elements of procedural protection already exist in Britain in the analogous context of utilities regulation, in the form of requirements to consult and publish service standards, and statutory duties to give reasons in determining certain types of dispute.[14] While there is a long way to go even in this familiar regulatory setting in achieving the kind of systematic proceduralism found in the United States,[15] there appears to be no reason why proceduralist principles should not be extended to processes of policy making and implementation in relation to public contracting. The case for tighter procedural controls governing appraising options reviews has been clearly stated by constitutional lawyers.[16] Following Lewis, given the continued denial of appropriate institutional deliberation of contractualization and privatization, what is needed is:

> . . . an evaluation technique . . . which can be regularly, if not routinely, applied to questions concerning service initiation, continuance, amendment or expansion. The strengths of privatisation, contracting out, franchising, user fees, public-private partnerships, etc need to be considered as a set of general principles and then applied to particular delivery systems once policies have been determined. This should happen in conjunction with users, carers, professionals of all sorts . . . The users of services must be regularly consulted on their views of the service with a commitment to change either the service itself or the delivery system where appropriate. Where public bodies deliver services, comparators can be developed with other public bodies delivering similar services.[17]

Such statutory procedures might be reinforced by the creation of a new institutional review mechanism in the form of a contracts commissioner or ombudsman who would report to Parliament, and whose remit would be to oversee the whole field of government contracting. The ombudsman would have jurisdiction over tendering procedures, make recommendations as to the circumstances in which contracting mechanisms should be adopted, investigate underlying causes

[13] A Standing Administrative Conference might be created (on analogy with the US Administrative Conference) in order to coordinate policy-making resources and help 'stimulate open, rational learning processes' – Harden and Lewis (n 11 above) 307; N Lewis, 'The Case for a Standing Administrative Conference' (1989) 60 *Political Quarterly* 421. 'The establishment of a Standing Advisory Committee or Conference on the machinery of government offers the best hope of instilling some form of institutional rational discourse into the UK governmental system' – ND Lewis, *Law and Governance: The Old Meets the New* (London: Cavendish Publishing, 2001) 137.

[14] T Prosser, 'Regulation, Markets, and Legitimacy', in J Jowell and D Oliver, (eds), *The Changing Constitution* (Clarendon Press: Oxford, 1994) 255–6.

[15] ibid 256.

[16] On the issue of what constitutes the irreducible core of government activity that should continue to be performed by the state, 'there is currently no constitutional apparatus which is equal to providing a serious debate with argument tested by counter-argument, the very least which could be expected when the very remains of the State are being picked over' – Lewis (2001), (n 13 above) 137.

[17] Lewis (2001), (n 13 above) 141–142.

of complaint, identify service failures and undesirable practices of contractors, and supervise the production of codes of practice, for example in relation to compensation for customers.[18]

There are many examples of the unregulated or under-regulated nature of contractualization processes in this sense in contemporary Britain. Most obviously, the PFI is remarkable for its apparent incoherence and lack of popular support amongst policy analysts, academics, and the public generally.[19] Yet there appears to be no constitutionally effective means of challenging or revising this policy, or of restricting its ever-widening application. While there has been no shortage of critical comment and discussion,[20] there continues to be real confusion and uncertainty over what is behind the Government's commitment to this form of public infrastructure financing. This policy might not have been adopted, or been developed in its present form given legally guaranteed procedures requiring scrutiny, consultation and debate. The same might be said of the policy on Academies, which New Labour has pursued into its third term of office with renewed zeal, but arguably without any proper opportunity for public deliberation and evaluation.[21]

Information and confidentiality

Information is of vital importance in enhancing responsiveness in the organization of public services.[22] The argument for greater access to information has both instrumental and normative dimensions, concerned respectively with increasing efficiency and (where appropriate) competition, and protecting administrative law values of fairness, accountability, and legitimacy.[23] The success of the attempt to control the pace and extent of contractualization through constitutional procedures is dependent at least in part on the wider availability of information about how policy is made and implemented. We saw in Chapter 8 how, once public contracting arrangements are established, information about the contract process must be available and in the public domain in order to hold the government to account and to assess its performance. While there will always be an incentive for politicians to conceal any evidence of a poor return for government expenditure that might indicate poor judgement,[24] the purchaser-provider split and associated contractual processes open up the possibility of increased transparency in this

18 ibid 143.

19 On the absence of effective opposition to the PFI in the NHS, see S Ruane, 'Acquiescence and Opposition: The Private Finance Initiative in the National Health Service' (2000) 28 *Policy and Politics* 411.

20 R Smith, 'PFI: Perfidious Financial Idiocy' (1999) 319 *British Medical Journal* 2.

21 *Independent* 13 September 2005.

22 M Aronson, 'A Public Lawyer's Responses to Privatisation and Outsourcing' in M Taggart, (ed), *The Province of Administrative Law* (Oxford: Hart Publishing, 1997) 58–63; see JA Weiss, 'Public Information', in LM Salamon, (ed), *The Tools of Government: A Guide to the New Governance* (Oxford: Oxford University Press, 2002).

23 ibid 60.

24 ibid.

regard. Information is also a necessary precondition for the effective operation of mechanisms of choice and voice, and for representing the interests of citizens and consumers on public service issues.

Even where a degree of transparency is achieved through the publication of guidance and criteria informing market testing, 'appraising options', and other competitive processes,[25] the problem remains of inadequate provision of information both to contractors and the interested public.[26] In the case of privatizations the details of asset valuations are often not disclosed. The practice in tendering for government contracts has been for basic contractual details such as performance specifications and prices to remain shrouded in secrecy. This accountability deficit has been especially acute in the case of PFI contracts for complex infrastructure projects such as hospitals and schools, with the Government's value-for-money claims being particularly difficult to evaluate in consequence. The making of effective choices between different forms of public service organization, the selection of the best type of contractual arrangement and of the contracting partner, and the accountability of decision makers for their actions, are all to some degree dependent on the quality and availability of information. Excessive secrecy in the processes of granting licences, privileges and contracts increases opportunities for fraud and corruption, as well as reducing the scope for optimal decision making and concealing errors and incompetence.

In addition there exist particular risks of anti-competitive practices and collusion among contractors in bidding for public contracts. Transparency of financial information is especially important in the case of concessions or franchises that are subject to periodic re-tendering, in order to prevent an unfair advantage for the incumbent provider.[27] Issues of information and accountability arise also at the post-contract stage, for example with regard to the publication of details of evaluation and award criteria, the debriefing of unsuccessful applicants, and the opportunity for those disappointed in the selection process to seek redress. Again these aspects are only partially and inadequately addressed in EU regulations and published government guidance. Generally, it is impossible properly to evaluate contractual performance when specifications, prices, and other contractual information are not in the public domain.[28] *Better Quality Services* (BQS) stated that departments must act on the presumption that 'contract prices may have to be

[25] As has been seen, the Better Quality Services (BQS) guidelines are no longer current. The BQS Handbook and Guide for Senior Managers are available on a Cabinet Office website which is being maintained 'for archive/historical purposes' only – see http://archive.cabinetoffice.gov.uk/eeg/1999/services.htm accessed 10 October 2005.

[26] In spite of the rhetoric (for example, under BQS the public was said to have a *right* to know how much government services cost, no matter who provides them) the disclosure of information was patchy in practice – Lewis (2001), (n 13 above) 127.

[27] D Heald, and N Geaughan, 'The Private Financing of Public Infrastructure' in G Stoker, (ed), *The New Management of British Local Governance* (London: Macmillan, 1999) 234.

[28] Audit Commission, *Realising the Benefits of Competition: The Client Role for Contracted Services* (London: Audit Commission, 1993).

disclosed', but there was never any requirement for contracts to be published in their entirety. The reluctance to make contractual information generally available is routinely justified by the argument that commercial confidentiality is necessary to protect competition, and to prevent the commercial advantage enjoyed by successful contractors being unfairly eroded. However, while there exists a tension between commercial confidentiality on the one hand, and transparency as to the conditions of the award of contracts and the performance of parties necessary for public accountability on the other, the view that the latter has to be 'traded off' against the former is difficult to sustain. The move to contract has arguably exacerbated the lack of transparency traditionally associated with British government.[29]

The problem with Freedom of Information (FOI) legislation in the common law countries generally is that the marking of documents 'commercial-in-confidence' is too readily accepted as a justification for non-disclosure.[30] In England and Wales the Freedom of Information Act 2000 confers a general right of access to information held by public authorities.[31] 'Public authority' includes any body, by order of the Secretary of State,[32] exercising functions of a public nature, or providing under a contract with a public authority any service whose provision is a function of that authority. 'Exempt information' includes information provided in confidence, where disclosure would constitute an actionable breach of confidence,[33] or where information constitutes a trade secret whose disclosure 'would, or would be likely to, prejudice the commercial interests of any person (including the public authority holding it').[34] A recent report of the Commons Work and Pensions Committee on Information Technology procurement concluded that civil servants rather than companies were usually responsible for concealing the details of projects. In meetings officials were more often likely to cite commercial confidentiality as a smokescreen than suppliers. Generally there is insufficient transparency in complex public procurement contracts, with a particular danger of ministers committing themselves to projects that are unworkable for short-term gain and political expediency.[35]

29 Lewis (2001), (n 13 above) 128–9.

30 Even under the relatively liberal Australian FOI regime, such documents are entitled to a range of privileges that defeat a major purpose of the legislation. Furthermore, FOI is limited to documentation, whereas the problem of information is wider. 'It is remarkable how wedded to confidentiality free marketers can be when they come to assess the information needs of government and the public as regards privatisation, the operation of privatised utilities, and outsourcing' – Aronson (n 22 above) 58. See M Frankel, *Freedom of Information: Some International Characteristics* (London: Campaign for Freedom of Information, 2002).

31 Freedom of Information Act 2000, s 1.

32 s 5.

33 s 41(1).

34 s 43(1) and (2). The protection of commercial interests under this exemption is significantly greater than originally proposed in the White Paper, '*Your Right to Know*' (Cm 3818, 1997), where the exemption would apply only if the company could prove that substantial harm would be caused by release of the information.

35 Commons Work and Pensions Committee, *Department of Work and Pensions Management of Information Technology Projects: Making IT deliver for DWP Customers*, Third Report Session 2003–2004, HC 311-I, 14 July 2004, (London: The Stationery Office, 2004) paras 93–94. One of the

Such governance deficiencies have been widely recognized and condemned by public lawyers. For example, Lewis argues that there is a need for a broader disclosure regime, underpinned by a guaranteed role for auditors and other monitoring bodies such as public accounts committees.[36] Such analyses are of direct relevance to the question of how to increase the responsiveness of the New Public Contracting. In the case of economic contracts, contract documents and information on contractor performance should be made publicly available, subject only to clear demonstration of a commercial or public interest in the information being kept secret.[37] In some situations there might be a general rule in favour of transparency in matters such as contract specification and award criteria. This might require restriction of the extent of FOI 'commercial-in-confidence' privileges. On more sensitive matters such as price, there could be a requirement for publication after a year or two of the contract's making.[38] In sum, 'FOI's present boundary line at the barrier marked "commercial: in confidence" needs adjustment where the information is of both commercial and governmental relevance.'[39]

Discussion

Over the past twenty five years in Britain, contracting regimes have served to restrict choice and foreclose debate among alternative options for the performance of a range of public service functions. In the economic realm, this has led to the over-prescription of contractual forms of organization, and exacerbated contract management problems. In the domains of public administration and social control also, policy-driven regulation has arguably resulted in the over-use, or inappropriate extension, of the contract mechanism. In addition to the absence of procedural constraints on the exercise of government discretion, the lack of

recommendations of the Committee is for the publication of Gateway Reviews, undertaken by the Treasury's Office of Government Commerce, on the progress of major procurement projects (recommendation 25, p 75). Currently these are secret with only two copies printed, on the justification that secrecy is necessary to ensure frankness in the reviews. The Committee found that the 2000 Act would have no effect on the disclosure of information relating to sensitive IT projects, and was highly unlikely to deter suppliers from bidding for public sector contracts – para 133.

36 'Departments should be prepared to reveal contract prices for services unless it can be shown that real harm would result to the department's, the contractor's or identified third party's competitive position' – Lewis (2001), (n 13 above) 128–9.

37 In Australia, the Administrative Review Council (ARC) recommended that the Commonwealth Freedom of Information Act 1982 be amended to the effect that all documents in the possession of the contractor relating to the contractor's obligations under the contract be deemed to be in the possession of the government agency. However, no change was thought necessary to s 45 of the Act, which provides for exemption from disclosure where such disclosure might found an action for breach of confidence – Administrative Review Council, *The Contracting Out of Government Services*, Report No 42 (Canberra: Commonwealth of Australia, 1998) 60. The preservation of the general law of breach of confidence in this section means that the courts would need to continue, under the reform suggested, to balance the FOI legislation against claims of confidentiality in deciding whether documents should be disclosed.

38 Aronson (n 22 above) 63.

39 ibid 70; C Finn, 'Getting the Good Oil: Freedom of Information and Contracting Out' (1998) 5 *Australian Journal of Administrative Law* 113.

information surrounding decision making processes has prevented proper public scrutiny of the government's justification for policy choices.

Again the PFI provides an obvious example. We saw in Chapter 7 that while the selection of this mode of procurement over other options is supposed to depend on detailed cost-benefit analysis, in particular as regards risk transfer to private investors and long-term consideration of the public interest, in many cases there is no practical alternative. PFI projects account for ninety of one hundred new and refurbished hospitals built under New Labour, and five hundred of five hundred and fifty schools, yet the proper evaluation of this major plank of current government policy continues to be hampered by lack of vital information on the awarding and operation of contracts.[40] Even the Commons Public Accounts Committee has failed to gain an understanding of the relationship between the profits earned by private investors in PFI projects and the risks they bear, concluding that Parliament has not been given the facts necessary to pass judgement on the benefits claimed by the Government for this form of procurement. In cases where the private partner has experienced financial difficulties, the risks supposedly transferred to the private sector appear to have been borne by the taxpayer.[41] The suspicion remains that the PFI cannot be justified in economic terms, and that it is a political project whose costs and ultimate purpose remain hidden from public view. On the more sanguine view that PFI is not fundamentally unsound or unjustifiable in principle, a more transparent evaluation procedure is still required in order to discriminate between good and bad applications of the policy, and to inform best practice in the design, letting, and management of PFI contracts.[42]

A responsive regulatory framework, by contrast, should maximize the scope for experimentation and adaptation on the part of bodies charged with the performance of public service functions, and encourage the development of a range of solutions appropriate to local circumstances and service delivery problems. Local

40 On commercial confidentiality impeding transparency in PFI prisons, see S Nathan, 'Prison Privatization in the United Kingdom', in A Coyle, A Campbell, and R Neufeld, (eds), *Capitalist Punishment: Prison Privatization and Human Rights* (London: Zed Books, 2003) 162. This despite the fact that PFI is arguably subject to greater public scrutiny than other forms of financing of public sector infrastructure, with 44 National Audit Office or public accounts committee reports since 2001 – *Guardian* 28 July 2004.

41 £35bn of new debt has been created by PFI projects over 12 years of the PFI. The cost to the public purse remains unknown – *Guardian* 27 July 2004. On the relative costs of PFI and more traditional financing of infrastructure in the NHS, see D Gaffney, AM Pollock, D Price, and J Shaoul, 'NHS Capital Expenditure and the Private Finance Initiative – Expansion or Contraction?' (1999) 319 *British Medical Journal* 48.

42 The Commons Work and Pensions Committee criticized the 'illusion of risk transfer'. In many IT contracts there was a failure to identify the commercial risks, and to price them accordingly. When risks were understood, there was a need to ensure that the private partners to whom they were transferred had the capability and authority to manage them – (n 35 above) para 69. One of the strongest criticisms of the notion of risk transfer in PFI contracts concerns the costs to the public purse of bankruptcy of the provider, since off-balance sheet funding does not necessarily (depending on how financial backing for the project has been arranged) prevent the cost ultimately being borne by the taxpayer.

councils and other public agencies should be free to choose the factors they wish to take into account in deciding public service priorities,[43] and the means by which policy objectives are to be pursued. Of course, this ideal is in direct conflict with the commitment to centralization and concentration of power within Whitehall that has characterized recent government policy on central-local relations, and which has underpinned the development of the New Public Contracting. Under prevailing constitutional arrangements it is difficult to envisage central government wishing or being able to guarantee the autonomy of local councils, education authorities, or health authorities in their public service roles.

Given such conditions, I have suggested that a modest but more practicable goal of legal reformers should be to develop mechanisms for structuring the exercise of discretion by ministers and officials through a combination of procedural and informational requirements governing both the making and implementation of policy on public services. In the debate about the legal governance of contractualization, however, it should be borne in mind that legal reform of whatever kind cannot automatically produce the practical organizational changes that are necessary for increased responsiveness. We saw in the conclusion to Chapter 10 that the goal of institutionalizing respect for values of openness, transparency, and accountability in decision making is unlikely to be achieved solely by means of law, but depends also on the reform of administrative practices within the whole range of public, private and independent sector organizations engaged in public service networks. Such institutionalization is a fundamental component of the hybrid reform strategy for increasing the responsiveness of public service organization, and hence of responsive regulation. An example of what may be achieved in this regard is provided by recent experience in Australia. Following an audit review that revealed major concerns with secrecy surrounding government contracting in the 1990s,[44] and in light of the general acknowledgement of lack of progress in achieving greater transparency through FOI legislation, the state of Victoria instituted a *policy* of disclosure of government contracts (as opposed to reluctant disclosure after FOI litigation).[45] What is required in Britain generally is a change of culture within government, and a positive commitment on the part of the Treasury and commissioning departments to greater transparency. This requires the institutionalizing of the assumption that information should be disclosed, with the onus being on the government to justify non-disclosure.

[43] Alder (n 10 above) 735.

[44] *Audit Review of Government Contracts, Contracting, Privatisation, Probity and Disclosure in Victoria 1992–1999: An Independent Report to Government* (Victoria: State Government of Victoria, 2000).

[45] N Seddon, 'The Victorian Audit Review of Government Contracts – Lessons Learned from the Kennett Era' (Public Sector Accountability and Governance Conference, University of Wollongong, 2000). The Victorian Government Purchasing Board now has a system for publishing contracts on the internet in summary form (less than AUD 100,000) and in full – see www.vgpb.vic.gov.au, accessed 8 October 2005.

Administrative contracts

Drawing on the analysis provided in Chapter 6, this section argues that while a clearer and stronger legal framework may be necessary in order to support the more effective operation of framework documents, such reform would not be appropriate in the case of PSAs, which should continue to be governed entirely within the political realm. The discussion here is brief, since the key points have been anticipated in earlier chapters.

Framework documents

We have seen how the original intention behind the creation of framework documents as an administrative mechanism was that they should be binding (albeit revisable) statements of the respective rights and responsibilities of parent departments and Next Steps agencies. However, this was not possible within prevailing constitutional arrangements due to the absence of separate legal personalities and the inability of the Crown to contract with itself.[46] The lack of independent legal status has meant that executive agencies in Britain remain subject to the direct exercise of ministerial authority.[47] In spite of the widely accepted principle of non-interference informing the original policy,[48] ministers and departments have routinely intervened in matters supposedly delegated to executive agencies. Public lawyers have unsurprisingly responded by arguing that the autonomy of agencies should be established on a firmer legal basis. The question for legal governance is how to achieve this, and how thereby to enhance the constitutional function of these administrative contracts.

We noted in Chapter 10 that one way of facilitating institutional depth and making these governance arrangements more 'contractual' would involve the creation of a public law normative framework, designed to structure the parties' negotiations and to provide incentives for performance. For example, an 'Internal Contracts Act' might specify rules of natural justice and fairness, accompanied by formal or informal enforcement or arbitration mechanisms.[49] The aim would be to increase the transparency and accountability of government, and to help preserve constitutional values associated with the 'separation of powers' of ministers and agencies. However, in addition to the difficulties already considered

46 I Harden, *The Contracting State* (Buckingham: Open University Press, 1992) 44.

47 K Walsh, *Public Services and Market Mechanisms: Competition, Contracting and the New Public Management* (Houndmills: Macmillan, 1995) 189; C Greve, 'Governance by Contact Creating Public-Private Partnership in Denmark' in Y Fortin and H Van Hassel, (eds), *Contracting in the New Public Management – From Economics to Law and Citizenship* (Amsterdam: IOS Press, 2000).

48 Harden (n 46 above) 27.

49 ACL Davies, *Accountability: A Public Law Analysis of Government By Contract* (Oxford: Oxford University Press, 2001) 206.

regarding the scope of application of a special public law, this strategy would arguably fail to address more fundamental constitutional deficiencies in the operation of British government. Adequate judicial scrutiny and legal enforcement of framework documents might require further constitutional reform, for example the establishing of the UK civil service on a statutory basis.[50]

Alternatively, framework legislation might regulate the process of creating executive agencies as separate legal entities with contracting powers and capacities.[51] The varied experience of corporatization among the common law countries, in particular New Zealand, demonstrates how distinct legal personalities may be established and governance through the private law of contract thereby enabled. In the UK, legislative reform might similarly be directed at changing the legal basis of the relationship between ministers and agencies, as opposed to superimposing institutional reforms on existing organizational structures. Were enforceable contracts of whatever kind to be adopted as a means of structuring administrative relations, it would still be necessary to avoid 'hard' contracting styles which are destructive of the trusting and cooperative relationships that are essential to effective government.[52]

Public Service Agreements

The position as regards Public Service Agreements (PSAs) is entirely different. The implication of the analysis presented in earlier chapters is that very little would be achieved here by a public law normative framework with formal rules (fairness, natural justice) structuring the parties' negotiations and governing enforcement and dispute resolution. Where disagreements between spending departments and the Treasury have occurred and been made public, the 'disputes' are not of a kind that could be resolved in an arbitral forum. Nor is there a case to be made in this context for clearer organizational separation, for example involving the creation of distinct legal personalities, in order to preserve constitutional values and the separation of powers. The best safeguard of the increased autonomy and devolution

[50] V Bogdanor, 'Ministers, Civil Servants and the Constitution' (1994) 29 *Government and Opposition* 676; ND Lewis, 'A Civil Service Act for the United Kingdom' [1998] PL 463; A Massey, 'In Support of a Civil Service Act' (2002) *Public Money and Management* (Oct–Dec) 6. For a contrary view see: G Jones, 'Against a Civil Service Act' (2002) *Public Money and Management* (Oct–Dec) 5. For a discussion of Bogdanor's radical proposal for more explicit contractualization of the relationship between ministers and officials, which would involve statutorily authorized delegation of powers to agencies and conversion of framework documents into legal contracts subject to judicial interpretation, see D Oliver and G Drewry, *Public Service Reforms: Issues of Accountability and Public Law* (London: Pinter, 1996) 145.

[51] Sir William Waldegrave argued during the summer of 1992 that problems of ministerial responsibility would be lessened if agencies were constituted as private companies – K Dowding, 'Managing the Civil Service' in R Maidment and G Thompson, (eds), *Managing the United Kingdom* (London: Sage, 1993) 256.

[52] On the hard and soft contracting styles adopted in different phases of the development of Danish contract agencies, see Greve (n 47 above) 49.

of powers 'promised' to spending departments under the Spending Review is likely to lie in regulating the publication and dissemination of information which relates to the attainment or failure to attain PSA targets. In other words, PSAs fall within the class of administrative relationships for which legal institutionalization in respect of the contract norms is wholly inappropriate. Since neither the effectiveness nor legitimacy of PSAs can be increased by strengthening contractual institutions, there is little point in treating the relationships as contractual, and the contractual label may as well be abandoned.

Social control contracts

As regards social control contracts, legal reform strategies need again to be tailored to the circumstances, with particular attention to the underlying causes of responsiveness deficits identified in Chapter 9. Two main types of deficiency have been distinguished. First, ineffectiveness in regulatory arrangements may be due to the lack of support of the basic norms of planning, consent, and choice that are necessary to constitute meaningful contractual relationships. I have suggested that Home-School Agreements fall squarely into this category. The failure to secure threshold conditions of contractual relations is reflected in the vague and general nature of the undertakings, the lack of credibility of commitments, and the confusion of identities and roles of the contracting parties. Any benefits that have resulted from these arrangements cannot be attributed to the contract mechanism. Given the weakness of the institutional foundations, any attempt to make the contracts legally enforceable, as originally envisaged in the 1997 Education Act which was repealed by the in-coming Labour government in that year, would be futile. There appears to be little point in maintaining the pretence of a contractual basis to these relationships.

Second, in instances where the minimum conditions of contractual relations have been established, the potential benefits of relational contracting may be undermined by damage to one or a number of the contract norms within or surrounding the relationship. I have suggested that problems of regulatory ineffectiveness in this sense are present to varying degrees in the design and operation of Jobseekers' Agreements, Youth Offender Contracts, and parenting contracts. The scope for repair of such deficiencies through legal institutionalization will now be considered.

Jobseekers' Agreements

We have seen how Jobseekers' Agreements might in theory operate to the benefit of unemployed claimants as well as the Government. In return for the jobseeker's commitment to seek employment in accordance with an agreed plan, the Jobcentre is required to act as a service broker in arranging for the provision of training opportunities, skills development, or other help in overcoming obstacles to employability. Where there is genuine reciprocity in the process of agreement and in the subsequent performance of the contract, the joint-maximizing potential of effective contractual relations might be realized. In practice, however, these contractual relationships have suffered from weakness or lack of support of various contract norms.

To recap, the problem as regards contract planning is that the agreement may be secured through a fundamentally coercive process in which there is no opportunity for genuine negotiation. The claimant may have little choice other than to sign the contract, while Jobcentre staff may be prevented by time and resource constraints from offering tailored services of any real help to the claimant in return. The legislative provisions for referrals of disputed issues to an adjudication officer and for further appeals do not control the process of negotiation of the agreement. As to performance, I have suggested that there is a lack of reciprocity in the quality of bindingness in these arrangements. Contractual commitments may indeed be enforced by the Jobcentre against the claimant through the threat of withdrawal of benefit, but not by the claimant against the Jobcentre for failure to deliver on its side of the bargain. Furthermore, the statutory disputes resolution procedure does not appear to provide adequate safeguards against inappropriate or illegitimate use of sanctions.

The key legal reform question is whether such problems of lack of mutuality and unfairness are remediable through a more explicit legal framework of rights and duties directed at redressing power imbalances in favour of the weaker party. There may be some scope for increasing the safeguards against the more obvious forms of unfairness through modification of the existing system of review and appeal. However, institutional strengthening by whatever means is unlikely to be successful where the public agencies which are responsible for implementing the schemes lack the powers or resources necessary to deliver employment services that are capable of benefiting jobseekers.

Parenting contracts

Provisions for parenting contracts under the Anti-social Behaviour Act 2003 may be analysed in a similar way. We saw in Chapter 9 how these contracts have been developed as a means of tackling social control problems in relation to both exclusion from school or truancy and criminal conduct and anti-social behaviour. Again, both parties (parents and YOTs or LEAs/governing bodies of schools) might theoretically benefit from a reciprocal agreement specifying the support which is to be provided by state agencies to parents to help enable them fulfil their responsibilities. As with the Jobseeker's Agreement, however, various contract norms are likely to be damaged or weakly represented in such arrangements. While parenting contracts are supposed to be voluntary, the agreements are negotiated against the background threat of application by the state agency to court for a compulsory parenting order or other penal measure, in the event that the parent either refuses to enter the contract or fails to abide by its terms. While this sanction enables the state agency to enforce the contract and thereby to bind parents to their commitments, there is no comparable mechanism available to parents for holding the agency to its side of the bargain. Not only is the relationship fundamentally lacking in reciprocity, but there is also the potential for unfairness due to the absence of procedural protections regarding state sanctions for 'breach of contract' by parents.

Again, the question for lawyers is whether the development of a framework of rights, duties, or procedures for redress would serve to strengthen the norms of consent and reciprocity, and thereby help establish the conditions of effective relational contracting. With regard to contract formation, the coercive environment of parenting contracts may be regarded as fundamentally inimical to the norm of consent which is necessary for willing agreement. On this interpretation, what is required is radical reform of the regulatory regime, for example by repealing legislative provisions requiring the court to take account of matters concerning compliance with the 'voluntary' contract in deciding whether to grant a formal parenting order. On a more sympathetic analysis of the responsive potential of current regulatory arrangements, the scope for genuine negotiation in the making of these contracts might be encouraged by administrative review mechanisms like those that apply in relation to the Jobseeker's Agreements. As regards performance of obligations by state agencies once contracts have been concluded, and fairness to parents in the threat and use of sanctions in the enforcement of compliance, a special administrative procedure for review and disputes resolution might also be necessary to restore reciprocity and to protect the interests of the weaker party. However, to the extent that the safeguards currently available to jobseekers are inadequate, it is difficult to see how they could operate effectively in the more overtly disciplinary context of parenting contracts.

Youth Offender Contracts

Youth Offender Contracts differ from all the examples of social control contracts so far considered in that the contractual process is triggered by criminal judicial proceedings. It may be recalled that referral to a Youth Offender Panel is a sentencing option available to the court in defined circumstances under the Youth Justice and Criminal Evidence Act 1999. Again, the operation of the norm of consent is heavily constrained by the circumstances in which the contract between the young offender and the state agency is agreed; the Panel having the power to refer the offender back to court for re-sentencing in the event of failure to agree a 'programme of behaviour' or to sign the resulting contract.

In one sense the relationship is even more obviously lacking in reciprocity than in the other social control contracts so far considered, since in this instance the state agency need undertake no contractual commitments of any kind to the offender.

While the interests of the offender are protected to some degree in the judicial referral process, there are no procedural safeguards that might ensure fairness in the deliberations and decisions of the Panel. As we have seen, the sanction of referral back to court for re-sentencing may be unfairly applied, and there is nothing to prevent the court passing a harsher sentence than if the referral order had not been made in the first place, thus punishing the offender for alleged failure to reach agreement. This would be in clear violation of the norm of propriety of means or proportionality. The potential for unfairness in Panel proceedings is rooted in the structural imbalance of power in the contractual relationship, as established in the present regulatory regime.

The most obvious way of rectifying deficiencies in the institutional environment of the contracting process would be to subject Panel deliberations to the safeguards that apply in other proceedings where criminal sanctions are at stake. Panels might be a required to inform the offender of her rights, and to keep a formal record of proceedings. Legal representation could be made available to advise on the terms of the contract. Provision could be made through legislative amendment for challenging the decisions of the Panel, or for complaint by the offender regarding treatment by the Panel. However, the formalization of proceedings in this way might be counter-productive in undermining relational conditions of trust and cooperation that are necessary for the scheme's success. Even were problems of unfairness in the agreement and the performance of the contract to be addressed through such legal reform, the fundamental problem of lack of mutuality and the structural imbalance of power would remain. The offender's contractual commitments may not be balanced by specific undertakings on the part of the state, for example to provide support that might be necessary to facilitate performance. Where the norm of reciprocity is weak, the offender is likely to see little difference between 'voluntarily' undertaken contractual commitments and being told what to do by a court. Whether this is so depends on the way in which the schemes are implemented in practice. We saw in Chapter 9 that there appears to be considerable variation between different regions, depending on factors such as the extent of local commitment to the schemes, the constitution of Panels, and the resources available to them. However, regardless of how well the schemes may be shown to operate in some cases, the lawyer's concern must be that the absence of proper safeguards means there is always a potential for future abuse.

Discussion

The conditions necessary for contract to serve responsively as a mechanism of social control may briefly be summarised. Firstly, effectiveness depends on the presence of relatively discrete norms of planning, consent, and limitation of choice that together enable the relationship to be structured in a contractual manner. Secondly, effectiveness is further dependent on maintaining an appropriate balance between all the essential contract norms governing the relationship. Where the contract norms are damaged or only weakly represented, regulatory objectives are unlikely to be attained.[53] Effectiveness in this sense is strongly associated with relational contracting and with fairness in the operation of contractual schemes. Whether institutional deficiencies in these contracting regimes are repairable by reform of the legal framework depends on the circumstances. Responsive legal governance cannot simply be grafted onto regulatory arrangements that are fundamentally lacking in the support of essential contract norms. The only viable reform options in such cases may be to modify the regulatory regime or, where this is regarded as impracticable or undesirable, to abandon the pretence that the policy has a genuinely contractual basis. Where responsiveness deficiencies are less deep-rooted, a legal reform strategy might aim at re-balancing the relationship between state agencies and individuals and thereby restoring the conditions of relational contracting. This might require a combination of: (1) legally guaranteed procedures for the representation of the individual's interests in the negotiation of the contract;[54] (2) legal safeguards against unfairness by the public agency in implementing the contract; and (3) legal mechanisms for enforcing the state's contractual obligations to the individual.[55]

One method of increasing the bindingness of undertakings of public agencies in social control contracts might be through development of the public law doctrine of legitimate expectation.[56] The effect of reform based on this doctrine would be to extend the supervisory jurisdiction of the courts beyond procedural matters to the enforcement of substantive obligations. According to this doctrine, which is an established part of the law throughout the EU and in some common law countries

[53] Where a policy can be shown empirically to have been successful in modifying behaviour relative to other more overtly hierarchical measures, this outcome may not be attributable to the specifically contractual operation of the regulatory regime. Even where the regime is judged effective in this narrow sense, there is the question of the cost of such success in terms of possible unfairness to individuals in the operation of schemes.

[54] For the argument that merits review and dispute resolution procedures are not sufficient to protect the individual's interests in welfare contracting in Australia, see T Carney and G Ramia, *From Rights to Management: Contract, New Public Management and Employment Services* (The Hague: Kluwer Law International, 2002). 'The question is what the law can do to secure equivalent outcomes for clients engaged in "negotiating" (mock) contracts as an element of a new personalised form of welfare. Can contracts between unequals be *rendered* fair?' – ibid 177.

[55] The success of Education Maintenance Allowance contracts in this regard is explained by the reciprocal nature of the arrangement. On the one hand the benefit to the state lies in reducing unemployment and increasing participation in post-16 education, while on the other hand, the pupil benefits by receiving payments in excess of those available for unemployment and is enabled to increase future employability. Mutuality is evident to both parties at the time of agreement.

[56] P Craig, 'Legitimate Expectations: A Conceptual Analysis' (1992) 108 LQR 79. Of course, in circumstances where the service user and provider are linked by a legally enforceable contract, such expectations are protected through the ordinary law of contract. In the commercial context private law protection may extend to cases where the parties are engaging in an activity, such as tendering, pursuant to the making of a contract – see *Blackpool and Fylde Aero Club v Blackpool BC* [1990] 3 All ER 25; JN Adams and R Brownsword, 'More in Expectation than Hope: The Blackpool Airport Case' (1991) 54 MLR 281.

such as Australia, private persons may be able to hold public agencies to their word or to a decision or course of action where the individual has a legitimate expectation that this will be the case. In the social control context, Lord Woolf has suggested that the 'prisoner's contract' agreed between the incarcerating establishment and new inmates might give rise to legitimate expectations on the part of the prisoner, thereby providing a platform for an application for judicial review even in the absence of private law rights. This might have the effect of making contractual undertakings indirectly enforceable.[57] However, at the present time there would be many legal difficulties in attempting to derive legitimate expectations from social control contracts.[58]

Generally, I have argued that a key role for responsive regulation is to help instil values of fairness, legality, rationality, and respect for human rights into the organizational structures of the public agencies that perform designated New Public Contracting functions. In some social control contracts, this objective might be achieved through a combination of formal and informal complaints and redress mechanisms aimed at encouraging the development of good administrative practice, backed ultimately by provisions for external supervision and control by the courts. However, the task of increasing responsiveness cannot be achieved solely through legal rights and duties. What is required is the institutionalization of the values associated with good administration, rather than just a mechanism for *ex post* disputes resolution. Furthermore, the dangers of compounding the organizational problems inherent in contracting regimes by imposing inappropriate legal institutional reforms should be emphasized. The use of contract as a mechanism of behaviour modification has arguably been least problematic where this has developed as part of professional practice in particular sectors such as education, probation, and social work, often in locally based initiatives. In such cases, the institutions necessary to support effective contracting are already present and no special legal reinforcement is required. Where central government is determined to adopt such schemes as a basis for national policy, the chances of success are likely to be maximized by a bottom-up rather than top-down approach to policy development and implementation. Whatever the legal means deployed in the attempt to enforce the state's contractual undertakings, a key objective in the design of regulatory schemes must be to ensure that state agencies have the resources necessary to discharge their side of the bargain.[59]

[57] See S Fredman and GS Morris, 'The Costs of Exclusivity: Public and Private Re-examined' [1994] PL 69, 85. Lord Woolf's suggestion in regard to prisoners' contracts was not developed in any depth – (Cm 1416, 1991) paras 12.120–129.

[58] One problem with all such reforms based on increasing the enforceability of the contractual commitments of public agencies at the instance of the other party concerns the situation where the social control function is performed by a private rather than public body. It would be anomalous, for example, if judicial review proceedings could be brought on this ground by those in public but not in private prisons – Fredman and Morris, ibid.

[59] This analysis mainly concerns the performance of the social control function by *public* agencies. Where social control functions are delegated under contract to *private* bodies, there is an additional

Economic contracts

The question of the proper role of legal institutions in the governance of economic contracts raises particular difficulties due to the complexity of contracting regimes and the multiplicity and competing nature of the interests of stakeholders. Here new forms of public service organization are posing major challenges to the regulating capacities of existing systems of both private and administrative law. In the following analysis I address this issue through separate consideration of three main axes of economic contracting regimes (see Chapter 7, Fig 6): the purchaser–provider relationship; the user–provider (contractor) relationship; and the citizen/user–public purchaser relationship. The focus in each case is on how the legal framework protects both particular interests and the more general public interest in the contractual organization of public services. The question is what type of legal or other regulatory reform is needed to increase the effectiveness of these contracting arrangements as presently conceived.

Purchaser–provider relationship

Whereas lack of institutional depth is a structural feature of both administrative contracts and social control contracts, economic contracts operate in the context of a stronger and more stable institutional environment. Contracts enforceable and unenforceable at private law will be examined in turn. In both instances the purchaser interest lies mainly in the quality of bindingness of contractual commitments, whereas the provider interest is more concerned with the fairness of the contracting process.

First, in the case of legally enforceable contracts, bindingness is assured by private law institutions in conjunction with the contract norms that have developed within particular relationships and sectors through custom, convention, and business practice. In public/private sector transactions, as in other economic exchanges, the legal framework enables the parties to plan their relationship and make mutual commitments against the background guarantee of judicial enforcement. However, we have seen in Chapter 7 how the ability of public purchasers to make full use of contract as a regulatory mechanism through the binding quality of contractual obligations ('contract compliance') is limited by domestic and EU law. In particular, legislation currently prevents local authorities from

potential for unfairness to the individual and increased danger of lack of public accountability. For example, in relation to the privatization of management of prisons, it is literally the freedom of individuals that is at stake rather than just the entitlement of individual consumers to public services. Government plans to transfer disciplinary regimes from Home Office controllers to directors of private prisons, ostensibly in order to enable them to compete on a level playing field, are likely to prove problematic in this regard – *Guardian* 3 June 2004; see P Carter, 'Managing Offenders, Reducing Crime: A New Approach' Prime Minister's Strategy Unit, January 2004.

taking account of 'non-commercial considerations' when awarding contracts.[60] This obstacle to implementing democratically mandated policy goals might easily be removed by repeal or amendment of the legislation, or by the exercise of powers of the Secretary of State to modify the list of non-commercial matters.[61] However, New Labour has shown no inclination to reverse the long-term trend towards contralization in the relationship between central and local government.

As regards provider or contractor interests, private law institutions may not in all cases provide sufficient support for the norms of reciprocity and power. This creates a potential for unfairness that has led to arguments for increased public law protections. It also raises the question of the adequacy of legal controls over the exercise of discretion by the public agency in the tendering, letting, and management of contracts. Firms which bid for public contracts have an obvious interest in all stages of the public contracting process. This overlaps with a public interest in ensuring that value-for-money is obtained transparently and through genuine competition, without fraud or corruption. A limited form of procedural regulation of competitive tendering is available at private law.[62] In addition, competitive tendering is regulated by domestic and EU law.[63] EU regulation does not mandate that public services should be provided through the market rather than directly by the state. Instead it aims to eliminate non-trade barriers to competition and to promote fairness in tendering for public contracts among member states where public services are subject to competition. Specified standards and procedures must be followed wherever the award of contracts for services exceeds certain amounts. In domestic law, there has been a trend towards increasing judicial control of tendering processes. Procurement decisions may be challenged in the High Court by way of judicial review. Where the contract has already been awarded, the court has power to set aside the decision or grant damages.[64] The courts have a central role in encouraging transparency and the free and open flow of information.[65] Generally, procedures for the award of contracts should be designed to be open and to encourage participation of affected interests.[66]

[60] Local Government Act 1988, s 17. See I Leigh, *Law, Politics and Local Democracy* (Oxford: Oxford University Press, 2000) 298–9; A Erridge and R Fee, 'Contract Compliance: National, Regional and Global Regimes' (1999) 27 *Policy and Politics* 199.

[61] Local Government Act 1998, s 19. However, such reform would not affect the operation at EU level of the public procurement regime and the decisions of the European Court to limit the use of 'additional specific conditions' to circumstances where there is no discrimination against bidders from Member States. The policy on contract compliance at both levels (domestic and European) would be more legitimate if it were more explicitly formulated after a full public debate – Davies (n 49 above) 22.

[62] *Blackpool and Fylde Aero Club v Blackpool BC* [1990] 3 All ER 25.

[63] S Arrowsmith, J Linarelli, and D Wallace, *Regulating Public Procurement: National and International Perspectives* (London: Kluwer International, 2000).

[64] S Arrowsmith, 'Judicial Review and the Contractual Powers of Public Authorities' (1990) 106 LQR 277.

[65] S Arrowsmith, 'Protecting the Interests of Bidders For Public Contracts: The Role of the Common Law' (1994) 53 *Cambridge Law Journal* 104; Aronson (n 22 above) 58.

[66] cf Prosser (n 14 above) 254.

Fairness to contractors in the award of public contracts might be increased through reform of the *ultra vires* doctrine, which currently enables the government to avoid liability by pleading fettering of discretion, or to escape bad bargains on grounds of incapacity. The capacity issue might be addressed by allowing the court discretion over whether or not to enforce the contract.[67] In relation to fettering of discretion, although the problem can be partially addressed through contractual price variation or standard terms, a more satisfactory solution might be found in flexible public law remedies of the sort provided in French law, which permits both modification of contract terms by the public authority and price adjustment by the contractor.[68] As regards contract performance, the question is how far the law protects the legitimate sphere of autonomy of the contractor and provides safeguards against unwarranted interference, which may result in inefficiency as well as unfairness. The arguments in favour of regulating the purchaser-provider relationship by extending the scope of judicial review, or through the development of a special public law of contract, were considered in Chapter 10. As we have seen, the main difficulty with the latter option – which would require the observance of more extensive good faith obligations in the performance of the contract than normally govern public procurement relationships – is its potential incompatibility with competitive tendering. The problem would remain of how to distinguish the circumstances in which the special law would and would not apply, particularly given the increasing range of economic contracts that involve competitive processes.

Second, in the case of economic contracts that are not legally binding, public lawyers have argued that the effectiveness of internal contractual relationships is compromised by the purchaser's inability to enforce the contract and to hold the provider to account for performance.[69] The argument here is that, in order for contracts to operate effectively, a special enforcement mechanism such as an arbitral tribunal is needed to help settle ongoing disputes and 'help the parties to treat their contracts as binding'.[70] However, the claimed existence of a problem of 'unenforceability' of internal contracts in the NHS, on which this prescription is based, is open to question.[71] The proposition that such formal enforcement and dispute resolution machinery should generally be applied to other 'internal' economic

[67] P Craig, *Administrative Law* (4th edn, London: Sweet and Maxwell, 1999) 150. In local government the problem has been partly mitigated through the Local Government (Contracts) Act 1997.

[68] W Wade and C Forsyth, *Administrative Law* (8th edn, Oxford: Oxford University Press, 2000) 336; Davies (n 49 above) 16.

[69] Davies (n 49 above) 52–3.

[70] ibid 178–9.

[71] Other research in the NHS has reached very different conclusions. One empirical study indicated a relatively high degree of bindingness associated with the use of non-statutory conciliation and arbitration procedures – I Harden and D Longley, 'National Health Service Contracts', in J Birds, R Bradgate, and C Villiers, (eds), *Termination of Contracts* (Chichester: John Wiley, 1995). Another study concluded that the main reason for the non-use of statutory arbitration was its unsuitability to resolving intractable disputes over resources with implications beyond individual contracts – D Hughes, J McHale, and L Griffiths, 'Settling Contract Disputes in the National

contracts, for example in local government, is particularly problematic.[72] The public law argument here underestimates the significance of economic incentives which encourage compliance and provide informal sanctions for breach of contract. For example, contracts between in-house providers and central government or local authority clients which result from market-testing or competitive tendering occur in a highly competitive or contestable environment. The ultimate sanction for contractor failure or poor performance is termination of the contract just as if it was legally enforceable. The function may then be outsourced in the subsequent re-tendering exercise.

Turning finally to the provider interest in legally unenforceable contracts, the main issue again, as with external contracts, concerns the potential for unfairness by the purchaser in dealings with internal contractors. The justification for a public law framework on this ground (ie that this is necessary to structure the exercise of discretionary powers by public agencies and thereby to protect the weaker party through natural justice norms) appears stronger than in regard to the supposed problem of lack of enforceability by the purchaser. As we have seen, the benefits of relational contracting can only fully be realized through adequate support of the contract norms of fairness and reciprocity. Public purchasing agencies should be guided by such norms and also observe a range of principles of good administration including natural justice in their dealings with internal providers. However, the suggestion that a public law normative framework should be applied in an internal enforcement and dispute resolution forum or 'arbitral tribunal',[73] and that formal hearings should be held to determine fault accurately and to consider whether difficulties should be handled cooperatively without resorting to sanctions,[74] is again highly problematic. Legalistic models of enforcement and dispute resolution derived from commercial practice may not be applicable within bureaucratic organizations such as the NHS, in which central management retains a paramount role both in establishing the general parameters of the contracting process and in deciding the approach taken to dispute resolution.[75] Far from indicating a governance deficiency, the structuring of behaviour through informal norms and the general shift to 'informal pathways' of dispute resolution may be regarded as a positive development, reflecting the rational adaptation of contractual institutions

Health Service: Formal and Informal Pathways' in R Flynn and G Williams, (eds), *Contracting for Health: Quasi-Markets and the National Health Service* (Oxford: Oxford University Press, 1997).

[72] For a detailed critique of Davies' argument, see P Vincent-Jones, 'Regulating Government by Contract: Towards a Public Law Framework?' (2002) 65 MLR 611.

[73] Davies (n 49 above) 70. [74] ibid 187.

[75] Structural pressures to compromise are inevitable, particularly given the intractability of many problems. The evidence of dispute resolution in all the empirical studies reveals the crucial role of hierarchical regulation in the internal market environment – J McHale, D Hughes, and L Griffiths, 'Conceptualizing Contractual Disputes in the National Health Service Internal Market' in S Deakin and J Michie, (eds), *Contracts, Cooperation and Competition: Studies in Economics, Management and Law* (Oxford: Oxford University Press, 1997) 206–7.

and dispute resolution mechanisms to deal with complex issues.[76] In short, the proposition that a public law of internal contracts would make such relationships more 'successful' must be regarded as dubious.[77] While the contract norms in these economic contracts may require further support, the form that this institutional strengthening should take remains highly debatable.

User–contractor relationship

Legal commentators addressing the accountability deficits that accompany contractualization have focused particularly on the relationship between private contractors and ultimate consumers of public services.[78] Apart from the clear need for adequate systems of redress of individual grievances, there are sound economic reasons for this concern. A fundamental purpose of outsourcing is to transfer responsibility for provision from government agencies to external parties. This objective might be undermined if remedies in respect of contractor performance were to lie against government agencies rather than the provider. The costs associated with the risk of legal action, handling complaints and paying compensation can theoretically be factored into the tender price. Contractors are also thereby subject to incentives to provide services in a fair and efficient manner, since this is likely to minimize complaints and maximize profits.[79] The question is how such citizen and consumer interests might better be protected, through what kind of legal reform. This section develops the suggestion made in the previous chapter that the best means of securing increased responsiveness on the part of public service providers to consumer needs is likely to lie in the adoption of a hybrid legal reform strategy, which both transcends the public/private divide and combines formal law with more informal institutional processes that operate within regulated organizations.

The idea that hybrid governance structures might be designed to regulate the relationships between the various parties engaged in public service networks following contractualization has recently been explored in Australia.[80] Here it has been argued that consumer protection arrangements under the Commonwealth Telecommunications Act 1997 may serve as a model for public services generally.[81] In this type of scheme, public purchasing agencies would specify, through

76 'The preference for informal solutions can be regarded as a rational attempt to find dispute-resolution processes that will adequately manage the types of disputes emerging in the NHS' – Hughes et al, (n 71 above) 111.

77 Davies (n 49 above) 185.

78 'Supervision of contracting power should not be available only at the suit of those who have failed to secure, or retain, a contract; the users of a service also have an interest in ensuring that there is no misuse of contracting power and that services provided pursuant to a contract are delivered' – Fredman and Morris (1994), (n 57 above) 79.

79 H Schoombee, 'Privatisation and Contracting Out – Where Are We Going?' in J McMillan, (ed), *Administrative Law Under the Coalition Government* (Canberra: AIAL, 1997) 142.

80 ibid.

81 Under the Commonwealth Telecommunications Act 1997, regulation of the liberalized telecoms markets is shared between government regulatory agencies (the Australian Competition and

terms of the contract with providers, performance standards in relation to such matters as internal and external customer complaints procedures and time limits for dealing with service requests and complaints.[82] As has been seen, human services are already governed to some degree by such standards which are designed to ensure satisfactory outcomes for service users. The scheme would provide for a monetary penalty (with minimum and maximum limits) payable by the contractor to the customer in the event of non-compliance with service standards. Self-enforcement through an informal, internal complaints mechanism would be backed by provision for complaint to an independent party such as an ombudsman, who could certify breach of the standard where the complaint was held to be justified.[83] Self-organization and self-financing of such schemes within service industries might encourage the development of effective complaint-handling mechanisms which would minimise the need for formal investigations.[84] The ombudsman's recommendation might be made enforceable in an industry-specific tribunal. In the event of non-payment or non-compliance by the contractor, the complainant would have an enforceable right of recovery in a court of law. The public law element in such regulation lies in the enforcement of service standards by the consumer without having to establish the existence of a contractual nexus, and in the initial process of investigation of the complaint and certification of breach of such standards. This element might be strengthened to include orders for corrective action to be undertaken by a provider.[85] The private law dimension lies in the monetary form of redress, and in the ultimate enforceability of the claim by civil action if necessary. To counter difficulties of third-party enforcement, the scheme might provide for enforcement on the consumer's behalf, whether by the public agency or a body representing the consumer interest.

Framework legislation could provide an adaptable template for the introduction of hybrid regulatory schemes of this nature, serving as a basis for the more specific development of standards, remedies, and procedures in particular human service

Consumer Commission and the Australian Communications Authority) and industry bodies: the Australian Communications Industry Forum is an industry-owned, operated and financed company, and the Telecommunications Industry Ombudsman is similarly self-funded by members of the scheme – see K MacNeill, 'Self-Regulation: Rights and Remedies – The Telecommunications Experience' in C Finn, (ed), *Sunrise or Sunset?* (Canberra: AIAL, 2000); A Stuhmcke, 'The Rise of the Australian Telecommunications Industry Ombudsman' (2002) 26 *Telecommunications Policy* 69.

82 In the case of services funded privately rather than publicly, ie in a regulated market rather than in quasi-market organization, similar conditions might be applied through terms contained in licences or operating agreements governing relationships between independent regulatory agencies and private or voluntary sector providers. The following argument on the need for citizen and stakeholder involvement in public contracting processes is valid also in such regulated market contexts.

83 The ombudsman role would be closer to that currently performed in private sector industries than existing public sector models – see M Seneviratne, *Ombudsmen: Public Services and Administrative Justice* (London: Butterworths, 2002) 55.

84 MacNeill (n 81 above) 255. In the telecoms scheme a 'complaint' becomes a 'dispute' if the manager in charge of the informal investigation is unable to resolve the matter to the satisfaction of the complainant.

85 Schoombee (n 79 above) 144.

sectors.[86] The implementation of service standards should be relatively straightforward, since the purchaser-provider contract already contains detailed service specifications and a range of other standards. Any legislation would then simply refer to the contract. The advantage of this reform compared with the simple extension of current ombudsman jurisdiction would consist in the ultimately enforceable nature of the right to payment, within a graduated self-enforcement structure aimed at making such formal recourse generally unnecessary. Such features also distinguish this proposal from current arrangements under public service charters in Britain for the payment of compensation to consumers for poor performance, which for a number of reasons are regarded as having been unsuccessful.[87]

The success of such a reform strategy would depend most obviously on the quality of contract management by public purchasing agencies.[88] Particular attention needs to be given to service specification and the definition of contractor obligations, and to monitoring, evaluating and reporting on contractor performance. Purchasers might be made responsible for specifying what contractual information should be available to service recipients and other members of the public, and how they are to gain access to that information. There are particularly strong public and citizen/consumer interests in the availability of, and access to, contractual information.[89] Additional responsibilities might be imposed on public agencies through the hierarchical dimension of contracting regimes, in anticipation of the obstacle under prevailing arrangements that many public bodies lack sufficient incentive or resources to undertake such extra burdens.

The responsiveness of any hybrid regulatory scheme also depends on the nature of service standards and on how they had been devised. The question of the nature and extent of public involvement in standard-setting and contract management raises the more general issue of the relationship between citizens/users and public purchasing agencies.

Citizen/user–public purchaser relationship

The relationship between the citizen or consumer and the public purchasing agency is of particular importance in quasi-market organization. In almost all

86 ibid 143–144; N Seddon, *Government Contracts: Federal, State and Local* (2nd edn, Sydney: Federation Press, 1999) 148.

87 G Drewry, 'Whatever Happened to the Citizen's Charter?' [2002] PL 9. The provisions for Financial Remedies for Maladministration, drawn up by the DWP, fall far short in various respects of what might be regarded as an adequate contractual system of redress for poor performance. Most notably, the compensation scheme is discretionary in nature. Ex gratia special payments are described in *Government Accounting* as 'payments which go beyond administrative rules or for which there is no statutory cover or legal liability'. www.jobcentreplus.gov.uk/pdfs/MaladministrationGuide.pdf, para. 8.

88 Schoombee (n 79 above) 'No remedy of whatever type could operate effectively unless there is *specificity* in relation to the obligations of the contractor, and *public disclosure* of those obligations', 142.

89 Seddon (n 45 above). A radical change in policy would be needed to remove the obstacle to public accountability that is currently posed by over-use of 'commercial-in-confidence' clauses.

cases of human services contracting, a public agency remains responsible for assessing individual needs and for commissioning or procuring appropriate services.[90] Administrative law remedies are available to the citizen/user who is dissatisfied with decisions made by the agency, in much the same way as under bureaucratic organization. The governance deficit here consists in the failure of these remedies to protect a range of citizen/user interests in the exercise of such discretion. In private law, the aggrieved service recipient has no remedy in contract against the purchasing agency,[91] and no rights against that body in respect of the contract between it and the provider. As we saw in the discussion of limits of private law reform strategies in the previous chapter, the option of making the public agency vicariously liable for the actions of the contractor would have various economic disadvantages as well as posing legal difficulties, for example concerning the measure of damages in actions between the public agency and the contractor.

The fundamental problem remains, then, how to connect citizens and consumers with the public purchasing functions that have been separated from service provision as a result of quasi-market organization.[92] In quasi-market organization there is a particular need to build 'publicness' into increasingly 'privatized' arrangements for public service provision.[93] In many public service quasi-markets where direct regulation is likely to be ineffective in promoting increased efficiency or equity, central government should play a role in improving the flow of information.[94] More particularly, the question is how consumers and citizens are represented in a range of 'demand decisions'.[95] As we saw in Chapter 8,

[90] For example, under the NHS and Community Care Act 1990, local authorities are under a duty to assess the needs of anyone who appears to be in need of community care services, and to decide whether such services should be provided (s 47).

[91] While there is no contractual nexus, actions may lie in tort and for breach of statutory duty.

[92] For all the disadvantages of unresponsive bureaucracy in the past, direct government tools potentially involve relatively strong linkages between citizens and government. While such tools have not always attracted popular support or public participation, indirect policy tools have been argued to pose greater problems for citizen involvement – Rathgeb Smith and Ingram (n 1 above) 570.

[93] L Stirton and M Lodge, 'Transparency Mechanisms: Building Publicness into Public Services' (2001) 28 JLS 471. In similar vein, Giddens argues that one of the aims of New Labour should be the 'forging of a more effective ideological position, which integrates the renewal of public services with a wider commitment to public institutions and the public sphere. This endeavour might be understood as a process of "publicization", distinct from privatization, but also from the traditional heavy reliance on the state sector' – A Giddens, *Where To Now For New Labour?* (Cambridge: Polity Press, 2002) 67. For a different but related concept of 'publicization', see J Freeman, 'Extending Public Law Norms Through Privatization' (2003) 116 *Harvard Law Review* 1285.

[94] 'An increase in information would allow greater competition, provide better protection for consumers and make it more likely that regulatory activity achieved its goals' – C Propper, 'Quasi-Markets and Regulation' in J Le Grand and W Bartlett, (eds), *Quasi-Markets and Social Policy* (Houndmills: Macmillan, 1993) 201.

[95] 'If "consumer sovereignty" is to be more than an empty slogan, then what is needed is a judicially-monitored public law procedural framework to surround sites of demand decisions, including requirements such as "notice and comment" for the establishment of service priorities, identification of customers and setting of performance standards' – Harden (n 46 above) 74.

these decisions concern the choice of outsourcing as a mode of provision, standard-setting, the specification of services in the contract, the selection of the contractor, and the allocation and rationing of resources.[96]

Firstly, with regard to the initial decision that a service should be contracted out to a private or non-profit body rather than provided directly, we established in the opening section of this chapter that citizen involvement and participation are crucial components in the design of legal procedures governing contractualization. Given the need to confine and structure the discretion of technical experts and politicians,[97] democratic values of probity, transparency and public deliberation must be built into processes of policy making and implementation.[98] Political legitimacy consists in the provision of maximum opportunity for deliberation over the merits of various forms of public service provision.[99] Lack of democratic involvement and of adequate public deliberation impacts directly on the quality of decision making, increasing the risk of inappropriate tool choice or instrument selection.[100]Minimum reforms here might involve procedures requiring public agencies to notify locally affected citizens of outsourcing plans, to consider the views of those who respond, and to provide reasons for contracting policy decisions. In addition, there exists considerable scope for innovation in the design of new fora of participation such as citizens' juries. The role of this type of representative body need not be confined to the implementation of policy, but might extend to consideration of fundamental decisions on policy direction over contracting out, privatization, and the PFI.[101] The overall regulatory design aim should be to mobilize in each public services context adequate substitutes for the qualities of consumer sovereignty and choice that make markets theoretically a superior form of organization.

Secondly, while there has been considerable debate on the legal governance of various public and private interests in the tendering and contract letting processes, relatively little attention has been accorded the issue of the role of citizens and consumers in setting standards, determining contract specifications, and managing

96 For an argument for 'enhanced proceduralism' in the utilities sector involving specific arrangements for consumer representation in regulatory processes as a means of redressing accountability deficits accompanying the loss of ministerial responsibility following privatization, see C Graham, *Regulating Public Utilities: A Constitutional Approach* (Oxford: Hart Publishing, 2000) 87.

97 Ch 5, above, on policy process and bad motives.

98 S Zifcak, 'Contractualism, Democracy and Ethics' (2001) 60 *Australian Journal of Public Administration* 86.

99 P Vincent-Jones, 'Contractual Governance: Institutional and Organisational Analysis' (2000) 20 OJLS 317; J Chalmers and G Davis, 'Rediscovering Implementation: Public Sector Contracting and Human Services' (2001) *Australian Journal of Public Administration* 74.

100 Public participation is necessary throughout the 'policy cycle', in evaluation as well as initial design – A Yeatman, 'Contracting Out and Public Values: A Symposium' (2001) 60 *Australian Journal of Public Administration* 71; DZ Robinson, 'Government Contracting for Academic Research' in BLR Smith and DC Hague, (eds), *The Dilemma of Accountability in Modern Government: Independence Versus Control* (London: Macmillan, 1971) 108–113.

101 Ch 8 above.

contracts.[102] The success of the type of hybrid regulation of the user–contractor relationship suggested earlier would be dependent on citizens becoming actively involved in the monitoring and enforcement of service standards. Again, consumer influence is dependent on access to information. Consumer councils are one mechanism for increasing consumer voice. There should also be systems for registering consumer views at the time of contract renewal, and on how contracts are to be managed generally. In appropriate circumstances there could be 'consumer input into the process of articulating some of the contract specifications or regulatory goals'.[103]

However, this begs the question of how service standards have been determined. An adequate hybrid regulatory scheme for human services would need to incorporate greater flexibility for public agencies in standard-setting and contract specification. The service standards in particular sectors might be collectively established through consultation between public agencies, consumers, and representatives of provider organizations. The ultimate objective of this procedure would be to render explicit for all interested parties the quality of services that consumers could reasonably expect, and the terms on which services would be provided. The standards thus established, including procedures for complaints handling and disputes resolution, might govern relationships between providers and consumers regardless of how the service was funded (ie publicly or privately) and of whether there existed a contractual nexus between consumer and service provider. This analysis is informed by the premise that the basic standards governing services such as social care and residential care for the elderly should be uniform across public and private sectors, rather than vary according to the ability to pay or the method of payment.[104] Of course, the advocacy of increased consumer and provider involvement in standard-setting processes is in tension with the centralizing spirit of contracting regimes as presently constituted. As with the decision to outsource, increased responsiveness will only come about if there is a significant reduction in central prescription.

Thirdly, we have already seen that quasi-market contracting opens up new possibilities (compared with traditional direct provision) for the better representation of citizen and consumer interests in regard to resource allocation and rationing. In one sense contracting out has made little difference to the rationing problem. The public purchasing agency remains responsible for assessing individual needs and for prioritizing resources among different types of claim. In the past the courts have been reluctant to interfere with resource allocation

102 Such dimensions were excluded from the terms of reference of the ARC investigation into contracting out – Administrative Review Council (n 37 above) para 1.9.

103 Harden (n 46 above) 60.

104 Where providers operate solely in the private sector and public agencies do not purchase services on behalf of consumers in quasi-market arrangements, regulation could not occur through a purchaser-provider contract.

decisions made by public authorities.[105] Rather than attempting to extend the scope of judicial control in the direction of review of the merits of such decisions,[106] a better legal reform strategy may be to structure the decision making processes involved in allocating resources and exercising discretion. This type of strategy is directed at building respect for the fundamental values of fairness, non-discrimination and public involvement into the operation of administrative systems. One benefit of the separation of purchaser and provider functions involved in contracting out is that the role of the public agency is clarified. This creates the potential for increased transparency in administrative processes. Specific procedures might be designed, appropriate to particular service settings, to promote such transparency and encourage participation on the part of citizens and stakeholders. The role of the courts would then be to ensure that such procedures had been properly followed, in accordance with established administrative law principles.[107]

New Labour has placed increased emphasis on empowering users of welfare services through a range of mechanisms such as citizens' juries, panels and other types of public forum. However, these devices appear to increase only marginally the influence of consumers in the decisions made by public purchasing agencies. They are not a substitute for supporting increased citizen involvement through democratic representative institutions.[108] The role of responsive law in the governance of the citizen/user–public purchaser relationship should be to guarantee procedures for representing the interests of citizens and service recipients in decision making by public agencies in respect of resource allocation, standard-setting, contract management and specification and, most fundamentally, the adoption of contracting out as a mode of provision. Responsiveness here implies a commitment to values of public participation and involvement that extend beyond fairness and

105 *R v Gloucestershire CC, ex p Barry* [1997] AC 584 (concerning the scope of local authority community care obligations under s 2(1) of the Chronically Sick and Disabled Persons Act 1970).

106 This tends to be the effect of 'rights-based' arguments – see E Palmer, 'Resource Allocation, Welfare Rights – Mapping the Boundaries of Judicial Control in Public Administrative Law' (2000) 20 OJLS 63. Allars contends that the traditional reluctance of courts in judicial review to interfere with government decisions concerning resource allocation needs to be addressed, but does not consider how, or with what implications – M Allars, 'The Commercialisation of Administrative Law' in S Kneebone, (ed) *Administrative Law and the Rule of Law: Still Part of the Same Package?* (Canberra: Australian Institute of Administrative Law, 1999) 167.

107 In *R v Cambridge HA, ex p B* [1995] 1 FLR 1055, [1995] 2 All ER 129, the Divisional Court and the Court of Appeal were in agreement that the health authority had not provided evidence of any prioritization policy informing the decision to refuse treatment. However, whereas for Laws J the authority had thereby acted unreasonably in failing to justify interference with B's right to life, Lord Bingham MR did not think the authority was required to provide such explicit justification. The common assumption here is that public authorities performing rationing functions should be required to give reasons for decisions and to make explicit their prioritization criteria.

108 In the education sector, see for example CM Farrell and J Jones, 'Evaluating Stakeholder Participation in Public Services – Parents and Schools' (2000) 28 *Policy and Politics* 251.

non-discrimination.[109] What this means in practice depends on the particular demand decision in question. The difficulties inherent in designing appropriate participation fora and legal governance frameworks are acknowledged.[110] But the purchasing function is one of the sites where the quality of administrative decision making might be improved, through specific procedural reforms aimed at increasing citizen and consumer involvement. If one of the principal goals of administrative law (alongside legality, accountability, rationality, integrity, and fairness) is participation, then 'participation in a court proceeding after the event is a poor substitute for democratic participation in the exercise of state power at the administrative level'.[111]

Redress of grievances

A fundamental aspect of the quest for responsiveness in the design of economic contracting regimes concerns the redress of grievances. The issue is posed particularly acutely in this context due to the complexity of multi-party relationships, the confusion caused by the proliferation of regulations applying to different public service sectors, and the general deterioration in the protection afforded certain citizens and consumers accompanying this form of contractualization. A 'grievance' may be defined for present purposes as a perception on the part of the consumer or citizen of a wrong or injustice, giving cause for complaint against the party believed to be responsible for the infliction of the harm.[112] Referring back to the discussion of the various interests of service recipients in contracting processes in Chapter 10, grievances may be associated most simply with dissatisfaction over quality or some other aspect of performance by the responsible service provider. They may concern perceived unfairness in decision making, for example in the award of places on educational and training courses, the withdrawal of services due to economic restructuring, or the withholding of services on the ground that the user no longer satisfies rationing criteria. The harm may take the form of contractors' reneging on promises that have given rise to legitimate expectations on the part of users that the services would continue to be provided indefinitely.[113] Or grievances may have more complex and deep-seated causes, for example concerning the nature of service standards and lack of control by consumers over specifications and terms of contracts between purchasers and providers.

109 Responsiveness in this context implies (beyond commitment to common values of good administration and fairness) additional processes of public deliberation and participation that are not expected to apply in the relationship between service recipients and private providers.

110 J Black, 'Proceduralizing Regulation: Part I' (2000) 20 OJLS 597.

111 M Aronson and B Dyer, *Judicial Review of Administrative Action* (2nd edn, Sydney: LBC Information Services, 2000) 144.

112 P Birkinshaw, *Grievances, Remedies and the State* (2nd edn, London: Sweet and Maxwell, 1994); N Lewis and P Birkinshaw, *When Citizens Complain: Reforming Justice and Administration* (Buckingham: Open University Press, 1993).

113 *R v North Devon HA, ex p Coughlan* [2000] 3 All ER 850; [2001] QB 213. In the most extreme cases the harm may involve deprivation of liberty, as in the unwarranted exercise of discretionary powers by contractors providing prison services. It is clear in both Australia and the UK that such decision making is subject to judicial review.

Procedures for the redress of grievances and disputes resolution in all public service fields are subject to detailed government guidance and regulations made in accordance with statutory frameworks. Statutory complaints and redress mechanisms vary depending on whether services are provided directly by central or local government, provided by a private company or voluntary organization under contract with a public body, or provided and funded entirely privately. The complexity of these regulations, complaints procedures, and redress mechanisms (for example in the health and social care sectors) is likely to have given rise to considerable confusion on the part of citizens as to where and how to pursue grievances.[114] There is a proliferation of regimes and central directions, with varying implications for citizen redress depending on the method of funding or the identity of the provider. Further problems associated with the centrally driven nature of the regulatory process concern the general lack of involvement and participation of stakeholders in standard-setting and enforcement, and the likely ineffectiveness of bureaucratic regulation in achieving its goals of improved redress and responsiveness in human services provision.

The Government has recently emphasized the need for informal or alternative disputes resolution (ADR) in the handling of grievances arising from the activities of government departments and executive agencies in cases where there exists a statutory right of appeal to a tribunal.[115] Similarly the National Audit Office, in its more general analysis of citizen redress in public services, has stressed the importance of informal complaints procedures located at the bottom of a metaphorical 'ladder of redress'.[116] While informed primarily by pragmatic efficiency and cost considerations, such sentiments are consistent with a responsive regulation approach which acknowledges the limits of law and legal processes in addressing regulatory problems.[117] There is widespread agreement among policy makers and academics as to the desirability of dealing with grievances in the first instance as close as possible to the site where the harm in question was supposed to have originated.

Both public agencies and non-state bodies engaged in human services networks are subject to various specific regulatory requirements concerning informal

114 See for example: Health Service Ombudsman for England, 'Making Things Better? A Report on Reform of the NHS Complaints Procedure in England', 10 March 2005. The Report reviews five key weaknesses in the current system and approach (para 23): complaints systems are fragmented within the NHS, between the NHS and private health care systems, and between health and social care; the complaints system is not centred on the patient's needs; there is a lack of capacity and competence among staff to deliver a quality service; the right leadership, culture and governance are not in place; just remedies are not being secured for justified complaints. www.ombudsman.org.uk/improving_services/special_reports/nhs_complaints/comp_c1.html accessed 9 October 2005. On the 'labyrinthine complexity' of redress applying to different consumers and service providers in the health care sector, see A Pollock and S Kerrison, 'Complaints as Accountability? The Case of Health Care in the United Kingdom' [2001] PL 115.

115 Department for Constitutional Affairs (DCA) *Transforming Public Services: Complaints, Redress and Tribunals* (Cm 6243, 2004).

116 National Audit Office (NAO) *Citizen Redress: What Citizens Can Do If Things Go Wrong With Public Services* (London: The Stationery Office, 2005) 8.

117 J Braithwaite, T Makkai, V Braithwaite, and D Gibson, *Raising the Standard: Resident Centred Nursing Home Regulation in Australia* (Canberra: Australian Government Publishing Service, 1993).

complaints procedures. In some cases but not others, where citizens have grievances that have not been satisfactorily resolved by such informal means, more formal internal and external redress mechanisms are available further up the ladder of redress including application to the Ombudsman and, at the apex of the hierarchy of remedies, judicial review.[118] The role of the Administrative Court as adjudicator of last resort in disputes involving public authorities is reinforced by the requirement that permission to proceed will not normally be granted until the applicant has exhausted alternative remedies.[119] This requirement has been reiterated by the Court of Appeal in *Cowl v Plymouth City Council*, in which Lord Woolf criticized the 'unfortunate culture' of 'over-judicializing' disputes in such cases.[120] This case illustrates the ineffectiveness of the remedial hierarchy – as presently constituted in the publicly managed nursing home sector – both in providing incentives for public officials to make decisions that are 'right first time', and (where errors are made or grievances occur) in ensuring that complaints are dealt with at a the lowest possible rung of the ladder of redress.[121] It further raises questions not only of institutional design and the relationship between the different

[118] For an analysis of the limited impact of judicial review on first-instance administrative decision-making, see S Halliday, *Judicial Review and Compliance with Administrative Law* (Oxford: Hart Publishing, 2004). ibid, 'The Influence of Judicial Review in Bureaucratic Decision-Making' [2000] PL 110; M Hertogh and S Halliday, (eds), *Judicial Review and Bureaucratic Impact* (Cambridge: Cambridge University Press, 2004); K Pick and M Sunkin, 'The Changing Impact of Judicial Review: The Independent Review Service of the Social Fund' [2001] PL 736.

[119] Civil Procedure Rules 1998 (SI 1998/3132).

[120] *Frank Cowl & Orrs v Plymouth City Council* [2002] 1 WLR 803 (CA); A Le Sueur, 'How to Resolve Disputes With Public Authorities' [2002] PL 203. The case involved a challenge to the legality of the council's decision to close down a residential care home. The seven resident applicants (aged between 77 and 92 apart from one aged 66, and all frail and in poor health) sought judicial review to quash the defendants' decision to close the home, at least three claiming that they had been given assurances by employees of Plymouth council that they would be able to stay in the home for the rest of their lives, and that they had a legitimate expectation that the council would be held to its promises. Affirming the decision of Scott Baker J at first instance that the claim should be rejected on the ground that there was insufficient evidence to establish that 'home for life' promises had been made, the Court of Appeal issued general guidance on the paramount importance of avoiding litigation wherever possible in disputes between members of the public and public authorities exercising powers on their behalf. Under the CPR the court must further the overriding objective of enabling the just disposal of cases through active management (CPR 1.4(1)), including encouragement of the parties to use any ADR procedure where appropriate (CPR 1.4(2)(e)). The parties could be required to explain the steps taken to resolve the dispute without the court's involvement, for example through complaints mechanisms, in an *inter partes* hearing.

[121] The appeal of the nursing home residents was dismissed subject to agreed terms going beyond what the Council was obliged to do under its statutory complaints procedure. When required to focus on the future well-being of the claimants, the parties had no difficulty in coming to an agreement which was ultimately annexed to the judgment and formed part of the order of the court. The terms of reference of the panel appointed to resolve the dispute included making recommendations to the Council's social services committee as to whether the home should be closed, taking account of the issue of whether any of the residents were promised a 'home for life', and the emotional, psychological, and physical health of the residents and the impact of a move upon them. The *Cowl* ruling emphasizes the necessarily residual role of judicial review even in disputes involving the provision of services by public bodies that are unambiguously public in character (leaving aside the separate issue of how far the decisions of private organizations are amenable to review on the basis of their performance of a

redress levels, but also of the responsiveness of regulatory arrangements in terms of knowledge on the part of citizens and consumers of complaints mechanisms, and their ability to express grievances through appropriate voice mechanisms.[122] The provision of information about grievance procedures and the existence of accessible channels of communication for complaints are essential prerequisites for the effective operation of remedial hierarchies.

The more fundamental problem for present purposes, however, concerns the lack of uniformity in regulatory schemes governing different modes of provision of public services, and the resulting unevenness in the protection of citizens' interests. To reiterate, informal grievance procedures vary depending on whether the decision-making body is a government department or agency, an independent provider delivering a public service under contract with a commissioning public agency, or a private body delivering a public service directly to the citizen. Judicial review is possible only where the decision complained of involves a government department or other public agency, or an independent body performing a public function as this term has been defined in law. The fact that the body in question provides services to third-party citizens under contract with a public agency is not by itself sufficient to render decision making amenable to judicial review. The result in such cases is that the relationship between the citizen and service provider may be regulated neither by contract nor by administrative law.[123]

There is a need for greater consistency in the protection of citizens' interests in human services regardless of the manner of delivery, the nature of funding, or the public or private identity of the service provider. All providers and other bodies performing public service functions in human services networks should have in place adequate complaints mechanisms and procedures through which grievances can be investigated and settlements reached wherever possible, prior to submission of disputes that cannot be so resolved to more formal adjudication and ultimate judicial determination. The overall regulatory objective of hybrid governance of the user-contractor relationship as suggested above should be to minimize grievances, complaints and disputes, and maximize performance through incentives for the decisions of both government and independent sector bodies to be made fairly and properly in the first instance.

The principal objection to such specific institutional reform is that to add a further layer of regulation to the governance of contracting would be excessively costly, bureaucratic and difficult to implement.[124] In addition, the proliferation

public function). Generally see M Adler, 'A Socio-Legal Approach to Administrative Justice' (2003) 25 *Law and Policy* 323.

122 Ombudsman's Annual Report for 2003–4 (2nd Report – 13 July 2004).

123 Where public services are privately funded and directly provided in the market, the apex of the remedial hierarchy is judicial enforcement of contractual rights and duties. The level of citizen protection in such cases may be superior in some respects while inferior in others, compared to that afforded under direct government provision or purchase-of-service contracting.

124 For a sceptical view of the prospects of complex regimes of administrative regulation in dealing with new governance problems, see C Harlow, 'Public Service, Market Ideology, and Citizenship'

of specific schemes for each different service sector might be both confusing for consumers and result in the unnecessary duplication of institutions dealing with very similar problems.[125] On the other hand, many of the elements necessary for this type of scheme are already present in some form in the regulatory environment (standards, complaints and disputes handling processes, etc). This strategy would solve some of the problems created by contracting, and would provide both redress for individual grievances, and a mechanism for holding contractors to account for unfairness and other deficiencies in decision making. It would serve also as a vehicle for the inculcation of the values of good administration within particular service sectors, through self-regulation backed ultimately by legal sanctions.

The guiding purpose of this type of regulation would be the improvement of management processes and decision making with a view to minimizing grievances and disputes.[126] The onus would be on organizations themselves to devise means by which standards, both substantive and procedural, could be satisfied. Responsive regulation would require escalation to more formal dispute resolution were the interests of service recipients not sufficiently met by self-regulation. This suggestion for reform takes account of the argument that a regulatory strategy based simply on standards, monitoring and sanctions for breach is likely to result in perverse incentives and game-playing that frustrate regulatory objectives and produce little or no benefit for service users.[127] The advantage of the proposed scheme is that it would be aimed at improving management processes and decision making with a view to minimizing disputes. A principal objective would be to create pressures on public agencies to observe procedural and substantive values.[128] 'The most efficient way for an organization to continuously reduce the injustice for which it is responsible will be dispute prevention rather than dispute resolution.'[129] The onus would be on organizations themselves to devise means by which substantive and procedural standards could be satisfied. Large organizations might be required to produce an annual report on their performance under such schemes. Responsive regulation would require a move to more formal dispute resolution were the interests of service recipients not sufficiently met by self-regulation. With regard to complaints that were upheld as a result of the disputes handling mechanism, the purpose would be not to punish the provider for breach of contract, but to make effective restoration to the users of public services who had been inconvenienced by the failure to perform in accordance with service

in M Freedland and S Sciarra, (eds), *Public Services and Citizenship in European Law – Public and Labour Law Perspectives* (Oxford: Oxford University Press, 1998) 54.

[125] A 'transaction-based' approach would be advantageous from the consumer point of view where there exist similar features across a diverse range of services or products – see MacNeill (n 81 above) 265.

[126] J Braithwaite, *Restorative Justice and Responsive Regulation* (Oxford: Oxford University Press, 2002): 'The most efficient way for an organization to continuously reduce the injustice for which it is responsible will be dispute prevention rather than dispute resolution', p 255.

[127] J Braithwaite, 'Rewards and Regulation', (2002) 29 JLS 12, 15.

[128] Aronson (n 22 above).

[129] Braithwaite (n 126 above).

standards.[130] At the apex of remedial hierarchies, the specifically human rights of citizens should be protected through obligations imposed on service providers in their contracts with public purchasers, combined with the adoption by the courts of a functional interpretation of the meaning of public authority in s 6(3)(b) of the Human Rights Act 1998.

Conclusion

The first task of responsive law should be to structure the exercise of discretion by ministers and government officials through procedural mechanisms and constraints operating at all levels of decision making on public services. These mechanisms should be designed to maximize the scope for public participation and deliberation with regard to contractualization. Where contract is adopted as a mode of organization and a form of regulation, the issue of legal and institutional reform should be approached with caution and with sensitivity to the particular circumstances. Throughout this book I have argued that functional differences between the three main types of the New Public Contracting mean that conclusions reached in one setting cannot be mechanically applied in another. Public contracting, in whatever form, requires *appropriate* institutional support for any potential for increased responsiveness to be realized. Accordingly this chapter has stressed the limits of law and of legal institutions in increasing responsiveness. Generally, there is a need for vigilance in guarding against juridification and the over-extension of legal governance into domains that are better regulated by other institutions and processes.

I have further suggested that the role of a responsive legal order should be to help embed principles of responsive administration within the organizational structures of the whole range of public and independent sector bodies engaged in public service networks. The commitment to institutional morality here is consistent with a broad administrative justice perspective in which the values of fairness and good administration are promoted through a variety of norms and mechanisms that generally inform decision making on matters of public interest.[131] In Selznick's terms, all such deliberations should be governed by the same 'process values' (eliminating bias, respecting natural justice, providing opportunities for reasoned argument, assuring accurate and reliable determination of facts, and upholding legal stability) that underlie more formal legal procedures.[132]

130 ibid 254.

131 P Craig, 'Three Perspectives on the Relationship Between Administrative Justice and Administrative Law' in R Creyke and J McMillan, (eds), *Administrative Justice – The Core and the Fringe* (Canberra: AIAL, 2000) 28; M Partington, 'Restructuring Administrative Justice? The Redress of Citizens' Grievances' (1999) *Current Legal Problems* 173–199.

132 P Selznick, *The Moral Commonwealth: Social Theory and the Promise of Community* (Berkeley: University of California Press, 1992) 738.

12

Conclusions and Policy Implications

This book has charted the increasing use of contract as a regulatory mechanism across a broad spectrum of economic and social relationships in Britain over the last twenty five years. Since New Labour came to power in 1997 the trend has accelerated. Contractual governance has spread rapidly beyond the spheres of economics and public administration into social policy. The experience of contractualization, however, has proved highly problematic. My overall conclusion is that, while there exists a potential for contracts to serve responsively in the performance of a range of public service functions,[1] in many cases contracting regimes have demonstrably failed or are at risk of failure.

The legitimacy deficit in the New Public Contracting consists in the lack of adequate opportunity for public deliberation in policy and decision making on public service issues. While there might be good arguments in favour of contractualization, these remain opaque and difficult to evaluate given the absence under the UK constitution of adequate procedures that promote accountability and transparency. Such governance deficiencies are intimately linked with problems of regulatory ineffectiveness. In economic contracting regimes, public authorities are under pressure to adopt forms of organization that may not be suited to the circumstances, or to the needs or preferences of citizens and consumers. I have suggested that the recent experience of contractual difficulties in fields as diverse as the procurement of schools and hospitals under the PFI and the contracting out of residential and nursing care services for vulnerable citizens begs the question whether these public service functions might be performed more effectively by the state directly. In administrative contracts and social control contracts, we have seen how regulatory problems stem from the weakness or imbalance of contract norms in relationships between parts of government and between state agencies and individual citizens.

This chapter summarizes the main arguments and findings concerning the failures of responsiveness of the New Public Contracting in contemporary Britain. Emphasizing the limits of contract as an instrument of public regulation, I conclude that the responsiveness of public contractual governance is dependent on

[1] See pp 357–361 below.

eight core conditions,[2] which are set out in detail in the next section. There follows a summary of policy recommendations for the institutional and organizational reform of particular contracting regimes. In the third section I consider the future of the New Public Contracting. Finally, I contrast New Labour's social contract rhetoric with the reality, and indicate the basic elements of an alternative vision of such a contract based on the commitment to social inclusion and democratic principles governing decision making on public services.

Conditions of responsive public contractual governance

The first four conditions may be described as relational (Fig 8). They refer to: (1) sensitivity on the part of regulators to the circumstances in which regulation occurs; (2) the presence in contractual relationships of norms of planning and consent necessary to support discreteness and presentiation; (3) the bindingness of obligations in those relationships, combined with norms of fairness and reciprocity; and finally (4) trust and cooperation in the performance of contracts.

Conditions of responsive public contractual governance	
Relational conditions	**Further institutional and organizational conditions**
(1) Regulatory sensitivity.	(5) Collective learning and institutional morality.
(2) Planning and consent norms.	(6) Citizen empowerment and consumer redress.
(3) Norms supporting bindingness, fairness, and reciprocity.	(7) Legal powers and resources of public agencies.
(4) Trust and cooperation in contract performance.	(8) Transparency, public deliberation and public accountability.

Figure 8. Theory of public contractual governance

[2] Like Macneil's contract norms, there is an element of arbitrariness in the number of such conditions and the manner in which they are presented. While there are overlaps with the dimensions of responsiveness in the general regulation literature outlined in ch 4, the conditions discussed here are peculiar to the public contracting environment.

These relational elements are necessary, but not sufficient, conditions of responsive regulation. Stable and cooperative relationships that benefit regulators and regulatees might be a mask for inefficiency, ineffectiveness, or fraud and corruption. The result in such a case would be to defeat the overall purpose of the regulatory regime. Again, the efficiency gains of relational contracting might be outweighed by disproportionate damage to other values such as equity or social justice, or harm to the interests of other stakeholders, such as consumers.

Accordingly, a further set of conditions of responsiveness must be specified, referring to institutional and organizational aspects of the design of contracting regimes. These concern: (5) the capacity of the system of governance to facilitate organizational learning and institutional morality among the various bodies engaged in public service networks; (6) the securing of citizen empowerment through appropriate fora of public participation, coupled with effective mechanisms for the redress of grievances; (7) the adequacy of legal powers and resources of public agencies charged with performing contractual regulatory functions; and finally (8) transparency, public deliberation and public accountability in both the design and implementation of contracting regimes. These eight conditions, which together constitute the basic elements of a theory of public contractual governance, will in turn briefly be considered and illustrated with examples drawn from the foregoing analysis.

Regulatory sensitivity

Chapter 3 established the importance of sensitivity on the part of regulators in contracting regimes to the circumstances in which regulation occurs. In particular, responsive regulators need to exercise fine judgment as to whether a more or less interventionist response is required, depending on the capacity of regulatees for self-regulation.[3] Regulatory sensitivity implies the existence of some degree of cooperation between regulators and regulatees in all forms of the New Public Contracting. In the case of economic contracts and social control contracts, this quality is necessary both in the hierarchical regulatory relationship between central government and public agencies, and in the contractual relationship between such agencies and the other contracting party.[4] Lack of regulatory sensitivity on the part of central government may be expected to have a negative impact on the capacity

3 J Braithwaite, *Restorative Justice and Responsive Regulation* (Oxford: Oxford University Press, 2002) 29; see ch 4, Fig 5.

4 Here there is an overlap with the specifically *contractual* norms that support trust and cooperation in the performance of contracts, further considered in point (4) below.

of public agencies to perform their contractual regulatory roles responsively.[5] Economic contracting regimes under the Conservatives in the era of CCT and compulsory market testing were characterized by regulatory *in*sensitivity. The generally less confrontational style adopted by New Labour since 1997 has not altered the underlying tensions in relationships between central government and local councils, health authorities, NHS Trusts, and other regulated entities which perform public service functions.

Regulatory sensitivity implies not only the general avoidance of adversarial relations and the minimum use of legitimate force,[6] but also the existence of active collaboration and partnership in regulatory relationships. This applies to the design and modification of contracting regimes as well as their practical operation. I have argued throughout this book that contracting regimes need to be designed and managed from the 'bottom-up', with greater involvement of professional groups and other stakeholders from the outset, rather than imposed from the 'top-down' in pursuit of the Government's pre-determined policy agendas.

Planning and consent

A second source of regulatory ineffectiveness and therefore of unresponsiveness in some instances of the New Public Contracting has been the failure to secure the threshold conditions of discreteness and presentiation that are the essence of functioning contractual relations. The norms of planning and consent are essential to any contract. Where these elements are absent, nothing of value is exchanged and there can be no possibility of welfare being jointly maximized by contractual means. Chapter 11 noted two obvious examples of the failure of planning in this sense: Home-School Agreements and Public Service Agreements (PSAs). In these cases, I have suggested that the use of contractual terminology is misleading and may as well be abandoned. The reason these arrangements are considered not to be contracts has nothing directly to do with the absence of the quality of legal enforceability. In neither case could legal reform directed at making the 'contracts' more enforceable be part of the solution to the governance deficiencies I have outlined.

We saw in Chapter 9 that social control contracts generally suffer from weak representation of the norms of consent and reciprocity in contract negotiation, rooted in the structural imbalance of power between state agencies and individual citizens in these relationships. I have suggested that further research is needed to determine

5 This dimension has been least problematic in the case of administrative contracts, where the bureaucratic and contractual elements in contracting regimes are combined in a relatively simple regulatory structure, and the relationships are solely between levels of government.

6 See ch 4, Fig 5. It should be emphasized that the quality of regulatory sensitivity does not rule out force and compulsion, but implies limits on the use of such measures to circumstances where they are necessary to achieve legitimate policy and regulatory goals – P Vincent-Jones, 'Values and Purpose in Government: Central-local Relations in Regulatory Perspective, (2002) 29 JLS 27.

how far the compulsive environment in which these agreements are concluded is fatal to their ability to deliver the welfare benefits associated with relational contracting, and whether the inherent imbalance of power is capable of being redressed through the institutional strengthening of these and other contract norms.

Bindingness, fairness, and reciprocity

Where the threshold conditions of contractual relations have been established (point (2) above), responsiveness is further dependent on the embedding of contractual institutions to an appropriate depth within public service relationships. On the one hand, contractual commitments must be credible and binding to the degree necessary to enable the parties to structure their relationships productively. On the other hand, the norms supporting the bindingness of obligations must be in equilibrium with those promoting fairness and reciprocity. We have seen how the failure or weakness of relational norms may be a source of problems for the public agency, for the other contracting party, or for both parties. The norm of reciprocity is particularly crucial to the success of government policies aimed at behavioural modification in the diverse fields of social security, education, criminal justice, and the control of deviance. Overall, institutional strengthening may be necessary to improve regulatory effectiveness,[7] and/or to provide safeguards against unfairness to the party in the weaker bargaining position. The question posed in Part III was how such institutionalization might best be achieved.

In the case of framework documents linking government departments and executive agencies, one option would be to subject these relationships to a specially created public law normative framework. However, I have suggested that a better alternative would be for framework legislation to regulate the process of creation of executive agencies as separate legal identities with contracting powers and capacities. As regards social control contracts, I argued in Chapter 11 that the contract norms might be strengthened through a combination of legally guaranteed procedures for representing the individual's interests in the negotiation of the contract, legal safeguards against unfairness by the public agency in implementing the contract, and legal mechanisms for enforcing the state's contractual obligations to the individual. If the contract norms of power, consent, and reciprocity cannot be restored by such means, there is little to distinguish contractual social control from the exercise of nakedly hierarchical authority, and we should dispense with the misleading and redundant terminology of contract. In the case of economic contracts recognized at private law, Chapter 7 took note of a range of solutions in mainstream legal debates designed to counter the problem of unfairness in

7 I have argued that, once the threshold conditions of contractual relations have been established, bindingness is not generally a problem for the party using the contract as an instrument of regulation. What remains problematic in contracts that are not legally enforceable, however, is the lack of reciprocity in the sense of the relative inability of the regulatee effectively to enforce the obligations undertaken by the state agency – see ch 8.

some purchaser–provider relationships. In the case of 'internal' economic contracts that are not recognized at private law, I have argued that while extra-legal sanctions are available to the public agency which compensate for the absence of legal enforceability, there remains a problem of unfairness to the service provider which should be addressed either through reform of the bureaucratic control structures within public service organizations or, where specifically legal reform can be shown to be necessary, by opening up relationships to existing systems of private law governance through the corporatization of provider entities.

Trust and cooperation in contract performance

A final relational condition of responsive regulation involves trust and cooperation in the performance of contracts. This implies an appropriate balance between discrete and relational norms within the contractual relationship and in its institutional environment for the duration of the contract. If these norms become damaged or otherwise cease to function properly, it cannot be expected that obligations will be fulfilled, or that the potential welfare benefits of contract will be realized. Much of this book has been devoted to analysing the success or failure of the state's regulatory efforts to secure conditions of contracting in which each party can trust with confidence in the cooperation of the other.[8] Severe damage to a number or all of the contract norms may result in the failure of a particular contract, and/or the total breakdown or unworkability of the contracting regime. The empirical socio-legal literature is replete with examples of transaction difficulties and costs associated with the undermining of trust and cooperation in economic contracts. I have suggested that the catastrophic failure of some PFI projects mirrors the problems that were encountered during the 1990s with the more overtly compulsory policy-driven programmes of CCT and market testing. Even where the damage to contract norms is less severe, and is expressed in less serious tensions in the management and operation of the contracts, the long-term consequences for the relationship may be disastrous. For example, the success of social control contracts is likely to be heavily dependent on the maintenance of high levels of trust and cooperation in the relationship between public agencies and individual citizens throughout the duration of the contract. Contracting regimes should be designed and managed in a way that not only avoids undermining the norms that support trust and cooperation, but also actively promotes those relational qualities.

Collective learning and institutional morality

The remaining conditions of responsiveness are concerned not directly with the relational or contractual dimensions of regulation, but with aspects of

[8] D Campbell and D Harris, 'Flexibility in Long-Term Contractual Relationships: The Role of Cooperation' (1993) 20 JLS 166, 184.

the institutional and organizational design of contracting regimes. We saw in Chapter 4 how the value of contractual exchanges may be enhanced through the capacity of regulatory schemes to facilitate collective learning among the various public, private, and voluntary bodies engaged in public service networks. Both regulating and regulated entities need to adapt within and learn from their environments, taking account of new information and adjusting their activities to core values and purposes. A hypothesis that might be tested in further research is that relationality (Fig 8(1)–(4)) and collective learning are closely related features of responsiveness, and that the latter is dependent on the former.[9] We have seen that a further factor contributing to the overall responsiveness of public services is institutional morality. Non-state bodies acquire responsibilities of ethical awareness and moral competence by virtue of their performance of specifically *public* service functions.[10] I suggested in Chapter 11 that the tailoring of 'remedial hierarchies' to the conditions prevailing in particular service sectors should help inculcate within public service industries values of good administration, fairness, and non-discrimination through self-regulation backed ultimately by legal sanctions. Institutional morality should be a feature also of the responsive operation of public agencies engaged in policy development and decision-making at the heart of government.

Citizen empowerment and consumer redress

A central argument of this book has been that responsiveness to citizen and consumer needs is essential to the success of economic contracting regimes. We saw in Chapter 10 how the concept of hybrid regulation may provide a key to developing effective complaints mechanisms and forms of redress of grievances, combining formal law and legal procedures with more informal institutional processes that operate within all organizations engaged in public service networks. The commitment to restorative justice requires that remedial hierarchies should serve to effect reparation to the citizens who have legitimate grievances in respect of the organization and provision of public services. I have suggested more fundamentally that citizen empowerment is dependent on the development of new voice mechanisms to counter the imbalance created by the emphasis in recent government policy on choice and exit. The decision whether a service should be outsourced or provided directly or under some other arrangement should be subject to 'notice and comment' and other publicity and consultation requirements. Standard-setting procedures in particular service sectors should be designed to

9 European Commission, *Framework 6 Integrated Project: 'Reflexive Governance in the Public Interest'* 2005–2010.

10 On the identity, loyalty and responsibilities of employees in network forms of organization, in the context of the blurring of the public/private divide, see J Rubery, J Earnshaw, M Marchington, F Lee Cooke, and S Vincent, 'Changing Organizational Forms and the Employment Relationship' (2002) 39 *Journal of Management Studies* 645.

involve both consumers and provider organizations. Specific representative institutions may be needed to enhance the legitimacy and responsiveness of decisions on rationing services, and to overcome the impasse presented by judicial reluctance to interfere with the merits of such decisions. I have argued that there exists considerable scope for innovation in the design of new fora of public involvement and participation, such as citizens' juries. The role of representative bodies need not be confined to the implementation of existing policy, but should extend to deliberation over fundamental issues of policy direction, for example concerning contracting out, privatization, Academies, and the PFI.[11] What is important is that the agendas for debate in such deliberative fora are locally and democratically determined, rather than imposed from above by central government in support of preconceived programmes of public service reform.[12]

Legal powers and resources of public agencies

Public agencies to whom responsibilities have been devolved in contracting regimes require appropriate legal powers and resources to perform their public service functions. Responsiveness in various senses might be increased through relaxation of current rules which disallow non-commercial considerations in the tendering and the award of contracts. The principle of subsidiarity requires that a wider margin of appreciation be permitted to local councils and other public agencies in making their own value and policy choices, and in deciding whether and how contract should be used as an instrument of regulation in their pursuit. We saw in Chapter 9 how the regulatory capacity of public agencies is also dependent on an appropriate level of resources, whether provided directly by central government or raised independently. The problem of lack of reciprocity in many social control contracts is exacerbated by resource constraints, which tend to inhibit public agencies such as Jobcentres and Youth Offender Panels making commitments and then delivering on their side of the bargain. In the case of local government, the shortage of resources is linked with the restriction of legal powers to raise revenues from local taxation. Contractual capacity in both senses must be built into the design of contracting regimes if they are to have any realistic chance of achieving their legitimate public service objectives.

Transparency, public deliberation, and public accountability

The qualities of transparency, public deliberation, and public accountability are vital to responsive public services. This condition is closely linked to that

[11] cf N Ryan, 'Reconstructing Citizens as Consumers: Implications for New Modes of Governance' (2001) 60 *Australian Journal of Public Administration* 104.

[12] On the inherent limitations of government public participation initiatives in major service sectors such as health, see R Rowe and M Shepherd, 'Public Participation and the New NHS: No Closer to Citizen Control?' (2002) 36 *Social Policy and Administration* 275.

concerning citizen empowerment. A major task of responsive law is to structure the exercise of discretion by ministers and officials through a combination of procedural and informational requirements. These would govern both the making of policy at the highest levels within government, and its implementation at lower levels by public agencies or authorities in particular instances. Such a legal framework should ensure that policy objectives are made explicit, and that policy formulation, development, and evaluation are subject to proper deliberation and public scrutiny. It should also ensure that official decision making is transparent, and that bureaucratic actors are properly accountable to legitimate sources of authority for their performance of public service functions. I argued in Chapter 11 that this requires the positive commitment at all levels of public administration to principles of open government and freedom of information. The making of effective choices between different forms of public service organization, the selection of the best type of contractual arrangement and of the contracting partner, and the accountability of decision makers for their actions, are all, to some degree, dependent on the quality and availability of information. Where it is decided that public services should be organized on a contractual basis, information about the contract process is vital for holding the government to account and for assessing its performance. The goal of institutionalizing respect for values of openness, transparency, and accountability in decision making on public services requires the radical reform of existing administrative practices and a challenge to the prevailing culture of secrecy within public sector organizations.

Summary of policy recommendations

Specific recommendations are as follows:

- Home-School Agreements fail to meet the threshold conditions of contractual relations. Since these regulatory arrangements appear to serve no useful purpose they should be abolished. The repeal of legislation would leave schools free to decide whether and how to implement their own contractual schemes, unencumbered by specific statutory requirements.
- Public Service Agreements (PSAs) fail to meet the threshold conditions of contractual relations. The pretence of a contractual basis to these relationships should be abandoned. The public accountability and transparency benefits accompanying the Spending Review process should be enhanced through regulatory measures directed at improving the quality and availability of performance information.
- The problem of the imbalance of power in relationships between government departments and executive agencies should be addressed by strengthening the contract norms supporting framework documents, either through a special public law of contract or by legislation regulating the process of creation of

executive agencies as independent legal entities with contracting powers and capacities.

- The problem of the potential for unfairness in legally enforceable economic contracts should be addressed through a combination of reform of certain aspects of the *ultra vires* doctrine, the introduction of flexible remedies in relation to the modification of contracts, and limited extension of the scope of judicial review.
- The problem of the potential for unfairness in 'internal' economic contracts should be addressed through reform of the bureaucratic authority structures within public service organizations, or where appropriate, through corporatization of provider entities.

More generally:

- Legal procedural reforms are needed to structure the exercise of official discretion in both the making of policy at the highest levels within government, and its implementation at lower administrative levels by public agencies or authorities in particular instances.
- There should be legally guaranteed procedures for representing the interests of citizens and consumers in decision making by public agencies in respect of a wide range of public service issues, including resource allocation, standard-setting, contract management, and most fundamentally the adoption of contracting out as a mode of organization.
- Freedom of contractual information should be enhanced by a combination of the amendment of current Freedom of Information (FOI) legislation in order to restrict the scope of the defence of 'commercial in confidence', and measures directed at combating the culture of secrecy and institutionalizing respect for values of openness, transparency, and accountability within government bodies.
- Contracting regimes should be designed and managed from the 'bottom-up' – ie with the greatest possible involvement of professional groups and other stakeholders – rather than imposed by government from the 'top-down'. They should be implemented in a way that not only avoids undermining the norms that support trust and cooperation in purchaser–provider and state–citizen relationships, but also seeks actively to promote those relational qualities.
- The capacity of public agencies to discharge the responsibilities delegated to them in contracting regimes should be enhanced through the removal of legal restrictions on the use of contract as an instrument for the achievement of democratically mandated policy goals, and by the grant of appropriate legal powers. Public agencies should either be allocated the resources necessary to enable them to discharge their contractual regulatory functions, or where appropriate have the legal power to raise revenues from independent sources.

- Remedial hierarchies should be carefully tailored to the conditions prevailing in particular service sectors, in order to both provide redress of individual grievances and to help inculcate within public service industries values of good administration, fairness, and non-discrimination.
- Further research should investigate the link between organizational or collective learning by bodies performing public service functions on the one hand, and relationality as a quality of regulatory relationships in public service networks on the other hand. This research might test the hypothesis that that the latter is a necessary condition of the former.
- Further research should investigate how far the structural imbalance of power in social control contracts threatens the success of these regulatory arrangements, and whether this inherent deficiency may be repaired by strengthening the contract norms by legal or other institutional means.

The future of the New Public Contracting

What of the future of the New Public Contracting? From a rational policy perspective, this ought to depend on how far the above conditions of responsiveness can be secured through general procedural reforms combined with the repair of institutional weaknesses that have been identified within particular contracting regimes. We have seen how, given the existence of appropriate public fora for the determination of policy goals, the potential of the New Public Contracting as a mode of regulation lies in its mixture of coercive and non-coercive, direct and indirect, and automatic and non-automatic regulatory elements. The fundamental question is whether the relational qualities that have been argued to characterize business and other private exchanges can be secured within complex contracting regimes, such that the maximization of the parties' welfare through contractual exchange is combined effectively with the attainment of legitimate public regulatory objectives.

The greatest challenges in this regard have undoubtedly arisen in the economic arena, due to the complexity of the task of regulatory coordination and the multiplicity of stakeholders with interests in contractual processes. We saw in Chapter 7 how economic contracting regimes tend to be particularly cumbersome, complex, and convoluted in operation.[13] The question is whether these regimes are capable of succeeding where bureaucracies and markets have failed; or rather, given that all governance arrangements are imperfect, whether in

[13] 'The more complex and convoluted the tool, the more separate actors are involved, the more difficult it is likely to be to manage. Some tools are more cumbersome to operate than others. While they may promise great efficiency and effectiveness in theory, they are unlikely to deliver it in practice because of the managerial difficulties they pose' – LM Salamon, 'The New Governance and the Tools of Public Action: An Introduction' in ibid (ed), *The Tools of Government: A Guide to the New Governance* (Oxford: Oxford University Press, 2002) 24.

any particular case this mode of economic coordination is better than the next worst alternative.[14] Some of the conditions for the responsive provision of public services might better be secured through properly constituted and regulated markets than through complex schemes of policy-driven regulation involving quasi-markets and purchase-of-service contracting. However, the devolution of decision-making functions to individual consumers in markets removes precisely that element of public control and direction that may be necessary to achieve fundamental social policy objectives, such as protecting vulnerable citizens, combating social exclusion, and reducing the damaging impact of widening economic and social inequalities on society more generally. As we have seen, ultimately there can be no individual 'exit' from the social problems associated with the deteriorating health, education, and housing conditions of marginalized or disadvantaged sectors of the population. While acknowledging that there are no easy answers to the question of how public services should be funded, provided and regulated, I have suggested that legal procedural reforms directed at improving the quality of deliberation in policy and decision making should at least help to address the issue of choice of mode of organization in a more rational and transparent manner than has recently been possible.

In the absence of a radical change in political direction, however, or of constitutional or procedural legal reforms controlling the pace and extent of contractualization, the drift to privatization is likely to continue. Economic contracting regimes as presently constituted appear to be a transitional stage from bureaucratic organization to ever-more privatized forms of public service provision. The not-so-hidden agenda of economic contracting regimes since the beginning of the 1980s has been to shift functions traditionally performed by government towards the outer boundaries of the 'public' relative to the 'private' sphere. The apparently neutral aim of improving public services by whatever means delivers best value is in tension with the more fundamental policy goals of reducing public sector borrowing, improving domestic productivity, and increasing international competitiveness by transferring responsibilities for funding and provision to the private and non-profit sectors. The real objective has been not to recuperate the poor performance of government providers, but to change the basic mode of organization of public services. The deployment of regulatory instruments including competition, corporatization, and choice in conjunction with contracting regimes is playing a major part in this process. I suggested in Chapter 8 that the more that consumers are brought into direct relationship with non-state providers, for example through vouchering, user-fees, co-payments and direct payments, the more the arrangement begins to resemble a regulated market rather than a quasi-market. Even if the responsibility for delivery of some sensitive

[14] RH Coase, *The Firm, the Market, and the Law* (Chicago: University of Chicago Press, 1988); C Wolf, *Markets or Governments: Choosing Between Imperfect Alternatives* (2nd edn, Cambridge, Mass: MIT Press, 1993).

public services is brought back under state monopoly control, the general trend may be irreversible. We have seen that, in the longer term, the trend may be away from regulated *public* contracting towards regulated *private* contracting in the organization and provision of public services, accompanied by an increased blurring of the boundary between regulated markets for public services and wholly private services.

A new social contract

This book has highlighted the glaring disparity between the social contract rhetoric adopted by New Labour and the reality of the New Public Contracting. The promise to 'deliver greater trust, transparency, responsibility and responsiveness' in the relationship between government and citizens is far from being achieved.[15] The continuing failure on the part of government properly to spell out policy purposes on public services, and the absence of public involvement and deliberation at a deep level in debates over processes of contractualization and privatization, reflect fundamental deficiencies in legal and political governance in contemporary Britain. As with the war in Iraq, there appears to have been a general lack of transparency and integrity in the manner in which policies involving Academies, Foundation Hospitals, and the PFI have been developed and implemented.

A new social contract between all levels of government and citizens is needed to address this deficit in political legitimacy, and to help promote a culture of openness in which the complex issues surrounding the contractualization and privatization of public services can be fully and properly debated. Ian Harden's public law vision of the 'new contract' some fifteen years ago was that this should be understood as a claim of citizens, based on the rule of law, not to be dependent on discretionary public power for the things necessary for individual autonomy.[16] My concluding argument, by contrast, is that the new social contract might better be conceived as a claim on the part of citizens and consumers *not to be excluded from* processes of decision making by public agencies in regard to a broad range of public service issues.[17] More than simply providing a bulwark against arbitrary public power and the exercise of discretion, this vision implies a regulatory role for law in guaranteeing the conditions in which choices and decisions may be made in as democratic and rational a manner as possible, at any given moment of time, about how government is organized and public services are provided, about how these functions

[15] *A New Contract for Welfare: New Ambitions for Our Country*, Green Paper, (Cm 3805, 1998) para 30.

[16] I Harden, *The Contracting State* (Buckingham: Open University Press, 1992).

[17] cf CB Macpherson, 'The Maximization of Democracy'; 'A Political Theory of Property' in *Democratic Theory: Essays in Retrieval* (Oxford: Clarendon Press, 1973).

are regulated, and about the policy purposes and values underlying regulatory interventions.[18]

This social contract should be built on an understanding of the inherent limits of purposive intervention in regulated social systems.[19] Policy making and evaluation should be seen as experiments in practical reason based on the pursuit of legitimate policy purposes rather than as technical exercises. Policy conjectures should be subject to continuous testing, review and evaluation, to assess whether they have worked, and if so to understand how and why.[20] The experience of other countries or systems should serve not as a template, but to prompt critical introspection and policy learning. A responsive policy process should aim to maximize deliberation and scrutiny of arguments and claims made by advocates of particular positions, exposing ambiguities or ambivalence, and teasing out different layers of meaning.

Finally, the new social contract implies a positive role for the nation state in identifying and removing practical obstacles to the enjoyment by all citizens of the benefits of that contract. Where individuals are disenfranchised by poverty, disability, or other forms of economic and social disadvantage they are less likely to be able or willing to participate in democratic processes.[21] This requires a commitment on the part of the state to securing minimum standards of universality, quality, and continuity in the provision of essential public services. Where such services are organized on a quasi-market or market basis, the state should have a continuing responsibility for overseeing provision and maintaining minimum standards of availability and security. Where an especially high value is placed on continuity and security, either the services should be provided directly, or the state should be prepared to underwrite the risks associated with privatization and contractualization.[22] As we have seen, quasi-market organization and

[18] See MC Dorf and CF Sabel, 'A Constitution of Democratic Experimentalism' (1998) 98 *Columbia Law Review* 267; J Dryzek, *Deliberative Democracy and Beyond: Liberals, Critics and Contestations* (Oxford: Oxford University Press, 2000); O Gerstenberg and C Sabel, 'Directly-Deliberative Polyarchy: An Institutional Ideal for Europe' in C Joerges and R Dehousse, *Good Governance in Europe's Integrated Market* (Oxford: Oxford University Press, 2002).

[19] R Mayntz, 'Governing Failures and the Problem of Governability: Some Comments on a Theoretical Paradigm' in J Kooiman, (ed), *Modern Governance: New Government-Society Interactions* (London: Sage Publications, 1993).

[20] I Sanderson, 'Evaluation, Policy Learning and Evidence-Based Policy Making' (2002) 80 *Public Administration* 1, 19; R Klein, 'Self-Inventing Institutions: Institutional Design in the UK Welfare State' in RE Goodin, (ed), *The Theory of Institutional Design* (Cambridge: Cambridge University Press, 1996).

[21] Effective citizen participation in decision making on public services requires the rebalancing of current inequalities of power in this regard – see S Arnstein, 'A Ladder of Citizen Participation' (1969) 35 *Journal of American Institute of Planners* 214.

[22] This happens effectively in the case of PFI bankruptcies, so there is no reason in principle why central government should not accept the economic risks associated with private provision in fields such as nursing home care.

other forms of privatization create a potential for certain harms to individual and public interests for which no legal remedy or other form of redress may be expected adequately to compensate. The question of the nature of the state's involvement in, and responsibility for, the organization of public services remains fundamental.

Bibliography

BOOKS AND ARTICLES

Aalders, M., and Wilthagen, T., 'Moving Beyond Command-and-Control: Reflexivity in the Regulation of Occupational Health and Safety' (1997) 19 *Law and Policy* 415.

Abbott, B., Blackburn, R., and Curran, J., 'Local Authority Privatisation and Markets for Small Business' (1996) 22 *Local Government Studies* 72.

Adams, D., and Hess, M., 'Alternatives to Competitive Tendering and Privatisation: A Case Study from the Australian Health Industry' (2000) 59 *Australian Journal of Public Administration* 49.

Adams, J., and Brownsword, R., 'Privity and the Concept of a Network Contract' (1990) 10 *Legal Studies* 12.

—— 'Contract, Consideration and the Critical Path' (1990) 53 *Modern Law Review* 536.

—— 'More in Expectation than Hope: The Blackpool Airport Case' (1991) 54 *Modern Law Review* 281.

Adler, M., 'A Socio-Legal Approach to Administrative Justice' (2003) 25 *Law and Policy* 323.

Administrative Review Council, *Government Business Enterprises and Commonwealth Administrative Law*, Report No. 38 (Canberra: Commonwealth of Australia, 1995).

—— *The Contracting Out of Government Services*, Report No. 42 (Canberra: Commonwealth of Australia, 1998).

Admiraal, R.J., and Jan van Helden, G., 'Benchmarking in the Dutch Waste-Water Treatment Sector' (2003) *Public Money and Management* (April), 113–118.

Airo-Farulla, G., 'Public and Private in Australian Administrative Law' (1992) 3 *Public Law Review* 186.

—— 'Administrative Law and "Governance" ', in Finn, C. (ed.), *Sunrise or Sunset? Administrative Law in the New Millennium* (Canberra: Australian Institute of Administrative Law, 2000), 268.

Alder, J., 'Legality and Democracy in Local Government From the Perspective of Judicial Review', paper for *Local Government and the Rule of Law* conference, University of Bristol, April 2000.

—— 'Incommensurable Values and Judicial Review: The Case of Local Government' [2001] *Public Law* 717.

Allars, M., 'Citizenship Rights, Review Rights and Contractualism' (2001) 18 *Law in Context* 79.

—— 'Private Law But Public Power: Removing Administrative Law Review From Government Business Enterprises' (1995) 6 *Public Law Review* 44.

—— 'The Commercialisation of Administrative Law', in Kneebone, S. (ed.) *Administrative Law and the Rule of Law: Still Part of the Same Package?* (Canberra: Australian Institute of Administrative Law, 1999), 146.

Allison, J.W.F., 'Theoretical and Institutional Underpinnings of a Separate Administrative Law', in Taggart, M. (ed.), *The Province of Administrative Law* (Oxford: Hart Publishing, 1997), 71.

Almqvist, R., ' "Management by Contract": A Study of Programmatic and Technological Aspects' (2001) 79 *Public Administration* 689–706.

Althaus, C., 'The Application of Agency Theory to Public Sector Management', in Davis, G., Sullivan, B. and Yeatman, A. (eds.), *The New Contractualism?* (Melbourne: Macmillan, 1997), 137.

Aman, A.C., 'Administrative Law for a New Century' in Taggart, M.(ed.), *The Province of Administrative Law* (Oxford: Hart Publishing, 1997), 90.

Amato, G., 'Citizenship and Public Services – Some General Reflections', in Freedland, M., and Sciarra, S. (eds.), *Public Services and Citizenship in European Law – Public and Labour Law Perspectives* (Oxford: Oxford University Press, 1998), 145.

Annas, G., 'Patients' Rights to Managed Care – Exit, Voice and Loyalty' (1997) 337 *New England Journal of Medicine* 219.

Arnstein, S., 'A Ladder of Citizen Participation' (1969) 35 *Journal of American Institute of Planners* 214.

Aquina, H., and Bekke, H., 'Governance in Interaction: Public Tasks and Private Organisations', in Kooiman, J. (ed.), *Modern Governance: New Government-Society Interactions* (London: Sage Publications, 1993), 159.

Aronson, M., and Dyer, B., *Judicial Review of Administrative Action* (2nd ed.) (Sydney: LBC Information Services, 2000).

Aronson, M., 'A Public Lawyer's Responses to Privatisation and Outsourcing', in Taggart, M.(ed.), *The Province of Administrative Law* (Oxford: Hart Publishing, 1997), 40.

Arrighetti, A., Bachmann, R., and Deakin, S., 'Contract Law, Social Norms and Inter-Firm Cooperation' (1997) 21 *Cambridge Journal of Economics* 171.

Arrowsmith, S., 'Judicial Review and the Contractual Powers of Public Authorities' (1990) 106 *Law Quarterly Review* 277.

—— 'Protecting the Interests of Bidders For Public Contracts: The Role of the Common Law' (1994) 53 *Cambridge Law Journal* 104.

—— 'Public Procurement as an Instrument of Policy and the Impact of Market Liberalisation' (1995) 111 *Law Quarterly Review* 234.

—— 'The EC Procurement Directives, National Procurement Policies and Better Governance: The Case for a New Approach' (2002) 27 *European Law Review* 3.

Arrowsmith, S., Linarelli, J., and Wallace, D., *Regulating Public Procurement: National and International Perspectives* (London: Kluwer International, 2000).

Ascher, K., *The Politics of Privatisation: Contracting Out Public Services* (Houndmills: Macmillan, 1987).

Ashton, T. , Cumming, J., McLean, J., McKinely, M. and Fae, E., *Contracting For Health Services In New Zealand: A Report For The World Health Organization* (WHO 2002).

Asenova, D., and Beck, M., 'The UK Financial Sector and Risk Management in PFI Projects: A Survey' (2003) *Public Money and Management* (July), 195–202.

Atiyah, P.S., 'The Modern Role of Contract Law', in *Essays On Contract* (Oxford: Oxford University Press, 1986), 1.

Audit Commission, *Realising the Benefits of Competition: The Client Role for Contracted Services* (London: Audit Commission, 1993).

—— *Making Markets: A Review of the Audits of the Client Role for Contracted Services* (London: Audit Commission, 1995).

Audit Review of Government Contracts, *Contracting, Privatisation, Probity and Disclosure in Victoria 1992–1999: An Independent Report to Government* (Victoria: State Government of Victoria, 2000).

Aulich, C., 'Cultural Change and Bureau Capture: Reform in an Australian Local Government System', conference paper for *Public Services Under Labour: Markets or Democracy?*, Cardiff Business School, April 1998.

Austin, R., 'Administrative Law's Reaction to the Changing Concepts of Public Service', in Leyland, P. and Woods, T. (eds.), *Administrative Law Facing the Future: Old Constraints and New Horizons* (London: Blackstone Press Ltd, 1997), 21.

Ayres, I., and Braithwaite, J., *Responsive Regulation: Transcending the Deregulation Debate* (Oxford: Oxford University Press, 1992).

Baggott, R., 'By Voluntary Agreement: The Politics of Instrument Selection' (1986) 64 *Public Administration* 51.

Bahle, T., 'The Changing Institutionalization of Social Services in England and Wales, France and Germany: Is the Welfare State On the Retreat?' (2003) 13 *Journal of European Social Policy* 5.

Baldwin, R., 'Governing With Rules: The Developing Agenda', in Richardson, G., and Genn, H. (eds.), *Administrative Law and Government Action: The Courts and Alternative Mechanisms of Review* (Oxford: Clarendon Press, 1994), 157.

—— 'The Next Steps: Ministerial Responsibility and Government by Agency' (1988) 51 *Modern Law Review* 622–8.

Baldwin, R., Scott, C., and Hood, C., 'Introduction', in Baldwin, R., Scott, C., and Hood, C. (eds.), *Regulation* (Oxford: Oxford University Press, 1998).

Baldwin, R., and Cave, M., *Understanding Regulation: Theory, Strategy, and Practice* (Oxford: Oxford University Press, 1999).

Ball, R., Heafey, M., and King, D., 'Private Finance Initiative: A Good Deal for the Public Purse or a Drain on Future Generations?' (2000) 29 *Policy and Politics* 95.

Barnes, M., 'Users as Citizens: Collective Action and the Local Governance of Welfare' (1999) 33 *Social Policy and Administration* 73–90.

Barnes, M., and Prior, D., 'Spoilt for Choice? How Consumerism Can Disempower Public Service Users' (1995) 15 *Public Money and Management* 53.

Barnett, P., and Jacobs, K., 'Policy-making in a Restructured State: The Case of the 1991 Health Reform Policy in New Zealand' (2000) 59 *Australian Journal of Public Administration* 73.

Barron, A., and Scott, C., 'The Citizen's Charter Programme' (1992) 55 *Modern Law Review* 526.

Barrowclough, D., 'Public Television Quasi-Markets in New Zealand and the UK', in Bartlett, W., Roberts, J.A., and Le Grand, J. (eds.), *A Revolution in Social Policy: Quasi-Market Reforms in the 1990s* (Bristol: The Policy Press, 1998), 257.

Bartlett, W, 'Quasi-Markets in Educational Reforms', in Le Grand, J., and Bartlett, W. (eds.)(1993), 125.

Bartlett, W., and Harrison, L., 'Quasi-Markets and the National Health Service Reforms', in Le Grand, J., and Bartlett, W. (eds.)(1993), 68.

Bartlett, W., and Le Grand, J., 'The Theory of Quasi-Markets', in Le Grand, J., and Bartlett, W. (eds.)(1993), 15.

Bartlett, W., Propper, C., Wilson, D., and Le Grand, J. (eds.), *Quasi-Markets in the Welfare State: The Emerging Findings* (Bristol: SAUS, 1994).

Bartlett, W., Roberts, J.A., and Le Grand, J. (eds.), *A Revolution in Social Policy: Quasi-Market Reforms in the 1990s* (Bristol: The Policy Press, 1998).

Bastiani, J., *Home-School Contracts – Opportunities or Threats* (London: Royal Society of Arts, 1996).

Beale, H., and Dugdale, T., 'Contracts Between Businessmen: Planning and the Use of Contractual Remedies' (1975) 2 *British Journal of Law and Society* 45.

Beerman, J., 'The Reach of Administrative Law in the United States', in Taggart, M. (ed.), *The Province of Administrative Law* (Oxford: Hart Publishing, 1997), 171.

Beetham, D., *Bureaucracy* (Buckingham: Open University Press, 1996), (2nd ed.)

Bell, J., Boyron, S., and Whittaker, S., *Principles of French Law* (Oxford: Oxford University Press, 1998).

Beloff, M.J., 'Judicial Review – 2001: A Prophetic Odyssey' (1995) 58 *Modern Law Review* 143.

Benington, J., 'The Modernization and Improvement of Government and Public Services' (2000) *Public Money and Management* (April-June), 3.

Bennett, C., and Ferlie, E., 'Contracting in Theory and In Practice: Some Evidence From the NHS' (1996) 74 *Public Administration* 49.

Bernstein, L., 'Opting Out of the Legal System: Extralegal Contractual Relations in the Diamond Industry' (1992) XXI *Journal of Legal Studies* 115.

—— 'Merchant Law in a Merchant Court: Rethinking the Code's Search for Immanent Business Norms' (1996) 114 *University of Pennsylvania Law Review* 1765.

Bevan, G., 'Legal Aid: A Case Study in Quasi-Market Failure', in Bartlett, W., Roberts, J.A., and Le Grand, J. (eds.) (1998), 219.

Beyleveld, D., and Pattinson, S., 'Horizontal Applicability and Horizontal Effect' (2002) 118 *Law Quarterly Review* 623.

Birkinshaw, P., 'By Command of Her Britannic Majesty's Government: Let There Be Government By Contract', conference paper for *The Constitutional Implications of Participation*, Sheffield, September 9–12 1997.

—— *Grievances, Remedies and the State* (2nd ed.)(London: Sweet and Maxwell, 1994).

Bishop, P., and Preston, N. (eds.), *Local Government: Public Enterprise and Ethics* (Sydney: The Federation Press, 2000).

Black, J., 'Constitutionalising Self-Regulation' (1996) 59 *Modern Law Review* 24.

—— 'Reviewing Regulatory Rules: Responding to Hybridisation', in Black, J., Muchlinski, P., and Walker, P., *Commercial Regulation and Judicial Review* (Oxford: Hart Publishing, 1998), 123.

—— 'Proceduralizing Regulation: Part I' (2000) 20 *Oxford Journal of Legal Studies* 597.

—— 'Proceduralizing Regulation: Part II' (2001) 21 *Oxford Journal of Legal Studies* 33.

—— 'Decentring Regulation: The Role of Regulation and Self-Regulation in a "Post-Regulatory" World' (2001) *Current Legal Problems* 103.

—— 'Enrolling Actors in Regulatory Systems: Examples from UK Financial Services Regulation' [2003] *Public Law* 63–91.

Blair, A., 'Home-School Agreements: A Legislative Framework for Soft Control of Parents' (2001) *Education Law Journal* 79.

Blair, A., and Waddington, M., 'The Home-School "Contract": Regulating the Role of Parents' (1997) 9 *Education and the Law* 291.

Blair, T., The Courage of Our Convictions: Why Reform of the Public Services is the Route to Social Justice (London: Fabian Society, 2002).

Bogdanor, V., 'Ministers, Civil Servants and the Constitution' (1994) 29 *Government and Opposition* 676.

Boston, J., Dalziel, P., and St John, S. (eds.), *Redesigning the Welfare State in New Zealand* (Auckland: Oxford University Press, 1999).

Boston, J., 'Purchasing Policy Advice: The Limits to Contracting Out' (1994) 7 *Governance* 1.

—— 'Inherently Governmental Functions and the Limits to Contracting Out', in Boston, J. (ed.), *The State Under Contract* (Wellington: Bridget Williams Books, 1995), 78.

—— 'The Use of Contracting in the Public Sector – Recent New Zealand Experience' (1996) 55 *Australian Journal of Public Administration* 105.

—— 'Preface', in Boston, J. (ed.), *The State Under Contract* (Wellington: Bridget Williams Books, 1995), ix.

—— 'The New Contractualism in New Zealand: Chief Executive Performance Agreements', in Davis, G., Sullivan, B., and Yeatman, A. (eds.), *The New Contractualism?* (Melbourne: Macmillan, 1997), 180.

—— (ed.), *The State Under Contract* (Wellington: Bridget Williams Books, 1995).

Boston, J., Martin, J., Pallot, J., and Walsh, P., *Public Management – The New Zealand Model* (Oxford: Oxford University Press, 1996).

Bovis, C., *EC Public Procurement: Case Law and Regulation* (Oxford: Oxford University Press, 2006).

Bowerman, M., and Ball, A., 'Great Expectations: Benchmarking for Best Value' (2000) *Public Money and Management* (April–June), 21.

Boyne, G., 'Bureaucratic Theory Meets Reality: Public Choice and Service Contracting in U.S. Local Government' (1998) 58 *Public Administration Review* 474.

—— 'External Regulation and Best Value in Local Government' (2000) *Public Money and Management* (July–Sept), 7.

—— 'Public and Private Management: What's the Difference?' (2002) 39 *Management Studies* 97..

—— 'Processes, Performance and Best Value in Local Government' (1999) 25 *Local Government Studies* 1.

Boyne, G., Gould-Williams, J., Law, J. and Walker, R., 'Plans, Performance Information and Accountability: The Case of Best Value' (2002) 80 *Public Administration* 691.

Bovaird, T., and Halachmi, A., 'Learning from International Approaches to Best Value' (2001) 29 *Policy and Politics* 451.

Bradley, A. W., and Ewing, K. D., *Constitutional and Administrative Law* (Harlow: Pearson Education, 2003).

Braithwaite, J., 'The Nursing Home Industry', in Reiss, A., and Tonry, M. (eds.), *Organizational Crime: Crime and Justice – A Review of Research*, Vol. V. (Chicago, Il: University of Chicago Press, 1993).

—— 'Accountability and Governance under the New Regulatory State' (1999) 58 *Australian Journal of Public Administration* 90.

Braithwaite, J., *Restorative Justice and Responsive Regulation* (Oxford: Oxford University Press, 2002).

—— 'Rewards and Regulation', (2002) 29 *Journal of Law and Society* 12.

Braithwaite, J., 'Meta Regulation for Access to Justice', Presentation to *General Aspects of Law* (GALA) Seminar Series, University of California, 13th November 2003. www.law.berkeley.edu/centers/kadish/gala03/Braithwaite%20Kent.pdf

Braithwaite, J., Makkai, T., Braithwaite, V., and Gibson, D, *Raising the Standard: Resident Centred Nursing Home Regulation in Australia* (Canberra: Australian Government Publishing Service, 1993).

Braithwaite, J., and Braithwaite, V., 'The Politics of Legalism: Rules Versus Standards in Nursing-Home Regulation' (1995) 4 *Social and Legal Studies* 307.

Braithwaite, J., and Pettit, P., *Not Just Deserts: A Republican Theory of Criminal Justice* (Oxford: Oxford University Press, 1990).

Bramley, G., 'Quasi-Markets and Social Housing', in Le Grand, J., and Bartlett, W. (eds.)(1993), 154.

Braucher, J., 'Contract Versus Contractarianism: The Regulatory Role of Contract Law' (1990) 47 *Washington and Lee Law Review* 697.

Bregman, E., and Jacobson, A., 'Environmental Performance Review: Self-Regulation in Environmental Law', in Teubner, G., Farmer, L., and Murphy, D. (eds.), *Environmental Law and Ecological Responsibility: The Concept and Practice of Ecological Self-Organization* (Chichester: John Wiley & Sons, 1994), 208.

Broadbent, J., and Laughlin, R., 'Contracts, Competition, and Accounting in Health and Education: An Example of Juridification at Work?', in Deakin, S., and Michie, J. (eds.), *Contracts, Cooperation and Competition: Studies in Economics, Management and Law* (Oxford: Oxford University Press, 1997), 214.

Brownsword, R., 'From Cooperative Contracting to a Contract of Cooperation', in Campbell, D., and Vincent-Jones, P. (eds.), *Contract and Economic Organisation: Socio-Legal Initiatives* (Aldershot: Dartmouth, 1996), 14.

—— *Contract Law: Themes for the Twenty-first Century* (London: Butterworths, 2000).

Buxton, R., 'The Human Rights Act and Private Law' (2000) 116 *Law Quarterly Review* 48.

Campbell, D., 'The Social Theory of Relational Contract: Macneil as the Modern Proudhon' (1990) 18 *International Journal of the Sociology of Law* 75.

—— 'The Relational Constitution of the Discrete Contract', in Campbell, D., and Vincent-Jones, P. (eds.), *Contract and Economic Organisation: Socio-Legal Initiatives* (Aldershot: Dartmouth, 1996), 40.1996a

—— 'Socio-Legal Analysis of Contract' in P. Thomas (ed.) *Socio-Legal Studies* (Aldershot: Dartmouth, 1997).1997a

—— 'Ian Macneil and the Relational Theory of Contract', in Campbell, D. (ed.), *Selected Papers of Ian Macneil* (London: Sweet and Maxwell, 2001).

Campbell, D., and Harris, D., 'Flexibility in Long-Term Contractual Relationships: The Role of Cooperation' (1993) 20 *Journal of Law and Society* 166.

Campbell, D., and Vincent-Jones, P. (eds.), *Contract and Economic Organisation: Socio-Legal Initiatives* (Aldershot: Dartmouth, 1996).

Cane, P., *An Introduction to Administrative Law* (3rd ed.) (Oxford: Clarendon Press, 1996).

—— 'Mapping the Frontiers', in Birks, P. (ed.), *The Frontiers of Liability* (Oxford: Oxford University Press, 1994), 137.

Capen, E., Clapp, R., and Campbell, W., 'Competitive Bidding in High Risk Situations' (1971) 23 *Journal of Petroleum Technology* 641.

Carney, T. and Ramia, G., 'Contractualism and Citizenship: Rivals or Bedfellows?' (2001) 18 *Law in Context* 8.

—— *From Rights to Management: Contract, New Public Management and Employment Services* (The Hague: Kluwer Law International, 2002).

Carr, H., Sefton-Green, D., and Tissier, D., 'Two Steps Forward for Tenants?, in Cowan, D., and Marsh, A. (eds.), *Two Steps Forward: Housing Policy into the New Millennium* (Bristol: Policy Press, 2001), 157.

Carter, N., and Greer, P., 'Evaluating Agencies: Next Steps and Performance Indicators' (1993) 71 *Public Administration* 407.

Carter, P., 'Managing Offenders, Reducing Crime: A New Approach', Prime Minister's Strategy Unit, January 2004.

Casson, M., *The Economics of Business Culture: Game Theory, Transaction Costs, and Economic Performance* (Oxford: Oxford University Press, 1991).

Challis, L., Day, P., Klein, R., and Scrivens, E., 'Managing Quasi-Markets: Institutions of Regulation', in Bartlett et al (eds.) (1994), 10.

Chalmers, J. and Davis, G., 'Rediscovering Implementation: Public Sector Contracting and Human Services' (2001) *Australian Journal of Public Administration* 74.

Charny, D., 'Nonlegal Sanctions in Commercial Relationships' (1990) 104 Harvard Law Review 375.

Chen, M., 'The Reconfiguration of the State and the Appropriate Scope of Judicial Review', in Boston, J. (ed.), The State Under Contract (Wellington: Bridget Williams Books, 1995), 112.

Christiansen, P.M., 'A Prescription Rejected: Market Solutions to Problems of Public Sector Governance' (1998) 11 *Governance* 273.

Coase, R. H., *The Firm, the Market, and the Law* (Chicago: University of Chicago Press, 1988).

Cohen, S., *Visions of Social Control: Crime, Punishment, and Classification* (Cambridge: Polity Press, 1985).

Collins, H., 'Ascription of Legal Responsibility to Groups in Complex Patterns of Economic Integration' (1990) 53 *Modern Law Review* 731.

—— 'Competing Norms of Contractual Behaviour', in Campbell, D., and Vincent-Jones, P. (eds.), *Contract and Economic Organisation: Socio-Legal Initiatives* (Aldershot: Dartmouth, 1996), 67.

—— *Regulating Contracts* (Oxford: Oxford University Press, 1999).

—— *The Law of Contract* (London: Butterworths/LexisNexis, 2003).

Common, R.K., 'Privatisation Through Contracting: The View From Local Government in the United States' (1994) 20 *Local Government Studies* 379.

Considine, M., 'Contract Regimes and Reflexive Governance: Comparing Employment Service Reforms in the United Kingdom, the Netherlands, New Zealand and Australia' (2000) 78 *Public Administration* 613.

—— 'Markets, Networks and the New Welfare State: Employment Assistance Reforms in Australia' (1999) 28 *Journal of Social Policy* 183.

—— *Enterprising States: The Public Management of Welfare to Work* (Cambridge: Cambridge University Press, 2001).

Considine, M., 'The End of the Line? Accountable Governance in the Age of Networks, Partnerships, and Joined-Up Services' (2002) 15 *Governance* 21.

Cooper, T., 'Ethical Issues in Citizen Participation and Representation in Local Government', in Bishop and Preston (eds.), 2000.

Cope, S., and Goodship, J., 'The Audit Commission and Public Services: Delivering for Whom?' (2002) *Public Money and Management* (Oct–Dec) 33.

Council of Europe, *The Role of Competitive Tendering in the Efficient Provision of Local Services* (Strasbourg: Council of Europe Press, 1993).

Cowan, D., and Marsh, A., 'Making Connections', in Cowan, D., and Marsh, A. (eds.), *Two Steps Forward: Housing Policy into the New Millennium* (Bristol: The Policy Press, 2001), 363.

Cox, R.H., 'The Consequences of Welfare Reform: How Conceptions of Social Rights are Changing' (1998) 27 *Journal of Social Policy* 1.

Coyle, A., Campbell, A., and Neufeld, R. (eds.), *Capitalist Punishment: Prison Privatization and Human Rights* (London: Zed Books, 2003).

Craig, P., 'Legitimate Expectations: A Conceptual Analysis' (1992) 108 *Law Quarterly Review* 79.

——*Administrative Law* (4th ed.)(London: Sweet and Maxwell, 1999).

——'Contracting Out, The Human Rights Act and the Scope of Judicial Review' (2002) 118 *Law Quarterly Review* 551.

——'Three Perspectives on the Relationship Between Administrative Justice and Administrative Law', in Creyke, R., and McMillan, J. (eds.), *Administrative Justice – The Core and the Fringe* (Canberra: AIAL, 2000), 28.

Crawford, A., 'Contractual Governance of Deviant Behaviour' (2003) 30 *Journal of Law and Society* 479.

Crawford, A., and Newburn, T., *Youth Offending and Restorative Justice: Implementing Reform in Youth Justice* (Cullompton: Willan, 2003).

——'Recent Developments in Restorative Justice for Young People in England and Wales: Community Participation and Representation' (2002) 42 *British Journal of Criminology* 476.

Crawford, A., and Burden, T., *Integrating Victims in Restorative Youth Justice* (Bristol: Policy Press, 2005).

Cutler, T., and Waine, B., 'Managerialism Reformed? New Labour and Public Sector Management' (2000) 34 *Social Policy and Administration* 318.

——'Advancing Public Accountability? The Social Services "Star" Ratings' (2003) *Public Money and Management* (April) 125–8.

——'Performance Management – The Key to Higher Standards in Schools?' (2001) *Public Money and Management* (April–June), 69–72.

Daintith, T., 'A Regulatory Space Agency?' (1989) 9 *Oxford Journal of Legal Studies* 534.

——'The Techniques of Government', in Jowell, J. and Oliver, D. (eds.), *The Changing Constitution* (Clarendon Press: Oxford, 1994).

——'Regulation by Contract: The New Prerogative' (1979) *Current Legal Problems* 41.

——'Regulation', *International Encyclopedia of Comparative Law* (1997) Ch 10.

——'State Power', in Newman, P. (ed.), *The New Palgrave Dictionary of Economics and the Law* Vol 3 (P-Z), 524 (London: Macmillan, 1998).

Daintith, T., and Page, A., *The Executive in the Constitution: Structure, Autonomy and Internal Control* (Oxford: Oxford University Press, 1999).

Davies, A.C.L., *Accountability: A Public Law Analysis of Government By Contract* (Oxford: Oxford University Press, 2001).

Davies, H., Nutley, S., and Smith, P., 'Introducing Evidence-based Policy and Practice in Public Services', in Davies, H.T., Nutley, S.M., and Smith, P.C. (eds.), *What Works? Evidence-based Policy and Practice in Public Services* (Bristol: The Policy Press, 2000), 1.

Davis, G., Sullivan, B., and Yeatman, A. (eds.), *The New Contractualism?* (Melbourne: Macmillan, 1997).

Davis, G., 'Implications, Consequences and Futures', in Davis, G., Sullivan, B. and Yeatman, A. (eds.), *The New Contractualism?* (Melbourne: Macmillan, 1997), 224.

Day, P., and Klein, R., 'Steering but not Rowing?' ESRC Whitehall Programme project briefing 4.

——*Accountabilities: Five Public Services* (London: Tavistock, 1987).

DeHoog, Ruth Hoogland, and Salamon, L.M., 'Purchase-of-Service Contracting', in Salamon, L.M., (ed.), *The Tools of Government: A Guide to the New Governance* (Oxford: Oxford University Press, 2002).

De Schutter, O., and Deakin, S., 'Reflexive Governance and the Dilemmas of Social Regulation', in (eds.), De Schutter, O., and Deakin, S. (eds.), *Social Rights and Market Forces: Is the Open Coordination of Employment and Social Policies the Future of Social Europe?* (Bruxelles: Bruylant, 2005).

De Schutter, O., and Deakin, S. (eds.), *Social Rights and Market Forces: Is the Open Coordination of Employment and Social Policies the Future of Social Europe?* (Bruxelles: Bruylant, 2005).

de Smith, S.A., Lord Woolf, and Jowell, J., *Judicial Review of Administrative Action* (London: Sweet and Maxwell, 5th ed 1995).

Deacon, A., 'An Ethic of Mutual Responsibility?: Towards a Fuller Justification for Conditionality in Welfare', in Beem, C., and Mead, L. (eds.), *Welfare Reform and Political Theory* (New York: Russell Sage Foundation, 2005).

——'Justifying Conditionality: The Case of Anti-Social Tenants' (2004) 19 *Housing Studies* 911.

Deacon, A., and Mann, K., 'Agency, Modernity and Social Policy' (1999) 28 *Journal of Social Policy* 413–435.

Deakin, N., and Walsh, K., 'The Enabling State: The Role of Markets and Contracts' (1996) 74 *Public Administration* 33.

Deakin, N., and Wright, A. (eds.), *Consuming Public Services* (London: Routledge, 1990).

Deakin, S., Lane, C., and Wilkinson, F., 'Contract Law, Trust Relations, and Incentives for Co-operation: A Comparative Study', in Deakin, S., and Michie, J. (eds.), *Contracts, Cooperation and Competition: Studies in Economics, Management and Law* (Oxford: Oxford University Press, 1997), 105.

Deakin, S., and Michie, J., 'The Theory and Practice of Contracting', in Deakin, S., and Michie, J. (eds.), *Contracts, Cooperation and Competition: Studies in Economics, Management and Law* (Oxford: Oxford University Press, 1997), 1.

Deakin, S., and Wilkinson, F., 'Contracts, Cooperation and Trust: The Role of the Institutional Framework', in Campbell, D., and Vincent-Jones, P. (eds.), *Contract and Economic Organisation: Socio-Legal Initiatives* (Aldershot: Dartmouth, 1996), 95.

Dean, M., 'Governing the Unemployed Self in An Active Society' (1995) 24 *Economy and Society* 559.

—— 'Liberal Government and Authoritarianism' (2002) 31 *Economy and Society* 37–61.

—— *Governmentality: Power and Rule in Modern Society* (London: Sage Publications, 1999).

Domberger, S., *The Contracting Organization: A Strategic Guide to Outsourcing* (Oxford: Oxford University Press, 1998).

—— 'Economic Regulation Through Franchise Contracts', in Kay, J., Mayer, C., and Thomson, D. (eds.), *Privatisation and Regulation: The UK Experience* (Oxford: Clarendon Press, 1986), 269.

Domberger, S., and Hall, C., 'Contracting for Public Services: A Review of the Antipodean Experience' (1996) 74 *Public Administration* 129.

Domberger, S., Meadowcroft, S.A., and Thompson, D., 'Competitive Tendering and Efficiency: The Case of Refuse Collection' (1986) 7 *Fiscal Studies* 69.

Domberger, S., and Rimmer, S., 'Competitive Tendering and Contracting in the Public Sector: A Survey' (1994) 1 *International Journal of the Economics of Business* 440.

Donahue, J., *The Privatization Decision: Public Ends, Private Means* (New York: Basic Books, 1989).

Donnelly, C., 'Leonard Cheshire again and Beyond: Private Contractors, contract and S. 6(3)(b) of the Human Rights Act' [2005] PL 785.

Dorf, M.C. and Sabel, C.F., 'A Constitution of Democratic Experimentalism' (1998) 98 *Columbia Law Review* 267.

Dorbeck-Jung, B., 'Towards Reflexive Responsibility. New Ethics for Public Administration', in Hondeghem, A. (ed.), *Ethics and Accountability in a Context of Governance and New Public Management* (Amsterdam: IOS Press, 1998), 45.

Dowding, K., 'Managing the Civil Service', in Maidment, R., and Thompson, G. (eds.), *Managing the United Kingdom* (London: Sage, 1993), 236.

Drewry, G., 'The Citizen and the New Contractual Public Management: The Quest for New Forms of Accountability and A New Public Law', in Fortin, Y. and Van Hassel, H. (eds.), *Contracting in the New Public Management – From Economics to Law and Citizenship* (Amsterdam: IOS Press, 2000), 255.

—— 'Whatever Happened to the Citizen's Charter?' [2002] *Public Law* 9.

Dryzek, J., *Deliberative Democracy and Beyond: Liberals, Critics and Contestations* (Oxford: Oxford University Press, 2000).

Dunleavy, P. *Democracy, Bureaucracy and Public Choice – Economic Explanations in Political Science* (Hemel Hempstead: Harvester Wheatsheaf, 1991).

Dunleavy, P., and Hood, C., 'From Old Public Administration to New Public Management' (1994) 14 *Public Money and Management* (Jul–Sep) 9–16.

Dunsire, A., 'Holistic Governance' (1990) 5 *Public Policy and Administration* 4.

—— 'A Cybernetic View of Guidance, Control and Evaluation in the Public Sector', in Kaufman, Franz-Xavier (ed.), *The Public Sector: Challenge for Coordination and Learning* (New York: Walter de Gruyter, 1991), 325.

—— 'Modes of Governance', in Kooiman, J. (ed.), *Modern Governance: New Government-Society Interactions* (London: Sage Publications, 1993), 21.

—— 'Tipping the Balance: Autopoiesis and Governance' (1996) 28 *Administration and Society* 299.

Dwyer, P., 'Conditional Citizens? Welfare Rights and Responsibilities in the Late 1990s' (1998) 18 *Critical Social Policy* 493–517.

Easton, S., 'The Meaning of Citizenship', in Willett, C., (ed), *Public Sector Reform and the Citizen's Charter* (London: Blackstone Press Ltd, 1996), 11.

Edgeworth, B., *Law, Modernity, Postmodernity: Legal Change in the Contracting State* (Aldershot: Ashgate, 2003).

Eisner, M., *Regulatory Politics in Transition* (Baltimore: John Hopkins University Press, 2000).

Elliott, M., '*Coughlan*: Substantive Protection of Legitimate Expectations Revisited' [2000] *Judicial Review* 27.

—— *The Constitutional Foundations of Judicial Review* (Oxford: Hart Publishing, 2001).

Elsenar, M.,'Law, Accountability and the Private Finance Initiative in the National Health Service' [1999] *Public Law* 35.

Erridge, A., and Fee, R., 'Contract Compliance: National, Regional and Global Regimes' (1999) 27 *Policy and Politics* 199.

Erridge, A., and Greer, J., 'Partnerships and Public Procurement: Building Social Capital Through Supply Relations' (2002) 80 *Public Administration* 503.

Escott, K., and Whitfield, D., *The Gender Impact of CCT in Local Government*, EOC Research Discussion Series No. 12 (Manchester: Equal Opportunities Commission, 1995).

Etzioni, A., *The Spirit of Community* (New York: Crown Books, 1993).

—— *The New Golden Rule* (New York: Basic Books, 1996).

Farrar, J., and McCabe, B., 'Corporatisation, Corporate Governance and the Deregulation of the Public Sector Economy' (1995) 6 *Public Law Review* 24.

Farrell, C.M. and Jones, J., 'Evaluating Stakeholder Participation in Public Services – Parents and Schools' (2000) 28 *Policy and Politics* 251.

Fee, R., 'Contract Compliance: Subnational and European Influences in Northern Ireland' (2002) 12 *Journal of European Social Policy* 107.

Fee, R., Maxwell, P., and Erridge, A., 'Contracting for Services: A Double Jeopardy? An Analysis of Contract Compliance in the Context of European and UK Social and Public Procurement Policy' (1998) 13 *Public Policy and Administration* 79.

Feintuck, M., *Accountability and Choice in Schooling* (Buckingham: Open University Press, 1994).

—— *'The Public Interest' in Regulation* (Oxford: Oxford University Press, 2004).

Ferguson, R.B., 'The Adjudication of Commercial Disputes and the Legal System in Modern England' (1980) *British Journal of Law and Society* 141.

Ferlie, E., Ashburner, L., Fitzgerald, L., and Pettigrew, A., *The New Public Management in Action* (Oxford: Oxford University Press, 1996).

Finn, C. (ed.), *Sunrise or Sunset? Administrative Law in the New Millennium* (Canberra: Australian Institute of Administrative Law, 2000).

Finn, C., 'Getting the Good Oil: Freedom of Information and Contracting Out' (1998) 5 *Australian Journal of Administrative Law* 113.

Flynn, R., and Williams, G. (eds.), *Contracting for Health: Quasi-Markets and the National Health Service* (Oxford: Oxford University Press, 1997).

Flynn, R., Williams, G., and Pickard, S., *Markets and Networks: Contracting in Community Health Services* (Buckingham: Open University Press, 1996).

France, G., 'Healthcare Quasi-Markets in a Decentralised System', in Bartlett, W., Roberts, J.A., and Le Grand, J. (eds.) (1998), 155.

Frankel, M., *Freedom of Information: Some International Characteristics* (London: Campaign for Freedom of Information, 2002).

Fox, A., *Beyond Contract: Work, Power and Trust Relations* (London: Faber and Faber, 1974).

Fredman, S., and Morris, G.S., 'The Costs of Exclusivity: Public and Private Re-examined' [1994] *Public Law* 69.

Freedland, M., 'Government by Contract and Public Law' [1994] *Public Law* 86.

—— 'Public Law and Private Finance – Placing the Private Finance Initiative in a Public Law Frame' [1998] *Public Law* 288.

—— 'Law, Public Services, and Citizenship – New Domains, New Regimes?', in Freedland, M. and Sciarra, S. (eds.), *Public Services and Citizenship in European Law – Public and Labour Law Perspectives* (Oxford: Oxford University Press, 1998), 1.

Freedland, M., and King, D., 'Contractual Governance and Illiberal Contracts: Some Problems of Contractualism as an Instrument of Behaviour Management by Agencies of Government' (2003) 27 *Cambridge Journal of Economics* 465.

Freedland, M., and Sciarra, S. (eds.), *Public Services and Citizenship in European Law – Public and Labour Law Perspectives* (Oxford: Oxford University Press, 1998).

Freeman, J., 'The Private Role in Public Governance' (2000) 75 *New York University Law Review* 543.

—— 'Private Parties, Public Functions and the New Administrative Law' (2000) 52 *Administrative Law Review* 814.

—— 'Extending Public Law Norms Through Privatization' (2003) 116 *Harvard Law Review* 1285.

—— 'Collaborative Governance in the Administrative State' (1997) 45 *UCLA Law Review* 1.

—— 'The Contracting State' (2000) 28 *Florida State University Law Review* 155.

Friedman, L. M., 'On Regulation and Legal Process', in Noll, R. G. (ed.), *Regulatory Policy and the Social Sciences* (Berkeley: University of California Press, 1985).

Fulbrook, J., 'The Job Seekers' Act 1995: Consolidation with a Sting of Contractual Compliance' (1995) 24 *Industrial Law Journal* 395.

Fuller, Lon L., 'The Forms and Limits of Adjudication' (1978) 92 *Harvard Law Review* 353.

Gaffney, D., Pollock, A.M., Price, D., and Shaoul, J., 'NHS Capital Expenditure and the Private Finance Initiative – Expansion or Contraction?' (1999) 319 *British Medical Journal* 48–51.

Gains, F., 'Implementing Privatization Policies in "Next Steps" Agencies' (1999) 77 *Public Administration* 713.

Galligan, D., *Due Process and Fair Procedures: A Study of Administrative Procedures* (Oxford: Clarendon Press, 1996).

—— 'Procedural Rights in Social Welfare', in Coote, A. (ed.), *The Welfare of Citizens – Developing New Social Rights* (London: IPPR, 1992), 55.

Garcia, E.M., 'Public Service, Public Services, Public Functions, and Guarantees of the Rights of Citizens: Unchanging Needs in a Changed Context', in Freedland, M., and

Sciarra, S. (eds.), *Public Services and Citizenship in European Law – Public and Labour Law Perspectives* (Oxford: Oxford University Press, 1998), 57.
Garland, D., 'The Limits of the Sovereign State: Strategies of Crime Control in Contemporary Society' (1996) 36 *British Journal of Criminology* 445.
Gaster, L., *Quality in Public Services: Managers' Choices* (Buckingham: Open University Press, 1995).
Gauld, R., 'Beyond New Zealand's Dual Health Reforms' (1999) 33 *Social Policy and Administration* 567.
Geddes, M., and Martin, S., 'The Policy and Politics of Best Value: Currents, Crosscurrents and Undercurrents in the New Regime' (2000) 28 *Policy and Politics* 379.
Gerstenberg, O., and Sabel, C.F., 'Directly-Deliberative Polyarchy: An Institutional Ideal for Europe', in Joerges, C., and Dehousse, R., *Good Governance in Europe's Integrated Market* (Oxford: Oxford University Press, 2002).
Geuss, R., *Public Goods, Private Goods* (Princeton: Princeton University Press, 2001).
Gewirtz, S., Ball, S.J., and Bowe, R., *Markets, Choice and Equity in Education* (Buckingham: Open University Press, 1995).
Gibson, D., and Means, R., 'Policy Convergence: Restructuring Long-Term Care in Australia and the UK' (2000) 29 *Policy and Politics* 43.
Giddens, A., *The Third Way: The Renewal of Social Responsibility* (Cambridge: Polity Press, 1998).
—— *Where To Now For New Labour?* (Cambridge: Polity Press, 2002).
Gillette, Clayton P., 'Opting Out of Public Provision' (1996) 73 *Denver University Law Review* 1185.
Goddard, R., 'Enforcing the Hypothetical Bargain: Sections 459–461 of the Companies Act 1985' (1999) 20 *Company Lawyer* 66.
Goldberg, V., 'Regulation and Administered Contracts' (1976) 7 *The Bell Journal of Economics* 426.
Goldhamer, H., and Shils, E., 'Types of Power and Status' (1939) 45 *American Journal of Sociology* 171.
Goldsworthy, D., *Setting Up Next Steps – A Short Account of the Origins, Launch and Implementation of the Next Steps Project in the British Civil Service* (London: HMSO, 1991).
Goodin, R.E., 'Structures of Mutual Obligation' (2002) 31 *Journal of Social Policy* 579.
—— 'Institutions and Their Design', in Goodin, R.E. (ed.), *The Theory of Institutional Design* (Cambridge: Cambridge University Press, 1996), 1.
—— 'Structures of Mutual Obligation' (2002) 31 *Journal of Social Policy* 579–596.
Gouldner, A.W., 'The Norm of Reciprocity' (1960) 25 *American Sociological Review* 161.
Graham, C., *Regulating Public Utilities: A Constitutional Approach* (Oxford: Hart Publishing, 2000).
—— 'Self-Regulation', in Richardson, G., and Genn, H. (eds.), *Administrative Law and Government Action: The Courts and Alternative Mechanisms of Review* (Oxford: Clarendon Press, 1994), 189.
Granovetter, M., 'Economic Action and Social Structure: The Problem of Embeddedness' (1985) 91 *American Journal of Sociology* 481.
Gregory, R., and Hicks, C., 'Promoting Public Service Integrity: A Case for Responsible Accountability' (1999) 58 *Australian Journal of Public Administration* 3.

Greener, I., 'Understanding NHS Reform: The Policy-Transfer, Social Learning, and Path Dependency Perspectives' (2002) 15 *Governance* 161.

Green-Pedersen, C., 'New Public Management Reforms of the Danish and Swedish Welfare States: The Role of Different Social Democratic Responses' (2002) 15 *Governance: An International Journal of Policy, Administration, and Institutions* 271.

Greer, P., 'The Next Steps Initiatives: An Examination of Agency Framework Documents' (1992) 70 *Public Administration* 89.

—— *Transforming Central Government: The Next Steps Initiative* (Buckingham: Open University Press, 1994).

Greve, C., 'Governance by Contact Creating Public-Private Partnership in Denmark', in Fortin, Y. and Van Hassel, H. (eds.), *Contracting in the New Public Management – From Economics to Law and Citizenship* (Amsterdam: IOS Press, 2000), 49.

—— 'Exploring Contracts As Reinvented Institutions in the Danish Public Sector' (2000) 78 *Public Administration* 153.

Griffiths, L., and Hughes, D., 'Purchasing in the British NHS: Does Contracting Mean Explicit Rationing?' (1998) 2 *Health* 349.

Gunningham, N., and Rees, J., 'Industry Self-Regulation: An Institutional Perspective' (1997) 19 *Law and Policy* 363.

Gunningham, N., Grabosky, P., with Sinclair, D., *Smart Regulation: Designing Environmental Policy* (Oxford: Clarendon Press, 1998).

Gunningham, G., and Sinclair, D., 'Designing Environmental Policy', in Gunningham, N., Grabosky, P., with Sinclair, D., *Smart Regulation: Designing Environmental Policy* (Oxford: Clarendon Press, 1998), 375.

Guest, D., 'Is the Psychological Contract Worth Taking Seriously?' (1998) 19 *Journal of Psychological Behaviour* 649.

Habermas, J., *Between Facts and Norms: Contributions to a Discourse Theory of Law and Democracy* (Oxford: Polity Press, 1996).

Haines, F., *Corporate Regulation: Beyond 'Punish or Persuade'* (Oxford: Clarendon Press, 1997).

—— *Corporate Regulation: Beyond 'Punish or Persuade'* (Oxford: Clarendon Press, 1997).

Hall, P.A., and Soskice, D. (eds.), *Varieties of Capitalism: The Institutional Foundations of Comparative Advantage* (Oxford: Oxford University Press, 2001).

Halliday, S., *Judicial Review and Compliance with Administrative Law* (Oxford: Hart Publishing, 2004).

—— 'The influence of Judicial Review in Bureaucratic Decision-Making' [2000] *Public Law* 110.

Halligan, J., 'New Public Sector Models: Reform in Australia and New Zealand', in Lane, Jan-Erik (ed.), *Public Sector Reform: Rationale, Trends and Problems* (London: Sage Publications, 1997), 17.

Handler, J.F., 'Social Citizenship and Workfare in the US and Western Europe: From Status to Contract' (2003) 13 *Journal of European Social Policy* 229.

Hancher, L., and Moran, M. (eds.), *Capitalism, Culture and Economic Regulation* (Oxford: Clarendon Press, 1989).

Harden, I., *The Contracting State* (Buckingham: Open University Press, 1992).

Harden, I., and Lewis, N., *The Noble Lie: The British Constitution and the Rule of Law* (London: Hutchinson, 1986).

Harden, I., and Longley, D., 'National Health Service Contracts', in Birds, J., Bradgate, R., and Villiers, C. (eds), *Termination of Contracts* (Chichester: John Wiley, 1995).

Harlow, C., ' "Public" and "Private" Law: Definition Without Distinction', (1980) 43 *Modern Law Review* 240.

—— 'Accountability, New Public Management, and the Problems of the Child Support Agency' (1999) 26 *Journal of Law and Society* 150.

—— 'Public Service, Market Ideology, and Citizenship' in Freedland, M., and Sciarra, S. (eds.), *Public Services and Citizenship in European Law – Public and Labour Law Perspectives* (Oxford: Oxford University Press, 1998), 49.

Harlow, C., and Rawlings, R., *Law and Administration* (London: Butterworths, 1997).

Harries, A., and Vincent-Jones, P., 'Housing Management in Three Metropolitan Local Authorities: The Impact of CCT and Implications for Best Value' (2001) 27 *Local Government Studies* 69.

Harris, B., 'The "Third Source" of Authority for Government Action' (1992) 109 *Law Quarterly Review* 626.

Harris, N., *Law and Education: Regulation, Consumerism and the Education System* (London: Sweet and Maxwell, 1993).

Hartley, K., and Huby, M., 'Contracting-out Policy: Theory and Evidence', in Kay, J., Mayer, C., and Thomson, D. (eds.), *Privatisation and Regulation: The UK Experience* (Oxford: Clarendon Press, 1986), 284.

Hawkins, K., 'The Use of Legal Discretion: Perspectives from Law and Social Science', in Hawkins, K. (ed.), *The Uses of Discretion* (Oxford: Clarendon Press, 1992), 11.

Heald, D., and Geaughan, N., 'The Private Financing of Public Infrastructure', in Stoker, G. (ed.), *The New Management of British Local Governance* (London: Macmillan, 1999), 222.

Healy, J., 'The Care of Older People: Australia and the United Kingdom' (2002) 36 *Social Policy and Administration* 1.

Heron, E., and Dwyer, P., 'Doing the Right Thing: Labour's Attempt to Force a New Welfare Deal Between the Individual and the State' (1999) 33 *Social Policy and Administration* 91.

Hertogh, M., and Halliday, S. (eds.), *Judicial Review and Bureaucratic Impact* (Cambridge: Cambridge University Press, 2004).

Hindess, B., 'A Society Governed by Contract?', in Davis, G., Sullivan, B. and Yeatman, A. (eds.), *The New Contractualism?* (Melbourne: Macmillan, 1997), 14.

Hirschman, A., *Exit, Voice and Loyalty: Responses to Decline in Firms, Organizations and States* (Cambridge, Mass: Harvard University Press, 1970).

Hoggett, P., *Modernisation, Political Strategy and the Welfare State* (Bristol: SAUS, 1990).

—— 'New Modes of Control in the Public Service' (1996) 74 *Public Administration* 9.

Hogwood, B., Judge, D., and McVicar, M., 'The Audit of Accountability – Agencies and their Multiple Constituencies', ESRC Whitehall project briefing 12, http://ncl.ac.uk/geps/about/politics/whitehall/riefings/briefing12.html, accessed 20th August 2003.

Hood, C., *The Tools of Government* (London: Macmillan, 1983).

—— 'A Public Management for All Seasons' (1991) 69 *Public Administration* 3–19.

—— 'The "New Public Management" in the 1980s: Variations on a Theme' (1995) 20 *Accounting, Organizations and Society* 93.

Hood, C., 'Which Contract State? Four Perspectives on Over-Outsourcing for Public Services' (1997) 56 *Australian Journal of Public Administration* 120.

——'Individualized Contracts for Top Public Servants: Copying Business, Path-Dependent Political Re-Engineering – Or Trobriand Cricket?' (1998) 11 *Governance* 443.

Hood, C., James, O., Scott, C., Jones, G., and Travers, T., *Regulation Inside Government: Waste-watchers, Quality Police and Sleaze-busters* (Oxford: Oxford University Press, 1999).

Hood, C., James, O. and Scott, C., 'Regulation of Government: Has It Increased, Is It Increasing, Should It Be Diminished?' (2000) 78 *Public Administration* 283.

Howells, G.,'The Potential and Limits of Consumer Empowerment by Information' (2005) 32 *Journal of Law and Society* 349.

Hoyes, L. and Means, R., 'Markets, Contracts and Social Care Services: Prospects and Problems', Bornat, J., Pereira, C., Pilgrim, D., and Williams, F. (eds.), *Community Care* (London: Open University Press, 1993).

Hughes, D., 'The Reorganization of the NHS – The Rhetoric and the Reality of the Internal Market' (1991) 54 MLR 88.

Hughes, D., McHale, J., and Griffiths, L., 'Settling Contract Disputes in the National Health Service: Formal and Informal Pathways', in Flynn, R., and Williams, G. (eds.), *Contracting for Health: Quasi-Markets and the National Health Service* (Oxford: Oxford University Press, 1997), 98.

——'Do Quasi-markets Evolve? Institutional Analysis and the NHS' (1997) 21 *Cambridge Journal of Economics* 259.

Hunt, M., 'Constitutionalism and the Contractualisation of Government', in Taggart, M. (ed.), *The Province of Administrative Law* (Oxford: Hart Publishing, 1997), 21.

——'The Horizontal Effect of the Human Rights Act' [1998] *Public Law* 423.

Hyndman, N., and Eden, R., 'Rational Management, Performance Targets and Executive Agencies: Views From Agency Chief Executives in Northern Ireland' (2001) 79 *Public Administration* 579.

James, O., 'Business Models and the Transfer of Businesslike Central Government Agencies' (2001) 14 *Governance* 233.

Janisch, H., and Levi, R., 'Criminal Justice From the Bottom-Up: Some Thoughts on Police Rulemaking Processes, in Taggart, M.(ed.), *The Province of Administrative Law* (Oxford: Hart Publishing, 1997), 243.

Jessop, B., *State Theory: Putting the Capitalist State in its Place* (Cambridge: Polity Press, 1990).

——'The Regulation Approach, Governance and Post-Fordism: Alternative Perspectives on Economic and Political Change?' (1995) 24 *Economy and Society* 307.

Jewell, T., and Steele, T. (eds.), *Law in Environmental Decision-Making: National, European, and International Perspectives* (Oxford: Clarendon Press, 1998).

Johnes, G., and Cave, M., 'The Development of Competition Among Higher Education Institutions', in Bartlett et al (eds.) (1994), 95.

Jones, G., 'Against a Civil Service Act' (2002) *Public Money and Management* (Oct–Dec) 5.

Jones, K., and Williamson, K., 'The Birth of the Schoolroom' (1979) 6 *Ideology and Consciousness* 59.

Jordan, G., 'From Next Steps to Market Testing: Administrative Reform as Improvisation' (1994) 9 *Public Policy and Administration* 21.

Jorgensen, T.B., 'Modes of Governance and Administrative Change', in Kooiman, J. (ed.), *Modern Governance: New Government-Society Interactions* (London: Sage Publications, 1993), 219.

Kaufman, Franz-Xavier (ed.), *The Public Sector: Challenge for Coordination and Learning* (New York: Walter de Gruyter, 1991).

Kelman, S.J., 'Contracting', in Salamon, L. M., (ed.) *The Tools of Government: A Guide to the New Governance* (Oxford: Oxford University Press, 2002).

Kelsey, J., *Rolling Back the State: Privatisation of Power in Aotearoa/New Zealand* (Wellington: Bridget Williams Books, 1993).

Kendall, J., 'Of Knights, Knaves and Merchants: The Case of Residential Care for Older People in England in the Late 1990s' (2001) 35 *Social Policy and Administration* 360–375.

—— 'The Mainstreaming of the Third Sector into Public Policy in England in the Late 1990s: Whys and Wherefores' (2000) 28 *Policy and Politics* 541.

Kettl, D., *Sharing Power: Public Governance and Private Markets* (Washington D.C.: The Brookings Institution, 1993).

—— 'Measuring Performance When There Is No Bottom Line', in Boston, J. (ed.), *The State Under Contract* (Wellington: Bridget Williams Books, 1995), 160.

—— 'Managing Indirect Government' in Salamon, L.M., (ed.) *The Tools of Government: A Guide to the New Governance* (Oxford: Oxford University Press, 2002),

King, D., *In the Name of Liberalism: Illiberal Social Policy in the United States and Britain* (Oxford: Oxford University Press, 1999).

Kirkpatrick, I., and Lucio, M., 'Introduction: The Contract State and the Future of Public Management' (1996) 74 *Public Administration* 1.

Klein, R., 'Self-Inventing Institutions: Institutional Design in the UK Welfare State', in Goodin, R.E. (ed.), *The Theory of Institutional Design* (Cambridge: Cambridge University Press, 1996), 240.

—— 'Learning From Others; Shall the Last be the First?' (1997) 22 *Journal of Health Politics, Policy and Law* 1267.

Knapp, M., Wistow, G., Forder, J., and Hardy, B., 'Markets for Social Care: Opportunities, Barriers and Implications', in Bartlett et al (eds.) (1994), 123.

Knill, C., and Lehmkuhl, D., 'Private Actors and the State: Internationalization and Changing Patterns of Governance' (2002) 15 *Governance* 41.

Kooiman, J. (ed.), *Modern Governance: New Government-Society Interactions* (London: Sage Publications, 1993).

—— 'Social-Political Governance: Introduction', in Kooiman, J. (ed.), *Modern Governance: New Government-Society Interactions* (London: Sage Publications, 1993), 1.

Koppen, I., 'Ecological Covenants: Regulatory Informality in Dutch Waste Reduction Policy, in Teubner, G., Farmer, L., and Murphy, D. (eds.), *Environmental Law and Ecological Responsibility: The Concept and Practice of Ecological Self-Organization* (Chichester: John Wiley & Sons, 1994), 185.

Lange, B., 'Regulatory Spaces and Interactions: An Introduction' (2003) 12 *Social and Legal Studies* 411.

Lane, Jan-Erik (ed.), *Public Sector Reform: Rationale, Trends and Problems* (London: Sage Publications, 1997).

Langrod, G., 'Administrative Contracts: A Comparative Study' (1955) 4 *American Journal of Comparative Law* 325.

Laughlin, R., 'Accounting Control and Controlling Accounting: The Battle for the Public Sector?, Sheffield University Management School Discussion Paper No.92.29 (1992).

Laughlin, R., and Broadbent, J., 'Accounting and Law: Partners in the Juridification of the Public Sector in the UK?' (1993) 4 *Critical Perspectives on Accounting* 337.

Lee, S., and Woodward, R., 'Implementing the Third Way: The Delivery of Public Services Under the Blair Government' (2002) *Public Money and Management* (Oct–Dec), 49.

Legard, R., Woodfield, K., and White, C., *Staying Away or Staying On? A Qualitative Evaluation of the Education Maintenance Allowance* (DfEE Research Report RR256, 2001).

Lenoble, J., 'Open Method of Coordination and Theory of Reflexive Governance', in De Schutter, O., and Deakin, S. (eds.), *Social Rights and Market Forces: Is the Open Coordination of Employment and Social Policies the Future of Social Europe?* (Bruxelles: Bruylant, 2005), 19.

Lenoble, J., and Maesschalck, M., *Toward a Theory of Governance: The Action of Norms* (London: Kluwer Law International, 2003).

Le Grand, J., 'Competition, Cooperation, or Control? Tales from the British National Health Service' (1999) 18 *Health Affairs* 27.

—— 'Further Tales from the British National Health Service' (2002) 21 *Health Affairs* 116.

Le Grand, J., and Bartlett, W. (eds.), *Quasi-Markets and Social Policy* (Houndmills: Macmillan, 1993).

Le Sueur, A., 'How to Resolve Disputes With Public Authorities'.[2002] *Public Law* 203.

Leigh, I., *Law, Politics and Local Democracy* (Oxford: Oxford University Press, 2000).

Lewis, N., 'The Case for a Standing Administrative Conference' (1989) 60 *Political Quarterly* 421.

—— 'Reviewing Change in Government: New Public Management and Next Steps' [1994] *Public Law* 105.

—— *Choice and the Legal Order: Rising Above Politics* (London: Butterworths, 1996).

—— 'The Case for a Standing Administrative Conference' (1989) 60 *Political Quarterly* 421.

—— 'A Civil Service Act for the United Kingdom' [1998] *Public Law* 463.

—— *Law and Governance: The Old Meets the New* (London: Cavendish Publishing, 2001).

Lewis, N., and Birkinshaw. P., *When Citizens Complain: Reforming Justice and Administratation* (Buckingham: Open University Press, 1993).

Lewis, M. and Hartley, J., 'Evolving Forms of Quality Management in Local Government: Lessons From the Best Value Pilot Programme' (2001) 29 *Policy and Politics* 477.

Lindblom, C., *The Intelligence of Democracy: Decision-making Through Mutual Adjustment* (New York: Free Press, 1965).

Lo, S., and Aryee, S., 'Psychological Contract Breach in a Chinese Context: An Integrative Approach' (2003) 40 *Journal of Management Studies* 1005.

Local Government Management Board, *CCT Information Service Survey Report* (London: LGMB, 1994).

Local Government Association, *Local Compact Guidelines* (London: NCVO, 2000).

Loughlin, M., 'Innovative Financing in Local Government: The Limits of Legal Instrumentalism – Part I', [1991] *Public Law* 372.

—— 'Innovative Financing in Local Government: The Limits of Legal Instrumentalism – Part II' [1991] *Public Law* 568.

—— 'The Restructuring of Central-Local Government Relations', in Jowell, J., and Oliver, D. (3rd edition)(eds.), *The Changing Constitution* (Oxford: Clarendon Press, 1994), 261.

—— 'The Restructuring of Central-Local Government Relations', in Jowell, J., and Oliver, D. (4th edition)(eds.), *The Changing Constitution* (Oxford: Clarendon Press, 2000), 137.

—— 'Courts and Governance', in Birks, P. (ed.), *The Frontiers of Liability* (Oxford: Oxford University Press, 1994), 91.

—— *Legality and Locality: The Role of Law in Central-Local Government Relations* (Oxford: Clarendon Press, 1996).

—— 'Understanding Central-Local Government Relations' (1996) 11 *Public Policy and Administration* 48.

—— *Sword and Scales: An Examination of the Relationship Between Law and Politics* (Oxford: Hart Publishing, 2000).

Lumley, F., *Means of Social Control* (New York: Century, 1925).

Macaulay, S., 'Non-Contractual Relations in Business: A Preliminary Study' (1963) 28 *American Sociological Review* 55.

—— 'Elegant Models, Empirical Pictures, and the Complexities of Contract' (1977) 11 *Law and Society Review* 507.

—— 'The Reliance Interest and the World Outside the Law School's Door' (1991) *Wisconsin Law Review* 247.

—— 'An Empirical View of Contract' (1985) *Wisconsin Law Review* 465.

—— 'Relational Contracts Floating on a Sea of Custom? Thoughts About the Ideas of Ian Macneil and Lisa Bernstein' (2000) 94 *Northwestern University Law Review* 775.

—— 'The Real and the Paper Deal: Empirical Pictures of Relationships, Complexity and the Urge for Transparent Simple Rules', in Campbell, D., Collins, H., and Wightman, J. (eds.), *Implicit Dimensions of Contract: Discrete, Relational, and Network Contracts* (Oxford: Hart Publishing, 2003), 51.

Mackintosh, M., 'Flexible Contracting? Economic Cultures and Implicit Contracts in Social Care' (2000) 29 *Journal of Social Policy* 1.

—— 'Trading Work: Discourses of Internal Exchange in the Economic Culture of Local Government' (1997) 12 *Public Policy and Administration* 17.

MacIntyre, C., 'From Entitlement to Obligation in the Australian Welfare State' (1999) 34 *Australian Journal of Social Issues* 103.

Macneil, I.R., 'Power of Contract and Agreed Remedies' (1962) 47 *Cornell Law Quarterly* 495.

—— 'The Many Futures of Contracts', (1974) 47 Southern California Law Review 691.

—— *The New Social Contract* (Yale University Press, 1980).

Macneil, I.R., 'Values in Contract: Internal and External', (1983) 78 *Northwestern University Law Review* 340.

—— 'Exchange Revisited: Individual Utility and Social Solidarity' 96 *Ethics* 567.

—— 'Political Exchange as Relational Contract' in B. Marin (ed.), *Generalized Political Exchange* (Frederick A. Praeger: Colorado, 1990).

—— 'Relational Contract Theory: Challenges and Queries', (2000) 94 *Northwestern University Law Review* 877.

—— 'Contracting Worlds and Essential Contract Theory', (2000) 9 *Social and Legal Studies* 431.

MacNeill, K., 'Self-Regulation: Rights and Remedies – The Telecommunications Experience', in Finn, C. (ed.), *Sunrise or Sunset?* (Canberra: AIAL, 2000).

Macpherson, C. B., *Democratic Theory: Essays in Retrieval* (Oxford: Clarendon Press, 1973).

Maguire, M., 'Ethics in the Public Service', in Hondegem, A. (ed), *Ethics and Accountability in a Context of Governance and New Public Management* (Amsterdam: IOS Press, 1998).

Maile, S. and Hoggett, P., 'Best Value and the Politics of Pragmatism' (2001) 29 *Policy and Politics* 509.

Martin, J., 'Contracting and Accountability', in Boston, J. (ed.), *The State Under Contract* (Wellington: Bridget Williams Books, 1995), 36.

—— 'Contractualism in New Zealand', in Fortin, Y. and Van Hassel, H. (eds.), *Contracting in the New Public Management – From Economics to Law and Citizenship* (Amsterdam: IOS Press, 2000), 67.

Martin, S.J., 'Implementing Best Value: Local Public Services in Transition' (2000) 78 *Public Administration* 209.

Martin, S., 'Re-evaluating Public Service Improvement: The Early Impacts of the Best Value Regime' (2001) 29 *Policy and Politics* 447.

Martin, S., and Davis, H., 'What Works and For Whom? The Competing Rationalities of Best Value' (2001) 29 *Policy and Politics* 465.

Martin, S., and Boaz, A., 'Public Participation and Citizen-Centred Local Government: Lessons From the Best Value and Better Government for Older People Pilot Programmes' (2000) *Public Money and Management* (April–June), 47.

Massey, A., 'In Support of a Civil Service Act' (2002) *Public Money and Management* (Oct–Dec) 6.

Mayntz, R., 'Governing Failures and the Problem of Governability: Some Comments on a Theoretical Paradigm', in Kooiman, J. (ed.), *Modern Governance: New Government-Society Interactions* (London: Sage Publications, 1993), 9.

McBarnet, D., and Whelan, C., 'The Elusive Spirit of the Law: Formalism and the Struggle for Legal Control' (1991) 54 *Modern Law Review* 848.

McDermont, M., 'The Elusive Nature of the "Public Function": Poplar Housing v Donoghue' (2003) 66 *Modern Law Review* 113.

McGuire, L., 'Service Delivery Contracts: Quality for Customers, Clients and Citizens', in Davis, G., Sullivan, B. and Yeatman, A. (eds.), *The New Contractualism?* (Melbourne: Macmillan, 1997), 102.

McHale, J., Hughes, D., and Griffiths, L., 'Conceptualizing Contractual Disputes in the National Health Service Internal Market', in Deakin, S., and Michie, J. (eds.), *Contracts, Cooperation and Competition: Studies in Economics, Management and Law* (Oxford: Oxford University Press, 1997), 195.

McLean, J., 'The Crown in Contract and Administrative Law' (2004) 24 *Oxford Journal of Legal Studies* 129.

Mead, L., 'Citizenship and Social Policy: T. H. Marshall and Poverty', in Paul, E., Miller, F., and Paul, J. (eds.), *The Welfare State* (Cambridge: Cambridge University Press, 1997), 197–230.

Means, R., Hoyes, L., Lart, R., and Taylor, M., 'Quasi-Markets and Community Care: Towards User Empowerment?', in Bartlett et al (eds.) (1994), 158.

Mellon, E., 'Executive Agencies in Central Government', in A. Harrison (ed.), *From Hierarchy to Contract* (Oxford: Transaction Books, 1993), 14.

Michie, J., *Public Services Yes. Euro No* (London: New Europe Research Trust, 2002).

Midwinter, A., and McGarvey, N., 'In Search of the Regulatory State: Evidence From Scotland' (2001) 79 *Public Administration* 825.

Miller, A.S., 'Government Contracts and Social Control: A Preliminary Inquiry' (1955) 41 *Virginia Law Review* 27.

—— 'Administration by Contract: A New Concern for the Administrative Lawyer' (1961) 36 *New York University Law Review* 957.

Miller, P., and Rose, N., 'Governing Economic Life' (1990) 19 *Economy and Society* 1.

Montgomery, J., *Health Care Law* (2nd ed.)(Oxford: Oxford University Press, 2003).

Moran, M., *The British Regulatory State: High Modernism and Hyper-Innovation* (Oxford: Oxford University Press, 2003).

Morgan, B., 'The Economization of Politics: Meta-Regulation as a Form of Nonjudicial Legality' (2003) 12 *Social and Legal Studies* 489.

Morison, J., 'The Government-Voluntary Sector Compacts: Governance, Governmentality, and Civil Society' (2000) 27 *Journal of Law and Society* 98.

—— 'Democracy, Governance and Governmentality: Civic Public Space and Constitutional Renewal in Northern Ireland' (2001) 21 *Oxford Journal of Legal Studies* 287.

Morris, P., 'Legal Regulation of Contract Compliance: An Anglo-American Comparison' (1990) 19 *Anglo-American Law Review* 87.

Morrison, E., and Robinson, S., 'When Employees Feel Betrayed: A Model of How Psychological Contract Violation Develops' (1997) 22 *Academy of Management Review* 226.

Muetzelfeldt, M., 'The Facilitative State and the Symbolic Potency of Mutual Obligation' (2001) 60 *Australian Journal of Public Administration* 99.

Mulgan, R., ' "Accountability": An Ever-Expanding Concept?' (2000) 78 *Public Administration* 555.

—— 'Comparing Accountability in the Public and Private Sectors' (2000) 59 *Australian Journal of Public Administration* 87.

—— 'Contracting Out and Accountability' (1997) 56 *Australian Journal of Public Administration* 106.

—— *Holding Power to Account* (London: Palgrave, 2003).

Nader, L., and Nader, C., 'A Wide Angle on Regulation: An Anthropological Perspective', in Noll, R. G. (ed.), *Regulatory Policy and the Social Sciences* (Berkeley: University of California Press, 1985).

Nathan, S., 'Prison Privatization in the United Kingdom', in Coyle, A., Campbell, A., and Neufeld, R. (eds.), *Capitalist Punishment: Prison Privatization and Human Rights* (London: Zed Books, 2003), 162.

Nelken, D., 'The Use of "Contracts" as a Social Work Technique' (1987) 40 *Current Legal Problems* 207.

Newdick, C., 'The NHS in Private Hands? Regulating Private Providers of Health Services' (2000) 3 *Current Legal Issues* 1.

Newman, J., ' "What Counts Is What Works"? Constructing Evaluations of Market Mechanisms' (2001) 79 *Public Administration* 89.

Newman, J., Raine, J., and Skelcher, C., 'Transforming Local Government: Innovation and Modernization' (2001) *Public Money and Management* (April–June), 61.

Niskanen, W., *Bureaucracy and Representative Government* (Chicago, Il: Aldine-Atherton, 1971).

Nonet, P., and Selznick, P., *Law and Society in Transition: Toward Responsive Law* (Harper Torch Books, 1978).

North, D.C., *Institutions, Institutional Change and Economic Performance* (Cambridge: Cambridge University Press, 1990).

O'Malley, P., 'Uncertain Subjects: Risks, Liberalism and Contract' (2000) 29 *Employment and Society* 460.

—— *Risk, Uncertainty and Government* (London: Glasshouse Press, 2004).

OECD, *Responsive Government: Service Quality Initiatives* (Paris: Organisation for Economic Cooperation and Development, 1996).

OECD, *Governance in Transition* (Paris: OECD, 1995).

Offe, C., 'Designing Institutions in East European Transitions', Goodin, R.E., (ed.), *The Theory of Institutional Design* (Cambridge: Cambridge University Press, 1996), 199.

Ogus, A., 'Rethinking Self-Regulation' (1995) 15 *Oxford Journal of Legal Studies* 97.

—— *Regulation: Legal Form and Economic Theory* (Oxford: Clarendon Press, 1994).

Oliver, D., *Government in the United Kingdom: The Search for Accountability, Effectiveness and Citizenship* (Milton Keynes: Open University Press, 1991).

—— 'Common Values in Public and Private Law and the Public/Private Divide' [1997] *Public Law* 630.

—— 'The Underlying Values of Public and Private Law', in Taggart, M. (ed.), *The Province of Administrative Law* (Oxford: Hart Publishing, 1997), 217.

—— *Common Values and the Public-Private Divide* (London: Butterworths, 1999).

—— 'Functions of a Public Nature under the Human Rights Act' [2004] *Public Law* 329.

Oliver, D., and Drewry, G., *Public Service Reforms: Issues of Accountability and Public Law* (London: Pinter, 1996).

Oquendo, A.R., 'Deliberative Democracy in Habermas and Nino' (2002) 22 *Oxford Journal of Legal Studies* 189.

Orts, Eric W., 'Reflexive Environmental Law' (1995) 89 *Northwestern University Law Review* 1227.

Ormsby, M.J., 'The Purchaser/Provider Split: A Report From New Zealand' (1998) 11 *Governance* 357.

Osborne, D., and Gaebler, T., Reinventing Government: How the Entrepreneurial Spirit is Transforming the Public Sector (Reading, Mass: Addison-Wesley, 1992).

Painter, J., and Goodwin, M., 'Local Governance and Concrete Research: Investigating the Uneven Development of Regulation' (1995) 24 *Economy and Society* 334.

Palmer, E., 'Should Public Health Be a Private Concern? Developing a Public Service Paradigm in English Law' (2002) 22 *Oxford Journal of Legal Studies* 663.

—— 'Residential Care: Rights of the Elderly and the Contracts (Rights of Third Parties) Act 1999' (2000) 22 *Journal of Social Welfare and Family Law* 461.

—— 'Resource Allocation, Welfare Rights – Mapping the Boundaries of Judicial Control in Public Administrative Law' (2000) 20 *Oxford Journal of Legal Studies* 63.

Palmer, E., and Sunkin, M., 'Needs: Resources and Abhorrent Choices' (1998) 61 *Modern Law Review* 401.

Parker, C., *The Open Corporation: Effective Self-Regulation and Democracy* (New York: Cambridge University Press, 2002).

Parker, C., Scott, C., Lacey, N., and Braithwaite, J. (eds.), *Regulating Law* (Oxford: Oxford University Press, 2004).

Parker, D., and Hartley, K., 'The Economics of Partnership Sourcing Versus Adversarial Competition: A Critique' (1997) 3 *European Journal of Purchasing and Supply Management* 115.

Partington, M., 'Restructuring Administrative Justice? The Redress of Citizens' Grievances' (1999) *Current Legal Problems* 173–199.

Pateman, C., *The Problem of Political Obligation: A Critical Analysis of Liberal Theory* (Chichester: John Wiley and Son, 1979).

Paterson, J., 'Trans-science, Trans-law and Proceduralization' (2003) 12 *Social and Legal Studies* 525.

Pendlebury, M.W., 'Management Accounting in Local Government' (1994) 10 *Financial Accountability and Management* 117.

Perri 6, 'Giving Consumers of British Public Services More Choice: What Can Be Learned From Recent History?' (2003) 32 *Journal of Social Policy* 239.

Peters, B. G., 'Contracts as a Tool for Public Management: Their Strange Absence in North America', in Fortin, Y. and Van Hassel, H. (eds.), *Contracting in the New Public Management – From Economics to Law and Citizenship* (Amsterdam: IOS Press, 2000), 33.

—— 'The Politics of Tool Choice', in Salamon, L. M., (ed.) *The Tools of Government: A Guide to the New Governance* (Oxford: Oxford University Press, 2002).

Pettit, P., *Republicanism: A Theory of Freedom and Government* (Oxford: Blackwell, 1997).

—— 'Institutional Design and Rational Choice', in Goodin, R.E. (ed.), *The Theory of Institutional Design* (New York: Cambridge University Press, 1996).

Phillipson, G., 'The Human Rights Act, "Horizontal Effect" and the Common Law: A Bang or a Whimper? 62 (1999) *Modern Law Review* 824.

Picard, E., 'Citizenship, Fundamental Rights, and Public Services', in Freedland, M., and Sciarra, S. (eds.), *Public Services and Citizenship in European Law – Public and Labour Law Perspectives* (Oxford: Oxford University Press, 1998), 83.

Pick, K., and Sunkin, M., 'The Changing Impact of Judicial Review: The Independent Review Service of the Social Fund' [2001] *Public Law* 736.

Poirier, J., 'The Functions of Intergovernmental Agreements: Post-Devolution Concordats in a Comparative Perspective' [2000] *Public Law* 134.

Polidano, C., 'The Bureaucrat Who Fell Under a Bus: Ministerial Responsibility, Executive Agencies and the Derek Lewis Affair in Britain' (1999) 12 *Governance* 201.

Pollock, A., *NHS plc: The Privatisation of our Heatlh Care* (London: Verso, 2004).

Pollock, A., and Kerrison, S.,'Complaints as Accountability? The Case of Health Care in the United Kingdom' [2001] *Public Law* 115.

Potter, J., 'Consumerism and the Public Sector: How Well Does the Coat Fit?' (1988) 66 *Public Administration* 149.

Powell, W., 'Neither Market Nor Hierarchy: Network Forms of Organization' (1990) 12 *Research in Organizational Behaviour* 295.

—— 'Hybrid Organizational Arrangements: New Form or Transitional Development?' (1987) *California Management Review* 67.

Power, M., *The Audit Society: Rituals of Verification* (Oxford: Oxford University Press, 1997).

—— 'Evaluating the Audit Explosion' (2003) 25 *Law and Policy* 185.

Prager, J., 'Contracting Out Government Services: Lessons from the Private Sector' (1994) 54 *Public Administration Review* 176.

Preston, N., 'Public Sector Ethics: What Are We Talking About', in Bishop, P. and Preston, N. (eds.), *Local Government: Public Enterprise and Ethics* (Sydney: The Federation Press, 2000).

Prideaux, S., 'New Labour, Old Functionalism: The Underlying Contradictions of Welfare Reform in the US and UK' (2001) 35 *Social Policy and Administration* 85.

Prior, D., Stewart, J., and Walsh, K., *Citizenship: Rights, Community and Participation* (London: Pearson Professional, 1995).

Propper, C., 'Quasi-Markets, Contracts and Quality in Health and Social Care: The US Experience', in Le Grand, J., and Bartlett, W. (eds.)(1993), 35.

—— 'Quasi-Markets and Regulation', in Le Grand, J., and Bartlett, W. (eds.) (1993), 183.

—— 'The Demand for Private Health Care in the UK' (2000) 19 *Journal of Health Economics* 855.

Propper, C., and Bartlett, W., 'The Impact of Competition on the Behaviour of National Health Service Trusts', in Flynn, R., and Williams, G. (eds.), *Contracting for Health: Quasi-Markets and the National Health Service* (Oxford: Oxford University Press, 1997), 14.

Prosser, T., 'Regulation, Markets, and Legitimacy', in Jowell, J. and Oliver, D. (eds.), *The Changing Constitution* (Clarendon Press: Oxford, 1994), 237.

—— *Law and the Regulators* (Oxford: Clarendon Press, 1997).

—— 'Public Service Law: Privatization's Unexpected Offspring' (2000) 63 *Law and Contemporary Problems* 63.

Pryor, S., 'The Responsible Prisoner: An Exploration of the Extent to which Imprisonment Removes Responsibility Unnecessarily and an Invitation to Change', Autumn 2001, www.homeoffice.gov.uk/docs/the_responsible_prisoner.pdf

Radford, M., 'Competition Rules: The Local Government Act 1988' (1988) 51 *Modern Law Review* 747.

Rathgeb Smith, S., and Ingram, H., 'Policy Tools and Democracy', in Salamon, L. M., (ed.), *The Tools of Government: A Guide to the New Governance* (Oxford: Oxford University Press, 2002).

Rawlings, P., and Willett, C., 'Consumer Empowerment and the Citizen's Charter', in Willett, C., (ed), *Public Sector Reform and the Citizen's Charter* (London: Blackstone Press Ltd, 1996), 25.

Rawlings, R., 'Concordats of the Constitution' (2000) 116 *Law Quarterly Review* 257.

Reddel, T., 'Beyond Participation, Hierarchies, Management and Markets: "New" Governance and Place Policies' (2002) 61 *Australian Journal of Public Administration* 50.

Rehfuss, J., 'The Competitive Agency: Thoughts From Contracting Out in Great Britain and the United States' (1991) 57 *International Review of Administrative Sciences* 465.

Reichard, C., ' "Kontraktmanagement" Experiences With Internal Management Contracts in German Local Government', in Fortin, Y. and Van Hassel, H. (eds.), *Contracting in the New Public Management – From Economics to Law and Citizenship* (Amsterdam: IOS Press, 2000), 127.

Rhodes, R.A.W., *Understanding Governance: Policy Networks, Governance, Reflexivity and Accountability* (Buckingham: Open University Press, 1997).

—— 'Interorganizational Networks and Control: A Critical Conclusion', in Kaufman, Franz-Xavier (ed.), *The Public Sector: Challenge for Coordination and Learning* (New York: Walter de Gruyter, 1991), 525.

Richards, S., and Rodrigues, J., 'Strategies for Management in the Civil Service: Change of Direction' (1993) 13 *Public Money and Management* No. 2, 33.

Richardson, G., 'The Legal Regulation of Process', in Richardson, G., and Genn, H. (eds.), *Administrative Law and Government Action: The Courts and Alternative Mechanisms of Review* (Oxford: Clarendon Press, 1994), 105.

Ringeling, Arthur B., 'European Experience with Tools of Government', in Salamon, L.M., (ed.), *The Tools of Government: A Guide to the New Governance* (Oxford: Oxford University Press, 2002),

Robbie, K., and Wright, M., 'Local Authorities, Compulsory Competitive Tendering and Buy-Outs' (1996) 22 *Local Government Studies* 127.

Robinson, David Z., 'Government Contracting for Academic Research', in Smith, Bruce L.R., and Hague, D.C. (eds.), *The Dilemma of Accountability in Modern Government: Independence Versus Control* (London: Macmillan, 1971), 103.

Robinson, M., 'Contract Budgeting' (2000) 78 *Public Administration* 75.

Roe, M., 'Chaos and Evolution in Law and Economics' (1996) 109 *Harvard Law Review* 641.

Rose, N., 'Government, Authority and Expertise in Advanced Liberalism' (1993) 22 *Economy and Society* 283.

—— *Powers of Freedom: Reframing Political Thought* (Cambridge: Cambridge University Press, 1999).

Rose, N., and Miller, P., 'Political Power Beyond the State: Problematics of Government' (1992) 43 *British Journal of Sociology* 173.

Ross, M., 'Article 16 E.C. and Services of General Interest: From Derogation to Obligation?' (2000) 25 *European Law Review* 22.

Rowe, R., and Shepherd, M., 'Public Participation and the New NHS: No Closer to Citizen Control?' (2002) 36 *Social Policy and Administration* 275–290.

Ruane, S., 'Acquiescence and Opposition: The Private Finance Initiative in the National Health Service' (2000) 28 *Policy and Politics* 411.

Rubery, J., Earnshaw, J., Marchington, M., Lee Cooke, F., and Vincent, S., 'Changing Organizational Forms and the Employment Relationship' (2002) 39 *Journal of Management Studies* 645.

Rummery, K., and Glendinning, C., 'Access to Services as a Civil and Social Rights Issue: The Role of Welfare Professionals in Regulating Access to and Commissioning Services for Disabled Older People Under New Labour' (2000) 34 *Social Policy and Administration* 529.

Ryan, N., 'Reconstructing Citizens as Consumers: Implications for New Modes of Governance' (2001) 60 *Australian Journal of Public Administration* 104.

—— 'The Competitive Delivery of Social Services: Implications for Program Implementation' (1995) 54 *Australian Journal of Public Administration* 353.

Sabel, C. F., 'Learning by Monitoring; The Institutions of Economic Development', in Smelser, N. J., and Swedberg, R. (eds.), *The Handbook of Economic Sociology* (New York: Russell Sage Foundation, 1994).

Sako, M., *Prices, Quality and Trust: Inter-Firm Relations in Britain and Japan* (Cambridge: Cambridge University Press, 1992).

Salamon, L.M., (ed.) *The Tools of Government: A Guide to the New Governance* (Oxford: Oxford University Press, 2002).

—— 'The New Governance and the Tools of Public Action: An Introduction', in Salamon, L.M., (ed.), *The Tools of Government: A Guide to the New Governance* (Oxford: Oxford University Press, 2002).

—— 'The Tools Approach and the New Governance: Conclusion and Implications', in Salamon, L.M., (ed.) *The Tools of Government: A Guide to the New Governance* (Oxford: Oxford University Press, 2002).

Sanderson, I., 'Performance Management, Evaluation and Learning in "Modern" Local Government' (2001) 79 *Public Administration* 297.

—— 'Evaluation, Policy Learning and Evidence-Based Policy Making' (2002) 80 *Public Administration* 1.

Saunders, P., 'Mutual Obligation, Participation and Popularity: Social Security Reform in Australia' (2002) 31 *Journal of Social Policy* 21.

Sauter, W., 'Universal Service Obligations and the Emergence of Citizens' Rights in European Telecommunications Liberalization', in Freedland, M., and Sciarra, S. (eds.), *Public Services and Citizenship in European Law – Public and Labour Law Perspectives* (Oxford: Oxford University Press, 1998), 117.

Savas, E.S., *Privatizing the Public Sector: How To Shrink Government* (Chatham House, 1982).

Sbragia, A., 'Governance, the State, and the Market: What is Going On?' (2000) 13 *Governance: An International Journal of Policy and Administration* 243.

Schanze, E., 'Symbiotic Contracts: Exploring Long-Term Agency Structures Between Contract and Corporation', in Joerges, C. (ed.), *Franchising and the Law: Theoretical and Comparative Approaches in Europe and the United States* (Baden-Baden: Nomos Verlagsgesellschaft, 1991, 67.

Schoombee, H., 'Privatisation and Contracting Out – Where Are We Going?', in McMillan, J. (ed.), *Administrative Law Under the Coalition Government* (Canberra: AIAL, 1997), 135.

Scott, C., 'Privatization, Control, and Accountability', in McCahery, J., Picciotto, S., and Scott, C. (eds.), *Corporate Control and Accountability* (Oxford: Clarendon Press, 1993), 231.

—— 'The "New Public Law" ', in Willett, C., (ed), *Public Sector Reform and the Citizen's Charter* (London: Blackstone Press Ltd, 1996), 43.

—— 'The Juridification of Regulatory Relations in the UK Utilities Sector', in Black, J., Muchlinski, P., and Walker, P. (eds), *Commercial Regulation and Judicial Review* (Oxford: Hart Publishing, 1998), 19.

—— 'Accountability in the Regulatory State' (2000) 27 *Journal of Law and Society* 38.

—— 'Analysing Regulatory Space: Fragmented Resources and Institutional Design' [2001] *Public Law* 329.

—— 'Private Regulation of the Public Sector: A Neglected Facet of Contemporary Governance' (2001) 29 *Journal of Law and Society* 56.

—— 'Speaking Softly Without Big Sticks: Meta-Regulation and Public Sector Audit' (2003) 25 *Social and Legal Studies* 203.

Seal, W., and Vincent-Jones, P., 'Accounting and Trust in the Enabling of Long-Term Relations' (1997) 10 *Accounting, Auditing and Accountability Journal* 406.

Seddon, N., *Government Contracts: Federal, State and Local* (Sydney: Federation Press, 1999) (2nd ed.).

—— 'Activity Agreements – Are They Contracts?', in Creyke, R., and Sassarella, M. (eds.), Targeting Accountability and Review (Canberra: AIAL, 1998), 82.

—— 'Is Accountability a Cost of Contracting Out?', in Finn, C. (ed.), *Sunrise or Sunset? Administrative Law in the New Millennium* (Canberra: AIAL, 2000), 37.

—— 'The Victorian Audit Review of Government Contracts – Lessons Learned from the Kennett Era', (Public Sector Accountability and Governance Conference, University of Wollongong, 2000).

—— 'Commentary: Privatisation and Contracting Out – Where are We Going?', in McMillan, J. (ed.), *Administrative Law Under the Coalition Government* (Canberra: AIAL, 1997), 146.

Self, P., *Government by the Market? The Politics of Public Choice* (Houndmills: Macmillan, 1993).

Selznick, P., 'Self-Regulation and the Theory of Institutions', in Teubner, G., Farmer, L., and Murphy, D. (eds.), *Environmental Law and Ecological Responsibility: The Concept and Practice of Ecological Self-Organization* (Chichester: John Wiley & Sons, 1994), 395.

—— 'Focussing Organizational Research on Regulation', in Noll, R.G. (ed.), *Regulatory Policy and the Social Sciences* (Berkeley: University of California Press, 1985).

—— *The Moral Commonwealth: Social Theory and the Promise of Community* (Berkeley: University of California Press, 1992).

Seneviratne, M., *Ombudsmen: Public Services and Administrative Justice* (London: Butterworths, 2002).

Shand, D., 'NPM: An International Perspective', Public Finance Foundation Review (1995) No 7 (August), 6.

Shapiro, M., 'Administrative Law Unbounded: Reflections on Government and Governance' (2001) 8 *Indiana Journal of Global Governance Studies* 369.

Shaver, S., 'Australian Welfare Reform: From Citizenship to Supervision' (2002) 36 *Social Policy and Administration* 331–345.

Shaw, K., Fenwick, J., and Foreman, A., 'Compulsory Competition for Local Government Services in the UK: A Case of Market Rhetoric and Camouflaged Centralism' (1995) 10 *Public Policy and Administration* 63.

Shearing, C., 'A Constitutive Conception of Regulation', in Grabosky, P., and Braithwaite, J. (eds.), *Business Regulation and Australia's Future* (Canberra: Australian Institute of Criminology, 1993), 67.

Sheaff, R., Pickard, S. and Smith, K., 'Public Service Responsiveness to Users' Demands and Needs: Theory, Practice and Primary Healthcare in England' (2002) 80 *Public Administration* 435.

Simon, H.A., 'Organizations and Markets' (1991) 5 *Journal of Economic Perspectives* 25.

—— 'Rational Decision-Making in Business Organizations (1979) 69 *American Economic Review* 493.

Sitkin, S.B., and Roth, N.L., 'Explaining the Limited Effectiveness of Legalistic "Remedies" for Trust/Distrust' (1993) 4 *Organization Science* 367.

Smith, B.L.R., and Hague, D.C. (eds.), *The Dilemma of Accountability in Modern Government: Independence Versus Control* (London: Macmillan, 1971).

Smith, B.L.R., 'Accountability and Independence in the Contract State', in Smith, B.L.R., and Hague, D.C. (eds.), *The Dilemma of Accountability in Modern Government: Independence Versus Control* (London: Macmillan, 1971), 3.

Smith, R., 'PFI: Perfidious Financial Idiocy' (1999) 319 *British Medical Journal* 2.

Snape, S., 'Contracting Out Local Government Services in Western Europe: Lessons from the Netherlands' (1995) 21 *Local Government Studies* 642.

Sommerlad, H., ' "I've Lost the Plot": An Everyday Story of Legal Aid Lawyers' (2001) 28 *Journal of Law and Society* 335.

Steele, J., 'Participation and Deliberation in Environmental Law' (2001) 21 *Oxford Journal of Legal Studies* 415.

Steuerle, Eugene C., and Twombly, Eric C., 'Vouchers', in Salamon, L.M., (ed.), *The Tools of Government: A Guide to the New Governance* (Oxford: Oxford University Pressm, 2002).

Stewart, J., 'The Limitations of Government by Contract' (1993) 13 *Public Money and Management* (No.3).

—— 'Purchaser-Provider – Are the Purchasers Ready for It?' (1999) *Australian Journal of Public Administration* 105.

Stinchcombe, A., 'Contracts as Hierarchical Documents', in Stinchcombe, A., and Heimer, C.A. (eds.), *Organization Theory and Project Management: Administering Uncertainty in Norwegian Offshore Oil* (Oslo: Nowegian University Press, 1985).

Stirton, L., and Lodge, M., 'Transparency Mechanisms: Building Publicness into Public Services' (2001) 28 *Journal of Law and Society* 471.

Stott, T., 'Market Testing and Beyond: Privatisation and Contracting Out in British Central Government' (1994) XI V *Teaching Public Administration* 36.

Street, H., *Governmental Liability: A Comparative Study* (Cambridge: Cambridge University Press, 1953).

Stuhmcke, A., 'The Rise of the Australian Telecommunications Industry Ombudsman' (2002) 26 *Telecommunications Policy* 69.

Sullivan, M., and Drakeford, M., 'Devolution, Divergence and Social Policy' (2005) 3 *Wales Journal of Law and Policy* 7.

Sutcliffe, F., 'Contracting Out Public Services: UK Policy *v* EC Law' (1993) 22 *Anglo-American Law Review* 337.

Taggart, M., 'The Province of Administrative Law Determined?' in Taggart, M.(ed.), *The Province of Administrative Law* (Oxford: Hart Publishing, 1997), 1.

Talbot-Smith, A., Gnani, S., Pollock, A., and Gray, D., 'Questioning the Claims from Kaiser' (2004) 54 *British Journal of General Practice* 415.

Tang, A., 'The Changing Role of Government in Community Services: Issues of Access and Equity in Administrative Review' (1997) 56 *Australian Journal of Public Administration* 95.

Tenbensel, T., 'Health Prioritisation as Rationalist Policy-Making: Problems, Prognoses and Prospects' (2000) 28 *Policy and Politics* 425.

Teubner, G., 'Substantive and Reflexive Elements in Modern Law' (1983) 17 *Law and Society Review* 239.

—— 'Introduction to Autopoietic Law', in Teubner, G. (ed.), *Autopoietic Law: A New Approach to Law and Society* (1987).

Thomson, W., 'Realising Rights Through Local Service Contracts', in Coote, A. (ed.), *The Welfare of Citizens – Developing New Social Rights* (London: IPPR, 1992), 129.

Thorelli, H., 'Networks: Between Markets and Hierarchies' (1986) 7 *Strategic Management Journal* 37.

Torfing, J., 'Workfare With Welfare: Recent Reforms of the Danish Welfare State' (1999) 9 *Journal of European Social Policy* 5.

Torres, L., and Pina, V., 'Changes in Public Service Delivery in the EU Countries' (2002) *Public Money and Management* (Oct–Dec), 41.

Travers, P., 'Quasi-Markets for the Social Services' (1995) 54 *Australian Journal of Public Administration* 346.

Trebilcock, M.J., 'Can Government Be Reinvented?', in Boston, J. (ed.), *The State Under Contract* (Wellington: Bridget Williams Books, 1995).

Turpin, C., *Government Procurement and Contracts* (Harlow: Longman, 1989).

—— *British Government and the Constitution – Text, Cases and Materials* (5th ed.)(London: Butterworths, 2002).

Vandenberghe, V., 'Educational Quasi-Markets: The Beligan Experience', in Bartlett, W., Roberts, J.A., and Le Grand, J. (eds.) (1998), 79.

Vermeulen, A., 'Contract Management in the Netherlands' (1988) 54 *International Review of Administrative Sciences* 201.

Vere, D., 'Training and Enterprise Councils: Putting Business in the Lead', in Harrison, A. (ed.), *From Hierarchy to Contract* (Oxford: Transaction Books, 1993).

Vincent-Jones, P., 'Contract and Business Transactions: A Socio-Legal Analysis', (1989) 16 *Journal of Law and Society* 166.

—— 'Hybrid Organization, Contractual Governance, and Compulsory Competitive Tendering in the Provision of Local Authority Services', in Deakin, S., and Michie, J. (eds.) (1997), 143.

—— 'Responsive Law and Governance in Public Services Provision: A Future for the Local Contracting State' (1998) 61 *Modern Law Review* 362.

Vincent-Jones, P.,'Competition and Contracting in the Transition from CCT to Best Value: Towards a More Reflexive Regulation?' (1999) 77 *Public Administration* 273.

——'The Regulation of Contractualisation in Quasi-Markets for Public Services' (1999) *Public Law* 303.

——'New Labour and the New Contract: Law and Social Relations in the Age of Privatisation', Professorial Lecture 17 November 1999.

——'Contractual Governance: Institutional and Organisational Analysis' (2000) 20 *Oxford Journal of Legal Studies* 317.

——'Central-Local Relations Under the Local Government Act 1999: A New Consensus?' (2000) 63 *Modern Law Review* 84.

——'Contracting for Public Services: Trust, Accountability and Consumer Participation in UK Local Authority Quasi-Markets', in Fortin, Y. and Van Hassel, H. (eds.) (2000), 143.

——'From Housing Management to the Management of Housing: The Challenge of Best Value', in Cowan, D., and Marsh, A. (eds.), *Two Steps Forward: Housing Policy Into the New Millennium* (2001) (Bristol: Policy Press, 2001), 241.

——'The Reception of Ian Macneil's Work on Contract in the UK' (Introduction to edited collection), in D. Campbell (ed.), *Selected Papers of Ian Macneil* (London: Sweet and Maxwell, 2001), 67.

——'Values and Purpose in Government: Central-local Relations in Regulatory Perspective, (2002) 29 *Journal of Law and Society* 27.

——'Regulating Government by Contract: Towards a Public Law Framework?' (2002) 65 *Modern Law Review* 611.

——'Citizen Redress in Public Contracting for Human Services' (2005) 68 *Modern Law Review* 887.

Vincent-Jones, P., and Harries, A., 'Partnership and Cooperation in Contracting Out Local Authority Refuse Collection Services: A Case Study', in Montanheiro, L., et al (eds.), *Public and Private Sector Partnerships in the Global Context*, (Sheffield: Pavic Publications, 1995), 632.

——'Limits of Contract in Internal CCT Transactions: A Comparative Study of Buildings Cleaning and Refuse Collection in "Northern Metropolitan" ', in Campbell, D., and Vincent-Jones, P. (eds.), (1996), 180.

——'Conflict and Cooperation in Local Authority Quasi-Markets: The Hybrid Organisation of Internal Contracting Under CCT, (1996) 22 *Local Government Studies* 187.

——'CCT, Conflict and Cooperation in Local Authority Quasi-Markets', in Bartlett, W., Roberts, J.A., and Le Grand, J. (eds.), (1998), 19.

——'Tenant Participation in Contracting for Housing Management Services: A Case Study', in Cowan, D., (ed.), *Housing: Participation and Exclusion*, (Aldershot: Dartmouth Publishing Company, 1998), 41.

Vincent-Jones, P., Campbell, D., Harries, A., and Seal, W., *Conflict and Cooperation in Contracting for Professional Services: A Comparative Study*, (ESRC Final Report, 1998).

Waddan, A., 'Redesigning the Welfare Contract in Theory and Practice: Just What Is Going On in the USA?' (2003) 32 *Journal of Social Policy* 19.

Wade, H.W.R., 'Horizons of Horizontality' (2000) 116 *Law Quarterly Review* 217.

Wade, W., and Forsyth, C., *Administrative Law* (8th ed) (Oxford: Oxford University Press, 2000).

Waldegrave, W., *The Reality of Reform and Accountability in Today's Public Service* (London: Public Finance Foundation, 1993).

Walker, B., and Davis, H., 'Perspectives on Contractual Relationships and the Move to Best Value in Local Authorities' (1999) 25 *Local Government Studies* 16.

Walsh, K., 'Quality and Public Services' (1991) 69 *Public Administration* 7.

—— *Public Services and Market Mechanisms: Competition, Contracting and the New Public Management* (Houndmills: Macmillan, 1995).

Walsh, K., and Davis, H., *Competition and Service: The Impact of the Local Government Act 1988* (London: HMSO, 1993).

Walsh, K., Deakin, N., Spurgeon, P., Smith, P., and Thomas, N., *Contracting for Change: Contracts in Health, Social Care, and Other Local Government Services* (Oxford: Oxford University Press, 1997).

Watts, A.G., 'Applying Market Principles to the Delivery of Careers Guidance Services: A Critical Review', in Bartlett, W., Roberts, J.A., and Le Grand, J. (eds.) (1998), 239.

Weber, M., *The Theory of Social and Economic Organization*, translated by Henderson, A.M., and Parsons, T. (London: Collier-Macmillan, 1947).

Wegener, A., 'Management Contracts in International Comparative Perspective: Experience From Leading-Edge Local Governments', in Fortin, Y. and Van Hassel, H. (eds.), *Contracting in the New Public Management – From Economics to Law and Citizenship* (Amsterdam: IOS Press, 2000), 107.

Weiss, J. A., 'Public Information', in Salamon, L. M., (ed.), *The Tools of Government: A Guide to the New Governance* (Oxford: Oxford University Press, 2002).

White, S., 'Social Rights and the Social Contract: Political Theory and the New Welfare Politics' (2000) 30 *British Journal of Political Science* 507–532.

Whitmore, H., 'Administrative Law Reform: A Personal Recollection' (2001) 8 *Australian Journal of Administrative Law* 144.

Whittaker, S., 'Unfair Contract Terms, Public Services and the Construction of a European Conception of Contract' (2000) 116 *Law Quarterly Review* 95.

Wightman, J., *Contract: A Critical Commentary* (London: Pluto Press, 1996).

—— 'Intimate Relationships, Relational Contract Theory, and the Reach of Contract' (2000) 8 *Feminist Legal Studies* 93.

Williams, T., 'Local Government Role-Reversal in the New Contract Culture', in Bennett, R.J. (ed.) *Local Government in the New Europe* (London: Belhaven Press, 1993), 95.

Williamson, O.E., *Markets and Hierarchies: Analysis and Antitrust Implications* (New York: Free Press, 1975).

—— 'Transaction-Cost Economics: The Governance of Contractual Relations' (1979) 22 *Journal of Law and Economics* 233.

—— *The Mechanisms of Governance* (Oxford: Oxford University Press, 1996).

Wilson, E., and Doig, A., 'The Shape of Ideology: Structure, Culture and Policy Delivery in the New Public Sector' (1996) *Public Money and Management* 53 (April–June).

Wirth, W., 'Responding to Citizens' Needs: From Bureaucratic Accountability to Individual Coproduction in the Public Sector', in Kaufman, Franz-Xavier (ed.), *The Public Sector: Challenge for Coordination and Learning* (New York: Walter de Gruyter, 1991), 69.

Wonnacott, C., 'The Counterfeit Contract – Reform, Pretence and Muddled Principles in the New Referral Order' (1999) 11 *Child and Family Law Quarterly* 271.

Wolf, C., *Markets or Governments: Choosing Between Imperfect Alternatives* (Cambridge, Mass: MIT Press, 1993) (2nd ed.).

Woolf, Lord, 'Judicial Review: A Possible Programme for Reform' [1992] *Public Law* 221.

—— '*Droit Public* – English Style' [1995] PL 57

Yeatman, A., 'Contracting Out and Public Values: A Symposium' (2001) 60 *Australian Journal of Public Administration* 71.

—— 'Interpreting Contemporary Contractualism', in Dean, M., and Hindess, B. (eds.). *Governing Australia: Studies in Contemporary Rationalities of Government* (Cambridge: Cambridge University Press, 1998), 227.

—— 'The New Contractualism: Management Reform or a New Approach to Governance', in Weller, P. and Davis, G. (eds.), *New Ideas, Better Government* (Sydney: Allen and Unwin, 1996).

Yeatman, A., and Owler, K., 'The Role of Contract in the Democratisation of Service Delivery' (2001) 18 *Law in Context* 34.

Zifcak, S., 'Contractualism, Democracy and Ethics' (2001) 60 *Australian Journal of Public Administration* 86.

—— New Managerialism: Administrative Reform in Whitehall and Canberra (Buckingham: Open University Press, 1994).

UK OFFICIAL PUBLICATIONS

Command papers

Cabinet Office, *Modernising Government*, White Paper, (Cm 4310, 1999).

Cabinet Office, *Next Steps Report 1997*, (Cm 3889, 1998).

Department of Education and Employment, *Excellence in Schools*, (Cm 3681, 1997).

DETR, *Modern Local Government: In Touch With the People*, White Paper, (Cm 4014, 1998).

DfEE, *Excellence in Schools*, White Paper, (Cm 3681, 1997).

DSS, *A New Contract for Welfare: New Ambitions for Our Country*, (Cm 3805, 1998).

DSS, *A New Contract for Welfare: Partnership in Pensions*, (Cm 4179, 1998).

DSS, *A New Contract for Welfare: Principles into Practice*, (Cm 4101, 1998).

DSS, *A New Contract for Welfare: The Gateway to Work*, (Cm 4102, 1998).

DSS, *A New Contract for Welfare: Support for Disabled People*, (Cm 4103, 1998).

Efficiency and Effectiveness in the Civil Service, (Cm 8616, 1982).

Fulton Report, *The Civil Service*, (Cmnd 6380, 1968).

HM Treasury, *Prudent for a Purpose: Building Opportunity and Security for All, 2000 Spending Review: New Public Spending Plans 2001–2004, July 2000* (Cm 4807, 2000), para. 1.2.

HM Treasury, *Competing for Quality – Buying Better Public Services*, White Paper, (Cm 1730, 1991).

HM Treasury, *Public Private Partnerships* (London: HMSO, 2000).

HM Treasury, *Public Services for the Future: Modernisation, Reform, Accountability*, (Cm 4181, 1998).

HM Treasury, *Setting New Standards: A Strategy for Government Procurement*, (Cm 2840, 1995).
Home Office, *Compact on Relations Between Government and the Voluntary and Community Sector in England*, (Cm 4100, 1998).
Home Office, *Compact: Getting It Right Together*, (Cm 4100, 1998).
Home Office, *Justice for All*, White Paper, (Cm 5563, 2002).
Home Office, *No More Excuses – A New Approach to Tackling Youth Crime in England and Wales*, (Cm 3809, 1997).
Home Office, *No More Excuses – A New Approach to Tackling Youth Crime in England and Wales*, White Paper, (Cm 3809, 1997).
Home Office, *Respect and Responsibility – Taking a Stand Against Anti-Social Behaviour*, White Paper, March 2003.
The Citizen's Charter: Raising the Standard, (Cm 1599, 1991).
The Next Steps Agencies Review 1992, (Cm 2111, 1992).
Widdicombe Report, *Report of the Committee of Inquiry into the Conduct of Local Authority Business*, (Cmnd 9797, 1985/86).
Woolf Inquiry, (Cm 1456, 1991).

Parliamentary papers

National Audit Office, *Managing the Relationship to Secure a Successful Partnership in PFI Projects*, HC 275 (2001–02).
Parliamentary Commissioner for Administration (Fourth Report) *Annual Report* HC 196 (1995–96).
HC Select Committee on *maladministration and redress* (HC Paper (1994–95) no 112).
Parliamentary Commissioner for Administration, *Investigation of Complaints Against the Child Support Agency* (Third Report) HC 135 (1994–5).
HC Select Committee 5th Report, *on target? Government by measurement* (HC Paper (2002–03) no 62-)
HC Select Committee the public service ethos, 7th Report (HC Paper (2001–02) no 263).
HC Select Committee, on *ombudsman issues* 3rd Report (HC Paper (2002–03) no 448).
HC Select Committee, on *review of the public sector obmudsmen in England* 3rd Report (HC Paper (1999–2000) no 612).
HC Select Committee on *implementation of the best value framework* 11th Report (HC Paper (1997–98) no 705).
HC Select Committee on local government finance (HC Paper (1998–99) no 78–1).
HL Select Committee on relations between central and local government, rebuilding trust (HL Paper (1995–95) no 97).
Treasury and Civil Service Committee on *civil service management reform: The next steps* (HC Paper (1987–88) no 494).
Treasury Select Committee, 3rd Report (HC Paper (2000–01) no 73).
HC Treasury Select Committee, on *spending review 2000* 9th Report (HC Paper (1999–2000) no 483).
HC Treasury Select Committee, on *the Private Finance Initiative* 6th Report (HC Paper (1995–96) no 146).

Other official publications

Cabinet Office (Better Regulation Task Force), *Principles of Good Regulation* (London: Cabinet Office, 2003).

Cabinet Office, *Better Quality Services: Guidance for Senior Managers* (London: The Stationery Office, 1998).

Cabinet Office, *Better Quality Services: Handbook* (London: The Stationery Office, 1998).

Cabinet Office, *Service First: The New Charter Programme* (London: The Stationery Office, 1998).

Department of Health, *Care Homes for Older People: National Minimum Standards* (London: The Stationery Office, 2002).

Department of the Environment, *Competing for Quality: Competition in the Provision of Local Services – A Consultation Paper* (1991).

HM Treasury, *Private Opportunity, Public Benefit – Progressing the Private Finance Initiative* (1995).

HM Treasury, *Review of Civil Procurement in Central Government* (P Gershon) (London: The Stationery Office, 1999).

HM Treasury, *The Private Finance Initiative – Breaking New Ground* (1993).

HM Treasury/Cabinet Office, *Comprehensive Spending Review on Efficiency in Civil Government Procurement Expenditure* (London: HMSO, 1998).

Treasury Taskforce, *Partnerships for Prosperity – The Private Finance Initiative* (1997).

Index

The manufacturer's authorised representative in the EU for product safety is Oxford University Press España S.A. of el Parque Empresarial San Fernando de Henares, Avenida de Castilla, 2 – 28830 Madrid (www.oup.es/en or product.safety@oup.com). OUP España S.A. also acts as importer into Spain of products made by the manufacturer.

www.ingramcontent.com/pod-product-compliance
Lightning Source LLC
LaVergne TN
LVHW011903200926
848484LV00002B/517
* 9 7 8 0 1 9 9 2 9 1 2 7 4 *